This will be an indispensable working tool, not just for specialists, in one of the central fields in contemporary political economy.

Wolfgang Streeck, Max Planck Institute for the Study of Societies, Cologne

Presenting an impressive range of authors and perspectives, this Handbook succeeds at delivering a comprehensive mapping of financialization studies. It is imaginatively organised and manages to bring coherence to this untidy and rapidly growing research field. This inevitably critical collection of chapters not only covers the reach and effects of finance, but also conveys some hope for future definancialization.

Julie Froud, Professor of Financial Innovation, University of Manchester

This book is a major contribution to the study of financialization. There has been an explosion in the term's use across a wide range of disciplines, which indicates the concept's usefulness. The book collates contributions from those disciplines, documenting how financialization helps understand both the "big picture" and developments in specific fields. It immediately establishes itself as the defining reference on financialization

Thomas Palley, independent economist, Washington, DC

THE ROUTLEDGE INTERNATIONAL HANDBOOK OF FINANCIALIZATION

Financialization has become the go-to term for scholars grappling with the growth of finance. This Handbook offers the first comprehensive survey of the scholarship on financialization, connecting finance with changes in politics, technology, culture, society and the economy.

It takes stock of the diverse avenues of research that comprise financialization studies and the contributions they have made to understanding the changes in contemporary societies driven by the rise of finance. The chapters chart the field's evolution from research describing and critiquing the manifestations of financialization towards scholarship that pinpoints the driving forces, mechanisms and boundaries of financialization.

Written for researchers and students not only in economics but from across the social sciences and the humanities, this book offers a decidedly global and pluri-disciplinary view on financialization for those who are looking to understand the changing face of finance and its consequences.

Philip Mader is a Research Fellow at the Institute of Development Studies (Brighton, UK) and program convenor of the MA in Globalisation, Business and Development. His research focuses on development and the politics of markets. His PhD from the Max Planck Institute for the Study of Societies and the University of Cologne was published as *The Political Economy of Microfinance: Financializing Poverty* (Palgrave, 2015) and was recognized with the Otto Hahn Medal and the German Thesis Award.

Daniel Mertens is Professor of International Political Economy at the University of Osnabrück. Prior to that, he was an assistant professor at Goethe University Frankfurt and a visiting scholar at Northwestern University. He received his PhD from the Max Planck Institute for the Study of Societies and the University of Cologne. His work ranges from the politics of credit markets and banking to analyses of the modern tax state and has been published in outlets such as the *Journal of European Public Policy, New Political Economy* and *Competition & Change*.

Natascha van der Zwan is Assistant Professor in Public Administration at Leiden University. She does comparative and historical research on financialization and pension systems, investment rules and regulations, and pension fund capitalism. Her article "Making Sense of Financialization" (*Socio-Economic Review*, 2014) has become a key article in scholarship on financialization and is widely used in university courses. Dr Van der Zwan holds a PhD in Political Science from the New School for Social Research.

THE ROUTLEDGE INTERNATIONAL HANDBOOK OF FINANCIALIZATION

Edited by *Philip Mader, Daniel Mertens and Natascha van der Zwan*

Routledge
Taylor & Francis Group

LONDON AND NEW YORK

First published 2020 by Routledge

2 Park Square, Milton Park, Abingdon, Oxon OX14 4RN
605 Third Avenue, New York, NY 10017

Routledge is an imprint of the Taylor & Francis Group, an informa business

First issued in paperback 2021

Publisher's Note

The publisher has gone to great lengths to ensure the quality of this reprint but points out that some imperfections in the original copies may be apparent.

Cover image: Hendrik Frederik Carel ten Kate, 1844, Satire op de aansporing tot deelneming in de (zogenaamde) vrijwillige 3% geldlening van 1844 (blad 5), The Hague. Courtesy of: Rijksmuseum, Amsterdam.

British Library Cataloguing in Publication Data
A catalogue record for this book is available from the British Library

Library of Congress Cataloging-in-Publication Data
A catalog record has been requested for this book

ISBN: 978-1-138-30821-3 (hbk)
ISBN: 978-1-03-217463-1 (pbk)
DOI: 10.4324/9781315142876

Typeset in Bembo
by Taylor & Francis Books

CONTENTS

Contents

Contents

Contents

Contents

ILLUSTRATIONS

Figures

Tables

CONTRIBUTORS

Manuel B. Aalbers is professor of Human Geography at KU Leuven/University of Leuven (Belgium) where he leads a research group on the intersection of real estate, finance and states, spearheaded by a grant from the European Research Council. He has also published on financialization, redlining, social and financial exclusion, neoliberalism, mortgage markets, the privatization of social housing, neighborhood decline and gentrification. He is the author of *Place, Exclusion, and Mortgage Markets* (Wiley-Blackwell, 2011) and *The Financialization of Housing: A Political Economy Approach* (Routledge, 2016) and the editor of *Subprime Cities: The Political Economy of Mortgage Markets* (Wiley-Blackwell, 2012).

Lisa Adkins is Professor of Sociology and Head of the School of Social and Political Sciences at the University of Sydney. She is also an Academy of Finland Distinguished Professor (2015–2019). Her contributions to the discipline of sociology are in the areas of economic sociology, social theory and feminist theory. Recent publications include *The Time of Money* (Stanford University Press, 2018), *The Post-Fordist Sexual Contract: Working and Living in Contingency* (with Maryanne Dever, Palgrave, 2016) and *Measure and Value* (with Celia Lury, Wiley, 2012). She is joint Editor-in-Chief of *Australian Feminist Studies* (Routledge/Taylor & Francis).

Rob Aitken is a Professor in the Department of Political Science at the University of Alberta. His research lies at the intersection of cultural economy, governmentality and the social studies of finance. His most recent book, *Fringe Finance*, was published by Routledge in 2015.

Mareike Beck recently completed her PhD entitled *German Banking and the Rise of Financial Capitalism, A Case of Extraverted Financialisation* at the University of Sussex. She also has co-published with Julian Germann an article in *Globalizations* on managerialism in Germany.

Bruno Bonizzi is Senior Lecturer in Finance at the University of Hertfordshire Business School. He researches and has published on financial integration, financialization and pension funds, with particular reference to the context of emerging economies.

Sarah Bracking is Professor of Climate and Society, School of Global Affairs, King's College London, and Honorary Senior Research Associate at the University of Johannesburg. She is editor of *Corruption and Development* (Palgrave, 2007); co-editor of *Valuing Development, Environment and Conservation* (Routledge, 2019); and author of *Money and Power* (Pluto, 2009) and *The Financialisation of Power in Africa* (Routledge, 2016).

Benjamin Braun is a Senior Researcher at the Max Planck Institute for the Study of Societies in Cologne and a member (2019–2020) of the Institute for Advanced Study in Princeton. He has published widely on the political economy of central banking, with a particular focus on central bank communication and on the central bank–finance nexus. In his current research, he focuses on the political economy of asset management.

Eve Chiapello holds a chair in the "Sociology of the transformation of capitalism" at EHESS (School for Advanced Studies in Social Sciences), Paris, France. Her present work is about the financialization of public policies, on which she has organized a series of international conferences with Universität Hamburg. She received the Anneliese Maier Research Award 2016 from The Humboldt Foundation. She has published the following books: *Artistes versus Managers* (Métaillé, 1998), *The New Spirit of Capitalism* (Verso 2005, with Luc Boltanski, first French edition 1999), translated into nine foreign languages, *Management Tools* (Cambridge University Press, 2019, with P. Gilbert, first French edition 2013), translated into English and Spanish, and numerous articles in international peer-reviewed journals.

Brett Christophers is Professor in the Department of Social and Economic Geography, Uppsala University. He is the author or co-author of six books, including most recently *The Great Leveler: Capitalism and Competition in the Court of Law* (Harvard University Press, 2016); *Economic Geography: A Critical Introduction* (with Trevor J. Barnes, Wiley-Blackwell, 2018) and *The New Enclosure: The Appropriation of Public Land in Neoliberal Britain* (Verso, 2018).

Nathan Coombs is Lecturer in Economic Sociology at the University of Edinburgh. He is founding co-editor of the journal *Finance and Society* and his current research focuses on post-crisis regulatory technologies. He has published his work in *Economy and Society, International Review of Economics Education, Journal of Cultural Economy, The European Legacy*, and *Journal of Political Ideologies*. His book, *History and Event*, was published by Edinburgh University Press in 2015.

Jean Cushen is a lecturer and director of postgraduate teaching and learning within the Business School of Maynooth University (MU). Jean's research focuses on financialization, human resource management (HRM) and the labor process.

Kavita Datta is Professor of Development Geography and Director of the Centre for the Study of Migration at Queen Mary University of London. Her research spans development and economic geography, and migration studies, contributing to critical understandings of transnational migration, financialization and migrants' financial practices. In addition to publishing numerous journal articles, Kavita is author of *Migrants and their Money: Surviving Financial Exclusion in London* (Polity Press, 2012), co-author of *Global Cities at Work: New Migrant Divisions of Labour* (Pluto Press, 2010) and co-editor of *Housing Finance in Developing Countries* (Routledge, 1999).

Christoph Deutschmann, born 1946, is Professor Emeritus and former Chair of Sociology at the University of Tübingen, Germany. His research interests and publications are in the fields of economic sociology, the sociology of work, and social theory.

Laura Deruytter is a researcher and FWO Fellow at Cosmopolis – Centre for Urban Research at the Vrije Universiteit Brussel. For her PhD research, she examines the changing nexus between finance and local governments in Belgium, with a focus on municipalities' engagement with financial markets through municipal companies and publicly owned banks. Laura holds a MSc in Geography from Ghent University. She is also editor of *AGORA*, Dutch-Flemish Magazine for Socio-Spatial Issues, and board member of FairFin, an NGO for sustainable and just finance.

Sheila Dow is Emeritus Professor of Economics at the University of Stirling, Scotland, and Adjunct Professor of Economics at the University of Victoria, Canada. Her main academic focus has been on raising methodological awareness in the fields of macroeconomics, money and banking, and the history of economic thought (especially Hume, Smith and Keynes). While her career has primarily been in academia, she has worked for the Bank of England and the Government of Manitoba, and as special advisor on monetary policy to the UK Treasury Select Committee. Her most recent book is *Foundations for New Economic Thinking* (Palgrave Macmillan, 2012).

Gerald Epstein is Professor of Economics and a founding Co-Director of the Political Economy Research Institute (PERI) at the University of Massachusetts Amherst. Epstein has written articles on numerous topics including financialization, financial crisis and regulation, and the political economy of central banking and financial institutions. He is the author, most recently, of *What's Wrong with Modern Money Theory: A Policy Critique* (Palgrave, 2019) and *The Political Economy of Central Banking: Contested Control and the Power of Finance* (Elgar, 2019). In recent years he has been the recipient of two INET grants on the financial system and monetary policy.

Ismail Ertürk is Senior Lecturer in Banking at Alliance Manchester Business School, The University of Manchester. His research interests are financialization, banking, financial regulation, post-crisis central banking, corporate governance and cultural political economy. He has co-authored and co-edited four books – on financialization, banking crisis and regulation, and post-crisis central banking – and numerous interdisciplinary academic articles. He has undertaken advisory work for companies and government institutions internationally. He has held various international visiting teaching and research positions. He regularly appears in international media including BBC and Bloomberg to comment on finance and economy.

Rodrigo Fernandez is a senior researcher at the Centre for Research on Multinational Corporations (SOMO). Previously he was a postdoc (2011–2013) at the University of Amsterdam and at KU Leuven/University of Leuven (2013–2019). Rodrigo has published on offshore financial centers, shadow banking, real estate and financialization. In his current research, he focuses on the financialization of non-financial corporations.

Jan Fichtner is postdoctoral researcher in the CORPNET project at the University of Amsterdam. His research interests lie in the interdisciplinary field of International Political Economy, particularly Global Finance, and cover index funds, the concentration of corporate ownership and control, structural power, financialization, hedge funds, and offshore financial centers. He is co-author of "Hidden power of the Big Three? Passive index funds, re-concentration of corporate ownership, and new financial risk", which has won the David P. Baron award for the best paper published in *Business & Politics* in 2017.

Ben Fine is Emeritus Professor of Economics at the School of Oriental and African Studies, University of London, UK, and Visiting Professor, Wits School of Governance, University of Witwatersrand, South Africa.

Daniela Gabor is Professor of Economics and Macro-Finance at the University of the West of England, Bristol. She holds a PhD in banking and finance from the University of Stirling (2009). Since then, she has published on central banking in crisis, on the governance of global banks and the IMF, on shadow banking and repo markets.

Vincent Guermond is a PhD researcher in the School of Geography at Queen Mary University of London. His research focuses on remittance market formation and the everyday lived experiences of financial(ized) inclusion processes in the Global South amongst remittance recipients in Senegal and Ghana. His research interests are in the areas of the geographies of financialization, marketization and financial inclusion, digital financial inclusion, work and social reproduction and the political economy of the migration–development nexus.

Olivier Godechot is Research Professor in Sociology (Sciences Po and OSC-CNRS) and the Co-Director of MaxPo research center, Paris, France. He is interested in the study of labor markets, especially finance and academic labor markets, as a means to understand the development of unequal exchange relations at work and their impact on the dynamics of inequality. He recently published *Wages, Bonuses and Appropriation of Profit in the Financial Industry* (Routledge, 2017).

Felipe González is assistant professor at the School of Government and Communication of the Universidad Central de Chile, Santiago. His postdoctoral project investigates the escalation of social conflict surrounding student debt, with a special focus on the emergence of social movements of debtors. He is editor – together with Aldo Madariaga – of *Economic Sociology, the Electronic European Newsletter*, edited by the Max Planck Institute for the Study of Societies in Cologne, Germany (period 2018–2019). Some of his publications include "Crédito, deuda y gubernamentalidad financier en Chile" (*Revista Mexicana de Sociología*) and "Where are the Consumers? Real Households and the Financialization of Consumption" (*Cultural Studies*).

Max Haiven is Canada Research Chair in Culture, Media and Social Justice at Lakehead University in Northwest Ontario and co-director of the ReImagining Value Action Lab (RiVAL). He writes articles for both academic and general audiences and is the author of books including *The Radical Imagination: Social Movement Research in the Age of Austerity* (with Alex Khasnabish, Zed, 2014), *Cultures of Financialization: Fictitious Capital in Popular Culture and Everyday Life* (Palgrave, 2014) and, most recently, *Art after Money, Money after Art: Creative Strategies Against Financialization* (Pluto, 2018).

Brooke Harrington is Professor of Sociology at Dartmouth College in the United States. Her research examines the social underpinnings of markets, and for the past dozen years has focused on professionals in offshore finance. She is the author of *Capital without Borders* (Harvard, 2016), winner of an American Sociological Association Outstanding Book Award (section on Inequality, Poverty & Mobility). Her articles have appeared in peer-reviewed journals such as *Human Relations, Socio-Economic Review, Social Psychology Quarterly* and *Family Business Review*, as well as in the *Washington Post*, the *Guardian*, and the *Atlantic*. Her PhD was awarded by Harvard University.

Reijer Hendrikse is a postdoctoral researcher at the Vrije Universiteit Brussel, Belgium. His research interests are broadly centered around the dynamic interlinkages between corporate and state structures, with a focus on finance, business services and technology. In 2015 Reijer received his PhD from the University of Amsterdam for his dissertation "The long arm of finance: Exploring the unlikely financialization of governments and public institutions." Amongst other subjects, Reijer has published on the financialization of local authorities and universities, the rise of financial technology, and the evolution of neoliberalism.

Ariane Hillig is a Lecturer in Economics at Goldsmiths, University of London. Her doctoral research in Economics and Finance took place at The Open University Business School. Prior to that, Ariane was a visiting lecturer in Germany and worked several years in the private sector. Her current research interests are centered on the impact of financialization on everyday life. In particular, she is interested in interdisciplinary approaches in studying financialization, combining social theory, finance, cultural and political economy. These interests are also reflected in her recent publication: "Everyday financialization: The case of UK households" (*Environment and Planning A*).

Annina Kaltenbrunner is Associate Professor in the Economics of Globalisation and the International Economy at Leeds University Business School. Her research focuses on financial processes and relations in emerging capitalist economies. She has published on financial integration, currency internationalization and macroeconomic policy, among others, in the *Cambridge Journal of Economics, Development & Change, Environment and Planning A, the Post Keynesian Journal of Economics, and New Political Economy*. She has participated in several large externally funded projects and is currently collaborating with the Brazilian Central Bank on currency regionalization and regional payment systems.

Ewa Karwowski is senior lecturer in economics at Hertfordshire Business School and senior research associate at the University of Johannesburg. Before joining University of Hertfordshire, she was a faculty member at Kingston University, London. Ewa holds a PhD from SOAS, University of London. She has worked as consultant for international organizations (OECD, ILO), including as ODI fellow in the National Treasury, South Africa. Her research interests include finance and development, the financialization of firms, and Kaleckian economics. Ewa is board member of the Post-Keynesian Economics Society, part of the International Initiative for Promoting Political Economy and member of Reteaching Economics.

Samuel Knafo is a Senior Lecturer in the Department of International Relations at the University of Sussex. He is the author of *The Making of Modern Finance: Liberal Governance and the Gold Standard* (Routledge, 2013). He has recently published various articles on shareholder value, financialization and the place of managerialism within neoliberalism.

Karsten Kohler is a lecturer in International Political Economy at King's College London. His research interests include open-economy macroeconomics, financial and business cycles, financialization and inequality.

Karen Lai is Associate Professor at the Department of Geography, Durham University. Her research interests include geographies of money and finance, market formation, service sectors, global city networks and financial center development. Her recent project examines everyday financialization through the knowledge networks of financial advisors and consumers. She is currently working on two projects regarding the global financial networks of investment banks and law firms, and how FinTech could be reshaping the roles of financial centers. She is on the Executive Committees of the Global Network on Financial Geography (FinGeo) and the Economic Geography Research Group of the Royal Geographical Society (with Institute of British Geographers). She is also on the journal editorial boards of *Geoforum* and *Geography Compass* (Economic section).

Paul Langley is Professor of Economic Geography at Durham University, UK. His publications include *Liquidity Lost* (Oxford University Press, 2015), *The Everyday Life of Global Finance* (Oxford University Press, 2008), and *World Financial Orders* (Routledge, 2002). His present research focuses on the emergence and stabilization of new forms of finance in the wake of the global financial crisis, including "FinTech," "green finance," and "social finance."

Christina Laskaridis is a Research Fellow at Duke University's Center for the History of Political Economy and Doctoral Researcher in Economics at SOAS, University of London. Research interests include financial globalization, debt and monetary debates in historical perspective, and the International Monetary Fund. Christina Laskaridis was a member of the Hellenic Parliament's Debt Audit Commission.

Lena Lavinas has a PhD in Economics from the University of Paris. She is Professor of Welfare Economics at the Federal University of Rio de Janeiro. Most of her research focuses on the design of social policies and their impact on poverty reduction and inequality; on comparative analysis of welfare regimes in Latin America; on socio-economic development in Brazil and Latin America; and on labor markets and gender issues. Her recent publications include "The collateralization of social policy under financialized capitalism" (*Development and Change*, vol. 49 issue 2, Forum, 2018) and *The Takeover of Social Policy by Financialization: The Brazilian Paradox* (Palgrave Macmillan, 2017).

Jeanne Lazarus is a tenured CNRS research fellow at the CSO in Sciences-po (Paris). Her research has focused on relationships between bankers and customers in French retail banks. She has also conducted research on the sociology of money and the consumption and monetary practices of the impoverished. She is currently studying the public policies surrounding individual money management in particular via education programs aimed at improving financial literacy, directives, and regulations regarding the commercialization of financial products and credit. She published *L'Epreuve de l'argent* in 2012, and edited several special issues on banking, credit and money management.

Nathan Legrand is a political scientist whose fields of study focus on sovereign debt, the labor movement and the alterglobalization movement. He currently works for the Committee for the abolition of illegitimate debts (CADTM) in Belgium.

Philip Mader is a Research Fellow at the Institute of Development Studies (Brighton, UK) and program convenor of the MA in Globalisation, Business and Development. His research focuses on development and the politics of markets. His PhD from the Max Planck Institute for the Study of Societies and the University of Cologne was published as *The Political Economy of Microfinance: Financializing Poverty* (Palgrave, 2015) and was recognized with the Otto Hahn Medal and the German Thesis Award.

Michael A. McCarthy is an Assistant Professor of Sociology at Marquette University. There he writes and teaches on the state, capitalism, and social theory. His recent book is *Dismantling Solidarity: Capitalist Politics and American Pensions since the New Deal* published with Cornell University Press in 2017. The project he is currently undertaking explores the politics of public finance.

Daniel Mertens is Professor of International Political Economy at the University of Osnabrück. Prior to that, he was an assistant professor at Goethe University Frankfurt and a visiting scholar at Northwestern University. He received his PhD from the Max Planck Institute for the Study of Societies and the University of Cologne. His work ranges from the politics of credit markets and banking to analyses of the modern tax state and has been published in outlets such as the *Journal of European Public Policy, New Political Economy* and *Competition & Change*.

Sebastian Möller is a Political Economy researcher at the Institute for Intercultural and International Studies (InIIS) and Program Coordinator for the Master Political Science and the Master International Relations at the University of Bremen. He conducts a PhD project on the use of interest rate derivatives by British, German and Austrian local governments with a particular focus on modes of financial intermediation. Sebastian holds a MA in Political Science from Goethe University Frankfurt and a BA in History and Political Science from the University of Wuppertal and has been a visiting researcher at Manchester Business School and Johannes Kepler University Linz.

Johnna Montgomerie is a Reader in International Political Economy and Head of Department in European and International Studies at King's College London She has written extensively on financialization, debt, austerity and the household; most recently in *Geoforum*, with Daniela Tepe-Belfrage "Cultures of debt resistance." Her most recent policy focused book *Should We Abolish Household Debt?* is published by Policy and an experimental collection *Critical Methods in Political and Cultural Economy*, published by Routledge.

Andreas Nölke is Professor of Political Science with a particular focus on International Relations and International Political Economy at Goethe University (Frankfurt). He also is associated with the Centre for the Study of Globalisation and Regionalisation/CSGR at the University of Warwick. Before joining Goethe University, he taught at the universities of Konstanz, Leipzig, Amsterdam and Utrecht. He has published in journals such as the *Review of International Political Economy, World Politics, Business and Politics*, the *European Journal of International Relations*, the *Review of African Political Economy*, the *Socio-Economic Review* and the *Journal of Common Market Studies*.

Stefano Pagliari is a Senior Lecturer in the International Politics Department at City, University of London. His research covers a number of themes related to international political economy and comparative political economy, with a particular focus on the political economy of financial regulation. He has edited together with Eric Helleiner and Irene Spagna the volume *Governing the World's Biggest Market. The Politics of Derivatives Regulation After the 2008 Crisis* (Oxford University Press).

Johannes Petry is an ESRC Doctoral Research Fellow and PhD Candidate in International Political Economy in the Department of Politics and International Studies at the University of Warwick. His work focuses on the political economy of securities exchanges and their role in capital market development. In his current research project, he analyses the development of capital markets in China, their internationalization and integration into global capital markets, and the role of exchanges in these processes. His research interests include the comparative and interdisciplinary analysis of financial markets, systems and crises as well as the political economy of emerging markets.

Jeff Powell is Senior Lecturer in Economics at the University of Greenwich, with research interests in finance and development, financialization and monetary economics. He is a member of the Institute of Political Economy, Governance, Finance and Accountability (PEGFA). Jeff is a founding member of the UK network of pluralist economists, Reteaching Economics.

Signe Predmore is a PhD Candidate in Political Science at University of Massachusetts Amherst. She is an interdisciplinary scholar with a background in anthropology and interest in feminist and critical race approaches to political economy. Her research concerns the contentious politics around trade policy, and the post-2008 gender diversity agenda in finance.

Sunanda Sen was Professor of Economics Jawaharlal Nehru University in New Delhi. She has also been a visiting professor at several universities in Europe, USA and UK. Her publications include a large number of books and articles in reputed journals. Her most recently published books include *The Changing Face of Imperialism: Colonies to Contemporary Capitalism* (Routledge, 2018) and *Dominant Finance and Stagnant Economies* (Oxford University Press, 2014). A former National Fellow of the Indian Council of Social Science, she was also a Joan Robinson Memorial Lecturer at Faculty of Economics, Cambridge. She is a Life member at Clare Hall, Cambridge, UK, and Research Associate at the Levy Institute of Economics, USA.

Dimitris P. Sotiropoulos is a Senior Lecturer in Finance at The Open University Business School. Prior to that he worked as lecturer and researcher in academic institutions in the United Kingdom, Germany, and Greece. His research interests are focused on the political economy of finance, the social aspects of risk management and the history of financial innovation. He has published three books, the most recent one being *The Political Economy of Contemporary Capitalism and Its Crisis: Demystifying Finance* (Routledge, 2013). His papers in journals and edited volumes cover research areas in business history, history of economic thought, and political economy.

Engelbert Stockhammer is professor of International Political Economy at King's College London. His research areas include macroeconomics, financialization, distribution and growth, and economic policy in Europe. He has published more than 60 articles in peer-refereed journals and is ranked among the top five percent of economists worldwide by REPEC. Recent books include *Wage-Led Growth. An Equitable Strategy for Economic Recovery* (Palgrave Macmillan, 2013).

Dennis Stolz obtained his PhD degree in Geography at the National University of Singapore. His thesis "Philanthro-capitalism and the production of space" cross-fertilises his interests in the geographies of money and finance with works in the Marxian political economy tradition. His interest in capitalist development in Asia stems from earlier work experience in the region; after completing his masters in economic geography at the Goethe-University in Frankfurt am Main, he worked at the German Society for International Cooperation in New Delhi, India. He has also held positions at the Deutsche Börse Group and the Financial Times Deutschland. Currently, he works for an economic development agency in Düsseldorf.

Matthias Thiemann is Assistant Professor at Sciences Po Centre d'Etudes Européennes. He is also an external fellow at the Research Center SAFE (Sustainable Architecture for Finance in

Europe), Goethe University Frankfurt. His work focuses on the regulation of financial markets pre- and post-crisis, its structural settings and the constrained agency of regulators in these circumstances. His work has appeared, inter alia in the *American Journal of Sociology*, the *Review of International Political Economy* and the *Journal of European Public Policy* and most recently in the book *The Growth of Shadow Banking: A Comparative Institutional Analysis* (Cambridge University Press, 2018).

Paul Thompson is Professor of Employment Studies in the School of Management at the University of Stirling, Scotland. He researches on the links between financialized business models and work and employment outcomes, and more generally on the changing nature of capitalism, managerial regimes and worker resistance. His extensive work has been published in seven languages and he is Convener of the International Labour Process Conference.

Eric Toussaint is a historian and political scientist with a PhD from the universities of Paris VIII and Liège. He is spokesperson for the CADTM (Committee for the abolition of illegitimate debt) international network. He is the author of a dozen of books, including *The Debt System: A History of Sovereign Debts and their Repudiation* (Haymarket, 2019) and *Bankocracy* (Resistance Books, 2015). Several of his books have been published in a dozen languages and have become reference works: *Debt, the IMF, and the World Bank: Sixty Questions, Sixty Answers* (Monthly Review, New York, 2010) and *The World Bank: A Critical Primer* (Pluto, 2008). He has taken part in producing two manuals for conducting citizens' audits and was a member of the Hellenic Parliament's Debt Audit Commission and the Ecuadorian Debt Audit Commission.

Arjen van der Heide is postdoctoral research fellow at the Max Planck Institute for the Study of Societies. He obtained his PhD from the University of Edinburgh, studying the emergence of new modes of risk management in contemporary British life insurance. His current research focuses on the evolution of trading in European sovereign debt.

Natascha van der Zwan is Assistant Professor in Public Administration at Leiden University. She does comparative and historical research on financialization and pension systems, investment rules and regulations, and pension fund capitalism. Her article "Making sense of financialization" (*Socio-Economic Review*, 2014) has become a key article in scholarship on financialization and is widely used in university courses. Dr. Van der Zwan holds a PhD in Political Science from the New School for Social Research.

Yingyao Wang is Assistant Professor of Sociology at the University of Virginia. Her research interests include the sociology of bureaucracy, state–market relations, public finance, development, and sociological analysis of the elites. She is currently working on projects related to the Chinese statecraft, political corruption, street-level taxation, and the subnational logic of global investment. Besides her empirical work, she also writes about social and organizational theory.

Beat Weber is an economist and political scientist at Oesterreichische Nationalbank, the central bank of Austria. He lives in Vienna. In studying the political economy of money and finance, he recently focused on monetary theory. His book *Democratizing Money? Debating Legitimacy in Monetary Reform Proposals* (Cambridge University Press, 2018) contains a critical examination of various monetary reform proposals.

Hadas Weiss is Tomás y Valiente Fellow at the Madrid Institute for Advanced Study, researching social aspects of contemporary capitalism in Israel, Germany and Spain. She has published in various anthropology and cross-disciplinary journals, and is the author of *We Have Never Been Middle Class: How Social Mobility Misleads Us* (Verso, 2019).

Gertjan Wijburg is assistant professor of Urban Planning and Economic Geography at Utrecht University, the Netherlands. Previously, he was a PhD Candidate and teaching assistant at the KU Leuven/University of Leuven (Belgium). He has published on real estate, financialization, (urban) political economy and modern architecture.

Kevin L. Young is Associate Professor in the Department of Political Science at the University of Massachusetts Amherst. His work focuses on international political economy, especially the operation of interest group coalitions and elite networks. He is the author (with Thomas Hale and David Held) of *Gridlock: Why Global Cooperation is Failing When it is Most Needed* (Polity Press, 2013), and has published work in *Review of International Political Economy, Public Administration, Regulation and Governance, Socio-Economic Review* and *International Studies Quarterly*.

1

FINANCIALIZATION: AN INTRODUCTION

Philip Mader, Daniel Mertens and Natascha van der Zwan

Introduction[1]

In countries across Asia, variations on a parable are told. A group of blind men encounter an elephant and, having never "seen" one before, one boldly reaches out, feels the elephant's leg, and tells the others that it is very much like a tree. A second touches its side, and reports that the elephant is, in fact, quite like a wall; a third touches the trunk and finds it is a big snake; another touches the tail (a rope); another its tusk (a spear); and so on. Depending on the variant, the parable ends either with the blind men disagreeing about the nature of the beast, perhaps even coming to blows over it, or with them wisely conferring on what they have learned, understanding that each was only partially correct, and recognizing that only together could they fully comprehend the beast.

At times, in the financialization literature, one might have been reminded of this parable; certainly not in the sense of scholars being blind or ignorant of others' perspectives, but in the sense of very different approaches having led them to divergent claims about the nature of financialization. This has involved tendencies to regard financialization as primarily, or *essentially*, one particular thing: as the increasing power of financial interests over politics, as the growing dominance of financial logics or "shareholder value," as changes in the spatial organization of the global economy, as the reconfiguration of society and the class system, or as the mutation of culture and how we relate to ourselves. Yet these are not mutually exclusive, and only together give the whole picture.

Arguably, the existence of many different approaches within financialization scholarship has also been central to the term's wide reception and uptake in recent years, particularly since the 2007–2008 Great Financial Crisis. Financialization has become the go-to term among a growing field of scholarship that studies the vastly expanded role played by finance in contemporary politics, economy and society. The concept of financialization itself has also expanded, evolving from a rather niche term used by critical scholars into one that increasingly informs research across and beyond the social sciences and humanities. We aim for this book to advance financialization studies, whose constitution as a field this volume documents, by bringing into conversation a wide range of perspectives from across disciplines and schools, in order to better understand the nature of the beast – and, to an extent, to make sure we are still talking about the same beast. As the contributions to this Handbook make clear, to work in a transdisciplinary way first requires an understanding of the specific contributions that particular (other) disciplines can make.

For this book, we have sought to reflect the breadth and depth of the financialization field, not just by including contributions from a wide range of disciplines (see especially Parts A and B) – except, alas, mainstream economics, which remains as ignorant of financialization as it remains at a loss for convincing explanations of financial crises[2] – but also by distinguishing different sets of perspectives on financialization. These include more structural and spatial ones (Part C), more agency-oriented and political ones (Part D), and more technological and cultural ones (Part E). With this, the Handbook invites readers to look over and across established horizons. And, in a world in which finance is often, by the public as well as some scholars, still largely equated with Anglo-America and with the financial system narrowly defined, we endeavor for the Handbook to reflect the highly spatially and segmentally variegated financializations that different institutions, people and societies are entangled with. Participants in financialization include not just bankers, investors and wealth managers in "high finance" and on Wall Street, but also microcredit borrowers and welfare recipients in the global South, mid-sized cities' municipal authorities, state-owned enterprises, multinational corporations and philanthropic organizations, which are all connected through a branching web of financial claims.

While aiming to broaden horizons, we also hope for this volume to help more clearly situate and delineate financialization and define its boundaries. This means to check a potentially harmful tendency toward the term being applied loosely, with "financialization" increasingly – to exaggerate only somewhat – being seen anywhere and everywhere there has lately been social, economic, political or cultural change. Simply to diagnose ever-more "financializations of" particular things and "financializations in" particular places risks devaluing the core conceptual currency of financialization studies. This is why we must take up the challenge brought by Brett Christophers (2015), to articulate more clearly "the limits to financialization." We would argue that to maintain its value, financialization studies must more clearly than ever distinguish – connect yet contrast clearly – its objects of interest from the other "elephants in the room," which include but are not limited to: commodification, marketization, globalization, neoliberalization, privatization, digitalization and precarization. In other words, financialization scholars must recognize and highlight financialization as but one "tendency among tendencies" in the transformation of capitalist societies,[3] which has both causes and effects in other contemporaneous processes (see e.g. Davis and Walsh 2017).

Our aim for this introduction is to offer a broad map on which financialization studies can be plotted across the academic disciplines that have contributed to it, showing its emergence and growth (Section 1), and then providing an overview of the commonly proposed definitions of financialization and clarifying our own position on them (Section 2). Our chapter ends with an outline of the various contributions to this volume (Section 3), followed by a brief outlook for the field (Section 4).

Financialization: a brief history of the field

The enormous popularity of the concept of financialization has led to an outpouring of publications over the past decade. Since 2010, the number of annually published journal articles on financialization has more than quadrupled, to almost 400 (Web of Science 2019; see also Figure 1.1). Book publications, while smaller in number, have followed a similar trend: while only a handful of books existed in the early years of the 21st century, now more than a dozen books on financialization are published each year (WorldCat 2019).[4] Financialization has also entered public discourse through the works of people like academic-turned-politician Yanis Varoufakis (2011) and journalists Rana Foroohar (2016) and Nicholas Shaxson (2018). They have taken the social-scientific concept and placed it center stage in their own popular narratives of "finance capitalism." Should these trends continue, financialization – that "wonky but apt moniker picked up by academics" (Foroohar 2016: 6) – could very well enter mainstream vocabularies.

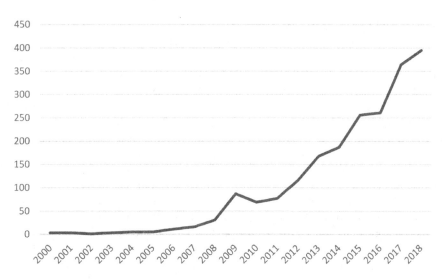

Figure 1.1 Journal articles with topic financialization by year
Source: Figure 1.1 reports the number of articles published in the years 2000–2018 that have either "financialization" or "financialisation" listed as keyword. The data presented here were collected from the *Social Science Citation Index* (Web of Science 2019). A search on article topics with either "financialization" or "financialisation" generated 2.112 article titles, which were subsequently grouped by year.

The speed and scale at which financialization scholarship has grown over the past decade invites us to take stock of its development. According to John Bellamy Foster, the origins of the term, which first appeared in the early 1990s, are "obscure" (Foster 2007: 1).[5] Many diagnoses of financialization in this period drew parallels to an earlier period of economic and political domination by "finance capital" and rentier classes around the turn of the 20th century, written about by Lenin, Rudolf Hilferding, Michał Kalecki and John Maynard Keynes. They also sought to highlight the differences and explain why the end of the post-war "Golden Age" of capitalism had given rise to financial expansion. The earliest figurations of the research enterprise, such as in the works of Harry Magdoff and Paul Sweezy (1987), explained the increasingly central role of finance and particularly debt as a response to the stagnation that ended the post-World War II American boom, and argued that America was becoming a "casino society." However, contrary to what many of their contemporary Keynesians thought, Magdoff and Sweezy's Marxian perspective suggested that the growth of financial markets was not undermining or replacing the production of goods and (non-financial) services, and rather increasingly becoming a prerequisite for it.

Exemplary for the subsequent manifestations of financialization scholarship is the collection *Financialization at Work* by Ismail Erturk and co-editors (2008), whose selection of contributions reveals the grounding of the concept in the history of economic thought. Erturk et al. took cues from John Maynard Keynes, early 20th century economic historian and philosopher R.H. Tawney, and corporate governance theorists (and F.D. Roosevelt advisors) Adolph Berle and Gardiner Means, as well as their agency-theoretical critics Michael Jensen and Eugene Fama, whose works fueled the neoliberal counterrevolution in economics. The contributions of financialization scholars leading into the mid-2000s reflected the different perspectives on financialization that characterized the scholarship from its very beginning: the critical accounting approach of the Manchester School, represented for instance by Julie Froud and collaborators (2000); the Regulationist approach exemplified by Robert Boyer's (2000) work; the heterodox economics of Engelbert Stockhammer

(2004) and Gerald Epstein (2005); the corporate governance perspectives of William Lazonick and Mary O'Sullivan (2000); and the cultural economy approaches of Randy Martin (2002) and Paul Langley (2004), to give some examples.[6] Some of the most influential conceptualizations of the term originated in this early scholarship, including the widely-employed definitions offered by Epstein (2005), Krippner (2005) and Stockhammer (2004; see also the next section of this chapter).

The scholarship on financialization entered a new phase in the years following the Great Financial Crisis, as the events of 2007–2008 served as a wake-up call, or reminder of the destructive scale and power of financial systems, prompting a much wider scholarly reckoning with finance and an increased usage of the term financialization. Moving away from public corporations and "financial markets" in the abstract, scholars scrutinized a host of financial actors – including but not limited to institutional investors and investment vehicles – and a host of different markets – bond markets, commodity markets, housing markets, welfare markets, and so on (see e.g. Aalbers 2008; Dixon and Sorsa 2009; Finlayson 2009; Montgomerie 2009; Fichtner 2013; Gospel et al. 2014). Finally, scholars also became more attuned to the variegated nature of the financialization process, focusing on places beyond Anglo-America (e.g. Engelen and Konings 2010; French et al. 2011). This led to the now-commonplace understanding that financialization cannot be reduced *simpliciter* to a global isomorphism towards Anglo-American finance capitalism but needs to be understood in relation to national/local contexts on the one hand and the global capitalist system on the other, even as the latter undeniably bears the historical legacy of US hegemony (Konings 2011). Illustrative in this regard are the works by Daniela Gabor (2010) on Eastern Europe, Lena Rethel (2010), Iain Hardie (2012) and Bruno Bonizzi (2013) on emerging economies, and the wide geographical reach of the FESSUD project (see FESSUD Studies in Financial Systems 2013).

This trend of broadening the scope of financialization studies has continued into the contemporary period, in which scholars have had to deal with the resilience of finance and financialization post-crisis; what one might call the "strange non-death" of financialization (cf. Crouch 2011). In recent years, we have gained a more thorough understanding of the driving forces of continued financialization, not least thanks to a growing scholarship on the role of the state and other "non-financial" actors (e.g. Nölke et al. 2013; Van der Zwan 2017). The scholarship has highlighted the inflections of finance with areas such as the food system (Clapp and Isakson 2018), the environment (Bayliss 2014; Ouma, Johnson and Bigger 2018), national treasuries (Lagna 2016; Fastenrath, Schwan and Trampusch 2017) and international development (Mader 2015; Mawdsley 2018; Storm 2018): often not merely as an intrusion, but also as a tool wielded by some players within these arenas. Noteworthy are also the ways in which scholars are exploring the boundaries of the concept by tackling theoretically and empirically complex manifestations, such as offshore finance, shadow banking and other frontlines of financial engineering (Ban and Gabor 2016; Botzem and Dobusch 2017).

The growth of the financialization scholarship coincided with its diffusion across academic disciplines. While (heterodox) economics and geography together account for the largest share of published articles on financialization, other fields – such as anthropology, accounting studies, development studies, political science and sociology – also have a clear presence in the scholarship (see Figure 1.2). The broad appeal of the concept might be explained by the subject's sheer complexity: each approach highlights aspects of financialization that other disciplines are less inclined or able to grasp. At the same time, the importance of interdisciplinary journals such as *Competition & Change* or *Socio-Economic Review* for this scholarship also signals how financialization *defies* disciplinary boundaries.

Over time, however, we can also observe a growing concern for the continued usefulness, or value, of the concept, driven by diagnoses of the dilution of the term as a result of its diffusion (cf. Christophers 2015; Aalbers 2020). In other words, the spread of the financialization concept

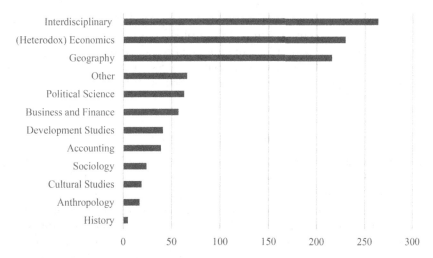

Figure 1.2 Articles with topic financialization by discipline
Note: Figure 1.2 presents the number of articles with the topic "financialization" or "financialisation" in journals that have published at least five such articles between 2000 and 2019 for each academic discipline, using data collected from the *Social Science Citation Index* (Web of Science 2019). Each journal was categorized as belonging to a particular discipline, based on title words. In case of doubt, we read the journal's mission statement to establish with which academic discipline(s) the journal self-identified. The category "interdisciplinary" contains journals such as *Competition & Change* or *Socio-Economic Review*, which list more than one academic discipline, as well as a host of Marxist journals. The category "other" contains journals that defied easy categorization, such as journals of industrial relations or agricultural studies.

across disciplinary boundaries brings risks. One such risk is *conceptual dilution*: if the adoption of the concept in different academic fields requires a more generic understanding of what financialization means, then the concept could atrophy to become a meme (an object passed on by mere imitation) without meaning. Another, opposite, risk is that of *solidification*: if one standardized definition becomes the norm for scholarship on financialization in a particular sub-field or school of thought, and a too rigid understanding of financialization leads to the blind-men problem and failure to recognize or account for new mutations of finance.

Ultimately, the growth of financialization studies reflects the need for an analytical vocabulary that captures key empirical developments in contemporary capitalism. Yet, the growth of financialization studies simultaneously warrants a more critical question: if rooted in such disparate academic fields and approaches, what unites this body of scholarship? While impossible to do justice to the variety within the scholarship, we can identify three shared affinities. First, financialization scholars depart from an understanding of finance as not subservient to the productive economy but as an autonomous realm that increasingly influences and even dominates other realms of society. Financialization scholars recognize and seek to understand and explain this emancipation of finance. Second, they almost uniformly assess this development as a negative one. Their point of departure is critique, not acceptance, of the empirical developments they analyze, which they often link to other socio-economic and political developments, such as rising inequality, macroeconomic instability, social precarity, and loss of democratic accountability. Third and finally, financialization scholars study finance not only, or even primarily, as an economic issue. Unlike those who work in mainstream finance traditions, financialization scholars, including those departing from (heterodox) economics, connect changes in finance with other shifts in politics, economics, social relations and culture, and articulate these as causes and consequences. It is precisely this recognition of finance as part of a socially created world that has enabled financialization scholarship to proceed in "explicit opposition to the Panglossian view of modern mainstream economics that financial markets, warts and all, provide the best possible mode of social regulation" (Storm 2018: 304). The embedding of finance within society, epistemologically as well as politically, is cardinal to financialization studies' power of critique.

Defining financialization

Defining what financialization actually is has been a key concern for both proponents and critics of the term. Repeatedly designated as "too broad" or "too vague," definitional issues have followed the financialization concept from its inception. What has contributed to this concern is the very success of definitions that have proven to be sufficiently encompassing to allow different approaches to tie in. This is particularly true for Gerald Epstein's seminal and deliberately broad notion that "financialization means the increasing role of financial motives, financial markets, financial actors and financial institutions in the operation of the domestic and international economies" (Epstein 2005: 3). Arguably, some of its building blocks raise definitional issues themselves, but Epstein's formulation certainly facilitated the consolidation of the field by providing a definitional handle that suited a wide range of research endeavors. In comparison, the similarly oft-quoted definition of financialization as "a pattern of accumulation in which profits accrue primarily through financial channels rather than through trade and commodity production" provided by Greta Krippner (2005: 174), was much more specific and attuned to particular empirical material. It triggered a debate over the relative weight of financial profits – or "profit financialization" – in the economy and within non-financial firms (see e.g. Nölke and Perry 2007; Van Treeck 2009; Christophers 2018). Other definitions also signal specific theoretical traditions, as for instance with a Marxist understanding of financialization as the "increasing incorporation of IBC [interest-bearing capital] into the circuits of capital" (Fine 2013: 62; *contra* Lapavitsas 2011).

Table 1.1 summarizes the definitions given in the most-frequently referenced contributions to financialization studies. One way to map this landscape of definitions is to distinguish roughly between three levels of analysis (Van der Zwan 2014): *macro*-level approaches, which usually focus on the transformation of capitalist accumulation or changes in macroeconomic aggregates and often engage with a state/market-dichotomy in processes of financialization; *meso*-level analyses, which put (mostly non-financial) corporations center stage and examine issues of ownership and control as well as changing corporate relations with financial markets; and *micro*-level approaches, which highlight how (mostly) non-elite actors are implicated in a "financiali-zation of daily life," zooming in on financial practices and rationalities in, for instance, saving and borrowing. This threefold heuristic helps to organize definitional issues and approaches, even though the borders between the levels of analysis are not always rigid.

Concerns about the definitional trade-off between breadth and depth – producing either a vague notion of financialization or a plethora of fine-tuned definitions – are evident in three types of critiques. The first is prominently articulated by Ewald Engelen's (2008) warning of *conceptual stretching* (Sartori 1970), which enabled scholarship to produce a vast amount of "financialization of" accounts, albeit through frequently neglecting the conceptual value added as well as questions of historical specificity. The second point of critique emerges from scholars' distinct treatment of financialization, sometimes as *explanandum* (what is to be explained), sometimes as *explanans* (the explanation) and sometimes as intervening mechanism between cause and effect – a point most forcefully made by Manuel Aalbers. According to Aalbers (2020: 2), the imprecision of concepts like financialization stems from the very empirical complexities they

Table 1.1 Main definitions of financialization

Author (Year)	Definition of financialization	Main level of analysis
Epstein (2005: 3)	"the increasing role of financial motives, financial markets, financial actors and financial institutions in the operation of the domestic and international economies"	Macro
Krippner (2005: 174)	"a pattern of accumulation in which profits accrue primarily through financial channels rather than through trade and commodity production"	Macro
Boyer (2000: 121)*	process by which "all the elements of national demand bear the consequences of the dominance of finance"	Macro
Tang & Xiong (2010: 3)	"process [...] through which commodity prices became more correlated with prices of financial assets and with each other"	Macro
Martin (2002: 43)	"insinuates an orientation toward accounting and risk management into all domains of life"	Micro
Stockhammer (2004: 720)	"increased activity of non-financial businesses on financial markets, [...] measured by the corresponding income streams"	Meso
Palley (2008: 29)	"(1) elevate the significance of the financial sector relative to the real sector; (2) transfer income from the real sector to the financial sector; and (3) contribute to increased income inequality and wage stagnation"	Macro
Froud et al. (2006: 4)	"changes induced by the rhetoric of shareholder value [which] sets firms and households utopian objectives such as value creation by management intervention for giant firms or security through stock-market saving for households"	Meso-Micro
Froud et al. (2000: 104)	"a new form of competition which involves a change in orientation towards financial results but also a kind of speed up in management work"	Meso
Aalbers (2008: 149)	"capital switching from the primary, secondary or tertiary circuit to the quaternary circuit of capital [...]; that is, the rise of financial markets not for the facilitation of other markets but for the trade in money, credit, securities, etc."	Macro
Orhangazi (2008: 864)	"designate[s] the changes that have taken place in the relationship between the non-financial corporate sector and financial markets"	Meso

Notes: Selection based on articles carrying "financialization" or "financialisation" in title, and Google Scholar citations > 500, last accessed Feb. 14, 2019; *derived, no explicit definition of financialization given and does not carry "financialization" in title.

aim to analytically make sense of: "While this may initially create more confusion, it also reflects an, often implicit, acknowledgement that we do not live in a closed system in which causations are linear, one-dimensional, and single-scalar." A third set of critiques takes issue with the simplistic transfer of conceptualizations based on Anglo-American capitalism to other parts of the world. While few would deny the power of the Anglosphere, expressed in part through the location of dominant financial centers, the universalization of the Anglophone trajectory towards financialization simply does not do justice to empirical developments elsewhere. This concern for contextualization mainly informs scholarship aimed at identifying variegated trajectories of financialization among both advanced and emerging or developing economies (e.g. Engelen and Konings 2010; Lapavitsas and Powell 2013; Karwowski and Stockhammer 2017; Mertens 2017).

Reflecting these critiques, we refrain from offering yet another novel definition or conceptualization of financialization. Instead, we argue that to be most valuable, definitions or conceptualizations of financialization that are adopted or proposed by scholars should follow particular principles. They should be: 1) *limiting*, in the sense of helping us recognize what is financialization and what is not; 2) *mechanism-oriented*, in the sense of clarifying the linkage of cause and effect; and 3) *contextual*, in the sense of making clear what contexts they claim validity for. *Limiting* conceptualizations will make explicit how the empirical phenomena under study relate to, but are not the same as, those already covered by other terms in our conceptual vocabulary, such as marketization or commodification, which is important for counteracting the risk of conceptual stretching and dilution. *Mechanism-oriented* articulations of financialization link effects to causes, bearing in mind Aalbers' (2019) injunction to recognize causation as often non-linear, multi-dimensional, and multi-scalar. An orientation to mechanisms produces research that moves beyond description, association or correlation, and instead counteracts unfounded assertions that certain things (places, sectors, domains of life, and so on) are, or have become, "more financialized," by forcing a clarification of *how* and *why* this happened. Finally, *contextualization* means more than just to acknowledge the fact that financialization takes different forms in different places, and that what is true for Anglo-America is not true everywhere. Insightful research compares the "apples and oranges" (Locke and Thelen 1995) of financialization, thus accounting for the difference in meaning that financialization may have across time and space, while clarifying what roots disparate financial phenomena have in common.

Lastly, moving beyond concepts and definitions, we argue that financialization researchers must work with an eye to clarifying the significance of their findings, from an academic perspective as well as, above all, from a wider societal perspective. This means to answer clearly the "so what?" question: what does it mean, in the bigger picture, to recognize and understand a particular facet of financialization? How is it significant, also for those outside the academy, including policymakers?[7] It means to be clear about what part of the whole – the elephant, as it were – one's own research comprises, and what it says about the whole.

Organization of the Handbook

The 40 contributions to this Handbook are individual pieces of the multifaceted whole of financialization studies. As parts of a pluralistic endeavor to grapple with financialization, the contributions to this volume differ in terms of their conceptualization of finance and money, the nature of state–economy relations, and even the ontological and epistemological foundations of the subject matter. As outlined above, this plurality is both a blessing and a challenge for financialization scholarship – and this is especially true for any effort to give orientation to those approaching financialization studies from the outside, as scholars or students entering the field.

The six sections of the Handbook thus articulate different "ways of seeing" financialization, beginning with Part (A), foundational questions about finance and financialization; (B) different methodological and epistemological approaches; (C) perspectives that emphasize the structural and spatial dimensions; (D) perspectives that emphasize agency, actors and politics; (E) perspectives that examine the technological and cultural manifestations of financialization; and, finally, (F) questioning how stable or unstable financialized societies and financialization itself are.

Part A takes the questions raised by this introduction forward and shows how scholarly understandings of finance and financialization have evolved over time in different disciplinary traditions. *Brett Christophers and Ben Fine* (2) shed light on the useful and problematic parts of financialization-as-concept, with a conversation focused on a key theme of classical and Marxist political economy – value, and how it is created – in the historical transformation of capitalism. They foreground the accumulation dimension, whereas *Christoph Deutschmann* (3) discusses the sociological underpinnings of where value comes from. He asks about the tensions between financialization and the entrepreneurship that capitalism needs in order to sustain, which raises the question: is finance more "parasitic" than constitutive, in its relationship with capitalist societies?[8] The complex interactions between the "financial" and the "real" economy also figure in critical business studies, which adopted the concept of financialization early. *Ismail Erturk* (4) introduces the "primacy of shareholder value" as a linchpin of this debate, focusing on the factors that shape non-financial corporations in contemporary capitalism. Shareholder value was welcomed by many in the economics profession as a potential driver of greater efficiency among firms; but as *Sheila Dow* (5) reminds readers, the promised benefits of shareholder value require a naively benign, liberal, view of how the financial sector works. From a Post-Keynesian perspective, the fundamental uncertainties and instabilities that finance produces need to be the starting points for any economic story of financialization. Wrapping up Part A, *Paul Langley* (6) focuses on the reworking of life itself by finance, revealing the power relations that emerge when financial logics and techniques reshape cultures and subjectivities, pushing us to consider the transformative impact of finance on everyday human lives and even "more-than-human life."

How can one study such a thing as financialization? The contributions to Part B showcase the methodological diversity of the scholarship and the types of findings that particular analytical tools can generate. To some extent, these chapters also reveal the difficulties of accurately taxonomizing the beast as rooted in different tools, conceptual lenses and empirical-analytical strategies. *Eve Chiapello* (7), for instance, illustrates the strengths of "a socio-technical angle," directing our view toward the sociological study of the instruments and *dispositifs* at work in finance. This "means looking into the actual operations performed by the 'workers' of financialization," which comprise a wide variety of organizational actors (p. 85). Similarly, *Hadas Weiss*' (8) introduction to the anthropological study of financialization emphasizes the agents and agencies that ground finance in lived human lives, highlighting how ethnographic fieldwork helps illuminate the contribution of professional *and* non-professional financial practices to financialization. It is often through such lenses that feminist and gender studies reveal, as *Signe Predmore* (9) shows, how financialization not only reflects masculine hegemony but also produces distinctly gendered (and colored) distributional effects. Yet seminal progress in the study of financialization here also stems from analyses that link micro- and macro-level dynamics through a focus on the interstices of production and reproduction. This is equally true for approaches in political science that analyze the politics of financial regulation, the financial industry's power and the diffusion of pro-finance sentiments among both elite and non-elite actors. *Stefano Pagliari and Kevin Young* (10) highlight these political mechanisms, making the case for financialization studies to open itself up to large-n empirical tests that also move beyond the Anglo-American focus of much of the literature. *Dimitris Sotiropoulos and Ariane Hillig* (11) introduce heterodox economic approaches to financialization, and, juxtaposing Post-Keynesian and Marxist approaches, advocate for a more historical approach to financialization, in contrast with the partial analyses that (even non-mainstream) economists have traditionally foregrounded. *Mareike Beck and Samuel Knafo* (12) conclude Part B with a complementary argument: that historiography has proven an important tool in coming to terms with the processes we now recognize as financialization, but that a more radical approach is needed to adequately historicize the social practices of finance. Their illustrative analysis of the emergence of liability management in the United States closes the loop with the "actual operations" of finance that Chiapello foregrounded.

Both Part A and Part B thus set the stage by introducing the lenses and tools that the contributions to the subsequent sections apply. Part C – Structures, Spaces and Sites of Financialization – centers on, broadly speaking, structural views of financialization, with chapters that highlight the macro-economic and -political drivers; they map and explain the commonalities and differences produced through a finance that is increasingly global, but still far from amorphous or placeless. Part C begins with contributions from Post-Keynesian and critical macroeconomics that present evidence on how financialization is not only spatially refracted, but also fundamentally shaped by the imbalances of global economic *and* political structure. *Engelbert Stockhammer and Karsten Kohler* (13) employ the concept of macroeconomic demand regimes to examine how different economies have been shaped by uneven processes of financialization, above all distinguishing the emergence of export-driven and debt-driven demand regimes in advanced capitalist countries. *Ewa Karwowski* (14), meanwhile, examines the variegated character of financialization in emerging economies, analyzing different scales of financial activity from international capital flows to the presence of financial centers, and critically engages with policy prescriptions to "deepen" finance for economic development. In the same vein, *Bruno Bonizzi, Annina Kaltenbrunner and Jeff Powell* (15) highlight the "subordinate" mode in which emerging capitalist countries have integrated into the world economy. The hierarchical nature of both global monetary and production relations, they argue, makes for a specific form of financialization that differs from the dynamics observable in advanced capitalist economies. These findings inherently raise questions about the role of the state and varying state capacity in shaping processes of financialization. As *Yingyao Wang* (16) demonstrates with reference to original evidence from the Chinese case, an emerging scholarship is exposing how states have actively provided the institutional infrastructure that undergirds processes of financialization. State transformations, legal reforms and jurisdictional specificities also loom large in three critical domains, analyzed in economic geography, that give more insight into the structural and spatial dimensions of financialization. Firstly, exposing the key importance of residential and commercial real estate in different stages of financialization, *Manuel Aalbers, Rodrigo Fernandez and Gertjan Wijburg* (17) shed light onto the urban underpinnings of debt-driven accumulation regimes. Secondly, *Sarah Bracking* (18) reflects on the role played by finance in changing nature–society relations and, incidentally, examining a range of issues from carbon policies to weather management, offers conceptual clarity to distinguish financialization from commodification. Thirdly, *Rodrigo Fernandez and Reijer Hendrikse* (19) examine offshore financial circuits, where "the world's dominant capital stocks and flows are today habitually routed and deposited" (p. 224), which showcase the intricate interweaving of territoriality and state sovereignty with financial power.

The complementary counterpart to these structurally–spatially focused contributions follows, in Part D, with chapters that foreground the actors, power relations and political processes at work in the "rise of finance." To begin, *Benjamin Braun and Daniela Gabor* (20) zoom in on the role of central banks, examining their infrastructural power and increasing "infrastructural entanglement" with shadow banking and shadow money markets, as they govern financial systems. These feedback loops between public and private power in the transformation of finance and society feature throughout the subsequent chapters. As *Johannes Petry* (21) for instance shows, securities exchanges, which are commonly understood as "mere" public marketplaces, have in fact become global corporations that organize, govern, and shape capital markets, making them both drivers of financialization and actors who are forced to respond to it. *Jan Fichtner* (22) examines the power relations at play in corporate financialization, by reviewing how corporations are reshaped by institutional investors, such as private equity funds, hedge funds, mutual funds, and the (highly concentrated) passive index fund industry. An intimate understanding of financial investors also is offered by *Brooke Harrington's* (23) examination of trusts, which, she explains, have been instrumental to the internationalization of capital and the creation of the secrecy-based offshore finance system. Trusts also often serve as vehicles for philanthropic investment, which channels a growing share of capital flows into developing countries, as *Dennis Stolz and Karen Lai* (24) discuss. They examine the "philanthropy-finance-development complex" that links (public and private) financial institutions and foreign aid with private foundations for impact investing, thus deepening global financial integration. At the other end of these financial flows, often, are households that, over the past decades, have become increasingly dependent on the financial services of different forms, as *Felipe González* (25) reflects with the case of micro-credit among poorer households. His chapter revisits the interactions between these and consumer financial service providers, which include payday lenders, microfinance institutions and department stores. As *Lena Lavinas'* chapter (26) shows, this financialization of poorer households in the Global South has been intimately linked with a continuing transformation of welfare systems that has effectively "collateralized" social policy as the basis for new credit relationships.

In debates over actors and power, however, the agency of labor, both organized in trade unions and more widely, as a social class, has remained notably absent. Only a few contributions on the impact of financialization on labor in the firm context (see e.g. Appelbaum and Batt 2014; Gospel, Pendleton and Vitols 2014) have sought to move beyond workers as mere passive victims of financialization, driven into financial traps and subordinated power positions. We sought to deepen and further encourage financialization research to fill this gap by studying the much more complex and multifaceted role of labor, via the *Essay Forum*, which features contributions from *Paul Thompson and Jean Cushen, Kavita Datta and Vincent Guermond, Lisa Adkins,* and *Michael McCarthy* (27). They conclude Part D with four short essays that discuss wage stagnation, migrant labor, workers' savings and the household as a site of financialization.

As these contributions already imply, financialization studies has nuts to crack that transcend structure and agency, and has to make sense of a wide range of cultural and technological changes. The contributions to Part E, therefore, ask about the meanings and technologies that underlie financial practices and the imaginaries involved in processes of becoming "financialized." Part E begins with a wide-ranging contribution by *Max Haiven* (28) that outlines the relationship of financialization with culture, looking across four dimensions, from the workplace culture of the financial sector to the production of contemporary visual art. If one will, *Nathan Coombs and Arjen van der Heide* (29) add a fifth dimension, focused on valuation cultures, which arise from the valuation (and valuing) of risk through developments in quantitative risk management techniques, culminating in the elevation of macroprudential regulation as a core societal concern. The notion of risk also lies at the heart of *Rob Aitken's* chapter (30) on the cultural economy of financial subjectivity, which examines how financialization redefines how the self is governed. By pointing to two procedural logics – configuration and selection – he maintains that financial subjectivity is not uniform, but fundamentally heterogenous and uncertain. A core node in these processes of financialization in the everyday life sphere is the "household," as *Johnna Montgomerie* (31) shows in her examination of household debt. In mortgage markets, for instance, an indebted landlord does not assume the same position in the hierarchical financial system as a middle-class homeowner or a subprime borrower; different households are required to work and manage their respective positions in the financial system. As *Jeanne Lazarus* (32) explains, financial literacy education, as one of the most common policy responses to financialization, has also served financialization by individualizing financial problems and seeking to re-make households and individuals as financial subjects who can behave and perform adequately. Neither are policymakers free from having to adapt their behaviors to financialized reality: as *Laura Deruytter and Sebastian Möller* (33) show, in producing public policy, local authorities engage in increasingly financialized practices as they manage municipal debts in accordance with the precepts of ever-more sophisticated financial norms and instruments.

Despite many differences in approach, one commonality among many contributions is an implicit search for political contestation or pushback against the expansion of finance. Financialization scholars generally agree that the processes examined here are unstable and have harmful distributional consequences; but it is less obvious where counter-movements or countervailing policies exist or where they should come from. Part F therefore is devoted to exploring the instabilities, discontents and possibilities of challenging and undoing financialization. First, *Olivier Godechot* (34) opens with a discussion of the link between financialization and rising inequality. The exploding incomes of financial professionals and the rise of within-firm inequality, he argues, are the key drivers of growing inequality; and inequality, in turn, has also reinforced financialization. *Andreas Nölke* (35) illuminates how financialization has posed challenges to the legitimacy and viability of democratic rule: "too big to fail" financial institutions, the increasingly networked character of finance, and its growing technical complexity have negatively affected the input and output dimensions of democratic legitimacy, contributing to the slow-burning crisis of Western democracies. In a similar vein, *Gerald Epstein* (36) argues that finance, particularly in the Anglo-American context, has gained power over modern societies in inverse proportion to how much it contributes to their well-being; these societies are, he alleges, dominated by a "Bankers' Club" that holds a commanding position within the polity. With recourse to Keynes and Minsky, and using examples from India, *Sunanda Sen* (37) highlights the ingrained economic instabilities that financialization produces, especially through corporate investment decisions and commodity speculation, and hitting small producers and consumers the most. Opening the discussion on the possibility of reforms and pushback, *Beat Weber*'s chapter (38) critiques monetary reform strategies as a means of undoing financialization. Critically engaging with models such as Bitcoin and proposals based on Modern Monetary Theory, Weber argues that effective policies seeking to de-financialize must rather focus on fiscal policy and financial regulation. This, however, does also not appear straightforward: as *Matthias Thiemann* (39) shows, post-crisis regulatory efforts have not aimed at tackling financialization; rather, macro-prudential regulation aims to stabilize and revive finance-led growth. In contrast, finally, to the generally pessimistic tone of these chapters, the last chapter explores collective strategies of resistance. *Christina Laskaridis, Nathan Legrand and Eric Toussaint* (40) review a long history of struggles against illegitimate debts, using this to highlight strategies for effectively challenging the power of creditors. With history thus in support, financialization appears less inevitable, and possible futures open.

Conclusion

The possible futures for financialization will also determine the future directions of financialization studies. The tendency of capital to find spatial-temporal fixes (Harvey 2007[1982]) will most likely feed back on the phenomenon under scrutiny and on the extent to which scholars will have to adjust the concepts and tools displayed in this Handbook. And if financialization has effects that are social causes for resisting it, as some of the final chapters suggest, financialization studies will study these. For now, the need to push the geographical borders of financialization studies is undiminished, with more countries integrating ever more deeply into the global financial system. This will provide a further test for how well established concepts, often developed to capture the realities of Anglo-America or the wider global North, travel across time and institutional contexts. We would expect to see a greater emphasis on the role of both ideas and interests in shaping the politics of (de)financialization, moving beyond the simple dichotomy of expansion or reversal, and exposing the contradictions and uncertainties inherent in the evolution of contemporary finance.

Certainly, we can contend that the financialization literature has grown more attuned to the many complexities and ambivalences, thereby not any longer seeing a nail everywhere because of the hammer that financialization-as-concept is. This is even more important as scholarship approaches the technical issues arising within rapidly evolving financial markets, clustering around new tendencies such as digital monies or fintech innovations. The key challenges for the field, however, ultimately do not look so different from those over a decade ago when Ewald Engelen (2008: 118) noted:

> [i]f the financialization community [...] embarked upon a constructive conversation between the different research communities that have crystallized around different empirical concepts and different causal mechanisms, the future may well hold great successes in store for the concept of financialization.

This book, we hope, has significantly furthered that conversation. The evolution of real-world events, to which the academic community and scholarly trends usually react, will continue to shape it. As for how much future financialization, as well as the study of it has, the next financial crisis will tell.

Notes

1 We would like to thank Bruno Bonizzi, Deborah Mabbett, Johannes Petry and Michael Schwan for helpful comments on this chapter as well as Marlene Willimek for her untiring editorial assistance. All contributors and the team at Routledge deserve thanks for making this project possible.
2 For possible beginnings, see Lagoarde-Segot (2017).
3 We owe this notion to a long-past conversation with a contributor to this Handbook, Dimitris Sotiropoulos.
4 A search on Worldcat.org for books with either "financialization" or "financialisation" in their title results in 775 hits. After filtering out double entries and other erroneous results, 145 titles remain.
5 Foster traces the early usage of the term to the near-simultaneous writing of Italian political economist and historian Giovanni Arrighi (1994) and the Republican-leaning American political commentator Kevin Phillips.
6 For the simultaneously thriving "social studies of finance" see e.g. Knorr Cetina and Preda (2005) as well as Callon et al. (2007).
7 We thank Bruno Bonizzi for suggesting we add this important element.
8 See also Bezemer and Hudson (2016) and Sotiropoulos et al. (2013) on this tension.

Bibliography

Aalbers, M., 2008. The Financialization of Home and Mortgage Markets. *Competition and Change*, 12(2), pp. 148–166.
Aalbers, M., 2020. Financialization. In: D. Richardson, N. Castree, M.F. Goodchild, A.L. Kobayashi and R. Marston (eds.) *The International Encyclopedia of Geography: People, the Earth, Environment, and Technology*. Oxford: Wiley.

Appelbaum, E. and Batt, R., 2014. *Private Equity at Work: When Wall Street Manages Main Street*. New York: Russel Sage.

Arrighi, G., 1994. *The Long Twentieth Century. Money, Power, and the Origins of Our Times*. New York: Verso.

Ban, C. and Gabor, D., 2016. The Political Economy of Shadow Banking. *Review of International Political Economy*, 23(6), pp. 901–914.

Bayliss, K., 2014. The Financialization of Water. *Review of Radical Political Economics*, 46(3), pp. 292–307.

Bezemer, D. and Hudson, M., 2016. Finance Is Not the Economy: Reviving the Conceptual Distinction. *Journal of Economic Issues*, 50(3), pp. 745–768.

Bonizzi, B., 2013. Financialization in Developing and Emerging Countries: A Survey. *International Journal of Political Economy*, 42(4), pp.83–107.

Botzem, S. and Dobusch, L., 2017. Financialization as Strategy: Accounting for Inter-organizational Value Creation in the European Real Estate Industry. *Accounting, Organizations and Society*, 59, pp. 31–43.

Boyer, R., 2000. Is a Finance-led Growth Regime a Viable Alternative to Fordism? A Preliminary Analysis. *Economy and Society*, 29(1), pp. 111–145.

Callon, M., Millo, Y. and Muniesa, F., (eds.) 2007. *Market Devices*. Oxford: Blackwell.

Christophers, B., 2015. The Limits to Financialization. *Dialogues in Human Geography*, 5(2), pp. 183–200.

Christophers, B., 2018. Financialisation as Monopoly Profit: *The Case of US Banking*. Antipode (online first).

Clapp, J. and Isakson, S.R., 2018. Risky Returns: The Implications of Financialization in the Food System. *Development and Change*, 49(2), pp. 437–460.

Crouch, C., 2011. *The Strange Non-Death of Neoliberalism*. Cambridge: Polity.

Davis, A. and Walsh, C., 2017. Distinguishing Financialization from Neoliberalism. *Theory, Culture & Society*, 34(5–6), pp. 27–51.

Dixon, A. and Sorsa, V., 2009. Institutional Change and the Financialisation of Pensions in Europe. *Competition & Change*, 13(4), pp. 347–367.

Epstein, G., 2005. Introduction: Financialization and the World Economy. In idem, ed., *Financialization and the World Economy*. Cheltenham: Edward Elgar, pp. 3–16.

Engelen, E., 2008. The Case for Financialization. *Competition and Change*, 12(2), pp. 111–119.

Engelen, E. and Konings, M., 2010. Financial Capitalism Resurgent: Comparative Institutionalism and the Challenges of Financialization. In G. Morgan, J.L. Campbell, C. Crouch, O.K. Pedersen and R. Whitley (eds.), *The Oxford Handbook of Comparative Institutional Analysis*. Oxford: Oxford University Press, pp. 601–624.

Erturk, I., Froud, J., Johal, S., Leaver, A. and Williams, K., (eds.) 2008. *Financialization at Work. Key Texts and Commentary*. Abingdon: Routledge.

Fastenrath, F., Schwan, M. and Trampusch, C., 2017. Where States and Markets Meet: The Financialisation of Sovereign Debt Management. *New Political Economy*, 22(3), pp. 273–293.

Faroohar, R., 2016. *Makers and Takers: The Rise of Finance and the Fall of American Business*. New York: Crown Business.

FESSUD Studies in Financial Systems, 2013, http://fessud.eu/studies-in-financial-systems/. Last accessed: March 1, 2019.

Fichtner, J., 2013. Hedge Funds: Agents of Change for Financialization. *Critical Perspectives on International Business*, 9(4), pp. 358–376.

Fine, B., 2013. Financialization from a Marxist Perspective. *International Journal of Political Economy*, 42(4), pp. 47–66.

Finlayson, A., 2009. Financialisation, Financial Literacy and Asset-Based Welfare. *The British Journal of Politics and International Relations*, 11(3), pp. 400–421.

Foster, J., 2007. The Financialization of Capitalism. In: *Monthly Review*, 58(11), pp. 1–12.

French, S., Leyshon, A. and Wainwright, T., 2011. Financializing Space, Spacing Financialization. *Progress in Human Geography*, 35(6), pp. 798–819.

Froud, J., Haslam, C., Johal, S. and Williams, K., 2000. Shareholder Value and Financialization: Consultancy Promises, Management Moves. *Economy & Society*, 29(1), pp. 80–110.

Froud, J., Johal, S., Leaver, A. and Williams, K., 2006. *Financialization and Strategy. Narrative and Numbers*. London: Routledge.

Gabor, D., 2010. *Central Banking and Financialization: A Romanian Account of How Eastern Europe Became Subprime*. Houndmills: Palgrave Macmillan.

Gospel, H., Pendleton, A., and Vitols, S. (eds.) 2014. *Financialization, New Investment Funds, and Labour. An International Comparison*. Oxford: Oxford University Press.

Hardie, I., 2012. *Financialization and Government Borrowing Capacity in Emerging Markets*. Houndmills: Palgrave Macmillan.

Harvey, D., 2007/1982. *The Limits to Capital*. London: Verso.

Karwowski, E. and Stockhammer, E., 2017. Financialisation in Emerging Economies: A Systematic Overview and Comparison with Anglo-Saxon Economies. *Economic and Political Studies*, 5(1), pp.60–86.

Knorr Cetina, K. and Preda, A., 2005. *The Sociology of Financial Markets*. Oxford: Oxford University Press.

Konings, M., 2011. *The Development of American Finance*. New York: Cambridge University Press.

Krippner, G., 2005. The Financialization of the American Economy. *Socio-Economic Review*, 3(2), pp. 173–208.

Lagna, A., 2016. Derivatives and the Financialisation of the Italian State. *New Political Economy*, 21(2), pp. 167–186.

Lapavitsas, C., 2011. Theorizing Financialization. *Work, Employment & Society*, 24(4), pp. 611–624.

Lapavitsas, C. and Powell, J., 2013. Financialisation Varied: A Comparative Analysis of Advanced Economies. *Cambridge Journal of Regions, Economy and Society*, 6, pp. 359–379.

Lagoarde-Segot, T., 2017. Financialization: Towards a New Research Agenda. *International Review of Financial Analysis*, 51, pp. 113–123.

Langley, P., 2004. In the Eye of the 'Perfect Storm': The Final Salary Pensions Crisis and the Financialisation of Anglo-American Capitalism. *New Political Economy*, 9(4), pp. 539–558.

Lazonick, W. and O'Sullivan, M., 2000. Maximizing Shareholder Value. A New Ideology for Corporate Governance. *Economy and Society*, 29(1), pp. 13–35.

Locke, R. and Thelen, K., 1995. Apples and Oranges Revisited: Contextualized Comparisons and the Study of Comparative Labor Politics. *Politics & Society* 23(3), pp. 337–367.

Mader, P., 2015. *The Political Economy of Microfinance*. London: Palgrave Macmillan.

Magdoff, H. and Sweezy, P., 1987. *Stagnation and the Financial Explosion*. New York: Monthly Review Press.

Martin, R., 2002. *Financialization of Daily Life*. Philadelphia, PA: Temple University Press.

Mawdsley, E., 2018. Development Geography II: Financialization. *Progress in Human Geography*, 42(2), pp. 264–274.

Mertens, D., 2017. Putting 'Merchants of Debt' in their Place: The Political Economy of Retail Banking and Credit-based Financialisation in Germany. *New Political Economy*, 22(1), pp. 12–30.

Montgomerie, J., 2009. The Pursuit of (Past) Happiness? Middle-class Indebtedness and American Financialisation. *New Political Economy*, 14(1), pp.1–24.

Nölke, A. and Perry, J., 2007. The Power of Transnational Private Governance: Financialization and the IASB. *Business and Politics*, 9(3), pp. 1–25.

Nölke, A., Heires, M. and Bieling, H.-J., 2013. Editorial: The Politics of Financialization. *Competition & Change*, 17(3), pp. 209–218.

Orhangazi, Ö., 2008. Financialisation and Capital Accumulation in the Non-financial Corporate Sector: A Theoretical and Empirical Investigation on the US Economy: 1973–2003 *Cambridge Journal of Economics*, 32 (6), pp. 863–886.

Ouma, S., Johnson, L. and Bigger, P., 2018. Rethinking the Financialization of 'Nature'. *Environment and Planning A: Economy and Space*, 50(3), pp.500–511.

Palley, T.I., 2008. Financialization: What It Is and Why It Matters. In Hein, E., Niechoj, T., Spahn, H.-P. and Truger, A., (eds.) *Finance-Led Capitalism: Macroeconomic Effects of Changes in the Financial Sector*. Marburg: Metropolis, pp. 29–60.

Rethel, L., 2010. Financialisation and the Malaysian Political Economy. *Globalizations*, 7(4), pp. 489–506.

Sartori, G., 1970. Concept Misformation in Comparative Politics. *The American Political Science Review*, 64 (4), pp. 1033–1053.

Shaxson, N., 2018. *The Finance Curse: How Global Finance is Making Us All Poorer*. London: The Bodley Head.

Sotiropoulos, D.P., Milios, J. and Lapatsioras, S., 2013. *A Political Economy of Contemporary Capitalism and its Crisis: Demystifying Finance*. London/New York: Routledge.

Stockhammer, E., 2004. Financialisation and the Slowdown of Accumulation. *Cambridge Journal of Economics*, 28(5), pp. 719–741.

Storm, S., 2018. Financialization and Economic Development: A Debate on the Social Efficiency of Modern Finance. *Development and Change*, 49(2), pp. 302–329.

Tang, K. and Xiong, W., 2010. Index Investment and the Financialization of Commodities. *NBER Working Paper* No. 16385.

Van der Zwan, N., 2014. Making Sense of Financialization. *Socio-Economic Review*, 12(1), pp. 99–129.

Van der Zwan, N., 2017. Financialisation and the Pension System: Lessons from the United States and the Netherlands. *Journal of Modern European History*, 15(4), pp. 554–578.

Van Treeck, T. (2009): The Political Economy Debate on 'Financialization' – A Macroeconomic Perspective. *Review of International Political Economy*, 16(5), pp. 907–944.

Varoufakis, Y., 2011. *The Global Minotaur: America, the True Origins of the Financial Crisis and the Future of the World Economy*. London: Economic Controversies.

Web of Science, 2019. *Social Science Citation Index*. Philadelphia, PA: Clarivate Analytics.

PART A

Finance and Financialization: Taking Stock

2

THE VALUE OF FINANCIALIZATION AND THE FINANCIALIZATION OF VALUE

Brett Christophers and Ben Fine

BC: Among the most forceful and compelling of the various arguments for the value of the concept of financialization is the thesis that in recent decades, capitalism has changed, and that the financialization concept helpfully captures one of the most significant vectors of this transformation. I am thinking in particular here of the types of definition of financialization offered by Greta Krippner (2005), Till van Treeck (2009) and Costas Lapavitsas (2013), where financialization is understood fundamentally in terms of a shift in the weighting of the capitalist economy toward financial forms of revenue and profit, whether or not those happen to be realized by the financial sector per se. It is striking, however, that some of the most forthright champions of the idea that capitalism has changed in this way – that it has, in a word, been financialized – nonetheless cling to an essentially *un*changed (Marxian) understanding of value.[1] Lapavitsas, in my view, is one such; John Bellamy Foster (2008) is clearly another. For these scholars, following Marx, there are essentially two types of labour under capitalism. There is productive labour, which produces value, and thus wealth; and there is unproductive labour, which does not. And the finance sector and the labour embodied within it are, in this schema, fundamentally unproductive. Hence Lapavitsas' claim, as per the title of his book (Lapavitsas 2013), that finance – and financialization – entails *profiting without producing* (value), or in other words profiting by extracting value that is exclusively produced elsewhere in the economy. But isn't this contradictory, or, at the very least, paradoxical? Is it in fact credible that capitalism has been financialized, while capitalist value – capitalism's *sine qua non* – has not?

BF: This raises a whole sheaf of questions bearing upon, but not limited to, the question of financialization. First is what is value and how is it produced (see Fine and Saad Filho 2018 for an account). Classically, within the Marxist tradition, it is only produced by wage labour dedicated to the purpose of producing commodities for profit. This entails a sharp distinction between (productive) labour as the source of value and other labours, not least those in exchange (including finance); even though these labours engage in real activities bringing about the forms in which values (e.g. commodities) or claims to values (e.g. assets) circulate and even appropriate some portion of the (surplus) value that has been produced. Further, labour in finance, and in many other activities, can facilitate the productivity of the labour that does produce value, as can a good climate, heavy oppression of the workforce, and any number of other factors whether involving labour or not.[2]

19

This inevitably gives rise to any number of corresponding theories of what value is or is not, and what or who produces it or not. But the classic Marxist position is as stated, and the more or less rise and influence of finance does not render it productive, any more than climate change now means we produce less "value" in the Marxist sense even though we are degrading the environment itself (in ways that could, nonetheless, be evaluated). Indeed, understanding value in this narrow way is crucial in analysing the excesses of both finance and the environment, albeit in their very different if occasionally overlapping ways (as in trading in futures in green energy).

In short, the line has to be drawn somewhere between what produces value and what does not. For the latter, as with finance, it is a matter of uncovering how it relates to (surplus) value production, distribution and circulation in its own ways. This will be different for different elements of finance (private household mortgaging as opposed to currency dealing or trading in state debt) as well as for the non-financial as such (e.g. rental payments which does not mean land or housing produces value).

Many have criticized Marxism for this tight notion of value, including those within the Marxist tradition itself, primarily because value is seen as an inadequate concept for explaining price formation. As it were, the myriad of factors that affect price then become contributors to value in their own right, reducing it to some sort of select theory of supply and demand. Value and price become synonymous and so value is not needed at all. Value is challenged with every existing and new complexity that capitalism throws at us, financialization or otherwise (and especially with the rise of so-called immaterial labour of which finance is a part). The alternative I adopt is to acknowledge that the increasingly complex forms, not determinants, taken by the circulation of value (not least with proliferation of financial assets, forms of credit, etc.) are precisely that, and no more; but their circulation needs to be traced out in how they relate (surplus) value to its forms with real effects.

But note that, even within this Marxist tradition over the source of value, there can be differences over how it is appropriated through financialization – with my position being that it is primarily from surplus value produced by workers whereas Lapavitsas places more emphasis on the appropriation of wages (value) through exploitative credit relations (Fine 2013). The point in common is that finance does not produce value even though it receives it as a surplus. The same is true of profits and rents but the forms and mechanisms are different.

The second issue is how to demarcate different periods of capitalism in general, and financialization in particular (see Beck and Knafo, in this volume). Here, there is more controversy about how to do this in principle than is to be found in the demarcations of those principles into different states of capitalism in practice, depending on how differences between the earliest forms of competitive capitalism and its monopolistic successor are specified (e.g. around Fordism), with a subsequent post-war boom leading to globalization and state interventionism. In general, none of these periodizations questioned positions on what is value so there is no reason why financialization should. Contemporary definitions of neoliberalism as a period of capitalism, focusing on its class character, its market ideology, or its economic policies, also seem to run orthogonally to how value is understood (and produced). Indeed, the financialization literature outside of Marxism has been remarkably disinterested in what is the source of value as such, and hence whether financialization contributes to it or not (with the notable exception of national income accounts; see p. 00).[3]

Third, then, my own definition of financialization sees it in terms of expansion of what Marx called interest bearing capital (IBC), i.e. capital in exchange that expands the production and circulation of surplus value. Whilst not producing surplus value, it at most facilitates accumulation (although susceptible to financial crises) but is distinct from simple credit as a loan that facilitates the circulation of value (as opposed to its immediate accumulation).

Thus, I could lend you a fiver and you could repay me. I could even charge interest, and then set up a business in consumer credit. If so, though interest is paid, like retailing on credit, I would not expect my profit rate to be excessive in reflecting that payments to underpin my profits come from simple credit relations.

With IBC, it is different as I am not simply advancing consumer credit but a loan that the borrower intends to use to generate profit. For Marx, IBC was primarily advanced for industrial development but, under financialized neoliberalism, it has been extended to, and intensified within, more or less each and every aspect of economic and social reproduction – not so much mortgaging or consumer credit as such, for example, as trading in the proliferating types and volumes of assets that can be formed out of these and any other exchange dealings involving (securitisable) streams of revenues.

Unlike other capitals in exchange (wholesaling and retailing for example), IBC is not susceptible to the competitive tendency for an equal rate of profit with other capitals – but this might be taken up later in our conversation. As such, financialization in this narrow sense is not new – Marx was able to identify it! What is new is the extent to which such financialization has gained purchase over what has been termed economic and social reproduction, financialization of everyday life, as it has been called (see Langley, in this volume). And, returning to the earlier issue of periodization, how reproduction is governed, with value at its core, is what tends to define one period of capitalism as opposed to another, although, as mentioned, which aspect of reproduction is taken as decisive varies across specifications. For me, neoliberalism is fundamentally underpinned by financialization although by no means reducible to it (Bayliss et al. 2020). To some degree, in its own focus, this has been brilliantly brought to the fore in Brett's own work in highlighting the material and ideological basis for redefinition of national accounts to incorporate finance as a contribution to GDP, as a service, as opposed to simply being an (unproductive) transfer (Christophers 2013; Assa 2017).

So, the paradox, if not contradiction, to which Brett points, is resolved by seeing financialization in how it is attached to the restructuring of the production, distribution and circulation of (surplus) value as opposed to its direct creation. Moreover, more generally, the narrow theoretical definition of financialization as IBC allows it to avoid the amorphous and unstructured definition arising from Epstein (2005) in which financialization is seen simply as more of finance and its effects.

BC: If I understand Ben correctly, his own preferred approach to financialization, or at least to operationalizing it as a valuable concept, moves us away from the types of understandings of financialization with which I opened the chapter. As I said, for Krippner (2005), Van Treeck (2009) and others, financialization refers to a post-1970s shift in the capitalist regime of accumulation (in certain countries), specifically whereby financial channels of profit generation come substantially to the fore. That is not what I hear Ben saying. He is suggesting that financialization is better understood as related to developments in the realm of *governance* of social and economic reproduction. In short, social and economic reproduction increasingly comes to be governed *by finance*.

This suggestion prompts two immediate thoughts. The first – unexpected! – is that, rightly or wrongly, I see interesting echoes of *Régulation* theory here. For regulationists, capitalism can be conceptualized in terms of a mode of production on the one hand and a mode of regulation on the other; the latter "acts to guarantee that the dominant [mode of production] is reproducible in the medium term, through the accommodation, mediation and normalization of crisis tendencies" (Peck and Tickell 1992: 349). Is Ben's governance of social and economic re-production not the same as, or broadly equivalent to, the regulationists' regulation/governance of the mode of production (I'll come back to the differentiating "re" shortly)? If it is, then it strikes me that Ben's own take on financialization is actually not dissimilar from Robert Boyer's (2000) influential theorization of a "finance-led growth regime," which is not something I had considered before.

The expansion of interest-bearing capital to gain increasing purchase over economic and social reproduction – with, as Ben says, value at its core – is, from this standpoint, a specific incarnation of Boyer's more general financialization of the mode of regulation via the imposition of what he refers to as "financial norms."

The second thought, connected to this, and again one that had not occurred to me previously, is that Ben's understanding of financialization is therefore not only fundamentally different from say Krippner's or Van Treeck's (as well as Lapavitsas's), but close to – and more interestingly, a sort of amalgam of – the other two main "schools" of financialization theory. As several people have noted (e.g. Van der Zwan 2014), although there are innumerable different definitions of financialization, it is just about possible to identify three primary schools: the structural shift in patterns of accumulation school (i.e. Krippner, Van Treeck, etc.) the school focused on the shift in corporate imperatives toward a more singular focus on shareholder value (Froud et al. 2000); and the school focused on finance's colonization of "noneconomic" lifeworlds (Martin 2002). In its focus on the governance of social and economic reproduction, Ben's definition of financialization connects to both the second and third approaches. With Froud et al. (and, as mentioned, Boyer, who also emphasizes the ascendancy of shareholder value), it addresses finance's strategic influence over the operations of all types of capital (firm) (see Erturk, in this volume). And with Randy Martin (2002), it addresses finance's growing influence over social *re*production as well as economic (value) production (see Aitken, in this volume).

In any event, Ben makes the interesting observation that financialization conceived this way is not *per se* new – Marx himself identified the role of interest-bearing capital in expediting the production and circulation of surplus value – and that what is new rather, presumably since the 1970s or so, is the massive expansion of interest-bearing capital's governmental scope. Ben does so in the context of discussing the issue of periodization: how reproduction is governed being, he suggests, what tends to differentiate one period of capitalism from another (which I might say is again a very regulationist way of viewing things). I think this question of periodization is terribly important, and for two reasons.

Firstly, as Ben's own discussion intimates, it is actually impossible to define financialization *without* being explicit about questions of periodicity. Alessandro Vercelli (2013), in a strangely underappreciated discussion of financialization, is excellent on this point. As he says, financialization tends to be periodized in three different ways in the literature: as a "unique" historical episode (these, in my view, tend to be the shallowest, most historically myopic treatments of financialization; and they are remarkably common); as a recurring phenomenon, occurring in waves, as in the work of Giovanni Arrighi (1994) and Carlota Perez (2002); or as a long-run, albeit historically and geographically uneven, process or tendency. As Vercelli shows, one cannot talk meaningfully about what financialization is without specifying its temporal scope and historical specificity (or otherwise). And although he hedges his bets somewhat – claiming that "the three options do not exclude each other" (Vercelli 2013: 21) – I read Vercelli's own approach to periodicity as very much of the third type. Specifically, he sees financialization as a secular tendency that is intrinsic in the very development of capitalist relations, as embodied in the centuries-long history of financial innovations designed to remove "constraints to the flexibility of economic transactions" and, in the process, to "extend the set of exchange options in time, space, and contents" for those who introduce such innovations (Vercelli 2013: 19).

This brings me to the second reason why I think periodization is important. There is a more-or-less universal tendency in the literature on financialization to treat it – whatever "it" is – as a departure, unique *or* recurring, from a (non-financialized) norm. Financialization is "other" to some "normal" capitalism. But is it? Not if Vercelli is right. Not if we follow Ben in framing financialization in terms of the expansion of the (systemically inherent) governance function of interest-bearing capital. And not if we adopt, as we well might, Hyman Minsky's perspective on these matters. To be sure, Minsky's famous instability hypothesis does not refer to a generic capitalism but, as Vercelli (2013: 37) observes, to "a mature stage of the evolution of capitalism in which credit and finance play a crucial role" – "money manager capitalism." Nevertheless, for Minsky, capitalism *in general* is, so to speak, financialized. "Capitalism," he wrote (1967: 33), "is essentially a financial system." Finance does not so much organize, or govern, the economy; it *is* the economy. This is why I think the idea of financialization as some sort of radical departure from a non-financialized norm is so misleading. I suspect this latter way of looking at things is rooted in the enormous influence of national accounting in shaping how we view the economy. Since it was uncommon to think about "the economy" as a coherent totality before the birth of national accounting in the mid-twentieth century (Mitchell 1998), the economy pictured in early national accounts became, in effect, and entirely arbitrarily, our historic base-line, our fixed understanding of what a "normal" capitalist economy looks like. But of course it was *not* normal. In particular, in the diminished role and power afforded to finance capital within that postwar economy, it was radically *abnormal* – perhaps even unique – in *longue durée* terms. Too often, it seems to me, discussions of contemporary financialization are constrained by that distorted historical imagination of capitalist normality. If, after Minsky, capitalism is inherently financial, there can arguably *be* no such thing as financialization, unless we understand the latter as merely a periodic intensification of what is already integral.

What is also integral, as Ben says, is value, and this is where I want to finish – by circling back to the thorny question of value creation. As far as I can tell, Ben does not resolve the paradox with which I opened the chapter so much as deny it exists. He does so by firmly bracketing off value creation from financialization. The latter, by his argument, involves restructuring of those processes whereby surplus value is produced, distributed and circulated. Finance, suitably engineered (e.g. through financialization), can make surplus production more (or less) efficient; but it does not par-ticipate in the creation of the value of which the surplus is a residual part, even as it shapes the conditions of that creation. Hence there *is* nothing paradoxical or contradictory about believing capitalism has changed – financialized – while value has not. My question, though, is whether we *can* comfortably bracket off value creation from finance (and financialization). Given the weight of profit now generated through financial channels, does a theory – classical Marxism – according to which finance is unproductive of value still hold water; still make sense? Is the value of financial commodities indeed merely "fictitious," and financial labour thus extraneous to value-producing labour? Some heretics (e.g. Bryan et al. 2015) suggest not. As I understand it, however, this remains Ben's view. I'd like to push him on this issue.

BF: I can see Brett is trying to put me in a box in terms of my understanding of financiali-zation, either by what I am or what I am not, and he offers plenty of scope by which to do this ranging across different authors and approaches. I see myself, though, not so much as same or different but as seeking to reconstruct critically the understandings of financialization on broader, deeper and sounder theoretical and historical bases – rendering his further questions highly salient.

So for financialization to serve as a critical point of departure for contemporary capitalism, it definitely must be attached to economic *and* social reproduction in the way that is acknowledged by Epstein. But it is equally necessary to unpick the amorphous notion that financialization is anything involving (the idea of) money. I do take Marx's longstanding theory of IBC as at the heart of financialization, in the narrow sense – in that IBC has expanded enormously both intensively (within existing activities) and extensively (to new areas of applications) over the past three decades. This is a bit like defining monopoly capital in terms of large-scale factory produc-tion and concentrated markets. But the stage of monopoly capitalism has to look far beyond the narrow economic definition to the social relations, structures, agencies and processes on which it is influential (and, by the same token in Brett's terms, transform what value is, or can be, historically and socially; not just a lump of labour, but its situation).

I would not myself put this in terms of financialization as governance (despite talking of governing previously) precisely because of the taint of Régulation theory that comes with it, as Brett points out. Thus, under the so-called Fordist regime (covering the Keynesian period), we had regulation through mass production and consumption and collective bargaining. The now for-gotten, putative successor to Fordism, so-called post-Fordism, was based on flexible-specialization, that is, small-scale niche, customer bespoke, production. Now we have undue regulation by finance. To be harsh, Régulation tends to dress up select grand empirical observation as (inevitably self-supporting) theoretical framing. This is just too theoretically and empirically rigid for the var-iegated natures and patterns of economic and social reproduction under neoliberalism let alone the previously delineated regimes of accumulation. It cannot deal with the contradictory tensions and the exceptions to its abstract framings, although credit must go to Aglietta (1976, 1995 and 1998) if not Boyer for putting finance as a governing aspect on the agenda, and at an early moment, Gutt-man (2008) for a neat account. In short, neither neoliberalism, nor financialization that underpins it, is homogenizing and conducive to simple and/or single modes of "regulation."

Unsurprisingly, then, given its reach of influence through economic and social reproduction, there should be a proliferation of definitions and approaches to financialization that Brett high-lights which, from my perspective, tend to conflate it in the narrow sense, as IBC, with its effects in the broader sense of being embedded in economic and social reproduction. My own approach to the latter depends again upon critical reconstruction of what I take to be invaluable contribu-tions. I use a range, if not sequence, of conceptualizations, involving distinctions between *commodification* as such, as with privatization, *commodity form* (streams of revenue which can be securitized, as with but not confined to mortgages) and *commodity calculation* where exchange as such is not present but in which the ethos of (neoliberal) management serves as a mimic of what is taken to be market control. The trajectories of these forms globally, nationally and sectorally across reproduction have been highly diverse but remorseless, with all forms expanding but with a tendency of movement from commodity calculation to commodity form, and from commodity form to commodification. In the British health system, for example, commodity calculation has recently been increasingly used to assess performance. This has led to allocation of funds on this basis (without the presence of a market as such) or commodity form. And, in turn, the way has been paved for private sector provision of health services alongside public provision, and hence commodification, itself with potential for financialization (Bayliss et al. 2020).

In this light, the temporality of financialization can be located in terms of the troika Brett raises of episodes, trends or recurring cycles (note the plurals, as each can be variegated as well as sequential and simultaneous). For the cycles, the work of Arrighi is key. There can be no doubt that the presence of finance is closely linked to all cycles under capitalism, both leading and following as well as intensifying. But I would be wary of linking this to an abstract theoretical logic as if night follows day, just as ups follow downs. Cyclical movements and the role (of which forms) of finance within them is fundamentally historical, just as the thirties is not the noughties. The "trend" over the past thirty years (how long before something is a trend?) is something much more than the quantitative and qualitative (in terms of sorts and integration of assets) expansion of finance in terms of the expansion of its intensive and extensive roles in economic and social reproduction. By the same token, nor is financialization an episode any more than we would apply this or the other such temporal monikers to the Keynesian period, to monopoly capitalism or even to imperialism. Financialization underpins the contemporary neoliberal stage of capitalism, episodically (in day-to-day policymaking for example), cyclically (in financially induced crises) and secularly (the financialization of everyday life) – although the passage from the 1930s to the 1970s witnessed significantly different trajectories around the presence and effects of finance than subsequently, not least with (US) deregulation, end of Bretton Woods, etc.

This does not mean that financialization, in the narrow sense of IBC, does not precede neoliberalism, just as monopolies, colonial wars and the like preceded imperialism. Otherwise, Marx could hardly have devoted so much of Volume III of *Capital* to finance and how to broach it both theoretically and empirically. And, of course, Minsky, as Brett observes, and Keynes emphasised the significance of finance (albeit reduced to money supply and demand in Keynesianism although Keynes himself praising Marx's M-C-M′ formula for his own purposes). I could not then agree more that finance is normally, indeed inevitably, a part of the capitalist economy. But it is not a normal part of the economy in the way that material factors in general and commodities (including labour power) are in two senses. First, it is not fixed, but fluid by nature in the roles and forms that it takes and, second, in a sense more fundamental, yes it is structurally distinct by being derived from money and its functions. This means what and how it is part of the economy is complex and wide-ranging, and this has been the basis on which the notion of financialization has inevitably prospered. So, yes again, financialization has been the "intensification of what is already integral" as Brett says, but it has also involved extensification to economic and social reproduction.

And, once again, Brett pushes on the issue of value theory, and both presents and questions my position with some acumen. I wonder what the answers would be from those who would usurp rather than modify my position. Where exactly do the boundaries of (surplus) value creation lie (theoretically as well as empirically/historically)? Which parts of finance are value creating, and which not, and when did this become so (when national income accounting said so, or non-financial firms started speculating, households began to hold more assets and credit cards, etc.)? How do we distinguish between the creation of this (surplus) value and its distribution or destruction (immanent in commodity and fictitious forms)? And why stop at finance in terms of value creation, since there is also domestic labour, prosumerism, corruption, tax evasion/avoid-ance, exchange rate fluctuations, and so on, each of which affects, or effects, pricing as well as who gets what? So I am not sure whether those who would set aside traditional value theory because finance appropriates and putatively creates value are at all secure in their alternative, even if they have told us what it is. And, *in extremis*, as with performativity, there is a tendency to lose the attachment of value to material processes altogether. As Brett correctly observes, if over-looking the role of value theory, "there *is* a capitalist system, increasingly structured by markets, with a history certainly sculpted *in part* by economic discourses and their instantiation in different calculative technologies, but the dynamics of which are clearly irreducible to those ideas and indeed represent an ineluctable framework for comprehending those ideas and their potential significance" (Christophers 2013: 11–12). In a nutshell, my work, with others, has sought to address economic discourses and their instantiation through careful theoretical and empirical reconstruction of the variegated structures, relations, processes and agencies through which the financialization of (surplus) value is integral with (the cultures of) neoliberal economic and social reproduction (see Fine 2017, for a synopsis with references to further literature).

BC: Ben is of course right that there is nothing straightforward about rethinking value and value theory in the light of financialization. There is not, and never has been, an easy answer to his question of where exactly the boundaries of (surplus) value creation lie. Marx himself found this to be true: his discussions of precisely where productive labour ends and unproductive labour begins were tortured and ultimately a bit unconvincing.[4] But if we think value theory remains indispensable, including in helping understand financialization, such questions cannot be dodged. Indeed, one might say that if financialization (as a set of real-world processes) has value, then it is at least partly in compelling us to confront these questions.

Personally, in any event, I am less and less satisfied with the traditional view that finance in general is unproductive of value; in other words, I tend to sympathize with those such as Bryan et al. (2015) who increasingly question convention on this point. My own approach to these matters is pretty simple (Christophers 2018a). It is to go back to Marxian basics: for I am not at all sure that allowing for movement in the boundaries of value creation necessarily means, as Ben suggests, setting aside traditional value theory *tout court*. As I read him, Marx said value is produced whenever people produce commodities for market exchange under conditions of capitalist production, i.e. as wage labourers. It's as simple as that. In Marx's (1863) own words, it's all about "the social relations of production, within which the labour is realized. ... [T]he productive labourer produces commodities for the buyer of his labour-power."[5] What value is *not* about is "the material characteristics of labour" or "the nature of its product." So, says Marx: "An actor, for example, or even a clown ... is a productive labourer if he works in the service of a capitalist (an entrepreneur) to whom he returns more labour than he receives from him in the form of wages."

If a clown can produce value, why not someone working in finance? It doesn't matter, surely, if the commodity they create for sale is a product (say a credit default swap) or a service (e.g. advice on a corporate takeover). As I see it, the only parts of finance that categorically do not involve value creation are those where commodities are merely being exchanged rather than produced. And here's the interesting thing about the past few decades. They have seen not just financialization but also – perhaps even as a feature *of* financialization? – a marked shift in the sources of finance sector revenues and profits away from pure exchange-based capital gains and toward other models of income generation such as premia and, in particular, fees (Christophers 2015). Which is to say, the categorically unproductive component of finance, in Marxian value terms, is becoming less and less important. I think that's significant.

In my view, scholars' reluctance to consider such heresies, and to think afresh about finance and value more generally, frequently stems from two common conflations. The first is a conflation of Marxian value with value in a more vernacular sense. We resist financializing value – countenancing that finance creates it – because we think of value as something inherently "good." Essentially we think of it as, in Marxian terms, *use* value, and thus as beneficial to society; as, generally, *valuable*. But, for Marx, it is not. A commodity can bear Marxian value but have little or no positive social use. "The use-value of the commodity in which the labour of a productive worker is embodied," Marx writes, "may be of the most futile kind." (Credit default swap, anybody?!) The capitalist could scarcely care less: she is "little concerned" with "the use-value of the product of this labour as such, since for the capitalist the product is a commodity (even before its first metamorphosis), not an article of consumption." Hence the capitalist's contempt for the unproductive labourer who "produces for him a mere use-value." Society, of course, lauds the producer of "mere" use-values. So does Marx: what this producer produces is good. But *value*? No. A productive labourer, one who by definition produces value, is "a labourer who produces wealth *for another*. His existence only has meaning as such an instrument of production for the wealth of others." His/her existence is one of exploitation. Hence: "It is a misfortune to be a productive labourer." To suggest that finance produces value, in short, is to suggest that financiers produce wealth for finance capital. Is that really such a stretch? It is not to suggest that finance is "good."

The second problematic conflation is of value and price. Returning to Ben's comments just above: corruption, tax evasion/avoidance, exchange rate fluctuations and the like may, as he says, affect pricing and who gets what; but that does not mean they affect, or indeed effect, value. Price – both the price of the products of labour and the price of labour-power per se – reflects the social construction of worth in markets, and, insofar as we think of the "right" price as the one equating to the value produced, markets can and do *mis*price. The fact that in many countries today banks and bankers, respectively, make outsized profits and wages does not mean (or mean accepting) that they are disproportionately value-creating. It could instead mean, and I think often it probably does mean, that the market competition required to effect equalization of profit rates across different sectors of the economy is lacking, and has been for decades (Christophers 2016). Specifically, in such cases, the hypothesis would be that banks make monopoly profits under-pinned by monopoly pricing underpinned, in turn, by monopoly power; the increased finance sector competition necessary to erode these monopoly profits has not materialized. In fact one could argue that in countries such as the United Kingdom and United States of America, this – persistent monopoly profit – is what post-1970s financialization, understood after Krippner (2005) as a shift in the capitalist regime of accumulation, is fundamentally about (Christophers 2018b).

Seen this way, it is perhaps possible by way of conclusion for me to say something speculative about the future prospects of financialization, as a real-world "thing" if not the scholarly discourse. The end of financialization as we know it would require at a minimum, I suggest, the end of the monopoly power of today's leading financial institutions; the latter would be a necessary, if not sufficient, condition. Unless and until this monopoly power is broken, there will be no end to the ability of the finance sector to extract disproportionate profits, and no end to its ability to thwart efforts to halt – still less roll back – the intensive and extensive expansion of interest-bearing capital to which Ben refers.

BF: On value once more, there are those that push its discursive, performative nature, although I suspect Brett rejects the idea that putting financial services into national accounts as such makes it productive of value. And there are those, towards which he is leaning, who see it as somewhat, but less, fluid (and not just in Marx's sense of taking different commodity, money and productive forms over its circulation and reproduction). I stick at the point that finance is structurally part of *exchange*, divided from *value* creation as labour exercised under capitalist production. This view itself derives from the elementary form of the commodity as use and (exchange) value, from the latter side of which monetary and financial relations have developed (prodigiously, both intensively and extensively, with financialization).

Even so, I accept Marx is ambiguous and even inconsistent over his (unfinished) work on (un)productive labour reflecting his critical reconstruction of others but, more fundamentally, the tension between the individual and the social productivity of labour (from the perspective of capital, it needs to be a source of surplus value as opposed to its appropriation). Of course, all sorts of individual labours (including my own dealings in house purchases, pensions and savings) can be individually productive (for me) but this does not make them socially productive. Agreed, this has nothing to do with whether what is done is good or bad, or the nature of the use value more generally. Clowns produce surplus value for their employers by producing jocular entertainment but the financiers make clowns out of us all by appropriating their share but do not add directly to what is to be shared.

As already argued, if put another way, it is not what is done that determines value production but the relations under which it is done. Exchange relations cannot be production relations and so cannot create value just as a catalyst does not find itself a part of an outcome of the chemical reaction in which it participates and for which its presence may even be essential. By contrast the clown does produce jokes, and value if under capitalist relations. Only in the imaginary model of exchange equilibrium of mainstream economics can exchange produce value with no production at all!

From this, all capital (and labour) in exchange is unproductive but it takes two forms, one of which is subject to a tendency for equalization with the rate of profit (merchant capital for Marx) and one which is not (IBC). Returns in the financial sector necessarily structurally combine equalized and non-equalized elements, profitability and interest, respectively. They are hard to distinguish in practice (as with the different forms of rent) although financialization is deeply engaged in integrating them and expanding the presence of IBC. But this means there is no reason for competition to equalize returns in finance with those in industry and, as Brett observes, "competition" (not least state support and regulation) has been prodigiously favourable to finance over the period of neoliberalism and its Global Financial Crisis (GFC), during which returns fell to -5% before almost immediately being restored to 20%.

In addressing future prospects, Brett's final paragraph reminds me of my favourite quote in the wake of the GFC, attributed to Sir Josiah Stamp, richest private individual in the UK in the interwar period, founder of Imperial Chemical Industries (ICI), board member of the Bank of England, and more:

> Banking was conceived in iniquity and was born in sin. The bankers own the earth. Take it away from them, but leave them the power to create money, and with the flick of the pen they will create enough deposits to buy it back again. However, take it away from them, and all the great fortunes like mine will disappear and they ought to disappear, for this would be a happier and better world to live in. But, if you wish to remain the slaves of bankers and pay the cost of your own slavery, let them continue to create money.

There is, though, more and worse to being such a slave today than during the interwar period. For, to return to periodization, it is worth recalling (and I am old enough to have been there at the time), for progressives (and others), the post-war boom seemed to offer a choice between continuing reform, variously described as social compacting and welfarism (in which we all became Scandinavian), and social revolution. In Marxist terms, economic and social reproduction was increasingly being socialized through the state (and its remorseless increase in spending on welfare and industrial interventions) with the equally remorseless expansion of multinational corporations potentially undermining such progress. With the mild exception of the lower rates of growth associated with the market-based banking systems of the USA and the UK (as opposed to the bank-based systems of West Germany and Japan), finance did not appear to figure at all as a major factor, with the same applying to the prospects for the modernization of developing countries as far as post-colonial developmental states were concerned.

Neither side of the reform/revolution divide is to be congratulated on its foresight. For, if putting financialization in other terms than previously, in the current period of capitalism the processes of economic and social reproduction have been increasingly socialized through (private) finance as opposed to the state (although the latter has aided and abetted). The result has been a corresponding loss of popular participation (especially of organized labour) as it was rolled back and neoliberal institutional forms and control rolled out. In the academic field, this is not adequately addressed by what might be termed an "X-minus, finance-plus" approach, whether X be social policy, social compacting, industrial policy or developmental state (whatever their merits for the bygone period of capitalism to which they owe their analytical origins). In short, the study of financialization is as imperative as it is omnipresent; the more grounded in other questions big and small, the better.

Notes

1 It should be stated at the outset that this chapter is focused squarely on political-economic rather than sociological or normative understandings of value.
2 See, for example, the debate over whether bees (as representative of the environment and/or nature) produce value or not in Kallis and Swyngedouw (2018).

3 Although tracing profitability, and its proximate numerical causes, has raised a number of measurement conundrums within Marxism over what is (un)productive and how it should be treated.

4 See the section on "Productive and unproductive labour" in the manuscript "Results of the immediate process of production" (the originally planned but ultimately discarded Part Seven of volume one of *Capital*, usually included today as an appendix thereof); and chapter 4 of *Theories of Surplus Value* (Marx 1863), the "fourth volume" of *Capital*.

5 All quotations from Marx in this paragraph and the following two are from chapter 4 of Marx (1863).

Bibliography

Aglietta, M., 1976. *Régulation et crises du capitalisme*. Paris: Calmann-Levy.

Aglietta, M., 1995. *Macroéconomie financière*. Repères n° 165, Paris: La Découverte.

Aglietta, M., 1998. *Le capitalisme de demain*. Paris: Fondation Saint-Simon.

Arrighi, G., 1994. *The long twentieth century: money, power and the origins of our times*. New York: Verso.

Assa, J., 2017. *The financialization of GDP – implications for economic theory and policy*. Routledge Advances in Heterodox Economics. London and New York: Routledge.

Bayliss, K., B. Fine, M. Robertson and A. Saad Filho, 2020. *Neoliberalism, financialisation and welfare: the political economy of social provision in the UK*. Cheltenham: Edward Elgar, forthcoming.

Bellamy Foster, J., 2008. The financialization of capital and the crisis. *Monthly Review*, 59(11), pp. 1–19.

Boyer, R., 2000. Is a finance-led growth regime a viable alternative to Fordism? A preliminary analysis. *Economy and Society*, 29(1), pp. 111–145.

Bryan, D., Rafferty, M. and C. Jefferies, 2015. Risk and value: finance, labor, and production. *South Atlantic Quarterly*, 114(2), pp. 307–329.

Christophers, B., 2013. *Banking across boundaries: placing finance in capitalism*. Chichester: Wiley-Blackwell.

Christophers, B., 2015. Value models: finance, risk, and political economy. *Finance and Society*, 1(2), pp. 1–22.

Christophers, B., 2016. *The great leveler: capitalism and competition in the court of law*. Cambridge, MA: Harvard University Press.

Christophers, B., 2018a. Risking value theory in the political economy of finance and nature. *Progress in Human Geography*, 42, pp. 330–349.

Christophers, B., 2018b. Financialisation as monopoly profit: the case of US banking. *Antipode*, 50(4), pp. 864–890.

Epstein, G., 2005. Introduction: financialization and the world economy. In G. Epstein (ed.) *Financialization and the World Economy*. Cheltenham: Edward Elgar, pp. 3–16.

Fine, B., 2013. Financialisation from a Marxist perspective. *International Journal of Political Economy*, 42(4), pp. 47–66.

Fine, B., 2017. A Note towards an approach towards social reproduction. Unpublished manuscript, Available at: http://iippe.org/wp/wp-content/uploads/2017/01/sroverviewben.pdf [Accessed 14 February 2019].

Fine, B. and A. Saad Filho, 2018. Marx 200: the abiding relevance of the labour theory of value. *Review of Political Economy*, 30(3), pp. 339–354.

Froud, J., Haslam, C., Johal, S. and K. Williams, 2000. Shareholder value and financialization: consultancy promises, management moves. *Economy and Society*, 29(1), pp. 80–110.

Guttman, R., 2008. *A Primer on finance-led capitalism and its crisis*. Available at: https://regulation.revues.org/5843 [Accessed 14 February 2019].

Kallis, G. and E. Swyngedouw, 2018. Do bees produce value? A conversation between an ecological economist and a Marxist geographer. *Capitalism, Nature, Socialism*. 29(3), pp. 36–50.

Krippner, G., 2005. The financialization of the American economy. *Socio-Economic Review*, 3(2), pp. 173–208.

Lapavitsas, C., 2013. *Profiting without producing: how finance exploits us all*. London: Verso.

Martin, R., 2002. *Financialization of daily life*. Philadelphia, PA: Temple University Press.

Marx, K., 1863. *Theories of surplus value*. Progress Publishers, Available at https://www.marxists.org/archive/marx/works/1863/theories-surplus-value/index.htm [Accessed 14 February 2019].

Minsky, H., 1967. Financial Intermediation in the money and capital markets. In G. Pontecorvo, R. Shay and A. Hart (eds), *Issues in banking and monetary analysis*. New York: Holt, Rinehart and Winston, pp. 33–56.

Mitchell, T., 1998. Fixing the economy. *Cultural Studies*, 12(1), pp. 82–101.

Peck, J. and A. Tickell, 1992. Local modes of social regulation? Regulation theory, Thatcherism and uneven development. *Geoforum*, 23(3), pp. 347–363.

Perez, C., 2002. *Technological revolutions and financial capital: the dynamics of bubbles and golden ages.* Cheltenham: Elgar.

Van der Zwan, N., 2014. Making sense of financialization. *Socio-Economic Review*, 12(1), pp. 99–129.

Van Treeck, T., 2009. The political economy debate on 'financialization' – a macroeconomic perspective. *Review of International Political Economy*, 16(5), pp. 907–944.

Vercelli, A., 2013. Financialization in a long-run perspective: an evolutionary approach. *International Journal of Political Economy*, 42(4), pp. 19–46.

3

ENTREPRENEURSHIP, FINANCE AND SOCIAL STRATIFICATION

The Socio-Economic Background of Financialization[1]

Christoph Deutschmann

Introduction

Since the last decades of the 20th century, the development of advanced capitalist economies was characterized by two major trends: first, a continuous and extraordinary growth of financial wealth, surpassing by far the growth of nominal GDP. In connection with this, the so-called FIRE-sector (financial services, insurance and real estate) has steadily increased its relative contribution to total economic value creation and employment, and became a dominant source of profit generation; these developments were to be observed in the US as well as in other OECD countries (Krippner 2005; Piketty 2014; Guttmann 2016). Political economists and economic sociologists have coined the term "financialization" to circumscribe these changes. Second, a long lasting decline of real economic growth rates, which was combined with rising unemployment, and stagnating or shrinking real mass incomes (Brenner 2006; Streeck 2017). As we know today, the global financial crisis of 2007/2008 did not result in a marked change of these trends. Even after 2007, no lasting contraction of the overall value of global financial assets could be observed. After a short recession, the volume of financial wealth and bank balances continued to rise, though at a much slower pace. At the same time, the recovery of the real economy in the US as well as in Japan and Europe was more sluggish than it used to be in earlier business cycles.

Is there a relationship between the two trends, and – if yes – how are they related to each other? Since the financial crisis of 2007/2008 the phenomenon of financialization is receiving broad scientific and public attention. It should be recalled, however, that the scientific literature on financialization is not that new at all, and can look back on a tradition of at least 20 years before the big crisis. As early as in the mid-1980s, Susan Strange warned of the dangerous consequences of the deregulation of global financial markets in the aftermath of the breakdown of the Bretton Woods system in 1973. Still, what she focused on was less the spectacular expansion of the financial sector itself, but rather the heightened volatility of global capital markets, and the resulting general uncertainty in commodity and labor markets. As Strange viewed it, the global economy became more and more similar to a "casino" – a casino, however, not built for entertainment, and one that allowed no one to escape (Strange 1986).

Most later analyses of financialization agree with Strange that the suspension of the gold-convertibility of the Dollar by the Nixon Government in 1971, the subsequent transition to floating foreign exchange rates, and the gradual abolition of national capital controls were key events initiating the process of financialization. The new volatility of foreign exchange rates gave rise to the spread of new financial instruments, such as derivatives, options, futures, and credit default swaps, originally designed to hedge traders and investors against unforeseeable market turbulences, but afterwards developing a life of their own as vehicles of speculation. The opening of global capital markets, which was continued by Margaret Thatcher's "big bang" in 1986, and the subsequent European deregulation of capital markets (for an overview Helleiner 1995; Bieling 2013), enabled capital now to move freely across borders. Banks saw themselves faced with an *El Dorado* of global investment opportunities, offering much more promising prospects than the conventional, nationally based savings and credit business. Viewed from this angle, financialization appeared as a process that had been initiated largely by regulatory changes regarding financial markets. Following this line of analysis, several researchers have highlighted the role of political decisions, and their intended and unintended consequences in promoting the financialization process. For instance, Greta Krippner showed how the financialization of the US economy unfolded as an unintended consequence of a number of discrete policy decisions, aiming to settle unresolved distributional conflicts under conditions of fading economic growth (Krippner 2011; see Pagliari and Young, this volume).

However, as it turned out soon, the focus on macro-level political decisions alone was not sufficient to understand the full complexity of the financialization phenomenon. The bird's eye view of political economy had to be supplemented by analyses of changes on lower system levels, to grasp the full societal impact of the phenomenon. Researchers developed different perspectives and approaches, focusing on at least three levels: macro-conditions of capital accumulation, the corporate level and the "shareholder revolution" evolving here, and the changed role of finance in private life (Van der Zwan 2014). Moreover, the influence of neoliberal ideologies in promoting financialization, and the structural changes of the political system due to the rising power of financial interests and investment banks, became key issues of research (Fox 2009; Mizruchi 2010). The "increasing role of financial motives, financial markets, financial actors and financial institutions," which Gerald Epstein put into the center of his widely cited definition of financialization (Epstein 2005: 3), indeed was something that seemed to permeate most spheres of society after the late 1980s. Not only the US and the UK, but most other advanced capitalist societies were implicated into these developments too. To gain a deeper sociological understanding of them, multilevel analyses appear most promising. It is this approach that I am going to follow here, aiming to open the view on the structural socio-economic conditions of the financialization phenomenon, which apparently have been neglected in the literature so far. It is the interaction between micro conditions of economic action and the changes of social stratification that appears vital to understand financialization (cf. also Deutschmann 2011a, 2019).

My focus will be on the factors contributing to the spectacular increase of financial wealth and financial assets over the last 30 years, in which the trend towards financialization is becoming most visible. According to figures from the McKinsey Global Institute, total global financial assets (including equity, government bonds, financial bonds, corporate bonds, securitized loans, non-securitized loans) grew from US $12 trillion in 1980, to $56 trillion in 1990, $119 trillion in 2000, and $206 trillion in 2007. This meant a rise of "financial depth" (the ratio of debt and equity outstanding to GDP) from 1.2 in 1980 to 2.6 in 1990, 3.1 in 2000, and 3.5 in 2007. After a short decline due to the financial crisis, the aggregate value of assets continued to grow to $ 225 trillion in 2012, which, however, meant a decline in financial depth to 3.1 due to the higher increase of GDP (McKinsey Global Institute 2013: 2). The overall rise in the value of assets as well as of "financial depth", nevertheless, remains remarkable. How could this happen? Basically, there are two types of explanations offered in the literature. The first one interprets financialization as a process of upward income redistribution, pushing up the share of capital incomes at cost of wages, public revenues and transfer incomes. The second explanation emphasizes the self-referential elements of financialization, due to speculative inflation of assets and spectacularly growing leverage of the financial sector. As a result, the financial sector decoupled itself from the development of the real economy. I will discuss the two approaches in turn, then – in the next chapter – turning to the relationship of both developments to the decline of real growth and its socio-structural conditions.

Upward Redistribution and Speculative Inflation of Assets as Key Elements of Financialization

To analyze the redistributive effects of financialization, the distinction between effects arising at the macro-, meso- and micro-levels is helpful. Considering the macro-level, it often has been shown that the deregulation of financial markets after the end of the Bretton Woods system in 1973 prepared the ground for the spread of a new type of global market actors: investment banks, mutual funds, hedge funds, rating agencies. Due to their growing transnational mobility and their tremendous capital resources, and backed by the influence of an ascendant ever-present neo-liberal ideology, these actors were able to exert massive pressures on the national states. National states increasingly found themselves in a position of having to compete for the favor of financial investors, thereby more and more copying the competitive behavior of private corporations (e.g. Davis 2010). To attract investors, many governments cut corporate taxes and tax rates on high incomes. In the 20 key OECD countries, the average corporate tax rate fell from 44% in 1985 to 29% in 2009; in the East European transformation economies, the tax reductions after 1990 were even more marked (Genschel and Schwarz 2011: 356). Moreover, the deliberate institution of tax havens by the UK, US and many other governments opened vast opportunities to evade taxation altogether. To discover and exploit these opportunities, an entire industry of accounting firms and consultancies developed, offering their services to corporations and wealthy individuals (Harrington 2016).

The redistributive effects of these developments were considerable. The erosion of tax revenues forced governments to cut social expenditures, public investments and to downsize public sector personnel; as a consequence, large parts of the population had to accept lower transfer payments, and a deterioration of the quality and quantity of public services. Moreover, governments decided to privatize public property and public corporations in sectors such as energy, transport, health, education on a large scale, thus obeying the pressure of investors to open new outlets for their idle capital. The consequences for employees and clients often were negative too. Despite privatizations, the trend towards rising sovereign debts could not be stopped and was even reinforced by the restrictive monetary policies of central banks in the G7-countries, which kept real interest rates above growth rates from the 1980s to the early 2000s. Again, investors profited from this in the form of rising interest revenues from state bonds. Due to the depressing impact of public austerity policies and high interest rates, unemployment rose in many countries, and the market position of labor and unions deteriorated. The redistributive consequences were spectacular, as a declining trend of wage to national income ratios in all G7-countries since the 1980s showed (SVR 2012: 322; see Adkins, this volume).

A key development on the meso-level was the so-called "shareholder revolution", starting in the US and then gradually spreading to the UK and the European continent (Fligstein 1990; Useem 1993). Since the 1970s, investment funds and institutional investors became the dominant party on the owner's side in many public companies; moreover, with the spread of "private equity," the grip of investors even extended to mid-sized and small family firms. This led to marked changes in the structure of corporate governance (Erturk, in this volume). The ideology of "shareholder value" and the portfolio theory of the firm gained influence on managerial theory and practice. Increasingly, managers were considered less to be skilled professionals, and more agents of shareholder value maximization. Increasing the value of the owner's portfolio by leveraged buyouts, stock repurchases, mergers and acquisitions became a top priority of business strategy (Fligstein 2008; Dobbin and Jung 2010). These changes occurred not only in the US and the UK, but also in the once firmly integrated business systems such as the German one, where the financialization of corporate governance – nevertheless – remained less pronounced (Deeg 2012; Faust 2012).

In practice, the impact of the influence of investment funds and institutional investors on corporate governance varied, depending on strategies and time horizons of investors, and the degree of their involvement in concrete management decisions (Fichtner, in this volume). However, to comply with the expectations of their clientele, and to perform well in a strongly competitive environment, fund managers often pressed corporate managers to pay out higher dividends, or, alternatively, to buy back shares of their own company in order to boost share prices (Lazonick 2010). Moreover, for corporate managers it became vital to meet the profit targets agreed upon with the owners, because the market value of the firm would decline if profits came under the projected rate. The overall result of these imperatives was a decline in the internal funds disposable for corporate management, which were curtailed further by soaring bonuses and salaries for managers themselves. Often, this had negative consequences not only for process and product innovation, but for many employees too, who were faced with personnel downsizing, wage and benefit cuts, and longer working hours (Epstein 2005; Mizruchi 2010; Van der Zwan 2014). Under financialization, capital largely drew back from its former functions of promoting innovations and industrial efficiency, focusing instead on the aim of maximizing personal wealth of capital owners and managers, in this sense developing "parasitic" (Sayer 2016) traits. Thus, the bottom-up redistribution processes to be observed at the macro-level were reinforced by parallel mechanisms on company level.

The financialization of everyday life revealed itself in a marked rise of private household debt to be observed in particular in the US (Phillips 2006; Montgomerie 2013) and in the UK, though not likewise in continental European countries such as France, Germany or Austria. The growth of household debt developed in connection with the institutional and organizational changes on company and macro-levels. Given the cuts to public welfare programs and transfer payments, the worsening employment situation and declining real wages, it is no surprise that many consumers took recourse to additional credit to maintain their standards of living, and were supported in this by the "democratization" of finance in parallel with the deregulation of the banking sector. With Colin Crouch (2009), one could speak of a regime of "privatized Keynesianism", with private credit cards, mortgage and pension schemes now taking over the former functions of the Keynesian welfare state to stabilize effective demand, though not in a sustainable way. Again, the redistributive implications of this shift from public to private Keynesianism are evident, as the rise of household debts – of course – went in parallel with a rise of interest obligations for large parts of the population. However, the changes in the structure of private finances cannot be interpreted solely as an aftereffect of the retreat of the welfare state and of declining real wages. They were also the result of autonomous changes of popular consumer and investor cultures. Not only consumer credit and mortgage debts mushroomed, but so did stock and mutual fund ownership. A "mass investment culture" (Harmes 2001; Fligstein and Goldstein 2015) emerged and gained ground even in the lower middle classes. Investment and consumption no longer seemed to be alternatives for many families, but occurred at the same time. Neoliberal politics did its part to promote the dream of ever-increasing wealth thorough promoting "financial literacy" and self-discipline as the keys to self-advancement (Lazarus, this volume). Since the Reagan era, stock ownership was propagated as a panacea for the solution of social problems; later, G.W. Bush would come up with his ideology of "ownership" society (Davis 2010). Though the dubious character of such enactments came to the fore in the financial crisis, there can be no doubt that the financialization of everyday life had a pervasive impact on individual value orientations and lifestyles even before (see Aitken, this volume).

Summing up, there is considerable evidence that the financialization of the advanced capitalist economies went in parallel with strong bottom-up redistribution effects (see also Roberts and Kwon 2017). A major factor contributing to higher income inequality and greater wage disparities was the size of the financial sector itself, due to the privileged pay conditions of its employees (see Godechot, this volume).

However, a growth of financial assets as spectacular as shown by the above-cited McKinsey figures certainly cannot be explained by bottom-up redistribution *alone*. Here, the second element mentioned above comes into play, which explains the increase in financial depth from a speculative inflation of assets, and a tremendous increase of financial leverage mediated by the circulation of a large variety of new financial "products." As pointed out above, national governments, with the US and the UK taking a leading role and many EU governments joining, actively dismantled the regulatory framework of financial markets. Bank laws were liberalized, shadow banking tolerated, capital resource requirements relaxed, firewalls between credit and investment banking demolished, transparency prescriptions watered down, offshore centers created, hedge funds allowed to develop, and so on. For the financial industry, this opened a chance to overcome the constraints of its traditional credit and saving business, and to engage in new and promising fields, such as global investment banking and the marketing of financial innovations. New vehicles of financial speculation such as derivatives, options, futures, credit default swaps, collateralized debt obligations (CDOs), asset backed securities (ABS) pushed financial leverage up to unprecedented dimensions. Dubious credits and bonds of all kinds were securitized and sold, following the logic of the "greater fool theory."[2] Ratings, securities and balances no longer were simply indicators of creditworthiness; rather, in the context of the speculative mania developing they became signals to justify ever increasing financial leverage. As a result, the financial sector decoupled from the real economy and developed according to a self-referential logic (Guttmann 2016). As the authors of the above cited McKinsey analysis found, only 28% of the rise in global financial depth between 1995 and 2007 came from credits for households and nonfinancial corporations, and 10% from the sovereign bond market. Some 62% of the increase of financial depth, on the other hand, was due to higher equity market valuations and financial system leverage (McKinsey Global Institute 2013: 17). As the authors emphasize, financial expansion was much more pronounced in the developed economies than in the emerging ones, as the level of financial depth in the former is roughly twice as high as in the latter, and substantially above the global average of 3.1 in 2012.[3]

With hindsight, it is evident that such an expansion could not sustain. However, when the bubble ultimately burst in 2007/2008, it turned out that it had become too big to let it collapse. Governments and central banks intervened with massive "rescue" programs to stabilize faltering banks. Interest rates were dropped down to zero or even negative levels; "Quantitative Easing" policies pumped additional liquidity into the financial sector, and continue to do so up to the present day. This helped to bring about an immediate stabilization, with the consequence, however, of making the dissociation of finance from the non-financial economy permanent. Viewed from this perspective, financialization is based not merely on redistribution, but has taken the character of a lasting, politically guaranteed inflation of financial assets. Perhaps one could speak of a super-bubble; nevertheless it remains a bubble. Imagine that, by some accident, the entire superstructure of inflated assets and derivative financial products would wither away with one stroke, with the exception only of primary accounts of states, firms and households. Would that really do so much harm to the non-financial "rest" of society?

Growth, Entrepreneurship and the Collective Elevator Effect: Socio-economic Contradictions underlying Financialization

It appears strange that among the explanations offered for financialization just one is lacking, which orthodox economics textbook models treat as the "normal" one. According to such models, financial expansion should reflect a growing and flourishing real economy requiring additional capital to finance promising innovations and future projects, and, hence, increasing the demand for credit and capital. As stated above, the opposite is the case. Today, there is abundant evidence that the process of financialization of the advanced industrial economies went along with a long-term decline of real economic growth and investment, which developed after the erosion of the often cited "Fordist" model of capitalism in the 1970s.[4] What is lacking up to the present, however, is a consistent theory about the slowdown of the real economy, and the interaction of the two developments. Did the slowdown of the real economy go back to a decline of productivity, or to a profit squeeze due to sticky wages and too strong unions, or to a combination of both factors – as some commentators have alleged? Is a somewhat modified version of the Marxian theory of the falling rate of profit required to explain the slowdown, as Robert Brenner (2006) suggested? Do we have to identify the causes of the crisis in the demise of the former "Fordist" regime of production, resulting in lasting mismatches between production and consumption, as the authors of the regulation school (for an overview see Boyer and Saillard 2002) are arguing? Or should we take recourse to some version of "long wave" theories, either of economic innovations, or of hegemonic political regimes (e.g. Arrighi and Silver 1999)? Certainly, most of these approaches have contributed valuable insights (Beck and Knafo, in this volume). However, a point that seems to be neglected in most of them (except the last-mentioned long wave theories) is the key role of economic innovation for profit and growth, and of the socio-economic conditions underlying the innovative process in capitalist economies. What I offer in this last section of my chapter is an outline of an alternative sociological approach, focusing on the socio-economic conditions of innovation and their internal contradictions, which could bring more light into the interaction between financial expansion and real economic slowdown (cf. also Deutschmann 2011a, b, 2019).

Some few preliminary remarks on the concept of economic growth are in order. Usually, growth is decomposed into absolute growth of real social product due to a rising population and workforce, and per capita growth due to higher productivity. Only per capita growth is "true" growth, as it implies a higher income per person. Per capita growth, however, should not be equalized with higher *physical* productivity; it does not simply mean "more of the same." What is vital, rather, are *innovations* resulting in a higher *value* of output. Innovations can take many forms: new products, new technologies, new systems of organization or logistics, discovery of new markets; they involve applied as well as basic technologies or products. It is extremely difficult to measure the contribution of innovation to value creation; only money has the numinous capacity to commensurate private property rights over a totality of vastly heterogeneous, and ever changing, objects of value. Therefore, textbook quantitative economic models such as $y\ growth = x\ capital + u\ labor + v\ knowledge$ are not sufficient for understanding the micro-dimension of the innovation process. Of course, capital, labor and knowledge are required to generate innovations, but the real question obviously is: *What kind* of capital, labor, knowledge precisely? As Schumpeter, Knight and Hayek have emphasized, such questions cannot be answered on the basis of abstract models, but only of the context-dependent expertise of the historical actors. A general theory of innovations would be a contradiction in terms, since product as well as process innovations are something that by definition cannot be predicted based on nomological knowledge.

What is possible, nevertheless, are sociological theories about entrepreneurs as a particular category of social actors and the typical social circumstances generating them. "Entrepreneurs" in the widest sense of actors promoting innovations include not only firm owners and self-employed persons but also all those taking entrepreneurial "functions" such as managers and qualified employees, if we follow Schumpeter further. Entrepreneurs, of course, need professional expertise and technical training. Nevertheless, what they are doing is not simply to "apply" given technical or academic knowledge. Higher education and scientific expertise will not necessarily produce entrepreneurship and, hence, also not growth.[5] It is the mission of entrepreneurs to make use of given knowledge in a *new* way, and to transform inventions into marketable "innovations". They strive to exploit the chances of a given market constellation, thereby employing not only scientific and academic knowledge, but also creativity and practical intuition. In the case of success, profit emerges as a premium on a temporary monopoly, which the successful entrepreneur enjoys.

To perform in the market, the entrepreneur – first of all – needs a strong personal motivation. What drives entrepreneurial action, if he/she is not simply a rational hedonist (as Schumpeter had emphasized)? To a large degree, it is the quest for social advance, mainly not through acquired formal qualifications, but through competitive performance on the market. The capitalist entrepreneur as a historically new type of actor, of course, does not fall from heaven. Entrepreneurship can arise only in the context of a particular class structure, which, in some sense, shows the characteristics of a "double-bind": on the one hand, it is characterized by a marked inequality of wealth; on the other hand, it leaves at least some room for the underprivileged to advance across class lines individually thanks to extraordinary market performance. Indeed, in contrast to pre-modern class structures, which ascribed class membership to social origin, the capitalist class dichotomy leaves individual affiliation to both main classes (worker and capitalist) formally open and social mobility across classes possible. Although actual chances for social advance mostly are low, the formal openness can encourage individual ambitions to rise. The relative openness of the capitalist class structure without doubt is a key variable motivating entrepreneurial action, and – even more so – generating "entrepreneurs" as a social category itself. The polarization of classes opens up room for intense competition, with entrepreneurs competing to exploit the creative potentials of labor with the aim of profit, and workers competing for subsistence and social rise too.

A factor that heats up these competitive pressures is population growth, which is a typical phenomenon in periods of rapid capitalist expansion. A growing population is a further structural factor vital for entrepreneurship, as nascent entrepreneurs concentrate strongly on the younger and middle cohorts (GEM 2014). The ideal constellation for capitalist growth is a strongly uneven distribution of wealth, in combination with a large, poor and *juvenile* population striving for social advancement; conversely, an ageing population will have a negative impact on growth.

Not all unpropertied people are receptive to the quest for social advance to the same degree. The members of the "underclass" are generally not, as are people in the traditional working-class milieus, who tend to develop a defensive and collective stance about their interests. However, individuals in the lower middle classes, including not only the self-employed, but also the "new" middle classes of white collar and qualified blue-collar workers, tend to view their prospects for individual social rise in a more positive light. To bridge the gap between their ambitious personal objectives and their mostly limited resources, they often take recourse to "innovative" ways of adaptation, sometimes on the boundaries of legality,[6] as the American sociologist Robert K. Merton (1965) had observed already in his classic studies of social anomie. To put it briefly: The paradoxical, open-as-well-as-closed structure of capitalist classes generates structural tensions which, in turn, induce processes of striving for social upward mobility in the middle and lower middle layers of society. The extraordinary efforts of entrepreneurs and employees, driven by the stick of competition as well as by the carrot of social rise, in turn, secure the continued profit-ability of capital. The innovative dynamics of capitalism and, hence, growth, can be explained largely from this constellation.

It would be short-sighted to hypothesize a simple empirical correlation between total, struc-tural as well as individual, mobility and growth. Mobility can have an upward as well as downward trajectory, thus the effect of total mobility on growth as a macro variable is largely indeterminate (Breen 2014: 465). What appears more relevant is *structural* mobility, implying a collective rise or descent of entire groups or layers within the social structure, either through individual careers or intergenerational succession. If a group advances collectively, this is a symptom of individual performance getting rewarded at a large scale, and experiences of market success outweighing those of failure. Structural upward mobility, therefore, can be interpreted as a factor indicating as well as promoting growth; conversely, the impact of structural down-ward mobility on growth will be negative. There is much evidence that historical periods of structural upward mobility are characterized by high growth rates. A spectacular example are the three decades after World War II, which were indeed "golden" ones for the advanced Western economies (Western Europe, North America, Japan), as the white collar middle and service classes expanded considerably at the cost of blue collar worker positions. Ulrich Beck (1992) coined the concept of a collective "elevator-effect" to describe these developments. At the same time, growth rates soared to historically unprecedented heights (Piketty 2014).

However, likewise, it is clear that structural upward mobility as a factor promoting growth cannot continue indefinitely. Not everybody can join the wealthy classes, since this would mean the end of the capitalist polarization of classes and hence of the capital market. Society needs Indians too, not only chiefs. Wealth is always contingent upon debt, the value of assets depending precisely upon the availability of solvent debtors who can service the claims of capital. With continuing structural upward mobility, therefore, an increasing mismatch in the capital markets tends to arise. On the one hand, the social structure becomes top-heavy, and the wealth even of the upper middle classes, all the more so of the elites, increases. The volume of rent-seeking financial assets soars accordingly, paving the ground for actors such as mutual funds and invest-ment banks to develop and to serve the needs of a larger and larger clientele. On the other hand, the entrepreneurial potentials to redeem the assets decrease, as the social reservoir of those still eager to advance, and to incur debts and risks for advancing their career shrinks, due to the col-lective elevator effect. This applies even more in the case of a parallel decline in population. The successful and their descendants may still be career oriented, but they no longer have a stringent motive for taking the personal risks of an *entrepreneurial career*. The accumulation of wealth in the hands of the successful gives them an edge over subsequent social risers. The intergenerational transmission of fortunes and educational privileges (Piketty 2014) exacerbates this effect, as it tends to close the channels of upward mobility. For those not belonging to privileged networks, and lacking access to credit, resources and education, the chances are dwindling. Nascent real econ-omy entrepreneurs, when asking banks for credit, often cannot compete with the apparently superior profitability of financial investments. At the same time, firm-internal entrepreneurs feel frustrated by the tough cost regime and the short-term profit targets that are characteristic in financialized firms. As a consequence, the gospel of social rise, and, with it, of growth, loses credibility even for many of the qualified in the younger generation (Blossfeld et al. 2005).

Thus, as financial assets grow, the entrepreneurial potential required to secure the profitability of capital tends to decline, with the result of declining real growth rates. Indeed this is exactly what seems to have happened after the 1980s in the advanced industrial economies, in the US as well as in Europe. While financial wealth grew up to unprecedented dimensions, social upward mobility went down (for the US see Noah 2012, for Europe Byrne 2005, Grabka and Frick 2008), and so did growth. On the one hand, financialization was a response to the erosion of real entrepreneurship. In some sense, it meant to substitute self-referential financial "innovation", making use of the "performative" effects of financial models (McKenzie and Millo 2008), for innovation in the real economy. On the other hand, financialization contributed to the further erosion of real entrepreneurship due to its demotivating effects on social risers. With ever-increasing concentration of wealth in the top income groups, the negative impact on upward mobility and growth became even stronger, as internationally comparative studies have shown. In his study on 13 OECD countries, Corak found that "countries with higher inequality of incomes also tend to be countries in which a greater fraction of economic advantage and disadvantage is passed on between parents and children" (Corak 2013: 2). Lippman et al. (2005) reached similar conclusions in their study on entrepreneurship, based on data on 60 industrial, emerging and developing countries provided by the "Global Entrepreneurship Monitor" (GEM) research network. The data show that the relative frequency of nascent entrepreneurs is much lower in the industrially advanced countries, as compared to emerging and developing ones. Moreover, the authors analysed the correlation between wealth inequality and nascent entrepreneurship and distinguished between necessity- and opportunity-based entrepreneurship, the first one being driven by the sheer absence of alternative livelihood options, the other one by perceived economic chances. As it turns out, the frequency of necessity-based entrepreneurship tends to increase linearly with wealth inequality, while the correlation of wealth inequality with opportunity based entrepreneurship showed a curvilinear pattern, with nascent entrepreneurship declining again beyond a medium level of inequality. As the authors conclude, it appears that only "moderate levels of inequality do help opportunity based entrepreneurship to flourish. Countries with high levels of inequality do not experience as much opportunity entrepreneurship, because people lack the resources and information required to take advantage of opportunities essential for such activity" (Lippman et al. 2005: 15).

Conclusions

The above discussion pinpoints how the success of capitalism at promoting social advance on a large scale undermines the chances for subsequent entrepreneurs and social risers, with the consequence of an erosion of innovation and growth. The decay of entrepreneurial spirit often happening in the third or fourth generations of entrepreneurial dynasties, which Thomas Mann highlighted in his novel on "The Buddenbrooks", is repeating itself at the collective level (cf. Deutschmann 2008). Financialization, be it in its redistributive or in its speculative forms, can be interpreted as an unintended response of the capitalist system to this dilemma. In some sense, it can be interpreted as an "innovative" reaction of the banking sector to declining profits in its traditional business; at the same time, it tends to exacerbate the problem due to its discouraging effects on real entrepreneurship.

Financialization, indeed, represents a "new mode of accumulation", as capital is accumulated no longer via innovation and entrepreneurial "creative destruction" in the Schumpeterian sense. On the one hand, capital takes the character of a power-based, "parasitic" claim on the productive resources of the economy, restoring in some sense the "feudal" past of capitalism as it redistributes resources ruthlessly upward (Neckel 2010; Sayer 2016). On the other hand, because such a redistribution will eventually encounter economic and political limits (and resistances); a way out lies in the politically safeguarded inflation of assets, which seems to work smoothly and to offer almost unlimited horizons, as the money-creating potential of central banks and the financial system is infinite. However, there is a price to be paid for this option too. First, reflating financial assets by central bank money means to push the rate of interest on loans to zero or negative values. With loans bearing negative real (or even nominal) interest rates, Keynes' "euthanasia of the rentier" looms large, as safe options for capital placement no longer deliver returns. Still, this mostly harms small middle-class savers, not big investors, and it does not signal the end of the capital market. However, the remaining markets – in particular stocks and real estate – are exposed even more to the risk of bubbles, and higher volatility. Second, and above all, capital departs from the real altogether, and takes refuge in a virtual and imaginary one. Similar to the pathology of "stinginess" described by Georg Simmel in his classic analyses (1989: 322f.), the rentier contents her-/himself with the obsession of what he *could do* with her/his money, while withdrawing from an innovative and transformative role in the real world. This may not yet come down to an "end" of capitalism, as Wolfgang Streeck (2016) has suggested, but financialized capitalism can no longer be legitimate as a social order promoting innovation and mass welfare.

Notes

1 I am greatly indebted to Phil Mader and Felipe Gonzalez for helpful comments to this article.
2 As John Lanchester explains, everybody who bought such titles knew it was crazy. However, he/she could count on meeting an even "greater fool" to whom the titles could be sold with a profit (Lanchester 2012: 129).
3 In 2012, the level of financial depth amounted to 4.6 in the US, 4.5 in Japan and 3.7 in Western Europe. By contrast, it amounted to 2.3 in China, 1.5 in the Middle East, 1.5 in other emerging Asia countries and India (McKinsey Global Institute 2013: 19).
4 Global per capita real output fell from an annual average growth rate of 2.5 percent between 1950 and 1980 to 1.7 percent between 1981 and 2012. In Europe it fell from 3.4 percent to 1.8 percent in the same periods, in America from 2.0 percent to 1.3 percent (Piketty 2014: 94).
5 Though nascent entrepreneurs show a comparatively high percentage of university graduates in Europe (ca. 5 percent), there are more than 3 percent nascent entrepreneurs among the low skilled too; in Germany nascent entrepreneurship is even higher among the low skilled than among university graduates (OECD 2013: 50).
6 An actual example is Uber, whose innovative business model is confronted with accusations of violating legal standards of safety and social security.

Bibliography

Arrighi, A. and Silver, B., 1999. *Chaos and Governance in the Modern World System.* Minneapolis: University of Minnesota Press.

Beck, U., 1992. *Risk Society. Towards a New Modernity.* London: SAGE.

Bieling, H., 2013. European Financial Capitalism and the Politics of (De)-financialization. *Competition and Change,* 17(3), pp. 283–298.

Blossfeld, H., Klijzing, E., Mills, M. and Kurz, K., 2005. *Globalisation, Uncertainity and Youth in Society.* London: Routledge.

Boyer, R. and Saillard, Y. (eds.), 2002. *Régulation Theory. The State of the Art.* London: Routledge.

Breen, R., 2014. Social Mobility in Europe. In: Grusky, D. and K. Weisshaar.,(eds.), *Social Stratification. Class, Gender and Race in Sociological Perspective,* Fourth Edition. Boulder, CO: Westview, pp. 464–479.

Brenner, R., 2006. *The Economics of Global Turbulence. The Advanced Capitalist Economies from Long Boom to long Downturn 1945–2005.* London: Verso.

Byrne, D., 2005. *Social Exclusion,* Second Edition. New York: Open University Press.

Corak, M., 2013. Income Inequality, Equality of Opportunity, and Intergenerational Mobility. Discussion Paper No. 7520, July 2013. Bonn: Institute for the Study of Labor (IZA).

Crouch, C., 2009. Privatized Keynesianism: An Unacknowledged Policy Regime. *The British Journal of Politics and International Relations* 11, pp. 382–399.

Davis, G., 2010. After the Ownership Society: Another World is Possible. In: M. Lounsbury and P. Hirsch (eds.), *Markets on Trial: The Economic Sociology of the U.S. Financial Crisis, Part B.* Bingley: Emerald, pp. 331–358.

Deeg, R., 2012. Financialization and Models of Capitalism: A Comparison of the UK and Germany. In: C. Lane and G. Wood (eds.), *Capitalist Diversity and Diversity within Capitalism.* London: Routledge, pp. 121–149.

Deutschmann, C., 2008. Die Finanzmärkte und die Mittelschichten: der kollektive Buddenbrooks-Effekt. *Leviathan* 36(4), pp. 501–517.

Deutschmann, C., 2011a. Limits to Financialization. Sociological Analyses of the Financial Crisis. *European Journal of Sociology* LII(3), pp. 347–389.

Deutschmann, C., 2011b. A Pragmatist Theory of Capitalism. *Socio-Economic Review* 9/1, pp. 83–106.

Deutschmann, C., 2019. *Disembedded Markets. Economic Theology and Global Capitalism.* London: Routledge.

Dobbin, F. and Jung, J., 2010. The Misapplication of Mr. Michael Jensen: How Agency Theory brought down the Economy and why it might again. In: M. Lounsbury and P. Hirsch (eds.), *Markets on Trial: The Economic Sociology of the U.S. Financial Crisis, Part B.* Bingley: Emerald, pp. 29–64.

Epstein, G., 2005. Introduction: Financialization and the World Economy. In: G. Epstein (ed.), *Financialization and the World Economy.* Cheltenham: Edward Elgar, pp. 3–17.

Faust, M., 2012. The Shareholder Value Concept of the Corporation and Co-determination in Germany: Unresolved Contradictions or Reconciliation of Institutional Logics? In: C. Lane and G. Wood (eds.), *Capitalist Diversity and Diversity within Capitalism.* London: Routledge, pp. 150–188.

Fligstein, N., 1990. *The Transformation of Corporate Control.* Cambridge: Harvard University Press.

Fligstein, N., 2008. The Finance Conception of the Firm. In: I. Erturk, J. Froud, S. Johal, A. Leaver and K. Williams (eds.), *Financialization at Work.* London: Routledge, pp. 307–318.

Fligstein, N. and Goldstein, A., 2015. The Emergence of a Financial Culture in American Households 1989–2007. *Socio-Economic Review* 13(3), pp. 575–601.

Fox, J., 2009. *The Myth of the Rational Market* New York: Harper Collins.

Genschel, P. and Schwarz, P., 2011. Tax Competition: A Literature Review. *Socio-Economic Review* 9(2), pp. 339–370.

GEM, 2014. *Global Entrepreneurship Monitor. 2013 Global Report.* J. Ernsto Amorós and N. Bosma, Universidad del Desarollo and Global Entrepreneurship Association, Utrecht University.

Grabka, M. and Frick, J. 2008. Schrumpfende Mittelschicht – Anzeichen einer dauerhaften Polarisierung der verfügbaren Einkommen. *DIW-Wochenbericht* 10/2008. Berlin: Deutsches Institut für Wirtschaftsforschung (DIW).

Guttmann, R. 2016. *Finance led Capitalism. Shadow Banking, Re-Regulation, and the Future of Global Markets.* New York: Palgrave Macmillan.

Harmes, A., 2001. Mass Investment Culture. *New Left Review* 9 (May-June), pp. 103–124.

Harrington, B., 2016. *Capital without Borders. Wealth Managers and the One Percent.* Cambridge, MA: Harvard University Press.

Helleiner, E., 1995. Explaining the Globalization of Financial Markets: Bringing States Back. *Review of International Political Economy* 2(2), pp. 315–341.

Krippner, G., 2005. The Financialization of the American Economy. *Socio-Economic Review* 3, pp. 173–208.

Krippner, G., 2011. *Capitalizing on Crisis: The Political Origins of the Rise of Finance.* Cambridge, MA: Harvard University Press.

Lanchester, J., 2012. *Whoops! Why Everybody Owes Everyone and No One Can Pay.* London: Simon and Schuster.

Lazonick, W., 2010. Innovative Business Models and Varieties of Capitalism: Financialization of the U.S. Corporation. *Business History Review* 84, pp. 675–702.

Lippman, S., Davis, A. and Aldrich, H., 2005. Entrepreneurship and Inequality. In: L.A. Keister (ed.), *Entrepreneurship.* Amsterdam: Elsevier, pp. 3–32.

McKenzie, D. and Millo, Y., 2008. Performativity and the Black Scholes Model. In: I. Erturk, J. Froud, S. Johal, A. Leaver, K. Williams (eds.), *Financialization at Work.* London: Routledge, pp. 269–281.

McKinsey Global Institute 2013. *Financial Globalization: Retreat or Reset?* McKinsey&Company.

Merton, R., 1965. *Social Theory and Social Structure,* Ninth Rev. and Enl. Edition. New York: Free Press.

Mizruchi, M., 2010. The American Corporate Elite and the Historical Roots of the Financial Crisis in 2008. In: M. Lounsbury and P. Hirsch (eds.), *Markets on Trial. The Economic Sociology of the US Financial Crisis, Part B.* Bingley: Emerald, pp. 103–140.

Montgomerie, J., 2013. America's Debt Safety-Net. *Public Administration* 91(4), pp. 871–888.

Neckel, S., 2010. Refeudalisierung der Ökonomie. Zum Strukturwandel der kapitalistischen Wirtschaft. *MPIfG Discussion Paper* 10/6, Max Planck-Institute for the Study of Societies, Cologne.

Noah, T., 2012. *The Great Divergence: America's Growing Inequality Crisis and What we can do about it.* New York: Bloomsbury Press.

OECD/The European Commission, 2013. *The Missing Entrepreneurs. Policies for Inclusive Entrepreneurship in Europe.* OECD Publishing.

Phillips, K., 2006. *American Theocracy. The Peril and Politics of Radical Religion, Oil, and Borrowed Money in the 21th Century.* London: Penguin.

Piketty, T., 2014. *Capital in the Twenty-First Century.* Cambridge: The Belknap Press of Harvard University Press (Original: *Le capital au XXIe siècle*, Paris 2013, Éditions du Seuil).

Roberts, A. and Kwon, R., 2017. Finance, Inequality and the Varieties of Capitalism in Post-industrial Democracies. *Socio-Economic Review* 15(3), pp. 511–538.

Sayer, A., 2016. *Why we Can't Afford the Rich.* Bristol: Policy Press.

Simmel, G., 1989. *Philosophie des Geldes*, Gesamtausgabe Band 6. Frankfurt/M: Suhrkamp.

Strange, S., 1986. *Casino Capitalism.* Oxford: Blackwell.

Streeck, W., 2016. *How Will Capitalism End? Essays on a Failing System.* London: Verso.

Streeck, W., 2017. *Buying Time. The Delayed Crisis of Democratic Capitalism*, Second Edition. London: Verso (Original: *Gekaufte Zeit*, Frankfurt/M 2013: Suhrkamp).

SVR, 2012. *Jahresgutachten des Sachverständigenrates zur Begutachtung der gesamtwirtschaftlichen Entwicklung* 2012/13.

Useem, M., 1993. Shareholder Power and the Struggle for Corporate Control. In: R. Swedberg (ed.), *Explorations in Economic Sociology.* New York: Russell Sage Foundation, pp. 308–334.

Van der Zwan, N., 2014. Making Sense of Financialization. *Socio-Economic Review* 12, pp. 99–129.

4

SHAREHOLDER PRIMACY AND CORPORATE FINANCIALIZATION

Ismail Erturk

Introduction

As Engelen (2008), Van der Zwan (2014) and Christophers (2015) indicate in their own distinctive theoretical contexts in reviewing the financialization literature, financialization studies emerged at a rupture in the history of capitalism when corporate governance at Anglo-Saxon firms had gone through a revolutionary change between the 1970s and 1990s. This has sparked off, from the beginning of the 2000s, a thematically coherent body of academic work from various disciplines on corporate financialization that critically engages with this discursive and political phenomenon in present day capitalism which has given us the neoliberal project of shareholder value maximization principle that is homogeneous as doctrine but inconsistent and heterogeneous as practice. Also commonly referred to as shareholder primacy, the shareholder value maximization principle advocates the idea that the purpose of the firm is to prioritize the financial interests of the shareholders, providers of capital to the firm. The purpose of the firm is a contested subject in corporate law studies and economics. The historic evolution of the owner-managed private firm to the professionally managed public firm has required the formulation of explicit corporate governance codes and principles that socio-economically organize the contractual relationship between owners (principals) and managers (agents). In this context a stakeholder perspective defines the purpose of the firm to equally serve employees, owners, customers, and the wider society. In the neoliberal era the shareholder value maximization principle has become the dominant corporate governance practice that has gained legitimacy through management education and consultancy recipes.

In this chapter, the first section will discuss the literature on corporate financialization in the 1990s and early 2000s where critical social science literature from political economy to economic sociology, from French Regulation School to the UK critical management studies have problematized the historical logic and sustainability of shareholder value primacy in the evolution of capitalism. The major contribution of this early body of work to the study of capitalistic firm is the analytical and conceptual formulation of the fact that the competition between firms has shifted from product markets to stock markets – the Chandlerian (Chandler 1977) competitive capitalistic firm producing innovative products in a socially cohesive socio-economic order is being replaced by the agency theorists' financially engineered firm that generates cash flows first and foremost for its shareholders at the expense of social cohesion for its all stakeholders.

When the financialized capitalism of shareholder primacy-driven firms, as its critics anticipated, regularly produced stock market crashes, corporate scandals and worsening inequality, politics and society did not respond equally forcefully to overturn the rule of shareholder primacy. The second section in this chapter will survey the literature on corporate financialization that documents its failure in delivering its socio-economic promises and critically engage with the underlining causes of its survival and expansion into non-market, non-profit organizations like universities and mutually owned banks. The third section of the chapter will comment on the criticism of the shareholder primacy after the Great Financial Crisis that now includes insiders in financialized capitalism and economists at international institutions like OECD and central banks.

The Rise of Shareholder Primacy and Firms Competing in the Stock Market

The literature on corporate financialization is primarily a critical engagement with the shareholder value maximization principle that the neoliberal economic ideology has codified and normalized as universally efficient and ideal firm behavior in present-day capitalism, against the background of the structural changes in the US firms' decline in competitiveness and the concurrent rise of dispersed ownership in the 1970s. The analytical codes and the implicit political choices of the academic proponents of the shareholder value maximization principle originate from neo-classical economics' imaginaries of market efficiency and self-correcting markets but expand these imaginaries to capital markets (valuation of firms) and the market for managerial labor (agency theory). As such the academic discipline that the shareholder value maximization principle is most closely associated with is financial economics, a discipline that is accommodated primarily in finance departments of business schools with close institutional links to the practice of management through consultancy, and MBA education and has flourished as business schools have proliferated globally since the 1980s (Mizruchi and Kimeldorf 2005).

Jensen (1993), one of the most prominent financial economists associated with the shareholder primacy, has called shareholder primacy a revolutionary managerial practice in the history of capitalism that has shifted the location of firm competitiveness from production cycles to the external stock market valuation processes. Jensen describes this shift as the key driver of what he calls the "modern industrial revolution" that is believed by the theorists and practitioners of modern finance theory to have revitalized the US firm's competitiveness.

This revolutionary shift in firm behavior in present-day US capitalism is acknowledged by the early contributors to corporate financialization literature (Fligstein 1993; Lazonick and O'Sullivan 1996; Froud et al. 2000; Crotty 2003). This new hegemonic governance mode by capital markets is seen as suppressive for innovation by Lazonick and O'Sullivan (1996). Crotty (2003) declared it as the end of the Golden Age of US capitalism and the historically progressive relationship between capital and labor. For Fligstein (1993) a new period of socio-economic stability replaced the Golden Age which would last until an inevitable major stock market crash occurred. This new paradigm of shareholder primacy is seen as an unrealizable project that only a handful of capital light firms are capable of delivering by Froud et al. (2000). The theoreticians of the French Regulation school too agreed with the US and the UK scholarship on financialization that *les trente glorieuses* that had been the socio-economic outcome of the Fordist accumulation regime with its own peculiar mode of regulation for social cohesion was replaced by a new regulation regime where the shareholder primacy-driven governance model plays a decisive role (Aglietta 1998; Boyer 2000; Grahl and Teague 2000). Aglietta (1998), who is theoretically more sensitive to finance amongst the French Regulation School, tends to see socially cohesive stabilizing forces in the financialized governance by shareholder pension funds in this post-Fordist finance-led growth regime. Boyer (2000), however, is more agnostic and sees a high probability potential for instability in an economy driven by financialized firm behavior.

Krippner (2005) introduces a methodological dimension to the literature on financialized firm behavior and produces a set of empirical data on accumulation of profit at the US firms. From this empirical content she concludes that financialization has solved the low profitability crisis of the US corporations in trade and production by creating sources of profit through financial channels in a globalized economy. Whereas Boyer (2000) theoretically and Froud et al. (2000) operationally see corporate financialization as unsustainable and fragile in present-day capitalism, Krippner (2005) is less inclined to think that financialized firm behavior and accumulation of capital through financial channels is under threat from capital market instability.

Corporate financialization has survived the dot.com crisis and the Enron corporate scandal just as it did the leveraged buyout crash in 1989. The defining characteristic of financialized corporate behavior, competing in stock market in share price, has survived even the 2007 crisis. Crotty's (2003) and Froud et al.'s (2000) analyses below, explaining what competition in stock market means, are, therefore, still very much relevant today.

> I stress two aspects of the changing relation between financial markets and large NFCs. The first is a shift in the beliefs and behavior of financial agents, from an implicit acceptance of the Chandlerian view of the large NFC [non-financial corporation] as an integrated, coherent combination of illiquid real assets assembled to pursue long-term growth and innovation, to a "financial" conception in which the NFC is seen as a "portfolio" of liquid subunits that home-office management must continually restructure to maximize the stock price at every point in time.
>
> *(Crotty 2003: 272)*

Froud et al. (2000) translate this stock market competition into the accounting language and point out how a financialized firm competing in stock market prioritizes the residual income-based measures of corporate success, return to shareholders, as opposed to the earnings-based measures that derive from product market performances like sales growth. This revolutionary rise of financial logic in measuring firm competitiveness through valuation in stock market resonates strongly in the early literature on corporate financialization.

> Equally, the parties to this debate share a concept of the firm as a bundle of investment projects and reduce the economy to one micro level, as the sum of the investment projects made by all the firms. In micro terms, the capital market is the more or less exclusive focus of interest with little reference to product or labor markets.
>
> *(Froud et al. 2000: 89)*

The success and realism of the shareholder value maximization principle in practice was questioned by Froud et al. (2000) through accounting-based research across firms operating in different industries. Then after the dot.com crash of 2001 Fligstein (2005) expected the death of shareholder primacy because all previous conceptions of control in the socio-economic history of the US firms had ended after a stock market crash.

> The shareholder value conception of control began with the merger movement from 1979–1987... A conception of control is not just a cognitive framework that suggests how to make money. It helps define and is defined by the social relationships between competitors, suppliers, customers, employees, financial markets, and governments.

These strategies and the social relationships they are embedded in have moved in cycles of approximately 20–25 years for the past 130 years.

(Fligstein 2005: 228)

In the very core of the shareholder value primacy doctrine lies the belief that the interests of the managers and the shareholders in modern public companies with distributed ownership can be resolved through optimal contracts between the owners (principals) and the managers (agents) where such contracts involve equity-based remunerations, mostly stock options, for the managers (Jensen and Meckling 1976; Fama 1980). The shareholder primacy doctrine promotes two purely economically legitimized beliefs about valuation technologies in stock markets: stock markets are the only disciplining mechanisms to enforce economically and socially optimal firm competition in a market economy and they are also the most efficient form of governance solving the agency problem in publicly owned companies. The post-war Golden Age of capitalism, on the other hand, was conceived as an economy with a corporate governance system where firms with priorities firmly anchored in product markets are led by managers pursuing product market defined objectives like market share and growth (Berle 1962; Galbraith 1967). Neo-classical economists like Jensen and Meckling (1976) and Fama (1980) led a counter argument to managerialism by offering theoretical solutions to the agency problem in historically evolving large firms with institutional shareholders.

This purely economic approach to corporate governance at modern firms has drawn criticism from law and economics scholars like (Stout 2001) and (Ireland 1999) who argued that there was no legal basis for the shareholder primacy notion of the firm. Stout (2001) explains that shareholders in limited liability companies cannot claim property rights on assets owned by the corporate legal entity. Ireland (2001) goes further to demonstrate that shareholders in modern corporations hardly provide capital and they are passive owners selling and buying shares in stock market. They are rentiers of the kind described by interwar writers like R.H. Tawney or John Maynard Keynes (see Ertürk et al. 2008). Paranque, too, explains the legitimacy of agency theory by politics of the shareholder value maximization principle: "Within this system, management appears to be the central figure in terms of running the system, under the cover of creating shareholder value" (Paranque 2017: 688). The shareholder value primacy idea, however, has managed to survive and has even expanded (the British government exercised its ownership rights in the banks it bailed-out through a shareholder primacy framework) in spite of its critics and the consecutive financial crises in the 2000s. Consequently the next generation of corporate financialization literature has studied its survival and proliferation in present-day capitalism.

Survival of the Shareholder Primacy after its Spectacular Failures in the 2000s

The early literature on corporate financialization in the 1980s and 1990s was about the transformation of Chandlerian managerial capitalism into shareholder primacy capitalism where firms compete in stock markets. In such a capitalism stock markets have become bubble producing giant financial mechanisms, making long-term shareholder value creation a rhetoric rather than a realizable managerial goal and, at the same time, undermining wage-led sustainable economic growth. The survival of the shareholder value primacy after the burst of the dot.com bubble and the scandalous collapse of Enron in 2001, after enriching managers and destroying shareholder value, has directed corporate financialization research into mostly empirical investigations on the gap between the rhetoric and the reality in financialized firms, and the further expansion of the shareholder primacy into new economic and social fields. This post-dot.com crisis corporate financialization literature research can be grouped under three headings: a) underinvestment and lack of long-term value creation in financialized firms; b) cultural logics of corporate financialization; and c) expansion of corporate financialization practices into non-public business organizations and non-profit public institutions.

Underinvestment and Lack of Long-term Shareholder Value Creation in Financialized Firms

For Dobbin and Zorn (2005) the Enron corporate governance scandal, which revealed an accounting malfeasance that was unprecedented in the modern corporate history of the US, was a consequence of financialized firm behavior. If Enron was unique in fraudulent behavior and financial engineering to alchemically transform an asset heavy utility firm into an asset light new economy stock market phenomenon, it was not unique in failing to create long-term shareholder value. Fligstein and Shin (2007), in their empirical work that examines data in 62 industries over 17 years between 1984 and 2000 in the US, found that financialized firms pursuing shareholder value maximization have not achieved shareholder value creating growth in profitability. Another study by Ertürk et al. (2005) on long-term value creation by the US and the UK firms, using data on total shareholder return, return on capital employed and growth in sales at S&P 500 and FTSE 100 firms between 1983 and 2002, found that financialized firms cannot create sustainable long-term value for shareholders.

Not only can financialized firms not create shareholder value over the long term, their short-term value creation is mostly due to the ebb and flow created by institutional funds in stock markets, and they do not create a strong economic base for innovation either. Lazonick and Tulum (2008) demonstrate that Research and Development (R&D) in technology companies was undermined by financialized business models. In order to achieve shareholder value maximization some leading bio-pharma companies returned cash to the stock market in the form of dividends and share buybacks, which in some cases, like in Merck and Pfizer, exceeded the R&D spending. Lazonick (2010) found similar patterns in leading information and communication technology companies like Microsoft, IBM, Cisco Systems, Intel, and Hewlett-Packard. Based on his empirical findings over a period of 30 years Lazonick and his co-authors argue that financialized businesses have undermined the US economy's innovative potential and restricted its economic growth by replacing retain and reinvest corporate behavior of the post-war Golden Age with downsized and distributed financialized behavior to pursue shareholder value maximization.

Milberg (2008) and Milberg and Winkler (2010) found that the US companies in general prioritize stock market performance at the expense of long-term productive growth not just through financial decisions by managers, like share buy-backs and higher dividends, but also through re-organizing labor and production circuits through global supply chains involving production decisions of out-sourcing and off-shoring. Milberg and Winkler's (2010) findings support earlier heterodox economists Stockhammer's (2004) and Orhangazi's (2008) econometrics-based empirical findings that at industry and macroeconomic levels financialized firm behavior does not favor growth generating investments in productive capacity. Fernandez and Hendrikse (2015) complement the aggregated macroeconomic findings of Milberg and Winkler (2010) by a case study approach on Apple's global supply chains and shareholder primacy-driven business model. Success in profits and stock market valuation at the firm level, as in the case of Apple, does not create socially progressive macroeconomic stability and growth. The result is a US economy with a chronic government budget deficit, low wages and increasing income and wealth inequality.

If internationally organized technology firms with successful performance in stock market do not necessarily form a base for macroeconomically successful economies, then how do low margin businesses of nationally organized retail companies fare socio-economically? Baud and Durand (2012) study low margin businesses of large global retail firms by following on Milberg's (2008) framework that analyses profit accumulation through a strategy of globalization and financialization. They find that product market weaknesses, low sales growth and low profit margins, at domestic markets did not stop such low technology companies from playing the shareholder primacy game. Baud and Durand's empirical work, using financial accounting data between 1990 and 2007, shows that a strategy of globalization followed by financialization has allowed the world's leading ten retailers, that include Walmart, Tesco, Carrefour, to increase return on equity and share price. Financialization at these big retailers involved investing in financial assets and paying higher percentages of profits to the financial sector through interest rates, dividends and share buybacks. This financialized success of retailers came at the expense of lower wages for the workers in the industry, financial distress for their suppliers and lower capital expenditure in the business.

Cultural Economy of Corporate Financialization

Corporate financialization is more than a political-economy phenomenon. Froud et al. (2006) carry out a linguistic and accounting case study of General Electric to demonstrate how financialized firms communicate with stock markets through carefully constructed performative narratives about corporate strategy. Business school researchers like Froud et al. (2006) and Andersson et al. (2010) who study financialized firm strategy by analyzing accounting data, stock market equity analysts' sell-side reports and by critically reviewing mainstream corporate strategy literature, introduce a cultural economy perspective where managers use narratives, developed for equity analysts and investors, to actively influence the share price of the companies they manage. Andersson et al. (2008) analyze the financial accounts of S&P 500 firms between 1990–2006 and find that they have used fair value accounting rules for acquisitions and share buybacks to report higher cash ROCE to influence share price and to finance future acquisitions. In a later study Andersson et al. (2010) introduce nuances into the cultural economy approach to the financialized firm behavior by describing patterns of contingent conditions where managers develop narratives for variable motifs of investors under variable conditions of stock market trajectories. Other examples of managerial narratives where legitimate but selective use of accounting data played a significant role to influence the stock market valuation of and therefore shareholder value creation at firms are given by Froud et al. (2004) and Newberry and Rob (2008) by using case studies of Enron and Telecom (NZ) Ltd respectively. A different cultural economy approach in studying corporate financialization is Haiven's (2014) work on Walmart. Haiven (2014) discusses Walmart's cultural financialized success that delivers shareholder value not through an analysis of accounting data and corporate strategy documents but through a Foucauldian analysis regarding Walmart's deep cultural penetration into low-income consumers' lives.

Other cultural economy approaches to corporate financialization argue that the expansion of financialized firm logic can follow a constitutive dialectic through cultural processes. For example, super structural technologies like accounting and valuation can play a constitutive role in entrenching and spreading financialized logic in firms as well as changing the nature of the work organization (see Chiapello, in this volume). Ezzamel et al. (2008) examine a US manufacturing company to argue that the external pressure from investors in stock market translate into internal performance metrics expressed in management accounting language, an organizational cultural form that is different from the financial accounting that most other researchers on corporate financialization have used, which restructures the work organization. Ezzamel et al. (2008) expand shareholder value primacy studies into a new territory where accounting figures are not simply data exhibiting the realization of shareholder value but are in fact used to constitute internally a shareholder value-driven firm by facilitating restructuring of the organization and work. Botzem and Dobusch (2017) demonstrate the constructionist aspects of the accounting representations in financialized business models in the German real estate industry by investigating the accounting practices at a German real estate firm between 2005 and 2007.

Expansion of Corporate Financialization Practices into Non-public Companies and Universities

The demutualization of building societies and the privatization of utilities in the UK have introduced financialized management behavior into non-public, hitherto stakeholder-driven business organizations. Klimecki and Willmott (2009) show how two small demutualized building societies – Northern Rock and Bradford&Bingley in the UK – had to be bailed out by taxpayers' money during the 2007 crisis when their financialized business models failed. Institutional investors like pension funds and private equity investors can promote financialized firm behavior through direct ownership of firms. Allen and Pryke (2013) demonstrate that utility firms that are privately owned by consortia of institutional investors, infrastructure funds, investment banks and sovereign wealth funds are managed by the same financial logic as stock market listed companies with distributed ownership. At such privately owned firms the goal of the management favors financial return to funds in the form of dividends at the expense of consumers who cannot change their water supplier and therefore become a captive source of cash flow to institutional investors.

Like water the provision of higher education can become financialized too as Engelen et al. (2014) and Eaton et al. (2016) argue in their respective studies of the Dutch and the US universities. Engelen et al. (2014) examine the financial scandal involving the use of interest rate derivatives by Dutch universities. The transfer of ownership of real estate from the state to the Dutch universities in 1995 and the following introduction of financial metrics to measure economic efficiency of teaching and research internally and to orient Dutch universities toward international competition, according to Engelen et al. (2014), caused a unique case of financialization in Dutch universities. Eaton et al. (2016) argue that US higher education institutions, too, have become financialized in their own unique way. They analyze four types of financial transactions by all types of US universities: 1) revenues from endowment investments; 2) interest paid on debt by non-profit public and private colleges; 3) profitability of equity financing in private colleges; 4) interest paid on student loans. When costs and returns from debt and investments are analyzed the wealthier US colleges benefit more than the poorer ones, allowing the fewer students of the wealthier colleges to receive better educational infrastructure. Eaton et al.'s findings at the US universities support Engelen et al.'s findings in the Netherlands that financialization in higher education spreads through social networks of professionals with a finance background who are increasingly employed in university management.

Shareholder Primacy Ten Years after the Great Financial Crisis

As the literature on corporate financialization has argued since the 1980s, shareholder primacy-driven firms compete in the stock market. Share buybacks and corporate restructuring narratives that involve serial mergers and acquisitions have immediate effect on the share price and produce short-term unsustainable shareholder value creation. A decade after the 2007 crisis prominent corporate insiders and technocrats at the leading supranational and national institutions have joined the academic critics of the shareholder value maximization principle and are critical about the macroeconomic consequences of an economic order driven by firms that are guided by a corporate governance model of shareholder value primacy.

In the aftermath of the Great Financial Crisis and the generally accepted distributional and allocative failures of quantitative easing and other unconventional monetary policy initiatives of central banks, the insiders from the corporate and financial world, and the economists at the leading international institutions have joined the critical academics in criticizing the shareholder value primacy as the cause for low private investments and dysfunctional capital markets. The International Corporate Governance Network (ICGN), which has 600 members in over 50 countries representing institutional investors with global assets under management in excess of US$26 trillion, publicly acknowledged the failure of the shareholder primacy-led corporate governance system after the Great Financial Crisis (ICGN 2008). The CEO of Blackrock, the world's largest asset manager, joined this chorus of respectable critics of financialized firm behavior and publicly expressed his views by writing an open letter in April 2015 to the boards of the S&P 500 companies in the US:

> ... corporate leaders have responded with actions that can deliver immediate returns to shareholders, such as buybacks or divided increases, while under-investing in innovation, skilled workforces or essential capital expenditures necessary to sustain long-term growth.
>
> *(Fink 2015)*

Andrew Haldane (May 2015), the Chief Economist of the Bank of England, who is somewhat rare among the regulators in expressing critical views on mainstream economics, agrees with Fink (2015). His empirical study of the macroeconomic consequences of the behavior of shareholder primacy-driven firms showed that private investments have suffered from such firm behavior. The President of Dallas Federal Reserve, Richard Fisher, too agrees that financialized firm behavior is a major obstacle to the desired functions of the transmission channels in monetary policy:

> Currently, much of the monetary base has piled up in the form of excess reserves of banks who have not found willing or able borrowers. Other forms of surplus cash are lying fallow on the balance sheets of businesses or being deployed in buying back shares and increasing dividend pay-outs to buttress company stock prices.
>
> *(Fisher 2013: 7)*

The OECD economists (2015: 31) joined this growing number of non-academic critics of financialized firm behavior: "stock markets currently reward companies that favor dividends and buybacks and punish those that undertake more investment ... which creates higher hurdle rates for investment in the current uncertain environment."

Since the Great Financial Crisis the historically low interest rates under quantitative easing allow stock market listed companies to borrow at very cheap rates in bond markets to buy back their own shares to create "shareholder value." Table 4.1 shows that there has been a significant increase in share buyback activity in the US after 2009 as S&P 500 went sharply upwards, fueled by three consecutive quantitative easing programs, reaching USD 485.39 billion in 2014. As a result of high levels of share buybacks net equity issuance in the US has been negative since 2008. Net equity issuance has always been negative since 2002 in the US (see Fichtner, in this volume) but what is significant after 2008 is that quantitative easing was meant to encourage firms to raise capital to invest in economic growth. Instead the US firms have been borrowing in bond markets at low long-term interest rates that quantitative easing has created (see the net bond issuance column in Table 4.1) to finance share buybacks. Consequently lower equity base

Table 4.1 Share Buybacks, Equity Issuance and Net Bond Issuance in the US

	US share buybacks $bn	Equity issuance $bn	US net equity issuance $bn	Net bond issuance $bn
2002	116.38	67.91	-48.47	162.38
2003	108.85	60.80	-48.05	221.08
2004	163.12	101.71	-61.42	76.20
2005	280.91	87.08	-193.83	88.61
2006	381.15	106.87	-274.28	177.04
2007	506.23	113.78	-392.46	126.53
2008	361.04	66.11	-294.94	104.50
2009	135.56	87.71	-47.85	285.47
2010	287.09	96.80	-190.29	251.03
2011	384.20	107.29	-276.91	140.62
2012	361.24	124.10	-237.14	368.23
2013	462.57	175.20	-287.37	341.15
2014	485.39	160.05	-325.34	373.14

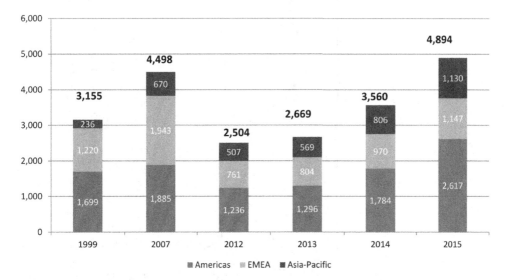

Figure 4.1 Global Announced Mergers and Acquisition Deals (US$bn)

arithmetically results in higher return on equity and higher earnings per share, two key performance metrics that boost share prices of firms in the stock market.

As the review of the corporate financialization literature has shown, the shareholder primacy-driven firms also tend to do high-premium mergers and acquisitions in rising stock markets by using their own inflated valuation and the cash generated from the operations to buy other companies. The global announced mergers and acquisitions deals have now exceeded the pre-crisis 2007 level of US$4.5 trillion and reached almost US$5 trillion in 2015 (see Figure 4.1). The share of the North and South America region, where the US is the biggest market, is the highest since 2012 at a value of US$2.6 trillion.

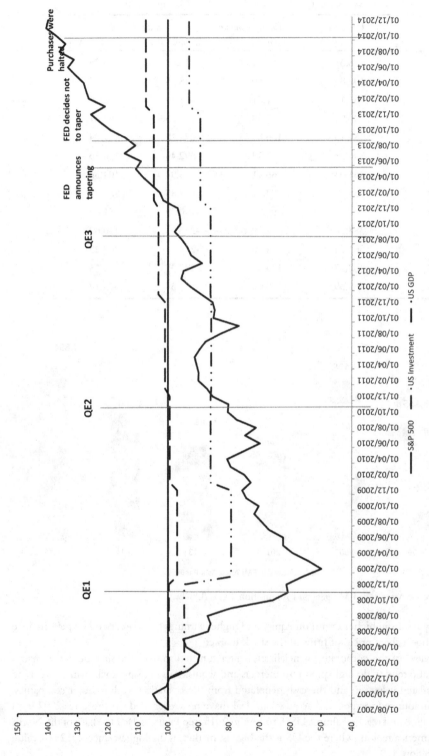

Figure 4.2 US Real GDP, S&P 500 and Private Investments as a percentage of GDP

The financialized firm behavior – especially in the US where quantitative easing by the Federal Reserve was both nationally and globally significant in size – clearly obstructs the intended transmission mechanisms in such monetary expansion policies and diverts capital overwhelmingly to unproductive share buy-backs and mergers and acquisitions. Figure 4.2 shows that the US share prices reacted quicker and with more enthusiasm than both real GDP and private investments to the Fed's three quantitative easing programs between 2008 and 2012. While S&P 500 is about 40 percent higher than its pre-crisis level at the end of 2014 the real GDP is only about 7 percent higher but more significantly private investments are still some 7 percent below the pre-crisis level. Seven years of extraordinary monetary policy have given the US a stock market boom but not investment and growth booms. The economic models of central banks that underpin the unconventional monetary policy since the GFC are deaf and blind to the findings of the literature on corporate financialization since the 1980s (see Braun and Gabor, in this volume). Although we have seen institutional macroeconomists and some key fund managers recently finally acknowledging the malign macroeconomic consequences of the shareholder primacy in present-day capitalism, we have not seen a similar critical debate amongst central bankers about how quantitative easing may be thwarted by financialized firm behavior. The most crucial cognitive challenge for central bankers today should be to discover corporate financialization and its relevance for monetary policy.

Conclusion

From the 1980s onwards the literature on corporate financialization has been mostly critical about the neoliberal project of shareholder primacy that was promoted as the corporate governance solution to the broken post-war managerial capitalism. The shareholder value maximization principle, also known as shareholder primacy, has shifted the competition of firms from product markets to stock markets and the agency theory legitimized this shift by introducing and promoting equity-based remuneration contracts between shareholders and managers. A series of significant financial crises and corporate scandals since the late 1980s that have been the consequences of stock market competition by firms have shown that the economic and social promises of shareholder primacy have not been achieved and are not realistic. However, the idea and practice of shareholder primacy has managed to survive all its failures as political support for it has not been withdrawn in spite of its cumulative social and economic costs. Individually there have always been firms that could demonstrate shareholder value creation over short to medium periods if not over the long term. The evidence from the literature covered in the second section of this chapter, however, shows that such value creation is accidental rather than causal as the growing size of funds that flood the stock markets tend to swell the share prices rather than managerial action. Consequently the sum of individually "successful" firms in stock markets do not aggregate to an economy with high private investments and sustainable wage-led growth. Although increasingly some leading technocrats and investors publicly criticize shareholder primacy, there is no meaningful political agenda to reform the financialized relationship between firms and capital markets. The future of literature on corporate financialization could be to investigate the resilience of the shareholder primacy in political and cultural terms.

Bibliography

Aglietta, M., 1998. Capitalism at the turn of the century: Regulation theory and the challenge of social change. *New Left Review*, November–December, pp. 41–90.

Allen, J. and Pryke, M., 2013. Financialising household water: Thames Water, MEIF, and 'ring-fenced' politics. *Cambridge Journal of Regions, Economy and Society*, 6(3), pp. 419–439.

Andersson, T., Gleadle, P., Haslam, C. and Tsitsianis, N., 2010. Bio-pharma: A financialized business model. *Critical Perspectives on Accounting*, 21(7), pp. 631–641.

Andersson T., Haslam C., Lee E. and Tsitsianis N., 2007. Financialized accounts: A stakeholder account of cash distribution in the S&P 500(1990–2005). *Accounting Forum*, 31(3), pp. 217–232.

Andersson, T., Haslam, C., Lee, E. and Tsitsianis, N., 2008. Financialization directing strategy. *Accounting Forum*, 32(4), pp. 261–275.

Bank for International Settlement, September 2015. *BIS Quarterly Review*. Available at: www.bis.org/publ/qtrpdf/r_qt1509.pdf [Accessed 17 February 2018].

Baud, C. and Durand, C., 2012. Financialization, globalization and the making of profits by leading retailers. *Socio-Economic Review*, 10(2), pp. 241–266.

Berle, A., 1962. Modern functions of the corporate system. *Columbia Law Review*, 62(3), pp. 433–449.

Botzem, S. and Dobusch, L., 2017. Financialization as strategy: Accounting for inter-organizational value creation in the European real estate industry. *Accounting, Organizations and Society*, 59, pp. 31–43.

Boyer, R., 2000. Is a finance-led growth regime a viable alternative to Fordism? A preliminary analysis. *Economy and Society*, 29(1), pp. 111–145.

Chandler, A.D., 1977 *The Visible Hand. The Managerial Revolution in American Business*. Cambridge, MA: Belknap Press.

Christophers, B., 2015. The limits to financialization. *Dialogues in Human Geography*, 5(2), pp. 183–200.

Crotty, J., 2003. The neoliberal paradox: The impact of destructive product market competition and impatient finance on nonfinancial corporations in the neoliberal era. *Review of Radical Political Economics*, 35(3), pp. 271–279.

Dobbin, F. and Zorn, D., 2005. Corporate malfeasance and the myth of shareholder value. *Political Power and Social Theory*, 17, pp. 179–198.

Eaton, C., Habinek, J., Goldstein, A., Dioun, C., Santibáñez Godoy, D.G. and Osley-Thomas, R., 2016. The financialization of US higher education. *Socio-Economic Review*, 14(3), pp. 507–535.

Engelen, E., 2008. The case for financialization. *Competition & Change*, 12(2), pp. 111–119.

Engelen, E., Ertürk, I., Froud, J., Johal, S., Leaver, A., Moran, M., Nilsson, A. and Williams, K., 2011. *After the Great Complacence: Financial Innovation and Politics of Financial Reforms*. Oxford: Oxford University Press.

Engelen, E., Fernandez, R. and Hendrikse, R., 2014. How finance penetrates its other: A cautionary tale on the financialization of a Dutch university. *Antipode*, 46(4), pp. 1072–1091.

Ertürk, I., Froud, J., Johal, S., Leaver, A. and Williams, K., 2005. Pay for corporate performance or pay as social division. *Competition and Change*, 9(1), pp. 49–74.

Ertürk, I., Froud, J., Johal, S., Leaver, A. and Williams, K., 2008. General introduction: Financialization, coupon pool and conjuncture. In: Ertürk, I. et al. (eds.), *Financialization: Key Texts and Commentary*. London: Routledge.

Ezzamel, M., Willmott, H. and Worthington, F., 2008. Manufacturing shareholder value: The role of accounting in organizational transformation. *Accounting Organizations and Society*, 33(2–3), pp. 107–140.

Fama, E.F., 1980. Agency problems and the theory of the firm. *Journal of Political Economy*, 88(2), pp. 288–307.

Fernandez, R. and Hendrikse, R., 2015. The financialisation of Apple. Available at: https://www.researchgate.net/publication/283289637_Rich_corporations_poor_societies_The_financialisation_of_Apple [Accessed 20 November 2016].

Fink, L., 14 April2015. BlackRock CEO Larry Fink tells the world's biggest business leaders to stop worrying about short-term results. *Business Insider*. Available at: http://www.businessinsider.com/larry-fink-letter-to-ceos-2015-4?IR=T [Accessed 10 July 2015].

Fisher, R.W., 2013. Horseshift! (With Reference to Gordian Knots). Remarks before the National Association of State Retirement Administrators 59th Annual Conference, August 5, 2013. Available at: http://www.dallasfed.org/news/speeches/fsher/2013/fs130805.cfm [Accessed August 17 2014].

Fligstein, N., 1993. *The Transformation of Corporate Control*. Cambridge, MA: Harvard University Press.

Fligstein, N., 2005. The end of (shareholder value) ideology? *Political Power and Social Theory*, 17, pp. 223–228.

Fligstein, N. and Shin, T., 2007. Shareholder value and the transformation of the US economy, 1984–2000. *Sociological Forum*, 22(4), pp. 399–424.

Froud, J., Haslam, C., Johal, S. and Williams, K., 2000. Shareholder value and financialization: Consultancy promises, management moves. *Economy and Society*. 29(1), pp. 80–110.

Froud J., Johal S., Papazian V. and Williams K., 2004. The temptation of Houston: A case study of financialisation. *Critical Perspectives on Accounting*, 15(6–7), pp. 885–909.

Froud, J., Leaver, A., Johal, S. and Williams, K., 2006. *Financialization and Strategy: Narrative and Numbers*. London: Routledge.

Galbraith, J.K., 1967. *The New Industrial State*. Boston, MA: Houghton Mifflin.

Grahl, J. and Teague, P., 2000. The Regulation School, the employment relation and financialization. *Economy and Society*, 29(1), pp. 160–178.

Haiven, M., 2014. *Cultures of Financialization: Fictitious Capital in Popular Culture and Everyday Life*. Basingstoke and New York: Palgrave Macmillan.

Haldane, A., 22 May2015. Who owns a company? Speech delivered at University of Edinburgh Corporate Finance Conference. Available at: http://www.bankofengland.co.uk/publications/Pages/speeches/ 2015/833.aspx [Accessed 20 July 2015].

ICGN (International Corporate Governance Network), 2008. Statement on the Global Financial Crisis, 10 November, 2008. Available at: http://www.iasplus.com/en/binary/resource/0811icgn.pdf/view [Accessed 10 July 2015].

Ireland, P., 1999. Company law and the myth of shareholder ownership. *Modern Law Review*, 62(1), pp. 32–57.

Jensen, M.C. and Meckling, W.H., 1976. Theory of the firm: Managerial behavior, agency costs and ownership structure. *Journal of Financial Economics*, 3(4), pp. 305–360.

Jensen, M.C., 1993. The Modern Industrial Revolution, exit, and the failure of internal control systems. *The Journal of Finance*, 48(3), pp. 831–880.

Klimecki, R. and Willmott, H., 2009. From demutualisation to meltdown: A tale of two wannabe banks. *Critical Perspectives on International Business*, 5(1–2), pp. 120–140.

Krippner, G.R., 2005. The financialization of the American economy. *Socio-Economic Review*, 3(2), pp. 173–208.

Lazonick, W. and O'Sullivan, M. 1996. Organization, finance and international competition. *Industrial and Corporate Change*, 5(1), pp. 1–49.

Lazonick, W., 2010. Innovative business models and varieties of capitalism: financialization of the U.S. corporation. *Business History Review*, 84 (Winter), pp. 675–702.

Lazonick, W. and O'Sullivan, M., 2000. Maximizing shareholder value: a new ideology for corporate governance. *Economy and Society*, 29(1), pp. 13–35.

Lazonick, W. and Tulum, O., 2008. Biopharmaceutical finance and the sustainability of the biotech boom. Paper presented at Copenhagen, CBS, Denmark, June 2008. Available at: http://www2.druid.dk/con ferences/viewpaper.php?id=3577&cf=29 [Accessed 15 March 2018].

McKinsey&Company (December 2015). M&A 2015: New highs, and a new tone. Available at: https:// www.mckinsey.com/business-functions/strategy-and-corporate-finance/our-insights/m-and-a-2015-ne w-highs-and-a-new-tone [Accessed 26 January 2016].

Milberg, W., 2008. Shifting sources and uses of profits: sustaining US financialization with global value chains. *Economy and Society*, 37(3), pp. 420–451.

Milberg, W. and Winkler, D., 2010. Financialisation and the dynamics of offshoring in the USA. *Cambridge Journal of Economics*, 34(2), pp. 275–293.

Mizruchi, M.S. and Kimeldorf, H., 2005. The historical context of shareholder value capitalism. *Political Power and Social Theory*, 17, pp. 213–221.

Newberry, S. and Robb, A., 2008. Financialisation: Constructing shareholder value …for some. *Critical Perspectives on Accounting*, 19(5), pp. 741–763.

OECD (2015) *OECD Business and Finance Outlook 2015*. Available at: http://www.oecd.org/finance/ oecd-business-and-finance-outlook-2015-9789264234291-en.htm [Accessed 15 November 2015].

Orhangazi, O., 2008. Financialization and capital accumulation in the nonfinancial corporate sector: a theoretical and empirical investigation on the US economy, 1973–2004. *Cambridge Journal of Economics*, 32(6), pp. 863–886.

Paranque, B., 2017. The need for an alternative to shareholder value creation? The Ethomed student experience. *Research in International Business and Finance*, 39, pp. 686–695.

Stockhammer, E, 2004. Financialization and the slowdown of accumulation. *Cambridge Journal of Economics*, 28(5), pp. 719–741.

Stout, L.A., 2001. Bad and not-so-bad arguments for shareholder primacy. *South California Law Review*, 75, p. 1189.

Van der Zwan, N., 2014. Making sense of financialization. *Socio-Economic Review*, 12(1), pp. 99–129.

5

FINANCIALIZATION, MONEY AND THE STATE

Sheila Dow

Introduction

Financialization has heightened the importance of finance for socio-economic life. But different groupings of economists frame the financial sector, and its relationship with the real sector and with the state, very differently. The framing which presumes that free competition will produce the social-optimal outcome has been persistent, and persistently influential, supporting the interests of the financial sector. Although the crisis opened this framing up to public challenge, such that increasing attention, even among central banks, is being paid to socio-economic considerations (e.g. income distribution), addressing financialization continues to be hampered by the view that the financial sector is normally benign.

We will focus here particularly on the problem financialization poses for financial stability, and the scope for a regulatory response, from a Post-Keynesian perspective. This approach, which has a longstanding contribution to the analysis of financialization, differs from the dominant theoretical framework in economics, which is built on market pricing with true prices as the benchmark. The extension of reach of market pricing (stocks rather than bonds, bailing-in rather than bailing-out, etc.), which accompanies financialization, is welcome from this latter perspective. But, from a Post-Keynesian perspective, there cannot even in principle be 'true prices' since the future is seen to be fundamentally uncertain. The socio-economic structure and creative behaviour evolve in unpredictable ways, such that future values and risk cannot be quantified categorically. It follows that market pricing cannot be relied upon for socially optimal outcomes. Rather the state has a central role to play in impeding damaging market forces while supporting socially beneficial market forces.

However, the strength of the forces for financialization pose particular challenges for the state. Real economic activity relies on finance and a stable financial environment. But, while financialization has extended the reach in society of financial forces (including the potential availability of finance), they have developed in such a way as to be inherently unstable. For centuries the state has acted, to a greater or lesser extent, to temper that instability. But the extent of instability in the recent crisis, and the severity of its real consequences, have brought· the role of the state to the forefront of debate. Depending on how they frame finance, different economic approaches come to different conclusions on financial regulation.

How best through regulation and its enforcement can the state enable the positive features of financialization, and how best can it constrain its negative features? Is regulation always to be regarded as a constraint which reduces social welfare? Or can state involvement be a vehicle for protecting powerful financial interests? At different times and depending on perspective, the theory and practice of financial regulation have involved differing emphases on, and interpretations of, these two functions of enabling and constraining. The financial crisis has brought these different perspectives into sharp relief.

It may seem remarkable that we should still be asking whether the financial sector should have special regulation, so soon after the latest financial crisis and with the prospect of another one. Yet the debate continues, and indeed some post-crisis bank regulation is currently being rolled back in the US. So the argument for regulation still needs to be made. In this chapter we will go back to first principles in order to consider why the financial sector needs special regulation, beyond normal company regulation (see further Dow 1996, Kregel and Tonveronachi 2014). How these principles are applied depends on the context, which, in finance, is always evolving.

In particular, we must bear in mind the goals set for the monetary authorities in considering financial regulation. In the decades before the crisis, the authorities focused primarily on targeting inflation, drawing on monetary theory referring to money as bank deposits which in turn were understood as a multiple of reserves. But resulting monetary policy had the unintended consequence of adding fuel to an ongoing process of financialization which had been spurred on by neo-liberal efforts to deregulate the financial sector and to encourage public participation in it. In particular, the financial sector saw opportunities in developing new liquidity and credit instruments outside the regulatory net, i.e. in shadow banking.

However, since the crisis the authorities have been forced to prioritise dealing with the financial instability of the crisis and the economic stagnation which resulted from austerity fiscal policy. The monetary authorities now (formally or informally) still aim to promote monetary stability (controlling inflation), but increasingly also financial stability (the degree of volatility in asset prices, and financial conditions more generally) and economic stability.

How we discuss financial regulation depends on how we understand the way in which the financial sector operates and how it fits in with general economic processes. We will explore in particular four different approaches which vary in the extent to which they see governments intervening in finance: the neo-Austrian approach, the Sovereign-Money approach, the mainstream New-Keynesian approach and the Post-Keynesian approach. It is important to understand these different framings because they underpin different types of contribution by economists to the policy debate around financialization. The New-Keynesian approach dominates academic contributions, while in practice many recent policy developments actually follow closer to Post-Keynesian principles. At the same time, radical proposals from neo-Austrians and the Sovereign-Money approach are making headway, echoing the discourse of the 1930s (see Weber, in this volume).

Framing Finance

The theoretical perspectives to be outlined below are built on different understandings of the nature of economic and social relations, and in particular of how the financial system works in relation to the real economy. This understanding also determines how ideas are presented and perceived: the framing of finance. There can be framing differences within economics, ranging from differences in meaning of terms, through theoretical differences, to differences in policy recommendations. Framing is a necessary feature of discourse and, in turn is generated and transmitted by discourse. Reality is also framed by the institutional arrangements, conventions and habits which put some boundaries around the scope for acting on knowledge (see e.g. Rein and Schön 1993).

Framing can be performative in the sense of altering reality (see e.g. Mackenzie, Muniesa and Siu 2007). What is regarded as the most sound theoretical perspective influences the framing by policy-makers, finance specialists and by the general public. But it is in turn influenced by the more powerful political and economic forces, notably as exercised by the financial sector. Academic power structures, and thus the direction of research, may be influenced by the dominant framing by government. Government in turn may be influenced by the framing by the financial sector of government deficit finance. The general public may be influenced by government framing in their efforts to understand government policy.

For mainstream economics, finance is understood in terms of conceptual separations; science itself consists of separations, building deductivist models and testing them against independent facts. Deductivism involves establishing axioms (about rational behaviour) and deriving propositions from them within formal mathematical models which are, by definition, closed systems (where there is a strict separation between endogenous and exogenous variables). The key endogenous variable through which market processes operate is price, where market prices gravitate to 'true' prices; the greater the extent of financialization, the more significant is pricing for social and economic life. But a deterministic modelling account of market pricing and the notion of true prices in financial markets require the capacity to quantify risk which is captured in stochastic relationships (see e.g. Dow 2016a).

In contrast to the focus on separation in the mainstream approach, the Post-Keynesian approach emphasises conceptual interaction. This stems from a different way of understanding financial processes, but also a different way of approaching the building of knowledge about those processes. The Post-Keynesian approach to knowledge of financial markets does allow separation (or segmentation) as provisional within theoretical analysis, as a necessary feature of formal models where they are employed. But the framing of these markets emphasises pervasive uncertainty which means that pricing, while informed, is necessarily conventional. Correspondingly, while mainstream analysis uses a strict notion of rationality as its benchmark for behaviour, Post-Keynesian analysis considers behaviour as reasonable, or unreasonable, given uncertainty; 'rationality' itself is framed differently. Not only is evidence theory-laden, but it is also performative in driving conventional interpretations. Formal models are useful as aids to understanding, and contributors to knowledge, rather than constituting complete arguments as in mainstream economics. Other styles of reasoning, and input from other disciplines contribute to the economic analyst's (uncertain) understanding.

This framing of the economist's knowledge is paralleled in the economist's understanding of knowledge in the economy. Thus, while mainstream economists posit rational individualistic behaviour (possibly subject to constraints on rationality or information), Post-Keynesian economists posit behaviour which relies on social convention and is inevitably conditioned by sentiment, in the absence of certain knowledge. This view of market behaviour underpins Minsky's (1982, 1986) theory of financial instability (see Sotiropoulos and Hillig, in this volume).

Further, much can be learned about market behaviour from analysis framed within sociology (Preda 2007) and psychology (Tuckett 2011). Both of these disciplines include strands which, like mainstream economics, have an 'ideal type' of agent as a benchmark. But there is a much greater proportion of work than in economics which draws on a range of evidence as to how agents actually frame their decision-making (under conditions of uncertainty). This latter work feeds readily into the realist Post-Keynesian approach. The difference between mainstream and Post-Keynesian framing of the economist's knowledge and knowledge in financial markets is epitomised by the difference between new and old behavioural economics, respectively (Sent 2004). While the former challenges the rationality axioms on empirical grounds, the aim is to establish new axioms more consistent with the evidence, continuing the closed-system deductivist approach (Dow 2013a).

The monetary authorities frame financial markets in a variety of ways, depending on the audience: government, practitioner or the general public. Successful communication of the central bank's thinking is now a central plank of monetary policy (Geraats 2002). But central banks are also influenced by academic framing of financial markets. At one level, as an independent body, central banks are encouraged to present monetary and financial policy as a technical matter. It is important, then, to frame policy decision-making in a technical, academic way. This reflects the sociological power in economics of the (contested) mainstream idea that it is a technical (value-free) discipline.

But the authorities are influenced by mainstream economic thinking also at the institutional level. The whole idea of separating monetary policy decision-making from fiscal policy decision-making and from financial regulation and its enforcement stems from the conceptual separations discussed above. If, as Post Keynesians argue, monetary policy, fiscal policy and financial regulation and its enforcement are fundamentally interdependent, then institutionally separating them without mechanisms to allow cooperation and coordination can only lead to a suboptimal policy mix.

In the meantime, when policy is presented as the product of expertise, the general public are expected to accept it; indeed treating monetary and financial policy as technical discourages public engagement (see also Nölke, in this volume). Still, the support of economists for deregulating the financial sector has been seen as serving sectional interests, namely those with most to gain from financialization; widening distributions of income and wealth since the crisis are taken as supporting evidence. The economists' claim to be apolitical experts, which Post-Keynesians have long challenged, is being more widely questioned. While central bank communications may continue to be effective with the financial sector, which has a shared view of economists as technical experts, it is becoming less effective with the general public (see e.g. Earle, Moran and Ward-Perkins 2016).

It is with public discourse in mind that we start our discussion of different approaches to finance with two approaches which have to some extent (as in the 1930s) captured the public imagination. We then proceed to discuss the New-Keynesian approach which has dominated the mainstream theoretical input, and then the Post-Keynesian approach which, while not theoretically dominant, has had considerable impact on the policy discourse.

Four Approaches to Understanding Financialization, Money and the State

Opposing Views on the Role of the State with Populist Appeal: The Neo-Austrian Approach

This approach traditionally builds on the work of Ludwig von Mises and Carl Menger, and more recently Friedrich A. von Hayek, who explicitly advocated the privatization of money (Hayek 1976). Recent contributors (such as Lawrence White, Kevin Dowd, Taylor Cowen, Randall Kroszner and George Selgin) have long advocated free banking, and now blame the recent crisis on state involvement in finance (see e.g. Dowd 2009).

This approach aims to have as little government involvement in finance as possible, relying instead on market forces. The general approach is based on the idea that, even though knowledge, and thus asset pricing, are uncertain, individuals in the market have better knowledge to guide their decisions than does the state. So the role of the state is limited to making sure that markets operate competitively:

> If man is not to do more harm than good in his efforts to improve the social order, he
> will have to learn that ... where essential complexity of an organised kind prevails, *he*

cannot acquire the full knowledge which would make mastery of the events possible. He will therefore have to use what knowledge he can achieve, not to shape the results as a craftsman shapes his handiwork, but rather to cultivate a growth by providing the appropriate environment, as the gardener does for his plants.

(Hayek 1975: 42)

Neo-Austrians see state supply of money as a source of monetary instability, inflation being seen as the by-product of politically motivated increases in the money supply. They therefore argue for money to be supplied instead only by the banks in the form of deposits whose value would vary with the value of the banks' assets (which would further fuel financialization). Competition would then determine which bank's deposits were the most appealing to hold as money. There would no longer be any need for a central bank.

As far as finance is concerned, it is argued on the basis of historical study that financial instability in the past has actually been *caused* by state interference. In terms of the recent crisis, the argument is that the state's support of the banks created moral hazard: it encouraged them to take undue risks. If instead banks were allowed to fail if they invested unwisely, their customers would withdraw their deposits when they sensed trouble ahead. In other words the market would be a much more effective discipline on bank behaviour than any regulation (see e.g. Dowd 2009). The latest development to be inspired by this thinking is cryptocurrencies, designed to provide money and a payments system independent of government (Weber 2016).

Opposing Views on the Role of the State with Populist Appeal: The Sovereign-Money Approach

The second, Sovereign-Money, approach draws on the 1930s arguments (e.g. of Irving Fisher) for full-reserve banking (see Benes and Kumhof 2012), and has been developed in modern form more recently, led by Ben Dyson, Graham Hodgson, Tim Jackson and Frank van Lerven, within the Positive Money organization (see e.g. Dyson, Hodgson and Van Lerven 2016).

According to this approach, bank behaviour, influenced by moral hazard, is the specific root cause of the financial crises. Society's money is mostly in the form of bank deposits, so that deposits are continuously recycled through the banks as payments are settled. This gives the banks the freedom to expand credit at will, with increased money stocks the consequence. Rather than the money supply being controlled by the central bank, it is controlled by the banks: it is endogenous. Since monetary and financial instability are associated (as in the recent crisis) with credit cycles, the cure for both is for the state to take over from the banks the supply of money. Recently the emphasis has been on the possibilities for central banks to issue their own digital currencies (Dyson and Hodgson 2016).

Adopting a monetary theory of inflation, like the neo-Austrian approach, it is argued that state control of the money supply would allow direct control of inflation. Also, it is argued that the banks would no longer be able to cause financial instability. Having lost the power to create money, and the state support that historically has gone with that, banks would have to accept market discipline like other financial institutions. The Sovereign-Money proposal for the state to establish a monopoly over money would therefore eliminate banking as we know it, without further need for regulation, or even deposit insurance (see e.g. Jackson and Dyson 2012). Like for the neo-Austrians, bank liabilities would then vary in value along with the value of banks' assets, further fuelling financialization.

This proposal has much in common with proposals current in the 1930s for full reserve banking whereby banks would be required to back their deposits 100% by reserves with the central bank (see further Dow 2016b). There have been several variants of these proposals, but the basic principles are the same. In many cases, the vehicle for getting new money into the economy is via fiscal expenditure. In some cases, the system would allow for a negative rate of interest imposed by the state as a means of discouraging hoarding of money. In the case of Sovereign Money, the state would issue money rather than the banks, but the banks would administer it along the payments system. However, the central bank would also coordinate with government by tying money supply to both fiscal policy and to allocating resources to facilitate and direct bank lending in pursuit of social and environmental goals, as well as economic goals. The functions of the central bank are thus envisaged to be much broader than has recently been the case, while, by omission, regulation of the private financial sector, once stripped of traditional banking, is not discussed.

The New-Keynesian Approach

The New-Keynesian approach is built on the idea of asymmetric information (and other market imperfections) distorting free market processes, justifying countervailing state intervention. The key initial expression was Stiglitz and Weiss's (1981) application of this idea to rationing in the credit market. The leading figure has continued to be Joseph Stiglitz, who has emphasised the pervasiveness of market imperfections. The approach was generalized with application notably to the labour market, with other contributors including Bruce Greenwald and Gregory Mankiw. Current contributors who have applied the approach particularly to questions of financial instability and bank regulation are Charles Calomiris (2017) and Roger Farmer (2013).

The New-Keynesian approach is what we might call the current mainstream approach to financial regulation, in that it is the one which has lately dominated the theoretical literature and much of the policy debate. Like neo-Austrians and promoters of Sovereign Money, they share a monetarist view of inflation: that it is caused by changes in the supply of money (although that supply may not be exogenous). The previously dominant mainstream approaches (Monetarism, then New Classicism) shared the neo-Austrian view that efficient market forces would ensure financial stability. Indeed, because past and current mainstream approaches use models which focus on equilibrium, stability is built into them as the natural place for economies to settle. But there is the crucial difference from the neo-Austrian theory that market forces are portrayed as operating through pricing based on quantifiable risk.

However, the New-Keynesian approach argues that in practice markets do not work perfectly, so that state input is needed to ensure monetary and financial stability (Farmer 2013). In particular, they challenge the view, both of neo-Austrians and of the previous mainstream, that individuals have the knowledge for making the best market decisions. Fundamental uncertainty still does not feature; information on quantifiable risk may be concealed, but is always in principle available. But, in the absence of full knowledge about borrowers' riskiness, banks may ration credit. More significantly, in the run-up to the latest crisis, banks were unable to assess properly the riskiness of the complicated structured market products which ultimately proved to be highly risky. Critically for this approach, since it is in principle possible to measure the riskiness of any asset, given full information, one aim of regulation is to enhance information availability, addressing for example the factors leading credit rating agencies to distort their ratings (see Blinder and Stiglitz 1983, for an early formulation of this argument).

A further aim of regulation, as with the neo-Austrian approach, is to remove incentives to take on undue risk, notably the promise of central bank liquidity support. The New-Keynesian approach to regulation has thus focused on dealing with bank failure. There has been a push, for example, for banks to issue contingent convertible ('coco') bonds which would in times of crisis convert debt into equity. This reflects the mainstream view that, because they are continually priced in competitive markets, equity is more efficient than debt (especially illiquid bank loans, but also bonds).

Further along these lines, were banks to fail, they should be bailed in rather than bailed out, i.e. the risk of failure should be priced in to their liabilities. Such elements are seen to be desirable features of the resolution mechanisms (or 'living wills') advocated for banks, enhancing in turn the knowledge of risk on the part of depositors. Consistent with the New-Keynesian focus on moral hazard as a major cause of the recent crisis, there is some support for the Sovereign-Money policy of eliminating the traditional banking model by giving the state a monopoly of money production, an idea fuelled by the possibility of a central bank digital currency (Engert and Fung 2017).

There has been growing awareness of network effects, whereby risks associated with one institution or asset can spread to others; these effects are a form of externality with respect to decision-making by any one institution. This is a further form of market imperfection for which New Keynesians have advocated regulatory reforms following the crisis. But Calomiris (2017) offers a critique of reforms which have been adopted, as departing from New-Keynesian principles, the first of which, for him, is that

> Financial regulation should focus exclusively on bona fide objectives that relate to the performance of the financial sector, grounded in core economic concepts of externalities and information costs and supported by evidence that shows that the costs of regulation are justified by demonstrable benefits.
>
> *(Calomiris 2017: 61)*

The Post-Keynesian Approach

The Post-Keynesian approach builds on a long-standing concern with financialization (although not always using that term), dating from Keynes (1936: ch. 12) and Minsky (1982, 1986). Post-Keynesianism (sometimes termed 'fundamentalist Keynesianism') differs from the hydraulic Keynesianism of the neo-classical synthesis and from New Keynesianism, both in terms of understanding of economic processes and in terms of the methodological approach judged most suitable to illuminate this understanding (see e.g. Dow 2013b). Key figures have included Joan Robinson, Michal Kalecki, Nicholas Kaldor, Geoff Harcourt, Victoria Chick, Paul Davidson and Jan Kregel. Post Keynesians have led the modern analysis of financialization, including Eckhard Hein (2012, 2013), Özlem Onaran (see e.g. Onaran, Stockhammer and Grafl 2011), Thomas Palley (2016) and Engelbert Stockhammer (2004). Given the importance of this long-standing contribution to financialization studies, it will be explored in greater detail than the other approaches.

The Post-Keynesian approach differs from the others, not just in terms of its theory of money and finance, and the policy proposals which follow, but also in terms of their basis in the way in which the economy is understood.[1] In particular, the first three approaches involve conceptual separations: notably a separation between the state and the private sector, a separation between money and other assets, and a separation between money and finance on the one hand and the real economy on the other.

The state and the private sector are intertwined, not least in terms of the market for sovereign debt and thus the implementation of monetary policy (see Braun and Gabor, in this volume). More fundamentally, the state provides an institutional, legal and knowledge foundation for the private sector; indeed the state has evolved along with markets to meet society's needs. This is clear from the history of banking. As banking evolved, it became evident that banks operating at the firm level did not normally address the macro level. A central bank instead could see the macro consequences of banks' actions and either attempt to moderate these actions or act to moderate the consequences. Thus confidence in the system as a whole was provided by the central bank providing a lender-of-last-resort facility, so that the liquidity problems of one bank would not spread throughout the system, or indeed so that problems for the banking system as a whole would not cause a crisis. There was an implicit deal (a 'social contract') between the central bank and the banks that support would be guaranteed as long as banks accepted restrictive regulation and supervision to limit the need for support.

When this system worked well, the banks were able to supply society with a stable money asset in the form of bank deposits. Occasionally this kind of system could emerge endogenously without a state-run central bank, as in Scotland in the eighteenth century, when the older banks acted like a central bank towards the newer banks which threatened confidence in the system as a whole. Thus state-like institutions can evolve within the private sector if the state does not meet a need. While this might seem consistent with the neo-Austrian view of endogenous institutional evolution, their focus is on financial markets at the micro level, such that any bank failure can be dealt with by transferring deposits to sound banks. But if in fact there is scope for systemic bank failures, then market discipline is insufficient and, without emergence of a private sector central bank, the system will collapse, leaving society without money.

Post-Keynesianism in Relation to the Other Approaches

This need for a safe money asset is central to the Post-Keynesian theory of money and banking. Since, in contrast with the neo-Austrian and New-Keynesian approaches, Post Keynesians emphasise the importance of most of our knowledge being uncertain; in general it is not possible to calculate the riskiness of any asset. Rather than being concealed, as in the New-Keynesian approach, such measures are unknowable. For Post Keynesians, it is unwarranted under uncertainty to rely for financial stability on market pricing.

Further, where neo-Austrians and proponents of Sovereign Money envisage individuals making their own decisions about how to value their bank deposits, Post Keynesians argue that the ensuing uncertainty would make these deposits unsuitable as money. More generally, as Minsky (1986) argued, the unavailability of true risk measures means that market valuations rely heavily on conventional judgements and are thus subject to wild swings. Since upward swings encourage increased leveraging (i.e. exposure to risk of asset price collapse), the outcome is financial instability as judgements about risks go into reverse and fire-sales of assets make price falls even worse. This was Minsky's Financial Instability Hypothesis.

As society needs a safe asset to hold in times of crisis, or even of increased uncertainty about the value of other assets, money acts as a store of value, a necessary feature of a means of payment. It also acts as a unit of account, which provides a secure foundation for debt and labour contracts. But, while state-issued money normally performs these functions best, the financial sector is adept at providing near-moneys, particularly when the state attempts to control the supply of its own money. The state can attempt to separate its money from rivals by requiring taxes to be paid in it. But the state cannot enforce a separation between its money and other assets, as presumed by the Sovereign-Money approach. Financial history demonstrates the ways in which the financial sector generates assets which are close money-substitutes, bank deposits being a notable case in point. But financialization has promoted the emergence of an increasing variety of assets (such as asset-backed securities) and liquid markets in which they are traded, meeting liquidity needs outside the retail banking system.

There is at any time a spectrum of assets with differing degrees of 'moneyness', depending on the degree of confidence in the liquidity of any asset (including the reliability of its expected value). This will vary, not only with market conditions, but also with institutional arrangements such as what central banks accept as collateral. But near-monies in the form of securities are vulnerable to changing market conditions which can drastically reduce their liquidity. Given the (often opaque) increasing interconnectedness of these markets, the collapse in value of any one near-money can spread throughout the financial system. Not only does this call for tighter regulation of banks to limit exposure to such potential market collapses, but regulation needs to extend its coverage to shadow banks where financialization has encouraged the strongest growth.

The third separation which Post Keynesians avoid is between money and finance on the one hand and the real economy on the other. In the New-Keynesian approach in particular, the two only connect when there is a market imperfection, e.g. credit for real investment projects is rationed because of concealed information about risk. In the Post-Keynesian approach the interconnections are fundamental. Money has the capacity both to enable real activity and to constrain it. It enables by providing a safe asset as the basis for contracts and as a refuge from uncertainty. But by the same token it constrains by providing an alternative to positive expenditure decisions when uncertainty is high. Then effective demand is reduced, creating unemployment. In particular, Keynes argued that the short-termism of financial markets diverted finance from productive investment, with obvious real effects. Finally the financial sector also has real effects when it promotes inequality of income and wealth.

Financialization has strengthened these forces (see e.g. Hein 2012 and Palley 2016). Real capital accumulation has been inhibited by such factors (associated with financialization) as firms' increased reliance on external equity finance and the resulting increased focus of management on maintaining short-term shareholder value. While this reduced investment has weakened effective demand, financialization has supported increased consumption expenditure with household debt and housing wealth, at the same time increasing the financial vulnerability of lower-income households. Further, financialization has fuelled a secular increase in inequality of income and wealth, not just between labour and capital, but with a particular skew in favour of the top end of the range whose financial position has benefitted dramatically from the recent decades of financialization. These trends have been analysed and subjected to substantial empirical investigation by Post-Keynesian scholars. For example, Stockhammer (2004) explores the link between financialization and real investment, finding a positive empirical link for the US, the UK and France (though not Germany). Further, Hein (2013) identifies empirically the nature and sources of the falling labour share of income in a variety of economies during recent decades of increased financialization, while Onaran, Stockhammer and Grafl (2011) relate financialization to income distribution and real investment and consumption in the US (also see Godechot, in this volume).

In terms of the role of the state, Keynes advocated that policy (e.g. on monetary reform) should aim for the efficient promotion of individual liberty and social justice: 'The outstanding faults of the economic society in which we live are its failure to provide for full employment and its arbitrary and inequitable distribution of wealth and incomes' (Keynes 1936: 372). Keynes thus saw central banking as operating within a wider remit than the narrow inflation-targeting version of monetary stability. Central banks rather were to work side-by-side with government in pursuing their goals. His approach indicates an enhanced role for regulation, given the financial sector's capacity to provide near-money assets and its inherent tendency to be unstable and to promote a maldistribution of income and wealth.

The Post-Keynesian approach to regulation is not, as with the other approaches, to separate the state from the private sector, the former possibly with a monopoly on money supply and the latter relied upon to promote social welfare through competitive markets. Rather it is to accept the intertwined nature of public sector and private sector banking, to promote a mutually supportive relationship between the two, to regulate particularly closely the provision of money-assets to ensure their safety, and to be alert to ongoing needs for new regulation as the financial environment evolves. Since Post Keynesians focus on interconnectedness, the three goals of monetary stability, financial stability and economic stability are seen as interconnected, and therefore all are the business of the monetary authorities. Monetary stability is the least important, since a stable economy and stable financial conditions are the main ingredients of low inflation, the money supply being endogenous (see further Dow 2017a).

Concluding Reflections on Regulation in the Wake of the Crisis

All four approaches considered here have contributed to the discourse on financial regulation in the wake of the crisis. The neo-Austrian idea of the state completely withdrawing from finance gained little traction during the crisis given the palpable need for some form of state intervention, but their confidence otherwise in market discipline persists in some policy discussions. In the meantime, central banks are actively considering the Sovereign-Money idea of state issue of money, sidelining retail banks (spurred on by the possibilities for a state digital currency). While New-Keynesian theory has been a major force since it dominates in academic economics, it has not dominated policy in the wake of the crisis.

Many of the changes which have been discussed and even introduced in the wake of the crisis in fact appear instead to follow Post-Keynesian principles. New macroprudential regulation aims to ensure more prudent bank behaviour, e.g. imposing minimum capital ratios, leverage ratios and liquidity ratios. There is now also a much greater recognition of systemic risk which cannot be addressed at the level of individual banks. The scope for financial networks to spread financial instability is now monitored and stress tests are now routinely applied in an attempt to identify individual banks' vulnerability to adverse developments at the market level (see Aikman et al. 2018 for a review). Functional separation between retail and investment banking is a further measure, designed to focus central bank support only on those institutions which supply society's money. Other forms of market segmentation are being considered, with possibilities for state support; the particular contribution of savings banks, co-operative banks and credit unions is being recognised, and ideas for state-run development banks being pursued. Further there has been discussion of a global tax on financial transactions, building on the original idea for a Tobin tax. While for Post Keynesians such a tax would increase the social efficiency of the financial sector, it nevertheless faces fierce opposition in that it would reduce efficiency in profit-making.

While there is much in common between the understanding of the financial sector of policy-makers and Post Keynesians, the force of mainstream academic input has influenced central banks' conceptual framework. There is widespread support, backed up by non-Post-Keynesian theory, for focusing on eliminating central bank support for banks. Many regulatory reforms have therefore been driven by the continuance of the 'too-big-to-fail' problem (that failure of a big bank would pose an unacceptable systemic risk), without an appreciation of the full significance of uncertainty for systemic risk. Instead much emphasis continues to be placed on minimum capital requirements, relying on the mainstream notion of measurable risk of portfolios. Yet the recent crisis was largely the effect of increased financialization of bank strategies adopted in the face of previous increases in capital requirements (Chick 2013). Indeed, financialization has continued to be evident in shadow banking, which has expanded apace as a major source of credit and (apparent) liquidity, increasing systemic risk. The clear implication is that regulation needs to keep up, and continue to keep up, to encompass shadow banking as it evolves. The Financial Stability Board is addressing the monitoring of shadow banking, which is a first step, but regulatory action is urgently required. Such regulation will be challenging, not least given the nimbleness of the financial sector, but that is not an adequate argument for no regulation.

For the three non-Post-Keynesian approaches, financialization is only relevant insofar as it applies to bank credit creation. Aside from market imperfections to be reduced by policy, the focus is on the state as the source of banking problems which lead to financial crisis. By implication, without state support the financial sector would be more stable and better able to serve society's needs. Of the groupings we have discussed here, only Post Keynesians focus on concern with the nature, size and influence of the financial sector as a whole, particularly its capacity to cause instability and crisis with profound socio-economic consequences. The role of the state in curbing these tendencies is key. This involves the state, not only in constraining and segmenting financial activity, but also in a more positive vein providing the support necessary for a stable financial environment to serve the real economy.

Note

1 Post Keynesians share with the Sovereign-Money approach a broader role for the monetary authorities, and also the view that the money supply is endogenously determined by the banks. But otherwise the analysis of the financial sector is very different (see e.g. Fontana and Sawyer 2016).

Bibliography

Aikman, D., Haldane, A.G., Hinterschweiger, M. and Kapadia, S., 2018. Rethinking financial stability. *Bank of England Staff Working Paper* No. 712.

Benes, J. and Kumhof, M., 2012. The Chicago Plan revisited. *IMF Working Paper* WP/12/202.

Blinder, A.S. and Stiglitz, J.E., 1983. Money, credit constraints, and economic activity. *American Economic Review*, 73(2), pp. 297–302.

Calomiris, C.W., 2017. *Reforming Financial Regulation after Dodd-Frank*. New York: Manhattan Institute.

Chick, V., 2013. The current banking crisis in the UK: An evolutionary view. In G. Harcourt and J. Pixley (eds.). *Financial Crises and the Nature of Capitalist Money: Mutual Developments from the Work of Geoffrey Ingham*. London: Palgrave Macmillan, pp. 148–161.

Dow, S.C., 1996. Why the banking system should be regulated. *Economic Journal*, 104(436), pp. 698–707.

Dow, S., 2013a. Formalism, rationality and evidence: The case of behavioural economics. *Erasmus Journal for Philosophy and Economics*, 6(3), pp. 26–43.

Dow, S., 2013b. Methodology and Post-Keynesian economics. In G. Harcourt and P. Kriesler (eds.). *Handbook of Post-Keynesian Economics*. Oxford: Oxford University Press, vol. 2, pp. 80–99.

Dow, S., 2016a. Uncertainty: A diagrammatic treatment. *Economics: The Open-Access, Open-Assessment E-Journal*, 10(3), pp. 1–25.

Dow, S., 2016b. The political economy of monetary reform. *Cambridge Journal of Economics*, 40(5), pp. 1363–1376.

Dow, S., 2017a. Central banking in the 21st century. *Cambridge Journal of Economics*, 41(6), pp. 1539–1557.

Dow, S., 2017b. People have had enough of experts. *INET Symposium on Experts*. Available at: https://www.ineteconomics.org/perspectives/blog/people-have-had-enough-of-experts [Accessed 27 Feb. 2019].

Dowd, K., 2009. *Lessons from the Financial Crisis: A Libertarian Perspective*. Libertarian Alliance [online]. Available at: http://www.libertarian.co.uk/lapubs/econn/econn111.htm [Accessed 27 Feb. 2019].

Dyson, B. and Hodgson, G., 2016. *Digital Cash*. London: Positive Money.

Dyson, B., Hodgson, G. and Van Lerven, F., 2016. *Sovereign Money*. London: Positive Money.

Earle, J., Moran, C. and Ward-Perkins, Z., 2016. *The Econocracy: The Perils of Leaving Economics to the Experts*. Manchester: Manchester University Press.

Engert, W. and Fung, B., 2017. Central bank digital currency: Motivations and implications. *Bank of Canada Staff Working Paper* 2017–2016.

Farmer, R.E.A., 2013. Qualitative easing: A new tool for the stabilization of financial markets: The John Flemming Memorial Lecture. *Bank of England Quarterly Bulletin*, December(Q4), pp. 405–413.

Fontana, G. and Sawyer, M., 2016. Full reserve banking: more 'cranks' than 'brave heretics'. *Cambridge Journal of Economics*, 40(5), pp. 1333–1350.

Geraats, P.M., 2002. Central bank transparency. *Economic Journal*, 112, pp. F532–565.

Hayek, F.A., 1975. Full employment at any price. *Hobart Paper*, 45. London: IEA.

Hayek, F.A., 1976. *The Denationalization of Money*. London: IEA.

Hein, E., 2012. *The Macroeconomics of Finance-dominated Capitalism and its Crisis*. Cheltenham: Edward Elgar Publishing.

Hein, E., 2013. Finance-dominated capitalism and redistribution of income: A Kaleckian perspective. *Cambridge Journal of Economics*, 39(3), pp. 907–934.

Jackson, A. and Dyson B., 2012. *Modernising Money*. London: Positive Money.

Keynes, J.M., 1936. *The General Theory of Employment, Interest and Money*. London: Macmillan.

Kregel, J. and Tonveronachi, M., 2014. Fundamental principles of financial regulation and supervision. *FESSUD Working Paper Series*, no. 29.

Mackenzie, D., Muniesa, F. and Siu, L. (eds.), 2007. *Do Economists Make Markets? On the Performativity of Economics*. Princeton, NJ: Princeton University Press.

Minsky, H.P., 1982. *Inflation, Recession and Economic Policy*. Brighton: Wheatsheaf.

Minsky, H.P., 1986. *Stabilizing an Unstable Economy*. New Haven, CT: Yale University Press.

Onaran, Ö., Stockhammer, E. and Grafl, L., 2011. Financialisation, income distribution and aggregate demand in the USA. *Cambridge Journal of Economics*, 35(4), pp. 637–661.

Palley, T., 2016. *Financialization: The Economics of Finance Capital Domination*. New York: Springer.

Preda, A., 2007. The sociological approach to financial markets. *Journal of Economic Surveys*, 21(3), pp. 506–528.

Rein, M. and Schön, D.A., 1993. Reframing policy discourse. In: Fischer, F. and Forester, J. (eds.). *The Argumentative Turn in Policy Analysis and Planning*. Durham: Duke University Press, pp. 145–166.

Sent, E.-M., 2004. Behavioural economics: How psychology made its (limited) way back into economics. *History of Political Economy*, 36(4), pp. 735–760.

Stiglitz, J.E. and Weiss, A., 1981. Credit rationing in markets with imperfect information. *American Economic Review*, 71(3), pp. 393–410.

Stockhammer, E., 2004. Financialisation and the slowdown of accumulation. *Cambridge Journal of Economics*, 28(5), pp. 719–741.

Tuckett, D., 2011. *Minding the Markets: An Emotional Finance View of Financial Instability*. London: Palgrave Macmillan.

Weber, B., 2016. Bitcoin and the legitimacy crisis of money. *Cambridge Journal of Economics*, 40(1), pp. 17–41.

6

THE FINANCIALIZATION OF LIFE

Paul Langley

Introduction

The purpose of this chapter is to elaborate upon financialization research that draws on the post-structural theorizations of contemporary power relations provided by Michel Foucault and Gilles Deleuze. The intertwined theoretical projects of Foucault and Deleuze would perhaps seem an unlikely source of inspiration for understanding financialization. Neither theorist directly and consistently addressed questions of money and finance, nor could their writings several decades ago foretell the present significance of financialization processes. Nonetheless, Foucault and Deleuze feature widely across academic disciplines in critical accounts of financial markets and analyses of financialization.

The opening section below concentrates on the body of financialization research that to date has drawn most thoroughly on the post-structural theories of Foucault and Deleuze. Both theorists are sources of inspiration for research into the financialization of the everyday routines and rhythms of socio-economic life. Indeed, important reviews of the financialization literature characterize post-structuralism as an approach that is primarily concerned with everyday life (Van der Zwan 2014). Post-structuralism contributes to enriching critical understandings of how everyday life is becoming financialized, especially by furthering analysis of the ways in which governmental rationalities and techniques configure economies, cultures and subjectivities of speculation and indebtedness.

The second section of the chapter will suggest that Foucauldian and Deleuzean theorizations of power have the potential to facilitate a more wide-reaching agenda for research that includes, but also extends well beyond, everyday socio-economic life. Foucault and Deleuze are deployed individually or together across extant research into financial markets and financialization processes. They are also variously mobilized without and within Marxist political economy frameworks. Notwithstanding the diverse uptake of Foucault and Deleuze, they provide a coherent critical analytical agenda for the study of financialization that is rooted in their prescient theorizations of the distinctive character of contemporary power relations (Deleuze 1992, 1999; Foucault 1991, 2007, 2008). Foucault and Deleuze encourage a focus on the co-production of financial knowledge and techniques, on the one hand, and contemporary power relations, on the other. They can thereby further analyses of financialization processes that foreground how financial logics and techniques are incorporated into, and are constitutive of, the prevailing power relations that seek to control and secure life under neo-liberal capitalism. Foucault and Deleuze draw attention, in short, to the conditions under which the financialization of life becomes possible and, for the present at least, continues apace.

The third section of the chapter illustrates the potential of a wide-reaching post-structural agenda for research into the financialization of life. A body of scholarship is drawn together that – developing somewhat separately from the reception of Foucault and Deleuze into the financialization literature – centres on the co-production of the new life sciences and contemporary power relations. Key contributions to this scholarship already highlight the speculative qualities of the life sciences and their so-called "bio-economies", but tend not to explicitly acknowledge wider processes of financialization. What such scholarship is shown to begin to offer is an agenda for studying financialization processes that analyses the force of financial logics and techniques in the ordering of biological life. Moreover, by way of conclusion to the chapter, I point to possibilities for research into further and related modalities of the financialization of life, processes that include both the infrastructural conditions of life and more-than-human life.

Financialization and Everyday Life

In the wake of work by Marxist, post-Keynesian and institutional political economists that analyses the shifting balance between the financial and productive economies – including changes in corporate form and management prompted by the privileging of shareholder value – financialization research has been marked by a pair of related tendencies. First, the literature stresses how the reach of financialization processes extends well beyond the productive and corporate economies. Whilst clearly not without contestation or limit points (see Christophers and Fine, in this volume), financialization appears to be a set of voracious processes that crystalize financial logics and values across multiple domains. Uninterrupted, and actually deepened in the course of the global financial crisis (Davis and Williams 2017), financialization processes are now arguably being experienced more widely and acutely than ever.

Second, when developing critical understanding of financialization processes beyond the productive and corporate economies, scholars also tend to broaden the theoretical remit of financialization research beyond political economy frameworks. To be clear, political economy is typically not jettisoned altogether by financialization researchers, especially given the crucial insights that Marxism holds for understanding the character and content of capitalist finance. However, more-often-than-not and in one way or another, political economy approaches are challenged or nourished with concepts and ideas taken from the wider body of social theory. Illustrative in this respect is the tendency for reviews of the financialization literature to begin by providing an overview of political economy work before turning to cover research from different theoretical perspectives that is variously positioned as contrasting to, or complementary with, political economy research.

One important manifestation of the tendencies to broaden the empirical and theoretical remit of financialization research is the literature that studies how these processes are transforming the everyday routines and rhythms of socio-economic life (Erturk et al. 2009; French, Leyshon, and Wainwright 2011; Van der Zwan 2014). This is not to say that everyday socio-economic life does not feature in institutional and Marxist political economy accounts of contemporary capitalism (e.g. Crouch 2011; Lapavitsas 2011). What usually marks research into the financialization of everyday life, however, is a dissatisfaction with macroeconomic and structural accounts of change (Van der Zwan 2014: 111–112). To apprehend financialization processes as they are experienced, faced and felt by households and individuals, research therefore tends to turn to, and be informed by, a wider body of social theory that may include, but which usually extends beyond, political economy approaches.

Particular impetus has been given to research into the financialization of everyday life by the post-structural theorizations of power provided by Michel Foucault and Gilles Deleuze. Such theorizations of power feature, for example, in research that coalesces around the notion of "finance/security" (de Goede 2010). Influenced in particular by the lectures that Foucault (2007, 2008) originally delivered during the late 1970s at the Collège de France, research into finance/security emphasizes that financial logics and techniques loom large in the formulation and execution of the contemporary neo-liberal government of social and economic life as problems of security. This is because finance and security share an ontological conundrum – how to confront the uncertain future – and a shared epistemology of risk that is manifest in the deployment of risk management techniques and tools in order to render the future actionable in the present (Boy, Burgess and Leander 2011). It follows that the financialization of everyday life is a manifestation of a powerful governmental rationality and a range of risk management techniques that regard uncertain financial market circulations in positive and productive terms as vital to securing socio-economic life.

By analysing the changing socio-economic experiences and practices of households and individuals in relation to the development of neo-liberal governmental programmes, finance/security research has thus made a distinctive contribution to understanding financialization. The financialization of everyday life is understood primarily in relation to a particular regime of neo-liberal governmentalized power that, including market deregulation and the privatization and individualization of welfare, features the instantiation of techniques of self-government, or what Foucault (1991) terms "governmentality". In the USA and UK in particular, neo-liberal governmentality is shown to have positioned financial markets as crucial to securing the future wealth and wellbeing of the population (Aitken 2010; Langley 2008, 2015). Everyday routines and rhythms of saving and borrowing are transformed by extensive and intensive relations with the uncertain circulations of global financial markets. The choices confronted by "free" individuals and households are not over whether to invest in the markets or to take on debt, but how best to do so.

As a technology of self-government, mutual fund investment has become privileged, for example, over and above both retail deposit account saving and collective, state and employer-guaranteed retirement insurance. The meaning of "security" and "risk" is changed, then, and is no longer a matter of individuals and households making thrifty provision for a rainy day, or collectively insuring against future dangers. Such change is not simply a "shift" of risk from the state and corporations to households and individuals (e.g. Hacker 2008), but rather a rearticulation of risk and uncertainty as opportunities to be embraced via the markets by entrepreneurial investor subjects who seek to secure their future wealth and wellbeing. Moreover, mortgages and consumer credit have also come to be regarded as playing a positive role in facilitating the security and prosperity of all, and are differentially priced in terms of the creditworthiness of borrowers and associated default risks (Marron 2009). While the global financial crisis of over a decade ago starkly exposed the ways in which outstanding debt obligations and accompanying risks from everyday borrowing are repackaged into objects of securitization and speculation by wholesale financial markets, obligations and risks have also become an object for management and manipulation by debtor subjects themselves (Langley 2014).

The contribution of Foucault and Deleuze to the study of the financialization of everyday life is also apparent when these post-structural theorists are mobilized alongside Marx. For autonomist Marxists such as Maurizio Lazzarato (2012), for example, the credit–debt relation is held to have displaced the labour relation in neo-liberal capitalism, such that credit–debt relations between "owners" and "non-owners" of capital are becoming "the basis of social life" (pp. 13–36). And, in explicitly Deleuzean terms, the debt relations of households and individuals are said to feature the "machinic subjugation" of credit scoring techniques which "dismantles the self, the subject, and the individual", such that credit and creditworthiness can be differentially assessed and priced in terms of risk (p. 150). At the same time, and in more Foucauldian terms, the expansion of credit–debt relations is a governmentalized form of power that "breeds, subdues, manufactures, adapts, and shapes subjectivity" (p. 39). Debtor subjects are hailed who, animated by debt's moral economy of responsibility and guilt (pp. 135–161; see also Stimilli 2017), ceaselessly work on themselves and their finances in order to make good on their obligations and creditworthiness.

Without and within Marxist political economy approaches, then, Foucault and Deleuze have attuned researchers to the transformations of everyday socio-economic life wrought by the governmentalized force of financial logics and the operations of financial techniques and devices. Attention is drawn, in particular, to logics of speculation and indebtedness that advance economies of rent and value capture but which, at the same time, also install certain and ongoing financial futurities and (in)securities into the ordering of everyday life. The pervasive influence of the financial logic of speculation is, for instance, a triumph of the governmental rationale of "speculative security", in the terms favoured by the finance/security literature (de Goede 2012; Morris 2018). Volatile financial market circulations pose dangers to the security of the population that have to be mitigated, but their vicissitudes and indeterminacies also present opportunities that are vital to the dynamic production of future wealth and wellbeing across the population (Langley 2015). Not dissimilarly, from Haiven's (2014; Chapter X in this volume) primarily Marxist perspective, the speculative character of the financialization of everyday life advances because of the growing hold of imaginaries and techniques of "fictitious capital" over popular culture.

For autonomist Marxists, meanwhile, an emphasis on the logic of speculation and security obscures the significance of credit–debt as both an economic and governing relation under neo-liberal capitalism. From this perspective, it is the logic and techniques of indebtedness that prevail throughout everyday socio-economic life, and the intensification of socio-economic insecurity is an ever-present, structural condition of life (Lazzarato 2012). However, as Lisa Adkins (2017) persuasively argues, guilt-racked struggles with indebted life also feature a logic of speculation, as "debt society demands subjects who must constantly adjust to recalibrations of pasts, presents and futures as well as to changes in the relations between and across these states" (p. 448; also Konings 2018).

Rather than retrenching under the weight of its own contradictions or reaching its limits as populations become increasingly indebted, the financialization of everyday life continues apace at present. To extend Lauren Berlant's (2010) astute analysis of contemporary economy and society, the financialization of everyday socio-economic life is sustained by the "cruel optimism" of speculation, as "the predominance of finance … brings people together only to seem to take away what they thought they possessed" (Martin 2002: 16). Optimistic and hopeful promises of opportunities and better times to come that can be seized through speculation and entrepreneurship serve to absorb and dissipate the tensions and conflicts engendered by growing inequality and indebtedness.

Financialization and Post-structural Theories of Power

Given the influence of Foucault and Deleuze on contemporary social theory, it would be surprising if these post-structural thinkers were not present in a burgeoning financialization literature that continues to broaden its empirical and theoretical remit. In this section of the chapter, however, I want to suggest that Foucault and Deleuze provide for a coherent critical research agenda for the study of financialization. This is an agenda that includes, but also extends well beyond, the financialization of everyday socio-economic life. Consistent with analysing the financialization of everyday life through a focus on the relations between the socio-economic experiences of households and individuals and the programmes and techniques of neo-liberal government, this more wide-reaching agenda is rooted in the theorizations of the distinctive character of contemporary power relations that are offered by Deleuze (1992, 1999) and Foucault (1991, 2007, 2008).

The agenda for financialization research provoked by the post-structural power theories of Foucault and Deleuze is distinct from their influence on the so-called "social studies of finance" (SSF) (MacKenzie 2009; Coombs and Van der Heide, in this volume). A host of Deleuzean concepts animate this cross-disciplinary literature, including, concepts such as "diagram" (Aitken 2015), "virtuality" (Arnoldi 2004), "war machine" (Erturk, Leaver and Williams 2010), "fold" (Langley 2018a), and "rhizome" (Vlcek 2010). However, the core research agenda of SSF is to provide an alternative to atomised and institutional accounts of agency in financial markets that stresses the socio-technical, material and relational character of financial market action (see also Chiapello 2019, this volume). This is an agenda that typically springs from the Deleuzean concept of "assemblage" or "*agencement*", while some contributors to SSF turn to Foucault's concept of "*dispositif*" ("apparatus"), not least because it holds particular efficacy for analysing governmental actions during periods of financial crisis management (Langley 2015).

In contrast, the post-structural theories of power provided by Foucault and Deleuze prompt research into financialization processes that foregrounds the co-production of financial knowledge, on the one hand, and contemporary power relations, on the other. By way of illustration, consider again post-structural accounts of the financialization of everyday life. The prominence of finance across economy and society is not essentially new, but the present day reach of finance throughout everyday socio-economic life would seem to be of a different order (Erturk et al. 2009). Offering a better understanding of the conditions under which this is possible is, put simply, where the poststructuralism of Foucault and Deleuze comes in. Deployed without and within Marxist political economy approaches, Foucault and Deleuze provide for accounts of the financialization of everyday life that are rooted in a productive and relational theorization of power. As financialization penetrates deep into the spaces, routines and rhythms of socio-economic existence, Foucault and Deleuze prompt recognition that these processes cannot simply be traced to powerful class interests and the constraining actions of elites (cf. Davis and Williams 2017; Epstein, in this volume). Neither does the circulation of expert and popular financial knowledges serve the "ideological obfuscation" of elite and class interests (Haiven 2014: 13). Financial logics and techniques are instead held to be better understood in constitutive terms, and as governmental forces that configure everyday economies, cultures and subjectivities. Equally, while state and market institutions are certainly crucial to the financialization of everyday life (Van der Zwan 2014), from a post-structural perspective institutions are incorporated within a decentred and relational understanding of the rationalities, programmes and techniques of governmentalized power (Langley 2015).

What unites Deleuze and Foucault as theorists of power is their preoccupation with the particular mode of power that has taken hold in the wake of the disciplinary liberal societies of the mid-twentieth century (Foucault 1977). For Deleuze, a new "diagram" of power is in operation in the contemporary period (Deleuze 1999), one that he characterizes as "the societies of control" (Deleuze 1992). Power in the societies of control has a new and different spatial-temporal logic. It does not primarily work on individual bodies in a disciplinary and linear fashion, as they pass into and through relatively enclosed institutions such as the prison, factory, school, hospital, family and so on. Rather, control operates to "modulate" disaggregated and dissected "*dividuals*", that is, it works through "masses, samples, data, markets, or 'banks'" (Deleuze 1992: 4, *emphasis in original*). For Deleuze (1992), the spatial-temporal logic of the contemporary mode of power is such that "the man of control is undulatory, in orbit, in a continuous network", a subject required to confront the uncertainties of "*limitless postponements*" in "continuous variation" (p. 5, *emphasis in original*). Crucial to the emergence of the new power logic and computerized technologies of control societies is the shift from the factory to the corporation that accompanies the rise of "a capitalism of higher-order production" (p. 6), a capitalism of distributed supply chains, marketing and incessant regulation by market mechanisms.

For Foucault, meanwhile, the "contemporary system" of "biopolitics" and "governmentality" contrasts with previously dominant sovereign and disciplinary modes of power and forms of liberal administration (2007: 6–8). The contemporary system seeks to secure life itself (not the security of the state) (Foucault 2007, 2008), and to govern "at a distance" and through the apparently natural and uncertain processes that are "immanent to the population" (Foucault 1991: 100). Crucial to the power-knowledge relations of the contemporary system is the constitutive role of the biological and economic sciences. Thus, life and population are not only figured as the objects of government, but are understood as abstracted "processes of a naturalness specific to relations between men", including "what happens spontaneously when they … exchange, work, and produce" (Foucault 2008: 349). While liberal government includes juridical limits on sovereign power and legal guarantees of the rights of individuals, neo-liberal government is marked by a second set of limits on sovereign power that arise from the biological and economic sciences; that is, the supposedly "natural" laws and logics of the market. Neo-liberal governmentality, therefore, does not seek to standardize and synchronize individual bodies in and through the enclosed institutions of the disciplinary mode of power, but instead intervenes in the uncertain conditions that impact on the life of the population.

For Deleuze and Foucault, power relations that seek to control, secure and govern life entail important corporate, economic and market dynamics, but do not necessarily feature financial logics and techniques. Subsequent research by post-structural scholars of financialization has been required to variously show how financial logics and techniques are incorporated into, and are constitutive of, the configuration of contemporary power relations originally elucidated by Foucault and Deleuze. For those drawing more exclusively on these theorists – and largely setting aside Marxist political economy – such research has centred on the role of financial logics and techniques in the speculative security practices and governmental programmes of neo-liberal life (e.g. Aitken 2010; de Goede 2010, 2012; Langley 2008, 2015, Morris 2018). Meanwhile, for autonomist Marxists, Foucauldian and Deleuzean theorizations of power facilitate the identification of a change in the dominant logic of present day capital – i.e. the passing from profit (accumulated via commodity production and circulation) to rent and value capture that operates on the terrain of social reproduction. The engine of contemporary capitalism is understood to be "finance's subsumption of life" (Lucarelli 2010: 136). What post-structural theories of power explicitly prompt, then, is research into the financialization of life, or what might be termed, by way of shorthand, processes of "bio-financialization" (French and Kneale 2012; Lilley and Papadopoulos 2014).

Financialization of Biological Life

Although post-structural research into financialization processes has to date been pursued most thoroughly by work on everyday socio-economic life, the agenda for research into the financialization of life that develops from Foucauldian and Deleuzean theorizations of power is a more extensive and wide-reaching one. This section of the chapter will therefore mark out a modality of biofinancialization that is related to, but different from, the financialization of everyday socio-economic life. It will draw together a body of scholarship that has developed largely in parallel with, and somewhat divorced from, the reception of Foucault and Deleuze into the financialization literature. The body of scholarship in question is primarily found within the fields of science and technology studies, anthropology and the humanities, rather than within the heterodox economics, sociology, geography, cultural studies and political science disciplines which tend to dominate financialization research. What I want to show, however, is that this scholarship provides an entry point for researching financialization which analyses the force of financial logics and techniques in the ordering of biological life.

It is clearly the case that, as Deleuze (1992: 4) remarks when fleshing out the emergence of the societies of control, "the extraordinary pharmaceutical productions, the molecular engineering, the genetic manipulations … are slated to enter into the new process." However, one of the notable features of post-structural research into the new life sciences and rise of bio-technologies is that it has provoked and carried forward a debate over post-structural theorizations of power. The crux of debate is dissatisfaction with how Foucault and Deleuze characterized the reorientation of contemporary power relations as acting primarily on and through the dynamic abstractions of populations (e.g. rates of birth, death, disease, etc.) and "dividuals" (i.e. "masses, samples, data, markets, or '*banks*'") (Lemke 2011: 93–96). This is because contemporary biological science (e.g. genetics, reproductive technologies, transplant medicine) is transforming nature. As Thomas Lemke summarizes, biology is "no longer" only "a science of discovery that registers and documents life processes", but is becoming "a science of transformation that creates life and actively changes living organisms" (2011: 94–95). It follows that "life" is framed, controlled and secured somewhat differently from the theorizations of power provided by Foucault and Deleuze, not least because bodies are molecularized in ways that they did not anticipate or explore in any detail (Braun 2007).

The literature that centres on how contemporary bio-scientific knowledge goes hand in hand with the post-disciplinary power relations of neo-liberal capitalism thereby works with a more comprehensive theorization of the power relations that act on life, grounded in an appreciation of how understandings of biological life are currently changing. In this respect, it undergirds an expansive agenda for research into bio-financialization processes that has the potential to include the financialization of biological life. Key contributors to the critical literature on the life sciences interrogate the associated emergence of so-called "bio-economies". They commonly identify how the "commercialization" and "corporatization" of the new life sciences are powered by investments of capital and hope (e.g. Sunder Rajan 2012), but do not sufficiently relate this to the distinctive, financializing character of contemporary neo-liberal governmentality and capitalism. Kaushilk Sunder Rajan (2006), for example, offers an account of bio-medicine (especially genomics and pharmaceuticals) that, combining Foucault with Marx, draws out the dynamics of what he calls *Biocapital*. For Sunder Rajan, "biocapital" is the outcome of an uneasy relationship between "two simultaneous, distinct, yet mutually constitutive forms of capital, one directly dependent on the production of the commodity, the other speculative and only indirectly so" (p. 9). While "the manufacture and sale of therapeutic molecules" is key to the profitability of the Indian companies that feature strongly in Rajan's fieldwork, this is less the case for bio-tech companies in the United States where "valuation is more directly dependent on speculative capital" (p. 9).

For the Foucauldian Nikolas Rose (2006), meanwhile, when it is "Conducted at a molecular level, biology and medicine require long periods of investment" to fund equipment, laboratories, clinical trials and regulatory processes "before achieving a return" (p. 31). This reliance on long-term investment – "subject to all the exigencies of capitalization, such as the obligations of profit and the demands of shareholder value" – serves to shape "the very direction, organization, problem space, and solution effects of biomedicine and the basic biology that supports it" (pp. 32–33). Investments are made on the expectation of "bio-value"; that is, "the value to be extracted from the vital properties of living processes" that will deliver both improvements to human health and economic returns (pp. 32–33; see also Sunder Rajan 2012; Walby and Mitchell 2006). As "Biopolitics becomes bioeconomics" (Rose 2006: 32–34), then, it is "promissory capitalism" that comes to the fore.

Melinda Cooper's (2008) book *Life as Surplus* provides, meanwhile, perhaps the most provocative and suggestive account of the bio-economies of the new life sciences. Cooper combines theoretical insights from Marx and Foucault to analyse the intersections of biological processes and strategies of capital accumulation, especially their configuration in the bio-tech industry in the United States. While the life sciences carry forward the molecularization of human life as new opportunities for the appropriation of value by capital, they also install ecological and complex-systems thinking as core to the orderings of neo-liberal capitalism. The future-facing speculative logic of neo-liberal capitalism is, for Cooper, a result of the intersections of the power of the new bio-sciences with finance and the flowering of attendant beliefs in the adaptive capacities of human life that confront and transcend ostensible ecological and economic limits. Cooper (2008: 10) is thereby clear that "What neoliberalism seeks to impose is not so much the generalized commodification of daily life … as its financialization." Life is rendered valuable in terms of the "nonmeasurable, achronological temporality of financial capital accumulation" (p. 10), such that, for the life sciences in particular, "the financial markets have become the very generative condition of production, making it impossible to distinguish between so-called economic fundamentals and the perils and promises of speculation" (p. 24).

Cooper (2008) is thus something of an exception within a literature that typically identifies speculative logics as significant to bio-economies, but which tends not to explicitly relate the prevalence of these particular economic forces and drives to broader processes of financialization. Indeed, as Kean Birch (2017: 462) has recently argued, although existing research into the life sciences is certainly attentive to "'speculative' value in the bio-economy", it remains largely within "a theoretical framework built on notions of biological materiality, commodity production, and commodification." For example, even though for Cooper (2008: 25) "The drive to overcome limits and relocate in the speculative future is the defining movement of capital," she nonetheless holds that there is "one limit that capitalism never escapes – the imperative to derive profit." Speculative investments are typically understood to be essential to the production of the commercial life sciences, then, but are nonetheless regarded as something of an aberration from the creation of value that materializes in products, services, or intellectual property. Yet understanding the financialization of biological life as a modality of bio-financialization requires that greater attention is paid to the ways in which the future promises of "bio-value" (Rose 2006) are actually "constitutive of value in the present" (Birch 2017: 462), and how financial logics and techniques continue to produce and sustain life sciences firms as investable assets despite the overall dearth of products and services.

Conclusions

This chapter has explored research into financialization that, without and within Marxist political economy, has taken up the post-structural theorizations of power provided by Michel Foucault and Gilles Deleuze. It has suggested that Foucault and Deleuze offer a critical analytical agenda for the study of financialization, one that foregrounds how financial logics and techniques are incorporated into, and are constitutive of, the governmentalized power relations that seek to control and secure life under neo-liberal capitalism. The chapter has concentrated, in particular, on two modalities of the financialization of life: the financialization of everyday life that configures economies, cultures and subjectivities of speculation and indebtedness; and, the financialization of biological life that construes the molecularization of life by the new life sciences as fundamentally and perpetually speculative.

By explicating the financialization of biological life, the chapter has shown that limiting post-structural research to the financialization of everyday life is to conceive of the scope and dimensions of bio-financialization too narrowly, to think of "life" too restrictively and largely in terms of the concrete corporeality of individual bodies and abstracted populations. Yet, expanding the remit of research into the financialization of life in this way also runs up against the anthropocentric limitations of post-structural theories of power identified by Karen Barad (2007), amongst others, and their autonomist Marxist applications that neglect more-than-human nature in accounts of capitalist accumulation (Johnson 2017). There is a danger that research into the financialization of life is still framed too narrowly, then, when it is concerned only with how these processes are transforming both everyday life and biological life.

Debates that continuously develop and update post-structural theories of power are thus of considerable import for the financialization of life as a critical research agenda. Particularly pertinent in this regard is the debate that probes how neo-liberal governmental power variously works on more-than-human matter. In a recent intervention by Thomas Lemke (2015: 5), for instance, neoliberal government is said to act on "the interrelatedness and entanglements of men and things, the natural and the artificial, the physical and the moral." Such interventions have the potential to provide the theoretical grounding for the further extension of research into the financialization of life to include additional modalities of bio-financialization. Indeed, a broader research agenda of this kind is also the compelling ambition of autonomist Marxist analyses of "the logic of financialized (bio)capitalism" (Marazzi 2010: 66). As Lilley and Papadopoulos (2014: 972–975) suggest, bio-financialization processes can be understood to centre on "everyday life, subjectivity, ecology and materiality," flourishing precisely because they "extract value from reproduction, distribution and consumption as well as other activities and the material surroundings which do not directly belong to the immediate sphere of production."

There is, for instance, a well-established and growing literature in human geography on the financialization of urban infrastructures. Such material infrastructures are governed as strategically significant and "critical" to securing circulations and the life of the population (Aradau 2010), but research to date has only rarely explored these processes as a modality of bio-financialization (Langley 2018b), or as what we might term the financialization of the infrastructures of life. Similarly, consider the proliferation and growth of a host of markets for "green finance" that are heralded as crucial to the future of the planet. While accounts of the neo-liberal government of the environment as "neo-liberalizing natures" recognize that this "financializes the inherent productivity of nature" (Braun 2015: 1), it would seem apposite to analyse these processes in post-structural terms as another form of bio-financialization, the financialization of more-than-human life. Post-structural research into the financialization of life has already made an important contribution to the study of these processes in everyday socio-economic life. But it also has further and presently underdeveloped critical potential for interrogating the ordering force of financial logics and techniques, not least in relation to biological life, life's infrastructural conditions, and more-than-human life.

Bibliography

Adkins, L., 2017. Speculative futures in the time of debt. *The Sociological Review*, 65(3), pp. 448–462.
Aitken, R., 2010. *Performing Capital: Toward a Cultural Economy of Popular and Global Finance*. Basingstoke: Palgrave MacMillan.
Aitken, R., 2015. *Fringe Finance: Crossing and Contesting the Borders of Global Capital*. London: Routledge.
Aradau, C., 2010. Security that matters: Critical infrastructure and objects of protection. *Security Dialogue*, 41(5), pp. 491–514.
Arnoldi, J., 2004. Derivatives: Virtual values, real risks. *Theory, Culture & Society*, 21(6), pp. 23–42.
Barad, K., 2007. *Meeting the Universe Halfway: Quantum Physics and the Entanglement of Matter and Meaning*. Durham, NC: Duke University Press.

Berlant, L., 2010. *Cruel Optimism*. Durham, NC: Duke University Press.

Birch, K., 2017. Rethinking value in the bio-economy: Finance, assetization and the management of value. *Science, Technology and Human Values*, 42(3), pp. 460–490.

Boy, N., Burgess, J.P. and Leander, A., 2011. The global governance of security and finance. *Security Dialogue*, 42(2), pp. 115–122.

Braun, B., 2007. Biopolitics and the molecularization of life. *Cultural Geographies*, 14(1), pp. 6–28.

Braun B., 2015. New materialisms and neoliberal natures. *Antipode*, 47(1), pp. 1–14.

Cooper, M., 2008. *Life as Surplus: Biotechnology and Capitalism in the Neoliberal Era*. Seattle, WA: University of Washington Press.

Crouch, C., 2011. *The Strange Non-Death of Neoliberalism*. Cambridge: Polity Press.

Davis, A. and Williams, K., 2017. Introduction: Elites and power after financialization. *Theory, Culture & Society*, 34(5–6), pp. 3–26.

de Goede, M., 2010. Financial security. In J.P. Burgess (ed.) *The Routledge Handbook of the New Security Studies*. London and New York: Routledge, 100–109.

de Goede, M., 2012. *Speculative Security: The Politics of Pursuing Terrorist Monies*. Minneapolis, MN: University of Minnesota Press.

Deleuze, G., 1992. Postscript on the societies of control. *October*, 59, pp. 3–7.

Deleuze, G., 1999. *Foucault*. London: Continuum.

Erturk, I., Froud, J., Johal, S., Leaver, A. and Williams, K., 2009. *Financialization At Work: Key Texts and Commentary*. London: Routledge.

Erturk, I., Leaver, A. and Williams, K., 2010. Hedge funds as 'war machine': Making the positions work. *New Political Economy*, 15(1), pp. 9–28.

Foucault, M., 1977. *Discipline and Punish: The Birth of the Prison*. London: Allen Lane.

Foucault, M., 1991. Governmentality. In G. Burchell, C. Gordon and P. Miller (eds.) *The Foucault Effect: Studies in Governmentality*, Chicago, IL: University of Chicago Press, 87–104.

Foucault, M., 2007. *Security, Territory, Population, Lectures at the Collège de France, 1977–1978*. Basingstoke: Palgrave MacMillan.

Foucault, M., 2008. *The Birth of Biopolitics, Lectures at the Collège de France, 1978–1979*. Basingstoke: Palgrave MacMillan.

French, S. and Kneale, J., 2012. Speculating on careless lives: Annuitising the biofinancial subject. *Journal of Cultural Economy*, 5(4), pp.391–406.

French, S., Leyshon, A. and Wainwright, T., 2011. Financializing space, spacing financialization. *Progress in Human Geography*, 35(6), pp. 798–819.

Haiven, M., 2014. *Cultures of Financialization: Fictitious Capital in Popular Culture and Everyday Life*. Basingstoke: Palgrave MacMillan.

Hacker, J.S., 2008. *The Great Risk Shift: The Assault on American Jobs, Families, Health Care and Retirement and How You Can Fight Back*. Oxford: Oxford University Press.

Johnson, E.R., 2017. At the limits of species being: Sensing the anthropocene. *South Atlantic Quarterly*, 116 (2), pp. 275–292.

Konings, M., 2018. *Capital and Time: For a New Critique of Neoliberal Reason*. Redwood City, CA: Stanford University Press.

Langley, P., 2008. *The Everyday Life of Global Finance: Saving and Borrowing in Anglo-America*. Oxford: Oxford University Press.

Langley, P., 2014. Equipping entrepreneurs: Consuming credit and credit scores. *Consumption Markets & Culture*, 17(5), pp. 448–467.

Langley, P., 2015. *Liquidity Lost: The Governance of the Global Financial Crisis*. Oxford: Oxford University Press.

Langley, P., 2018a. The folds of social finance: Making markets, remaking the social. *Environment and Planning A: Economy and Space*, online early.

Langley, P., 2018b. Frontier financialization: Urban infrastructure in the United Kingdom. *Economic Anthropology*, 5(2), pp. 172–184.

Lapavitsas, C., 2011. Theorizing financialization. *Work Employment and Society*, 25(4), pp. 611–626.

Lazzarato, M., 2012. *The Making of the Indebted Man*. Los Angeles, CA: Semiotext(e).

Lemke, T., 2011. *Biopolitics: An Advanced Introduction*. New York: New York University Press.

Lemke, T., 2015. New materialisms: Foucault and the 'government of things'. *Theory, Culture and Society*, 32(4), pp. 3–25.

Lilley, S. and Papadopoulos, D., 2014. Material returns: Cultures of valuation, biofinancialisation and the autonomy of politics. *Sociology*, 48(5), pp. 972–988

Lucarelli, S., 2010. Financialization as biopower. In A. Fumagalli and S. Mezzadra (eds.) *Crisis in the Global Economy: Financial Markets, Social Struggles, and New Political Scenarios*. Los Angeles, CA: Semiotext(e).

MacKenzie, D., 2009. *Material Markets: How Economic Agents are Constructed*. Oxford: Oxford University Press.

Marazzi, C., 2010. *The Violence of Financial Capitalism*. Los Angeles, CA: Semiotext(e).

Marron, D., 2009. *Consumer Credit in the United States: A Sociological Perspective from the Nineteenth Century to the Present*. Basingstoke, UK: Palgrave MacMillan.

Martin, R., 2002. *Financialization of Daily Life*. Temple University Press.

Morris, J., 2018. *Securing Finance, Mobilizing Risk: Money Cultures at the Bank of England*. London: Routledge.

Rose, N., 2006. *The Politics of Life Itself: Biomedicine, Power and Subjectivity in the Twenty-First Century*. Princeton, NJ: Princeton University Press.

Stimilli, E., 2017. *The Debt of the Living: Ascesis and Capitalism*. Albany, NY: State University of New York Press.

Sunder Rajan, K., 2006. *Biocapital: The Constitution of Postgenomic Life*. Durham, NC: Duke University Press.

Sunder Rajan, K. (ed.), 2012. *Lively Capital: Biotechnologies, Ethics, and Governance in Global Markets*. Durham, NC: Duke University Press.

Van der Zwan, N., 2014. Making sense of financialization. *Socio-Economic Review*, 12(1), pp. 99–129.

Vlcek, W., 2010. Alongside global political economy – a rhizome of informal finance. *Journal of International Relations and Development*, 13(4), pp. 429–451.

Walby, C. and Mitchell, R., 2006. *Tissue Economies: Blood, Organs, and Cell Lines in Late Capitalism*. Durham, NC: Duke University Press.

PART B

Approaches to Studying Financialization

7

FINANCIALIZATION AS A SOCIO-TECHNICAL PROCESS

Eve Chiapello

Introduction

The purpose of this chapter is to propose a particular understanding of financialization, connected with a special approach to studying it. Financialization is often defined as a process of morphological transformation of capitalism, entailing the capture of resources by finance in the broadest sense through expansion of the financial markets, and a rise in the number and variety of financial operators. I propose a different definition taking into account the socio-technical elements involved. Financialization is understood in this article as a specific process of transforming the world, objects, organizations and the problems we encounter, by the introduction of "financialized" practices, theories and instruments. The first part examines this definition more closely, explaining its positioning in relation to other approaches to financialization. The second part proposes a series of concepts to guide any empirical research claiming to belong to the approach presented here.

Towards an Instrument-based Approach to Financialization

The way we define our understanding of financialization is inseparable from the research operations that document the phenomenon. As the "-ation" suffix suggests, financialization designates a process of change in which the object studied is transformed by "added finance". But the nature of this "addition" and the ways it is described differ depending on the approach taken.

Positioning the Socio-technical Definition of Financialization

Some researchers see financialization as a major shift in revenue and profit distribution between actors in the economic system (e.g. Epstein 2005; Krippner 2005) or at the level of a sector (e.g. Baud and Durand 2012). Others focus not on movements of capital but on the changes in actor configurations. They study the arrival, in a variety of organizational situations, of new financial actors or professionals assisting them who are able to extract significant revenues by virtue of their involvement in those situations (e.g. Erturk et al. 2008).

My approach to studying financialization is to focus not chiefly on the actors or changes in economic flows, but primarily on the practices and techniques being implemented. In most cases, the stakes concern changes in financial circuits channeling funds to economic agents.

Financial actors keep the financial markets in operation, and organize a financing circuit for the economy in which they play the leading role, collecting savings in various types of funds (e.g. investment funds, private equity funds) and investing in acquisitions of various types of assets. It is this kind of investment financing circuit that has grown substantially with financialization; analytically it must be distinguished from the credit circuits which are based on traditional banking intermediation (involving maturity transformations from deposits to loans) and also from the tax and public spending circuits (in which taxes or welfare contributions are used to finance public services or distribute replacement incomes).

With financialization, credit circuits and public circuits alike have become increasingly hybridized with the financial circuits: the banks have developed asset management activities and are offloading their loans via securitization; states and local authorities are issuing bonds (Lemoine 2017) and using a growing number of investment vehicles to conduct their policies (Chiapello 2017; Deruytter and Möller, in this volume). This approach to financialization focuses on the construction of these new circuits in which financial actors are the principal operators, on the forms of knowledge and knowhow used in these operations, and on the techniques – primarily financial and legal – that are necessary. What matters most here is *what* is done, said, and made, rather than *who* is doing, saying, and making it.

This approach is part of a more general rediscovery of the role of instruments and *dispositifs* [1] in economic sociology and political sciences (Hood 1993; Lascoumes and Le Gales 2004; Chiapello and Gilbert 2019). Through technicalities and devices, it makes it possible to propose a new definition of financialization as a specific process for transforming the world by practices, theories and instruments that originated in the financial sector, as a process of "colonization" by "financialized" techniques and practices (whose characteristics are described on p. 83), and to focus on the "work of financialization." Indeed, financializing requires considerable efforts from a wide variety of actors (audit firms, lawyers, rating agencies, fund managers, banks, consultants, but also governments, standard-setters, non-governmental organizations, think tanks and research institutes). It requires "investments in form" (Thévenot 1984) in systems of visibility creation, metrics, databases, development of theoretical conceptualizations, production of a large number of policy documents and laws, preparation of contracts, and setting up new organizations. The sociology of techniques and sciences has already provided many publications describing the role of certain calculations and devices in the rise of finance (MacKenzie and Millo 2003; MacKenzie 2006; Callon, Milo and Muniesa 2007; see review in Coombs and van der Heide, in this volume).

My approach to financialization interacts easily with other approaches that concentrate on financial actors and financial flows; it is through the implementation of a range of specific practices and instruments that financial actors are gaining power and capturing resources, and that the overall shapes of financial distribution are changing at the level of society as a whole. Nonetheless, techniques and ways of thinking clearly have a specific appeal and a capacity to circulate in partial independence of the professions whose core knowledge they constitute. This is what makes the distinction between the different approaches interesting and particularly relevant when, rather than directly concerning the financial world, an investigation concerns social spaces where very few financial professionals are to be found and the financial markets seem quite distant (as in the social sector or environmental matters). But financialization of these areas can also be observed in the arrival of approaches and techniques specific to finance, even when no financial actors are involved and there is not (yet) any significant change in financing circuits. I shall select several examples from these areas to point up these developments.

The distinction made above also enables to identify different degrees of financialization, depending on how active financial actors are in the situations and how much profit they extract from them. For example, it could be considered that a state of "weak financialization" is characterized by some changes in vocabulary and a few practices that have no real repercussions for activities, corresponding to a decoupling (Meyer and Rowan 1977) between discourses and practices, while a state of "strong financialization" exists where new financial circuits connected with private investors or financial markets have been created and are operating under financialized rules. Financializing an issue, an organization, an activity or a public policy consists of transforming the language and instruments that organize it, and importing practices and ways of thinking that come from the financial world. The transformation may remain superficial (weak financialization) or connect with the world of private finance (strong financialization). But what is common to all financialized situations is their reliance on a specific form of valuation which I call "financialized," described in the next section.

Financialized Valuation

Categorizing situations, things and people, ranking them, assigning value to various entities or actions, are all practices that enable actors to position themselves and join in certain courses of action. The notion of valuation designates the process of worth attribution. It draws attention to the fact that value is not intrinsic to the object but produced in the relationship between the object and the person who considers it valuable. It results from practical valuation activities. It involves first, identifying and selecting which objects deserve attention (and thus what escapes attention), and second, identifying what is valuable, i.e. the viewpoint from which objects are praised, estimating their "worth" within the chosen framework. This last operation can itself bring into play technical apparatuses of varying degrees of sophistication, and produce a quantification of value, possibly in monetary terms (on value, see also Christophers and Fine, in this volume).

I argue that financialization relies on specific modes of valuation that I call "financialized" and that relate to how beings and things are valued by financial actors, and the characteristics of the instruments they use to "measure" these "values." Financialized valuation is equipped by models, instruments and representations belonging to the explicit knowledge underpinning the approach and practices of finance professionals. This knowledge is taught and may be accessible from sources such as finance textbooks or professional literature. In a previous article I identified three main approaches to valuation in finance (Chiapello 2015) associated with three quantification conventions (Chiapello and Walter 2016): 1) the actuarial convention, which uses discounting to present value; 2) the mean-variance convention central to portfolio management techniques, which considers that any value can be expressed in terms of expectation (returns) and standard deviation ("risk"); 3) the market-consistent convention, which identifies value with market price.

The Actuarial Convention and the Forward-looking Investor's Viewpoint

The first valuation approach is equipped by the discounted cash flows (DCF) calculation method, which consists of forecasting the future economic flows that will be generated by using the object to be valued, and applying a discount to those flows to bring them to present value. This valuation method takes an ambivalent view of the future, since it defines value by future cash flows but is quick to reduce that value by applying a discount rate. It contrasts with a backward-looking conception of value, which considers that value lies in what has been done to or spent on it (a cost value, for example).

Although the two operations required for these calculations, anticipating future income flows and choosing a discount rate, offer considerable room for maneuver, the need to discount to present value is certainly one of the most firmly rooted central beliefs in financial calculations. Its strength is that it offers a socio-technical translation of the investors' viewpoint.

From this point of view, goods are seen as "capital goods" (goods in which capital is invested) and their value is related to their capacity as value-producers: an object is only worth buying (only "has value") if it generates returns that are higher than the amount initially invested. The capital provider's demand for liquidity is also incorporated into the calculation, as discounting embodies the idea that the investor should always consider not investing (and for example putting his money in an interest-bearing account instead) and recovering the money to invest elsewhere (Doganova 2017).

The Mean-variance Convention and the Risk-return Reduction

The second valuation approach uses probability-based statistics. Statistics arrived in the world of finance to solve a problem of value prediction: fluctuations in prices on the markets, and the occasionally high volatility even within a single day, were incompatible with the idea that prices have some objective foundation, and can be predicted. The solution was to consider it possible to describe stock market prices using mathematical expectations and volatility (standard deviation) (Walter 1996). This hypothesis then became generalized.

According to this second valuation technique, the value of anything can be reduced to a couple of indicators (risk and return). This information reduction highlights another aspect of the investor's viewpoint which is broadly summarized as the search for better returns or lower risks. Portfolio management models provide financial actors with easy techniques to manage investments and risks (or to believe that risks are managed). These ideas also paved the way for very strong assumptions about the special skills of financial actors, endowed with the ability to discern the most profitable investments (through examination of a wide universe of possible investments and application of models of investment choices) and diversify risks (Lockwood 2015).

The Market-consistent Convention and the Quest for Permanent Liquidity

Price has always been used as a source of valuation. Recently, however, it has acquired a substantially higher status. In finance theory, market value is not considered as one value among others, but as the "best estimation" of the "true" worth of goods. This approach relies on the efficient market hypothesis. Financial theory postulates that at any point in time, if the market is operating properly (i.e. is liquid and well-informed), the market price is equal to the "fundamental value" (Walter 1996). Market value goes further than other conventions concerning liquidity, since it is the immediately liquid value of the item. Saying that market value is the "best" possible estimate of the "true" worth gives both a moral and an epistemological foundation to the investors' demand for liquidity, hiding the fact that liquidity reduces their risks and allows them to break their connection with the targets of their investment at any time by demanding to recover their input.

The instrument-based approach to financialization means paying attention to the practices and tools that support and facilitate financial actors' involvement in a range of different situations, and their capture of resources. These practices and tools enact financialized valuation and materialize the investor's concern for return, risk and liquidity. The process of financialization should therefore be considered as "work", involving actors' deliberate efforts to distort practices by importing new thought frameworks backed up with financialized devices and re-organizing financial circuits in such a way that financialized rules can be applied. This financialization approach, methodologically, leads to the aim of describing and understanding this "work."

84

Methodological Consequences: Studying the Work of Financialization

Studying financialization from a socio-technical angle means looking into the actual operations performed by the "workers" of financialization. This is all the more important since they are constructing a highly opaque world made up of a network of complicated, non-standardized contracts involving a huge number of participants, and this network hides economic distributions and reinforces the power of the financial sphere (Epstein, in this volume).

A number of operations are required to financialize. I propose to classify them in three groups that can also be seen as logically ordered stages:

- *Problematization*: operations through which things and activities are redefined as questions of investment, which requires categorizing and interpreting the world using the words and perspectives of an investor;
- *Tangibilization*: operations through which ideas, expectations or promises take on an existence enabling them to be included in accounts or contracts;
- *Financial structuring*: operations which organize monetary flows, such that the doors are open to money managed by profit-seeking financial investors. Private finance professionals play two roles in theses circuits: either they act as professional service providers who receive fees for managing them (as fund managers) and servicing them (as accountants, lawyers or consultants); or they act as the target financial investors who are to be attracted and convinced to invest.

Problematization and tangibilization are generic operations that can be identified in many social processes, not only financialization. So is financial structuring, as there are many ways to channel money. But when the three types of operations are infused with financialized valuation, they are part of a financialization process. Muniesa et al. (2017) propose the word "capitalization" to designate the process of transforming things into objects of investment. They generally use this concept to address operations of the first two stages identified here, leaving largely unexplored the financial structuring stage, which is the most important to understand how this approach to financialization can connect with others which focus on changes in revenue distribution and the rise of financial actors.

These three categories of operation can also be used to determine the degree of financialization of any question: strong financialization requires financial structuring, whereas the weakest degree of financialization is characterized only by new forms of problematization.

Problematizing: Framing for Investors

Problematizing is an operation that establishes a subject as a problem to be solved. Construction of the problem is inseparable from suggestion of the appropriate type of solution. As research on social movements has shown, constructing a problem means framing it. This includes "diagnostic framing" (problem identification and attributions), "prognostic framing" (articulation of a proposed solution to the problem), and "motivational framing" (rationale for engaging in ameliorative collective action) (Snow and Benford 1988).

For financialization to develop, elements of the situations concerned must be presented as an investment problem, for example under-investment[2] requiring support from financial investors. Problematization is also the first step in the translation process according to actor-network theory (Callon 1986), i.e. the point at which certain actors establish themselves discursively an as obligatory passage point (OPP) in the network of relationships they were building. Similarly, financialized problematization constitutes financial actors as OPPs.

Problematization notably relies on discursive and ideological work, consisting of relabeling questions in terms of investment, capital, returns and risks, disseminating the new conceptualizations, enrolling actors in order to make them endorse the related analysis or proposals, etc. Financialization of social or environmental questions, for example, starts by calling the thing to be protected or encouraged "capital" (i.e. something valuable because it should generate returns in the future), and thus worthy of care and expenditure. For example, "human capital" is used to designate the stock of people's skills and knowledge, "natural capital" to designate the environment (see Bracking, in this volume). Social questions then become questions of investment in "human capital". Another way is to redefine things that are to be avoided and problems encountered as "risks," which thus affect future returns. This is observed in references to "environmental risks" and "climate risks." This language indicates probable losses, suggesting that it is necessary to both reduce and cover the risks – potentially using financial techniques.

Tangibilizing: Towards the Making of Assets and Liabilities

The second activity in the work of financialization is giving embodiment to these visions. This involves production of knowledge and expertise aiming to describe the new potential objects of investment, their qualities and the associated risks. The move to quantification can turn a general idea of "capital" into an identification of specific "assets" with the potential for risks and returns. The vocabulary of risk can also lead to the creation of new "liabilities." An asset, in the financial sense, is an entity that generates returns in the future. Creating one therefore means clarifying, and quantifying, the type of returns.

Tangibilization requires *explicitation* work (Linhardt and Muniesa 2011), setting the boundaries of the risk and capital, the types of returns, the expected services and benefits, and the associated risks. *Quantification* usually follows. Figures and models and monetary valuations of these new objects can be produced. This makes them visible, lending credibility to the theory that they are worthy of investment. This also means they can be included in reports, calculation of optimizations and investment decisions.

The explicitation work is based on input from the specialists in the issue being addressed. For example, the concept of "ecosystem services" initially based on descriptions by natural science specialists (ecologists and naturalists) has been a milestone along the path to valuation of something like "natural capital" and more detailed financial assessments seeking to assign monetary value to each service, involving different actors and forms of expertise.

Thanks to problematization, special narratives using the language of investment and its returns, of capital and its risks, make thinkable the possibility of attracting financial actors and persuading them to finance what is under-invested. Thanks to the tangibilization work, it is then possible to identify what is worth investment, assign values, and incorporate them into calculations. However, tangibilizing a potential return is not enough to ensure that private investors will actually come on board. To appeal to profit-seeking investors and move towards a stronger financialization stage, a third type of activities is required.

Structuring Monetary Flows: Financial Circuit Building Operations

This stage requires mobilization of specific competences, principally legal and financial, to bring about change in the regulatory frameworks and elaborate cleverly structured financial operations. Creating a financial circuit largely proceeds from the work of law-writing, defining entities which receive funds that are managed under certain criteria by certain people, signing contracts with other entities that organize monetary exchanges and lay down the terms for such transactions. The construction of a financialized circuit must be able to meet investors' demands for returns, lower risks, and liquidity. Another way of involving financial actors is to involve them in the management of these new circuits. Not only will they be paid for that, but they will instill their reasoning methods and their practices, and this will enhance their ability to convince fellow members of their world. The first thing needed to attract investors is to offer investment vehicles.

Creating Investment Vehicles: Securities, Contracts and Funds

A first possibility is to create securities, which are readily tradeable commodities. This means following the pattern of company shares that are "rights to future profits" sold to finance the company. For the newly identified types of social or environmental assets (such as human or health capital), it also means selling rights to future cash flows. Straightforward work on contract drafting may be enough to organize returns, as in the case of debt contracts that set out the rules for repayment and the applicable interest rate.

A second option is a more exotic type of contracting found in the social sector: the pay-for-success contracts called Social Impact Bonds (SIB) in the UK. These contracts encourage financial investors to put money into social projects which are, by definition, non-profitable – such as support programs to prevent prisoners re-offending. The trick is considering that if the social activity is well-managed, then the induced costs for the community will be lower (fewer re-offenders means less public expenditure in the future). It may thus be in the community's interest to promise the investor a return if the entity financed achieves its social objectives.

A third technique consists of creating funds, "pockets" of money managed by appointed fund managers and specifically dedicated to issues that are becoming financialized. These funds have the dual advantage of being both an investment vehicle for investors and a source of remuneration for professional financers. It is often difficult when examining financialized circuits to separate what is designed to attract investors by addressing their concerns about risk, returns and liquidity from what organizes remuneration for finance intermediaries.

Channeling and Creating Returns

An investment vehicle is founded on the promise of a financial return, but that promise is not always easy to keep. The financialization of new matters such as social and environmental issues therefore often requires work on economic models to orient them towards income generation. Financialization has notably given rise to the markets for impact-commodities (Barman 2015; Chiapello and Godefroy 2017; Bracking, in this volume). For example, negative effects are transformed into "pollution rights," while positive effects can become "carbon credits." Associations that support the unemployed could also consider selling "social impact certificates" to fund their activities. Note that government action is vital if these new impact-commodities are to be purchased and thus provide new resources. Their purchase can be declared compulsory (e.g. obligations to buy "pollution rights"), or governments may intervene on the market to influence their price.

Although these impact-commodities are not themselves financial securities, they are increasing with financialization. First, they are used to derive profit from unprofitable economic models in order to attract investors, who could also be remunerated in impacts, for example in the form of "certificates" they need to obtain to meet regulatory requirements, or to support claims of social responsibility. Second, they are based on financialized forms of valuation which claim that the value of a thing is measured by the services (impacts) it provides.

Another way to create returns involving governmental action is to offer tax incentives, for example to investors in ventures that are considered low-profit or too risky but nonetheless important for the common good, such as social enterprises, small innovative firms or social housing. Immediate tax-deductibility of a percentage of the amount invested offers an instant return that may compensate for poor returns in the longer term. Tax breaks are also an important way to persuade individuals and companies to give more to foundations (Lai and Stolz, this volume), or to put money into pension funds (Van der Zwan 2017; Fichtner, this volume). Foundations and pension funds are financialized forms of charities and pension schemes respectively, as they both rely on building up funds that seek investment on the markets and are professionally managed by asset managers. This type of policy "kills two birds with one stone": it attracts private funding into general public missions and develops professional fund management.

Reducing Risks

Returns and risks are in fact two sides of the same coin, since they are both indicators describing the same cash flows expected of an investment. So whenever products are structured in a way that generates returns, there are invariably conditions, and therefore risks, attached. A commitment by a state with a good credit rating to lease a building constructed via a Public–Private Partnership for 40 years is a relatively sure return, as is an immediate tax break or a waiver of income in a concession, while the signature of a Social Impact Bond in which payouts are conditional on achievement of social objectives suggests slightly greater risks. Portfolio theory has rationalized this investment choice, considering that for a high risk a high expected return is required, and conversely a low expected return should be associated with more certainty. The engineering work consists of creating acceptable risk-return balances that will appeal to investors.

Certain actions and measures exist solely to manage the question of risk, for example guarantee systems, credit insurance, or some uses of derivatives. Here again, the public authorities can play a role in production of the guarantee system. For example, they may themselves make contributions to guarantee funds securing loans to ventures considered too risky by private financers, as in the Juncker plan in Europe (Mertens and Thiemann 2019). This seems a good strategy for government in times of austerity: one euro spent on providing a guarantee is said to facilitate private money lending, and can also be re-used after reimbursement to guarantee another loan. This is a clear example of financialized public policy oriented towards investors' need for security, where the state spends money for them in the hope of orienting some of their funds into projects they would have ignored otherwise. It also creates another fund (a guarantee fund) that requires professional investment services.

Creating Liquidity

The ultimate demand from investors is for liquidity: even long-term-oriented investors pay a great deal of attention to the possibility of reselling their investment. Offering potential investors liquidity can thus be part of the work that must be done to make the new financing circuits operational, and this requires a specific sort of engineering. Organizing marketplaces or exchanges is one possible solution, but the products traded there must be known, regularly valued, and comparable so that participants can invest and divest, and manage their portfolios. This work has traditionally been done by specialized professionals (e.g. auditors, ratings agencies, data brokers, financial analysts) and usually requires government regulation. Building up investment funds should also be seen as a means of creating liquidity, by grouping several investments of a non-liquid nature, for example investments in small and medium enterprises, into a single investment vehicle. This vehicle purchases shares, makes loans, and signs contracts which cannot be simply sold on. However, shares in the vehicle are sold to investors, giving them rights to future profits. And these shares may be easier to sell.

Conclusion: Putting the Analytical Framework to Work

The three sets of operations making up the work of financialization (problematization, tangibiliza-tion, financial structuring) are relevant to describe the development of any new financialized circuit: not only concerning social or environmental questions, but also in more traditional situations, such as when a small family business is floated on the stock market or bought up by a Private Equity fund. Unpacking the process makes it easier to identify who is involved. It brings out the active involvement of professional groups who specialize in the techniques applied – and are also the people who have found support and prosperity in financialization (financiers, lawyers, auditors, consultants, assessors). These activities also enable them to move into new situations where they can establish a stronghold, advancing the associated process of colonization and value capture.

In the case of a firm's IPO, the operation is made possible because the enterprise concerned is considered as an object of investment whose purpose is to produce returns for the shareholders (instead of being considered as activities that supply jobs, or places where products or services are made, for example) (problematization). The development of financial valuation techniques and a world of professional experts in such valuation offers the required expertise for estimating the value of this investment, while consultants and analysts identify untapped reserves of value and growth potential, and stage "corporate products." They paint a glowing picture of the gains to be derived from such an acquisition project, backed up by their calculations and simulations (tangibilization). Finally, other actors create the connection with the world of finance (financial structuring). Various bankers set share issue prices, organize sales, etc. Investment funds become purchasers and the stock markets organize the liquidity of shares. The credit circuit, meanwhile, rather than directly funding the firm as is the case in traditional financial circuits, funds the financial holding companies that make acquisitions, enabling new shareholders to use the leverage effect to increase returns further.

Identification of these different operations means that, for a given case of local organizations or issues currently in the process of financialization, the level of financialization can be assessed regardless of whether only problematization has taken place, advanced tangibilization has taken place with quantifications and offers of expertise, or new financing circuits have been con-structed. On social questions, for example, the existence of a few Social Impact Bonds that have managed to attract a few investors is an indication of strong financialization at local level. At worldwide level, however, greater nuance is needed: a few successful experiments will not necessarily become generalized.

At systemic level, the financialization of an issue must be considered in the early or "weak" phases when it is essentially discursive. In such situations, a large body of grey literature may exist, metrics be proposed, standards developed, consultants be proposing their services, but in practice, apart from a few much-hyped experiments, the financial volumes involved are low. This is currently the case for Social Impact Bonds: much has been written about them, but they are still few in number, and are failing to attract many financial investors. They are widely dis-cussed but are making very little difference to the problems they are intended to solve. In many respects their role appears essentially ideological and the experiments that have succeeded, whatever the involvement and authenticity of the actors implementing them, can be accused of being no more than "proofs of concept" whose job is to support the ideological work and general legitimacy of financial activities. However, a low level of financialization can also be considered as the first step towards much greater financialization, as the innovations being tried out grow more common and the new financial circuits become better-established.

The progress of financialization depends on the issues concerned, the national spaces, the channels used and the resistance triggered by these projects. In social questions, strong financialization would mean a significant rearrangement of the welfare state – for example, a substantial shift towards a funded pension system (Van der Zwan 2017). Even supported by dominant groups of actors who have an interest in its development, either to gain legitimacy or profit, financialization is not inevitable (see the final Part of this Handbook). One advantage of the research approach proposed here is that it pays attention to the very large number of actors, expert assessments, technical and legal inventions, and public intervention needed to twist existing financing circuits and make more room for financial actors and their demands for returns. Extraction of value to the benefit of finance is only possible because these new assemblies hold and are cemented by laws, information systems, and networks of contracts. Close monitoring of these socio-technical processes enables us to follow the money, and also to better describe how, and how far, these arrangements are reshaping a whole range of activities, and the consequences that is having.

Notes

1 Michel Foucault uses the word *dispositif* that is often translated as "apparatus". "Device" or "arrangement" may also be used.
2 Golka (2019) gives a detailed description of the action frame that legitimized the rise of Social Impact Investing in the UK. One of narratives is chronic under-investment in social services, leading to a need that cannot be met solely by the state or charities.

Bibliography

Barman, E., 2015. Of principle and principal: Value plurality in the market of impact investing. *Valuation Studies*, 3(1), pp. 9–44.
Baud, C. and Durand, C., 2012. Financialization, globalization and the making of profits by leading retailers. *Socio-Economic Review*, 10(2), pp. 241–266.
Callon, M., 1986. Some elements of a sociology of translation: Domestication of the scallops and the fishermen of St Brieuc Bay. In: Law, J. (ed.). *Power, Action and Belief: A New Sociology of Knowledge*. London: Routledge and Kegan Paul, pp. 196–233.
Callon, M., Millo, Y. and Muniesa, F., 2007. *Market Devices*. London: Blackwell.
Chiapello, E., 2015. Financialisation of valuation. *Human Studies*, 38(1), pp. 13–35.
Chiapello, E., 2017. La financiarisation des politiques publiques. *Mondes en développement*, 45(2), pp. 23–40.
Chiapello, E. and Gilbert, P., 2019. *Management Tools: A Social Science Perspective*. Cambridge: Cambridge University Press.
Chiapello, E. and Godefroy, G., 2017. Judgment devices and market fragmentation: Why does the plurality of market classifications matter? *Historical Social Research*, 42(1), pp. 152–188.
Chiapello, E. and Walter, C., 2016. The three ages of financial quantification: A conventionalist approach to the financiers' metrology. *Historical Social Research*, 41(2), pp. 155–177.
Doganova, L., 2017. How to think about discounted value. In: Muniesa, F. et al. (eds.). *Capitalization. A cultural guide*. Paris: Presses de l'Ecole des Mines, pp. 37–46.
Epstein, G.A. (ed.), 2005. *Financialization and the World Economy*. Cheltenham: Edward Elgar Publishing.
Erturk, I., Froud, J., Johal, S., Leaver, A. and Williams, K. (eds.), 2008. *Financialization at Work. Key Texts and Commentary*. New York: Routledge.
Golka, P., 2019. *Financialization as Welfare. Social Impact Investing and British Social Policy, 1997–2016*. Springer International Publishing.
Hood, C., 1993. *The Tools of Government*. London: MacMillan.
Krippner G., 2005. The financialization of the American economy. *Socio-Economic Review*, 3(2), pp. 173–208.
Lascoumes, P. and Le Gales, P. (eds), 2004. *Gouverner par les instruments*. Paris: Presses de Science Po.

Lemoine, B., 2017. The politics of public debt financialization: (Re-)inventing the market for French sovereign bonds and shaping the public debt problem (1966–2012). In: Buggeln, M., Daunton, M. and Nützenadel, M. (eds.), *The Political Economy of Public Finance. Taxation, State Spending and Debt since the 1970s*. Cambridge: Cambridge University Press, pp. 240–261.

Linhardt, D. and Muniesa, F., 2011. Trials of explicitness in the implementation of public management reform. *Critical Perspectives on Accounting*, 22(6), pp. 550–566.

Lockwood, E., 2015. Predicting the unpredictable: Value-at-risk, performativity, and the politics of financial uncertainty. *Review of International Political Economy*, 22(4), pp. 719–756.

MacKenzie, D., 2006. *An Engine, Not a Camera: How Financial Models Shape Markets*. Cambridge, MA: MIT Press.

MacKenzie, D. and Millo, Y., 2003. Constructing a market, performing theory: The historical sociology of a financial derivatives exchange. *American Journal of Sociology*, 109(1), pp. 107–145.

Mertens, D. and Thiemann, M., 2019. Building a hidden investment state? The European Investment Bank, national development banks and European economic governance. *Journal of European Public Policy*, 26(1), pp. 23–43.

Meyer, J. W. and Rowan, B., 1977. Institutionalized organizations: Formal structure as myth and ceremony. *American Journal of Sociology*, 83(2), pp. 340–363.

Montagne, S., 2013. Investing prudently: How financialization puts a legal standard to use. *Sociologie du travail*, 55(1), e48–e66.

Muniesa, F., et al., 2017. *Capitalization. A cultural guide*. Paris: Presses de l'Ecole des Mines

Snow, D.A. and Benford, R.D., 1988. Ideology, frame resonance, and participant mobilization. *International Social Movement Research*, 1, pp.197–217.

Thévenot, L., 1984. Rules and implement: Investment in forms. *Social Science Information*, 23(1), pp. 1–45.

Van der Zwan, N., 2017. Financialisation and the pension system: Lessons from the United States and the Netherlands. *Journal of Modern European History*, 15(4), pp. 554–578.

Walter, C., 1996. Une histoire du concept d'efficience sur les marchés financiers. *Annales. Histoire, Sciences Sociales*, 51(4), pp. 873–905.

8

THE ANTHROPOLOGICAL STUDY OF FINANCIALIZATION

Hadas Weiss

Introduction

In one of anthropology's classic studies, Pierre Bourdieu (1979) observed Algeria in the 1960s as the institutions of global capitalism descended upon it. Challenging narratives of linear modernization, he showed Algeria's traditional social orders being reproduced. His ethnography also succeeded in defamiliarizing finance: making its logic overt rather than obscured by a seemingly self-evident reality. It did so particularly with respect to the financial demand that one sacrifice immediate interests for abstract future ones. This demand contradicted, for Algerian farmers, a prior state of being in which their work was organically linked to its returns. Credit, to be repaid with set interest rates, forced upon them an unwelcome sense of time laden with financial value that needs to be identified and calculated, as well as the necessity to organize their lives in relation to future opportunities. Bourdieu's study was an early indication of anthropology's capacity to problematize finance for readers whose lives would soon become intertwined in it.

Anthropologists have followed Bourdieu's lead in studying societies at the margins of the global economy, which contend with the superimposition of finance through institutions like the World Bank, the International Monetary Fund and development agencies. Reasserting the social productivity of non-financial debt in the form of mutual commitments and obligations (Peebles 2010; Graeber 2011), these anthropologists have specified the novelties of finance as intruding upon prior ways in which societies were organized. For example, Parker Shipton (2007, 2009, 2010) explained the failures of the Kenyan Luo to pay back farm-development loans coming from abroad because of their more fundamental debts: fathers-in-law expecting installments on marriage payments, school fee sponsors waiting for return favors, and so forth. Having to pledge ancestral land as collateral likewise contravened the Luo's treatment of land custody as intergenerational entrustment.

Studies of this kind approached finance by looking at the mindsets and relations of non-financialized subjects that come into contact with it. But these days, greater urgency resides in studying populations that can no longer interact with each other and with the institutions that govern their lives, let alone save, consume and insure, without the mediation of finance. According to Karen Ho (2015), an overemphasis on populations that contend with finance coming from the outside often leaves finance itself undertheorized, assumed to be an abstract and corrosive intrusion upon more authentic social relations. The goal should be to trouble such representations, reviving Bourdieu's original impulse of defamiliarizing what finance has normalized. A burgeoning anthropology of finance and financialization is doing just that.

Humans and human societies, anthropology's subject matters, are as variegated as the actual groups, practices and institutions that anthropologists venture out to study. If they are everywhere being reshaped in the mold of financial technologies, which penetrate public and private domains that had previously been closed off to them, it stands to reason that anthropologists would direct their attention to these very dynamics of financialization. Still, anthropologists are accustomed to surprised reactions when they proclaim to be studying finance and its ramifications. The perceived formalism of finance – represented as a technical procedure governed by objective rules and value-free conventions – removes it in popular imagination from the domains of "culture" and "emotion" to which anthropologists are usually confined.

It is precisely this kind of segregation, however, that anthropology contests, considering the economy and its (financial and non-financial) components as embedded in society. While it shares this conviction with other social sciences, anthropology's uniqueness is in the methodology through which it renders the embedded nature of the economy explicit. Namely, it makes use of ethnographic fieldwork, that is, a sustained study of specific societies or social institutions in a way that triangulates interview data with hermeneutic/textual analysis and participant observation of the things that people do in relation to the things they say. Such fieldwork brings the messiness of everyday life to the fore, in contrast to abstract attributions thereof. This messiness is singularly revealing with respect to the tidiness of finance, as represented in models that range from portfolio graphs through interest-rate calculations to actuarial charts. This is so because it subjects the abstractness of financial models to critical examination (see Chiapello, in this volume, on financialization as a socio-technical matter and Langley, in this volume, on the financialization of life).

There are, nevertheless, unique challenges to studying finance ethnographically, starting from the fact that many of its practitioners do not want to be studied. This forces the ethnographer to be creative in seeking out multiple sites to work in, and to painstakingly build informant networks with people from these sites (Souleles 2018). Long-term immersion in a bounded locality, allowing an intimate knowledge of how its residents live their lives, remains the bread and butter of ethnographic fieldwork. The anthropologist interested in finance can take advantage of this familiarity to trace how, and for what purposes, financial technologies are integrated into daily life.

This strategy is less feasible, however, in urban hubs, nor is it sensible when the technologies under consideration scale far beyond the household. Anthropologists are therefore opportunists in seeking out appropriate sites and events. They combine interviews with lay or professional actors, participant observation of financial transactions, seminars, consultancies, finance-related social gatherings or activities, and analysis of public and professional discourse on finance over time. Informed by an understanding of the broader logic of finance, their findings are thereupon made to speak back to, enrich or complicate this logic.

In conducting ethnographic fieldwork, anthropologists routinely observe the complexity, flux and plasticity of everyday life being manifested in people not taking recourse to financial intuitions or using financial services as prescribed. In itself, there is nothing surprising about this. The finance sector is quite vocal about over-indebtedness and inadequate or insufficient financial planning. Indeed, it is actively engaged in addressing such misuses of finance through lobbying for legislation and promoting financial literacy. But the finance sector also holds its own logic as the benchmark for a rationality that should apply to everyone. It therefore considers people's alternative uses or rejection of financial instruments and services as evidence of their faulty understanding, foresight or self-control. It further seeks ways of aligning people's attitudes and practices with those that finance prefigures. Ethnographic research, in contrast, unearths and elucidates the social logic encapsulated therein.

Far from amassing empirical evidence for how people appropriate financial technologies whose rules are pregiven, anthropologists approach finance itself as social, emerging out of the powers and dynamics of society and, in turn, reconfiguring these powers and dynamics. What is more, anthropologists do not set out to test financial hypotheses empirically, as this would leave the terms of inquiry to be set by the very powers that frame the dominant discourse on finance. Rather, they carefully observe what people care about, say and do with and through the financial instruments and services they use, as well as the financial or financialized institutions that influence their lives and relationships.

This allows anthropologists to challenge the formalism of finance by humanizing its procedures, by questioning its neutral-technocratic placement in the service of individual goals, by challenging its association with rationality, and by unearthing the social logic of people's apparent misuse of finance. I want to spend the rest of this chapter fleshing out these accomplishments with some examples. Illuminating thereby how anthropology accentuates aspects of finance that might otherwise go unnoticed, I will conclude by discussing the critical stakes in an anthropology of financialization.

Anthropological Approaches

Pushing the frontiers of ethnographic fieldwork to trading floors and central banks, anthropologists have studied finance managers in Paris, finance professionals in Shanghai, traders and brokers in Chicago and London, investment bankers on Wall Street, derivatives traders in Tokyo and central bankers in Germany, Malaysia and New Zealand, among others (Zaloom 2006; Ho 2009; Holmes 2013; Miyazaki 2013; Ortiz 2013; Rudnyckyj 2019). Their impulse has not been to give a human-interest backstory to what professionals do beyond their financial dealings, but rather to humanize these very dealings. This, against the backdrop of ideas about market efficiency, whereby prices are assumed to reflect all available information and signal to investors where they should allocate their money (Ortiz 2012). So, for example, Horatio Ortiz (2013, 2014) finds in his ethnographic study of finance professionals in Paris that their estimates of the value of shares and their convictions about these estimates are central to trades and investments, even as they stand in productive tension with their beliefs about how prices ultimately move.

Rather than venturing into the commanding heights of finance, however, most anthropologists draw on their experience studying local societies and the mundane habits and practices of non-professionals. They trace the changes brought about by financial technologies, infrastructures and institutions introduced into settings and interactions from which they were previously absent. Their studies challenge the formalism of finance, or the assumption that finance is devoid of independent objectives, a set of products and procedures through which individuals and institutions could pursue whatever objectives they happen to have (Shiller 2012). Permeating public discourse, this assumption turns finance into a shorthand for the ways in which states and firms, households and publics harness capital for the accomplishment of their respective goals. Consumer credit is paradigmatic of this discourse. It is commonly represented as being agnostic about the identity of its users and the purposes for which they use it, and by extension blameless for its repercussions, a mere instrument that allows one to purchase now things that one will pay for later (see Gonzalez, in this volume). Anthropologists demonstrate, in contrast, that like other instruments of finance, it targets and excludes certain populations in predictable ways. Most profoundly, the agents and agencies of finance shape the goals for which people use its instruments, while undermining others.

One example is the infrastructure projects undertaken through partnerships between governments and private (often transnational) corporations. Silent about the ways in which they would grease the wheels of accumulation, their orchestrators propagate the values of development, nationalism and growth to which their financing would contribute. Following such initiatives in the transportation infrastructure of India's Hooghley River, Laura Bear (2015, 2017) reveals them to be part of a transfer of fiscal control from the state to global commercial banks and international financial markets. Among members of the Indian public sector in the 1990s, debt relations had not been treated as monetary debts expected to be paid back. When the government abruptly demanded repayment with interest, it created a permanent state of crisis. Public sector jobs were hollowed out and development was pursued through precarious contract work. Once powerful waterfront unions turned into brokers of labor for private sector industries, and port bureaucrats conducted business through secretive personal friendships. State employees were pitted against informal workers in ways that prevented them from prioritizing their common grievances. These new divisions exacerbated the volatility of the market and the relationships it reconfigured; a crisis managed through additional austerity measures, and justified by dependence on global markets and credit-rating agencies.

Another example of finance shaping and undermining objectives is micro-financing initiatives, which are promoted as empowering and advancing women by giving them access to financial instruments, and instructing them on how to use finance to achieve their entrepreneurial goals. In her ethnography of microfinance in Paraguay, Caroline Schuster (2015) portrays these initiatives as driving women into a spiral of debt, repaying one loan with another. Financing schemes are deliberately steered toward groups of women who are rendered collectively responsible for their repayment. Loans are collateralized, in other words, with the creditworthiness of these women, which turns on peer pressure, shame, mutual support and reciprocity. Such financing presupposes that women, more than men, possess those qualities. But as Schuster shows, it goes a step further in forcing flexibility and a sense of obligation upon women: driving them into multiple business ventures and to recruiting family resources in order to repay the debt. Lending policies create and fix ideologies regarding women's domesticity and economic flexibility. As women use their debt relationships to buoy their businesses, many of these relationships are strained and broken by investments that fail.

Financial instruments are commonly advocated as contributing toward family care. This appears intuitive to the people who take out loans, save, insure and invest in order to give their children the chance of a better life or protect their loved ones from calamity. But far from finance consisting of neutral instruments for people pursuing such goals, financialization magnifies the family in people's minds as the institution through which these goals are to be accomplished (as opposed to, say, public risk-pooling). Financial markets grow through the circulation of capital, and have everything to gain by tapping into the capital nested in the family and its household assets. Anthropologists describe how the family is mobilized for financial gain rather than the other way around. Examples range from the commodification of family dependencies among the poor in India (Kar 2018) and Spain (Palomera 2014), through the pitting of families against each another as some take control of the over-indebted farms of others in rural America (Dudley 2000), to the selective supply of credit to vulnerable populations in Chile, obliging recipients to care privately for their vulnerable relatives (Han 2012).

Among the most poignant case studies are Deborah James's (2014, 2015) on post-Apartheid South Africa. She challenges the empowerment rhetoric of finance, as if by being placed in the hands of deprived black populations, it would help them consume previously inaccessible things and foster their upward mobility. But the credit that fuels the aspirations of black Africans, also amplifies the pressures under which they operate. The influx of transnational credit contributes to jobless growth and raises the costs of housing, education, medical aid and transport. The rising cost of marriage, in particular, intensifies the claims that extended-family members make on the resources of those who have any. Financial advice books and lectures induce them to withstand these pressures, warning people against their dependents and instructing them to partner up in stable nuclear families that encourage the achievements of their children. Far from being a means for the accomplishment of people's own aims, the aspirations promoted are those that would fortify the dominance of finance and accelerate financial market growth (see Lazarus, in this volume, on financial literacy). Meanwhile, people's ability to achieve the most far-reaching of these aspirations is curtailed.

If finance is draped in a veil of neutrality regarding the uses to which it is put, there are nevertheless values about which it is anything but agnostic. These are the values of independence, initiative and satisfaction maximizing along the lines of *homo economicus*, or economic man, with which it is commonly associated. The incentives, penalties and tailored products of financial engineering, policies and marketing campaigns are represented as nudging individuals to assume these traits, placing finance on the side of an enterprising and calculating rationality. Social scientists often take these representations at face value and seek, as counterpart to financial instruments, a calculating and entrepreneurial subjectivity among the people who use them. Ethnographic fieldwork, in contrast, begins with grounded research on what is actually expected of finance's subjects. I can attest from my observations of finance seminars and consultancies in Germany to how far these expectations sometimes stray from the encouragement of calculation and enterprise.

What I discovered (Weiss 2018a) was that even though financial literacy campaigns make a big show of empowerment, rehearsing the goals of skill building and enlightenment through knowledge, the messages they deliver are quite different. Advisers regale audiences and clients with evidence of their inadequacy to the task of managing finance as enterprising and calculating agents – attitudes that are best left to professionals. They portray the market as an unfriendly reality consisting of inflation and attendant dangers: an abstraction one can neither understand nor control. They harp on about how reckless it would be to give into personal impulse and risk-taking, which would lead one to spend money frivolously or invest it recklessly. Instead, they advise thrift and responsibility in committing one's resources toward the long term through diversified assets and in never biting off more debt than one can chew over time. Indeed, the finance sector can hardly allow savers to be as strategic and risk-taking as firms or professionals. It is far more desirable, from the standpoint of having to ensure the sustainable circulation of household capital, that individuals be diffident in insuring themselves and their families, reliable in taking on prudent real-estate debt that they will service at whatever cost, and steadfast in making regular payments into pensions and long-term savings products. Far from empowering individuals by stimulating their calculating rationality and entrepreneurial self-confidence, finance disempowers them by encouraging their fear of the future and compliant responsibility.

Even as the finance sector is vocal about associating finance with responsibility, it defines the exercise of responsibility according to its needs. If responsibility has a long and positive legacy as identified with work, frugality and risk avoidance, it is now being redefined as risk management in the form of financial planning (Weiss 2018b). Anthropologists relate finance to responsibilization, in the sense of putting citizens in charge of providing for their families and futures instead of relying on public arrangements to do this for them. A common example is the responsibilization that accompanies the liberalization of pension systems. Anthropologists have the methodological advantage of not merely naming it, as do other social scientists, but also tracing its application, reception and possible contestation.

One example is Anette Nyqvist's (2016) research in Sweden. The role of the Swedish state has been reformulated from the management of national finance and the pooling of citizens' risks, to the provision of information and skills to citizens. Drawing on observations and interviews with pension policy-makers and with soon-to-be retirees who fret about their future, Nyqvist shows how Swedes do not respond to this change in the ways that the state has intended.

Tasked with maximizing and supplementing their expected retirement annuities, they neither actively choose funds in the Premium Pension System, nor do they opt to work longer hours and/or longer into old age in order to optimize their financial security in later life. Confusing the government information they receive by mail with commercial advertising, they complain that they are ill equipped to handle their new responsibilities, and they lose trust in the government and its directives.

I found similar sentiments in my study of the financialization of the pension system in Israel (Weiss 2015), where I observed pension negotiations in which insurance agents walked uncomfortable clients through investment strategies. These clients understood very little about finance and wanted nothing to do with risk-management. They were willing to put aside portions of their income for retirement if they could afford it, but all they really wanted to know was that these deductions would provide them with security in old age; the very assurances that the new financial arrangements were designed not to give. Insurance agents would write off as irrationality and shortsightedness all of the responses I had witnessed. They included treating pensions as savings accounts, imagining them to be a state-guaranteed civic right, refusing to place one's money at risk, recoiling from the choice between investment products, blaming the government for the devaluation of savings and expecting retirements to reflect work-life sacrifices. Yet, these expectations were actually aligned with what the agents of capitalism have long promised: that self-reliant investment realized by working, paying taxes and putting money aside for the future would add up to economic wellbeing.

Ethnographic fieldwork provides the anthropologist with such opportunities to anchor the expectations of finance's subjects in the policies and structural conditions that shape them. This can be achieved by studying how financial policies have changed over time – as Caitlin Zaloom (2018) does by comparing mid-twentieth-century policies of financial planning in the USA to contemporary ones. She traces how old policies of near-term prudence have been replaced with long-term forecasts, which parents hoping to fund their children's higher education must now imagine and anticipate. Engaging with populations in distress gives insight into how these imaginations are strained. So, Ainur Begim (2018) shows for Kazakhstan how the selling of German life-insurance policies taps into nostalgia for the security of retirement in the Soviet era, while also seducing potential clients with the idea that they could recuperate it through low-yielding German bonds that they imagine to be safe and stable. Similarly, Mateusz Halawa (2015) shows for Warsaw how a mortgage credit boom fueled the expectations of young Poles for predictable personal progress, linked to their country's growing prosperity and encapsulated in the 30-year mortgage contracts they signed. But as the bubble burst and plunged them into negative equity, the synchronism of the market with their everyday lives came undone. So, too, the imagination of these homeowners transformed from one of being active in and gaining momentum by the market, to one of being vulnerable to its fluctuations and entrapped in its dictates.

By drawing out contesting expectations, anthropology also reveals how the very fact of financialization is problematic insofar as people believe that some things should remain out of bounds for finance. So, for example, with the financialization of water services in Italy, which has emerged as a counterpart to austerity, insofar as the depletion of public funds encouraged private investments in a public good. As soon as this happened, citizens took to the streets, burning their unreasonably high water-bills as a public act of protest. Describing their protests, Andrea Muehlebach (2017) finds points of comparison with the eighteenth-century food riots in England, which E.P. Thomson famously analysed as instances of historical agency in pursuit of a moral economy rather as the simple mob-like responses to economic stimuli that some historians considered them to be. Now as then, Muehlebach argues, anger is fuelled by what people perceive to be an assault on popular notions of justice and a fair price. These notions are grounded on a belief that water, as any other basic resource, is a commons that ought to be shared rather than exploited for profit.

Ethnographic fieldwork among populations using financial instruments in unanticipated ways allows anthropologists to identify cases in which finance is mobilized for goals to which it cannot contribute. Such are the socially productive goals set forth by development agencies that draw on finance. Tracking microenterprises in Cairo in the mid-1990s, Julia Elyachar (2005) describes how the money channeled from International Finance Institutions (IFIs) was designed to set the poor proletariat free from the shackles of the national economy to become entrepreneurs and launch their own businesses. IFIs preached a gospel of empowerment through debt, harnessing people's already existing informal social networks and real-life practices. They also championed culturally grounded production by lending to local NGOs and civil society organizations. But the only entrepreneurs to succeed were those that came from families of craftsmen who brought their markets with them. Officials, employees, and everyone else took what they could and used it to buy apartments so that they would be able to get married and start a family. They also forged order forms from public sector institutions in order to get their loans released from the bank. And they turned their microenterprises into shells for wealthy businessmen seeking new ways to escape taxes. Empowerment debt unleashed appropriation, then, without productive investment (see Lai and Stoltz, in this volume, on civil society and financialization).

Another example is from the United Kingdom, where the government issued a levy on banks whose irresponsible lending practices gave rise to widespread indebtedness. Presented as a remedy for harm, the levy turned out to operate more like a payment for a cash collection service. Observing debt advice organizations funded by this bank levy, Ryan Davy (2017) shows how it taxes the institutions that issue debt to the poor in order to provide these people with advice that cannot actually solve their problems. Debt advice organizations try to get the poor to accept debt repayment as their moral duty, encouraging them to honor their obligations and guiding them through punitive procedures for insolvency. Customers are made amenable to debt recovery, reducing thereby the costs of debt collection. The finance industry's intentions of remedying the harmful effects of financial instruments extend, in other words, only in so far as they are profitable.

The most dramatic instances of finance undermining its own stated goals are arguably those of the Microfinance Institutions (MFIs) that operate in the global south under the banner of economic empowerment. Anthropology paints a far bleaker picture. So it is with the proliferation of MFIs and financial technologies in the lives of the poor in Kolkata, India. They extract money from the poor by providing them with new financial products like health and life insurance or educational and housing loans to be repaid with interest, in the absence of decent public alternatives. Sohini Kar (2018) shows how inequalities among the borrowers are reproduced as MFI staff, practicing due diligence, bring their preconceptions of race, cast and religion into their assessments. They deem some less creditworthy than others, based on the very social norms that are already discriminating against women, minorities and migrants. What is more, the increasing financialization of these poor populations makes it important for creditors to preserve a punishing status quo in order to avert expensive crisis and social collapse. Because the poor lack material collateral, life insurance is MFIs' last resort for recovering loans from borrowers whose lives are precarious to begin with. While life insurance seems necessary to many in the face of high mortality rates, the pressure that borrowers face to repay their loans is so great that death is often their only means of escaping debt.

This is but a small selection of the growing corpus of anthropological studies that describe populations in different parts of the world that use financial instruments in distinct ways. Beyond the specific arguments they advance, they provide ethnographic accounts of the tensions and contradictions of financial technologies as they touch ground in everyday life, challenging the formalism of finance as represented by the finance sector. Half a century ago, Bourdieu defamiliarized finance by emphasizing the foreignness of its logic to the mindsets of Algerian peasants in the 1960s. Anthropologists today do the same by uncovering its operation among populations worldwide, as deriving from and acting back upon practices, institutions and structures of power.

The Stakes

Proponents of finance deflect attention from debt, volatility and crisis, by shifting the limelight toward the things that finance enables: the higher education that student loans finance, the home bought on mortgage, the car purchased on credit, the pension secured through long-term investment and so forth. The perception of finance as an efficient means of achieving whatever ends people use it for, helps fortify this association. But finance's link with people's aspirations also renders it susceptible to critique when these aspirations are not fulfilled. Finance professionals blame housing bubbles, over-indebtedness and impecunious retirements on people's misuse of financial instruments. Anthropology, in contrast, insists on the implication of finance in the goals it invokes and the practices it encourages, as well as in the institutions that activate it and necessitate its particular uses. Grounding finance in everyday life, ethnography makes explicit the agents and agencies that shape its logic.

This is perhaps easiest to spot in economic systems that hold the financialization of households at bay by pooling and managing risks for their citizens. Gustav Peebles (2011), who studied the financial arrangements in Sweden whose dismantling Nyqvist (2016) traces, found among its population a sense of freedom that comes from being free of personal debt. It encouraged and enabled Swedes not to be financially indebted to one another or even to their families upon reaching adulthood. Freedom was also attributed to their being free of the economic valuation of careers: ideally studying and working in whatever field they liked without financial considerations constraining their choices. Swedes expressed their fidelity to the public institutions that pooled and managed their resources to afford them this freedom, in the rigor with which they kept track of how their market transactions are taxed, debated to whom debt-forgiveness should be applied, and ejected vagrants and freeloaders outside the moral bounds of their community.

Such commitments are ever more conspicuous where private debt and saving strategies are newly introduced. This pushes people to negotiate the boundaries of public and private provisioning, as well as the extent of their own responsibility. My study of financial advice in Germany revealed that, to fulfill their charge of public service, advisors distinguish consumers who can use finance to their advantage from those who cannot and would therefore be better served by public arrangements. Where some people stand to gain by embracing risk, others are simply at-risk and in need of protection. Where some can save better by investing, others have to scale back. And where some can use debt as a wealth-building strategy, others are in danger of becoming over-indebted. But even those privileged enough to be able to buy a home or to lock away some of their savings in long-term investments, are well aware that these strategies carry risks and that there are no guarantees for their choices being the right ones. Financial advisors normalize the new demands of financial planning by couching them in popular rhetoric of personal responsibility. This, as many of Germany's current retirees see themselves as having exercised responsibility through work and thrift without further ado. That responsibility today translates into placing money in time-dated debt and saving instruments, with a range of risk and value prospects from which to choose according to specific lifecycle milestones, shows how far the term "responsibility" has been stretched (Weiss 2018b).

The anthropology of finance exposes, in other words, the seam lines of the capitalist social arrangements of which finance is part and into which it is often introduced as a stopgap, including its exclusions and the inequality and lack of agency it exacerbates.

Such seam lines are harder to pick out in fully financialized economies like the United States and the United Kingdom, where taking on debt and making financial investments are difficult if not impossible to avoid, and therefore more naturalized. There, financial instruments and strategies are popularly perceived as putting the house, the car, the credential or the retirement nest egg within popular reach, encouraging everyone to exert themselves in hunting them down. This motivates people to keep working and digging ever deeper into their pockets, even when the property or assets they procure turn out not to have the value they were counting on.

Financialization thereby brings about a social dynamism, which the finance sector represents as inclusive and enabling. This dynamism encompasses not only the debt-enabled affordability of consumption goods, but also the riskiness of financial strategies, the volatility of asset values and the perennial bubbles, booms and busts. Financialization is welcomed with a rhetoric of investment, as if its services and instruments are there to encourage and validate people's willingness to put money away, lock some of it up, assume long-term commitments, and service loans, for the sake of their aspirations for the future. That many of these investments fail to pan out gives pause to those who would underline finance's capacity to enrich and empower.

The finance sector allays such concerns by deflecting from finance toward its alleged abuses and abusers. Social scientists generally agree that such distinctions are nonsensical, insofar as finance is always already social and cannot be divorced from the ways in which it is deployed. But in order to make this point familiar and convincing, and to avoid ceding to finance its supposed formalism, we need empirical research that shows what finance presupposes, encourages and proscribes in specific settings. The anthropology of finance has already made great strides in this direction, and it is well poised to make many more.

Bibliography

Bear, L., 2015. *Navigating Austerity: Currents of Debt along a South Asian River*. Stanford, CA: Stanford University Press.

Bear, L., 2017. Alternatives to austerity: A critique of financialized infrastructure in India and beyond. *Anthropology Today*, 33(5), pp. 3–7.

Begim, A., 2018. How to retire like a Soviet person: Informality, household finances, and kinship in financialized Kazakhstan. *Journal of the Royal Anthropological Institute*, 24(4), pp. 767–785.

Bourdieu, P., 1979. *Studies in Modern Capitalism: Algeria 1960*. Trans. R. Nice. Cambridge: Cambridge University Press.

Davy, R., 2017. Polluter pays? Understanding austerity through debt advice in the UK. *Anthropology Today*, 33(5), pp. 8–11.

Dudley, K., 2000. *Debt and Dispossession: Farm Loss in America's Heartland*. Chicago, IL: The University of Chicago Press.

Elyachar, J., 2005. *Markets of Dispossession: NGO's, Economic Development, and the State in Cairo*. Durham: Duke University Press.

Graeber, D., 2011. *Debt: The First 5,000 years*. New York: Melville House.

Halawa, M., 2015. In New Warsaw: Mortgage credit and the unfolding of space and time. *Cultural Studies*, 29(5–6), pp.707–732.

Han, C., 2012. *Life in Debt: Times of Care and Violence in Neoliberal Chile*. Berkeley: University of California Press.

Ho, K., 2009. *Liquidated: An Ethnography of Wall Street*. Durham: Duke University Press.

Ho, K., 2015. Finance, anthropology of. In: Wright, J.D. (ed.). *International Encyclopedia of the Social and Behavioral Sciences*, 2nd edition, volume 9. New York: Elsevier, pp. 171–176.

Holmes, D., 2013. *Economy of Words: Communicative Imperatives in Central Banks*. Chicago, IL: Chicago University Press.

James, D., 2014. "Deeper into a hole?" Borrowing and lending in South Africa. *Current Anthropology*, 55 (S9), pp.17–29.

James, D., 2015. *Money from Nothing: Indebtedness and Aspiration in South Africa.* Stanford, CA: Stanford University Press.

Kar, S., 2018. *Financializing Poverty: Labor and Risk in Indian Microfinance.* Stanford, CA: Stanford University Press.

Miyazaki, H., 2013. *Arbitraging Japan: Dreams of Capitalism at the End of Finance.* Berkeley: University of California Press.

Muehlebach, A., 2017. The price of austerity: Vital politics and the struggle for public water in Southern Italy. *Anthropology Today*, 33(5), pp. 20–23.

Nyqvist, A., 2016. *Reform and Responsibility in the Remaking of the Swedish National Pension System: Opening the Orange Envelope.* New York: Palgrave Macmillan.

Ortiz, H., 2012. Anthropology of the financial crisis. In: Carrier, J. (ed.). *Handbook of Economic Anthropology*, 2nd edition. Northampton, MA: Edward Elgar, pp. 585–595.

Ortiz, H., 2013. Economic value: Economic, moral, political, global. *HAU: Journal of Ethnographic Theory*, 3(1), pp. 64–79.

Ortiz, H., 2014. The limits of financial imagination: Free investors, efficient markets, and crisis. *American Anthropologist*, 116(1), pp. 38–50.

Palomera, J., 2014. How did finance capital infiltrate the world of the urban poor? Homeownership and social fragmentation in a Spanish neighborhood. *International Journal of Urban and Regional Research*, 38 (1), pp. 218–235.

Peebles, G., 2010. The anthropology of credit and debt. *Annual Review of Anthropology*, 39, pp. 225–240.

Peebles, G., 2011. *The Euro and its Rivals: Currency and the Construction of a Transnational City.* Bloomington: Indiana University Press.

Rudnyckyj, D. 2019. *Beyond Debt: Islamic Experiments in Global Finance.* Chicago, IL: The University of Chicago Press.

Schuster, C.E., 2015. *Social Collateral: Women and Microfinance in Paraguay's Smuggling Economy.* Oakland: University of California Press.

Shiller, R.J., 2012. *Finance and the Good Society.* Princeton, NJ: Princeton University Press.

Shipton, P., 2007. *The Nature of Entrustment: Intimacy, Exchange, and the Nature of the Sacred in Africa.* New Haven, CT: Yale University Press.

Shipton, P., 2009. *Mortgaging the Ancestors: Ideologies of Attachment in Africa.* New Haven, CT: Yale University Press.

Shipton, P., 2010. *Credit between Cultures: Farmers, Financiers, and Misunderstanding in Africa.* New Haven, CT: Yale University Press.

Souleles, D., 2018. How to study people who do not want to be studied: Practical reflections on studying up. *Political and Legal Anthropology Review*, 41(S1), pp. 51–68.

Weiss, H., 2015. Financialization and its discontents: Israelis negotiating pensions. *American Anthropologist*, 117(3), pp. 506–518.

Weiss, H., 2018a. Popfinance: From the economic man to the Swabian housewife. *Hau: Journal of Ethnographic Theory*, 8(3), pp. 455–466.

Weiss, H., 2018b. Lifecycle planning and responsibility: Prospection and retrospection in Germany. *Ethnos*, 84(5), pp. 789–805.

Zaloom, C., 2006. *Out of the Pits: Traders and Technology from Chicago to London.* Chicago, IL: University of Chicago Press.

Zaloom, C., 2018. How will we pay? Projective fictions and regimes of foresight in US college finance. *Hau: Journal of Ethnographic Theory*, 8(1–2), pp. 239–251.

9

FEMINIST AND GENDER STUDIES APPROACHES TO FINANCIALIZATION

Signe Predmore

Introduction

This chapter provides an overview of feminist and gender studies approaches to financialization. These approaches allow us to consider not only the different effects of financial practices on women, but also the ways in which finance is intertwined with the development of gendered subjectivities. Feminist scholars encounter the privileging of masculinities in finance as not external or spurious, but integral to its practices. Furthermore, looking at gender enables analysts to draw connections between the macro-structural level of global finance and the micro-level of everyday life.

What does it mean to take a feminist approach to financialization? Feminist scholars often draw our attention to the ways that gender and race operate at all levels of analysis of political power, including the global. However, feminisms are diverse. Even the shallowest investigations of the literature will reveal deep contention around the label "feminist." Additionally, feminist work does not cover all research that adopts gender as a frame of analysis (Carpenter 2003), which is why I include both feminist and gender studies scholarship here (though I will not distinguish between them throughout). Yet the concept of gender emerged from feminist scholarship that used it to point out the social construction of women's marginalization, to problematize the idea of "women" as a singular and coherent population, and to illuminate the social processes of women's oppression (Butler 1990; Carver 2003). Feminist frameworks thus have the advantage of maintaining links between critical analysis and emancipatory politics. Also, as Ackerly and True (2018) have recently reasserted, much feminist inquiry is marked by a reflexivity that helps to reveal gendered power relations as they constitute politics as an object of study, but equally as important, as they constitute the formation of disciplinary academic knowledge. Finally, feminist analyses need not necessarily fix on gender as the most important analytic (Peterson 2003: 15) but also look to race, sexuality, class, and ability as aspects that define intersectional subjectivities as well as political and social dynamics.

I organize my review around three prominent themes in this scholarship: 1) the distributional effects of crises and austerity policies, which are generally more severe for women and people of color; 2) the hegemonic masculine norms pervasive throughout both "high" and "everyday" finance, along with the women's inclusion initiatives that have emerged in response to criticism of these norms; and 3) the financialization of social reproduction and "everyday life," two distinct but related concepts. The three areas I highlight are by no means separable; I draw them out singularly here in order to emphasize their value as contributions to the collective knowledge about financialization. Indeed, they overlap and inform one another to a great extent, and some authors incorporate them all. The latter part of the chapter suggests important considerations for future feminist studies of financialization.

Financial Crisis, Austerity, and Resistance

Given the salience of crises and austerity policies as consequences of financialization, much feminist work concerns their distributional effects, which generally disadvantage women and people of color. This is an extensive literature that I can only briefly allude to here. Van Staveren (2002), Young (2003), and Elson (2014) exemplify some of the work on the disproportionate gender effects of the Latin American debt crisis of the 1980s and the Asian financial crisis of the late 1990s. Elson (2014: 191–192) describes how in Mexico and other Latin American countries, structural adjustment policies imposed by the IMF contracted the job market. Gendered cultural norms about work led to men's unemployment being compensated by entry of women into employment in different areas of production, particularly the garment and electronics industries, as well as informal spheres. However, in general, women worked at lower pay and in worse conditions. Roberts and Elias (2018: 286) indicate some of the variation in these kinds of distributional impacts, for example, the Philippines followed a trend similar to the Latin American one described above, where men's unemployment increased but "feminized" sectors were more resilient. In South Korea, by contrast, women's unemployment rose dramatically compared to men's after the Asian crisis. These examples demonstrate the importance of both the cultural and material contexts in determining gender-based differentiations in distributional impacts.

With the 2008 global financial crisis, analysts of gendered distributional effects turned to Europe and the US. Feminist scholars describe how macroeconomic policy biases undergird the crisis and disproportionately impact women. Young et al. (2011) identify "risk bias," which encourages the move from collectivization of risk to individualization, for example the depletion of low-income housing funds coupled with policy encouraging high interest rate mortgages. In addition, lending practices themselves are biased, as an extensive literature explores (Hyman 2011; Gill & Roberts 2011; Dymski et al. 2013). In the US case, researchers note that women, especially women of color, made progress to overcome historical barriers to credit access, only to become more likely to be holders of subprime mortgage loans (Dymski et al. 2013). Gill and Roberts (2011: 166) find that women were overrepresented among US subprime borrowers by a rate of 29%. Young et al. (2011) also examine a macroeconomic "creditor bias" that favors bailouts for creditors but offers little assistance for debtors (see Epstein, this volume). It can be supposed that because women have more subprime loans, they have likewise experienced more foreclosure, although this has yet to be empirically demonstrated (Baker 2014). Foreclosure pushes many families into homelessness, compounds an already existent gender wealth gap (where women have limited savings and asset ownership), and eliminates a crucial financial cushion for many households at a time of social safety net erosion (Ibid.). Although US housing debt played a uniquely central role in the crisis, financialization of housing markets exposes women to similar risk elsewhere. In Ireland, for example, female-headed households were 2.6 times more likely to be in mortgage related arrears around the time of crisis (Wöhl 2017: 147).

As far as policy responses to the financial crisis go, feminist scholars have exposed gendered effects of stimulus and recovery efforts. For example in Germany, where post-crisis recovery was comparatively swift, male-dominated sectors (ex. industry) benefitted more from supposedly "gender-neutral" tools like extension of temporary work benefits (Annesley & Scheele 2011: 340). Likewise, in the US, initial drafts of Obama's 2009 stimulus plan, the American Recovery and Reinvestment Act, were centered on infrastructure, which tends to generate jobs in male-dominated sectors like industry and construction. Following critiques of this "gender-blind" oversight, the administration revised the plan to extend to health care and education (Enloe 2013).

However, the main focus of feminist study of post-crisis economic policy has been on the gendered effects of austerity, which are documented at the national level through a plethora of case studies (Karamessini & Rubery 2014; Kantola & Lombardo 2017). As in earlier crises in the developing world, austerity impacts employment rates and conditions for women. For example, the 2012 Spanish labor reforms diminished care-related flexibility and parental leave benefits (Lombardo 2017). In the UK, budget cuts to service the public debt impacted women who are more heavily employed in public sector jobs and therefore experienced more layoffs (Annesley & Scheele 2011; Enloe 2013). Many observers recognize that shrinking public services often add to the social reproductive labor that women disproportionately bear. Enloe (2013: 94) emphasizes that the worst impacts of UK austerity policies were felt by single parents, 92% of which were women in 2011, in part because they could no longer rely on public services such as childcare. As with the financial crisis, post-crisis austerity policies are undergirded by macroeconomic policy bias towards commodification or privatization—the belief that the private sector is better at delivering services and benefits (Elson 2014). Privatization plays into financialization because it encourages those who cannot pay up front for access to services to take on securitized debt (Adkins 2015; Roberts 2016b). Moreover, crisis and austerity reverberate through webs of social relationships in ways that go far beyond the economic concerns of employment and access to resources. True (2018: 549) draws connections between post-crisis recession, austerity, and an uptick in reported domestic violence; she argues that gender-based violence increases when financial crises or economic reforms "disrupt gender roles and expectations linking male social identity and power to their breadwinner, head-of-household status."

Of course, those concerned by the gendered effects noted here have not just passively accepted the outcomes of crises and austerity. Feminists have put forth alternative women-centered policy plans, like Plan F in the UK and the US-based 2011 Women's Scholars Forum proposal (Enloe 2013: 89; Elson 2016). Women in Britain and Ireland have engaged in their own efforts to understand and resist the gendered impacts of austerity through "feminist economic research, feminist budgetary analysis, feminist media analysis, feminist labor activism, feminist public services activism" (Enloe 2013: 98–99; Wohl 2017). In several European countries, grassroots efforts have arisen to bypass slow or unsatisfactory responses to austerity by neoliberalized nonprofit women's organizations (Bassel & Emejulu 2017; Elomäki & Kantola 2017).

Feminist scholars also importantly continue to question what the concepts of "crisis" and "austerity" mask. Bassel and Emejulu (2017) note that framing the events of 2008 and beyond as a "crisis" reveals a divide between the experiences of the economically privileged, and many minority women's ongoing experiences of hardship (though they certainly recognize the disproportionate gender and racialized effects discussed above). Adkins (2015) calls for feminists to press beyond the familiar narratives that austerity exacerbates existing gender and racial inequalities, and that redistributive policies are the answer. She argues that feminists ought to focus less on the issue of income volume, but rather on how the role of wages has changed in the financialized economy. Given that wages are going largely to meet household needs through the purchase of securitized debt, this creates the "financially overexposed female subject who is locked into a whole lifetime of securitised debt repayment, whose household is dependent on securitised debt relations, and whose debts—if indexed against income—can never be repaid" (Adkins 2015: 44). Adkins' point resonates with Fishbein and Woodall's (2006) findings that as women's income increases, so does their likelihood, compared to men, of holding a subprime loan. In other words, increased wealth does not consistently protect women from the risks of financialization (Baker 2014).

Hegemonic Masculine Norms and Women's Inclusion

Another major contribution of feminist research on financialization is analysis of the masculine norms pervasive throughout financial services and practices. Whereas the concept of financialization points to the increasing influence of finance in the economy, the social norms that preside in this sector take on oversized significance. Feminist scholars who study these norms are grappling with the question of how social, organizational, and institutional culture affects macro-structural elements of finance (Le Baron 2010; Enloe 2013). Analysts of gender and financialization pay attention not only to women, but also to masculinities, and the interplay of masculine/feminine. In response to criticisms of the hypermasculinity of finance in the wake of the 2008 crisis, "gender diversity" or women's inclusion initiatives have emerged to address the paucity of women decision-makers in the sector. However, while crises may have the potential to challenge existing norms, they can also serve to reinforce them (Elson 2014: 198). Many feminist scholars look skeptically upon the idea of changing gender norms via inclusion; as Griffin (2013: 14) notes, the symbolic power of masculinity in finance does not necessarily depend on men's demographic overrepresentation. Furthermore, gender norms are critical not only to "high" finance, but also "everyday" financial practices in both the global North and South.

Two touchstones of the financialization scholarship on masculine norms are Marieke de Goede's (2005) work on the *longue durée* of gendered discourses of finance, and Connell's (1995; Connell & Wood 2005) work on hegemonic masculinities. De Goede examines eighteenth-century English political debate surrounding credit, describing how Daniel Defoe and others drew from representations of the goddess Fortuna to portray Lady Credit as seductive and tempting, also "capricious, unpredictable, irrational and inconsistent… in opposition to virtuous, honest, reliable and rational financial man" who must tame credit through techniques of self-regulation such as double entry bookkeeping (2005: 38). De Goede (2005: 39–41) argues that this gendered discourse still frames contemporary understanding of financial crises, evident through concepts like "irrational exuberance," which Alan Greenspan blamed for asset inflation, and which Nobel prize-winning economist Robert Shiller developed as a theme for his book on market dynamics.

Prior to De Goede's work, Connell adapted the Gramscian concept of hegemony to an understanding of gender roles to describe the normative underpinnings of the social practices of patriarchy. Hegemonic masculinity "embodied the currently most honored way of being a man, it required all other men to position themselves in relation to it, and it ideologically legitimated the global subordination of women to men" (Connell & Messerschmidt 2005: 832). Assassi (2009: 26–27) uses Connell's concept of hegemonic masculinity to explain how a naturalized, "common sense" male dominance and female subordination was firmly embedded in the roots of the modern financial system as it emerged in the nineteenth century. Yet there is no single homogenous masculinity that characterizes finance. Enloe (2013) for instance, takes a comparative look at financialized masculinities in the US, UK and Iceland, and finds that cultural connotations differ with national contexts. Nevertheless, there are shared trends among them; she finds "the welding of risk taking and short-term-goal-seeking to the most organizationally prized version of masculinity—especially when it is combined with a misogynist denigration of caution—can so warp any country's financial system that the economic security of an entire society is jeopardized" (Enloe 2013: 79).

Attitudes towards "risk" appear central to financialized gender norms. A simplistic binary notion of women as risk-averse and hypermasculine men as risk-tolerant has yielded various social manifestations, and also complications, within the world of finance. Fisher's (2015) ethnographic research on the first generation of women on Wall Street shows that from the 1970s to the early 2000s, a small group of women played on "natural feminine" attributes, like caring and risk-aversion, to gain opportunities particularly in research and brokerage. These were realms removed from the "masculinized areas of investment banking and trading" (Ibid.: 144). With the 2008 financial crisis, the discourse around women in finance shifted as some saw men's greed and impulsiveness in the market as partially to blame. Though young women paradoxically lost jobs in finance at this time, while young men's employment in the sector grew, the "business case" for gender equality was on the rise. Whereas previously, women had drawn on gender norms for employment in certain sectors of finance, post-crisis women were positioned as saviors of a *global* market, and were leveraging these narratives for leadership and positions in sectors from which they had previously been excluded (Ibid.: 151). Prugl (2016: 32) similarly notes that through the crisis there was a resignification of male risk-taking as a liability and female prudence as necessary. While "seemingly new because of the reversal of values" within the financial realm that previously stigmatized caution, the new "myth" actually draws on traditional gender roles that circumscribed women to a domestic support role for their male husbands, who had license to act in the public sphere. Research that grounds the gendered norms of finance in ethnographic detail is perhaps the most helpful in illustrating their complexity (Roth 2006; Ho 2009; Fisher 2015). Ho (2009: 321–322) presents a picture of Wall Street investors who believed they could "manage" risk through financial instruments like derivatives that would allow them to both reap high yields as well as redistribute the potential losses. Privilege and belief in industry intelligence made predominantly male financial managers unconcerned with potential negative consequences of their financial practices.

It is important to note the distinction between scholars looking at norms as socially constructed and subject to change or evolution, and behavioral economists who essentialize gendered traits like risk-taking as linked to hormones or biological sex (Apicella 2008; Coates & Herbert 2008). Feminists meet behavioral arguments with a range of attitudes. McDowell (2010), after initial skepticism about hormonally induced investment performance, encounters a neuro-economics report on the subject and comes around to a more accepting view of "testosterone capitalism," or the idea that biology plays a part in financial speculation. While granting that behavioral explanations may offer some limited insight into social conditions of the crisis, Griffin (2013: 25) critiques these approaches for failing to properly attend to contextual and historical practices of financial deregulation and the social creation of market incentives. Butler (1990) reveals that gender does not map onto a natural, distinct sexual dimorphism, but that sex as well as gender is a constructed category. Following her insights, we might understand efforts to ground attitudes toward risk in biology as an indication of the depth of cultural associations between risk and gender.

The narrative of women as saviors of financial markets has led to discourse and initiatives promoting women's leadership and inclusion in finance, what Hozic and True (2016: 18) refer to as "the 'spectre of gender' now ever present among transnational businesses, neoliberal governments, and elite women leaders." Some research considers financial oversight via women's leadership in state government. In this regard Iceland has drawn attention as a country that moved more women into leadership after the 2008 crisis, and then charted "a very different course" than many other European governments (Elson 2014: 203–204). But as Enloe (2013) points out, Iceland already had a comparatively narrow gender leadership gap (ranked fourth internationally) in the decades preceding the crisis, and this wasn't enough to forestall it. Regarding women's leadership in the private sector, one oft-cited moment is IMF director Christine Lagarde's speculation that had the investment firm Lehman Brothers instead been "Lehman Sisters," the financial crisis might have been handled differently (Prugl 2016). True (2016) examines how "women's leadership manifestos" position women's inclusion in finance as a post-crisis "silver bullet." Roberts (2016a) describes "womenomics," "gender dividend" and "gender lens investing" as emerging frameworks designed to integrate women into profit-making ventures in business and finance. Targeted programs, with names like Girls Who Invest and Winning Women, have emerged in the private sector and non-profit world to expand the pipeline of female finance professionals. Overall, much critical feminist literature dismisses these initiatives as corporate capture of liberal feminist ideas, and holds out little hope that they will reform gendered norms or financial practices (Fraser 2009; Hozic & True 2016).

Gendered notions of risk in "high" finance are not the only focus of feminist scholars looking at financialized gender norms. Other gendered dichotomies inform the privileging of hegemonic masculinities, as well as "women as savior" narratives. These traits include (men's) hypermobility versus (women's) constrained mobility or locality, cool-headedness as opposed to emotionality, and individualism versus relational ethics (Young 2010; Mussell 2018). Gender norms also operate in the realm of "everyday" personal finance. Joseph (2013: 243) analyzes the way popular media in the global North construct femininity through financial attitudes by portraying women as either "impulsive shopaholics" or "paralyzed non-investors." In development contexts, gender norms that characterize women as risk-averse now position them as an ideal population for financial inclusion via microcredit loans (Maclean 2013). Cultural context also matters with regards to the way gender norms are implicated in microfinance. Karim (2008: 10) examines how microcredit among the Bangladeshi rural poor relies on women fulfilling the traditional role as "custodians of family honor," and microfinance institutions use "pre-existing social practices" to ensure repayment by surveilling women's conduct and shaming men for women's debts. I turn to a broader look at feminist studies of the financialization of everyday life in the next section.

The Financialization of Social Reproduction and Everyday Life

Feminist and gender studies scholars use social reproduction and "everyday life" as two distinct but related approaches to financialization. While work on social reproduction grows squarely out of a feminist political economy tradition, the "everyday International Political Economy" (IPE) literature (Hobson & Seabrooke 2009; Langley 2008) is the product of critical—but not explicitly feminist—scholars. For Bakker & Gill (2003: 32) social reproduction is a broad concept that variously encompasses: 1) biological reproduction of the species, 2) reproduction of the labor force, and 3) reproduction of provisioning and caring needs. Those who study social reproduction often point to the ways that realms of the private and domestic—coded as feminine—have been partitioned as separate from the market, though the market is dependent on and intertwined with them. Analysts of everyday IPE also look beyond elite financial professionals, and beyond abstracts like "global flows," to the ways in which "ordinary" people are constitutive of the economy (Langley 2008; Hobson & Seabrooke, 2009: 293). Both social reproduction and everyday life approaches are concerned with what lies hidden in plain sight but is often neglected in political economy approaches to global markets. However, some feminist scholars criticize the everyday IPE literature for the lack of attention paid to household and reproductive labor, despite its apparent compatibility with, and intellectual debt to, feminist inquiry (Le Baron 2010; Elias & Roberts 2016; Redden 2018). At the same time, several have adopted the everyday approach in their own work, or attempted to bridge the gap between social reproduction and everyday IPE literatures through concepts like Elias and Roberts' (2016) "feminist global political economy of the everyday" (Allon 2014; Redden 2016).

The financialization of social reproduction largely concerns the particular role that household debt takes in the contemporary era. In the first place, this entails the fact that debt has become necessary for many households to meet the costs of social reproduction, including food, healthcare, housing, and education. This marks a change from past economic crises, wherein many women compensated for a shortfall in resources predominantly by taking on more labor, both paid and unpaid, rather than entering into debt (Roberts 2016b). Rising personal and household debt is problematic in one sense because "women and their households become fully exposed to what money may do on financial markets, and they shoulder the risks of this exposure" meaning that for many, an already insecure situation may become all the more so (Adkins 2015: 44). Secondly, there is a structural change in the role of the household in patterns of accumulation. Previously, households primarily contributed to profit via reproduction of labor. Now, as households enter into debt to meet their needs, "many reproductive activities have now become immediate sites of capital accumulation" (Federici 2014: 233). Because financialized social reproduction points to this structural change, Roberts argues that it is a more effective conceptual framework for exploring feminist concerns about current economic arrangements than the analysis of gendered impacts of austerity policies, discussed above (2016b: 139–140). She also points to potential system level effects in that wider household exposure to securitized debt can make financial crises worse.

Others point to qualitative, affective ramifications of this new financialized role for the household. It is here some have built a bridge with the everyday life literature. In "everyday" analyses, financialization often operates as a logic of discipline, in the sense of a Foucauldian governmentality (Hobson & Seabrooke, 2009; Van der Zwan 2014: 102). Most notably among feminist adaptations of the framework, Allon (2014: 13) sees a "feminization of finance" in "the ordinary and normalised presence of financial capitalism at the level of domesticity and home-life as well as the gendered entrepreneurial subjectivities that are increasingly brought to bear on those domains." Building on the observation that the home has become a financial object, she describes how sweat equity, economic management and future-oriented financial calculation have become new forms of domestic labor, and in turn "redefine what 'women' are and can be" (Ibid.: 13). Because the financialization of everyday life works at the level of individual subjectivities and household roles, this poses a stark challenge to feminist efforts at reform and resistance through policy and leadership (Elson 2014: 200; Adkins 2015).

One of the most institutionalized ways that financialization of everyday life and social reproduction proceeds is through microfinance. This is recognizable especially in the global South as a vast development studies literature attests (see Bateman & Maclean 2017 for a recent critical overview). However, financial instruments created for the developing world are also migrating northwards, where they continue to address the economically and socially excluded by serving as a sorting mechanism for the deserving and undeserving poor, and to integrate finance as "a code of self and citizenship in the conduct of everyday life" (Randy Martin in Baringa 2014: 27). Microfinance is a vehicle of financialization, on the one hand, due to the big banks and private investors that are funding the loans distributed by microfinance institutions, and are accumulating profit via the interest from loan repayment (Giron 2015; Duvendack & Mader 2017). However, a focus on microfinance as financialization of social reproduction highlights the role of the debt incurred by microloan recipients in meeting households needs. Additionally, microfinance is a process of financialization of everyday life in that it conditions gendered subjectivities and responsibilities. For example, many have noted that microfinance imposes new entrepreneurial subjectivities on women, which are compounded by continued efforts to ensure that women attend to the work of social reproduction (Young 2010; Schuster 2015; Khandelwal & Freeman 2017). The concepts of social reproduction and everyday life allow feminists to apprehend these multitudinous effects of financialization in the lives of women.

Conclusion

To conclude, I offer two suggestions for the further development of feminist research on financialization. First, this work should continue to mine the insights that come from reflexivity. By this, I refer to the elements of a feminist research ethic as delineated by Ackerly and True (2018: 262–263). These include:

> sceptical scrutiny of our research questions, our disciplines and methods; inclusionary inquiry, considering all possible sources and sites of knowledge; explicitly choosing a deliberative moment to reflect on possible biases, exclusions and forms of marginalization; and conceptualizing the field as a collective intrinsically related to knowledge production and social struggles outside scholarship.
>
> *(Ackerly & True 2018: 260)*

In the existing literature, this orientation is more evident in some work; Bassel and Emejulu (2017) use Black feminist frameworks and epistemologies to portray minority women as "experts on their own lives" and thus offer an alternative to the narrative of minority women as "devalued victims" of crisis and austerity (Hill Collins 2017). Nicola Smith (2016), through a queer studies perspective, urges reflection on the centrality of "the household" in feminist political economy and financialization studies. She reminds us that heteronormativity is integral to narratives about responsibility for crisis, which "draw upon imaginaries not just of market activity, but also of the 'private' spheres of family, intimacy and sexuality" (236). As these examples demonstrate, reflexivity can involve interrogating assumptions implicit in foundational concepts and dominant perspectives. The impacts of this can be fruitful for wider scholarship on financialization as well. This is already apparent, for example where scholars have pressed beyond the question of how financialization differently affects gendered subjects to ask how centering approaches to gender can impact understandings of financialization. Out of this a body of research has developed that applies performative approaches to finance, drawing on the work of Judith Butler (1990), even while its substantive focus is not limited to gender (De Goede 2003; Aitken 2007).

My second suggestion is for scholars to remain attentive to places where financialization scholarship not explicitly concerned with gender could productively engage with insights from feminist research. Caution is warranted in endeavors to bridge these intellectual divides because feminist work may not share the same underlying assumptions or translate easily into conversation, particularly with orthodox IPE work (Peterson 2018). Nevertheless, there are opportunities for dialogue. To name just one, I see the literature on women's inclusion in finance as highly relevant to Baker's (2018) discussion of the social purpose of finance. Baker argues that the inability of key actors (central bankers, academic economists, and staff of international regulatory bodies) to define a coherent social purpose for finance has contributed to "macroprudential minimalism," or lack of robust financial regulation in the wake of the 2008 crisis (see Thiemann, this volume). Baker is largely focused on the ontologies that are constitutive of economic policy. However his definition of social purpose as an "intersubjective consensus" between elites and the public on the normative role of finance as part of broader social and economic systems certainly leaves room to consider private and non-profit women's leadership initiatives like those discussed above in the section on norms and inclusion. Feminist interrogations pose a challenge to Baker's theory by suggesting that a concerted and to some degree successful effort has been made, through phenomena like gender lens investing and inclusion programs like JP Morgan's Winning Women, to define the social purpose of finance through the promotion of gender equality and women's empowerment. Yet this definition, as critical feminists have noted, could also provide cover for keeping reform limited. Creating avenues for some women to share in the gains of the financial sector neither addresses the financialization of social reproduction, nor the disproportionate impacts of crisis and austerity on marginalized populations. In sum, gender is not merely a micro-level concern divorced from the macro-structural level, and financialization scholarship on the whole should continue to inquire about how social structures connect these levels of analysis.

Bibliography

Ackerly, B. and True, J., 2018. With or without feminism? Researching gender and politics in the 21st century. *European Journal of Politics and Gender*, 1(1–2), pp. 259–278.

Adkins, L., 2015. What can money do? Feminist theory in austere times. *Feminist Review*, 109, pp. 31–48.

Aitken, R., 2007. *Performing Capital: Toward a Cultural Economy of Popular and Global Finance*, New York: Palgrave Macmillan.

Allon, F., 2014. The feminisation of finance: Gender, labour and the limits of inclusion. *Australian Feminist Studies*, 29(79), pp. 12–30.

Annesley, C. and Scheele, A., 2011. Gender, capitalism and economic crisis: Impacts and responses. *Journal of Contemporary European Studies*, 19(3), pp. 335–348.

Apicella, C.L., Dreber, A., Campbell, B., Gray, P.B., Hoffman, M., and Little, A.C., 2008. Testosterone and financial risk preferences. *Evolution and Human Behavior*, 29, pp. 384–390.

Assassi, L., 2009. *The Gendering of Global Finance*. New York: Palgrave Macmillan.

Baker, A.C., 2014. Eroding the wealth of women: Gender and the subprime foreclosure crisis. *Social Service Review*, March 2014, pp. 59–91

Baker, A., 2018. Macroprudential regimes and the politics of social purpose. *Review of International Political Economy*, 25(3), pp. 293–316

Bakker, I. and Gill, S., 2003. *Power, Production and Social Reproduction*. New York: Palgrave Macmillan.

Baringa, E., 2014. Microfinance in a developed welfare state: A hybrid technology for the government of the outcast. *Geoforum, 51*, pp. 27–36.

Bassel, L. and Emejulu, A., 2017. *Minority Women and Austerity: Survival and Resistance in France and Britain*. Bristol: Policy Press.

Bateman, M. and Maclean, K. (eds.), 2017. *Seduced and Betrayed: Exposing the Contemporary Microfinance Phenomenon*. Albuquerque: University of New Mexico Press.

Butler, J., 1990. *Gender Trouble*. New York: Routledge.

Carpenter, C., 2003. Gender theory in world politics: Contributions of a non-feminist standpoint? *International Studies Review*, 4(3), pp. 153–165.

Carver, T., ed. 2003. "Forum: Gender and International Relations" *International Studies Review*, 2003(5), pp. 287–302.

Coates, J.M. and Herbert, J., 2008. Endogenous steroids and financial risk taking on a London trading floor. *Proceedings of the National Academy of Sciences of the United States of America*, 105, pp. 6167–6172.

Connell, R.W., 1995. *Masculinities*. New York: Oxford University Press.

Connell, R.W. and Messerschmidt, J.W., 2005. Hegemonic masculinity: Rethinking the concept. *Gender & Society*, 19(6), pp. 829–859.

Connell, R.W. and Wood, J., 2005. Globalization and business masculinities. *Men and Masculinities*, 7(4), pp. 347–364.

De Goede, M., 2003. Beyond Economism in International Political Economy. *Review of International Studies*, 29(1), pp. 79–97.

De Goede, M., 2005. *Virtue, Fortune and Faith: A Genealogy of Finance*. Minneapolis: University of Minnesota Press.

Duvendack, M. and Mader, P., 2017. Poverty reduction or the financialization of poverty? In Bateman, M. and Maclean, K. (eds.), *Seduced and Betrayed: Exposing the Contemporary Microfinance Phenomenon*. Albuquerque: University of New Mexico Press, pp. 33–48.

Dymski, G., Hernandez, J. and Mohanty, L., 2013. Race, gender, power, and the US subprime mortgage and foreclosure crisis: A meso-analysis. *Feminist Economics* 19(3), pp. 124–151.

Elias, J. and Roberts, A., 2016. Feminist global political economies of the everyday: From bananas to bingo. *Globalizations*, 13(6), pp. 787–800.

Elomäki, A. and Kantola, J., 2017. Austerity politics and feminist resistance in Finland: From established women's organizations to new feminist initiatives. In Kantola, J. and Lombardo, E. (eds.), *Gender and the Economic Crisis in Europe: Politics, Institutions and Intersectionality*. Cham, Switzerland: Palgrave Macmillan, pp. 231–256.

Elson, D., 2014. Economic crises from the 1980s to the 2010s: A gender analysis. In Rai, S.M. and Waylen, G. (eds.), *New Frontiers in Feminist Political Economy*. New York: Routledge, pp. 189–212.

Elson, D., 2016. Plan F: Feminist plan for a caring and sustainable economy. *Globalizations*, 13(6), pp. 919–921.

Enloe, C., 2013. *Seriously! Investigating Crashes and Crises as if Women Mattered*. Berkeley: University of California Press.

Federici, S., 2014. From commoning to debt: Financialization, microcredit and the changing architecture of capital accumulation. *The South Atlantic Quarterly*, 113(2), pp. 231–244.

Fishbein, A. J. and Woodall, P., 2006. *Women are Prime Targets for Subprime Lending: Women Are Disproportionately Represented in High-Cost Mortgage Market*. Report, Washington, DC: Consumer Federation of America.

Fisher, M., 2015. Wall Street women: Professional saviors of the global economy. *Critical Perspectives on International Business*, 11(2), pp. 137–155.

Fraser, N., 2009. Feminism, capitalism, and the cunning of history. *New Left Review*, 56, pp. 97–117

Gill, S. and Roberts, A., 2011. Macroeconomic governance, gendered inequality and global crises. In Young, B., Bakker, I. and Elson, D. (eds.), *Questioning Financial Governance from a Feminist Perspective*. New York: Routledge, pp. 155–172.

Giron, A., 2015. Women and financialization: Microcredit, institutional investors, and MFIs. *Journal of Economic Issues*, 49(2), pp. 373–396.

Griffin, P., 2013. Gendering global finance: Crisis, Masculinity, and Responsibility. *Men and Masculinities*, 16(1), pp. 9–34.

Hill Collins, P., 2017. Foreword, in Bassel, L. and Emejulu, A., *Minority Women and Austerity: Survival and Resistance in France and Britain*. Bristol: Policy Press, pp. xi–xv.

Ho, K., 2009. *Liquidated: An Ethnography of Wall Street*. Durham, NC: Duke University Press.

Hobson, J. M. and Seabrooke, L., 2009. Everyday international political economy. In Blyth, M. ed., *Routledge Handbook of International Political Economy: IPE as a global conversation*, New York: Routledge.

Hozic, A. and True, J., 2016. Making feminist sense of the global financial crisis. In Hozic, A.A. and True, J. (eds.), *Scandalous Economics*. New York: Oxford University Press

Hyman, L., 2011. *Debtor Nation: The History of America in Red Ink*. Princeton, NJ: Princeton University Press.

Joseph, M., 2013. Gender, entrepreneurial subjectivity, and pathologies of personal finance. *SocPol: Social Politics*, 20(2), pp. 242–273.

Kantola, J. and Lombardo, E. (eds.), 2017. *Gender and the Economic Crisis in Europe: Politics, Institutions and Intersectionality*. Cham, Switzerland: Palgrave Macmillan.

Karamessini, M. and Rubery, J. (eds.), 2014. *Women and Austerity: The Economic Crisis and the Future for Gender Equality*. New York: Routledge.

Karim, L. 2008. Demystifying micro-credit: The Grameen Bank, NGOs, and neoliberalism in Bangladesh. *Cultural Dynamics*, 20(5), pp. 5–29.

Khandelwal, M. and Freeman, C., 2017. Pop development and the uses of feminism. In Bateman, M. and Maclean, K. (eds.), *Seduced and Betrayed: Exposing the Contemporary Microfinance Phenomenon*. Albuquerque: University of New Mexico Press, pp. 49–68.

Langley, P., 2008. *The Everyday Life of Global Finance: Saving and Borrowing in Anglo-America*. London: Oxford University Press.

Le Baron, G., 2010. The political economy of the household: Neoliberal restructuring, enclosures, and daily life. *Review of International Political Economy*, 17(5) pp. 889–912.

Lombardo, E., 2017. Austerity politics and feminist struggles in Spain: Reconfiguring the gender regime? In Kantola, J. and Lombardo, E. (eds.), *Gender and the Economic Crisis in Europe: Politics, Institutions and Intersectionality*. Cham, Switzerland: Palgrave Macmillan, pp. 209–230.

Maclean, K., 2013. Gender, risk and micro-financial subjectivities. *Antipode*, 45(2), 455–473.

McDowell, L., 2010. Capital culture revisited: Sex, testosterone, and the city. *International Journal of Urban and Regional Research*, 34(3), pp. 652–658.

Mussell, H., 2018. Who dares to care? (in the world of finance). *Feminist Economics*, 24(3), pp. 113–135.

Peterson, V.S., 2003. *Critical Rewriting of Global Political Economy: Integrating Reproductive, Productive, and Virtual Economies*. London: Routledge.

Peterson, V.S., 2018. Problematic premises: Positivism, modernism and masculinism in IPE. In Roberts, A. and Elias, J. (eds.), *Handbook on the International Political Economy of Gender*. Northampton, MA: Edward Elgar,

Prugl, E., 2016. Lehman Brothers and Sisters: Revisiting gender and myth after the financial crisis. In Hozic, A.A. and True, J. (eds.), *Scandalous Economics*. New York: Oxford University Press, pp. 21–40.

Redden, S., 2016. What's on the line?: Exploring the significance of gendered everyday resistance within the transnational call center workplace, *Globalizations*, 13(6), 846–860.

Redden, S., 2018. Feminist Engagements with 'Everyday Life.' In Roberts, A. and Elias, J. (eds.), *Handbook on the International Political Economy of Gender*. Northampton, MA: Edward Elgar, pp. 159–170.

Roberts, A., (2016a) Finance, financialization, and the production of gender. In Hozic, A.A. and True, J. (eds.), *Scandalous Economics*, New York: Oxford University Press, pp. 57–75

Roberts, A., (2016b) Household debt and the financialization of social reproduction. *Research in Political Economy*, 31, pp. 135–164.

Roberts, A. and Elias, J., 2018. Financial crises in historical perspective. In Roberts, A. and Elias, J. (eds.), *Handbook on the International Political Economy of Gender*. Northampton, MA: Edward Elgar, pp. 281–310.

Roth, L.M., 2006. *Selling Women Short: Gender Inequality on Wall Street*. Princeton, NJ: Princeton University Press.

Schuster, C.E., 2015. *Social Collateral: Women and Microfinance in Paraguay's Smuggling Economy*. Berkeley: University of California Press.

Smith, N., 2016. Towards a queer political economy of crisis. In Hozic, A.A. and True, J. (eds.), *Scandalous Economics*. New York: Oxford University Press

True, J., 2016. The global financial crisis's silver bullet: Women leaders and 'leaning in'. In Hozic, A.A. and True, J. (eds.), *Scandalous Economics*. New York: Oxford University Press, pp. 41–56.

True, J., 2018. Gendered states of punishment and welfare meets the political economy of violence against women. *Capital & Class*, 42(3), pp. 547–551.

Van Staveren, I., 2002. Global finance and gender. In Scholte, J.A. and Schnabel, A. (eds.), *Civil Society and Global Finance*, New York: Palgrave Macmillan, pp. 228–246.

Van der Zwan, N., 2014. Making sense of financialization. *Socioeconomic Review*, 12(1), pp. 99–129.

Wöhl, S., 2017. The gender dynamics of financialization and austerity in the European Union—The Irish case. In Kantola, J. and Lombardo, E. (eds.), *Gender and the Economic Crisis in Europe: Politics, Institutions and Intersectionality*. Cham, Switzerland: Palgrave Macmillan, pp. 139–160.

Young, B., 2003. Financial crises and social reproduction: Asia, Argentina and Brazil. In Bakker, I. and Gill, S. (eds.), *Power, Production and Social Reproduction*. New York: Palgrave Macmillan.

Young, S., 2010. Gender, mobility and the financialization of development, *Geopolitics*, 15, pp. 606–627.

Young, B., Bakker, I. and Elson, D., 2011. *Questioning Financial Governance from a Feminist Perspective*. New York: Routledge.

10

HOW FINANCIALIZATION IS REPRODUCED POLITICALLY

Stefano Pagliari and Kevin L. Young

Introduction

While most analyses of financialization in the literature have focused on primarily the economic and social dimensions of this phenomenon, it is increasingly recognized that financialization is also a political phenomenon. Recent scholarship has investigated the multiple political roots that explain the rise of finance, such as the structural crises of the 1970s, and the associated deregulation of financial services across many jurisdictions in recent years (Johnson and Kwak 2010; Krippner 2011; Hopkin and Alexander Shaw 2016; Witko 2016). Scholars have come to recognize that financialization is a political phenomenon not only for its roots in political decisions and processes, but also for its consequences over the political processes and the design of public policies. The central contention explored in this contribution is that financialization is creating the conditions for its own deepening by conditioning the regulatory environment in which it is situated.

Focusing on the financial regulatory politics in particular, this review of the literature on the political implications of the financialization of the economy will highlight how this process has influenced the political power and preferences of four sets of domestic actors identified in the literature as influencing the design of regulatory policies: the financial industry, the state, non-financial corporates, and households and individuals. From this perspective, the financialization of the economy can be understood as creating the conditions for its own reproduction not only by strengthening the power of the financial industry but also by broadening the pro-finance clientele among public officials, the rest of the business community, and society at large.

How has the literature explored empirically this claim regarding the political consequences of financialization? We focus on the challenges associated with empirically examining how the conditions supporting financialization are reproduced politically. We will highlight how existing scholarship has approached this topic from a methodologically pluralist orientation, relying on and benefiting from a variety of different methods. The analytical eclecticism (Sil and Katzenstein 2010) that characterizes much of this literature and the diversity of approaches have been functional to bring to the surface and highlight a number of different important cases and mechanisms through which financialization is reproduced politically.

At the same time, only few studies have explored the political consequences of different facets of financialization and the implications for its political reproduction in a systematic way.

In general single case studies designed to generate hypotheses and thick description regarding institutional detail and political processes associated with financialization tend to dominate within this literature. On the contrary, instances of empirical hypothesis testing remain limited and few larger-N works have examined the implications of financialization over the political process. Studies are broadly conversant with one another, but together often have different directional results. As a result, we argue that the evidence in support of the political reproduction of financialization is still limited.

In what follows below, we describe the recent research on how or whether financialization has affected the policy-shaping power of the financial industry itself, the preferences and engagement of both state actors and non-financial corporates as well as individuals. Finally, the contribution reflects upon the methodological strengths and limitations of this literature.

Financialization and the Power of the Financial Industry

The literature that has investigated the political origins of financialization has acknowledged how the financial industry has not been a passive bystander in the design of the policies that have contributed to the financialization of the economy. The focus of this scholarship has predominantly been on the US. Since the 1970s, different segments of the financial industry have thrown their weight behind the removal of existing regulatory constraints introduced in previous decades in the US and other key jurisdictions which constrained the scope of financial intermediation (Krippner 2011). In more recent decades, financial industry groups have been pushing for deregulatory policies that have enabled the growth of financial innovations that contributed significantly to the Global Financial Crisis of 2008–2009 (Johnson and Kwak 2010). These changes in the financial regulatory environment have played a key role in enabling the growth in size and profit share of the financial industry vis-à-vis other economic sectors in the economy of many industrial countries (Epstein and Power 2002).

There are two main competing perspectives to explain how the power of the financial industry may have expanded in parallel with the role of finance in the economy. First, the growth in the size of the financial industry in the economy has broadened the financial resources that financial firms and associations can deploy to lobby policymakers in the design and implementation of financial regulatory policies (Hacker and Pierson 2010; Johnson and Kwak 2010). As the financial sector gets richer it is better able to advocate for more of its preferences to be realized, and thus to defend its privileged position. For instance, the financial contributions by the financial industry to fund US elections increased by more than 13 times between 1990 and 2016, outpacing the growth in lobbying expenditures by numerous other sectors.[1]

Second, the active deployment of financial resources to lobby policymakers is not the only channel through which the financial industry has been theorized as capable of shaping regulatory policies. Building upon a long-standing body of work on "structural power" within political economy (Lindblom 1977; Culpepper 2015), different scholars have claimed that the structural dependence of the state on the financial industry for controlling access to credit as well as purchasing government debt enables these actors to influence the agenda of policymakers even in the absence of active lobbying (Strange 1988). As Bell and Hindmoor have argued "governments typically need to anticipate and seriously consider the demands of banks because bank lending is a critical determinant of overall levels of investment and economic performance" (Bell and Hindmoor 2014: 3).

From this perspective, the process of financialization can be understood as having reinforced the structural power of the business community and constrained the capacity for states to regulate financial markets and institutions, because the state itself has become dependent on continued financial sector expansion (Baker 2010; Culpepper and Reinke 2014). Bell and Hindmoor have argued that the fact that before the global financial crisis the financial sector in the comprised 8.3% of the GDP, employed more than 300,000 people in, and accounted for 25% of Corporation Tax Revenue contributed to its political clout vis-à-vis British authorities and the emergence of a "light-touch" regulatory regime (Bell and Hindmoor 2017). Moreover, this structural prominence of finance in the UK and US has been described by these authors as contributing to the reproduction of financialization after the crisis. To Bell and Hindmoor, "[t]his state–finance nexus in the US and UK now inhibits fundamental reform of finance" (Bell and Hindmoor 2015: 26) and the structural power of business groups can explain "government's caution about capital regulation in the immediate aftermath of the 2008 crisis" (Bell and Hindmoor 2017: 104), as major banks made the case that more stringent capital rules would result in lower levels of lending to the real economy and therefore lower growth.

At the same time, some recent literature in the aftermath of the crisis has challenged the notion of finance's structural prominence in the economy necessarily leading to a regulatory policy environment favorable to the financial industry. For example, contrary to the hypothesis that countries with a highly financialized economy would be less likely to engage in strong regulatory reforms following the crisis because of the power of the financial industry to block reform initiatives, Young and Park's (2013) analysis of 30 advanced capitalist countries finds regulatory authorities from highly financialized countries have been the most proactive in re-regulating their banking sectors in the immediate aftermath of the crisis, as they sought to exploit a window of opportunity for banking reforms.

Other explanations have been provided in the post-crisis literature to explain why even in countries with dominant financial sectors, financial industry groups have not been able to consistently stall reforms in the aftermath of the global financial crisis. For instance, the perceptions of government policymakers (Bell and Hindmoor 2014), the institutional configuration of the financial sector and the level of competition that banks face from other financial intermediaries in providing credit to businesses (Howarth and Quaglia 2013) are considered critical for translating structural prominence into structural power. So too is the salience of financial regulatory issues, which is understood to influence the incentives for policymakers to challenge the policy preferences of banks (Bell and Hindmoor 2017; for a different perspective see Keller 2018). For example, the prominence of an industry is not necessarily automatically understood as options are being considered by policymakers.

In sum, while the process of financialization may be associated with an increase in the prominence the financial industry, the capacity of financial firms to leverage this position is not automatic but rather contingent on a number of factors.

Financialization of the State and Financial Regulation

While theories of financial power discussed in the previous section have placed the emphasis squarely on the influence of the financial industry over the design of regulatory policies, a central theme in the literature of financialization concerns how states agencies themselves have been central actors in promoting the expansion of financial markets for reasons that cannot be subsumed to the interests of finance (DeRuytter and Möller, this volume; Wang, this volume). For instance, Krippner (2011) has discussed how the origins of the current age of financialization in the US can be traced to the decision of the US government to respond to the stagnation of the US economy and fiscal pressures in the late 1970s by lifting the interest rate ceiling and later abandoning it in order to reinvigorate the economy while avoiding unpopular redistributive policies.

At the same time, the mechanisms though which public authorities have facilitated the expansion of finance have not been limited to their traditional role as regulators. On the contrary, the literature on financialization has detailed a wide range of cases where other types of public actors themselves have become key participants in financial markets. For instance, in numerous cases public entities have encouraged the expansion of financial intermediation by providing legal and economic guarantees of new kinds of financial instruments (Pacewicz 2013), such as in the case of the government-sponsored enterprises which played a key role in the development of mortgage-backed securities in the US (Quinn 2017).

Most importantly, recent decades have witnessed an expansion in the range of public actors directly involved in the financial markets. For instance, government agencies tasked with managing sovereign debt have come to rely increasingly on financial market techniques and instruments that mirror the operations of private funds (Fastenrath, Schwan and Trampusch 2017), including a greater use of derivatives to manage and in some cases hide the official debt levels (Lagna 2016). Different countries have created state asset management bodies (Wang 2015; Helleiner and Lundblad 2008) to invest a large amount of financial assets in the financial markets. The way central banks pursue their monetary policy objectives has come to rely on financial institutions borrowing against collateral, as well as on financial practices from the private sector, notably mark-to-market techniques, margin calls and hair-cuts (Gabor and Ban 2016; Braun 2018; Braun and Gabor, this volume). Moreover, at the municipal level, local authorities in numerous US cities have also begun to create bonds similar to structured asset-backed securities to finance local development projects (Pacewicz 2013).

Overall, these examples of public actors relying on financial markets, financial indicators and financial instruments have been interpreted in the literature as amounting to a deep transformation in the relationship between the state and finance, which different scholars have labeled as "financialization of the state" (Wang 2015; Braun 2018; Wang, this volume). Most importantly, some of these works have started to theorize how these transformations in the relationship between public actors and finance may have implications for the design of public policies and the reproduction of the financialization of the economy.

First, Braun has theorized how the greater market-based agency of state actors has created new forms of dependencies of the state on the financial markets which have enhanced the political power of finance. Braun labels this form of power "infrastructural power" arguing that "whereas structural power operates via policymakers' expectation that harming business will harm economic performance, infrastructural power operates via policymakers' expectation that curtailing markets will curtail the effectiveness of their own, market-based policy instruments" (Braun 2018: 16). This form of infrastructural power was evident in the aftermath of the global financial crisis when the European Commission tried to tax repo markets and rein in securitization. These regulatory proposals were opposed not only by different interests within the financial industry but also by the European Central Bank, which remained dependent on these financial infrastructures for the implementation and transmission of monetary policy (Braun 2018).

Second, the financialization of the state might be understood as enhancing the influence of those public actors most closely related to finance. In particular, the analysis of the financialization of urban development by Pacewicz (2013) shows that the greater reliance on exotic municipal bonds to finance local development projects elevated the status of those development professionals who engineered this transformation. These individuals in turn had an incentive to promote further reliance on financial tools and practices to maintain their professional status, even if these were not necessarily aligned with the interest of the state. Meanwhile DeRuyter and Möller in this volume show that financialization has changed how public administrators and local policymakers operate at the local municipal level. They argue that government behavior has transformed from traditions of risk-averse conservative financial administration of local affairs into a process of active debt management.

Third, the financialization of the state can be regarded as shaping future policies by changing the mindset and operational culture of different public actors. In his analysis of Norwegian municipal owners of hydroelectric utilities, Løding (2018: 2) argues that the "modeling of organizational solutions on securities markets has become embedded in the municipal toolkit as a commonsense policy option to resolve core policy issues". As more public entities embrace financial solutions as rational ways to conduct statecraft, the public sector management therefore takes on a financialized rationality that facilitates the further integration of the state into financial markets (Løding 2018). Municipal governments have been active participants in this process, though not under conditions of their own choosing – a point shown in Peck and Whiteside's (2016) study of Detroit, and as DeRuytter and Möller (this volume) argue in the case of the overall rationalities and technologies of city-level financing.

In sum, these works have suggested how the state's greater reliance on financial practices and instruments can contribute to the reproduction of financialization by generating new dependencies on financial markets, shifting the bureaucratic incentives of key public authorities, as well as influencing the mindset of public officials. As Pacewicz succinctly puts it, "public policies have transformed financial markets, but reliance on financial markets can also transform political institutions in ways that promote further financialization" (Pacewicz 2013: 413). Similarly to the literature on financial power, it is worth noting that the vast majority of the studies investigating the impact of financialization in shaping the incentives and preferences of state actors has focused on illustrative case studies, and these claims have not been tested more systematically.

Financialization of Non-financial Firms and Financial Regulation

Non-financial firms are another set of actors whose relationship with finance has been presented within the literature on financialization as facing significant transformations in recent decades. During this period, non-financial firms have increasingly become dependent on finance beyond the simple provision of credit to include a wider range of financial services and resources, such as derivatives to hedge commercial risks and exchange rate volatility (Carroll and Fennema 2002; Carroll, Fennema and Heemskerk 2010; Mizruchi 2013). Even more significant transformations concerning the relationship between finance and non-financial firms occurred on the other side of the balance sheet. In this respect, empirical research has uncovered a systematic growth of financial assets on the balance sheets of non-financial corporations (Crotty 2002; Stockhammer 2004), a rise in the provision of financial services to the customers of non-financial corporations (Baud and Durand 2012), and the growing tendency of non-financial corporations to generate profits through financial channels rather than through the production of goods and services (Krippner 2005). Moreover, the literature has detailed how financial metrics and imperatives have come to play in the evaluation of corporate performance, such as the emphasis on maximizing shareholder value at the expense of other stakeholders such as employees (Lazonick and O'Sullivan 2000; Fligstein and Shin 2007; Cutler and Waine 2010). In sum, the literature on financialization has claimed that the lines between financial and non-financial firms have become progressively blurred. As Krippner argues, "Non-financial corporations are beginning to resemble financial corporations – in some cases, closely" (Krippner 2005: 202).

To what extent have these trends also influenced the politics of financial reforms? One claim is that the preferences of NFCs have changed. For instance, Van der Zwan (2019) identifies the position of different business groups in the financialized political economy as a key factor informing their policy preferences regarding occupational pensions' reforms. Her analysis of the mobilization of business groups around pension reforms in the Netherlands and the US shows that despite the long-standing differences between these two, the predominance of capital

funding as the main method of financing for occupational pensions shifted the policy preferences of business groups from the reduction of "social risks" associated with old age to the
reduction of "financial risk" deriving from capital funding. These changes have in some cases
heightened the conflict between non-financial and financial business groups, as demonstrated by
the business opposition in both the Netherlands and the US to legislative proposals to increase
corporate disclosure of their pension liabilities and to the harmonization of determining how
pension liabilities should appear on corporate accounts.

Other works instead have highlighted how in recent years the preferences of non-financial
firms have often converged with those of finance. When engaging in financial regulatory
debates in the aftermath of the global financial crisis, non-financial corporates often expressed
positions aligned with the financial industry; for instance, a variety of retail, energy, medical
research, manufacturing firms, as well as firms and industry associations from different sectors
have mobilized around parts of Dodd-Frank such as the provision in the US legislation limiting
the proprietary trading activities in the federally insured banking institutions (so-called Volcker
Rule), regulation of derivatives markets, the creation of a Consumer Financial Protection
Agency, or the regulation of money market funds (Pagliari and Young 2014; Baines 2017).
Going beyond these examples, Young and Pagliari have mapped the policy preferences of non-
financial and financial firms across a variety of regulatory issues in the US, EU, and other
industrialized countries and found that the financial sector has received significant support from
the rest of the business community, and that this business solidarity is stronger in finance than
for other sectors (Young and Pagliari 2017).

An argument advanced in the existing literature is that the financialization of non-financial
companies has broadened the support of pro-finance positions within the business community.
For instance, Baines (2017) argues that the financialization of the agri-food industry in the US
has expanded the range of forces opposing far-reaching regulatory reforms to counter the
financialization of these markets. The fact that large-scale farmers in the US have come to
integrate extensively financial derivatives into their day-to-day operations might explain the fact
that these groups have often joined forces with major banks that dominate the derivatives
markets in calling for a more limited regulatory intervention (Baines 2017).

Another mechanism through which the financialization of non-financial firms can be
understood as influencing the political process has been theorized by Callaghan (2015). In her
analysis of corporate governance reforms in the UK, Callaghan has argued that the introduction
of reforms expanding markets makes it more difficult for those companies that stand to lose
from this process to mobilize "because issue salience declined after the implementation of rules
and because market-enabling rules enhance the capacity of market forces to penalize those who
attempt to contravene them" (Callaghan 2015: 16). As Callaghan puts it, "market-enabling
arrangements endured not only because beneficiaries grew stronger. Marketization also engendered
decreasing opposition" (Callaghan 2015: 15).

Overall, the literature reviewed in this section presents compelling arguments for why the
greater penetration of the financial sector in the non-financial corporate world has influenced
the politics of financial reforms by broadening the pro-finance clientele within the business
community and weakening the capacity of those firms that stand to lose from financialization to
mobilize. It is noticeable, however, how while the economic consequences of the financialization of non-financial companies have been investigated in a systematic way by a number of
studies (for instance, see Tori and Onaran 2018), existing empirical analyses of claims reviewed
in this section regarding the political consequences of the same phenomenon have mostly
focused on individual sectors and policies in a single country.

The Financialization of Everyday Life and its Political Consequences

A final side of financialization that has attracted significant attention in the literature concerns the ways in which the rise of finance in the economy has come to have a direct effect on individuals and households, in what has been described in the literature as the "financialization of everyday life" (Martin 2002; Langley 2008; Langley, this volume). Financial developments such as the diffusion of credit cards and expansion of other securitized products bundling together of stream of future repayments from car loans and credit card debt have expanded the access of households to credit, as well as linked household borrowing with global capital markets (Erturk, Froud, Johal, Leaver and Williams 2007; Montgomerie 2009; Montgomerie, this volume). Moreover, a series of transformations such as tax breaks for investment into mutual funds and changes in the retirement system in many countries have increased the extent to which individuals and households come to rely on tradable financial securities to secure their future position (Clark, Thrift and Tickell 2004). While in the early post-war period only four percent of American adults owned stocks, by 2005 about one half of US households and one third of individual adults owned stock market equities either directly or indirectly (Harrington 2008; Richardson 2010).

To what extent have these transformations detailed in the literature on the "financialization of everyday life" also affected the policymaking process and design of financial regulatory policies? One important perspective within the existing literature has described the financialization of the economy as transformative for the identity and preferences of the individuals that find themselves increasingly exposed to the vagaries of financial markets. Fligstein and Goldstein for example depict the emergence of a "finance culture", where households not only become more fluent in financial language but also shift their orientation towards financial activities and become "more willing to take financial risks, including increasing indebtedness as a means to support their lifestyle" (Fligstein and Goldstein 2015: 576). Along the same lines, Langley has argued that the process of financialization entails a transformation in the perception of individuals towards financial risk and the "summoning up of the investor subjects" (Langley 2006: 929; Aitken, this volume).

From this perspective, this shift in the identity of financialized individuals has been presented as reshaping their policy attitudes and creating the perception of a growing link with the interests of finance capital. More specifically, Harmes hypothesizes that "by transforming tens of millions from passive savers into 'active' investors" whose personal wealth is tied to financial markets, the financialization of the economy is vastly expanding the constituency in favour of neoliberal policies "such as capital mobility, price stability, low capital-gains tax and shareholder value" (Harmes 2001a: 122). Along the same lines, Watson has argued that the way that pensions have transformed has contributed to the emergence of an important constituency backing the continuation of financialization (Watson 2008). The enmeshment of financial asset ownership by households is also seen, by some, to affect the relative power of particular kinds of financial institutional forms – such as mutual funds (Harmes 2001b), and, for example, by virtue of the way they manifest in diffuse forms of social control within the marketplace (Davis 2008; Fichtner, Heemskerk and Garcia-Bernardo 2017; Fichtner, this volume). This more direct exposure of individuals to financial activities creates a potential for a "split personality" dilemma for political subjectivity under conditions of financialization. In terms of policy preferences, those policies that may benefit an individual or household as investors – such as policies to promote shareholder value maximization in the management of companies – may affect them adversely as workers (Harmes 2001b).

But what is the empirical evidence that the greater engagement of households and individuals with the financial markets has effectively influenced the attitude of individuals over economic policies? Here the literature to date has relied heavily on survey data, to systematically test hypotheses. For instance, Cotton Nessler and Davis (2012) analyse survey data to investigate the link between stock ownership, political beliefs and party affiliation in the US, between 2000 and 2008 and find a conditional and small effect of stock ownership on identification with the Republican Party. Through another analysis of US survey data, Fligstein and Goldstein likewise find the greater use of financial services has brought a shift in cultural norms and attitudes towards risk and debt. In particular they find that middle and upper middle class households "have responded to income inequality by more actively managing their financial situations and adopting a more thoroughly financial mindset," taking on a more aggressive attitude towards risk-taking and engaging more financial activities (Fligstein and Goldstein 2015: 577). Yet Fligstein and Goldstein also find that working-class individuals have not become more willing to accept high levels of risk or to rely on debt to support their lifestyles. Pagliari, Phillips and Young (2018) have similarly examined the extent to which the holding of financial securities has shaped the preferences of individuals towards different financial policies and fostered a convergence with the preferences of the financial industry. Their analysis shows how in the aftermath of the financial crisis US households owning financial assets expressed less support for the Dodd-Frank reforms than those who do not report financial asset ownership, and that these patterns persisted years after the crisis as well. Again, the overall effect is concentrated mostly among higher-income households.

If the more widespread ownership of financial asset can be associated with the emergence of new constituencies backing the expansion of the financial markets as theorized by the financialization literature, the magnitude of this change is so far modest and varies significantly across different socio-economic classes (Fligstein and Goldstein 2015). Only recently have such survey analyses engaged with questions of actual support or opposition to financial regulatory reform (e.g. see Young and Yagci 2018). All such survey studies to date have examined patterns within the US, reflecting data availability and the strengths of survey methodology in that country. In general there is enormous potential in assessing how financialization may be conditioning the attitudes of the public. While nationally representative samples of a given population, whether inside or outside the US and UK, are often costly, there is every opportunity to examine hypotheses related to attitudinal orientations toward financialization through a variety of methods. For instance, Stanley (2014) departs from survey analysis and uses focus groups of UK citizens to examine how elite-driven narratives of austerity translate into shared popular subjectivity surrounding the financial crisis, its causes, and its aftermath.

Conclusion

Any large-scale socioeconomic transformation will have elements of self-reinforcement if it is to be durable across time and changing circumstances. Increasingly, scholars have made the point that financialization creates the conditions for its own reproduction by altering the political landscape. It is only very recently that scholars have begun to explore empirically the ways in which this occurs, and which of the manifold aspects of financialization's dynamics relate to its political reproduction.

In this chapter we have discussed the ways in which the financialization process may be building its own constituencies of political support. How financialization is reproduced politically is a complex question, and we have broken this down into four mechanisms. As a macro-structural phenomenon financialization conditions its own regulatory environment by strengthening the resources that the financial industry can deploy, it draws in both public authorities and non-financial corporates as strategic supporters, and the financialization of "everyday life" alters political subjectivity in ways conducive to political support. Overall, these four mechanisms suggest that the financialization of the economy can be understood as a process creating the political conditions for its own reproduction.

Yet despite an analytically eclectic orientation and an array of new empirical studies, the literature on financialization has yet to fully mature. As Krippner has argued in the case of the broader literature on financialization, "enthusiasm for the concept of financialization has run far ahead of serious attempts to establish evidence for this phenomenon" (Krippner 2011: 23). Along the same lines, while the literature has focused mostly on seeking to theorize how financialization may plant the seeds for its own continuation and advancement, only a few studies have opened these claims to empirical scrutiny. This can perhaps be explained by the methodological challenges of researching financialization's political reproduction, which are considerable. It is worthwhile commenting on this in light of future efforts to better understand these processes.

In particular, two main methodological traits of this literature are worth noting. First, the majority of claims regarding financialization's political consequences, as documented above, are single case studies seeking to illustrate how dynamics associated with financialization have expanded to new domains and reshaped the policymaking process. This is a natural starting point in the presence of new developments that have yet to be properly theorized. However, the prevalence of case studies providing a thick description of a particular event or phenomenon and developing new hypotheses from its analysis has rarely been followed by attempts to empirically *test* a particular hypothesis or set of hypotheses against new data.

A second important characteristic of this literature concerns its geographical focus. The literature on financialization has highlighted how this phenomenon operates differently in different locales, even while some contend that it is a quintessentially global phenomenon (Christophers 2012). Yet, the majority of the literature has been focused on the political economy of the United States and a few more advanced capitalist countries. While financialization per se is often subject to quantitative measurement (Epstein and Jayadev 2005; Tomaskovic-Devey and Lin 2011; Maxfield, Winecoff and Young 2017), only few works have to date adopted a large- or medium-N approach to study financialization's political reproduction across different institutional contexts.

As a result, there is a lot that is still unknown about how financialization proceeds, and in particular how much of its political reproduction is due to institutional inertia versus the active agency of stakeholders seeking to buttress its continuation. While the literature reviewed in this contribution has suggested a number of important avenues for further research, the state of the existing empirical literature suggests that claims concerning the political consequences of financialization over the design of regulatory policies should not be overstated. The more that is learned about how this process works, the more that the process appears to be multifaceted, complex and highly conditional on an array of institutional conditions not under the complete control of the financial industry.

Note

1   https://www.opensecrets.org/industries/totals.php?cycle=2018&ind=F.

Bibliography

Baines, J., 2017. Accumulating through food crisis? Farmers, commodity traders and the distributional politics of financialization. *Review of International Political Economy*, 24(3), pp. 497–537.

Baker, A., 2010. Restraining regulatory capture? Anglo-America, crisis politics and trajectories of change in global financial governance. *International Affairs*, 86(3), pp. 647–663.

Baud, C., and Durand, C., 2012. Financialization, globalization and the making of profits by leading retailers. *Socio-Economic Review*, 10(2), pp. 241–266.

Bell, S., and Hindmoor, A., 2014. Taming the city? Ideas, Structural power and the evolution of British banking policy amidst the great financial meltdown. *New Political Economy*, 20(3), pp. 454–474.

Bell, S., and Hindmoor, A., 2015. *Masters of the Universe, Slaves of the Market*. Cambridge, MA: Harvard University Press.

Bell, S., and Hindmoor, A., 2017. Structural power and the politics of bank capital regulation in the United Kingdom. *Political Studies*, 65(1), pp. 103–121.

Braun, B., 2018. Central banking and the infrastructural power of finance: The case of ECB support for repo and securitization markets. *Socio-Economic Review*, advance online, doi:10.1093/ser/mwy008.

Callaghan, H., 2015. Who cares about financialization? Self-reinforcing feedback, issue salience, and increasing acquiescence to market-enabling takeover rules. *Socio-Economic Review*, 13(2), pp. 331–350.

Carroll, W.K., and Fennema, M., 2002. Is there a transnational business community. *International Sociology*, 17(3), pp. 393–413.

Carroll, W.K., Fennema, M., and Heemskerk, E.M., 2010. Constituting Corporate Europe: A study of elite social organization. *Antipode*, 42(4), pp. 811–843.

Christophers, B., 2012. Anaemic geographies of financialisation. *New Political Economy*, 17(3), pp. 271–291.

Clark, G., Thrift, N., and Tickell, A., 2004. Performing finance: The industry, the media and its image. *Review of International Political Economy*, 11(2), pp. 289–310.

Cotton Nessler, N.C., and Davis, G.F., 2012. Stock ownership, political beliefs, and party identification from the "ownership society" to the financial meltdown. *Accounting, Economics, and Law*, 2(2).

Crotty, J., 2002. *The Effects of Increased Product Market Competition and Changes in Financial Markets on the Performance of Nonfinancial Corporations in the Neoliberal Era*. PERI Working Paper, Amherst, MA.

Culpepper, P.D., 2015. Structural power and political science in the post-crisis era. *Business and Politics*, 17(03), pp. 91–409.

Culpepper, P., and Reinke, R., 2014. Structural power and bank bailouts in the United Kingdom and the United States. *Politics & Society*, 42(4), pp. 427–454.

Cutler, T., and Waine, B., 2010. Social insecurity and the retreat from social democracy: Occupational welfare in the long boom and financialization. *Review of International Political Economy*, 8(1), pp. 96–118.

Davis, G.F., 2008. A new finance capitalism? Mutual funds and ownership re-concentration in the United States. *European Management Review*, 5(1), pp. 11–21.

Epstein, G., and Jayadev, A., 2005. The determinants of rentier incomes in OECD Countries: Monetary Policy, Financial Liberalization, And Labor Solidarity. In: Epstein, G. (ed.), *Financialization and the World Economy*. Northampton, MA: Edward Elgar, pp. 46–74.

Epstein, G., and Power, D., 2002. *The Return of Finance and Finance's Returns: Recent Trends in Rentier Incomes in OECD Countries, 1960–2000*. Research Brief (Vol. 2002–2002). Political Economy Research Institute.

Erturk, I., Froud, J., Johal, S., Leaver, A., and Williams, K., 2007. The democratization of finance? Promises, outcomes and conditions. *Review of International Political Economy*, 14(4), pp. 553–575.

Fastenrath, F., Schwan, M., and Trampusch, C., 2017. Where states and markets meet: The financialisation of sovereign debt management. *New Political Economy*, 22(3), pp. 273–293.

Fichtner, J., Heemskerk, E.M., and Garcia-Bernardo, J., 2017. Hidden power of the Big Three? Passive index funds, re-concentration of corporate ownership, and new financial risk. *Business and Politics*, 19(02), pp. 298–326.

Fligstein, N., and Goldstein, A., 2015. The emergence of a finance culture in American households, 1989–2007. *Socio-Economic Review*, 13(3), pp. 575–601.

Fligstein, N., and Shin, T., 2007. Shareholder value and the transformation of the U.S. economy, 1984–2000. *Sociological Forum*, 22(4), pp. 399–424.

Gabor, D., and Ban, C., 2016. Banking on bonds: The new links between states and markets. *JCMS: Journal of Common Market Studies*, 54(3), pp. 617–635.

Hacker, J., and Pierson, P., 2010. Winner-take-all politics: Public policy, political organization, and the precipitous rise of top incomes in the United States. *Politics and Society*, 38(2), pp. 152–204.

Harmes, A., 2001a. Mass investment culture. *New Left Review*, 9, pp. 103–124.

Harmes, A., 2001b. *Unseen Power: How Mutual Funds Threaten the Political and Economic Wealth of Nations*. Toronto: Stoddart Publishing.

Harrington, B., 2008. *Pop Finance: Investor Clubs and the New Investor Populism*. Princeton, N.J.: Princeton University Press.

Helleiner, E., and Lundblad, T., 2008. States, markets, and sovereign wealth funds. *German Policy Studies*, 4(3), pp. 59–82.

Hopkin, J., and Alexander Shaw, K., 2016. Organized combat or structural advantage? The politics of inequality and the winner-take-all economy in the United Kingdom. *Politics & Society*, 44(3), pp. 345–371.

Howarth, D., and Quaglia, L., 2013. Banking on stability: The political economy of new capital requirements in the European Union. *Journal of European Integration*, 35(3), pp. 333–346.

Johnson, S., and Kwak, J., 2010. *13 Bankers*. New York: Pantheon Books.

Keller, E., 2018. Noisy business politics: Lobbying strategies and business influence after the financial crisis. *Journal of European Public Policy*, 25(3), pp. 287–306.

Krippner, G.R., 2005. The financialization of the American economy. *Socio-Economic Review*, 3(2), pp. 173–208.

Krippner, G.R., 2011. *Capitalizing on Crisis: the Political Origins of the Rise of Finance*. Cambridge, MA: Harvard University Press.

Lagna, A., 2016. Derivatives and the financialisation of the Italian state. *New Political Economy*, 21(2), pp. 167–186.

Langley, P., 2006. The making of investor subjects in Anglo-American pensions. *Environment and Planning D: Society and Space*, 24(6), pp. 919–935.

Langley, P., 2008. *The Everyday Life of Global Finance: Saving and Borrowing in Anglo-America*. Oxford: Oxford University Press.

Lazonick, W., and O'Sullivan, M., 2000. Maximizing shareholder value: A new ideology for corporate governance. *Economy and Society*, 29(1), pp. 13–35.

Lindblom, C.E., 1977. *Politics and Markets: The World's Political and Economic Systems*. New York: Basic Books.

Løding, T.H., 2018. The financialization of local governments—the case of financial rationality in the management of Norwegian hydroelectric utilities. *Socio-Economic Review*. doi:10.1093/ser/mwy026.

Martin, R., 2002. *Financialization of Daily Life*. Philadelphia: Temple University Press.

Maxfield, S., Winecoff, W.K., and Young, K.L., 2017. An empirical investigation of the financialization convergence hypothesis. *Review of International Political Economy*, 24(6), pp. 1004–1029.

Mizruchi, M.S., 2013. *The Fracturing of the American Corporate Elite*. Cambridge, MA: Harvard University Press.

Montgomerie, J., 2009. American financialisation the pursuit of (past) happiness? Middle-class indebtedness and American financialisation. *New Political Economy*, 14(1), pp. 37–41.

Pacewicz, J., 2013. Tax increment financing, economic development professionals and the financialization of urban politics. *Socio-Economic Review*, 11(3), pp. 413–440.

Pagliari, S., Phillips, L.M., and Young, K.L., 2018. The financialization of policy preferences: Financial asset ownership, regulation and crisis management. *Socio-Economic Review*, advance online, doi:10.1093/ser/mwy027.

Pagliari, S., and Young, K., 2014. Leveraged interests: Financial industry power and the role of private sector coalitions. *Review of International Political Economy*, 21(3), pp. 575–610.

Peck, J. and Whiteside, H. 2016. Financializing Detroit. *Economic Geography*, 92(3), pp. 235–268.

Quinn, S., 2017. "The miracles of bookkeeping": How budget politics link fiscal policies and financial markets. *American Journal of Sociology*, 123(1), pp. 48–85.

Richardson, M. C., 2010. *Financial Stocks and Political Bonds: Stock Market Participation and Political Behavior in the United States and Britain*. Dissertation, University of Illinois at Urbana-Champaign.

Sil, R., and Katzenstein, P.J., 2010. Analytic eclecticism in the study of world politics: Reconfiguring problems and mechanisms across research traditions. *Perspectives on Politics*, 8(2), pp. 411–431.

Stanley, L., 2014. "We're reaping what we sowed": Everyday crisis narratives and acquiescence to the age of austerity. *New Political Economy*, 19(6), pp. 895–917.

Stockhammer, E., 2004. Financialization and the slowdown of accumulation. *Cambridge. Journal of Economics*, 28(5), pp. 719–741.

Strange, S., 1988. *States and Markets*. New York, NY: Continuum.

Tomaskovic-Devey, D., and Lin, K.-H., 2011. Income dynamics, economic rents, and the financialization of the U.S. economy. *American Sociological Review*, 76(4), pp. 538–559.

Tori, D., and Onaran, Ö., 2018. Financialization, financial development and investment. Evidence from European non-financial corporations. *Socio-Economic Review*, advance online, doi:10.1093/ser/mwy044.

Van der Zwan, N., 2019. The financial politics of occupational pensions: A business interests perspective. In: Oude Nijhuis, D. (eds). *Business Interests and the Development of the Modern Welfare State*. London: Routledge.

Wang, Y., 2015. The rise of the "shareholding state": financialization of economic management in China. *Socio-Economic Review*, 13(3), pp. 603–625.

Watson, M., 2008. Constituting monetary conservatives via the "savings habit": New Labour and the British housing market bubble. *Comparative European Politics*, 6(3), pp. 285–304.

Witko, C., 2016. The politics of financialization in the United States, 1949–2005. *British Journal of Political Science*, 46(02), pp. 349–370.

Young, K.L., and Yagci, A.H., 2018. Status quo conservatism, placation, or partisan division? Analysing citizen attitudes towards financial reform in the United States. *New Political Economy*, advance online, doi:10.1080/13563467.2018.1446923.

Young, K., and Pagliari, S., 2017. Capital united? Business unity in regulatory politics and the special place of finance. *Regulation & Governance*, 11(1), pp. 3–23.

Young, K., and Park, S.H., 2013. Regulatory opportunism: Cross-national patterns in national banking regulatory responses following the global financial crisis. *Public Administration*, 91, pp. 561–581.

11

FINANCIALIZATION IN HETERODOX ECONOMICS[1]

Dimitris P. Sotiropoulos and Ariane Hillig

Introduction

There is a general consensus both in mainstream and heterodox economics that the role of finance has increased in contemporary capitalist societies since the 1980s, discussions further fuelled by the 2007 financial meltdown. While mainstream economic approaches have attempted to reconsider the concepts of market efficiency and/or financial risk (for instance, see Blinder, Lo and Solow, 2012 and Shin, 2010), heterodox studies have relied on the term *financialization* to explain how changes in modern finance have become core elements in the transformations of contemporary capitalism. Financialization is one of the most widely used terms in heterodox studies. Coming up with a single and coherent definition is impossible since there is no definition which can be theoretically neutral or unbiased (see the introductory chapter by Mader, Mertens and Van der Zwan, in this volume). The success and the wide dissemination of the term comes thus at a price, as it has become imprecise, inexplicit, and quite often contradictory.

This chapter reviews and summarizes different research strategies employed within heterodox economic studies on financialization. Given the large volume of relevant research and the limited space of this chapter, it is impossible to include every single study on financialization. Since the focus lies on heterodox economics, we leave out from our analysis important studies from other social disciplines. Our aim is not to give an exhaustive review of the heterodox economic debates but to offer a general overview of the different research pathways that have been followed. This chapter critically reflects the way we interpret these debates, but it is not engaged in direct criticism of arguments with which we disagree or which we see as insufficient for an understanding of contemporary capitalism. In the following, Section 2 offers an account of post-Keynesian literature, Section 3 covers the Marxist literature, and Section 4 ends up with an indication of alternative approaches to studying modern finance.

The Post-Keynesian Paradigm

The Revenge of Rentiers

The central idea in post-Keynesian discussions is that the rise of finance is associated with the predominance of a particular economic elite (see Epstein, in this volume). Keynes described this

elite as a class of *rentiers or* "functionless investors" (Keynes, 1973: 376). To him, these individuals were akin to Ricardo's landowners, enjoying incomes founded on scarcity without any
real productive contribution. The term used earlier by Veblen to characterize the very same
group was *absentee owners* – the class that had managed to subordinate the regime of "traffic in
goods" to that of "trading of capital" (Veblen, 1958: 75). Taking the same analytical line,
Minsky introduced the term "money manager capitalism" to describe a version of capitalism
that is dominated by financial activities (Tymoigne and Wray, 2013: 245). There is a fast-
growing body of literature providing a systematic analysis of the current financialization of
capitalism in terms of the hegemony of this rentier group. Seen from this perspective, modern
financial developments are a consequence of social conflicts being resolved in ways that favour
absentee owners over the "productive" classes.

The main idea of this literature strand has been set out by Hein and van Treeck (2010) in an
income distribution type of argument. Financialization has reshaped firms' objectives. A dominance
of shareholders has subordinated management and worker preferences for (long-run) accumulation
of the firm to shareholders' preference for (short-term) profitability (see Erturk, in this volume).[2]
This shift in power relations to the benefit of shareholders feeds back on investment. Aspects such as
increasing dividend payments and share buybacks restrict the amount of internal funds available for
investment projects. The overall outcome has led to a new institutional setting based on profits
without investments: a finance-oriented rather than production-oriented economic system with the
financial sector gaining importance and absorbing a rising income share relative to the real sector. In
what follows, we discuss several aspects of this accumulation regime based on shareholder value
maximization as they have been developed in recent post-Keynesian research.

Financialization Crowds Out Physical Investment

The first literature group discussed here draws upon the post-Keynesian argument that financialization (the expansion of the financial sector) has a negative impact on traditional productive
purposes (Epstein, 2005; Onaran, Stockhammer and Grafl, 2011; Hein, 2013). The rise of
finance and the increasing orientation of the non-financial sector towards financial activities
implies a decline in physical investment, thus inducing poor and fragile economic growth, and
long-term stagnation in productivity (Tori and Onaran, 2017). This impact of financialization
on physical investment is approached from two perspectives.

On the one hand, studies in this literature strand draw on macroeconomic data to discuss the
phenomenon of financialization. Stockhammer (2004) uses annual macroeconomic data of the
non-financial business sector and offers econometric evidence that rentiers' income (that is,
interest and dividend income, which was used as a proxy for financialization) caused a slowdown in accumulation in the US and France (but not in the UK and Germany) between 1960
and 2000. Using also macroeconomic data from the early 1980s until 2005, van Treeck (2008)
provides econometric evidence that for some OECD countries the profit share and rentier
income have been decoupled from accumulation, reflected in the growth rate of the capital
stock of businesses. This study argues that the link that connects profit share and rentier income
with the accumulation of tangible capital has become very loose under financialization. Rather
than profit shares arising from accumulation in the real sector, it is related to high dividends and
a higher propensity to consume by the dividends' recipients.[3]

On the other hand, there is also post-Keynesian research that addresses the very same question
of crowding out from a micro-perspective using data at the firm level. Orhangazi (2008) analyzes
the effect of financialization (captured by financial profit and financial payout ratios) on the
investment behavior of non-financial corporations in the US, for the period of 1973–2003. The

author offers evidence that financial investment and profit opportunities have risen and directed funds away from real investment. Increased focus on financial markets has reduced the availability of internal funds for real investments and shortened the planning horizons of firm management. Demir (2009) analyzes financialization in non-financial companies in Argentina, Mexico, and Turkey in the 1990s with the same emphasis on firm-level data. This study also finds that companies prefer financial investments with a short-term investment focus in contrast to "irreversible" long-term fixed investments. Finally, Tori and Onaran (2017) show the impact of financialization on physical investment in certain Western European countries. By using panel data at the firm level for the period 1995–2015, they find evidence for a negative correlation between financial incomes (interests and dividends) and investment in fixed assets by non-financial corporations.

The literature strand introduced here constructs a dichotomy between the real and financial sector and states that growing investments into financial assets has led to declining investments in the real sector, hence, financialization crowds out physical investment. This shareholder value approach, however, has not gone unchallenged within post-Keynesianism. Dögus (2016) argues that the direction of causality is reversed. Rather than firms making fewer physical investments because of higher distributed dividends, they are able to generate higher dividends when investing more in financial assets. The shareholder value approach is also viewed critically by Kliman and Williams (2015) who question the possibility of financial investments crowding out real investments in an environment of rising availability of external finance. The authors show that in the US the share of profit invested in productive investments has not changed significantly since the 1980s.[4]

Financialization of the Household Sector

Post-Keynesian insights into the financialization of firms have been extended to the analysis of the household sector. This line of research accompanies the thriving studies on the financialization of everyday life in economic geography and economic sociology in the 2000s (see Gonzalez, in this volume).[5] Unlike the studies of the financialization of daily life that aim at offering a holistic account of the changes in household finance, post-Keynesian research is more narrowly focused on rising indebtedness, which is in fact only one part of the overall household balance sheet transformations. The main insight is that, because of financialization, output growth can be sustained at lower levels of real wage income than would otherwise be possible. Given the increases in income inequality, poorer households rely heavily on debt to keep up with social consumption norms, while richer households benefit from rising capital income (Onaran and Guschanski, 2017). In a comprehensive literature survey, Stockhammer (2015) also supports the idea that financialization is related to a debt-led growth regime in countries that do not pursue export-led growth (see also Stockhammer, in this volume).

Following this train of thought, Barba and Pivetti (2009) question the long run sustainability of a system that uses debt as a substitute for wage growth: at some point households will no longer be able to service debt and this will come with important macroeconomic implications such as a decline in economic growth. Kim, Setterfield and Mei (2015) provide some empirical evidence based on econometric analysis for US households since the 1950s, arguing that household debt accumulated for consumption is unsustainable in the long-run causing economic recessions. This line of argument is often connected to Minsky's financial instability hypothesis (Dymski, 2010; Bellofiore, 2011). Financial instability is defined as the tendency of economies to become unstable due to excessive debt levels. This includes economic units such as households moving from being mainly hedge financed (cash inflows satisfying principal and interest payments) towards speculative (income is only sufficient for interest payments) and then

Ponzi financed (income is sufficient for neither interest nor principal payments; Minsky, 2008). Placing income inequality at the heart of this reasoning about economic recessions, Kapeller and Schütz (2013) draw in a synthetic fashion upon Veblen, Keynes, and Minsky. According to their view, households move increasingly into speculative and Ponzi units due to debt being used to support household consumption in the context of stagnating wages, increasingly precarious work, and less welfare provisions.

The post-Keynesian line of research is enriched by an interesting twist in the argument with regard to household indebtedness offered by the analysis of Dymski, Hernandez and Mohanty (2013). The latter bring race and gender into the discussion and provide a more active role for financial intermediation. This study argues that the relatively more vulnerable position of women and minorities (having less secure jobs, fewer assets, and more insecure prospects) provides the setting for the creation of new exploitative lending instruments to the benefit of banks. Using data from the Survey of Consumer Finances (SCF, conducted by the Federal Reserve Board), Wolff (2014) sheds further light on the condition of US minorities. During the late 2000s relative indebtedness of middle-class households increased because of declining net wealth and income, rather than rising absolute indebtedness. In the wake of the 2007 financial meltdown, the elevated homeownership rates in the US and the associated high levels of relative indebtedness is linked to a rise in wealth inequality. This leaves some middle-class groups, such as the young, Hispanic, and black households, particularly vulnerable.

The post-Keynesian literature provides undoubtedly valuable insights into household financial behaviour and its impact on the macro-economy. In particular, it highlights the role of income inequality and the concomitant indebtedness of households due to debt being used as substitution for falling wages. This however results in an unequal treatment of the household balance sheet, neglecting the asset side of the balance sheet and thus presenting only a partial view of rising indebtedness (Michell and Toporowski, 2013). Moreover, despite interacting in a social and institutional structure which is influenced not only by structural economic changes but also by conflicting interests, norms, and conventions, expectations are not "crucial components" in post-Keynesian models but rather "it is the structural interconnections of sectors whose equilibria are not mutually consistent which generate unstable outcomes" (Dymski, 2012: 335). The post-Keynesian literature thus usually dispenses with going "into intricate detail of individual behaviour" in favour of studying the "interaction between various groups and classes of society based on received conventions" (Lavoie, 2015: 92). This interaction between various groups and sectors is picked up in the stock-flow literature.

The Stock-Flow Literature

The financial crisis of 2007 called into question the validity of many existing mainstream macro-modelling studies. It was in this context that the interest in stock-flow consistent (SFC) models was revived.[6] The structure of a SFC model is based on two types of matrices, the flow matrix and the stock matrix. Each matrix consists of a set of rows and columns: the rows represent several assets or commodities and the columns the sectors of the economy to be modelled. These two types of matrices together form a logical network that incorporates a rigorous accounting structure, which is stock-flow consistent (Godley and Lavoie, 2007).[7]

Generally, there are three broad categories in SFC modelling (Caverzasi and Godin, 2015). The first category uses the SFC framework to illustrate an argument and clarify its exposition about consistency and completeness. The second group, which reflects the great bulk of recent research, uses the SFC structure to set out a theoretical model of dynamic equations and solve it via simulation. The third category of models can be referred to as "fully empirical" and rely on econometric methods to estimate parameter values of the equations in line with Wynne Godley's (1996) original insights, who was one of the first post-Keynesian economists to establish macroeconomic SFC models. Research in the context of SFC modelling is mostly associated with the post-Keynesian school of thought, some of which is concerned with financialization.

SFC models enable the researcher to study aspects which are usually researched in isolation in the form of financial and real variables including credit and wealth as well as production and income. In one instance, Dallery and van Treeck (2011) show with a simple SFC model how the two historical phases of capitalism, the post-Second World-War "Fordist" regime and the recent "financialization" regime, differ with regard to the relationship between managers, workers and financial institutions. Whereas in the "Fordist" regime managers and workers are the dominant groups determining profitability, in the financialization regime shareholders put pressure on managers and workers to generate profits. In another instance, Botta, Caverzasi, and Tori (2015) model the shadow banking system using a SFC model, while Sawyer and Veronese Passarella (2017) explore, also in the context of a SFC model, how the theory of monetary circuits reflects the stylized features of financialization. Finally, there has been some stock-flow consistent modelling of the main post-Keynesian insight with regard to household indebtedness. Nikolaidi (2015) argues that securitisation and wage stagnation can jointly affect financial fragility and can be viewed as two main root causes of the global financial crisis.

While the studies in the previous two sections confirm the main stylized facts of financialization, such as a stronger focus on financial investment and rising indebtedness of households, Skott and Ryoo (2008) emphasize the need to avoid partial analyses and develop holistic accounts of financialization. It is, for example, essential to depict how firm's investment decisions interact with other sectors such as households and the government. With SFC models it is possible to overcome the limitations of partial analyses and study the interactions of different sectors at the same time. However, SFC models become increasingly complex when working with real data and often retreat to simulations with the help of assumed parameters (Lavoie, 2008).

Marxist Approaches

Underconsumptionist Approaches and Emphasis on the Rate of Profit

There has been a long tradition of Marxist approaches that refer to the rate of profit to analyze capitalist accumulation and crises. A significant share of Marxist explanations of financialization interprets developments in finance as a by-product of the historical trend in the profit rate. In this regard, the rise of finance is an unstable (and therefore temporary) solution to capitalism's long-term problem of underconsumption. The trend in the profit rate reflects capitalism's inability to absorb the final economic product. There are two alternative versions of the underconsumptionist argument.

The first interprets financialization as a result of high capitalist profitability. If profits are mostly saved and wages are relatively low in comparison to profits, the potential productive output cannot be absorbed when there is no rise in final consumption. Without any corrective action, capitalists are faced with a dearth of genuine investment-outlets and as a result build up excess capital. From this perspective, financialization appears as a remedy to lacking demand, recycling the excess consumption power from capitalists to workers in the form of debt and/or devolving into speculative activities. Similar to the post-Keynesian studies, financial innovation is argued here to have enabled households to take on debt to finance consumption while capitalists can conduct speculative investments resulting in asset price increases. This is clearly an advantageous situation for capitalists, because it solves the problem of surplus capital without jeopardizing capitalists' interests and income position. The only drawback is that financial recycling cannot be viewed as a permanent solution and adds to the fragility of the system, eventually resulting in financial bubbles followed by crises.[8] This analysis appears under various forms in the accounts offered by, among others, Husson (2012), Mohun (2013), Resnick and Wolff (2010).

The second version of the profit-rate explanation also argues from underconsumption but proposes low profitability as its cause. Due to squeezed wages (rather than, as above, high profits) and the concomitant low demand, output cannot be absorbed. The resultant poor profitability leads to stagnant and excess capital because capital can only be channelled into production at a declining rate. In the absence of other solutions that might boost demand, financial recycling becomes the means of intermediation, decongesting the accumulation of surplus capital. The argument here is essentially the same as in the previous scenario: financial debt and credit bubbles offer capital the easiest means for tackling declining profitability without incurring major costs (Bakir, 2015; Maniatis, 2012).

Some authors (Goldstein, 2009; Kotz, 2013; Dünhaupt, 2016), whilst remaining true to the overall spirit of the argument of underconsumption, link low profitability, in addition to low wage incomes (demand), to high values of constant capital already invested (overcapacity). Demand thus always lags behind productive capacity. Even as profit falls, there will be continuing investment which will add to the overall "amount" of capital. As a result, the productive capacity will exceed demand. This line of argument emphasizes over-investment of capital relative to realized profitability. It identifies an additional channel via which downward pressure is exerted on the profit rate: the numerator (i.e. the decrease in realized profit) is not the only thing that counts; so does the denominator (i.e. the increase in constant capital and the creation of overcapacity).

Many current approaches to financialization can be viewed as falling within the theoretical tradition outlined here in which "financialization is merely a way of compensating for the underlying disease affecting capital accumulation itself" (Foster and Magdoff, 2009: 18).[9] The notion of a lack of final demand and the associated conflicts over income between capitalists (and managers) and workers bear a striking resemblance with many post-Keynesian approaches already mentioned. However, the emphasis here falls on the rate of profit. To capture and discuss the long-term developments in capital accumulation, the calculation of the profit rate must commence before the 1970s or 1980s, which was when financialization is seen to have taken off. Given that such long-term macroeconomic series of national accounts exist only for the US or the UK, this train of research has necessarily narrowed its focus on these two countries.

Financialization as Income Expropriation

The idea that finance has a predatory element that "squeezes" other industrial or "productive" economic activities is also known to the Marxist tradition. At the start of the twentieth century—even before Keynes and Veblen had argued this—Hilferding (1981: 226) maintained that a form of capitalism was possible in which the industrial sector was subordinate to the financial sector. Although there is not the space here to give a proper account of Hilferding's point of view (which was greatly influenced by the historical conditions prevailing in Germany at that time), it is worth noting that his ideas have inspired a number of recent theorizations.

Fine, for instance, views neoliberalism as a capitalist regime that lays stress on "financial-speculative activities as opposed to industrial investment as an increasingly important source of profit" (Fine, 2010: 113; see Christophers and Fine, in this volume). One form of capital (the interest-bearing capital) predominates over all other forms (industrial etc.). In a similar fashion, Jessop (2015) argues that financialization comprises the growth of non-functioning rather than functioning capital, where non-functioning capital is capital which does not contribute to the growth of the real economy. Crotty (2005), as well, argues that in the case of the US, the increasing role of finance in the non-financial corporate sector resulted in decreasing capital accumulation and lower capital investment.

In the same train of thought, exploring the impact of financialization in a global perspective, Ivanova (2012) and Mah-Hui and Ee (2011) show in their studies how the global financial value chain has been transformed. Over-investment in the periphery and debt-driven consumption bubbles in the core illustrate the rising importance of "non-productive elements" such as finance (Ivanova, 2012: 67). Finally, Lapavitsas (2009) sees the financial expropriation of workers by capitalists and banks as an additional source of profit that has emerged in the sphere of circulation as a result of the poor level of real accumulation since the late 1970s.[10] Both post-Keynesian and the majority of Marxist approaches thus depict finance as dysfunctional developments within a capitalist society which take away resources from a productive into an unproductive sector.

Financialization: Taking Stock and Moving Forward

The analytical canvas of the existing heterodox approaches to financialization is huge. Despite the variety and the wealth of insights and empirical findings, arguably the great majority of the above-mentioned literature underestimates the autonomy of financial innovation in the workings of capitalist societies. Finance and its innate socio-technological developments (see Chiapello, in this volume) are mostly seen as passive and adjustable to external factors (e.g. wage squeeze, insufficient effective demand, over-accumulated fixed capital relative to demand etc.). Finance is thus often interpreted as *ahistorical*, in the sense that its own history as a social domain is merely a reflection of external economic developments. And yet, one major lesson from economic history is that financial innovation is effective, central, and immanent (but not passive) in the accumulation of capital (Kindleberger, 1984). This is indeed one of Marx's major contributions, a fact mostly overlooked. Finance in its contemporary version encompasses much more than accumulated liabilities and increased indebtedness. It presupposes substantial levels of investment, analytical research, and financial innovation and it is shaped by major institutional developments, economic strategies, social conflicts, and state regulations at the global level. All these elements have their own unique histories, institutional paces, and social temporalities.

There are attempts to offer an alternative analysis of financialization in a Marxist fashion, looking at ways finance transforms class and capital.[11] In a genuine interdisciplinary approach, Martin (2002, 2007, 2009) and Bryan and Rafferty (2006) treat financialization not as some sort of distortion or simply a shift in the balance of power between classes and the generation of economic volatility, but also as a tool in re-constituting our understanding of class as a formal economic category and class relations (Bryan, Martin and Rafferty, 2009; Bryan, Rafferty and Jefferis, 2015). The focus is thus on the "positive" side of social transformations; "positive" not in the sense that the rise of finance is de facto beneficial but that it is intertwined with a series of social and class transformations and cannot be undone. In a similar line of argument, Sotiropoulos, Milios and Lapatsioras (2013) argue that the rise of finance sets forth a technology of power (in which risk and its commodification play a central role) that changes the workings of contemporary capitalism. This anti-teleological line of research, arguing that there is not an ideal model of capitalism which has been sacrificed to finance, but rather assessing the ways in which capitalism transforms itself, offers an alternative line of research.

Notes

1 We would like to thank Paul Auerbach, Ewa Karwowski and Philip Mader for their comments on an earlier version of this chapter. The responsibility of any remaining errors or omissions is ours alone.
2 Quite influential has also been the intervention by Lazonick and O'Sullivan (2000) outlining the negative effects of shareholder value maximization. As we shall see below, this idea has become central in the post-Keynesian literature (see, for instance Dallery 2009; Cordonnier and Van de Velde 2015).
3 For a similar line of research, see Arestis, Gonzalez and Dejuan (2012), De Souza and Epstein (2014).
4 For a further criticism see Lysandrou (2011, 2016) who has stressed that it is both the demand and the supply of financial securities that is important in contemporary capitalism, thus, offering a somewhat different approach to understanding the role of financial innovation.
5 See for example Clark (2012), Coppock (2013), Langley (2008), Smith (2008).
6 For an excellent analysis of the history of SFC modelling see Smith (2018).
7 For a thorough description of the SFC modelling see Godley (1996) and Godley and Lavoie (2007).
8 It is quite striking that most of the abovementioned Marxist and post-Keynesian approaches rely on the concept of asset bubbles. This concept is from mainstream financial economics and indicates a situation in which the market price of an asset is much higher than its "fundamental value." The notion of fundamental or intrinsic value is however problematic because it is not theoretically neutral.
9 See also Brenner (2006), McNally (2009), Harvey (2010), Lazzarato (2012).
10 The discussed themes in this section do not fully reflect the analytical wealth of all relevant approaches. For instance, Arrighi (1999) argues that the modern neoliberal organization of capitalism is a reflection of the changing hegemonic position of the USA. Faced with declining profit opportunities in commodity markets, financial capital flows elsewhere in search for profits.
11 For an interesting attempt to rethink alternatives to contemporary capitalism see Auerbach (2016).

Bibliography

Arestis, P., Gonzalez, A.R. and Dejuan, O., 2012. Modelling accumulation: A theoretical and empirical application of the accelerator principle under uncertainty. *Intervention. European Journal of Economics and Economic Policies*, 9(2), pp. 255–275.

Arrighi, G., 1999. Globalization, state sovereignty, and the 'endless' accumulation of capital. In: D.A. Smith, D.J. Solinger and S.C. Topik (eds.), *States and Sovereignty in the Global Economy*. London and New York: Routledge, pp. 53–73.

Auerbach, P., 2016. *Socialist Optimism*. New York: Palgrave Macmillan.

Bakir, E., 2015. Capital accumulation, profitability, and crisis: Neoliberalism in the United States. *Review of Radical Political Economics*, 47(3), pp. 389–411.

Barba, A. and Pivetti, M., 2009. Rising household debt: Its causes and macroeconomic implications – a long-period analysis. *Cambridge Journal of Economics*, 33(1), pp. 113–137.

Bellofiore, R., 2011. From Marx to Minsky. In: H. Ganssmann (ed.), *New Approaches to Monetary Theory – Interdisciplinary Perspectives*. London and New York: Routledge, pp. 191–211.

Blinder, A.S., Lo, A.W. and Solow, R.M., 2012. *Rethinking the Financial Crisis*. New York: Russell Sage Foundation.

Botta, A., Caverzasi, E. and Tori, D., 2015. Financial-real side interactions in the monetary circuit: Loving or dangerous hugs? *International Journal of Political Economy*, 44(3), pp. 196–227.

Brenner, R., 2006. *The Economics of Global Turbulence*. London: Verso Books.

Bryan, D. and Rafferty, M., 2006. *Capitalism with Derivatives: A Political Economy of Financial Derivatives, Capital and Class*. New York and London: Palgrave Macmillan.

Bryan, D., Martin, R. and Rafferty, M., 2009. Financialization and Marx: Giving labor and capital a financial makeover. *Review of Radical Political Economics*, 41(4), pp. 458–472.

Bryan D., Rafferty M. and Jefferis, C., 2015. Risk and value: Finance, labor, and production. *South Atlantic Quarterly*, 114(2), pp. 307–329.

Caverzasi, E. and Godin, A., 2015. Post-Keynesian stock-flow-consistent modelling: A survey. *Cambridge Journal of Economics*, 39(1), pp. 157–187.

Clark, G.L., 2012. Pensions or property? *Environment and Planning A*, 4(5), pp. 1185–1199.

Coppock, S., 2013. The everyday geographies of financialisation: Impacts, subjects and alternatives. *Cambridge Journal of Regions, Economy and Society*, 6(3), pp. 479–500.

Cordonnier, L. and Van de Velde, F., 2015. The demands of finance and the glass ceiling of profit without investment. *Cambridge Journal of Economics*, 39(3), pp. 871–885.

Crotty, J., 2005. The Neoliberal Paradox: The impact of destructive product market competition and 'modern' financial markets on nonfinancial corporation performance in the neoliberal era. In: G. Epstein (ed.), *Financialization and the World Economy*. Cheltenham: Edward Elgar, pp. 77–110.

Dallery, T., 2009. Post-Keynesian theories of the firm under financialization. *Review of Radical Political Economy*, 41(4), pp. 492–515.

Dallery, T. and van Treeck, T., 2011. Conflicting claims and equilibrium adjustment processes in a stock-flow consistent macroeconomic model. *Review of Political Economy*, 23(2), pp. 189–211.

Demir, F., 2009. Financial liberalization, private investment and portfolio choice: Financialization of real sectors in emerging markets. *Journal of Development Economics*, 88(2), pp. 314–324.

De Souza, J. and Epstein, G., 2014. *Sectoral Net Lending in Six Financial Centres*. PERI Working Paper Series. No. 346. Amherst, MA: Political Economy Research Institute.

Dögus, I., 2016. *A Minskian Criticism on the Shareholder Pressure Approach of Financialisation*. ZÖSS Discussion Paper. No.1868–4947/53. Hamburg: Zentrum fuer Ökonomische und Soziologische Studien.

Dünhaupt, P., 2016. *Financialization and the Crises of Capitalism*. IPE Working Paper. No.67/2016. Berlin: Berlin Institute for International Political Economy.

Dymski, G., 2010. Why the subprime crisis is different: A Minskyan approach. *Cambridge Journal of Economics*, 34(2), pp. 239–255.

Dymski, G., 2012. Keynesian approaches to financial crisis. In: E. Hein and E. Stockhammer (eds.), *A Modern Guide to Keynesian Macroeconomics and Economic Policies*. Cheltenham: Edward Elgar, pp. 325–351.

Dymski, G., Hernandez, L. and Mohanty, L., 2013. Race, gender, power, and the US subprime mortgage and foreclosure crisis: A meso analysis. *Feminist Economics*, 19(3), pp. 124–151.

Epstein, G.A., 2005. *Financialization and the World Economy*. Cheltenham: Edward Elgar.

Fine, B., 2010. Locating financialisation. *Historical Materialism*, 18, pp. 97–116.

Foster, J.B. and Magdoff, F., 2009. *The Great Financial Crisis: Causes and Consequences*. New York: Monthly Review.

Godley, W., 1996. *Money, Finance, and National Income Determination*. PERI Working Paper Series. No.167. Annandale-on-Hudson, NY: Levy Economics Institute of Bard College.

Godley, W. and Lavoie, M., 2007. *Monetary Economics – An Integrated Approach to Credit, Income, Production and Wealth*. Basingstoke: Palgrave Macmillan.

Goldstein, J.P., 2009. An introduction to a unified heterodox macroeconomic theory. In: J.P. Goldstein and M.G. Hillard (eds.), *Heterodox Macroeconomics – Keynes, Marx and Globalization*. London and New York: Routledge, pp. 36–53.

Harvey, D., 2010. *The Enigma of Capital and the Crises of Capitalism*. London: Profile Books Ltd.

Hein, E., 2013. *The Macroeconomics of Finance-Dominated Capitalism – And its Crisis*. Cheltenham: Edward Elgar.

Hein, E. and van Treeck, T., 2010. 'Financialisation' and rising shareholder power in Kaleckian/post-Kaleckian models of distribution and growth. *Review of Political Economy*, 22(2), pp. 205–233.

Hilferding, R., 1981. *Finance Capital*. London: Routledge and Kegan Paul.

Husson, M., 2012. Where is the crisis going? In: F. Leplat and Ö. Onaran (eds.), *Capitalism: Crisis and Alternatives*. London: Resistance Books, pp. 11–39.

Ivanova, M.N., 2012. Marx, Minsky, and the Great Recession. *Review of Radical Political Economics*, 45(1), pp. 59–75.

Jessop, B., 2015. The symptomatology of crises, reading crises and learning from them: Some critical realist reflections. *Journal of Critical Realism*, 14(3), pp. 238–271.

Kapeller, J. and Schütz, B., 2013. Exploring pluralist economics: The case of the Minsky–Veblen cycles. *Journal of Economics Issues*, 47(2), pp. 515–523.

Keynes, J.M., 1973. *The General Theory of Employment, Interest and Money*. London: Macmillan.

Kindleberger, C.P., 1984. Financial institutions and economic development: A comparison of Great Britain and France in the eighteenth and nineteenth centuries. *Explorations in Economic History*, 21, pp. 103–124.

Kim, Y., Setterfield, M. and Mei, Y., 2015. Aggregate consumption and debt accumulation: An empirical examination of household behaviour. *Cambridge Journal of Economics*, 39(1), pp. 93–112.

Kliman, A. and Williams, S., 2015. Why 'financialisation' hasn't depressed US productive investment. *Cambridge Journal of Economics*, 39(1), pp. 67–92.

Kotz, D.M., 2013. The current economic crisis in the United States: A crisis of over-investment. *Review of Radical Political Economics*, 45(3), pp. 284–294.

Langley, P., 2008. *The Everyday Life of Global Finance: Saving and Borrowing in Anglo-America.* Oxford: Oxford University Press.

Lapavitsas, C., 2009. Financialised capitalism: Crisis and financial expropriation. *Historical Materialism*, 17, pp. 114–148.

Lavoie, M., 2008. Financialisation issues in a Post-Keynesian stock-flow consistent model. *Intervention. European Journal of Economics and Economic Policies*, 5(2), 331–356.

Lavoie, M., 2015. *Post-Keynesian Economics: New Foundations.* Cheltenham: Edward Elgar.

Lazonick, W. and O'Sullivan, M., 2000. Maximising shareholder value: A new ideology for corporate governance. *Economy and Society*, 29(1), pp. 13–35.

Lazzarato, M., 2012. *The Making of Indebted Man.* Los Angeles, CA: Semiotexte.

Lysandrou, P., 2011. Global inequality, wealth concentration and the subprime crisis: A Marxian commodity theory analysis. *Development and Change*, 42(1), pp. 183–208.

Lysandrou, P., 2016. The colonisation of the future: An alternative view of financialisation and its portents. *Journal of Post Keynesian Economics*, 39(4), pp. 444–472.

Mah-Hui, M.L. and Ee, K.E., 2011. From Marx to Morgan Stanley: Inequality and financial crisis. *Development and Change*, 42(1), pp. 209–227.

Maniatis, T., 2012. Marxist theories of crisis and the current economic crisis. *Forum for Social Economics*, 41 (1), pp. 6–29.

Martin, R., 2002. *Financialization of Daily Life.* Philadelphia: Temple University Press.

Martin, R., 2007. *An Empire of Indifference: American War and the Financial Logic of Risk Management.* Durham, NC: Duke University Press.

Martin, R., 2009. The Twin Towers of financialization: Entanglements of political and cultural economies. *The Global South*, 3(1), pp. 108–125.

McNally, D., 2009. From financial crisis to world-slump: Accumulation, financialisation and the global slowdown. *Historical Materialism*, 17(2), pp. 35–83.

Michell, J. and Toporowski, J., 2013. Critical observations on financialization and the financial process. *International Journal of Political Economy*, 42(4), pp. 67–82.

Minsky, H.P., 2008. *Stabilizing an Unstable Economy.* 2nd ed. New York: McGraw Hill.

Mohun, S., 2013. Rate of profit and crisis in the US economy: A class perspective. In: T. Michl, A. Rezai and L. Taylor (eds.), *Social Fairness and Economics: Critical Economic Theory in the Spirit of Duncan Foley.* London and New York: Routledge.

Nikolaidi, M., 2015. *Securitisation, Wage Stagnation and Financial Fragility: A Stock-flow Consistent Perspective.* GPERC Working Paper Series. No.14078. Greenwich: Greenwich Political Economy Research Centre.

Onaran, Ö. and Guschanski, A., 2017. Capital lessons: Labour, inequality and how to respond. *IPPR Progressive Review*, 24(3), pp. 152–162

Onaran, Ö., Stockhammer, E. and Grafl, L., 2011. Financialisation, income distribution and aggregate demand in the USA. *Cambridge Journal of Economics*, 35(4), pp. 637–661.

Orhangazi, Ö., 2008. Financialisation and capital accumulation in the non-financial corporate sector: A theoretical and empirical investigation on the US economy: 1973–2003. *Cambridge Journal of Economics*, 32(6), pp. 863–886.

Resnick, S. and Wolff, R., 2010. The Economic Crisis: A Marxian interpretation. *Rethinking Marxism*, 22 (2), pp. 170–186.

Sawyer, M. and Veronese Passarella, M., 2017. The monetary circuit in the age of financialisation: A stock-flow consistent model with a twofold banking sector. *Metroeconomica*, 68(2), pp. 321–353.

Shin, H.S., 2010. *Risk and Liquidity.* New York: Oxford University Press.

Skott, P. and Ryoo, S., 2008. Macroeconomic implications of financialisation. *Cambridge Journal of Economics*, 32(6), pp. 827–862.

Smith, G., 2018. *A Political Economy of Modern Finance and its Economic Consequences.* Unpublished doctoral thesis. The Open University: Milton Keynes.

Smith, S.J., 2008. Owner-occupation: At home with a hybrid of money and materials. *Environment and Planning A*, 40(3), pp. 520–535.

Sotiropoulos, D.P., Milios, J. and Lapatsioras, S., 2013. *A Political Economy of Contemporary Capitalism and its Crisis: Demystifying Finance.* London: Routledge.

Stockhammer, E., 2004. Financialisation and the slowdown of accumulation. *Cambridge Journal of Economics*, 28(3), pp. 371–404.

Stockhammer, E., 2015. Rising inequality as a cause of the present crisis. *Cambridge Journal of Economics*, 39 (3), pp. 935–958.

Tori, D. and Onaran, Ö., 2017. *The Effects of Financialisation and Financial Development on Investment: Evidence from Firm-Level Data in Europe*. GPERC Working Paper Series. No.44. London: Greenwich Political Economy Research Centre.

Tymoigne, E. and Wray, L.R., 2013. *The Rise and Fall of Money Manager Capitalism – Minsky's Half Century from World War Two to the Great Recession*. New York: Routledge.

van Treeck, T., 2008. Reconsidering the investment-profit nexus in finance-led economics: An ARDL-based approach. *Metroeconomica*, 59(3), pp. 371–404.

Veblen, T., 1958. *The Theory of Business Enterprise*. A Mentor Book. New York, NY: The New American Library of World Literature.

Wolff, E.N., 2014. Household wealth trends in the United States, 1983–2010. *Oxford Review of Economic Policy*, 30(1), pp. 21–43.

12

FINANCIALIZATION AND THE USES OF HISTORY

Mareike Beck and Samuel Knafo

Introduction

This chapter reflects on the uses of history for understanding financialization. By referring to "uses," we are primarily interested in the ways in which history has offered a resource for scholars to conceptualize or theorize financialization. The value of history partly lies in the opportunity it affords us to gain critical distance from the present. It makes it possible to relativize current financial developments in order to challenge assumptions we might have about what we take to be the salient features of financialization. In that respect, it is an invaluable resource to specify further what really stands out about recent financial developments and help us conceptualize it.

The turn to history, however, is fraught with difficulties when it comes to financialization. For this concept remains ill defined. The problem is that scholars have tried to cover too much with it. Seeking a concept that would encompass the great variety of financial developments that have taken place over the past 40 years across numerous countries and regions of the world, scholars have been forced to adopt vague and abstract notions. For only the most basic features can be taken as common denominators to define financialization when too many instances are involved. The result has been an underspecified concept that makes it difficult for scholars to know what to look for when historicizing financialization (Engelen 2008).

Take a well-known formulation, Epstein's definition of financialization as the "increasing role of financial motives, financial markets, financial actors and financial institutions in the operation of the domestic and international economies" (Epstein 2005: 3). Such a reference to financialization cannot help us to discriminate between different developments that relate to finance. Do all changes in the world of finance partake in the same process of financialization? It is difficult not to think so from Epstein's perspective. As a result everything and nothing seems to be relevant to the history of financialization, making it difficult to track its history. The concept is thus less useful as a framing device because it does not help us take decisions about what matters. It also makes the work of historicization less productive, because it is then impossible to see how history can inflect our theories of financialization. If a vague concept fits too easily the evidence because it is highly abstract, then it is not clear what can destabilize it. Historical findings always seem to fit the theory with the result that the work of historicization will have little impact on it.

We argue that the problem of history in the study of financialization is foremost a conceptual one. It pertains to the rigour we set for ourselves when framing historical analysis. We make our case in the first part of this chapter by surveying various historical perspectives on financialization and the ways in which they frame our understanding of this development. As we point out, scholars have traditionally looked through history to either find common patterns of financial development (Reinhart and Rogoff 2009) or periodize its trajectory. While these studies have offered great insights into the dynamics of financialization, they often downplay the significance of concrete financial practices *in their conceptualization of financialization* in favour of more abstract conceptions that emphasise generic financial logics of development.

In the second part of this chapter, we reflect on what is needed to frame the historical study of financialization in more productive ways. We argue that a more substantive conceptualization explicitly based on concrete financial practices is needed in order to turn financialization into a proper object of historical enquiry. This leads us to sketch a different approach to financialization. We make the case for considering the rise of liability management (LM) from the 1960s onwards as the defining feature of financialization. As we show, this practice developed by New York commercial banks enabled a much more aggressive approach to finance that profoundly transformed the way in which banks finance themselves and the power they can exert. By making it possible to raise great sums rapidly, it proved a vital advantage for banks in various corporate contests to capture all sorts of assets and fuelled the dramatic leveraging that supported the financial explosion of the 1980s.

Financialization and the Turn to History

Grasping the problem that history poses for studies of financialization requires that we start with the reasons that prompted academics to develop this concept in the first place. It was fleshed out in the 1990s when scholars began reflecting on whether the growing importance of finance in society was ushering a radically "new economy." With a broad range of actors turning to financial and speculative strategies, various scholars argued that we were witnessing the emergence of a new finance-led form of capitalist accumulation. The concept of financialization was then put forward as a means to reflect on the nature of these financial transformations and determine their broader societal significance (Van der Zwan 2014).

As it is often the case, the existence of what seemed to be a large-scale phenomenon encouraged scholars to look for large structural changes that could account for it. Many pointed to the economic crisis of the 1970s arguing that limited profits in production had incited investors to migrate towards more financial and speculative endeavours. In doing so, these authors challenged the mainstream idea that the economy allocates resources in an efficient manner. For scholars of financialization, finance was not simply a functional and neutral mediator tasked with reallocating unused capital for productive use. Depending on the way finance is organized, they argued, it has different socio-economic effects which can be detrimental to agents and sectors of the economy.

History proved to be of great help here to highlight the potentially destabilising impact of finance. Indeed, scholars of financialization often turned to a long tradition of historical critique that gravitated around two broad themes regarding the potentially dysfunctional nature of finance. The first was the recurrence of financial crises. A broad literature argued that finance is prone to speculative bouts, fuelled by the overvaluation of financial assets, that are ultimately unsustainable and lead to crisis (Minsky 1982). Because such financial bubbles clash with the image of the rational actor found in economics, much emphasis was placed on the irrationality of these financial manias (Kindleberger 2000). A second popular theme was the relationship of finance to production, or more specifically the alleged tendency of finance to undermine sound economic growth by diverting capital away from productive, and towards speculative, uses (Elbaum and Lazonick 1986; Cain and Hopkins 2001). Both themes thus served as an influential background for reflections on current financial transformations.

However, working with history required that some form of equivalency be established so that knowledge of the past could be used to understand the present. Why were developments in the nineteenth century or the 1920s relevant to the study of financialization? As we examine below, scholars of financialization have crafted four different perspectives on history on the basis of such equivalencies. The first three approaches (minskyian, world-systems and historical institutionalism) mobilized historical research by framing financialization as another instance of a recurrent pattern of development in history. The past thus served as a guide by helping us discern patterns that would be reproduced under financialization, even if on a different scale. The last approach (regulation theory) used a second strategy, periodising the history of finance in order to help bring out what is distinctive about financialization (see Christophers and Fine, in this volume). In what follows, we examine in turn these four approaches.

One of the most important sources of inspiration for the work on financialization has been the influential economist Hyman Minsky who used the repeated occurrence of financial crises as the basis for a cyclical analysis of the economy which placed finance at its centre. Minsky's main contribution was his financial instability hypothesis which posits that economic prosperity breeds financial instability by fuelling confidence and providing more and more license for people to speculate. As people find it easier to borrow money and leverage their operations in a context where there is sustained economic growth, they take on more risks. Financial institutions thus become increasingly leveraged through their speculative gambles as they borrow to make riskier deals. In the process, they sow the seeds for their own collapse as they make it harder to repay growing debts (Minsky 1982; see Sotiropoulos and Hillig, in this volume).

While Minsky's framework emphasises structural patterns, his analysis displays a keen sense of the specificity of each case of financial bubble and a pragmatic approach to dealing with them. As he demonstrates, financial innovations tend to blur the lines between investment and speculation for they necessarily mean entering unchartered territories with consequences that are impossible to predict. There is always a speculative dimension to these innovations and this explains why we need a historical approach to take account for how this plays out. This orientation has been reflected in the work produced by authors working in this tradition who have produced insightful writings on the evolution of financial markets and monetary policy. Nesvetailova, for example, (2007: 7) provides an impressive update of international crises in the 1990s and 2000s and of the financial innovations that "make it dangerously easy for today's financiers to disguise their growing share of borrowings as investments and often, misrepresent their liabilities as profits."

The risk for this approach, however, is to become overly fixated on the cycles of instability. The historical work is then cast as an instance of a familiar pattern that downplays the novelty of financialization. More importantly, a theoretical framework based on a recurrent pattern of capitalist development makes it difficult for the historical analysis to make a difference conceptually. For example it remains unclear how Minsky's analysis of US post war finance could frame our understanding of financialization. It is striking that most authors using Minsky usually abstract from Minsky's historical account of US post war finance to focus on his general schema of financial crisis (i.e. the more theoretical and portable aspect of his work). Wray, for example, discounts this analysis by collapsing financialization into a simple return to money manager capitalism which "restored conditions similar to those that existed in the run up to the Great Depression with a similar outcome" (Wray 2011: 7) as if nothing was fundamentally new. As a result, despite all its empirical richness, this body of work has often struggled to highlight what is distinctive about financialization.

A second perspective that focuses on historical patterns is loosely associated with the world systems approach. By contrast to the more economic focus of Minsky, this approach is concerned with the political and social implications of financial developments and draws from a broader vista to focus on the relationship between the rise and fall of great powers and its relationship to financial patterns of development (Braudel 1982; Germain 1997; Langley 2002; Wallerstein 2004).

One author who stands out in this tradition is Giovanni Arrighi who followed Fernand Braudel in making the argument that periods of financial expansion should be conceived as the twilight in a cycle of hegemony. They usually take place in dominant economic centres and announce their subsequent decline. To explain this pattern, Arrighi invokes the role of power relations and the way they underpin financialization. The cycle proceeds in three steps. Emerging economies initially rise in the world economy's hierarchy on the back of their competitive production. But when increased competition in the global economy becomes intense, making it harder for capitalists to do well at the level of production, powerful capitalists tend to move their money from production into speculative financial markets in search of higher profits (Arrighi 1994: 2003). For dominant economic centres where commerce flows, it is then tempting to exploit their position in the global economy as a taxing mechanism, using financial flows as a means to extract wealth from others. But what is advantageous in the short term proves to be detrimental in the long turn. Focusing on finance rather than production, their own economy becomes more fragile and less competitive. Coasting on the labour of others, they become increasingly dependent and sow the seeds of their decline.

Arrighi is part of a distinct scholarly tradition which casts financialization as a product of power because financialization can only be sustained on the back of significant economic imbalances. Here the emphasis differs significantly from Minsky who traces financial expansion and speculative investments back to the optimistic expectations of profitability in the real economy. By contrast, Arrighi sees financial expansion as a means for some privileged agents to compensate for difficulties in the material economy.

From this perspective, financialization has been framed as the last phase in a cycle of US hegemony. As many other authors (Hudson 2003; Gowan 1999; Panitch and Gindin 2012), Arrighi highlights the important role of the dollar in establishing power relations that have allowed the US to maintain the commercial imbalances that fuelled its financial expansion. As the dominant currency of the post war era, the US dollar has enabled this country to freely issue money to cover for trade imbalances. This resulted in a surplus of dollars accumulating in foreign countries which ended up being re-invested on US financial markets thus fuelling their speculative growth from the 1980s onwards (Krippner 2011). Starting with the "monetarist counterrevolution of 1979–1982" which pushed interest rates high up, Arrighi argues, the US successfully established itself as the centre of power rerouting capital flows towards the US where investors hope to benefit from high interests (2003: 50ff).

The theme of economic imbalances at the international level supporting the ability of the US to sustain stock market and housing bubbles is explored by a wide range of authors. Coming from a variety of theoretical traditions, they are in no way reducible to a world systems approach. However, they shed light on the same aspect of financialization: the relationships of power at the global level that have contributed in fuelling a generalized reliance on finance anchored in US financial markets (Schwartz 2008). However, this focus on global imbalances, as the key to the logic of this cycle, has again diverted the attention away from the specific origins of the practices generating financialization (for an insightful exception see Konings 2008). The focus on international flows may thus downplay the importance of financialization as a process. As Krippner points out, Arrighi "explains financialization as resulting from intensified intercapitalist and interstate competition" but does not establish "the existence of financialization" and what it means for the nature of the economy (Krippner 2005: 174).

A third approach which uses knowledge about historical patterns to conceptualize financialization has emerged from the comparative literature on finance that is influenced by what could be labelled historical institutionalism. In contrast to the world systems' focus on global power interplays, this literature emphasises the national level and the financial patterns that emerge from domestic institutions. To frame its analysis, this literature has commonly used the contrast between two broad ideal types of finance: an Anglo-Saxon model based on liberalism and freer markets and a continental model based on coordinated forms of finance where the state and banks play a key role in orchestrating development by allocating capital to the desired sectors of the economy.

Particularly influential here has been the work of Alexander Gerschenkron (1979) who highlighted the propensity of Anglo-Saxon countries towards speculation. He associated this feature with liberalism and the freedom given in these countries to financial intermediaries to invest where they wish to. From this perspective, financiers tend to gravitate towards speculative investments that bring big and fast rewards (even if this is more risky) but often undermine production in the process because the latter requires long-term commitments that are difficult for financiers to control. Gerschenkron explained Britain's liberalism as a result of its economic dominance. With limited competition from other countries, the British state had few incentives to get involved and to actively support the economy. By contrast, economies trying to catch up struggled to find capital and entrepreneurial leadership. As a result, states or banks were needed for these countries to compensate such shortcomings.

This idea has since been fleshed out by a wide range of authors (Zysman 1983; Vitols 2004). It is indeed a common theme in the literature that casts financialization as the product of a liberalization of finance opening the door for Anglo-Saxon (and speculative) practices to generalize themselves internationally. This process is often seen to represent a response to the crisis of the 1970s when economic stagnation fuelled a desire to liberalize the economy. With the removal of the constraints previously placed on finance, numerous economies would thus have witnessed Anglo-Saxon patterns of financial speculation. For these scholars, the "heart of the issue is whether the continental, consensus-oriented model of capitalism is gravitating towards the Anglo-Saxon, market-oriented model" (Lütz 2000: 149; cf. Hardie et al. 2013).

This comparative angle has been useful to reflect on specific trajectories of finance. But once more, the reliance on a recurrent pattern of historical development often led scholars to assimilate financialization to a pre-given ideal type. Instead of using comparative methods to contrast different trajectories of financial developments since the 1980s, this comparativist framework often became a means to reduce financialization to a variation on the Anglo-Saxon model of financial development. While there is much work in this tradition emphasising hybrid practices that reflect the perpetuation of domestic path-dependent institutions and practices (Deeg 2012), it has proven difficult to grasp financialization on its own term. Scholars too often end up with a conceptually fuzzy notion of a hybrid society "in-between" two models, neither of which seemed to capture well financialization.

The final perspective based on history has developed a different strategy to conceptualize financialization. Instead of looking at historical patterns to frame its analysis of finance, these scholars have sought to periodize financial developments. This has yielded a more productive framework to think about the specificity of financialization. By delineating different eras of capitalist development, scholars who rely upon it have been able to reflect more directly on the traits that demarcate financialization from previous regimes of accumulation. These accounts have usually borrowed from the classic tripartite periodization often found in political economy which frames the history of western capitalism in three broad periods: Liberalism in the nineteenth century, Fordism/Keynesianism in the post war era and neoliberalism starting in the late 1970s/1980. For this reason, this approach tends to examine the intricate relationship between neoliberalism, as a regime of governance, and financialization.

Of particular importance here has been the regulation school. It was among the first to reflect on the societal implications of the financial transformations of the 1990s and to look for a distinct systemic logic of accumulation behind them. With the sustained rise of the stock market in the 1990s, authors such as Robert Boyer (2000) and Michel Aglietta (2000) began to examine whether financial markets could become the engine that fuels economic growth. What struck them was the fact that speculative bubbles seemed to produce a wealth effect that might generate the demand needed to sustain economic growth. In particular, the sustained increases in the value of shares made it possible for shareholders to cash in their gains and finance further purchases (a dynamic which also played out in the 2000s with the rise of house prices). Were financial markets replacing the role previously carried out by Keynesian policy in sustaining demand? Following in these footsteps, numerous authors have thus become interested in private Keynesianism and more generally debt, as a motor of economic growth and whether this was sustainable (or not) (Brenner 2006; Montgomerie 2006; Crouch 2011).

While there is a considerable variety within this literature, the common feature that characterizes it is the desire to identify new patterns at the level of large economic aggregates that can establish the societal features of financialization. This has been developed in various directions either to highlight the distinct sources of capital accumulation (Duménil and Lévy 2004; 2011; Krippner 2005), or the ways in which financial priorities are entrenched in public and corporate governance, for example with the rise of shareholder value (Lazonick and O'Sullivan 2000; see Erturk, in this volume).

This focus on periodization has provided a neat conceptual framework to capture the rupture that financialization represents. Questions about the sources of aggregate demand or the ability of the stock market to power the economy are certainly of great significance to assess the transformative power of finance. However, this framing poses various problems for historical analysis. By exaggerating the coherency of each period, it often leads to functional accounts where everything seems to be well-coordinated. A concern with the reproduction of macro processes may help account for why a certain configuration remains stable over a defined period of time, but it makes it difficult to account for change or divergent trajectories. Furthermore, this approach tends to project what happens in a specific country, often the United States, onto others as if all national economies are going through the same motions. Finally, and more importantly, it has led scholars to think of financialization *at an aggregate level*. As a result, regulation school scholars often abstract from concrete financial practices in their conceptualizations of financialization in order to characterize the economy as a whole. In contrast, our next section will outline a different approach that builds more explicitly from financial practices (see also Chiapello, in this volume). Specifically, we will show how a focus on liability management (LM) can provide a useful historical framing for the analyses of financialization.

A Radical Historicist Perspective on Financialization

Whereas economics usually reduces history to a set of evidence we can use to test our theories, much of the literature on financialization has turned to history as a means to gain perspective. Yet too often, we have argued, the desire for a concept that fits a wide variety of cases and practices has led to highly abstract concepts that hinder historical research. Taking this problem into consideration, our main aim in defining financialization as a concept is not simply to provide an "accurate representation" of a historical transformation, but to frame the analysis in a sufficiently precise way so that we can think more clearly about it. This requires that we be specific about the practices involved in order to discriminate among different financial developments and put some of them "outside of the frame."

To move in this direction, we develop a radical historicist approach. This approach is based on the idea that theorization and conceptualization should be based on the work of historicization. Instead of relying on abstract heuristics and ontologies that are first defined in generic terms and then confronted to history, we use comparative analysis as a means to specify concepts by identifying what is distinctive about a given phenomenon. The more precise the object of analysis, the easier it is to develop rich comparisons that are insightful theoretically. In particular, clarity about the social practices involved enables us to compare more precisely a specific development with what existed previously and with other similar phenomena that can be found in other places.

One of the hypotheses that has been explored recently from such a perspective is that the trigger for financialization is related to the development of liability management (LM) (Knafo 2014; Beck 2019; Dutta 2019). LM represents a new practice developed by New York commercial banks to finance themselves. Instead of relying on their own capital or deposits, which accumulated at a relatively slow pace, they began to actively seek short-term loans on money markets in order to raise funds at a much greater and variable pace. Depending on their needs, they could dramatically increase in this way the funds at their disposal.

The impact of this practice on financial markets took place, we argue, in three stages. The origins of LM can be traced back to the 1960s when this practice was born as an emergency expedient in response to a funding crisis. US commercial banks then came under pressure because corporations began to systematically withdraw their cash deposited with commercial banks in order to invest these sums themselves on financial markets. At the time, commercial banks were unable to raise their interest rates to attract deposits because regulation Q capped the rate they were allowed to offer. Facing a funding crisis, some banks decided to borrow the funds they suddenly needed to finance their operations. They did so by tapping money markets through the issue of certificates of deposits (CDs), a short-term commitment to pay back a certain sum plus interest at a fixed date (Stigum 1983). What was initially a pragmatic solution to deal with a crisis soon proved to be a highly attractive practice that offered great flexibility for commercial banks keen to expand rapidly. It opened the door for banks to systematically rely on financial markets to fund their own operations

While a wide variety of scholars has commented on these certificates of deposits, and the rise of LM (Battilossi 2002; Schenk 2002), no one has tried to think systematically about their implications for our conception of financialization. Usually, LM is treated as a prelude for the real financial explosion of the 1980s. Its significance is then limited to that of a process that undermined the regulatory structure of financial governance in the US and led to the dismantlement of the Glass-Steagall system (see for example, Wray 2011 or Konings 2011). In other words, scholars too often refer to its destructive impact, but miss its vital role in reshaping the practices of global finance.

Here a historical perspective can offer profound insights. Before the advent of this practice, the trajectory of banking was dominated by the rise of deposit banking. Since the mid-nineteenth century, banks had been competing among themselves in order to build large reserves of deposits that could finance their operations. This focus on deposit banking reflected the relatively cheap and stable nature of these funds for banks and the large pool they provided for financing bank growth. In this context, LM would have appeared as a counterintuitive strategy. Raising money on money markets was expensive because it involved dealing with savvy investors who would ask for higher yields. It was also too risky since conditions on these markets can change suddenly.

142

Deposits by contrast represented a relatively secure strategy to get funding so that banks could primarily focus on what they cared for most: making profitable investments. This is why money markets were rarely used to finance banks. Instead they were employed by them to manage their short-term imbalances.

This all changed in the 1960s with the rise of LM. There was a growing sense then that the active management of liabilities could be as vital as strategies of investment. This meant multiplying the options for raising money, looking for different sources of funds and using different financial instruments, so as to make it easier to shift from one strategy to the next depending on the context. While it was a costly strategy to raise money, at least initially, the flexibility it provided would prove decisive in various corporate struggles. For example, it made it easy to raise money on a large scale by offering investors better terms than what other financial institutions, subject to tougher regulatory constraints, could offer. In this way, commercial banks were able to get the money where it was (notably tapping into the Euromarkets) by simply designing securities that would appeal to various classes of investors. In particular, LM was used by banks to circumvent the regulations of Glass Steagall and they exploited this freedom to prey on other parts of the financial system time and time again.

The second phase of financialization came in the 1970s when the growing reliance of banks on LM transformed the relationship between commercial banks and money markets. As we pointed out, this part of the financial system had previously served to manage the imbalances of banks and was home mostly to specialized discount houses and security traders. However, as banks started financing themselves more systematically on money markets, they attracted a wide array of investors, most notably institutional funds. This fuelled the incredible growth of these money markets. Particularly important was the emergence of money market funds. By pooling the money of small investors into funds, these funds enabled savers to invest in assets such as certificates of deposits and Treasury bills which had been previously reserved for bigger investors because of their high denominations. This dramatically increased the money available on money markets and thus the possibility for financial actors to finance their operations in this way.

The final phase in the rise of financialization took place in the 1980s. This is the period often seen as the key turning point. Its main feature, we argue, was not deregulation contrary to what is often believed. While the deregulation that marked this era was certainly significant, scholars too often miss the fact that deregulation was partly the product of an already changing financial system which left no choice for the American state but to adjust to banking practices that profoundly challenged its old paradigm of governance. Instead, we argue that the dominant feature of this decade was the realignment of capital markets with the rise of LM as investment banks began to take advantage, or simply respond, to the radical transformations of money markets. While the 1960s had witnessed the development of LM by commercial banks, the 1980s was marked by the attempts of investment banks to negotiate their own turn towards LM in order to take advantage of the new opportunities it offered.

Historically, the relationship of capital markets to money markets has been somewhat limited. Since money markets involved short-term lending they were risky for capital markets.[1] Investing in shares or bonds required long-term commitments which were too risky for money market financing. While security dealers did rely on call markets, they mostly did so to support their role as market makers and were expected to use their knowledge of the market to dispose rapidly of assets they purchased. Money markets were then used for short-term strategies with small margins, and were thus usually shunned by the biggest players on Wall Street (Meyers 1993).

The rise of LM and money market funds changed this in two important ways. First, the money market funds set out a different business model that could mobilize the resources that traditionally went to deposit banks and redirect them towards capital markets. The principle of a money market fund was to find assets with sufficiently high yields so as to offer promising returns to investors yet in a liquid form that resembled deposits. Buying treasury bills or certificates of deposits with higher interests made it possible to offer depositors better terms than what they could get from a savings account in a bank. Having learned to pool deposits in this manner, there was no reason to stop with short-term securities. The more promising cash flow of long-term debt, or riskier debt, proved highly attractive and helped channel resources onto capital markets. It is a principle that got spun off to reconfigure long-term lending in dramatic ways with the development of securitization and the use of derivatives. The practice became particularly attractive for investment banks because of their ability to use them to make risky investments while shifting much of the risks onto less savvy investors.

Second, the money markets offered the necessary means to negotiate this turn. For this required much more capital than what investment banks had at their disposal. Indeed, the work to produce attractive cash flows on the basis of pooling securities was a practice that was capital intensive. Investment banks, which became initially involved for example with securitization, had to hold onto assets for relatively longer periods of time in order to transform them into attractive securities. For this purpose, the resources of money markets became important to both purchase loans/assets for securitization and to help sell securities on credit to institutional funds or financial actors, such as Saving & Loans firms. The problem was particularly acute for investment banks because they had relatively little capital to rely on, by contrast to commercial banks, and thus had to find ways to raise money without placing too much stress on their reserves of capital. Investment banks thus turned to the dramatically expanding infrastructure of money markets to finance their operations.

This quick outline of a different history of financialization illustrates the use of starting from a more specific and concrete concept of financialization based on a specific financial practice. Thinking about financialization as a product of the rise and diffusion of LM allows to explore much more concretely the specific nature and implications of financialization. It is much easier to be precise about these processes when the referent is a simple practice instead of a wide set of social relations that confines us to generic claims about finance. As we have shown by comparing LM with modern deposit banking, one can get a rich conceptual account of financialization which helps us think not only about the distinctive nature of this development, but also about the concrete transformations of financialization itself as a process.

Many scholars may think that the downside for this precision is a poorer concept that only speaks to a narrow set of phenomena. This is why scholars are often resistant to think of macro social processes from the perspective of specific practices. Yet the value of starting from a specific practice is precisely that it *cannot account for the history that it frames*. Instead, it helps to specify what needs to be accounted for historically. It forces us to track the work that social agents had to do for this practice to be translated to different fields. In other words, the point of this conceptualization is to help structure our engagement with history, not to provide an explanation to account for it. LM is not an abstract ideal type that captures the essence of developments under financialization. Nor is it a substitute for history that explains in itself the transformation of money markets or investment banks. Instead, the purpose of a concept (or a theory) is to serve as a framing device to put history into perspective. This allows us to reflect on different developments we associate with financialization and how they are connected. By helping us understand how this practice opened new opportunities or forms of agency, we can analyse how it radically transformed the field of possibilities.

Conclusion: Towards a Historicist approach to Financialization

This chapter has reflected on the uses of history when analysing financialization. As we argued, historical perspectives on financialization have helped us reflect on what is at stake in the processes of financialization. Yet, too often they abstract from concrete financial practice when they conceptualize financialization. This results in concepts that entertain an indeterminate relationship towards history. Not only is it difficult to use them to make decisions about the historical evidence we confront, but they also make it difficult to determine how our research can impact our theories because our concepts are too vague and fit pretty much everything.

By contrast, we have argued that the distinctive features of financialization are rooted in a profound transformation of the way in which financial agents fund their operations allowing them to transcend limits of what previously seemed possible. In particular, the rise of liability management has led to a much more active and dynamic approach to liabilities which has fuelled a dramatic increase in leveraging among banks. The focus of financial institutions on issuing securities as a means to finance their own operations, rather than serving other economic agents, marks a radical departure that has profoundly inflected the workings of financial markets. It helped propel US finance and radically transform finance in other parts of the world. This suggests that financialization is largely the story of how finance started to revolve increasingly around money markets as a channel for financial actors to finance their operations. By exploring how new practices of funding tied to LM are connected historically to various phenomena associated with financialization, such as the explosion of debt, the revolution in over the counter derivatives, or the rise of corporate raiders, this approach promises a more organic understanding of financialization built on a precise account of the practices involved and the way they were mobilized to change society.

Note

1 Banks involved on capital markets historically focused on issuing securities which, while risky, involved a one-off moment that could be better controlled by banks at the time.

Bibliography

Aglietta, M., 2000. Shareholder Value and Corporate Governance: Some Tricky Questions. *Economy and Society*, 29(1), pp. 146–159.
Arrighi, G., 1994. *The Long Twentieth Century: Money, Power and the Origins of Our Times*. New York: Verso.
Arrighi, G., 2003. The Social and Political Economy of Global Turbulence. *New Left Review*, 20, pp. 5–71.
Battilossi, S., 2002. Banking with Multinationals: British Clearing Banks and the Euromarkets' Challenge, 1958–1976. In: S. Battilossi & Y. Cassis (eds.), *European Banks and the American Challenge: Competition and Cooperation in International Banking Under Bretton Woods*. Oxford: Oxford University Press, pp. 103–134.
Beck, M., 2019. *German Banking and the Rise of Financial Capitalism. A Case of Extraverted Financialisation*. PhD Dissertation. University of Sussex.
Boyer, R., 2000. Is a Finance-led Growth Regime a Viable Alternative to Fordism? A Preliminary Analysis. *Economy and Society*, 29(1), pp. 111–145.
Braudel, F., 1982. *Civilization and Capitalism, 15th-18th Century* (Vols I–III). Berkeley: University of California Press.
Brenner, R., 2006. *The Economics of Global Turbulence: The Advanced Capitalist Economies from Long Boom to Long Downturn, 1945–2005*. Verso.
Cain, P.J., & Hopkins, A.G., 2001. *British Imperialism: 1688–2000*. New York: Longman.
Crouch, C., 2011. *The Strange Non-Death of Neo-Liberalism*. Cambridge: Polity Press.
Deeg, R., 2012. Financialisation and Models of Capitalism: A Comparison of the UK and Germany. In: G. Wood and C. Lane (eds.), *Capitalist Diversity and Diversity within Capitalism*. London: Routledge, pp. 121–149.
Duménil, G., & Lévy, D., 2004. *Capital Resurgent: Roots of the Neoliberal Revolution*. Cambridge, MA: Harvard University Press.
Duménil, G., & Lévy, D., 2011. *The Crisis of Neoliberalism*. Harvard University Press.
Dutta, S.J., 2019. Sovereign Debt Management and the Transformation from Keynesian to Neoliberal Monetary Governance in Britain. *New Political Economy*. Published Online Ahead of Print: 11/06/2019. https://doi.org/10.1080/13563467.2019.1680961.

Elbaum, B., & Lazonick, W., 1986. *The Decline of the British Economy*. London: Clarendon Press.

Engelen, E., 2008. The Case for Financialization. *Competition & Change*, 12(2), pp. 111–119.

Epstein, G.A., 2005. *Financialization and the World Economy*. Cheltenham: Edward Elgar Publishing.

Germain R.G., 1997. *The International Organization of Credit: States and Global Finance in the World Economy*. Cambridge: Cambridge University Press.

Gerschenkron, A., 1979. *Economic Backwardness in Historical Perspective: A Book of Essays*. Cambridge, MA: Belknap Press.

Gowan P., 1999. *The Global Gamble: Washington's Faustian Bid for World Dominance*. London: Verso.

Hardie, I., Howarth, D., Maxfield, S., & Verdun, A., 2013. Banks and the False Dichotomy in the Comparative Political Economy of Finance. *World Politics*, 65(4), pp. 691–728.

Hudson, M., 2003. *Super Imperialism: The Origins and Fundamentals of U.S. World Dominance*. London: Pluto Press.

Kindleberger, C.P., 2000. *Manias, Panics, and Crashes: A History of Financial Crises* (4th ed.). New York: Wiley.

Knafo, S., 2014. Financial Crises and the Political Economy of Speculative Bubbles. *Critical Sociology*, 39 (6), pp. 851–867.

Konings, M., 2008. The Institutional Foundations of US Structural Power in International Finance: From the Re-Emergence of Global Finance to the Monetarist Turn. *Review of International Political Economy*, 15(1), pp. 35–61.

Konings, M., 2011. *The Development of American Finance*. Cambridge: Cambridge University Press.

Krippner, G., 2011. *Capitalizing on the Crisis: The Political Origins of the Rise of Finance*. London:Harvard University Press.

Krippner, G. R., 2005. The Financialization of the American Economy. *Socio-Economic Review*, 3(2), pp. 173–208.

Langley, P., 2002. *World Financial Orders: An Historical International Political Economy*. London and New York: Routledge.

Lazonick, W., & O'Sullivan, M., 2000. Maximizing Shareholder Value: A New Ideology for Corporate Governance. *Economy and Society*, 29(1), pp. 13–35.

Lütz, S., 2000. From Managed to Market Capitalism? German Finance in Transition. *German Politics*, 9(2), pp. 149–170.

Meyers, M., 1993. *Nightmare on Wall Street: Salomon Brothers and the Corruption of the Marketplace*. New York: Simon Schuster.

Minsky, H. P., 1982. The Financial-instability Hypothesis: Capitalist Processes and the Behavior of the Economy. In: C.P. Kindleberger, & J.-P. Laffargue (eds.), *Financial Crises. Theory, History and Policy*. New York: Cambridge University Press, pp. 13–39.

Montgomerie, J., 2006. The Financialization of the American Credit Card Industry. *Competition & Change*, 10(3), pp. 301–319.

Nesvetailova, A., 2007. *Fragile Finance: Debt, Speculation and Crisis in the Age of Global Credit*. Basingstoke: Palgrave Macmillan.

Panitch, L., & Gindin, S., 2012. *The Making of Global Capitalism: The Political Economy of American Empire*. London: Verso.

Reinhart, C.M., & Rogoff, K.S., 2009. *This Time is Different: Eight Centuries of Financial Folly*. Princeton, NJ: Princeton University Press.

Schenk, C., 2002. International Financial Centres 1958–1971: Competitiveness and Complementarity. In: S. Battilossi, & Y. Cassis (eds.), *European Banks and the American Challenge: Competition and Cooperation in International Banking Under Bretton Woods*. Oxford: Oxford University Press, pp. 74–102.

Schwartz, H., 2008. Housing, Global Finance, and American Hegemony: Building Conservative Politics One Brick at a Time. *Comparative European Politics*, 6(3), pp. 262–284.

Stigum, M.L., 1983. *The Money Market*. Homewood, IL: Dow Jones-Irwin.

Van der Zwan, N., 2014. Making Sense of Financialization. *Socio-Economic Review*, 12(1), pp. 99–129.

Vitols, S., 2004. From Banks to Markets: The Political Economy of Liberalization of the German and Japanese Financial Systems. In: W. Streeck, & K. Yamamura (eds.), *The End of Diversity: Prospects for German and Japanese Capitalism*. Ithaca, NY: Cornell University Press, pp. 240–260.

Wallerstein, I.M., 2004. *World-Systems Analysis: An Introduction*. Durham: Duke University Press.

Wray, L.R., 2011. Minsky's Money Manager Capitalism and the Global Financial Crisis. *International Journal of Political Economy*, 40(2), pp. 5–20.

Zysman, J., 1983. *Governments, Markets and Growth: Financial Systems and the Politics of Industrial Change*. Ithaca: Cornell University Press.

PART C

Structures, Spaces and Sites of Financialization

13

FINANCIALIZATION AND DEMAND REGIMES IN ADVANCED ECONOMIES[1]

Engelbert Stockhammer and Karsten Kohler

Introduction

Post-Keynesian economics (PKE) has long been concerned with the macroeconomic outcomes of financialization. On a theoretical level, there has been a debate under what conditions financialization can have expansionary effects on aggregate demand (Boyer 2000; Dutt 2006; Skott and Ryoo 2008). Empirical research on financialization has demonstrated negative effects on firm investment (Orhangazi 2008; Tori and Onaran 2018) and functional income distribution (Dünhaupt 2016; Kohler et al. 2019), but expansionary effects of household debt on consumption and of property prices on investment (Kim et al. 2015; Stockhammer and Wildauer 2016). Post-Keynesians have also developed a typology of macroeconomic regimes allowing for cross-country comparative analysis. They distinguish wage-led and profit-led (Bhaduri and Marglin 1990; Lavoie and Stockhammer 2013), as well as export-driven and debt-driven demand regimes (Hein 2013; Stockhammer 2016).

In this article, we adopt a Post-Keynesian (PK) approach to examine how different degrees of the financialization of households in the decade prior to the Great Financial Crisis (GFC) fostered the development of distinct demand regimes. Second, we analyze the interdependence and sustainability of these demand regimes. Lastly, we assess if the regime configuration that prevailed before the crisis has undergone changes in the post-crisis period. Our focus is on advanced countries, in particular Europe and the USA. We argue that in the Anglo-Saxon and southern European countries, financialization contributed to the development of a debt-driven demand regime, in which mortgage securitization and capital inflows facilitated property price inflation. The latter led to a boom in residential investment, rising household debt, and ultimately large current account deficits. Macroeconomic dynamics in eastern Europe were shaped by catching-up through foreign direct investment from northern Europe with worsening current account positions. Northern Europe, in contrast, relied on an export-driven demand regime with a weaker role for domestic financialization. The export-driven demand regime relies on the financialization of southern Europe and the Anglo-Saxon countries, which helped create export demand for northern Europe. We find that this configuration of demand regimes gives rise to divergent economic performance and macroeconomic instability. Despite some deleveraging in the Anglo-Saxon and southern Europe countries at the downturn of the financial cycle, the configuration that has contributed to the crisis has not fundamentally changed.

While the basic macroeconomic mechanisms that underpin export- and debt-driven demand regimes have been in place for a long time, we believe that the institutional configurations that allowed for the development of distinct export- and debt-driven demand have only been created since the 1980s. A key institutional pre-condition for the development of these interdependent regimes is the liberalization of international capital flows, which in Europe took the form of European Monetary Union. This allowed credit booms and trade imbalances to amplify and thus for the emergence of strong and persistent export and debt-driven demand episodes.

The article is structured as follows: the second section briefly introduces the post-Keynesian concept of demand regimes. The third section examines how different forms of financialization gave rise to different demand regimes in advanced economies. The fourth section compares the PK analysis to International Political Economy (IPE) and Varieties of Capitalism (VoC) approaches to the euro crisis. The last section concludes.

Demand Regimes

The concept of effective demand is the unifying theme for PKE (see also Dow, in this volume). In a situation of involuntary unemployment the level of effective demand will determine the level of output. In its analysis of demand regimes, PKE has highlighted the effect of changes in income distribution on effective demand through the distinction of wage-led vs. profit-led demand regimes (Bhaduri and Marglin 1990; Lavoie and Stockhammer 2013). If the expansionary effect of a rise in the wage share on consumption outweighs the negative effects on investment and net exports, the demand regime is called wage led, but if the net effect on aggregate demand is negative, it is profit-led. Empirical research on wage-led vs. profit-led demand regimes tends to find more evidence for wage-led than profit-led demand regimes, but generally concludes that the distributional effects on aggregate demand are rather modest (Hein 2014: 300–307).

Consequently, post-Keynesians have identified two additional growth models that have been empirically fruitful to analyze economic trajectories under neoliberal capitalism: debt-driven and export-driven growth (Hein 2013; Stockhammer 2016). As financialization involved rising levels of private debt due to financial innovations and easier access to credit, the possibility of a debt-driven demand regime has been analyzed by post-Keynesians from a macroeconomic point of view (Boyer 2000; Dutt 2006; Skott and Ryoo 2008). Expansionary effects on consumption can arise if the recipients of financial incomes have a comparatively high propensity to consume or if asset price inflation leads to wealth effects on consumption demand. On the other hand, financialization may have contractionary effects on consumption if rentiers have a lower propensity to consume than debtors, and if financialization redistributes income from workers to firms with a higher propensity to save. Rising property prices can have expansionary effects on residential investment through wealth effects. Contractionary effects on business investment may result from a loss of means of internal finance due to rising financial payouts or from a shift from real accumulation toward financial accumulation. In an empirical study, Stockhammer and Wildauer (2016) find positive effects of household debt on consumption, and of property prices on total investment. Regarding the effects of financial payments and financial income of non-financial corporations' investment decisions, the empirical literature mostly finds contractionary effects (Orhangazi 2008; Tori and Onaran 2017). If that is correct, a debt-driven regime would require that the expansionary effects on consumption and residential investment outweigh the contractionary effects on non-residential investment.

While the possibility of an export-driven demand regime is economically straightforward, its link to financialization may not be obvious. Post-Keynesians have argued that financial liberalization (for instance in the context of European integration) facilitates the development of an export-driven demand regime for competitive economies, as it eases the access of deficit countries to foreign credit (Storm and Naastepad 2015). Moreover, empirical research shows that export-driven demand regimes exhibit weak correlation with several dimensions of domestic financialization such as corporate leverage and the size of the financial sector (Karwowski et al. 2017). This suggests that export-driven regimes are domestically only weakly financialized themselves but rely on the financialization of their trading partners.

Importantly, debt-driven and export-driven demand regimes are interdependent. As the debt-driven model involves significant gross and net capital inflows that stimulate asset price inflation, domestic credit growth, and import demand, it effectively constitutes the mirror image of the export-driven demand regime, which relies on the debt-financed trade deficits of other countries. Thus, both debt- and export-driven demand regimes allow for growth but are intrinsically unstable, because they require increasing debt-to-income ratios. In the case of the debt-driven model it involves domestic private debt; in the case of the export-driven model it requires foreign debt of the trade partners.

Financialization and Demand Regimes

Financialization

Financialization is often measured by the size (Brown et al. 2017) or profitability (Krippner 2005) of the financial sector. However, cross-country studies (Karwowski et al. 2017) have shown that financialization has several dimensions and does not affect all economic sectors equally. Due to its multidimensionality, it cannot be reduced to measures that are related to the financial sector only. For instance, Karwowski et al. (2017) show that the category of market-based (as opposed to bank-based) financial systems, that is often used in the VoC literature as a measure of financialization, is correlated only with the financialization of firms, but not households. In contrast, we argue that it was precisely the financialization of households that has played the key role in determining demand regimes in the decade prior to the GFC. Domestic credit (and especially its growth in recent years) has been driven by mortgage credit, not credit to businesses. Thus, disregarding the financialization of households can be misleading when assessing country-specific financialization dynamics. In particular, the financialization of southern Europe is understated when focusing only on measures for the size or profitability of the financial sector (e.g. see Table 2 in Brown et al. 2017, where the financialization trends of most southern European countries are classified as stable or moderate).

We are specifically concerned with the impact of financialization on demand formation and the extent to which it has allowed for a debt-driven model. Thus, our analysis of financialization focuses on household debt and property prices.[2] We will measure this by the debt-to-net disposable income ratio for households and by real property prices (i.e. property prices relative to consumer prices). We argue that the debt-driven demand regime is intimately linked with the export-driven model via trade- and capital flows from the export-driven to the debt-driven countries. To measure the extent to which a country is export-driven, we use the current account-to-GDP ratio.

Following Stockhammer et al. (2016), we group advanced economies into northern Europe, southern Europe, the Anglo-Saxon countries, and eastern Europe. The country groupings are based on our explanation of the demand regimes in the decade before the GFC. We choose a few representative countries for each group. Northern Europe will be Germany, Austria, and the Netherlands. These are countries of the Germanic block within the Euro area. They all follow an export-driven model with limited domestic financialization (with the exception of the Netherlands, where household debt grew fast). Southern Europe will consist of Greece, Ireland, Italy, Portugal,[3] and Spain. These are the peripheral countries within the Euro area that were hit hard by the crisis (often called the GIIPS countries). We argue that these are debt-driven demand regimes that are strongly shaped by financialization. We further analyze the Anglo-Saxon countries USA and the United Kingdom that also exhibit the characteristics of debt-driven regimes but with some specificities that separate them from southern Europe. Lastly, the eastern European group consists of Poland, the Czech Republic, Slovakia, Hungary, and Slovenia. These are post-communist economies that have undergone a foreign direct investment (FDI)-based catching-up process after opening up to the West in the 1990s.

There are several potential issues. First, the delineation of groups is arbitrary at the border and one could include Scandinavian countries. Within the northern group, the Netherlands is an interesting intermediate case that has elements of an export-driven as well as of a debt-driven economy. Second, as regards the southern group, the question is whether Italy should be included or not. We include it but note that it does not display the characteristics of a debt-driven regime to the same extent as other countries in the group. Moreover, although geographically not part of southern Europe, we include Ireland as it belonged to the group of countries that were at the heart of the European sovereign debt crisis. It is sometimes classified as a liberal market economy by VoC (e.g. Hassel 2014). Amable (2003) classifies Ireland as part Continental European Capitalism, which corresponds to the coordinated model. We argue that it better fits into the southern group as its increase in household debt is much higher than that of the USA and UK, and because it does not dispose of a sovereign currency and is thereby constrained in its monetary autonomy.

Financialization and Demand Regimes in Advanced Economies

We cover the period before the crisis (2000–2008), as well as the post-crisis period (2008–2016). Table 13.1 describes the financialization of households in Europe and the USA, measured by changes in household debt and property prices. In the period before the crisis, household debt as percentage of the net disposable income of households increased by 23.7%-pts in northern Europe, 36.2%-pts in eastern Europe, 47.7%-pts in the Anglo-Saxon countries, and by a staggering 62.2%-pts in southern Europe. Household debt is to a large extent driven by house prices (see Aalbers et al., in this volume). In the pre-crisis period, these grew by 3.3% in real terms in northern Europe, but by considerable 52.9% in southern Europe, and by 60.5% in the Anglo-Saxon countries.

Overall, northern Europe experienced only a weak form of financialization of households in the pre-crisis period, with household debt and asset prices growing at comparatively low rates. An exception is the Netherlands which underwent a surge in household debt and house price inflation. The southern European and Anglo-Saxon countries, in contrast, experienced strong financialization with a marked increase in household debt and house prices. Eastern European countries had an intermediate form of financialization with household debt increasing more than in northern Europe, but less than in the southern and Anglo-Saxon countries.

Looking at the post-crisis period, we observe a strong reduction in household debt of -21.4%-pts and -11.7%-pts in the Anglo-Saxon and southern European countries, respectively. In the northern European countries, household indebtedness fell slightly by -2.9%-pts, while it moderately grew by 4.6% in eastern Europe. The trajectories observed in the Anglo-Saxon and southern European countries are also reflected in house prices which fell by -6.6% and -30.7%, respectively. Eastern Europe experienced declining house prices (-10.2%) despite its increase in

Table 13.1 Changes in the Financialization of Households, 2000–2016

	Δ Household Debt (%GDP)		Real House Prices, Growth (%)	
	2000–2008	2008–2016	2000–2007	2007–2016
Austria	14.4	1.8	-0.3	37.8
Germany	-17.1	-6.0	-12.8	18.2
Netherlands	74.0	-4.4	23.2	-17.8
Mean (northern Europe)	23.7	-29.8	3.3	12.7
Greece+	56.8	31.3	52.4	-43.8
Ireland★+	118.9	-51.9	70.8	-33.1
Italy	27.1	6.6	45.1	-26.1
Portugal	42.1	-11.7	-10.5	-13.8
Spain	66.0	-32.9	106.6	-36.6
Mean (southern Europe)	62.2	-11.7	52.9	-30.7
Czech Republic+~	37.2	9.0		-1.2
Hungary+	59.8	-28.7		-10.9
Poland+#	39.7	12.7		-9.9
Slovakia+	23.7	26.4		-4.7
Slovenia★+	20.5	3.5		-24.5
Mean (eastern Europe)	36.2	4.6		-10.2
United Kingdom	63.2	-18.2	85.7	-5.0
USA	32.3	-24.6	35.2	-8.3
Mean (Anglo-Saxon countries)	47.7	-21.4	60.5	-6.6
Total mean	43.9	-5.8	39.5	-12.0

Sources: OECD. Own calculations.

Notes: Δ denotes change over time. ★ Household debt data only from 2001. + Household debt data only until 2015. ~ House price data only from 2008. # House price data only from 2010. No data on house prices for Eastern European countries between 2000 and 2007.

household debt, indicating that the strong positive link between household debt and house prices that is so characteristic of the financialization era is less tight in these economies. Similarly, northern Europe experienced house price growth (12.7%) despite falling household debt, but at a comparatively moderate rate. However, most notable is the deleveraging of the southern and Anglo-Saxon countries in the post-crisis period, which is characteristic of the downturn phase of a financial cycle.

Table 13.2 summarizes the development of the external sector as captured by the current account balance in relation to GDP. It also provides average real GDP growth, as demand is a key determinant of net exports. In the pre-crisis years, we note a strong current account surplus in northern Europe of about 4.1% of GDP on average, combined with moderate GDP growth of 2.1%. The Netherlands exhibit strong current account surpluses despite a fast growth in household leverage, which suggests that its export performance overcompensated strong domestic demand growth. The Anglo-Saxon, eastern and southern European countries, in

Table 13.2 External Sector and GDP Growth, 2000–2016

	Current Account (%GDP), Average		Real GDP Growth (%), Average	
	2000–2007	2008–2016	2000–2007	2008–2016
Austria	1.7	2.4	2.4	0.7
Germany	2.8	6.8	1.6	1.1
the Netherlands+	7.7	8.1	2.3	0.6
Mean (northern Europe)	4.1	5.8	2.1	0.8
Greece★	-9.8	-6.4	4.0	-3.3
Ireland#	-1.7	-0.1	6.0	2.2
Italy	-0.6	-0.5	1.5	-0.8
Portugal	-9.4	-4.2	1.5	-0.4
Spain	-6.0	-1.7	3.8	0.0
Mean (southern Europe)	-5.5	-2.8	3.4	-0.4
Czech Republic	-4.1	-1.2	4.5	1.3
Hungary	-7.3	1.1	3.8	0.8
Poland+	-4.6	-3.2	4.2	3.2
Slovakia+	-7.2	-2.1	5.7	2.3
Slovenia	-1.7	1.8	4.3	0.2
Mean (eastern Europe)	-5.0	-0.7	4.5	1.6
United Kingdom	-1.9	-3.6	2.8	1.0
USA	-4.7	-2.7	2.7	1.3
Mean (Anglo-Saxon countries)	-3.3	-3.2	2.7	1.2
Total mean	-3.1	-0.4	3.4	0.7
Total standard deviation	4.6	3.9	1.4	1.5

Sources: Current account: AMECO; GDP: OECD. Own calculations.

Notes: ★ Data only from 2002. + Data only from 2004. # Ireland's 2015 GDP growth rate of 25.6% was excluded from the average as it was mostly driven by changes in the residency of several multinational corporations.

contrast, exhibited large current account deficits of -3.3%, -5% and -5.5% of GDP, respectively. In southern Europe, the deficit is clearly linked to strong GDP growth. In the post-crisis period, the qualitative pattern of current account imbalances persists, but the cross-country variance declined somewhat (as indicated by a lower standard deviation of 3.9 compared to 4.6 in the pre-crisis period). This slight decrease in current account imbalances is entirely due to the reduction of current account deficits in southern and eastern Europe. These two groups managed to reduce their deficit to about -2.8% and -0.7% of GDP, respectively, while the northern European economies even increased their current account surplus to about 5.8% of GDP on average. In the southern European countries, this decrease is partly due to the severe decline in import demand in the wake of harsh austerity measures (average GDP growth was -0.4% in the post-crisis period). It is noteworthy that the Anglo-Saxon countries, despite being at the center of the financial crisis in its first years, did not manage to reduce their current account deficits significantly as they realized above average growth rates in the post-crisis period.

Our examination of changes in financialization of households and the external sector suggests that the demand regime of the northern European countries is based on a strong export orientation with weak dynamics of financialization (with the exception of the Netherlands). Stockhammer et al. (2016) further show that the northern European countries maintained a relatively stable share of manufacturing in GDP, while other European economies underwent de-industrialization. Together with comparatively moderate levels of inequality, this configuration creates a stable environment in which long-term finance allows firms to invest in high value-added goods for the export market, while domestic consumption and residential investment play a secondary role. With respect to the post-crisis experience, we note that the northern European countries have reinforced their export orientation. While household indebtedness and property prices are on the rise, the dynamics are quantitatively nowhere near the boom the southern European and Anglo-Saxon countries underwent prior to the crisis.

The southern countries experienced a strong wave of financialization of households with sharply increasing levels of household debt and a property price boom in the period before the crisis. While some authors point to rising inequality as the key driver behind the surge in US household debt (Barba and Pivetti 2009), household indebtedness in southern Europe seems to have been driven by asset price inflation as changes in income inequality were comparatively moderate. The strong growth in asset prices and private credit was partly caused by gross and net portfolio credit flows from northern Europe and the Anglo-Saxon countries (Lane and McQuade 2014; Hale and Obstfeld 2016). The resulting boom in consumption and residential investment was accompanied by large current account deficits. The experience of the southern European countries before the crisis thus fits well into the PK category of debt-driven demand. The post-crisis development was strongly shaped by the deleveraging of households in a context of weak macroeconomic performance due to harsh austerity packages. Due to their membership in the European Monetary Union (EMU), these countries could not resort to quantitative easing to support expansionary fiscal policy (Stockhammer 2016). Moreover, the period prior to the crisis was characterized by a marked de-industrialization (Stockhammer et al. 2016) rendering these economies very vulnerable to adverse shocks to their debt-driven domestic demand model. As a result, house prices collapsed, and aggregate income decreased severely, resulting in a reduction of current account deficits.

The Anglo-Saxon countries exhibit a similar demand regime to the southern European countries but with some noteworthy differences. They have experienced a slightly less pronounced but still remarkable process of financialization, reflected in strong household debt growth coupled with a property price bubble that stimulated private consumption demand and residential investment. The resulting boost to import demand led to a deficit position in the current account. Different from the southern European countries, high levels of inequality in these countries arguably contributed to the surge in household debt, as workers tried to keep up with social consumption norms despite constant or declining real wages. In the post-crisis period, the Anglo-Saxon countries experienced a strong deleveraging of households, even surpassing the development in southern Europe. Property prices dropped as well, though less dramatically than in southern Europe. A remarkable difference in the post-crisis development of the Anglo-Saxon and southern European countries concerns the current account. While the southern countries significantly reduced their deficits, the Anglo-Saxon countries maintained their large deficit position. There are at least two reasons for this phenomenon. First, the Anglo-Saxon countries were more successful in fighting the 2009 recession by means of expansionary fiscal policy supported by accommodative monetary policy. Monetary policy sovereignty is an important pre-requisite for such an approach and constitutes a key difference to the situation of the southern EMU members (Stockhammer 2016). Second, while the Anglo-Saxon countries also underwent de-industrialization prior to the crisis, they maintained their role as global financial centers. This sustained domestic import demand and allowed for a smooth flow of foreign capital financing their external deficits. From a PK perspective, the Anglo-Saxon countries clearly fall into the category of a debt-driven demand regime.

The eastern European countries experienced a medium wave of financialization of households prior to the crisis. While household debt did play a role, it was (with the exception of Hungary) not as marked as in the southern European and Anglo-Saxon countries. The increase in household debt has slowed down in the period after the crisis when property prices fell. The current account deficit significantly improved in the post-crisis period. Overall, the Eastern European countries underwent quite different dynamics compared to the Anglo-Saxon and southern European countries with which they share the current account deficit position. The opening of the financial account in conjunction with the privatization of formerly public enterprises created a boom in foreign ownership. Stockhammer et al. (2016) argue that more important than household debt was a surge in FDI inflows that modernized parts of industry and subsumed them into German commodity chains. A part of these FDI inflows came from northern Europe, where firms were actively outsourcing segments of production to reduce production costs. This process has helped build a competitive productive structure in eastern Europe but went hand in hand with current account deficits prior to the crisis. Thus, while eastern Europe is linked to the export-driven model, it is characterized by a dependent catching up process with some elements of a debt-driven growth process (see Bonizzi et al., in this volume).

Table 13.3 provides a summary of our classification of demand regimes. We conclude that the financialization of households has played a key role for the development of a debt-driven demand regime in southern Europe and the Anglo-Saxon countries. This is due to the strong impact of rising property prices on (residential) investment and of household debt on consumption demand (Stockhammer and Wildauer 2016). The northern European countries with limited financialization of households, on the other hand, were able to deepen their export-driven demand regime with a suppressed role for domestic demand. We argue that these demand regimes are interdependent. The export-driven model relies on debt-financed imports from abroad. The southern European countries received gross portfolio capital inflows (from Anglo-Saxon as well as from northern countries (Hale and Obstfeld 2016)) that pushed asset price inflation and helped finance a boom in consumption, residential investment, and ultimately imports. Lastly, the eastern European countries are dependent on the northern countries as they have become more integrated into international supply chains that are dominated by the latter.

This configuration of demand regimes has fostered divergent economic performance and gives rise to macroeconomic instability. The debt-driven model is intrinsically unstable as it is prone to a domestic debt crisis once the property prices bubble bursts. This is indeed what happened in southern Europe. In countries that can sustain asset prices via quantitative easing and external finance due to their role as financial centers, the bust may be less dramatic. This is what we observe in the Anglo-Saxon countries. However, as these economies were not forced to undertake a fundamental revision of their debt-driven model, another financial crisis may lurk in the near future. For the export-driven northern economies this will have negative feedback effects as they rely on the import demand of their trading partners. Overall, the interrelation of debt- and export-driven demand regimes is an unstable configuration with little prospects for sustainable macroeconomic performance over longer periods.

Interdisciplinary Perspectives: Comparing PKE, IPE, and VoC

How does our PK analysis compare to other strands of political economy research, namely International Political Economy (IPE) and Varieties of Capitalism (VoC) approaches? Within the IPE literature on the euro crisis, there have been some attempts to fuse Marxist inspired analyses of the state and class relations with an economic analysis that draws on Marxist, as well

Table 13.3 Summary of Demand Regimes

Countries	Demand Regime	Key Characteristics			Post-crisis Trajectory
		Financialization	External Sector	Industry and Finance	
Austria, Germany, the Netherlands	Export-driven	Moderate	Current account surpluses	Industrial centres	Reinforcement of export-orientation; moderate financialization of households
Greece, Italy, Ireland, Portugal, Spain,	Debt-driven	Household debt; property price bubble	Current account deficits	De-industrialization	Strong asset price deflation; deleveraging of households; reduction of current account deficit; contractionary fiscal policy
United Kingdom, United States	Debt-driven	Household debt; property price bubble	Current account deficits	Financial centres; de-industrialization	Strong deleveraging of households; asset price deflation; quantitative easing
Czech Republic, Hungary, Poland, Slovakia	Dependent catching up	Financial liberalization; stock market bubble	Current account deficits	FDI-driven industrialization	Strong reduction of current account deficits

as on post-Keynesian arguments. Becker and Jäger (2012) as well as Ryner (2015) offer a contradistinction between export-oriented versus financialized economies similar to ours and, indeed, draw on a similar post-Keynesian literature, while maintaining a Marxist-inspired regulationist framework. Similar to our approach, Heyes et al. (2012) identify export-led growth and finance-led growth as two interdependent accumulation strategies and argue that financialization has led to a weakening of worker's bargaining power through rising indebtedness. Blyth (2016) emphasizes the interdependence of the export-driven northern European and the debt-driven southern group. He points to the unsustainability of the export-driven model, but does not link his analysis to financialization. Finally, a number of contributions have highlighted the importance of household debt for domestic demand formation in Anglo-Saxon countries as opposed to export-oriented regimes (Crouch 2009; Watson 2010), without however analyzing the interaction between the two regimes.

Thus, there is some overlap between IPE and PKE analyses of the decade prior to the crisis, but also differences. While several IPE scholars use the notion of a finance-led growth regime, they fail to analyze the exact channels through which financialization boosts aggregate demand. This is sometimes due to a supply-side focus in Marxist-inspired IPE. Moreover, the macroeconomic interdependence of different demand regimes, while visible in Blyth (2016), has not been fully integrated into the IPE framework, which continues to lack more comprehensive accounts of aggregate demand formation. Overall, however, we see complementarities between PKE and IPE with potential for mutual benefit (Stockhammer and Köhler 2014).

VoC proponents analyze the developments in Europe leading up to the crisis as the result of the interaction of the core countries with coordinated wage bargaining and the peripheral countries with weak bargaining coordination in a fixed exchange rate regime without central (European) fiscal policy (Hall 2014; Johnston et al. 2014; see Nölke 2016 as a survey). Northern countries with coordinated wage bargaining systems were able to maintain competitiveness; southern countries with less coordinated wage bargaining systems experienced a loss of competitiveness. The decline in competitiveness in the periphery is explained as the result of lack of wage restraint in the non-tradeable sectors among which public-sector wages are singled out as the main culprit. Current account imbalances are thereby analyzed as result of cost differences, and there is little concern for financialization.

Recently, some VoC authors have made a step towards a greater consideration of aggregate demand and finance. Baccaro and Pontusson (2016) embrace the PK idea of different demand-driven growth models. They provide an analysis of growth models of four European countries prior to the crisis, but with a stronger focus on export performance than on financialization.

Overall, there are differences in the analytical framework and some agreements as well as some disagreements. While VoC requires internal coherence and external competitiveness for a viable model, we regard the debt-driven and export-driven models as unstable in the longer term. VoC regards labor relations as the key institutional structure that shapes models of capitalism, whereas we highlight that financialization has played a key role in the neoliberal era. Overall, VoC has a strong focus on supply-side factors, albeit in a much richer form than mainstream economics, but has no systematic analysis of demand formation. While recently there have been efforts to move away from the supply-side focus (Baccaro and Pontusson 2016), it remains to be seen whether demand regimes can be integrated into the VoC framework without losing its internal coherence.

Conclusion

This chapter took a macroeconomic perspective by linking financialization to the post-Keynesian notion of demand regimes. First, we argued that the degree to which households are financialized partly determines if countries adopt a debt-driven demand regime or an export-driven demand regime. Examining the decade prior to the crisis (2000–2008), we found that while northern European economies deepened their export-driven model with only moderate financialization, southern and Anglo-Saxon countries developed a debt-driven model with a key role for the financialization of households in the form of household debt and property price inflation. Eastern Europe only experienced a moderate level of financialization, and its economic development was strongly shaped by catching-up through FDI-based industrialization.

Second, we argued that the export-driven and the debt-driven demand regime are intimately linked to each other, but ultimately unstable. The export-driven model relies on debt-financed imports abroad. The debt-driven economies receive capital inflows from the surplus economies financing their boom in consumption, residential investment, and ultimately imports. This configuration of demand regimes in advanced economies has fostered divergent economic performance and gives rise to macroeconomic instability. The debt-driven model is intrinsically unstable as it is prone to a domestic debt crisis once the bubble in property prices bursts. The export-driven model hinges on the macroeconomic performance of its trading partners, which it partly undermines through destabilizing capital flows.

Third, we showed that, the pre-crisis configuration has not fundamentally changed. While the southern and eastern European countries have managed to reduce their current account deficits somewhat, the Anglo-Saxon countries have maintained their deficits and the northern European countries have even increased their surpluses. There has been some deleveraging in the Anglo-Saxon and southern European countries, which was contractionary in southern Europe. This is characteristic of the downturn phase of the financial cycle and illustrates that debt-drivenness can go both ways. Deleveraging thus does not by itself imply a revision of the debt-driven model.

Our approach has some overlap with recent IPE contributions that have highlighted financialization, but we place a stronger focus on demand formation. Moreover, we share the comparative approach of VoC by employing a topology of regimes but highlight the importance of financialization and identify instabilities rather than functional complementarities. The contribution of PKE to the analysis of financialization consists of its macroeconomic framework and its theory of demand regimes. Its relative weakness is its lack of a theory of the state and power relations between political actors. We note the following topics for future research: first, different sectors may experience financialization at different points in time. While we have, looking backward, emphasized the role of household debt, future crisis may center on business debt. Second, the position of countries in the international hierarchy of currencies matters, in financial crisis even more so than during the boom. Third, state policies not only shape institutions that may foster or channel financialization, but they also play a critical role for economic performance through their expenditures, which may stabilize or even constitute demand regimes. Here, different social coalitions and political settlements may result in different uses of the proceeds of a debt-driven boom as well as in different government strategies in the event of crisis. Future research on comparative capitalisms will have to balance the institutional and demand formation analysis.

Notes

1 We would like to thank Daniel Mertens, Brigitte Young and Natascha van der Zwan for helpful comments. All remaining errors are the authors'.
2 While household debt in advanced economies also includes consumer credit, student loans, and loans for medical bills, mortgage debt typically constitutes the lion's share (Zabai 2017: Table 1).
3 Hein (2013) classifies Portugal and Italy as domestic demand-led demand regimes.

Bibliography

Amable, B., 2003. *The Diversity of Modern Capitalism*. Oxford: Oxford University Press.
Baccaro, L. and Pontusson, J., 2016. Rethinking comparative political economy: The growth model perspective. *Politics & Society*, 44(2), pp. 175–207.
Barba, A. and Pivetti, M., 2009. Rising household debt: Its causes and macroeconomic implications – a long-period analysis. *Cambridge Journal of Economics*, 33, pp. 113–137.
Becker, J. and Jäger, J., 2012. Integration in crisis: A regulationist perspective on the interaction of European varieties of capitalism. *Competition and Change*, 16(3), pp. 169–187.
Blyth, M., 2016. Policies to overcome stagnation: The crisis, and the possible futures, of all things euro. *European Journal of Economics and Economic Policies: Intervention*, 13(2), pp. 215–228.
Bhaduri, A. and Marglin, S., 1990. Unemployment and the real wage: The economic basis for contesting political ideologies. *Cambridge Journal of Economics*, 14, pp. 375–393.
Brown, A., Spencer, D.A. and Veronese Passarella, M., 2017. The extent and variegation of financialisation in Europe: A preliminary analysis. *Revista de Economía Mundial*, 46, pp. 49–69.
Boyer, R., 2000. Is a finance-led growth regime a viable alternative to Fordism? A preliminary analysis. *Economy and Society*, 29(1), pp. 111–145.

Crouch, C., 2009. Privatised Keynesianism: An unacknowledged policy regime. *The British Journal of Politics and International Relations*, 11, pp. 382–399.

Dünhaupt, P., 2016. Determinants of labour's income share in the era of financialisation. *Cambridge Journal of Economics*, 41(1), pp. 283–306.

Dutt, A., 2006. Maturity, stagnation and consumer debt: A Steindlian approach. *Metroeconomica*, 57(3), pp. 339–364.

Hall, P., 2014. Varieties of capitalism and the Euro crisis. *West European Politics*, 37(6), pp. 1223–1243.

Hale, G. and Obstfeld, M., 2016. The euro and the geography of international debt flows. *Journal of the European Economic Association*, 14(1), pp. 115–144.

Hassel, A., 2014. Adjustments in the Eurozone: Varieties of capitalism and the crisis in southern Europe. *LEQS Paper No. 76/2014*. Available at: http://www.lse.ac.uk/europeanInstitute/LEQS%20Discussion %20Paper%20Series/LEQSPaper76.pdf [Accessed 13 Jan. 2019].

Hein, E., 2013. The crisis of finance-dominated capitalism in the Euro area, deficiencies in the economic policy architecture, and deflationary stagnation policies. *Journal of Post Keynesian Economics*, 36(2), pp. 325–354.

Hein, E., 2014. *Distribution and Growth after Keynes. A Post-Keynesian Guide*. Cheltenham: Edward Elgar.

Heyes, J., Lewis, P. and Clark, I., 2012. Varieties of capitalism, neoliberalism and the economic crisis of 2008, *Industrial Relations Journal*, 43(3), pp. 222–241.

Johnston, A., Hancké, B. and Pant, S., 2014. Comparative institutional advantage in the European sovereign debt crisis. *Comparative Political Studies*, 47(13), pp. 1771–1800.

Karwowski, E., Shabani, M. and Stockhammer, E., 2017. Financialization: Dimensions and determinants. A cross-country study. *Kingston University Economics Discussion Papers 2017–1*. Available at: https://ep rints.kingston.ac.uk/37295/1/2017_001.pdf [Accessed 13 Jan. 2019].

Kim, Y.K., Setterfield, M. and Mei, Y., 2015. Aggregate consumption and debt accumulation: An empirical examination of US household behaviour. *Cambridge Journal of Economics*, 39(1), pp. 93–112.

Kohler, K., Guschanski, A., and Stockhammer, E., 2019. How does financialisation affect functional income distribution? A theoretical clarification and empirical assessment, *Cambridge Journal of Economics*, 43, pp. 937–74.

Krippner, G., 2005. The financialization of the American economy. *Socio-Economic Review*, 3, pp. 173–208.

Lane, P.R. and McQuade, P., 2014. Domestic credit growth and international capital flows. *Scandinavian Journal of Economics*, 116(1), pp. 218–252.

Lavoie, M. and Stockhammer, E., (eds.) 2013. *Wage-led Growth. An Equitable Strategy for Economic Recovery*. Basingstoke: Palgrave McMillan.

Nölke, A., 2016. Economic causes of the Eurozone crisis. The analytical contributions of comparative capitalism. *Socio-Economic Review*, 14(1), pp. 141–161.

Nölke, A. and Vliegenthart, A., 2009. Enlarging the varieties of capitalism: The emergence of dependent market economies in East Central Europe. *World Politics*, 61(4), pp. 670–702.

Orhangazi, Ö., 2008. Financialisation and capital accumulation in the non-financial corporate sector: A theoretical and empirical investigation on the US economy: 1973–2003. *Cambridge Journal of Economics*, 32, pp. 863–886.

Skott, P. and Ryoo, S., 2008. Macroeconomic implications of financialisation. *Cambridge Journal of Economics*, 32, pp. 827–862.

Ryner, M., 2015. Europe's ordoliberal iron cage: Critical political economy, the Euro area crisis and its management. *Journal of European Public Policy*, 22(2), pp. 275–294.

Stockhammer, E., 2016. Neoliberal growth models, monetary union and the Euro crisis. A post-Keynesian perspective. *New Political Economy*, 21(4), 365–379.

Stockhammer, E. and Köhler, K., 2014. Linking a post-Keynesian approach to critical political economy: Debt-driven growth, export-driven growth and the crisis in Europe. In Jäger, J. and Springler, E. (eds.). *Asymmetric Crisis in Europe and Possible Futures: Critical Political Economy and Post-Keynesian Perspectives*. New York: Routledge, pp. 34–49.

Stockhammer, E., Durand, C. and List, L., 2016. European growth models and working class restructuring: An international post-Keynesian political economy perspective. *Environment and Planning A*, 48(9), pp.1804–1828.

Stockhammer E. and Wildauer R., 2016. Debt-driven growth? Wealth, distribution and demand in OECD countries. *Cambridge Journal of Economics*, 40(6), pp.1609–1634.

Storm, S. and Naastepad, C.W.M., 2015. NAIRU economics and the Eurozone crisis. *International Review of Applied Economics*, 29(6), pp. 843–877.

Tori, D. and Onaran, Ö., 2018. Financialization, financial development and investment. Evidence from European non-financial corporations. *Socio-Economic Review*. Advance access, https://doi.org/10.1093/ser/mwy044 [Accessed 28 Nov. 2019].

Watson, M., 2010. House price Keynesianism and the contradictions of the modern investor subject. *Housing Studies*, 25(3), pp. 413–426.

Zabai, A., 2017. Household debt: Recent developments and challenges. *BIS Quarterly Review*, March 2017, pp. 39–54.

14

ECONOMIC DEVELOPMENT AND VARIEGATED FINANCIALIZATION IN EMERGING ECONOMIES

Ewa Karwowski

Introduction

One of the main strengths of financialization as a concept is its potential for interdisciplinary research (Aalbers 2015). In this spirit, the chapter brings together different debates from economic geography, political economy and heterodox economics, addressing the underlying structures and spatial sites of variegated financialization. The focus here is on the Global South, and specifically on emerging economies (EMEs), where financialization is acknowledged to take on a distinct character, shaped by the interaction of international and domestic forces. While the distinctiveness of financialization in EMEs has been discussed for some time, producing important studies on the changing nature of financial markets and institutions within specific countries (Rethel 2010; Correa, Vidal & Marshall 2012; Ashman & Fine 2013), there are few comparative accounts across a larger number of poorer countries or regions.[1]

This chapter discusses financialization with respect to dimensions, which are important for EMEs, on three geographical scales: the urban (or city) level, the nation state and the international scale. In this way, links are created across different research strands since typically the changing nature of finance is discussed either in the context of financial centres, highlighting the interaction of city and international scales, or financial liberalization, focusing on the integration of domestic economies into international financial structures. These financialization dimensions are: (1) financial liberalization, (2) financial globalization, (3) the presence of globally operating companies, (4) the financialization of the financial sector, (5) non-financial companies (NFCs), (6) households and (7) the state as well as (8) asset price inflation and (9) the existence of financial centres.

The chapter takes stock of these dimensions across 20 EMEs. Acknowledging the origins of financialization research as an agenda focusing on the US and UK as well as the peripheral character of financialization in the Global South (see Bonizzi, Kaltenbrunner and Powell in this volume) the empirical evidence is compared with measures for the two largest Anglo-Saxon economies.[2] The comparative analysis suggests that particularly EMEs in Asia are showing strong signs of financialization on the city, national and international scales. In contrast, these signs appear – maybe surprisingly in the light of economic history – much less pronounced in Latin America, while Central and Eastern Europe (CEE) and South Africa can be placed between these two extremes. Variegation also comes strongly to the fore within regions. While the experience of financialization in East Asia generally has a strong international dimension, where financial liberalization attracted foreign capital inflows, China and India are important exceptions. Both countries shied away from pushing financial liberalization and promoting foreign inflows to the same extent as their regional peers.

Locating Financialization in the Global South

Analyses of financialization in poorer countries only started gaining visibility by the 2010s once the financialization research agenda had grown and broadened. Frequently, however, such studies merely replicated empirical work previously done for the US. Nevertheless, there is a long-standing tradition – in theory and policy – of scrutinizing the role of finance in development (Kalecki 1951[1993]; Shaw 1973; McKinnon 1974). The financialization literature as it emerged within critical accounting, heterodox economics, cultural political economy and economic geography stresses the inherently unstable nature of financial processes in capitalist economies (see Sen, in this volume). Thus, it is deeply suspicious of claims that growth and innovation in the financial sector will bring about economic prosperity or development. Here, financialization is at least implicitly understood to be a type of structural transformation through which productive structures lose out or become subordinated to financial accumulation.

Historically, the backlash against the financial repression hypothesis is a predecessor of debates on financialization in the Global South, predating broader financialization debates. Given the importance of these earlier debates, it is worthwhile to recount them in some detail. They strongly focus on financial liberalization, which entails domestic financial deregulation as well as capital account opening, as the key dimension. Shaw (1973), Gurley & Shaw (1955) and McKinnon (1974) put forward the thesis that overregulated financial markets, which they argued were "repressed," were holding back growth and development in poor countries. Interest rate and credit controls were the major culprits behind a misallocation of capital in their view. Interest rate controls meant rates were administratively set too low, and adversely affected household saving and hampered credit extension for investment. Credit controls, referring to governments favouring certain economic sectors to receive this subsidised credit over others, arguably led to inefficient allocation of scare capital resources. Financial liberalization was proclaimed to be the cure since higher interest rates and credit allocation by market forces would incentivise household saving, allow for larger credit volumes and support more (and more efficient) private investment.

The financial repression hypothesis rejected the Keynesian view that industry should be favoured over finance, which was dominant in the immediate post-war era and embodied in the Bretton Woods system of fixed exchange rates. This orthodox Keynesian view also fed the belief that desired economic outcomes such as economic catching-up of poor regions could be engineered through good policies. The post-war economic "golden age" came to a turbulent end in rich countries with stagflation in the 1970s. By that time, in developing economies many had also become disillusioned with the promise of catching-up (Leys 1996). The 1970s brought about a reconsideration of economic thinking and the financial repression hypothesis emerged as part of a broader shift towards market liberalization (Loiz 2017). McKinnon's and Shaw's ideas became dominant in the 1980s with "getting interest rates right" an integral part of the World Bank's development policy toolkit by the end of the decade (Long 1991: 169).

Claims that higher real interest rates would induce more saving were empirically shaky at best (Ostry & Reinhard 1992; Ogaki et al. 1996; Loiz 2017). Nonetheless, more and more countries embraced inflation targeting via high interest rates beginning in the early 1990s, emulating New Zealand's example.[3] But high interest rates in emerging economies are a major driver of state financialization in the Global South since they open up avenues for financial accumulation to domestic capital potentially at the expense of supporting productive enterprise (Karwowski forthcoming), while feeding the international search for yield of (mostly rich-country) financial investors (Bonizzi 2017).

The pro-liberalization debate shifted focus in the 1990s, arguing that fostering credit extension would increase future growth (Levine & King 1993; Levine 2005). Financial deepening – so the modified claim – would support economic growth. The volume of credit, initially measured by investment credit and later replaced by general credit measures – in total GDP represented financial depth. An open capital account was seen as an important part of this liberalization. The argument for freeing up international financial flows was one of efficiency (Stiglitz 2000). Foreign inflows could be an important additional source of investment funding and simultaneously force domestic institutions – private firms and public authorities – to be more efficient. Thus, financial globalization, meaning the growth in cross-border financial investment, was encouraged by international financial institutions as part of the Washington Consensus. Thus, while public policies can introduce and support financialization at a national level, affecting firms' operations and citizens' lives domestically, international phenomena such as financial globalization or the Washington Consensus actively shaped domestic policies in turn (see also Wang, in this volume).

Frequent financial crises in emerging economies especially since the 1990s have generated a backlash against financial liberalization and financial globalization. Open capital accounts allowed for increasing foreign inflows which were often short-term and easily reversible (such as in East Asia during the 1990s, Corsetti, Pesenti & Roubini 1998; Stiglitz 2000). Thus, especially heterodox economists viewed them with suspicion since they had the potential to generate asset price inflation, plunging a country into financial and exchange rate crises once the unsustainable nature of price rises becomes apparent (Kregel 1998; Dymski 1999; and Arestis & Glickman 2002).

The East Asian crisis was crucial to illustrate the flaws in policies pushing for capital account openness. Many of the affected economies, such as Hong Kong, Singapore, South Korea and Taiwan, had become high-income countries in the late 1980s/early 1990s, accomplishing the until today very rare miracle of economic catching-up with the OECD world. But it was these dynamic and at the time strongly growing countries that faced severe currency and financial crises in 1997/1998. Importantly, their fundamentals, especially their growth performance, government deficits and debt levels alongside their export positions, were strong and backed by prudent policies. Thus, if financial globalization ended in tears even for the Asian "Tigers" (Arestis & Glickman 2002), financial liberalization was clearly a flawed policy, requiring substantial domestic regulation and supervision (Kawai et al. 2005).

Financialization scholars warn of financial sector deregulation and, in the context of developing regions, especially of hastily opening up capital accounts. Crucially, they regard not only short-term inflows with caution, but also point to the presence of foreign banks or companies as risk factors, since these corporations tend to transfer their financialized practices, meaning more short-term and often financial instead of productive investment, into the local economy (see dos Santos 2013 on banks and Rossi 2013 on non-financial corporations).

The realisation that households' relationship with the financial sector was also changing came relatively late. One of the core signs is high and rising debt burdens (Cynamon & Fazzari 2008; Kus 2012; Alvarez 2015). Mainstream economists tend to regard increasing household credit volumes in emerging and developing parts of the world uncritically. They are put down as signs of financial deepening, meaning financial development. This disregards difference in types of credit and considerations about debt sustainability. Especially household borrowing does not build up productive capacity, and instead potentially worsens financial fragility. Thus, recent expansion in emerging economies' household debt is increasingly seen with caution even by the financial press (Wheatly 2018).

Since financial centers host internationally operating companies, functioning as nodes between the national and global financial spheres, they constitute a core dimension of financialization. The foundations of the research agenda on financial centers were laid in Friedman's world cities hypothesis, further developed by Sassen (1991) and her work on global cities, which shifted the focus from manufacturing to producer services. Sassen singled out London, New York and Tokyo. Until today, New York and London – or NYLON – are the leading financial centers (Wójcik 2013). This research tradition stresses the competition among cities and their hierarchical relationships, while a network research agenda emerged in parallel, emphasising the linkages among cities and their positions as nodes in an international web of money and power (Amin & Thrift 1992). A milestone in terms of empirical data, capturing these international linkages, is the Global and World Cities project, mapping the relationships across hundreds of cities internationally (Beaverstock et al. 2000; Taylor 2004). Cities in the Global South are part of this effort and visibly play a lesser – if growing – role in comparison to their rich-country counterparts.

Having understood these dimensions, measuring the extent to which emerging economies have been affected by changes on these dimensions, as the next section does, will reveal the overall extent of financialization in the Global South as well as variations across countries.

Measuring Financialization in EMEs

This section discusses the measures that capture the different dimensions of financialization in EMEs. Table 14.1 provides an overview of the proposed indicators, stating the dimension measured, the scale addressed, and the sources used. The analytical focus are the years since the Global Financial Crisis of 2007–2008, providing the latest snapshot of countries' financialization across nine dimensions. Where possible, given data availability, average values for the years 2008–2017 are reported.

The term EME is not well defined in the literature, and loosely refers to middle-income countries undergoing economic transformation, for instance, from planned to free-market economy (Kvint 2009). The choice of the 20 emerging economies considered reflects existing literature on financialization in the Global South and emerging economies (see Karwowski & Stockhammer 2017 for an overview) and data limitations.[4] The following countries are included in the analysis: Argentina, Brazil, Chile, Colombia and Mexico from Latin America; China (together with Hong Kong), India, Indonesia, Malaysia, Singapore, South Korea and Thailand, representing Asia; the Czech Republic, Hungary, Poland, and Russia are included for CEE; Saudi Arabia and Turkey are the only two economies from the Middle East and North Africa (MENA)[5] region for which data could be gathered, while South Africa is the only African country in the sample. These 20 economies can be broadly seen as emerging economies. Hong Kong, Singapore, South Korea together with most of the CEE economies are high-income economic entities and have been so for a while. Nevertheless, given their relatively recent experience with economic catch-up they tend to be perceived as EMEs especially by financial investors. This is illustrated by their proneness to contagion during financial crises in other EMEs.

On the international scale, financial liberalization is an important indicator of financialization. This type of deregulation can be captured using the Chinn–Ito financial openness index (Chinn & Ito 2006). Financial liberalization goes hand in hand with financial globalization. The Lane & Milesi-Ferretti database is used to measure the stock of assets owned by foreign investors. All

Table 14.1 Financialization Dimensions and Indicators

Financialisation Interpresentation	Scale	Indicator	Source
Financial liberalization	International	Ito-Chinn openness index	Chinn Ito & 2017
Foreign financial inflows		Stock of foreign liabilities (portfolio investment, FDI and other financial inflows)	Lane & Ferretti 2011
Presence of global companies		Number of companies among top 300 listed global companies by operational revenue across ten sectors	Osiris
Household financialization	Nation state	Household debt (% of GDP)	BIS
NFC financialization		NFC debt (% of GDP)	BIS
Financial sector financialization		Financial market capitalization (% of GDP)	World Bank
Government financialization		Net interest rate margin	World Bank
House price volatility		Real house price indices (2010 = 100), coefficient of variation	BIS
Global financial centres	City	The Global Financial Centres Index	Z/Yen Group Limited
		Global Command and Control Centres	GaWC Research Network

types of assets are considered, not just short-term financial investment, since the presence of foreign companies can also induce domestic companies to embrace more financialized behaviour. Finally, inspired by the global production networks literature, the Osiris database is used to assess the presence of globally operating companies headquartered in each of the analysed countries. Large listed companies are more likely to be exposed to shareholder demands or integrated into networks, which cater towards generating shareholder value.

On the national level, to assess the financialization of the domestic financial sector, the World Bank's measure of stock market capitalization as share of GDP is employed. Debt volumes for NFCs and households are also used to detect sectoral financialization. The two measures are inspired by Hyman Minsky, who argued that debt should be assessed relative to the income stream of an economic unit, providing an indication of how easily debt burdens can be paid back (see Sotiropoulos and Hillig, this volume). GDP is an estimate of a country's ability to generate cash flow, which in turn is crucial to pay off debt obligations. The Bank for International Settlement (BIS) provides data on the market value of sectoral debt as share of GDP. The level of domestic net interest margins is utilised as proxy for state financialization, given the impact of monetary policy on domestic accumulation patterns. Central banks do not determine interest rate margins directly, and they are rather an outcome of the interplay between monetary policy and domestic financial structures, both influenced by international capital flows. Nevertheless, tight monetary policy is likely to translate into larger margins (Borio et al. 2015). This means that high rates set by central banks are associated with larger financial accumulation by the financial sector. This might of course be a symptom of an uncompetitive – because concentrated – financial sector where banks and other private lenders are able to charge high interest rates while paying low rates on deposits. Given the crucial role of the central bank as regulator such a situation is however still, at least partially, an outcome of monetary and financial-sector policies (see Dow, this volume). Finally, house price bubbles signal financialization. The BIS provides historical series of real house price indices, used here to calculate the volatility of residential real estate prices.[6]

Considering indicators to document global financial center status, two measures have been included, one capturing the hierarchical dimension of cities' relationships among each other, another accounting for the role these centers play as nodes in a global network. The first aspect is represented by the Global Financial Centres (GFC) Index, which combined so-called "objective evidence" and "subjective assessment" across 92 cities. The former include infrastructure measures, but also perception indicators such as the World Bank's Ease of Doing Business or the Corruption Perceptions Index, the latter is based on questionnaire responses. The top financial center is quoted for each of the included countries and its global position. The second measure is derived from the Globalization and World Cities Research Network at Loughborough University. The project assesses the importance of cities as Global Command and Control Centres (GCCC). The number of financial headquarters present in 2012 is the relevant measure.

Of course, the presented measures will not be able to capture financialization dynamics exhaustively. Longitudinal and qualitative studies of changing international, domestic and urban financial patterns would give us additional insights into the structural transformation brought about. Therefore, the analysis presented here captures financialization across nine different dimensions by generating a dashboard of measures, which should ideally be read alongside qualitative studies.

Comparing Variegated Financialization Across and Within Regions

When comparing measures of financialization in EMEs a strong degree of variegation can be observed across but also within regions. Table 14.2 provides the nine dimensions of financialization for our sample economies, showing relative positions through color coding. Values ranked within the top quartile of an indicator are highlighted in black to symbolize a strong degree of financialization (high). Positions in the second quartile are highlighted in dark grey (medium high), while the lower ranks are represented by light grey (medium low). Values that indicate the least degree of financialization (low) for a given indicator are marked in off-white. The US and UK are included only as points of reference. Both would rank "high" or "medium high" on almost all of these indicators, with house price volatility and the net interest rate margin (in the post-2008 period) as notable exceptions.

Amongst the represented regions, Asia shows the strongest evidence of financialization with an average of seven out of ten dimensions of financialization for each country flagged in black or dark grey. It is followed by South Africa – the only African economy in the sample – with five indicators showing up as medium high or high. In CEE, countries typically show signs of high or medium high financialization according to only four indicators, and both Latin America and the two MENA region countries show even fewer signs. Variegation is also present within regions, and especially clearly in Asia and Latin America. While Hong Kong shows signs of financialization across all indicators except for interest rate margins, signs of the phenomenon are very weak in Indonesia

The opposite is true for Latin America. Whereas Chile reaches levels of financialization across these dimensions comparable to Asian economies, Argentina shows hardly any signs of finan-cialization. Some unifying patterns within individual regions also emerge. The indicators reveal that high interest rates are a major driver of financialization in Latin America. This has been documented in the past (see Becker et al. 2010; Kaltenbrunner & Painceira 2017). In Asia, the main driver in most countries is the interplay between financial liberalization and globalization.

Table 14.2 Financialization Indicators across 20 Emerging Economies and Three Scales

Scale	International level			Nation-state level					City level	
Indicator	Openness index	Financial inflows	Global companies	Fin market cap (% GDP)	NFC debt (% GDP)	Household debt (% GDP)	Net interest rate margin	House price volatility	GFC index	GCCC (no of HQs)
	2008–2015	2008–2011	2017	2008–2015	2008–2017	2008–2017	2008–2015	2008–2017	2017	2012
Argentina	0.1	56.6	6	10	13.4	5.4	5.60	n/a	90 (Buenos Aires)	n/a
Brazil	0.4	59.5	55	50	42.5	22.0	5.26	16.2	63 (Sao Paulo)	5 (Sao Paulo)
Chile	0.8	114.2	19	106	84.3	36.0	3.95	8.9	n/a	2 (Santiago)
Colombia	0.4	56.2	14	52	32.4	21.1	6.29	14.8	n/a	2 (Bogota)
Mexico	0.7	69.5	19	36	19.9	14.5	5.65	3.9	73 (Mexico City)	1 (Mexico City/ Monterry)
China	0.2	41.8	312	55	134.0	30.9	2.93	3.6	6 (Shanghai)	15 (Beijing)
Hong Kong, China	1.0	915.0	46	1000	185.9	60.5	2.06	23.7	3 (Hong Kong)	21 (Hong Kong)
India	0.2	46.9	69	73	49.5	9.5	3.03	20.7	60 (Mumbai)	10 (Mumbai)
Indonesia	0.5	58.2	19	38	18.1	15.1	6.01	2.7	62 (Jakarta)	5 (Jakarta)
Malaysia	0.3	104.8	20	133	62.2	62.8	2.73	18.0	55 (Kuala Lumpur)	6 (Kuala Lumpur)
Singapore	1.0	753.7	22	232	95.1	53.1	1.77	7.3	4 (Singapore)	6 (Singapore)
South Korea	0.6	75.9	87	85	101.3	81.1	2.49	1.7	22 (Seoul)	13 (Seoul)

Scale	International level			Nation-state level					City level	
Indicator	Openness index	Financial inflows	Global companies	Fin market cap (% GDP)	NFC debt (% GDP)	Household debt (% GDP)	Net interest rate margin	House price volatility	GFC index	GCCC (no of HQs)
	2008-2015	2008-2011	2017	2008-2015	2008-2017	2008-2017	2008-2015	2008-2017	2017	2012
Thailand	0.2	85.5	28	77	47.5	59.8	3.12	7.0	61 (Bangkok)	6 (Bangkok)
Czech Republic	1.0	104.1	2	22	56.7	29.3	2.85	6.0	58 (Prague)	n/a
Hungary	1.0	295.5	3	17	84.3	30.4	3.76	12.9	72 (Budapest)	1 (Budapest)
Poland	0.5	95.5	11	32	42.8	33.9	3.03	5.9	36 (Warsaw)	2 (Warsaw)
Russia	0.6	64.9	44	43	45.7	13.5	4.04	22.5	87 (St Petersburg)	3 (Moscow)
Saudi Arabia	0.7	50.8	11	63	38.8	11.1	2.86	n/a	77 (Riyadh)	7 (Riyadh)
Turkey	0.4	66.6	19	29	48.3	16.6	4.57	12.1	78 (Istanbul)	3 (Istanbul)
South Africa	0.2	88.1	26	228	33.2	39.0	3.02	3.9	48 (Johannesburg)	3 (Johannesburg/Cape Town)
UK	1.0	672.0	105	108	90.1	90.0	1.52	7.4	1 (London)	19 (London)
US	1.0	162.9	802	118	69.2	85.8	3.39	9.6	2 (New York)	30 (New York)

The International Dimension

There are three indicators that are used to capture the international dimension of financialization: financial liberalization, financial globalization and the presence of globally operating corporations. Considering financial liberalization, the openness index is high or medium high across almost all CEE countries, in the three richest Asian economies of the group (Hong Kong, Singapore and South Korea) and Indonesia, Chile and Mexico in Latin America as well as Saudi Arabia. The past decade coincided with a relative roll-back of financial liberalization in many EMEs. In 2015, conditions in Argentina, Chile and Colombia as well as Indonesia, Malaysia and Thailand were more restrictive then in the aftermath of the financial crisis. This was not the case in CEE. Here, the Czech Republic and Hungary were fully financially "open" throughout the period, earning the same score as the US and UK on the indicator, while Poland and Russia have furthered their financial liberalization. The openness of capital accounts among CEE countries is unsurprising since the region has traditionally been extremely welcoming to foreign financial inflows ever since the beginnings of its transformation towards capitalism, in many countries implemented as "big bang," an abrupt and fast liberalization.

Financial openness and foreign inflows seem to go hand in hand. Most countries that are open to inflows (relative to their peer group) also received a higher share of foreign capital measured as share of GDP. The only notable exceptions are Thailand and South Africa where financial openness is classified as very low while the presence of foreign capital is rather high. In the case of South Africa, this is peculiar since the country is regarded to be extremely financially open according to a rival index (the IMF's financial reforms index, scoring 0.85 of 1 in 2005). Notably, Hong Kong and Singapore have attracted more foreign capital (measured as share of GDP) than the UK, while Hungary's foreign capital liabilities exceed those of the US.

The presence of global companies – and their being headquartered in EMEs – does not seem to coincide with the two other international-level measures, financial liberalization and globalization. While CEE is a region open to foreign inflows, there are few globally operating companies incorporated there. Russia is the only exception, hosting 44 major companies that operate internationally. This result is driven by the country's strong resource endowments since the majority of these 40-odd Russian firms are engaged in the utilities (17 firms), energy (12), or basic materials (seven) sectors. Brazilian companies operating internationally have a similar profile (25 utilities and seven energy companies). However, Brazil alongside India and China does not seem particularly open to foreign capital, while itself being home to a large number of global companies. Of course, these three countries possess large domestic markets, facilitating the formation of home-based transnationally operating corporations. The smaller Asian economies in the sample – especially Hong Kong, Malaysia, Singapore, South Korea and Thailand – have also managed to support a notable number of globally operating corporations but unlike in China and India this coincided with large foreign capital inflows. While the US hosts by far the largest number of global companies (800+) among the sample countries, the UK's importance as base for international corporations appears much more modest (with only 105 companies incorporated there). The UK's close links to many off-shore centers can partially explain this observation (see Fernandez and Hendrikse, in this volume).

Nation-state Level

Table 14.2 also provides us with five indicators capturing dimensions of financialization on the national level. They correspond to the four domestic macroeconomic aggregates – the financial sector, non-financial firms, households and the government – plus a measure of asset price inflation in residential property.

The measure of financial sector financialization appears closely linked to the presence of globally operating companies in a country. All emerging economies in the sample that rank high or medium high on the former indicator also host a substantial number of global companies with the exception of Chile and Saudi Arabia. This result illustrates the links across geographical scales. Domestic capital markets can of course have a transnational dimension. Thus, US and UK stock markets attract large numbers of international companies – in the 1990s several major South African companies relocated to London once capital account restrictions were loosened, effectively becoming UK-based firms (Chabane et al. 2006). Hong Kong and Singapore, in turn, are regional financial hubs and function as off-shore financial centers. The former constitutes a gateway into China, still a relatively closed financial market. Thus, especially in recent years, the ties between Hong Kong and Shanghai, the prime mainland stock exchange in China, have strengthened backed by financial deregulation. For instance, since 2014 the Shanghai–Hong Kong Stock Connect enables foreign investors to buy selected Shanghai-listed stocks, while allowing Chinese investors to buy Hang Seng-listed equity (Prasad 2016; see Petry, this volume).

In recent years, the financial press has been concerned about rising debt in emerging economies, in particular among non-financial enterprises and households (Wheatley 2018). This most clearly affects Asia. Examining NFCs, debt burdens are indeed extremely high across most of the Asian countries in the sample. In Hong Kong, China, South Korea and Singapore corporate debt volumes (measured as share of GDP) exceed those in the two Anglo-Saxon economies (see Figure 14.1). Especially in China and Hong Kong, the expansion of corporate debt over the past decade has been enormous (70–90%). Only Chile, Mexico and Turkey experienced similar growth rates albeit from a much lower base.

Similar growth patterns are visible with respect to household debt, even though debt taken on by individuals is smaller than corporate debt (see Figure 14.2). Household debt is comparatively high across Asia, especially in South Korea, Malaysia, Hong Kong, Thailand and Singapore, but does not reach UK and US levels. However, household debt has been growing strongly over the last decade in the vast majority of emerging countries in the sample (South Africa, Hungary and India being notable exceptions); by contrast, individuals in the two Anglo-Saxon economies have reduced their overall debt. (see also Gonzalez, in this volume)

The net interest rate margin, gauging the financialization of government and its policies, provides quite a different picture from the other national-level measures employed in this analysis. The highest margins can overwhelmingly be found in Latin American countries. Indonesia is the only country from outside the region with similarly high interest margins.

House price volatility, capturing asset price inflation, is another indicator flagged as high or medium high in many of the Latin American economies included here (i.e. Brazil, Chile and Colombia). However, over the past decade it has been more severe in Hong Kong, Russia, India and Malaysia. It is noteworthy that asset price inflation shows up as low in South Africa. The country was one of the few emerging economies that experienced a similarly extreme real price inflation of residential housing as the US and UK in the run-up to the global financial crisis (see Karwowski 2018). Thus, similar to the two Anglo-Saxon economies the housing market in the country has been stagnant ever since the crisis, showing little price movement and therefore hardly any volatility.

The City Level

Finally, let us consider the position of emerging market financial centers in the global economy. The GFC index places all top financial centers in our sample firmly within the Asian economies.

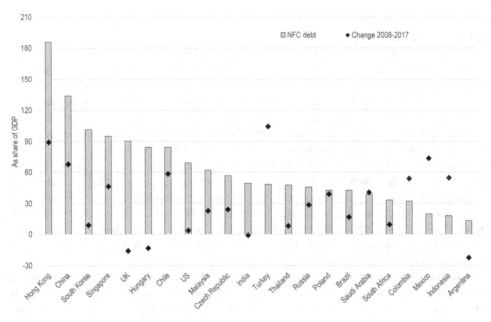

Figure 14.1 NFC Debt and its Growth for Selected Economies, 2008–2017
Source: Based on data from BIS, 2018

While London and New York lead the index, they are followed by Hong Kong and Singapore in positions three and four, respectively. Shanghai comes sixth and Seoul is ranked 22nd. The 2017 GFC index captures 92 and their relative positions. Thus, while Kuala Lumpur (55) and Mumbai (60) are labelled as medium high in our relative comparison, they make only the second half of this global city ranking. Among cities in the CEE region, Warsaw (36) and Prague (58) are classified as comparatively high on the index. Johannesburg ranks at position 48. When comparing to the GCCC indicator, based on network analysis, it becomes apparent that financial centers in CEE and Africa are in fact only weakly integrated into global financial networks. While all Asian financial metropoles hosted at least five headquarters of international financial companies in 2012, this number did not exceed an average of three for financial metropoles in CEE. In the case of South Africa, Cape Town appears as an important financial center alongside Johannesburg, each city being the seat of three international corporate headquarters. The GFC Index is a broader indicator than the GCCC indicator. However, its subjective assessment elements and limited global reach might overestimate the importance of cities included in the ranking as appears to be the case for Warsaw, for instance.

Conclusion

This chapter has argued that financialization is not merely a rich country phenomenon and that financialization theory has its roots in researchers' and policymakers' rejection of claims that growth and innovation in the financial sector will bring about economic prosperity and development. Thus, the rejection of the financial repression hypothesis is a key predecessor of financialization debates which is too often overlooked. To tackle this shortcoming, the chapter firmly locates financialization in the Global South by providing an overview of key dimensions of financialization across 20 EMEs. Using ten measures to take stock of financialization across and within developing

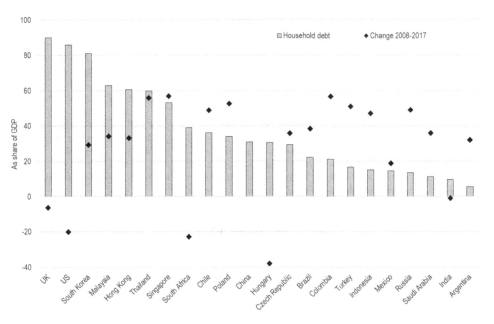

Figure 14.2 Household Debt and its Growth for Selected Economies, 2008–2017
Source: Based on data from BIS, 2018

regions, the variegation of the phenomenon is striking. This dashboard of financialization indicators illustrates the importance of spatial distinctiveness, local institutions, and history.

Among the EMEs in the sample, Asian economies (and in fact South Africa) show the greatest evidence of financialization overall, Latin American ones (together with Turkey and Saudi Arabia) are comparatively less financialized, with CEE somewhere in between the two regions. Distinct regional patterns can be observed: In Latin America tight monetary policy and high interest rate margins appear a crucial driver of financialization. Against the backdrop of the region's history of elevated inflation levels, high interest rates and margins make financial accumulation attractive, paving the way for financialization if productive investment appears less lucrative. Financial liberalization and globalization are the most important dimensions of financialization in CEE, a region that experienced "big bang"-type financial sector liberalization during the 1990s.

Intriguingly, Asia, a region known for its dynamic manufacturing capacity, exhibits strong signs of financialization on all three scales, the international, domestic and urban level. Asian financial centers have caught up visibly with London and New York over the past decade. Hong Kong, Singapore and Shanghai are close on NYLON's heels in the international rankings of leading financial cities. Asian companies rival US- and UK-based corporations operating internationally, by also becoming international players. But financialization remains a deeply problematic phenomenon. Therefore, strongly rising NFC and household debt alongside substantial house price volatility are worrying developments across Asia, which should be monitored and held in check otherwise they might lead to similar flare-ups of financial instability in Asian economies as the US and UK have experienced over the past two decades. Given the high levels of financial globalization among Asian EMEs financial disturbances in the region would have global consequences. The 2015/2016 jitters in the Chinese stock market, which prompted the US Federal bank to delay interest rate increases, might have been a first sign of this development.

Notes

1 Notable exceptions are Becker et al. (2010) studying the financialization of Brazil, Chile, Serbia and Slovakia as well as Karwowski & Stockhammer (2017) analysing the phenomenon across 17 EMEs.
2 A broad definition of the Global South is used here which encompasses all emerging economies and developing countries. EMEs also include countries in Central Eastern Europe which are generally regarded to be peripheral to the centres of global finance even if not always included in the term Global South.
3 More than half of the emerging economies in the sample have now adopted inflation targeting.
4 The author's intention was to also include the Baltic state and the Philippines but, since no BIS data was available, measures capturing financialization on the state level could not be compiled.
5 Admittedly, MENA is interpreted rather broadly.
6 If fewer than five years of data are available, the measure is not included. A shorter historical series allows less assessment of volatility using the coefficient of variation.

Bibliography

Aalbers, M.B. 2015. The potential for financialization. *Dialogues in Human Geography*, 5(2), pp. 214–219. https://doi.org/10.1177/2043820615588158
Abiad, A., Detragiache, E. and Tressel, T. 2008. *A New Database of Financial Reforms*. International Monetary Fund.
Alvarez, I. 2015. Financialization, non-financial corporations and income inequality: The case of France. *Socio-Economic Review*, 13(3), pp. 449–475.
Amin, A. and Thrift, N. 1992. Neo-Marshallian nodes in global networks. *International Journal of Urban and Regional Research*, 22, pp. 571–587.
Arestis, P. and Glickman, M. 2002. Financial crisis in Southeast Asia: Dispelling illusion the Minskyan way. *Cambridge Journal of Economics*, 26(2), pp. 237–260.
Ashman, S. and Fine, B. 2013. Neo-liberalism, varieties of capitalism, and the shifting contours of South Africa's financial system. *Transformation: Critical Perspectives on Southern Africa*, 81(1), pp. 144–178.
Baud, C. and Durand, C., 2011. Financialization, globalization and the making of profits by leading retailers. *Socio-Economic Review*, 10(2), pp. 1–26.
Bayliss, K. 2014a. The financialization of water. *Review of Radical Political Economics*, 46(3), pp. 292–307.
Bayliss, K. 2014b. Case study: The financialisation of water in England and Wales. FESSUD Working Paper no. 52.
Beaverstock, J.V., Smith, R.G. and Taylor, P.J. 2000. World city network: A new metageography. *Annals of the Association of American Geographers*, 90(1), pp. 123–134.
Becker, J., Jäger, J., Leubolt, B. and Weissenbacher, R. 2010. Peripheral financialization and vulnerability to crisis: A regulationist perspective. *Competition & Change*, 14(3–4), pp. 225–247.
BIS. 2018. *Data: Total Credit to the Non-financial Sector*, Basel: Bank for International Settlement (BIS).
Bonizzi, B. 2017. International financialisation, developing countries and the contradictions of privatised Keynesianism. *Economic and Political Studies*, 5(1), pp. 21–40.
Borio, C., Gambacorta, L. and Hofmann, B. 2015. The influence of monetary policy on bank profitability. BIS Working Papers, no. 514.
Carrington, J.C. and Edwards, G.T. 1979. *Financing Industrial Investment*. London: Macmillan.
Chabane, N., Goldstein, A., and Roberts, S. 2006. The changing face and strategies of big business in South Africa: More than a decade of political democracy. *Industrial and Corporate Change*, 15(3), pp. 549–577.
Chinn, M.D. and Ito, H. 2006. What matters for financial development? Capital controls, institutions, and interactions. *Journal of Development Economics*, 81(1), pp. 163–192.
Chinn, M.D. and Ito, H. 2017. *Notes on the Chinn-Ito Financial Openness Index, 2015 Update*. Available at http://web.pdx.edu/~ito/Chinn-Ito_website.htm
Correa, E., Vidal, G. and Marshall, W. 2012. Financialization in Mexico: Trajectory and limits. *Journal of Post Keynesian Economics*, 35(2), pp. 255–275.
Corsetti, G., Pesenti, P. and Roubini, N. 1998. *What Caused the Asian Currency and Financial Crisis? Part I: A Macroeconomic Overview* (NBER Working Paper Series No. 6833). Cambridge, MA: National Bureau of Economic Research.
Crotty, J. 2005. The neoliberal paradox: The impact of destructive product market competition and 'modern' financial markets on nonfinancial corporation performance in the neoliberal era. G.A. Epstein,

ed., *Financialization and the World Economy*. Cheltenham, UK /Northampton, MA: Edward Elgar, pp. 77–110.

Cynamon, B.Z. and Fazzari, S.M. 2008. Household debt in the consumer age: Source of growth–Risk of collapse. *Capitalism and Society*, 3(2), pp. 1–32.

dos Santos, P.L. 2013. A cause for policy concern: The expansion of household credit in middle-income economies. *International Review of Applied Economics*, 27(3), pp. 316–338.

Dymski, G.A. 1999. *Asset Bubbles and Minsky Crises in East Asia: A Spatialized Minsky Approach* (Research Paper Series). Department of Economics, University of California-Riverside.

Epstein, G.A. (ed.) 2005. *Financialization and the World Economy*. Cheltenham, UK ; Northampton, MA: Edward Elgar.

Farhi, M. and Borghi, R.A.Z. 2009. Operations with financial derivatives of corporations from emerging economies. *Estudos Avançados*, 23, pp. 169–188.

Friedmann, J. 1986. The world city hypothesis. *Development and Change*, 17, pp. 69–83.

Froud, J., Haslam, C., Johal, S. and Williams, K. 2000. Shareholder value and financialization: Consultancy promises, management moves. *Economy and Society*, 29(1), pp. 80–110.

Gurley, J.G. and Shaw, E.S. 1955. Financial aspects of economic development. *American Economic Review*, 45, pp. 515–538.

Hardie, I. 2011. How much can governments borrow? Financialization and emerging markets government borrowing capacity. *Review of International Political Economy*, 18(2), pp. 141–167.

Kalecki, M. 1951 [1993]. Report on the main current economic problems of Israel. J. Osiatynsky, ed., *Collected Works of Michal Kalecki*, Vol. V. Oxford: Oxford University Press.

Kaltenbrunner, A. and Painceira, J.P. 2017. The impossible trinity: Inflation targeting, exchange rate management and open capital accounts in emerging economies. *Development and Change*, 48(3), pp. 452–480.

Karwowski, E. 2015. The finance-mining nexus in South Africa: How mining companies use the South African equity market to speculate. *Journal of Southern African Studies*, 41(1), pp. 9–28.

Karwowski, E. 2018. Corporate financialisation in South Africa: From investment strike to housing bubble. *Competition & Change*, 22(4), pp. 413–436.

Karwowski, E. forthcoming. Towards (de-)financialisation: The role of the state. *Cambridge Journal of Economics*.

Karwowski, E. and Stockhammer, E. 2017. Financialisation in emerging economies: A systematic overview and comparison with Anglo-Saxon economies. *Economic and Political Studies*, 5(1), pp. 60–86.

Kawai, M., Newfarmer, R. and Schmukler, S.L. 2005. Financial crises: Nine lessons from East Asia. *Eastern Economic Journal*, 31(2), pp. 185–207.

Kregel, J. 1998. Yes, "it" did happen again—A Minsky crisis happened in Asia. Working Paper No. 234, Annandale-on-Hudson, NY: Levy Economics Institute of Bard College.

Kus, B. 2012. Financialisation and income inequality in OECD nations: 1995–2007. *The Economic and Social Review*, 43(4), pp. 477–495.

Kvint, V.L. 2009. *The Global Emerging Market: Strategic Management and Economics*. New York: Routledge.

Lane, P. and Milesi-Ferretti, G.M. 2011. *External Adjustment and the Global Crisis* (No. w17352). Cambridge, MA: National Bureau of Economic Research.

Lapavitsas, C. 2013. *Profiting without Producing: How Finance Exploits Us All*. London; New York: Verso.

Lazonick, W. and O'Sullivan, M. 2000. Maximizing shareholder value: A new ideology for corporate governance. *Economy and Society*, 29(1), pp. 13–35.

Levine, R. 2005. Finance and growth: Theory and evidence. In P. Aghion and S. Durlauf (eds.) *Handbook of Economic Growth* (Vol. 1). Amsterdam: Elsevier, pp. 865–934.

Levine, R. and King, R.G. 1993. Finance, entrepreneurship, and growth: Theory and evidence. *Journal of Monetary Economics*, 32, pp. 513–542.

Leys, C. 1996. *The Rise & Fall of Development Theory*. Nairobi: EAEP, East African Educational Publisher.

Loiz, K. 2017. The financial repression–liberalization debate: Taking stock, looking for a synthesis. *Journal of Economics Surveys*, 32(2), pp. 440–468.

Long, M. 1991. Financial systems and development. P. Callier (ed.), *Financial Systems and Development in Africa*. Washington: World Bank, pp. 159–172.

McKinnon, R.I. 1974. *Money and Capital in Economic Development*. Washington, DC: Brookings Institution.

Ogaki, M., Ostry, J.D. and Reinhart, C.M. 1996. Saving behaviour in low- and middle-income developing countries: A comparison. *IMF Staff Papers*, 43(1), pp. 38–71.

Ostry, J.D., and Reinhart, C.M. 1992. Private saving and terms of trade shocks: Evidence from developing countries. *IMF Staff Papers*, 39, pp. 495–517.

Philippon, T. 2007. Why has the U.S. financial sector grown so much? The role of corporate finance. NBER Working Paper, no. 13405, Cambridge, MA: National Bureau of Economic Research.

Phillips K. 1993. *Boiling Point: Democrats, Republicans and the Decline of Middle-Class Prosperity.* New York, NY: Random House.

Phillips, K. 1994. *Arrogant Capital: Washington, Wall Street, and the Frustration of American Politics* (1st ed.). Boston: Little, Brown and Co.

Prasad, E. 2016. *China's Economy and Financial Markets: Reforms and Risks* (Testimony). Brookings.

Rethel, L. 2010. Financialisation and the Malaysian political economy. *Globalizations*, 7(4), pp. 489–506.

Rossi, J.L.J. 2013. Hedging, selective hedging, or speculation? Evidence of the use of derivatives by Brazilian firms during the financial crisis. *Journal of Multinational Financial Management*, 23(5), pp. 415–433.

Sassen, S. 1991. *The Global City: New York, London, Tokyo.* Princeton, NJ: Princeton University Press.

Schaberg, M. 1999. *Globalization and the Erosion of National Financial Systems: Is Declining Autonomy Inevitable?* Cheltenham, UK; Northampton, MA, USA: Edward Elgar.

Shaw, E.S. 1973. *Financial Deepening in Economic Development.* London; New York, NY: Oxford University Press.

Stiglitz, J.E. 2000. Capital market liberalization, economic growth, and instability. *World Development*, 28 (6), pp. 1075–1086.

Stockhammer, E. 2004. Financialization and the slowdown of accumulation. *Cambridge Journal of Economics*, 28 (5), pp. 719–741.

Streeck, W. 2013. *Gekaufte Zeit*, Berlin: Suhrkamp.

Taylor, P.J. 2004. *World City Network: A Global Urban Analysis.* London: Routledge.

Wheatley, J. 2018. Financial markets under pressure as debt mounts. *The Financial Times*, 6 March 2018.

Wójcik, D. 2013. The dark side of NY–LON: Financial centres and the global financial crisis. *Urban Studies*, 50 (13), pp. 2736–2752.

World Bank. 1989. *World Development Report 1989.* Nairobi, Kenya: World Bank.

World Bank. 2017. *Financial Development and Structure Database. June 2017 Update.* Washington, DC: World Bank.

15

SUBORDINATE FINANCIALIZATION IN EMERGING CAPITALIST ECONOMIES

Bruno Bonizzi, Annina Kaltenbrunner and Jeff Powell

Introduction

In the explosion of literature on financialization, there is a much smaller but growing interest in what the phenomenon means for emerging capitalist economies (ECEs) (Bonizzi 2013; see also Karwowski, this volume). Much of the literature that focuses on the advanced capitalist economies (ACEs) lacks a clear theory of financialization. This absence becomes even more problematic when the lens is used to attempt to describe and understand changes in ECEs.

The theory of financialization adopted here draws a necessary distinction between processes which are cyclical in nature, and secular changes in the relations of capitalist accumulation (Powell 2018). The former are both temporally and spatially limited, with financialization giving way to de-financialization. The latter mark the emergence of a new stage of mature capitalism – financialized capitalism – wherein the passage of capital through its various forms – in Marxist terms, from money capital to productive capital to commodity capital, and back again – is occurring at the global level, rather than within the nation-state. The last two decades have witnessed the realization of this process, first theorized in the 1970s with the rise of the multinational corporation (Palloix 1975). Whereas this internationalization had previously been limited to financing and commodity circulation, it now includes the genuine internationalization of production itself. Within this transformation, finance plays a catalytic role in the extension, expansion and intensification of capitalist accumulation; at the same time, it is afforded unprecedented opportunities for exploitation and expropriation, both legal and otherwise.

Theorizing financialized capitalism as a global phenomenon in this way, requires us to confront how it emerges from and plays out across a hierarchical and uneven global landscape. This chapter holds that, for agents located in ECEs, the encounter with both cyclical processes and secular stage is from a subordinate position. This subordination is approached from two analytical vantage points. First, in relation to global production, ECE firms generally occupy subordinate locations in global production networks, providing cheap labor and raw, or at best, intermediate inputs. This structural subordination in global production, among other things, mediates ECEs' relations to financial markets, both as potential contenders for lead firm position, and power and position within the network itself.

Second, in relation to global finance, ECEs are structurally subordinated to ACEs, that is, both trade and the most liquid capital markets are denominated in the currency of ACEs. The hegemonic position of the capital markets of the ACEs, especially the US, is bound up with the dominant role of their currencies (Kaltenbrunner and Lysandrou 2017). ECE currencies, on the other hand, sit on the lower end of the hierarchy, a fact that fundamentally shapes their interaction with financial markets (Powell 2013; Prates and Andrade 2013; Kaltenbrunner 2015; Bonizzi 2017a).

In what follows, we attempt to advance our understanding of how subordinate financialization emerges from and plays out in the realms of production, circulation and finance in ECEs. In production, lead firms within cyclical limits may be able to capture profits across global production networks which can be used to pay dividends, buy back shares, boost management salaries or purchase financial assets, with possibly deleterious effects for fixed investment. Even where such financial artistry meets its limits, globalized firms must continue with their engagement with financial products which help them manage increasingly complex networks of uncertainty. Their subordination in international production means firms based in ECEs are able to capture less of the value created than firms higher in the hierarchy and must pay more to hedge macroeconomic risk. Their subordinate location in relation to markets and currencies means their rising engagement with financial markets, either as a result of their lead firm position or in an attempt to strengthen their position in the network, take on potentially different forms than those observed in ACEs (e.g. the relative importance of foreign currency debt). These forms bring with it increased volatility, external vulnerability and financial instability.

In circulation, strategies may emerge in ACEs wherein increased household indebtedness and/ or asset market inflation maintain aggregate demand. Lower levels of income and wealth in ECEs may circumscribe such a model, encouraging the turn to export-led growth, a pattern consistent with their subordinate position within global production networks. This, in turn, encourages the development of domestic financial markets and may put downward pressure on wages, benefits and taxes which underpin systems of social reproduction (e.g. health, education and unemployment insurance), encouraging a turn towards private welfare provision (see Lavinas, in this volume). Finally, ECEs' subordinate position in relation to money and capital markets means that capital inflows are predominantly short-term, seeking financial yields rather than assuming productive risk. The results are continued volatility, external vulnerability and subordination to the currencies of the ACEs, which themselves serve to further deepen domestic financialization. By highlighting the potentially negative implications, the chapter concludes that, while by no means pre-destined, financialization as experienced in ECEs may serve to further cement their subordinate position in the global structure.

Internationalization of Production

The first transformation of global capital accumulation considered crucial to conceptualize financialization phenomena in ECEs is the internationalization of production, that is, the creation of global networks of production, transforming value creation and labor relations. As the literature on Global Value Chains (GVCs) and Global Production Networks (GPNs) shows, large firms, more often than not originating from the capitalist core, have disaggregated production processes and distributed them over the globe ranging from loose relationships such as competitive customer-supplier relations to tight intra-firm relations (Gereffi et al. 2005). Although specifics depend on the actual configuration of the network, common to these geographically disaggregated production processes is the existence of uneven power relations and extraction of value from weaker parts of the chain which frequently concentrate on lower wage production (Bair 2005). These are often located in the Global South but also in ACE countries such as Spain, Italy or Portugal. While the actual generation of value is increasingly dispersed geographically, profits continue to be captured in the capitalist core (frequently parked in tax havens).

So far, the discussion of how this international reorganization of production shapes, and is in itself shaped by financialization has been rather limited (Powell 2019). In their seminal work, Milberg (2008) and Milberg and Winkler (2010) argue that US firms have generated higher profits due to the mark-ups generated from their powerful positions in GVCs/GPNs, towards both suppliers and workers, which has allowed them to sustain financialization processes through freeing up resources for financial investments. Baud and Durand (2012) add to this by highlighting the ability of lead firms to free cash and reduce financing costs by transferring the need to hold inventories onto their suppliers and extend supplier payment periods. Rather than reinvesting these profits in core activities, they are used to pay higher dividends, buy back shares to drive up stock prices, and pursue mergers and acquisitions. This argument is confirmed econometrically by Durand and Gueuder (2016) and Auvray and Rabinovich (2019) who show that US firms' offshoring decisions were related to the slowdown in gross fixed capital formation.

These changes in international production also have significant effects on ECE firms. On the one hand, although still limited, a few ECE firms (e.g. Tata from India or Embraer from Brazil) have turned themselves into global players and lead firms of global and regional production networks (Mathews 2006; UNCTAD 2007). In line with the argument above, the resulting pooling of profits in the head offices of these firms has generated resources (Toporowski 2009) which could be diverted into financial markets. More generally, their internationalization requires, and indeed enables, Non-Financial Corporations (NFCs) to operate in different financial markets and currencies to obtain funding, hedge currency and operational risks, and invest in financial assets. These new risks and opportunities require increased financial sophistication and tie NFCs' operations to (international) financial markets.

On the other hand, financialization can become a crucial factor in determining a firm's "competitiveness" both between lead firms and within the network itself (Graser 2010; Hiratuka and da Rocha 2015). For example, if global leadership is achieved through mergers and acquisitions both the cost of external financing and large cash holdings are important to take advantage of opportunities and/or fend off hostile takeovers. This is more likely in the case of ECE firms which do not start from a dominant position. Moreover, Randøy et al. (2001: 667) argue that "the global wave of mergers and acquisitions makes it important for companies to boost stock price in order to maintain influence after a potential merger and protect themselves from being taken over."

At the same time, internationalization becomes part and parcel of a more financially oriented firm strategy. Hiratuka and Sarti (2011) and Carmody (2002) show for Brazil and South Africa respectively that in several cases the internationalization of domestic firms aimed explicitly at becoming global players to boost their shareholder value and ability to leverage. This echoes results by Palpacuer et al. (2006) who show for large French agribusinesses that once exposed to international financial markets, further internationalization became an important element of "financial success." According to their results, large international (institutional) investors want global players which can diversify their assets and income streams and are powerful actors in the market. Similarly, Montalban and Sakinç (2013) argue that externalization and outsourcing are important consequences of shareholder value orientation, as these practices can decrease the level of capital used and increase returns on assets.

Whereas these processes are likely to be found in ACEs, this chapter contends that in the case of ECEs they will be mediated through their subordinate position in financial and product markets (Painceira 2011; Powell 2013; Kaltenbrunner and Painceira 2016). As to financial markets, whereas ACEs' firms can largely fund themselves in domestic financial markets and currencies, recent surges of ECEs' NFCs borrowing have been predominantly in foreign currency and on international financial markets (Bruno and Shin 2015; McCauley et al. 2015). This not only deepens their vulnerability to exchange rate changes but also ties them further to financial markets when attempting to hedge the resulting risk. As a result, several ECEs, such as Brazil, Mexico and Poland, have seen a substantial increase in domestic derivatives markets (Farhi and Borghi 2009). In several cases, such as the cellulose producer Aracruz in Brazil or the tortilla maker Gruma in Mexico, these operations also turned speculative and led to substantial losses in the international financial crisis of 2008.

At the same time, the predominance of debt issues on international financial markets (offshore), combined with a generally larger share of foreign investors in domestic debt markets, has deepened ECEs' vulnerability to international market conditions and required a more sophisticated management of the resulting risks. One distinct element of ECE firm financialization has been the substantial increase in cash holdings (Karwowski 2012; Powell 2013) which were, at least partly, precautionary (Demir 2009; Akkemik and Özen 2014). One could argue that international investors are more forceful in putting shareholder value pressures on domestic NFCs. These global operators with vast international portfolios can easily adjust their positions. This gives these institutions a higher possibility of "exit" hence putting pressure on domestic NFCs. Offshore issuance also means that the debt is issued under the law of the country of arbitration which reduces the influence of national legal systems and more generally the reach of the ECE state. Arguably, the terms of these debt contracts will be designed by the large international financial institutions intermediating and marketing the debt, which potentially endows them with an informational and operational advantage (e.g. with regards to their underlying risks).

Finally, there is some evidence that ECE firms' internationalization and increased financialization has interacted with the financialization of other sectors, although experiences vary from country to country and more research is needed. For example, the increased financial needs of ECEs have required increased financial sophistication from domestic banking systems and/or fostered foreign bank entry to fill the void. Reflecting another element of ECEs' financial subordination, foreign banks tend to have better access to international financial markets and experience and information on offshore markets which gives them an advantage over domestic banks (Pelletier 2018).

Internationalization of Circulation and Profit Realization

As production becomes internationalized, new issues emerge in the phase of profit realization. In the present conditions of increasing concentration and intensive exploitation of global productive networks, companies are capable of holding down labor costs; low wages in turn create the issue of ensuring adequate effective demand to allow profit realization and the continuation of capital accumulation. Financialization has in this sense been understood as a way to ease the problem of low demand and thus counter the potential stagnation tendencies of global capitalism (Magdoff and Sweezy 1987; Harvey 2011). This line of thought also finds echoes in the Post Keynesian and "Regulationist" literature that focuses on a "finance-dominated" accumulation regime where financial dynamics affect aggregate demand (Boyer 2000; Hein 2012; Stockhammer, in this volume).

In this line of thought, financialization can stimulate aggregate demand through two main channels: asset price inflation and increasing indebtedness. Rising asset prices – especially housing (Aalbers, Fernandez and Wijburg, this volume) – and increasing credit to households have been crucial to stimulate demand and sustain accumulation, through a combination of reduced saving and wealth effects on consumption (Cynamon and Fazzari 2008; Crouch 2009). At the global level, the location of production and realization of profits through these mechanisms do not have to coincide: surplus value extracted in one country may well be exported and realized as profit in another, where asset price inflation and indebtedness fuel demand. In an internationalized and financialized world economy, the mechanism that sustains aggregate demand and profit realization in individual countries can therefore be either (net) exports or debt-fueled consumption (Stockhammer, in this volume).

Financialization in ECEs needs to be understood in relation to these global patterns of circulation and profit realization. Many ECEs have relied on an export-oriented growth strategy, often as an explicit policy goal that came as part of Washington Consensus policies. Such a strategy however is not purely a matter of policy choice but reflects the restructuring of global production described in the previous section: in general, ECEs occupy a structurally subordinate position within GPNs, favoring a role as producer of primary commodities, intermediate goods, and consumer goods for export. ACEs, and chiefly the United States, have played the counterpart role of the importers, as "debt-financed excess spending from the capital gains of a housing boom turned Americans into the world's buyers of the last resort absorbing the export-led growth of Europe and of many emerging market economies" (Guttmann 2016: 140).

Export-led growth shapes the process of financialization in ECEs in particular ways. At first glance, there is evidence that this growth model reduces the scope for many financialized practices that are typically associated with debt-led economies. In most countries where exports are the key lever of aggregate demand, there is evidence that countries experience lower levels of household indebtedness and less pronounced real estate booms (Karwowski and Stockhammer 2017; Mertens 2017). Nevertheless, as discussed, financialization seen as a global secular phenomenon goes deeper than its cyclical quantitative manifestations. Its structural secular dimensions manifest in ECEs in a way that is mediated by their export-led structure.

Firstly, the proceeds from exports can be channeled towards domestic and international financial markets. As exporters in ECEs realize profits, subdued domestic demand may limit the opportunities for profitable investment. Just like in advanced economies, NFCs and wealthy individuals may then be led to invest in financial markets. As discussed above, there is evidence that NFCs have accumulated a growing share of assets in financial investments, often at the detriment of fixed capital formation (Demir 2007; Correa et al. 2012; Seo et al. 2012; Karwowski 2015; Tori and Onaran 2017). Furthermore, inequalities in the distribution of wealth and income fueled financial asset demand, as large profits were distributed in the hands of high-net worth individuals, fueling stock market booms in several ECEs (Akyüz 2017). A form of "elite financialization" developed in those countries where domestic financial rates of returns – e.g. high interest rates to attract capital inflows – made it possible for wealthier sections of the population to find remunerative savings vehicles (Becker et al. 2010; Araújo et al. 2012). Nevertheless, given the small capacity of ECEs' financial markets as well as their subordination in the global financial system, a large share of this wealth has been invested into ACEs (Lysandrou 2011; Goda et al. 2017).

Secondly, export-led growth has contributed to the accumulation of foreign exchange reserves, where central banks have intervened in the foreign exchange markets. In those countries which experienced current account surpluses – by accident or "neo-mercantilist" design – net exports directly fuelled the accumulation of reserves (Painceira 2009). But even in those "unsuccessful" export-led ECEs, which did not produce substantial current account surpluses, reserves accumulation proceeded on the back of substantial foreign capital inflows (Levy-Orlik 2014; Luna 2015). Accumulation of reserves paradoxically represents both a reaction to financialization dictated by export orientation, and its strengthening: they allow ECEs to act in foreign exchange markets, and thus contain exchange rate volatility, which can have severe destabilizing effects on exports; but they simultaneously represent wealth that is channeled to financial markets, through vehicles such as Sovereign Wealth Funds, in a way not dissimilar to the portfolio decisions of wealthy private investors (Monk 2011; Fichtner, this volume). As discussed further below, these reserves have also been instrumental in driving the development of domestic financial markets (Lapavitsas 2014; Painceira 2012).

Thirdly, financialization may provide ways to support export orientation through its engagement with households. Reforms of social security systems, involving greater reliance on financial markets, have been part of the restructuring of the economy towards export-led growth, often coming as a part of neoliberal "policy packages" (Cosar and Yegenoglu 2009; Becker et al. 2010; Correa et al. 2012; Lavinas 2017). Finance has therefore served as an engine to establish privatized forms of social reproduction, as the competitive pressures of export orientation and the need to keep a country's position within GPNs limit the scope for public provision of welfare. Through these reforms, including the expansion of private pension funds, pooled investment systems, and easier access to credit including for housing purchases, households in ECEs have come to depend to a greater extent on financial markets. Furthermore, credit extension can also work as a disciplining mechanism, undermining the resistance of indebted workers (Karacimen 2015; Mader 2015).

While export orientation represents a key tendency in the majority of ECEs, there have been exceptions. For example, there is evidence that in some ECEs forms of debt-financed consumption have taken place: household debt expansion has at least partly contributed to stimulate aggregate demand in South Africa (Newman 2014), Brazil (Lavinas 2017; Lavinas, this volume), Slovakia (Becker et al. 2010) and Malaysia (Rethel 2010). Finance has therefore worked as a "relief valve" for domestic aggregate demand even in ECEs, at least temporarily. It is not surprising therefore that indebtedness in ECEs has increased in the post-crisis period, as the US tempered its role as global "buyer of last resort," thus limiting the potential of export-led growth.

In sum, financialization can be understood as an aid to circulation and profit realization by stimulating aggregate demand globally. In this, ECEs have mainly – though not exclusively – played a role of exporters to debt-led economies, chiefly the US as the "buyer of last resort." The forms of financialization in ECEs are therefore fundamentally shaped by this phenomenon, as corporations and central banks accumulate wealth that is channeled towards financial assets, fostering the development of financial markets and financial innovation domestically, and households increasingly engage with financial markets to manage those activities necessary to social reproduction. The precise forms taken vary according to each nation's particular involvement with these structural features.

Internationalization of Finance

The final change in global capital accumulation we want to highlight is the tremendous increase in international financial markets, their changing nature, and ECEs' shifting and subordinate integration into them. Moreover, ECEs' integration into these global markets has also changed, in a process which could be considered the international aspect of financialization (Bortz and Kaltenbrunner 2017).

First, in line with the expansion of global finance, ECEs' external assets and liabilities rose from under 33% to more than 130% of their GDP between 1970 and 2013. Capital inflows and outflows rose from 3.52 per cent and 2.22 per cent of GDP in 1976–1985 to more than 6 per cent and nearly 8 per cent respectively in 2006–2015 (Bortz and Kaltenbrunner 2017).

Second, the nature of these flows has changed and has become highly complex, characterized by new instruments, markets and international actors. As to the actors, traditional investors in

ECEs (such as banks and dedicated funds) have been joined by a wide range of other actors, including institutional investors (pension, mutual and insurance funds) (Bonizzi 2017b) and new types of mutual fund investors such as exchange-traded funds and macro hedge funds (Aron et al. 2010; Jones 2012; Yuk 2012). Given the enormous size of these financial investors, even a small reallocation of their portfolio can have a substantial impact on capital flows to ECEs. Moreover, these different actors have diverse investment strategies and funding patterns, substantially increasing the complexity of foreign investment. With regards to the instruments and markets, foreign investors have gained access to a wider set of (domestic currency) assets, such as equities, derivatives, and local bond markets (Kaltenbrunner and Painceira 2015; Akyüz 2017). Kaltenbrunner and Painceira (2015) argue that the returns of these assets are often based on capital gains, rather than investment income, which potentially increases the volatility of capital flows and increases the importance of open and liquid financial markets for portfolio adjustment. In the case of domestic currency assets, the exchange rate becomes an important element of these capital gains, resulting in destabilizing feedback dynamics not only in asset prices but also the exchange rate.

Third, the relation between domestic actors and international financial markets has tightened considerably. NFCs from ECEs have become active players on international financial markets and internationalized their balance sheets. ECEs' banks have expanded internationally, partly accompanying the increase in outward FDI, partly offering their rich domestic clients new investment opportunities abroad, and partly on their own account (World Economic Forum 2012). In many ECEs household lending has surged, in several of them largely denominated in foreign currency (Gabor 2010).

In line with the argument of this chapter, these changes in ECEs' financial integration were shaped by their subordinate position in the international financial and monetary system which manifested itself both in the nature of their international financialization and its implications. As to the former, although ECE public actors could borrow increasingly in domestic currency (less so private ones which had to rely largely on international dollar funding as discussed above) and seemingly move away from their traditional "original sin," foreign financial flows to those countries have remained relatively volatile. They have been dominated by short-term financial return considerations rather than productive, long-term investment. One example are the notorious carry trade operations, where financial actors borrow in low interest rate currencies, such as the Japanese Yen or the US Dollar, and invest in high-interest ECE currencies, taking advantage of the interest rate differential and very often sustained periods of exchange rate appreciation caused by those same carry trade operations. These high interest rates and profitable exchange rate movements, in turn, are an expression of ECEs' international monetary subordination necessary to compensate for these currencies' lower standing in the international currency hierarchy.

Even long-term investors and those invested in domestic assets remain funded on international financial markets. This maintains their sensitivity to international market conditions and depreciation pressures on ECEs' assets and currencies as funds need to be repatriated in the future. For example, Bonizzi (2017b) shows that despite their longer time horizons pension fund investment in ECEs will not act as a stabilizing force due to their need to match their liabilities, which are predominantly located in the capitalist core. Finally, probably one of the clearest manifestations of ECEs' subordinated position in international finance has been the phenomenon of reserve accumulation. As mentioned in the previous section, rather than being channeled into the economy, billions of dollars have been absorbed by ECE central banks to protect against future capital outflows (and frequently to deal with the exchange rate volatility associated with both capital in- and outflows).

Though still quite limited, several authors have shown how these aspects of ECEs' financial integration have shaped domestic financialization processes. For example, volatile capital and exchange rate movements tighten economic actors', in particular NFCs', relations to derivatives and financial markets more generally (Coutinho and Belluzzo 1998; Correa et al. 2012; Akkemik and Özen 2014). Painceira (2011) shows convincingly, in the case of Brazil and South Korea, how reserve accumulation and consequent sterilization operations (the sale of short-term government bonds by the central bank to absorb the additional money created from its foreign exchange purchases) contributed to the financialization of banks (reflected in an expansion of balance sheets and increase in market funding) and households (through consumption loans). According to his argument, domestic banks used the sterilization bonds issued by the central banks to (a) increase their own short-term funding and (b) use this short-term funding to increase their lending to households.

In sum, in addition to changes in the international organization and realization of production, the changing nature of international financial markets themselves have contributed fundamentally to financialization processes in ECEs. On the one hand, this refers to the growing but subordinate nature of ECE financial integration, which is dominated by short-term capital flows that remain funded in ACE currencies. On the other hand, such integration has fundamentally shaped the financial practices of domestic agents, such as the holding of financial assets by NFCs and the expansion of bank loans for consumption.

Conclusions

This chapter has argued that ECEs' financialization emerges and is fundamentally shaped by the subordinate nature of their integration into the world economy. We have examined how this has played out across production, circulation and finance. In production, the global disaggregation of production networks, and ECE firms' emerging leadership and/or integration into these networks, has given rise to new financial practices and relations through the centralization of profits, and novel risks, opportunities and pressures. In circulation, ECEs' integration into a global system of surplus realization and the need to boost domestic demand through exports has provided impetus for the increased depth and sophistication of domestic financial markets and exerted pressures on systems of social reproduction. In finance, the increased size and complexity of international financial integration has drawn ECE agents, instruments, and markets deeper into the remit of global financial markets. In all three spheres, the chapter showed that these processes have been mediated by ECEs' subordinate position in global production and finance, which has both contributed to financialization in these countries (e.g. through the heightened volatility of domestic asset prices and the exchange rate) and given it its specific forms (e.g. the importance of foreign currency operations).

The argument has an important corollary. Not only has financialization been mediated by ECEs' global subordination, but these same processes of financialization may serve to cement or even deepen their subordination in the global hierarchy of nations. As shown in this chapter, financialization will benefit lead firms of global production networks, still located predominantly in ACEs, which are able to channel pooled profits into financial markets and deploy financialized strategies. The costs of engaging in GPNs will be relatively higher for ECE firms. At the same time, many of the ECE firms which have acquired global leadership and been able to profit from increasingly sophisticated financial markets have been from traditionally strong sectors such as mining and raw materials (at least in the case of Latin America and Africa), whereas other sectors involving high-risk innovation have suffered from the increased volatility and risk brought by financialized capitalism. From the perspective of circulation, insofar as financialization reinforces export orientation, this makes ECEs more vulnerable to the volatility of an ever more finance-dominated global demand, the relative decline of which has created several problems for ECEs in the post-crisis era. On the financial side, financialization has helped to maintain relatively high interest rates, and exacerbate external vulnerability and asset price volatility, rendering it yet more difficult to overcome subordination through attracting more stable long-term investment and/or developing domestic financial markets.

The implications of both cyclical processes of financialization and secular changes associated with financialized capitalism across the uneven hierarchy of global capitalism remain underexplored. More research is needed on the concrete ways in which the uneven nature of international finance and production are both shaped by and exacerbate changes in the financial relations and practices of global, regional and national economic actors.

Bibliography

Akkemik, K.A. and Özen, Ş., 2014. Macroeconomic and Institutional Determinants of Financialisation of Non-Financial Firms: Case Study of Turkey. *Socio-Economic Review*, 12(1), pp. 71–98.

Akyüz, Y., 2017. *Playing with Fire: Deepened Financial Integration and Changing Vulnerabilities of the Global South*. Oxford: Oxford University Press.

Araújo, E., Bruno, M. and Pimentel, D., 2012. Financialization against Industrialization: A Regulationist Approach of the Brazilian Paradox. *Revue de La Régulation. Capitalisme, Institutions, Pouvoirs*, 11(Spring).

Aron, J., Leape, J. and Thomas, L., 2010. Portfolio and Capital Markets in South Africa. Paper presented at the CSAE Conference 2010 Economic Development in Africa, 21–23 March, Oxford.

Auvray, T. and Rabinovich, J., 2019. The financialisation–offshoring nexus and the capital accumulation of US non-financial firms. *Cambridge journal of economics*, 43(5), pp. 1183–1218.

Bair, J., 2005. Global Capitalism and Commodity Chains: Looking Back, Going Forward. *Competition & Change*, 9(2), pp. 153–180.

Baud, C. and Durand, C., 2012. Financialization, Globalization and the Making of Profits by Leading Retailers. *Socio-Economic Review*, 10(2), pp. 241–266.

Becker, J., Jager, J., Leubolt, B. and Weissenbacher, R., 2010. Peripheral Financialization and Vulnerability to Crisis: A Regulationist Perspective. *Competition and Change*, 14(3–4), pp. 225–247.

Bonizzi, B., 2013. Financialization in Developing and Emerging Countries. *International Journal of Political Economy*, 42(4), pp. 83–107.

Bonizzi, B., 2017a. An Alternative Post-Keynesian Framework for Understanding Capital Flows to Emerging Markets. *Journal of Economic Issues*, 15(1), pp. 137–162.

Bonizzi, B., 2017b. Institutional Investors' Allocation to Emerging Markets: A Panel Approach to Asset Demand. *Journal of International Financial Markets, Institutions and Money*, 47, pp. 47–64.

Bortz, P.G. and Kaltenbrunner, A., 2017. The International Dimension of Financialization in Developing and Emerging Economies. *Development and Change*, 49(2), pp. 375–393.

Boyer, R., 2000. Is a Finance-led Growth Regime a Viable Alternative to Fordism? A Preliminary Analysis. *Economy and Society*, 29(1), pp. 111–145.

Bruno, V. and Shin, H.S., 2015. Global Dollar Credit and Carry Trades: A Firm-level Analysis. *BIS Working Paper*, 51.

Carmody, P., 2002. Between Globalisation and (post) Apartheid: The Political Economy of Restructuring in South Africa. *Journal of Southern African Studies*, 28(2), pp. 255–275.

Correa, E., Vidal, G. and Marshall, W., 2012. Financialization in Mexico: Trajectory and Limits. *Journal of Post Keynesian Economics*, 35(2), pp. 255–275.

Cosar, S. and Yegenoglu, M., 2009. The Neoliberal Restructuring of Turkey's Social Security System. *Monthly Review*, 60(11), pp. 36–49.

Coutinho, L.G. and Belluzzo, L.G.D.M., 1998. Financeirização da Riqueza, Inflação de Ativos e Decisões de Gasto em Economias Abertas. *Economia e Sociedade*, 11, pp. 137–150.

Crouch, C., 2009. Privatised Keynesianism: An Unacknowledged Policy Regime. *The British Journal of Politics & International Relations*, 11(3), pp. 382–399.

Cynamon, B.Z. and Fazzari, S.M., 2008. Household Debt in the Consumer Age: Source of Growth–Risk of Collapse. *Capitalism and Society*, 3(2), article 3.

Demir, F., 2007. The Rise of Rentier Capitalism and the Financialization of Real Sectors in Developing Countries. *Review of Radical Political Economics*, 39(3), pp. 351–359.

Demir, F., 2009. Financialization and Manufacturing Firm Profitability under Uncertainty and Macroeconomic Volatility: Evidence from an Emerging Market. *Review of Development Economics*, 13(4), pp. 592–609.

Durand, C. and Gueuder, M., 2016. The Investment–Profit Nexus in an Era of Financialisation and Globalisation. A Profit Centred Perspective. *Post Keynesian Economics Study Group Working Paper*, 1614.

Farhi, M. and Borghi, R., 2009. Operações com Derivativos Financeiros das Corporações de Economias Emergentes no Ciclo Recente. *Estudos Avançados*, 23(66), pp. 169–188.

Gabor, D., 2010. *Central Banking and Financialization: A Romanian Account of How Eastern Europe Became Subprime.* Basingstoke: Palgrave Macmillan.

Gereffi, G., Humphrey, J. and Sturgeon, T., 2005. The Governance of Global Value Chains. *Review of International Political Economy*, 12(1), pp. 78–104.

Goda, T., Onaran, Ö. and Stockhammer, E., 2017. Income Inequality and Wealth Concentration in the Recent Crisis. *Development and Change*, 48(1), pp. 3–27.

Graser, S., 2010. *Realwirtschaftliche und Finanzwirtschaftliche Internationalisierung: Die besondere Relevanz fuer Emerging Market Multinationals.* Wiesbaden: Gabler Verlag.

Guttmann, R., 2016. *Finance-Led Capitalism: Shadow Banking, Re-Regulation, and the Future of Global Markets.* Basingstoke: Palgrave Macmillan.

Harvey, D., 2011. *The Enigma of Capital: And the Crises of Capitalism.* London: Profile Books.

Hein, E., 2012. Finance-dominated Capitalism, Re-distribution, Household Debt and Financial Fragility in a Kaleckian Distribution and Growth Model. *PSL Quarterly Review*, 65(260), pp. 11–51.

Hiratuka, C. and da Rocha, M., 2015. Grandes Grupos no Brasil: Estrategias e Desempenho nos Anos 2000. *Ipea Texto para Discussao*, 2049.

Hiratuka, C. and Sarti, F., 2011. Investimento Direto e Internacionalizacao de Empresa Brasileiras no Periodo Recente. *Ipea Texto para Discussao*, 1610.

Jones, S., 2012. Macro Funds Seek Succour in Emerging Markets. *Financial Times*, 24th October.

Kaltenbrunner, A., 2015. A Post Keynesian Framework of Exchange Rate Determination: A Minskyan Approach. *Journal of Post Keynesian Economics*, 38(3), pp. 426–448.

Kaltenbrunner, A. and Lysandrou, P., 2017. The US Dollar's Continuing Hegemony as an International Currency: A Double-matrix Analysis. *Development and Change*, 48(4), pp. 663–691.

Kaltenbrunner, A. and Painceira, J.P., 2015. Developing Countries' Changing Nature of Financial Integration and New Forms of External Vulnerability: The Brazilian Experience. *Cambridge Journal of Economics*, 39(5), pp. 1281–1306.

Kaltenbrunner, A. and Painceira, J.P., 2016. International and Domestic Financialisation in Middle Income Countries: The Brazilian Case. *FESSUD Working Paper*, 146. Retrieved from http://fessud.eu/working-papers/#WP6.

Karacimen, E., 2015. Interlinkages between Credit, Debt and the Labour Market: Evidence from Turkey. *Cambridge Journal of Economics*, 39(3), pp. 751–767.

Karwowski, E., 2012. Financial Operations of South African Listed Firms: Growth and Financial Stability in an Emerging Market Setting. *iii conferencia international do ieSe*, Mozambique September. Retrieved from www.iese.ac.mz/lib/publication/III_Conf2012/IESE_IIIConf_Paper6.pdf

Karwowski, E., 2015. The Finance–Mining Nexus in South Africa: How Mining Companies Use the South African Equity Market to Speculate. *Journal of Southern African Studies*, 41(1), pp. 9–28.

Karwowski, E. and Stockhammer, E., 2017. Financialisation in Emerging Economies: A Systematic Overview and Comparison with Anglo-Saxon Economies. *Economic and Political Studies*, 5(1), pp. 60–86.

Lane, M.P.R. and Milesi-Ferretti, M.G.M., 2017. International Financial Integration in the Aftermath of the Global Financial Crisis. *IMF Working Paper*, 115.

Lapavitsas, C., 2014. *Profiting Without Producing: How Finance Exploits Us All.* London: Verso Books.

Lavinas, L., 2017. How Social Developmentalism Reframed Social Policy in Brazil. *New Political Economy*, 22(6), pp. 628–644.

Levy-Orlik, N., 2014. Financialisation in Unsuccessful Neo-Mercantilist Economies: External Capital Inflows, Financial Gains and Income Inequality. *Limes+*, XI(3), pp. 147–175.

Luna, V. M. I., 2015. Foreign exchange reserves accumulation in Latin America during the current crisis. *Economía Informa*, 392L, pp. 3–13.

Lysandrou, P., 2011. Global Inequality and the Global Financial Crisis: The New Transmission Mechanism. In: Michie, J. (ed.). *The Handbook of Globalisation*. Cheltenham: Edward Elgar, pp. 495–517.

Mader, P., 2015. *The Political Economy of Microfinance: Financializing Poverty.* Basingstoke: Palgrave Macmillan.

Magdoff, H. and Sweezy, P.M., 1987. *Stagnation and the Financial Explosion.* New York: Monthly Review Press.

Mathews, J.A., 2006. Dragon Multinationals: New Players in 21st Century Globalization. *Asia Pacific Journal of Management*, 23(1), pp. 5–27.

McCauley, R., McGuire, P. and Shushko, V., 2015. Dollar Credit to Emerging Economies. *BIS Quarterly Review*, December, pp. 27–41.

Mertens, D., 2017. Putting 'Merchants of Debt' in their Place: The Political Economy of Retail Banking and Credit-based Financialisation in Germany. *New Political Economy*, 22(1), pp. 12–30.

Milberg, W., 2008. Shifting Sources and Uses of Profits: Sustaining US Financialization with Global Value Chains. *Economy and Society*, 37(3), pp. 420–451.

Milberg, W. and Winkler, D., 2010. Financialisation and the Dynamics of Offshoring in the USA. *Cambridge Journal of Economics*, 34(2), pp. 275–293.

Monk, A.H.B., 2011. Sovereignty in the Era of Global Capitalism: The Rise of Sovereign Wealth Funds and the Power of Finance. *Environment and Planning A: Economy and Space*, 43(8), pp. 1813–1832.

Montalban, M. and Sakinç, M.E., 2013. Financialization and Productive Models in the Pharmaceutical Industry. *Industrial and Corporate Change*, 22(4), pp. 981–1030.

Newman, S., 2014. *Financialisation and the Financial and Economic Crises: The Case of South Africa.* Financialisation, Economy, Society & Sustainable Development (FESSUD) Project. Retrieved from https://econpapers.repec.org/paper/fesfstudy/fstudy26.htm

Painceira, J.P., 2009. Developing Countries in the Era of Financialisation: From Deficit Accumulation to Reserve Accumulation. *Research on Money and Finance Discussion Paper*, 4. Retrieved from http://ideas.repec.org/p/rmf/dpaper/04.html

Painceira, J.P., 2011. *Central Banking in Middle Income Countries in the Course of Financialisation: A Study with Special Reference to Brazil and Korea.* PhD Dissertation, SOAS, University of London.

Painceira, J.P., 2012. Financialisation, Reserve Accumulation and Central Bank in Emerging Economies: Banks in Brazil and Korea. *Research on Money and Finance Discussion Paper*, 38.

Palloix, C., 1975. *L'economie mondiale capitaliste*, Paris: François Maspero.

Palpacuer, F., Perez, R., Tozanli, S. and Brabet, J., 2006. Financiarisation et globalisation des stratégies d'entreprise: Le cas des multinationales agroalimentaires en Europe. *Finance Contrôle Stratégie*, 9(3), pp. 165–189.

Pelletier, A., 2018. Performance of Foreign Banks in Developing Countries: Evidence from Sub-Saharan African Banking Markets. *Journal of Banking & Finance*, 88, pp. 292–311.

Powell, J., 2013. *Subordinate Financialisation: A Study of Mexico and its Non-Financial Corporations.* PhD dissertation, SOAS, University of London.

Powell, J., 2019. Towards a Marxist Theory of Financialized Capitalism. In: Pew, P. et al. (eds.). *The Oxford Handbook of Karl Marx.* New York: Oxford University Press, pp 629–650.

Prates, D.M. and Andrade, R., 2013. Exchange Rate Dynamics in a Peripheral Monetary Economy. *Journal of Post Keynesian Economics*, 35(3), pp. 399–416.

Randøy, T., Oxelheim, L. and Stonehill, A., 2001. Corporate Financial Strategies for Global Competitiveness. *European Management Journal*, 19(6), pp. 659–669.

Rethel, L., 2010. Financialisation and the Malaysian Political Economy. *Globalizations*, 7(4), pp. 489–506.

Seo, H.J., Kim, H.S. and Kim, Y.C., 2012. Financialization and the Slowdown in Korean Firms' R&D Investment. *Asian Economic Papers*, 11(3), pp. 35–49.

Stockhammer, E., 2015. Rising Inequality as a Cause of the Present Crisis. *Cambridge Journal of Economics*, 39(3), pp. 935–958.

Toporowski, J., 2009. International Business and the Crisis. *Critical Perspectives on International Business*, 5(1/2), pp. 162–164.

Tori, D. and Onaran, Ö., 2017. Financialisation and Physical Investment: A Global Race to the Bottom in Accumulation? *Post Keynesian Economics Study Group Working Paper*, 1707.

UNCTAD, 2007. *Global Players from Emerging Markets: Strengthening Enterprise Competitiveness Through Outward Investment.* Geneva.

World Economic Forum, 2012. *Financial Development Report.* New York: World Economic Forum.

Yuk, P., 2012. The Rise of Emerging Markets ETFs. *Financial Times*, 18th October.

16

FINANCIALIZATION AND STATE TRANSFORMATIONS

Yingyao Wang

Introduction

One of the widely cited definitions of financialization refers to the phenomenon as "the increasing role of financial motives, financial markets, financial actors, and financial institutions in the operation of domestic and international economy" (Epstein 2005: 3). In this account of financialization, the object that was being financialized was foremost the economy.

The state, however, has remained largely underdeveloped in this flourishing literature on financialization. Few accounts and little evidence were available to assess what roles the state has played in financializing the economy and whether the state itself was an object of financialization, until recently. Beyond merely facilitating the expansion of financial markets by supplying policies, states actively participated in financial markets through making sovereign debts marketable (Hardie 2012; Davis and Walsh 2016; Lagna 2016; Fastenrath et al. 2017). Furthermore, states have strategically turned to finance for providing public goods and stimulating growth (Dixon and Sorsa 2009; Pacewicz 2013). Allegedly, financialization has been a rising paradigm of governance and a new form of statecraft that allowed some states to eschew altogether the politics associated with fiscal policy and reinvent their relationship with markets, in particular the financial market (see also Braun and Gabor, this volume).

Building on the above insights, this chapter deepens the examination of the interface between states and financial markets. It presses further on the distinctiveness of the state's engagement with finance and how it is different from other market actors. I submit that state transformation and financialization are endogenously connected. A thorough examination of the state–finance nexus requires treating states as ensembles of organizations and sets of powerful ideas that interact with the inner working of finance in complicated ways. To substantiate my argument that state and finance are enmeshed in each other, I uncover its three interrelated processes. First, the engagement of the state with finance has provided the state with opportunities for self-invention. Second, rebuilding the state in the image of finance altered the organizational makeup of the state. It has spawned nested principal-agent relationships within the state that further served as the institutional infrastructure for financial market expansion and innovation. Third, sovereign power of the state has leveraging effects on finance via various forms of sovereign promises and guarantees.

This chapter uses the transformation of the Chinese state as an example to develop the three propositions. I show that the Chinese state, in bringing the management of sovereign borrowing and state assets in line with principles of finance, has rebuilt itself into a shareholding state with an extensive system of state asset management. Within this sprawling system, inter-organizational relationships centering around shareholding, delegations, and mutual assurance served as the relational infrastructure for building financial markets. Finally, the omnipresence of sovereign backup by various levels of the Chinese state that permeated the state asset management system served to expand credit and leverage. The Chinese case by no means exclusively or uniquely exhibits the growing interdependence of state and finance that this chapter diagnoses for states around the world more broadly.

The Role of the State in Financialization

Much of the analysis of the financialization of the economy has stopped at the conceptual boundary between economics and politics. Financialization refers to transformations in the structure of the markets or the organization of capitalism, while the question of the state remains outside of the analytical purview. Scholarly discussion on the rise of finance in the broader context of neoliberalization and globalization did strive to include the realm of the political (Harvey 2007; Kotz 2010; Centeno and Cohen 2012), and this body of literature rightly argued that financialization has been accompanied by great transformations of state politics. However, research in this tradition tended to implicitly assume that finance expanded at the expense of the state. The contraction of the state was seen as symptomatic of a general net loss of political capacities under the sway of neoliberalism, for which state weakening was merely part of the definition. We were reminded that everywhere we turned, public sectors were privatized, fiscal spending of the state was constrained, and government regulations were curtailed. Losing assets and capacity, states were left toothless in the face of the rising global finance. Financialization, itself an intrinsic part of liberalization and globalization, only exacerbated the weakening of the state (Şiriner et al. 2016). Relatedly, the crowding-out of industry by finance eroded the jurisdiction and legitimacy of industrial policies that defined the strength of many of the once celebrated "developmental states" (Lechevalier et al. 2017). Global capital flows greatly narrowed the policy range of the national states in influencing domestic economies (Helleiner 2002). Finance-based calculation and reasoning submitted anything possible to (future) market valuations and have colonized the public sectors and legitimated decisions for their privatization (Chiapello 2015; Christophers 2017; Chiapello, this volume). In a word, financialization, arguably another transformative stage of capitalism, has been perceived to have further sealed the fate of the state.

Recent studies on the rise of finance began to consider states as having greater agency in relation to financialization. They asked what state policies have contributed to the rapid ascendance of finance. Scholars demonstrated that the rise of shareholder value as a guiding principle in restructuring firms and establishing corporate controls was first of all a response to state antitrust regulations (Fligstein 1990). Looking beyond firm-level changes, scholars observed that many national governments in the 1980s and 1990s put in place policy changes to lift capital controls, deregulate financial investments, and raise interest rates, which all attracted economic activities to finance (Iqbal and James 2002; Sherman 2009). By foregrounding the effects of policies, regulations, and laws in shaping market incentives, this group of studies found an entry to bring the state back into explaining financialization. This shows that state was not a passive recipient of financial influence but played facilitative roles in the growing dominance of finance.

Empirical and theoretical puzzles remained as to why states liberalized finance and whether this promotional role has exhausted all the ways in which the state and financialization were related to each other. The facilitation explanation treated state actions as external to the economy. It did not include state motives and political interests as forces in their own rights driving financialization. In the past several years, a growing body of scholarship has emerged to call for an extensive and intensive examination of the state–finance nexus by taking the question of the political seriously. Scholars asked why politicians and bureaucrats alike attempted to liberalize finance in the first place. They have drawn attention to the political motivations underpinning financial and monetary decisions (Krippner 2012; Davis and Walsh 2015; Trampusch 2015; Lagna 2016; Quinn 2017). This line of inquiry embedded the analysis of macro-level change in the specific political and social circumstances policymakers were embedded in. Crucially, policy elites were beholden to political and career concerns that were distinctive from those of economic actors. As a result, the new regulatory paradigm with regard to finance might well be less a grand strategy and more an accumulation of expedient solutions assembled to tackle concrete problems politicians and policymakers faced. Still another group of scholars elaborated on the state–finance linkages by examining the interface where states and financial markets intermingled. They looked beyond instances where state action passively legalized finance but forayed into sites, sectors, and situations in which states were active participants in the financial markets. States invested in the market. They also supplied financialized products, or even created financial markets that were previously nonexistent (Pacewicz 2013; Massó 2016; Livne and Yonay 2016; Gabor and Ban 2016; Fastenrath et al. 2017).

Two chief observations follow. First, states were active participants in the financial markets. States' participation in the markets was primarily achieved through the commercialization of sovereign debts. Issuing public debt by governments was hardly new. Yet scholars have identified that the extent to which governments have marketized and financialized their debts was unprecedented. A significant change was found in the growing proportion of "marketable" debts in governmental debt portfolios, and by extension, in the prevalent application of debt policy innovations. In examining the transformation of sovereign debt management in 23 OECD countries, research showed that, prior to 1980, governments sold their debts in the form of bonds with politically controlled interests and to targeted buyers with whom governments negotiated (Verdier 2000). Since the 1980s, governments have packaged sovereign obligations into marketable debts with interest rates determined by the supply and demand of the financial markets. Hoping to broaden their investor bases, governments designed the structures of national public debt markets in a way that they could create liquidity and allow speculations on risks of default (Massó 2016; Lemoine 2017). Aside from the general growth of the public debt market, specific institutional linkages with the financial markets have also developed between state organizations and state-sponsored programs. Departing from a mode of welfare funding through fiscal allocations, present welfare state institutions moved closer to financial markets. State agencies for pensions, housing, education, and healthcare have invested in the market, borrowed from the market, and subsidized market-based financing (Dixon and Sorsa 2009; Mertens 2017). Corporations investing on behalf of government agencies have proliferated in the financial markets and played variant roles in the food chain of securitization, serving as either issuers, underwriters, aggregators, or guarantors (Quinn 2017). Government bonds and debts have been increasingly integrated into the sophisticated architecture of financial engineering. Government debts could serve as bases for the creation of derivatives. Various national governments have freely employed debt-related derivatives to reduce borrowing cost and dress up government debts (Lagna 2016; Massó 2016). Government debts have also been used as collateral in shadow banking as observed in Europe's repo market (Gabor and Ban 2016; Braun and Gabor, this volume).

Second, financialization also provided strategic opportunities for governments to solve problems of a political nature (Krippner 2012; Quinn 2017). While governments became more vulnerable to the crisis-prone dynamics of the financial markets, they also gained access to a range of new tools and a new style of governance that allowed them to creatively cope with existing or prospective political conflicts. States to various degrees were autonomous fields beholden to political and bureaucratic objectives, among which fiscal solvency and political legitimacy were two primary concerns. Furthermore, states were also arenas in which political struggles took place among competing parties, ideological groups, and factions. In these conflicts, financialization can be seen as a political project for seeking fiscal solvency, bolstering political legitimacy, and defeating political rivals. For example, Quinn has demonstrated that financialization—in one of its pioneering places and powerhouses the United States—was driven as much by politics as by the force of the market. In tracing the origins of securitization, Quinn showed that the Johnson Administration in the 1960s, mired in political battles with the federal government over asset sales and the budget, reorganized its housing finance policy by severing Fannie Mae from the government and authorizing it to issue mortgage-backed securities. This policy change shifted governmental support of housing finance out of the purview of budget politics and thus defused political tensions revolving around distribution decisions (Quinn 2017; see also Aalbers, this volume). Similarly, a series of government policies enacted in the late 1970s and 1980s to deregulate financial markets, encourage inflows of foreign capital, and elevate monetary policy to be a central economic policy of the federal government as the result of politicians' reactions to intractable fiscal imbalances and stalled economic growth. Turning to the financial markets allowed policymakers to depoliticeize social and political dilemmas and shift the blame to the market (Krippner 2012).

Furthermore, financialization can also become a tool used in domestic political struggles. The arguments for the development of financial markets were used as weapons by political contenders to undercut the establishment, who allegedly benefitted from the current arrangement of public spending and the entrenched connections with the public sectors (Trampusch 2015). For example, using financial reasoning, Italian pro-market technocrats and center-left politicians attacked the traditional political and business elites who allegedly thrived on high public debt, the growth of the state-owned sector, and a concentrated structure of corporate ownership in the Italian economy (Lagna 2016). The challengers thus aimed to use the logic of financial efficiency to downsize the public sector and disperse ownership concentration.

In all the above cases, governments and political elites reacted to existential threats, whether political or fiscal, and used financial devices and markets to carve out innovative institutional space in which they could seek remedies and turn around the situation in their favor. Such reactions, expedient and practical from the outset, have quickly morphed and accumulated into paradigmatic solutions to political problems. In the past decade, governments were more conscious in their systematic usage of financial instruments and institutions as part of emergent political strategies and systems of governance. This process proceeded in tandem with the changing knowledge structure of the state. Development specialists, financial engineers, and risk managers have been recruited into the state to craft the technical and epistemic apparatus of governance through financial markets (Pacewicz 2013). Political decision-making has further shifted from democratic institutions to sites of technocracy (Streeck 2014; Vogl 2017). Taken together, this body of literature has shown that the relationship between financialization and state transformation was far more complicated than the victimhood argument suggests. In finance-mediated fashion, policy elites reconstituted statehood and reengineered statecraft to meet their political needs. By including the motives of the state, this budding literature cast new light on the origins, contexts, and implications of financialization.

Extending the State–Finance Nexus

Building on these insights, this chapter seeks to extend the inquiry into the state–finance linkages. I submit that there remains analytical room to unpack the processes through which state and finance transformed each other in the age of financialization. I argue that we can further unpack the conception and the organization of the state and ask specifically how state ideas, state organizations and state-making processes dovetailed with the expansive mechanisms of finance. In this spirit, the following questions are examined: first, how the state has built itself through building financial markets; second, how was the internal makeup of the state altered in the project of financialization; third, what is unique about the state as a market actor, and particularly, how the operation of sovereign power has shaped the relationship of the state with finance. Inquiries along these lines entail utilizing and redirecting political sociological tools previously deployed in analyzing state building to parse the causes, processes, and consequences of state transformations during financialization.

Market Building as State Building

State building and market building are recursive processes. By linking public finance to the financial markets, the state introduced new organizations, functions, expert groups, techniques, instruments, and ideas into its apparatus. These new institutions are not isolated add-ons. They are generative and can profoundly transform the parameters of state power. As states created state-backed but legally sanctioned market entities, a liminal category of actors, such as state asset management firms, sovereign wealth funds, state-owned investment firms, emerged in the space between full-blown corporations and governments (Clark et al. 2013; Mertens and Thiemann 2018; Vogel 2018). While marketization might have shrunk some functions of the state, the existence and multiplication of parastate organizations also pushed the boundaries of the states outwards and rendered the divisions between the state and the market increasingly murky. Furthermore, by building financial markets, states also invented new jurisdictions for state business—regulation and management. The need to reconcile the twin roles of the state as both a financial regulator and a market actor anticipates the need for continuous state rebuilding.

The Mutual Constitution of State and Finance Infrastructure

States are not monolithic wholes. States are ensembles of constituent organizations. Financialization boosts the status and power of some ministries, departments, agencies, and personnel bases at the expense of many others. Yet the transformation of the internal makeup of the state involves more than tipping the power balance between parts of the state. States are webs of political relations, constituted through nested principle-agent relationships, positions of intermediation, and acts of delegation. This relational infrastructure of the state can mesh with or can be geared towards building the architecture of financial markets. Primary activities that drove financialization, such as exercising shareholder controls in corporations or engineering complicated financial products, required setting up representative bodies or installing intermediary institutions. To understand how finance and the state mutually constituted each other at a deeper level thus entails investigation into the extent to which authority structure of the states or parastatal organizations supplied the infrastructure of finance or altered states' own relational infrastructures in accordance with the image of finance.

The Leveraging Power of Sovereigns

Westphalian notions of statehood conceive of states primarily through their existence as sovereigns. Sovereigns project supreme authority in given territories. Sovereigns have distinctive sets of capabilities, objectives, and concerns that render the state essentially unlike any other actors in the financial marketplaces. The baseline political potency of the state is defined by its capacity to ensure its existence and maintain some measures of institutional continuity. Therefore, sovereigns are concerned with any systemic risks including those growing in the financial markets that could arouse instabilities and pose existential threats to the continuation of the sovereigns.

Authority is the legitimate exercise of power. Legitimacy exists in the perception of those who are ruled or governed. Similar to the relational construction of authority, what underpins the functioning of any financial markets is a generalized confidence in its sovereign backup and thus its assorted promises about the future (Ingham 2004). In effect, the generalized inscription of sovereign confidence in finance can be translated into various forms of sovereign promises, which includes underwriting loans, backing up borrowing with tangible and intangible public assets, the enlisting of public confidence in certain financial products and the financial market in general, and the implicit assumptions about the unlikelihood of government defaults and about the likelihood of government bailout in the face of vaguely defined "systemic risk," which all can become indispensable parts of the financial structures and aid the construction of many financialized products (Knafo 2013). Resorting to government as the lender of last resort is the financial expression of sovereign power in action. To some extent, sovereigns per se can be defined through their capacity to declare states of emergency and the monopoly over final decisions (Schmitt, 2007). The exercise of sovereign power in finance has been observed in incidents of government guarantees, bailouts, and government-assisted recapitalization programs. Sovereigns aggravate confidence as much as risk. Finance prospers when confidence in the future is high. Governments thus have the unique ability to "leverage" finance, not only through securitizing techniques, but through the more nebulous and taken-for-granted popular assumptions about sovereigns' intentions to support financial activity and their capacity as the ultimate guarantors.

The Financialization of the Chinese State

This chapter uses the Chinese state to examine the above three propositions. The Chinese state can be considered as a strategic case to analyze the evolving linkages between state and finance. Typical of many late developers, China embraced financialization without following the exact routes of development seen in advanced economies. Capitalist forms of financing landed in the heart of a political economy that still maintained statist features. Compared to its counterparts, the Chinese state owned a large amount of state assets which added up to $23 trillion in 2010 on its sovereign balance sheet. State assets included hundreds of thousands of state-owned enterprises, four mammoth state-owned commercial banks, three development banks, tax revenues, land, foreign reserves, social security funds, infrastructures, and facilities. The abundance of such varied state assets heightened the state's managerial needs. The Chinese state has looked to harness financial reasoning and techniques to reinvent the state's role in managing its own assets and governing the growing financial markets in general. The financialization of the Chinese state has markedly reached a scope that far went beyond financializing its public debt.

Yingyao Wang

State Building through Market Building: Making the Chinese Shareholding State

As China attempted to modernize its state-owned enterprises, the idea of shareholder value made its way into the policy realm through the intellectual brokerage of the Chinese institutional economists (Wang 2015). Shareholder value was portrayed as a politically neutral concept that could be used to discipline the state-owned enterprises (SOEs). Candidate solutions for turning around loss-generating public sector companies flowered, ranging from competitive manager selection to technological upgrading to internationalization. The idea of using shareholder value to corporatize the state-owned enterprises became a serious issue when Chinese political elites attempted to reconcile the dilemma between averting privatization yet still harnessing market forces to modernize the public sector. The institutional economists and their sympathizers in the government argued that the problem with SOEs was not about the state ownership itself but the state's execution of rights as an owner. They lamented that the documentation of ownership in SOEs was immensely unclear. Although SOEs were nominally "owned" by the state, state ownership comprised vaguely defined obligations and responsibilities. As state asset loss became a top concern in society and government in the late 1990s, the shareholder value advocates advanced a financial diagnosis of the causes of state asset drain and offered corresponding solutions. The failure of the state to exercise shareholder rights occurred because there was no way to know how much state assets were really worth on the market since state asset transactions often went unmonitored and unmarketized (Wu and Qian 1993; Wu and Xie 1994; Zhou et al. 1994). The solution was to corporatize SOEs according to the financial conception of firms, crown the state as the shareholder with clearly designated rights, and build markets for state asset sales.

This array of diagnosis and prognosis struck the political leadership of the central government as both innovative and politically feasible. The reform of the public sector was carried out largely according to this plan since the only way to assess the worth of state assets was to build markets to measure and reflect their true value. The government carefully designed a financial market for this purpose. To prevent state ownership from being diluted, the stock market for the public sector was tiered in a way that the strategic parts of the state assets were off limit while the non-strategic ones were actively traded. As a result, SOEs enjoyed access to public means of fund raising without jeopardizing majority shareholding by the state.

The formation of the shareholding state set in motion a revolution of the way in which the state managed its assets. The revolution was both epistemic and organizational. More than preventing asset loss, the Chinese government expressly made raising the value of state assets an official objective of the government in 2013. This encouraged a transition in the mode of state asset management from "managing material assets" (*guanzichan*) to "managing capital." (*guanziben*). To fulfill this transition entailed an overhaul of state assets under the jurisdiction of different levels of government. Such efforts included reclassifying state assets in terms of their marketability, moving state assets which were previously out of the reach of the market into its realm, and transforming the government from a passive to an active institutional investor. This epistemic rethinking animated a new bout of organizational building in the Chinese state. A new body of state asset management organizations has mushroomed to marketize, capitalize, and financialize state assets (Wang 2015). They existed in the forms of asset management companies, trusts, investment groups, and holding companies. For lack of a better term, local governments called the aggregation of various asset management bodies and financing vehicles "financing platforms." On these platforms, local governments centralized and professionalized local state asset management where "creative" borrowing took place (Lu and Sun 2013).

The Mutual Constitution of State and Finance Infrastructure: The Multiplication of Financial Agents of the Chinese State

The imperative to craft the state asset management system not only changed the mission and identity of the Chinese state, it also altered the political relations and authority structures within the state. The rise of the Chinese shareholding state reorganized the relationship between the bureaucratic administration and the state-owned business from those of administrative domination to those of corporate control. This transformation however did not necessarily simplify control. Ministries and departments asserted themselves as owners of state business on behalf of the state. Layers of administrations were turned into chains of ownership ties (Wang 2015).

Yet bureaucratic shareholding had its own shares of problems. Administrative bodies were already burdened with day-to-day management of administrative issues. It was legally awkward and professionally inadequate for them to assume extra new roles as shareholders and investors. To address this issue, another stratum of organizations was created between the state administrations and the state firms. The newly created agents of the state were mostly registered as corporate entities and dedicated solely to the mission of asset management. They were designated as corporate offspring of ministries or holding companies in their own rights to solely focus on exercising shareholder rights and investing with state assets. As a result of all the above reorganizations, the Chinese state was remade in the image of a giant conglomeration.

The multiplication of the agents of the state became part and parcel of the institutional infrastructure for securitizing government debts. This phenomenon was especially salient at the local government levels. Chinese local government sought to use the local state asset management system as special purpose vehicles to support urban development, infrastructure, and public welfare projects. Because Chinese local governments were forbidden from borrowing directly from the banks or issuing bonds, they set up municipal investment companies which borrowed and invested on the government's behalf. On these local financing platforms, local governments packaged a wide range of state assets to be used as collateral in order to borrow from the banks. Leased public facilities, stakes in local state-owned companies, and tax revenues have all served as collateral. The most widely used kind of collateral was mortgaged public lands. Although land in China is owned by the central state, the sale and leasing rights remain in the hands of the local governments. Revenue from real estate development has become the largest source of projected income for local governments and has been aggressively tapped to secure loans. Local government financing platforms, operating between the banks and local governments, are the key avenues via which the state can borrow against its collateralized assets. Further, it is not uncommon for one municipal government to have multiple financing platforms, and for one financing platform to have multiple subsidiaries and spin-offs. The availability of more than one agent under local government control enabled government to shift debt obligations around between government controlled corporate entities and greatly smoothed refinancing. Overall, the chained and nested organizational structure of the financing platforms has bolstered financial innovation and heightened hidden risks, in many cases even to the exclusion of the knowledge of local officials themselves.

The Leveraging Power of Sovereigns: The Omnipresence of Government Backup

A generalized confidence in the likely unhindered use of its sovereign power by the Chinese state is implicit in the expansion of China's state asset management system. The sovereignty power has been extended in various practices of delegating and outsourcing the management of state assets to administrative agents and corporate entities. In China's financialized state, nested ownership and shareholding relationships are also relationships of guarantees. At the center of this edifice is the triangle constituted by interdependence among the central state, local governments, and state-owned commercial banks. Local governments routinely turn to state-owned commercial banks for credit. Both the general public and market participants assume that the central state would let neither the local governments nor the state banks go bankrupt. Fiscal transfer from the central to local governments is ready to be deployed. State-owned commercial banks continued to serve as indispensable vehicles of economic growth (Sanderson and Forsythe 2013; Stent 2016). These implicit sovereign promises undergird both excessive risk taking behavior and institutional innovation within the Chinese state.

The recapitalization of state-owned commercial banks and the expansion of China's shadow banking system illustrate the working of the sovereign effect. Throughout the 1990s, state banks were mired in non-performing loans due to their close ties to lossmaking SOEs. The accumulation of bad loans was a major obstacle for reforming China's banking system. The Ministry of Finance (MOF) stepped in to restructure two ailing state banks by transferring their bad loans to an account co-managed by the MOF. What the banks received however was not cash but "receivables" funded by MOF's future claims of the banks' dividends, income taxes, and interest-bearing bonds (Walter and Howie 2011). Altogether, MOF spent $32.6 billion on recapitalizing the four banks. The MOF's usage of IOU was an act of leveraged buyout, built on the self-fulfilling power of the sovereign authority.

Covert and overt sovereign promises also hovered over the rapid growth of China's shadow banking in the past decade. China's Shadow Banking industry is estimated to be worth $15 trillion up to mid-2018 (Bloomberg 2018). Different from regular banks that asked for assets as collaterals to make loans, shadow banks—the majority of them are trusts—rely on guarantees. Guarantees could come from a company, another trust company, or government agency, where the relationships between the three parties are poorly spelled out (Collier 2017). Thus, trust corporations or trust products issued by state-owned commercial banks have become desirable vehicles through which governments or private companies who have close government ties borrow money. Lenders for shadow banks assume that there is always government standing somewhere in the chain behind the loan. To save failing trusts, various local governments have stepped in to convince local banks to supply new loans or even force local companies to buy up bad assets. When economic growth lifted all boats, the sovereign promise was assumed rather than drawn upon. This presupposition has leveraged confidence in the future, which, when aggregated and interlocked, could systematically build up hidden risks in China's financial system.

Aware of the potential risks, Chinese central government has doubled its effort to place more stringent budgeting and auditing rules on local governments. It has put caps on local government loans, marketized local financing platforms, and banned the riskiest products in the shadow banking industry. Yet, with the developmentalist drive strong among local officials and local governments barred from issuing bonds on their own, the incentives for creative borrowing and financialization remain in place. The Chinese state, like many other states that have resorted to the financial markets to rejuvenate public financing, eventually will have to come to terms with the limitations in using financialization to bolster political legitimacy.

Conclusion

This chapter synthesized and extended the research on the role of the state in financialization. It has drawn attention to a rising body of research that shows states to be more than just promoters and facilitators of financial markets. States have used financial instruments and institutions to solve political problems associated with public finance. This new development in research on the state–finance nexus calls for more systematic examinations of how the financialization of the state has engendered new forms of statecraft and systems of governance.

To this end, this chapter invites financialization scholars to extend the inquiry into the state–finance linkages. I argue that there remains analytical space in which we can further unpack the conception and the organization of the state and ask specifically how state ideas, organizations, and processes have responded to the logic of finance. Using China as a strategic case study, I showed that the state and finance are even more endogenously connected to each other than is usually understood, in that the exercise of state power has been constitutive of the rise of finance. The logic of state and finance can mutually facilitate each other's reorganization and expansion. Concretely, endogenous linkages between state and finance were found in three processes: first, states strategically use their engagement with finance as opportunities for self-reinvention; second, state building in the image of finance alters the organizational makeup of the state and has spawned an array of parastatal organizations, as seen in China, which serve as infrastructure for the financial markets; third, the sovereign power of the state, exercised through sovereign promises and guarantees, has a leveraging effect on finance that expands both state power and financial risks. Cases from China's shareholding reform, local development financing, and the growth of its shadow banking industry illustrate the above propositions.

Overall, through highlighting the endogeneity of the development of the deepened state–finance linkages, this chapter has drawn attention to new challenges in regulating the financial market and disciplining the state. It invites more research on parallel national cases from which comparatively informed lessons might be drawn.

Bibliography

Bloomberg. 2018. Cracks are showing in China's shadow banking industry. Available at https://www.bloomberg.com/news/articles/2018-01-23/china-s-15-trillion-shadow-banking-edifice-showing-more-cracks [Accessed February 20, 2019].

Centeno, M.A. and Cohen, J.N., 2012. The arc of neoliberalism. *Annual Review of Sociology*, 38(1), pp. 317–340.

Chiapello, E., 2015. Financialisation of valuation. *Human Studies*, 38(1), pp. 13–35.

Christophers, B., 2017. The state and financialization of public land in the United Kingdom. *Antipode*, 49(1), pp. 62–85.

Clark, G.L., Dixon, A.D. And Monk, A.H.B., 2013. *Sovereign Wealth Funds: Legitimacy, Governance, and Global Power*. Princeton: Princeton University Press.

Collier, A., 2017. *Shadow Banking and the Rise of Capitalism in China*. New York, NY: Palgrave Macmillan.

Davis, A. and Walsh, C., 2015. The role of the state in the financialisation of the UK economy. *Political Studies*, 64(3), pp. 666–682.

Dixon, A.D. and Sorsa, V., 2009. Institutional change and the financialisation of pensions in Europe. *Competition & Change*, 13(4), pp. 347–367.

Eaton, C., Goldstein, A., Habinek, J., Kumar, M., Stover, T.L. and Roehrkasse, A., 2013. Bankers in the ivory tower: The financialization of governance at the University of California. Working Paper Series, Institute for Research on Labor and Employment, UC Berkeley.

Epstein, G., 2005. *Financialization and the World Economy*. Cheltenham, UK: Edward Elgar.

Fastenrath, F., Schwan, M. and Trampusch, C., 2017. Where states and markets meet: the financialisation of sovereign debt management. *New Political Economy*, 22(3), pp. 273–293.

Fligstein, N. 1990. *The Transformation of Corporate Control*. Cambridge, Mass: Harvard University Press.

Gabor, D. and Ban, C., 2016. Banking on bonds: The new links between states and markets. *JCMS: Journal of Common Market Studies*, 54(3), pp. 617–635.

Hardie, I., 2012. *Financialization and Government Borrowing Capacity in Emerging Markets*. London and New York: Palgrave Macmillan.

Harvey, D., 2007. *A Brief History of Neoliberalism*. Oxford: Oxford University Press.

Helleiner, E., 2002. Sovereignty, territoriality and the globalization of finance. In: D.A. Smith, D.J. Solinger and S.C. Topik (eds.) *States and Sovereignty in the Global Economy.* Abindgon: Routledge.

Ingham, G., 2004. *The Nature of Money.* Cambridge: Polity.

Iqbal, F. and James, W.E., 2002. *Deregulation and Development in Indonesia.* Westport: Greenwood Publishing Group.

Knafo, S., 2013. The politics of liberal financial governance and the gold standard. *New Political Economy,* 18(1), pp. 43–63.

Kotz, D., 2008. Neoliberalism and financialization. Paper presented at the Conference at the Political Economy Institute at University of Massachusetts Amherst.

Krippner, G.R., 2005. The financialization of the American economy. *Socio-Economic Review,* 3(2), pp. 173–208.

Krippner, G.R., 2012. *Capitalizing on Crisis: The Political Origins of the Rise of Finance.* Cambridge, MA: Harvard University Press.

Lagna, A., 2016. Derivatives and the financialisation of the Italian state. *New Political Economy,* 21(2), pp. 167–186.

Lechevalier, S., Debanes, P. and Shin, W., 2017. Financialization and industrial policies in Japan and Korea: Evolving institutional complementarities and loss of state capabilities. *Structural Change and Economic Dynamics,* 48, pp. 69–85.

Lemoine, B., 2017. The politics of public debt financialisation: (Re)Inventing the market for French sovereign bonds and shaping the public debt problem (1966–2012). In: M. Buggeln, M. Daunton and A. Nützenadel (eds.) *Taxation, State Spending and Debt Since the 1970s.* Cambridge: Cambridge University Press.

Livne, R. and Yonay, Y.P., 2016. Performing neoliberal governmentality: An ethnography of financialized sovereign debt management practices. *Socio-Economic Review,* 14(2), pp. 339–362.

Lu, Y. and Sun, T., 2013. Local government financing platforms in China: A fortune or misfortune? IMF Working Paper. Available at https://www.imf.org/en/Publications/WP/Issues/2016/12/31/Local-Government-Financing-Platforms-in-China-A-Fortune-or-Misfortune-41131 [Accessed February 20, 2019].

Massó, M., 2016. The effects of government debt market financialization: The case of Spain. *Competition & Change,* 20(3), pp. 166–186.

Martin, R., 2002. *Financialization of Daily Life.* Philadelphia: Temple University Press.

Mertens, D., 2017. Borrowing for social security: Credit, asset-based welfare and the decline of the German savings regime. *Journal of European Social Policy,* 27(5), pp. 474–490.

Mertens, D. and Thiemann, M., 2018. Market-based but state-led: The role of public development banks in shaping market-based finance in the European Union. *Competition & Change,* 22(2), pp. 184–204.

Pacewicz, J., 2013. Tax increment financing, economic development professionals and the financialization of urban politics. *Socio-Economic Review,* 11(3), pp. 413–440.

Quinn, S., 2017. The miracles of bookkeeping: How budget politics link fiscal policies and financial markets. *American Journal of Sociology,* 123(1), pp. 48–85.

Sanderson, H. and Forsythe, M., 2013. *China's Superbank: Debt, Oil and Influence: How China Development Bank is Rewriting the Rules of Finance.* Bloomberg Press.

Schmitt, C., 2007. *The Concept of the Political.* Chicago, IL: The University of Chicago Press.

Sherman, M., 2009. A short history of financial deregulation in the United States. Center for Economic and Policy Research Report. Available at http://cepr.net/publications/reports/a-short-history-of-financial-deregulation-in-the-united-states [Accessed February 20, 2019].

Şiriner, İ., Dobreva, J., Boz, Ç. (eds.) 2016. *Political Economy of Globalization: Financialization & Crises.* London: IJOPEC Publications.

Streeck, W., 2014. *Buying Time: The Delayed Crisis of Democratic Capitalism.* London: Verso.

Stent, J., 2016. *China's Banking Transformation: The Untold Story.* Oxford: Oxford University Press.

Trampusch, C., 2015. The financialisation of sovereign debt: an institutional analysis of the reforms in German public debt management. *German Politics,* 24(2), pp. 119–136.

Verdier, D., 2000. State and finance in the OECD previous trends and current change. *Politics & Society,* 28, pp. 35–65.

Vogel, S., 2018. *Marketcraft: How Governments Make Markets Work.* Oxford: Oxford University Press.

Vogl, J., 2017. *Ascendancy of Finance?* Cambridge: Polity.

Walter, C.E. and Howie, F.J., 2011. *Privatizing China: Inside China's Stock Markets.* Charlottesville, VA: Wiley.

Wang, Y., 2015. The rise of the 'shareholding state': Financialization of economic management in China. *Socio-Economic Review,* 13(3), pp. 603–625.

Wu, J. and Zhou, X., 1988. *A Comprehensive Design of China's Economic Reform.* Beijing, China: Zhanwang Publisher.

Wu, J. and Qian, Y., 1993. On corporatization. *Industrial Enterprise Management*, 8, pp. 38–42.

Wu, J. and Xie, P. 1994. Envision the debt restructuring between the Chinese SOEs and the banks. Paper Presented at the Jinglun Conference, published in Xiao Meng. 1999. *Debt Restructuring and Bankruptcy Procedure in the Reconstruction of Corporate Governance*. Beijing: Central Compilation and Translation Press.

Zhou, X., Lou, J. and Li, J., 1994. The managerial class and the ownership problem in microreform. Paper Presented at the Jinglun Conference, published in Xiao Meng. 1999. *Debt Restructuring and Bankruptcy Procedure in the Reconstruction of Corporate Governance*. Beijing: Central Compilation and Translation Press.

17

THE FINANCIALIZATION OF REAL ESTATE

Manuel B. Aalbers, Rodrigo Fernandez and Gertjan Wijburg

Introduction

Thomas Piketty's *Capital in the Twenty-first Century* (2014) has become one of the key books in contemporary economics and political economy. Although Piketty never mentions the financialization of real estate, his analysis of long-term developments as a "metamorphosis of capital" is indicative of financialization. His data show that in France and the UK the capital-to-income ratio followed a U-shaped curve in the period from the eighteenth to the twenty-first century. A stable capital stock in the range of 600 percent of income throughout the eighteenth and nineteenth centuries was largely based on agricultural land and increasingly from the colonial investment outlets. After WWI the ratio of capital-to-income declined dramatically, only to return from the 1970s onwards. This return towards a large capital-to-income ratio was largely propelled by real estate, i.e., again based on land, although now predominately on urbanized rather than agricultural land. From the 1950s to the 1990s Piketty's data show that real estate wealth as share of overall capital remained stable at 40 percent albeit increasing rapidly vis-à-vis income. In the last two decades, however, the size of real estate increased to 58 percent of the overall stock of wealth and 300 percent of annual income in 2010.

In this *longue durée* exposé of the transforming composition of capital, Piketty demonstrates that the present-day value of real estate in relation to the overall stock of capital and of income is truly without historical precedent. The explanation for the rising capital-to-income ratio, in Piketty's theory, lies in the overarching "laws" of capitalism. On the one hand, we find the decline of the economy of flows, the growth rate of national income, driven primarily by demographic change. On the other hand, we find the combination of a sustained savings rate and return on investment (R) larger than economic growth (G), i.e. R > G, that allows for the capital stock to grow relative to annual income or economic output. Therefore, the stock of capital inflated proportionately to the flows of income and production. What Piketty's laws point to is that the role of real estate, both residential and commercial, as store of value for the growing capital-to-income ratio, is expected to grow in the century ahead. This is where Piketty's wide-ranging theory about the nature of capitalism intersects with the interdisciplinary fields of not only real estate but also financialization studies.

Unfortunately, Piketty does not elaborate on the wider political economy implications of the growing role of housing wealth (beyond inequality). To appreciate both the socio-economic arrangements and consequences of the growing store of value function of real estate, we need to contextualize it in broader contemporary processes and debates and move out of the narrow methodological universe of economics. Elsewhere we have argued that the institutional and ideational structure under which the metamorphosis of capital takes place, is not a by-product of R > G but central to its development and should therefore be at the heart of the analysis that tries to understand its variegation across space and time (Fernandez and Aalbers 2017). Real estate has become more significant in the political economy of the last three decades, not primarily in terms of housing production, but rather as store of value.

The transformation of real estate under financialized capitalism is missing from Piketty's depiction of how capital has increasingly morphed into real estate. The shift from a production-oriented and wage-led post-war economy to a debt-led financialized accumulation regime in the age of financial globalization (Boyer 2000) is critical to understand the new centrality of real estate in the political economy not only in the global north but increasingly also in the global south (e.g. Rolnik 2013; Shatkin 2017). Under the conditions of financialization, real estate became dominant on the balance sheets of households (the property as an asset and the debt as a liability) and financial institutions (the loans as an asset that enable banks to borrow more on the liability side), thereby altering the power relations and conditioning behavior (Hudson 2012; Lazzarato 2012). Finance played a crucial role in this process as capital circulation in the post-war global economy was increasingly mediated *via* a select group of (globally operating) financial institutions and other intermediary channels (Sweezy 1994). With finance and real estate becoming increasingly interdependent, we can thus think of a "real estate–finance nexus" to denote the intensified connections between both sectors (Aalbers 2016).

In the chapter we first ask the question: Why is real estate an object of financialization? This chapter will discuss different answers to this question through a focus on both commercial real estate (offices, retail, etc.) and residential real estate (housing). We pay attention to the key role of mortgage markets – including a discussion of securitization – but also to the rise of investment vehicles such as private equity, hedge funds, listed funds and Real Estate Investment Trusts (REITs) in both residential and commercial real estate. Throughout the chapter, we discuss the role of the state in regulating and facilitating the financialization of real estate. Besides looking at different markets and "financialized" actors, we also show how the real estate–finance nexus (with the state as part of the equation) has allowed for different forms of real estate financialization.

Why is Real Estate an Object of Financialization?

Real estate has always been dependent on finance, whether one unit is purchased individually or as part of a larger portfolio. In the past (and we are consciously vague here, as this is different for different countries), real estate finance was offered through separate channels, i.e. separate from other banking and financial channels. Mortgaged homeownership, for example, was only possible if a large down-payment was made and the remainder of the housing price was typically financed through specialized institutions such as building societies, savings and loans institutions, *Bausparkassen, cajas,* savings banks and credit unions – in many countries general banks have only been allowed to be active in the mortgage market for a couple of decades. States typically treated these specialized mortgage lenders favorably in terms of conditions and taxes.

Real estate generally also acts as a highly valued form of collateral. Like precious pieces of art, real estate is considered to have a secure fixed value. But unlike art, real estate debt and rental income from real estate offer the advantages of scale, standardization, well-established calculative systems, fixed income (respectively interests-cum-instalments and rent) and a highly standardized institutional framework to collect future income streams (Fernandez and Aalbers 2016). Housing-based wealth, that is housing valued at current market prices minus debt, has risen to historically unprecedented heights, implying that real estate has become more important as store-of-value in the age of financialization. In the Eurozone, for example, housing-based wealth grew from €3.7 trillion in 1980 to €13.2 trillion in 1999 and €24.2 trillion in 2006 (BIS 2009; ECB 2006). Since the Great Financial Crisis, the surge in housing wealth stalled in the Eurozone, and reached a relatively stable plateau of roughly €22.5 trillion from 2007 to 2015 (ING 2016: 5). To put this into perspective, the EU market size for government bonds (€7.5 trillion) and EU stock market valuation (€7.2 trillion) combined was smaller than the stock of housing wealth in the EU in 2011, signalling its importance as store-of-value (EPRA 2013).

In fact, banks as well as private equity funds, REITs, housing investment funds and other non-bank financial institutions are increasingly interested in commercial real estate as well as rental housing. This is because real estate debt, as any other type of debt, serves as an investment outlet. Next to public debt from core economies, particularly US T-bills and bonds from blue chip companies, mortgages and real estate are strategic "fixed income" products for institutional investors such as pension funds. These three categories of investments are considered high-quality collateral (HQC).

There is a large and growing pool of liquidity seeking HQC, fed by four sources. Firstly, there is "money manager capitalism" (Minsky 1996) or "pension fund capitalism" (Clark 2000), which is characterized by the expanding investment portfolios of institutional investors (see Fichtner in this volume). Secondly, there is the "savings glut" (Bernanke et al. 2011), i.e. the recycling of the growing trade surplus of emerging economies of $5 trillion (BIS 2012). In the US, for example, the supply of HQC increased by $3.1 trillion between 1998 and 2002, and by $5.1 trillion between 2003 and 2007. The slice of the HQC pie that was acquired by non-residents increased from 22 percent in the first period to 55 percent in the second (Bernanke et al. 2011: 8). Thirdly, in recent years loose monetary policies such as quantitative easing sharply increased demand for HQC (Fernandez and Aalbers 2017). Fourthly, the rise in accumulated profits of transnational corporations in tax havens, amounting to approximately 30 percent of global GDP (Henry 2012), a direct sign of overaccumulation, points to the problematic nature of the absorptive capacity of capitalism in the face of rising corporate profits (Fernandez and Aalbers 2016; see Fernandez and Hendrikse in this volume).

Compared to alternatives, such as unsecured loans, the size of real estate and in particular mortgage markets, even if they are largely nationally bound, enabled investors to create a liquid marketplace that serves to diversify portfolios globally. Through a process known as securitization, mortgage lenders resell their mortgage portfolios in a secondary mortgage market, thereby cleaning up their balance sheets. The move to securitization is far from a global phenomenon, although it has also expanded to the global south (e.g. Pereira 2017), but the sale of, and trade in, mortgage-backed securities (MBS) has rapidly become a global market, with investors coming from almost any country in the world (Gotham 2006; Aalbers 2015). MBS, like REITs, are financial instruments that have de-linked real estate and place by making the intrinsically local and fixed nature of real estate into something liquid and therefore tradable on global financial markets (Gotham 2006, 2012).

Real estate provides a critical outlet for investments, i.e. it acts as "spatial fix" for an endemic state of overaccumulation (Harvey 1985). The absorption of capital by real estate is one of the defining characteristics of the current financialized, real estate-driven regime of accumulation (Fernandez and Aalbers 2016). Henri Lefebvre (1974), David Harvey (1985) and others have theorized the connections between urbanization and capitalism, arguing that the built environment has become essential to both creating and storing surplus value. Building on this literature,

Buckley and Hanieh (2014) have recently argued that in some cases, such as Dubai, urbanization can be seen as a process of financial re-engineering. Furthermore, it could be related to what Crouch (2009) has dubbed "privatised Keynesianism", i.e., both a way to fuel the economy by propping up consumption and to "compensate" labor for decades of negligible or even negative real income growth. In other words, the financialization of real estate resulted in asset-based wealth for the middle, and in some countries also working, classes. Yet, this now appears limited to some generations as younger people are increasingly excluded not only from permanent employment but also from (affordable) housing (Forrest and Yip 2011; Aalbers 2015).

It could be argued that the rise in mortgage debt is the key expression of the financialization of real estate, which is the focus of the next section. However, we can also witness the financialization of real estate in other domains, such as rental housing and commercial real estate – the focus of the subsequent section. Like mortgage debt and the securitization thereof, rental housing and commercial real estate are increasingly seen as investment classes, as assets that are typically considered low-risk while delivering a good return-on-investment compared to other such assets. The rise in mortgage debt and the entrance of "financialized" investment companies in the markets for rental housing and commercial real estate thus exemplify different forms of real estate financialization. Finally, real estate can be financialized in the stage of development and construction (Calbet i Elias 2017; Romainville 2017) or through the use of derivatives and social housing bonds by housing associations (Aalbers et al. 2017; Wainwright and Manville 2017).

Mortgage Markets

The twentieth century could easily be dubbed the century of the mortgage loan. A study of 17 selected advanced economies, including the US, Canada, Australia, Japan and 13 European states, covering the period 1870–2010, found that private-debt-to-GDP ratios remained in the range of 50–60 percent until 1980, but increased to 118 percent in 2010 (Jordá et al. 2014). Although this is noteworthy in itself and illustrative of the rapid rise of financialization since 1980, it is important to note that the debt explosion was primarily an explosion of mortgage debt. Non-mortgage lending remained stable between 1914 and 2010, always hovering between 41 and 46 percent of GDP. What did change was mortgage lending. Between 1870 and 2010 the ratio of mortgage-lending-to-GDP increased from less than 1 to around 7 (ibid.).

At the end of 2004, there was €4.5 trillion of outstanding mortgage loans in the European Union (EU) and €6.1 in the US. Twelve years and a severe crisis later, these figures stand at respectively €7.0 trillion and €9.8 trillion respectively (EMF 2017: 99). And while the mortgage-debt-to-GDP ratio in the US rose from 54 to 86 percent between 1998 and 2007, and subsequently dropped to 62 percent in 2012, the same figure for the EU rose from 32 to 47 and then 51 percent (EMF 2014: 74). In the most extreme case, the Netherlands, the figures are 84, 100 and 105 percent for the same years. At the other end of the spectrum, figures in Romania and Bulgaria stay well below 10 percent (Figure 17.1). In relative terms, small Cyprus saw the biggest increase in mortgage-debt-to-GDP: from 10 to 72 percent in the scope of eight years, even though the homeownership rate dropped from 91 to 74 percent (EMF 2014: 74). Housing prices declined in many OECD countries, most notably in Ireland where they almost halved since the end of 2007 (Figure 17.2). Other notable declines in house prices were recorded in Spain, Romania and Greece. On the other hand, house price continued to increase with more 30 percent in Norway, Turkey and Austria.

Mortgage markets are not just important due to their sheer volume, but also because most homeowners depend on them, because they fuel the economy, can be used as an "ATM" in some countries, both directly and indirectly (through equity withdrawal and so-called "wealth

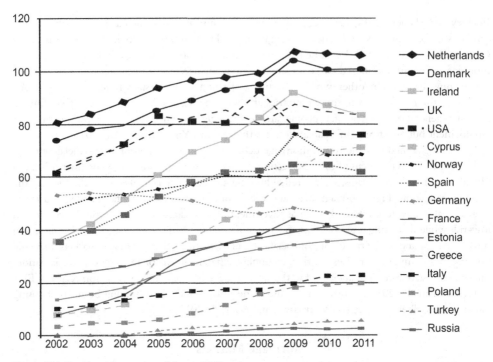

Figure 17.1 Residential mortgage debt to GDP ratio
Source: European Mortgage Federation National Experts, European Central Bank, National Central Banks, Eurostat, Bureau of Economic Analysis, Federal Reserve

effects'), and because they serve an ideological purpose in the neoliberal age. Mortgage markets – and credit markets more generally – have been de- and re-regulated in order to widen access to mortgage markets and thus to fuel economic growth and increase homeownership rates, and thereby further the neoliberal agenda of private property. It comes as no surprise then that important changes to the mortgage market took place earlier in the US than in the UK, and earlier in the UK than in most of continental Europe and elsewhere.

Throughout the history of mortgage markets there have been different kinds of institutions that originate mortgage loans. Historically, most of these institutions have been "depository institutions": lenders that not only make loans but also take deposits from savers. It may seem obvious that lenders need to accumulate deposits as a reserve from which to make loans, but this is not a necessity. It is also possible for a lender to acquire funding in other ways. "Non-depository institutions" may only need a small amount of "working capital" to originate loans if they sell these loans in the secondary mortgage market. Every time they sell a portfolio of loans they have freed up capital that they can use to originate new loans. The share of non-depository institutions grew markedly in the US between the 1980s and 2007, but much less so elsewhere.

Until a few decades ago most mortgage lenders were local or regional institutions. Today, most mortgage lenders are national lenders who tap into the global credit market. This is not so much the case because lenders are global financial institutions – most lenders are national in scope – but because they compete for the same credit in a global market. In the US, Fannie Mae and Freddie Mac, two government-sponsored enterprises that were meant to spur homeownership rates for low- and middle-income households, already introduced mortgage

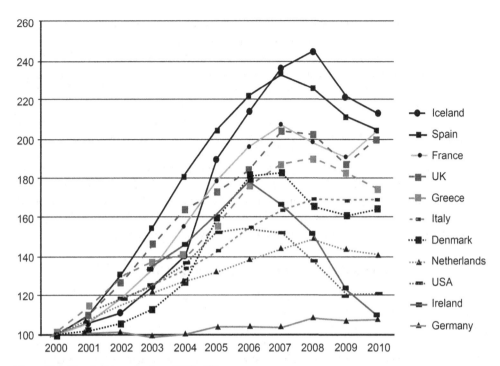

Figure 17.2 Nominal house prices, 2000=100
Sources: European Mortgage Federation, National Statistics Offices, OECD, ECB (for the euro area), US Bureau of Census

securitization in the 1960s. Gotham (2006, 2012) has studied the de- and re-regulation of the mortgage market and demonstrates how the US federal government, step-by-step, has enabled securitization, e.g. by the Financial Institutions Reform, Recovery and Enforcement Act (1989) that pushed portfolio lenders to securitize their loans and shift to non-depository lending. Mortgage portfolios could now be sold to investors anywhere in the world and because these investors thought mortgage portfolios were low-risk and there was a lot of money waiting to be invested, especially after the dot-com bubble crash (2000–2002), there was a great appetite for residential mortgage-backed securities (RMBS). In other words, the Savings & Loans crisis, the following bank merger wave (Dymski 1999), securitization, the entry of non-bank lenders, and the demand for low-risk investments together shaped the globalization and financialization of mortgage markets (Aalbers 2008).

There is a growing body of literature that tries to trace the trajectories of different national structures of securitization (Aalbers et al. 2011; Aalbers and Engelen 2015; Gotham 2006, 2012; Wainwright 2012, 2015; Walks and Clifford 2015). While strongly linked to the surge of financial innovation characteristic of post-Bretton Woods financial markets, securitization is in fact an old financial technique that can be traced back to the creation of proto-mutual funds in eighteenth-century Holland, which issued tradable shares on the back of aggregated life insurance premiums (Rouwenhorst 2005). In essence, today's structured financial products are based on the same principles. Opaque contracts are pooled and sold to a separate legal entity or special purpose vehicle (SPV), which in turn issues bonds to end investors to pay for the underlying assets. The investors receive parts of the cash flow generated by these contracts. In countries like Germany,

France and Denmark, covered bonds are used in a similar way, albeit with one difference: covered bonds remain on the balance sheets of the banks that issued them (Aalbers 2016).

As a result, the amount of information needed to assess the bonds on offer is radically reduced. For example, in mortgage contracts investors do not have to assess the quality of the mortgaged property, the socio-economic expectations of the neighbourhood or the creditworthiness of the mortgagee (Aalbers and Engelen 2015). They only have to assess the reliability of the originator (Is the mortgage granted by a prudential lender?), the sophistication of the structurer (Does the investment bank do a good enough job?), and the trustworthiness of the servicer (Is the servicer a reliable collector of the principal of the loan and interest?). As a result, it has become extremely uncommon for investors to look at the underlying portfolio of their securities, other than through aggregate data. Instead, all risk assessments have increasingly been delegated to rating agencies. These private organizations have a legal mandate to rate the creditworthiness of emitters of bonds and are remunerated for their work by the emitters on a fee-basis. The largest and best-known agencies are Standard & Poor's, Moody's and Fitch.

Commercial Real Estate and Rental Housing

Real estate is by definition spatially fixed, but during the last decades it has been remade into an increasingly liquid asset class (Van Loon and Aalbers 2017). The previous example of financialized mortgage markets has already illustrated that. Yet, portfolio trading among institutional investors and other large corporations is another important manifestation of real estate financialization. Real estate has always been an investment good for some fractions of capital, but in the contemporary, financialized economy, real estate is a key asset, in particular for institutional investors looking for mid- to long-term investment objects (increasingly through indirect investment in real estate) and a range of other "financialized" actors such as private equity firms and hedge funds who are interested in "buying low and selling high" and typically hold large real estate portfolios for a few years at a time.

Ever since the property boom of the 1990s, international investors are more active in both developed and developing countries. Commercial real estate markets are of particular interest because they are heavily tied to both national and international finance, but also because of the tension between location and liquidity. Financial liberalization in the 1980s not only resulted in the rise of mortgage debt; it also triggered property booms as new available credit was linked to the production of new "glitzy office space" in the new business districts of global cities like London, Paris and New York (Pryke 1994). However, since most of these building activities were speculative in nature, a severe property crisis followed and many property developers and investment banks plunged into bankruptcy (Lizieri 2009). With credit drying up and property prices dropping, new market opportunities emerged for those "financialized" actors seeking to profit from falling property prices by "buying low and selling high." American private equity firms and hedge funds entered the commercial markets and introduced new modes of profitability but also undermined long-term stability. Subsequently, the spread of such new "financialized" investment practices was further facilitated and regulated by public bodies of the state. The introduction of new tax regimes made it in various countries for instance possible to invest indirectly in investment vehicles such as listed real estate companies and REITs (Wijburg & Aalbers 2017b; Waldron 2018).

Real estate investment has become a standard investment class for households in many countries and wealth management by institutional investors increasingly relies on investments in commercial real estate. In many advanced capitalist countries, chiefly in Germany, Spain and the US but also in middle-income countries like Brazil, we see a range of funds recently entering also the rental housing market: private equity firms, hedge funds, REITs and publicly listed real estate firms. Like in the commercial markets, a shift from private equity to listed real estate can be observed here. We refer to the original acquisition of different forms of decommodified and not-fully commodified housing (public, social, cooperative, rent-stabilized and company housing) by private equity funds and other opportunistic investment funds as financialization 1.0. The subsequent phase 2.0 starts with the conversion to REITs and listed real estate firms (Wijburg et al. 2018) and is emerging as a trend beyond the cases discussed here (see Table 17.1 for an analytical distinction between financialization 1.0 and 2.0 as applied to housing).

The financialization of rental housing 1.0 in cities like New York and countries like Germany largely took place in the seven years before the global financial crisis (2000–2006) and is characterized by highly leveraged and complex financial deals to acquire decommodified and not-fully commodified housing. Financialization 1.0 is associated with short-term investment strategies of "buying low and selling high" (Holm 2010; Fields and Uffer 2016; Wijburg et al. 2018). Private equity firms and hedge funds operate in a financial web of multiple actors, loans and securitizations, which makes it difficult to conceptualize who really is the landlord and to whom tenants should address their grievances. Private equity firms have a short-term focus (three to five years), are highly leveraged (i.e., loaded with borrowed money and little equity) and typically invest little in maintenance (Diamantis 2013; Fields 2015).

However, in cities like New York and Berlin the financial expectations of the private equity firms often did not materialize. Making money on subsidized rental housing turned out to be harder than expected. Some of these firms simply have collapsed, others had to readjust their strategies: both rents and sales brought in less money than expected and buy- hold- and sell- plans had to be adjusted accordingly (Fields 2015; Fields and Uffer 2016). As a result of the crisis, accessing external finance, crucial for the business models of private equity and hedge funds, became so difficult that most were forced to sell off their portfolios (Aalbers 2016). However, financialization did not stop or halt; many private equity funds were converted into

Table 17.1 Investment strategies under the Welfare State, Financialization 1.0 and 2.0

Phase & Company Structure Characteristics	Welfare State: Social Housing Company	Financialization 1.0: Private Equity and Hedge Funds	Financialization 2.0: Listed Real Estate Companies/REITs
Principal activity	Providing affordable housing for low- and moderate-income households	Buying low and selling high	Managing and maintaining income-producing real estate assets
Debt structure	Fiscal and financial subsidies, bank loans	Low equity and high debt, often through offshore finance (highly leveraged)	Capital markets and offshore finance
Profit versus risks	Non-profit, long-term	High risks, high profits, short-term	Medium profits, low to medium risks, long-term
Tenants	Security of price and tenure	Insecurity of price and tenure	In/security of price and tenure

Source: expanded from Wijburg et al. 2018

REITs and listed real estate companies, and housing portfolios were sold directly to listed real estate funds (Wijburg and Aalbers 2017a). We refer to the take-over of housing portfolios by REITs and listed real estate funds as the financialization of rental housing 2.0.

Unlike private equity and hedge funds, REITs and listed real estate companies appear to adopt a long-term investment strategy to create stable cash flows for their shareholders (Lizieri 2009). They seek to create a "rentier structure" to optimize cash flows, rental incomes and capital gains through the sale of individual housing units (Moreno 2014). While shareholders expect a maximization of shareholder value, listed real estate companies typically seek returns of 4–6 percent annually and are thus devoted to creating continuous cash flow and operative income by renting out housing units and selling individual units at profitable prices (Heeg 2013; IEIF 2014). Furthermore, they seek to enhance the net value of the portfolio, for instance through focusing on core investment strategies, stimulating gentrification effects through modernizations and refurbishments, "gaming" rental regulations and teaming up with local authorities to coordinate neighborhood development (Beswick et al. 2016; Bernt et al. 2017; Wijburg et al. 2018). Since listed real estate companies and REITs typically hold a diversified portfolio they operate in different kinds of national and urban settings: recent examples have shown that REITs have now also appeared in the rental markets of countries as varied as Ireland, Canada, Spain and the autonomous territory of Hong Kong (Aveline-Dubach 2016; Garcia-Lamarca 2017; August & Walks 2018; Waldron 2018).

We argue that the shift towards financialization 2.0 does not signify a radical break with financialization 1.0, but rather a continuation with different means and strategies. For that reason, it must be emphasized that the boundaries between private equity and hedge funds on the one hand and REITs and listed real estate companies on the other are not as clear-cut as it seems. Some private equity funds were already involved in property management before they sold off their portfolios or before their IPO; some listed funds still adopt private equity techniques and divest the less profitable parts of their housing portfolio (Kofner 2012). Both private equity funds and listed real estate companies have become known for gaming rental regulations and for exploiting local opportunity structures (Bernt et al 2017; August & Walks 2018). Increasing evidence also shows how both private equity funds and listed real estate companies engage in a tight network of supporting financial intermediaries, thus extending their activities far beyond the reach of the real estate industry alone and also generating income through fees, commissions and mortgage securitization (Botzem and Dobusch 2017). Table 17.1 provides a summary of the investment strategies of REITs and listed real estate companies compared to both social housing companies emblematic of an active welfare state, and private equity and hedge funds.

The linking of real estate to the stock exchange (see Petry in this volume) denotes a fundamental transformation that is equally observable in residential and commercial real estate markets (Wijburg & Aalbers 2017b). More precisely, it entails a stage of capital accumulation in which real estate portfolios are treated as long-term investment objects for investment funds. Paradoxically, the long-term investment focus of these funds enables a short-term investment focus by buying and selling shares in these funds on the stock exchange. The rent paid by residential or commercial tenants, therefore, no longer merely circulates in the national economy where the real estate is located, but instead is absorbed by capital markets which squeeze out the rental potential from urban areas (Moreno 2014). The implication of this global trend is that the already existing ties between real estate and finance have further tightened (Wijburg et al. 2018). The financialization of real estate not only manifests itself through the expansion of securitized housing debt: the advent of corporate landlords is another manifestation of it.

Coda

Real estate, and housing finance in particular, is not simply one of the many objects of financialization; it is one of the central objects of financialization. The sheer size, both in the form of housing wealth and mortgage debt, is vast and its growing weight on the balance sheets of households, banks and other financial intermediaries mediated particular financialized practices and structured their behaviour during the manic phase of our economies all the way to the crash. Real estate as a carrier of practices of capital accumulation has a strong track record in creating instability (Kindleberger and Aliber 1978; Harvey 1985; Reinhart and Rogoff 2009). The debt-led accumulation model (see Stockhammer and Köhler in this volume), which underpins the financialization of real estate, producing tradable financial assets, feeding financial markets, on the one hand, and supporting private consumption on the other, is clearly not a formula for stability. However, this set of relations has been in the making for at least four decades. We did have a major crash that globally fed growing income and wealth inequality. But overall, the system was resilient and the real-estate/finance nexus remains the dominant model. With reference to Piketty (2014), we may thus expect that the "metamorphosis of capital" during the twenty-first century will increasingly coalesce with the financialization of real estate.

Real estate is not only central to the reproduction of the current highly financialized system (both as a form of collateral and a source for private consumption) but it also is its weak link. As real estate financing systems become more liberalized and global capital markets introduce cheaper mortgages and more leverage for real estate funds, private-debt-to-GDP ratios rise. This transforms real estate markets into Ponzi schemes (cf. Walks 2010). While it all works well as long as new entrants set foot on the property ladder and prices continue to rise, it falls apart once people cannot take on any more debt and housing prices fall, as they did in 2007–2010 in a range of countries where housing was highly financialized. As housing prices (P) rise faster than income (I), this is bound to break down somewhere down the road. Indeed, R > G and P > I are not only two expressions of the same long-term trend but both are also inherently politically enabled constructions as well as economically unstable in the long run.

Despite the fragility of the financial system in which the financialization of real estate occurs, a few disclaimers can still be made here. Long-term cycles of capitalism alternate between periods of booms-and-bust and "casino capitalism" and periods of relative stability, in which the flow of capital is less destructive and more stable. State authorities may contribute to this: they may regulate flows of capital differently, creating boundary conditions for the expansion of finance into real estate, and implementing tools of value capture to enforce private firms to also provide affordable housing (Fainstein 2016). From the side of capital a similar dynamic can be expected: the advent of financialization 2.0, under which long-term and steady growth is prioritized over speculative growth, already indicates that capital accumulation is shifting in the direction of more steady capitalist development in which footloose finance tempers itself.

Civil society and social movements may also mobilize resistance and contestation against the financialization of real estate: some local governments in cities such as Berlin, Barcelona and Amsterdam have already addressed de-financialization and affordable housing as major policy issues. Nevertheless, a structural "de-financialization" of real estate still appears hard to imagine in the current political conjuncture: debt and finance have so much penetrated into real estate markets, and policies that encourage high real estate remain accepted by the electorate, that a radical de-leveraging might be politically and economically impossible in the short run. In the longer run, however, we can think of the Polanyian pendulum swinging back towards de-commodification as the new housing crisis intensifies, producing ever stronger intergenerational and class divisions, altering the egalitarian, democratic and accessible city into a restricted, private, high class urban landscape. This social-economic and demographic transformation of the urban fabric in the age of financialization is unlikely to remain unchallenged as the patterns of winners and losers deepen.

Bibliography

Aalbers, M.B., 2008. The financialization of home and the mortgage market crisis. *Competition & Change*, 12(2), pp. 148–166.

Aalbers, M.B., 2015. The Great Moderation, the Great Excess and the global housing crisis. *International Journal of Housing Policy*, 15(1), pp. 43–60.

Aalbers, M.B., 2016. *The Financialization of Housing: A Political Economy Approach*. London: Routledge.

Aalbers, M.B. and Engelen, E., 2015. The political economy of the rise, fall, and rise again of securitization. *Environment and Planning A*, 47(8), pp. 1597–1605.

Aalbers, M.B., Engelen, E. and Glasmacher, A., 2011. Cognitive closure in the Netherlands: Mortgage securitization in a hybrid European political economy. *Environment and Planning A*, 43(8), pp. 1779–1795.

Aalbers, M.B., van Loon, J. and Fernandez, R., 2017. The financialization of a social housing provider. *International Journal of Urban and Regional Research*, 41(4), pp. 572–587.

August, M. and Walks, A., 2018. Gentrification, suburban decline, and the financialization of multi-family rental housing: The case of Toronto. *Geoforum*, 89, pp. 124–136.

Aveline-Dubach, N., 2016. Embedment of "liquid" capital into the built environment: The case of REIT investment in Hong Kong. *Issues & Studies*, 52, pp. 1–32.

Bernanke, B.S., Bertaut, C.C., Demarco, L., and Kamin, S.B., 2011. International capital flows and the return to safe assets in the United States, 2003–2007. *FRB International Finance Discussion Paper* no. 1014.

Bernt, M., Colini, L. and Förste, D., 2017. Privatization, financialization and state restructuring in East Germany: The case of "Am Südpark". *International Journal of Urban and Regional Research*, 41(4), pp. 555–571.

Beswick, J., Alexandri, G., Byrne, M., Fields, D., Hodkinson, S. and Janoschka, M., 2016. Speculating on London's housing future. *City*, 20(2), pp. 321–341.

BIS, 2009. EU housing statistics. *IFC Bulletin*, 31, pp. 111–120.

BIS, 2012. The great leveraging. *BIS Working Articles* no. 398.

Botzem, S. and Dobusch, L., 2017. Financialization as strategy: Accounting for inter-organizational value creation in the European real estate industry. *Accounting, Organizations and Society*, 59, pp. 31–43

Boyer, R., 2000. Is a finance-led growth regime a viable alternative to Fordism? A preliminary analysis. *Economy and Society*, 29(1), pp. 111–145.

Buckley, M. and Hanieh, A., 2014. Diversification by urbanization: Tracing the property-finance nexus in Dubai and the Gulf. *International Journal of Urban and Regional Research*, 38(1), pp. 155–175.

Calbet i Elias, L., 2017. *The Speculative Production of the City: Financialization, Housing and Berlin's Inner City Transformation*. PhD thesis. Berlin: Technische Universität Berlin.

Clark, G.L., 2000. *Pension Fund Capitalism*. Oxford: Oxford University Press.

Crouch, C., 2009. Privatised Keynesianism: An unacknowledged policy regime. *British Journal of Politics and International Relations*, 11(3), pp. 382–399.

Diamantis, C., 2013. *Abschlussbericht der Enquetekommission "Wohnungswirtschaftlicher Wandel und neue Finanzinvestoren auf den Wohnungsmärkten in NRW"*. Düsseldorf: Landtag Nordrhein-Westfalen.

Dymski, G.A., 1999. *The Bank Merger Wave: The Economic Causes and Social Consequences of Financial Consolidation*. Armonk, NY: Sharpe.

ECB, 2006. *Monthly Bulletin December*. ECB.

EMF, 2014. *Hypostat 2014*. Brussels: European Mortgage Federation.

EMF, 2017. *Hypostat 2017*. Brussels: European Mortgage Federation.

EPRA, 2013. *Stock Exchange Listed Property Companies: Building a Stronger Europe*. Brussels: European Public Real Estate Association.

Eurostat, 2011. *Annual National Accounts, Aggregates and Employment*. Brussels: Eurostat.

Fainstein, S., 2016. *The Just City*. New York: Cornel University Press.

Fernandez, R. and Aalbers, M.B., 2016. Financialization and housing: Between globalization and varieties of capitalism. *Competition and Change*, 20(2), pp. 71–88.

Fernandez, R. and Aalbers, M.B., 2017. Housing and capital in the 21st century: Realigning housing studies and political economy. *Housing, Theory and Society*, 34(2), pp. 151–158.

Fields, D., 2015. Contesting the financialization of urban space: Community organizations and the struggle to preserve affordable rental housing in New York City. *Journal of Urban Affairs*, 37(2), pp. 144–165.

Fields, D. and Uffer, S., 2016. The financialisation of rental housing: A comparative analysis of New York City and Berlin. *Urban Studies*, 53(7), pp. 1486–1502.

Forrest, R. and Yip, N.-M. (eds.), 2011. *Housing Markets and the Global Financial Crisis*. Cheltenham: Edward Elgar.

Garcıa-Lamarca, M., 2017. Housing dispossession and (re)surging rents in Barcelona: Financialised housing 2.0? Paper presented at the Finance, Crisis and the City: Global Urbanism and the Great Recession conference, Villa La Pietra, NYU Florence, 5–7 May.

Gotham, K.F., 2006. The secondary circuit of capital reconsidered: Globalization and the U.S. real estate sector. *American Journal of Sociology*, 112(1), pp. 231–275.

Gotham, K.F., 2012. Creating liquidity out of spatial fixity: The secondary circuit of capital and the restructuring of the US housing finance system. In Aalbers, M.B. (ed.), *Subprime Cities: The Political Economy of Mortgage Markets*. Oxford: Wiley-Blackwell, pp. 25–52.

Harvey, D., 1985. *The Urbanization of Capital. Studies in the History and Theory of Capitalist Urbanization*. Oxford: Blackwell.

Heeg, S., 2013. Wohnen als Anlageform: vom Gebrauchsgut zur Ware. *Emanzipation – Zeitschrift für sozialistische Theorie und Praxis*, 3(2), pp. 5–20.

Henry, J.S., 2012. The price of offshore revisited. *Tax Justice Network*, 22, pp. 57–168.

Holm, A., 2010. Privare heißt Rauben zur Ökonomie von Wohnungsprivatisierungen. *Zeitschrift Marxistische Erneuerung*, 21(83) 46–59.

Hudson, M., 2012. *The Bubble and Beyond: Fictitious Capital, Debt Deflation and Global Crisis*. Dresden: Islet.

IEIF, 2014. *Annuaire des sociétés immobilières cotées européennes. SIIC, REITs et foncières*. Paris: IEIF les publications

ING, 2016. *Household Wealth in Europe: Post-crisis Recovery Leaves Big Differences between Countries and Households*. Amsterdam: Economic and Financial Analysis, ING.

Jordá, Ò., Schularick, M. and Taylor, A.M., 2014. *The Great Mortgaging: Housing Finance, Crises, and Business Cycles*. Federal Reserve Bank of San Francisco Working Paper 2014–2023. Available at: http://www.frbsf.org/economic-research/files/wp2014-23.pdf [Accessed July 29, 2016].

Kindleberger, C. and Aliber, R., [1978] 2005. *Manias, Panics and Crashes: A History of Financial Crashes*. London: Wiley.

Kofner, S., 2012. *Aktuelle Geschäftsmodelle von Finanzinvestoren im Themenfeld Wohnungswirtschaftlicher Wandel und neue Finanzinvestoren*. Düsseldorf: Gutachten im Auftrag der Enquetekommission Wohnungswirtschaftlicher Wandel und Neue Finanzinvestoren auf den Wohnungsmärkten in NRW.

Lazzarato, M., 2012. *The Making of the Indebted Man: An Essay on the Neoliberal Condition*. Cambridge, MA: MIT Press.

Lefebvre, H., 1974. La production de l'espace. *L'Homme et la société*, 31(1), pp. 15–32.

Lizieri, C., 2009. *Towers of Capital. Office Markets & International Financial Services*. Oxford: Wiley-Blackwell.

Moreno, L., 2014. The urban process under financialised capitalism. *City*, 18(3), pp. 244–268.

Minsky, H.P., 1996. Uncertainty and the institutional structure of capitalist economies. *Journal of Economic Issues*, 30(2), pp. 357–368.

OECD, 2011. The evolution of homeownership rates in selected OECD countries: Demographic and public policy influences. *OECD Journal: Economic Studies*, 2011/1.

Pereira, A., 2017. The financialization of housing: New frontiers in Brazilian cities. *International Journal of Urban and Regional Research*, 41(4): 604–622.

Piketty, T., 2014. *Capital in the Twenty-First Century*. Cambridge, MA: Harvard University Press.

Pryke, M., 1994. Looking back on the space of a boom: (Re)developing spatial matrices in the City of London. *Environment and Planning A*, 26, pp. 235–264.

Reinhart, C. and Rogoff, K., 2009. *This Time is Different: Eight Centuries of Financial Folly*. Princeton, NY: Princeton University Press.

Rolnik, R., 2013. Late neoliberalism: The financialization of homeownership and housing rights. *International Journal of Urban and Regional Research*, 37(3), pp. 1058–1066.

Romainville, A., 2017. The financialization of housing production in Brussels. *International Journal of Urban and Regional Research*, 41(4), pp. 623–641.

Rouwenhorst, K.G., 2005. The origins of mutual funds. In W.N. Gotzmann and K.G. Rouwenhorst (eds.), *The Origins of Value: The Financial Innovations that Created Modern Capital Markets*. Oxford: Oxford University Press, pp.249–270.

Shatkin, G., 2017. *Cities for Profit: The Real Estate Turn in Asia's Urban Politics*. Ithaca, NY: Cornell University Press.

Sweezy, P., 1994. The triumph of financial capital. *Monthly Review*, 46(2), pp. 1–11.

Van Loon, J. and Aalbers, M.B., 2017. How real estate became "just another asset class": The financialization of the investment strategies of Dutch institutional investors. *European Planning Studies*, 25(2), pp. 221–240.

Wainwright, T., 2012. Building new markets: Transferring securitization, bond-rating, and a crisis from the US to the UK. In M.B. Aalbers (ed.), *Subprime Cities: The Political Economy of Mortgage Markets*. Oxford: Wiley-Blackwell, pp. 97–119.

Wainwright, T., 2015. Circulating financial innovation: New knowledge and securitization in Europe. *Environment and Planning A*, 47(8), pp. 1643–1660.

Wainwright, T. and Manville, G., 2017. Financialization and the third sector: Innovation in social housing bond markets. *Environment and Planning A*, 49(4), pp. 819–838.

Waldron, R., 2018. Capitalizing on the state: The political economy of real estate investment trusts and the "resolution" of the crisis. *Geoforum*, 90, pp. 206–218.

Walks, R.A., 2010. Bailing out the wealthy: Responses to the financial crisis, Ponzi neoliberalism, and the city. *Human Geography*, 3(3), pp. 54–84.

Walks, A. and Clifford, B., 2015. The political economy of mortgage securitization and the neoliberalization of housing policy in Canada. *Environment and Planning A*, 47(8), pp. 1624–1642.

Wijburg, G. and Aalbers, M.B., 2017a. The alternative financialization of the German housing market. *Housing Studies*, 32(7), pp. 968–989.

Wijburg, G. and Aalbers M.B., 2017b. The internationalization of commercial real estate markets in France and Germany. *Competition & Change*, 21(4), pp. 301–320.

Wijburg, G., Aalbers, M.B. and Heeg, S., 2018. The financialization of rental housing 2.0: Releasing housing into the privatized mainstream of capital accumulation. *Antipode*, 50(4), pp. 1098–1119.

18

FINANCIALIZATION AND THE ENVIRONMENTAL FRONTIER

Sarah Bracking

Financialization

The most common understanding of financialization, covered in the introduction of this book, is where finance becomes increasingly dominant in the economy in relation to production, generating more value over time. However, this observation at macro scale does not address how greater interest-bearing value is generated; how financialized commodities at the ecological frontier, and the markets in which they circulate, are made; and how far these circumstances generate patterns of engagement and resistances between people, "more-than-human" (Sullivan 2018) species and nature. This brief chapter will apply theories of financialization to see how far the traditional externalities of capitalism, other species and the living plants and ecosystems of "Nature" have been affected by financial rationality. Other living things are referred to here as "more-than-human" to reflect a necessary de-centering of the human in ecological analysis.

The role of finance in nature–society relations has grown from the 1990s and has been met by an increasing commentary in human and economic geography and related disciplines. These literatures are now vast, and cover how nature and finance are increasingly entrained in projects and practices of conservation (Sullivan 2013a, 2013b); environment (Cooper 2010; Loftus and March 2015) and specific sectors such as weather management (Pryke 2007; Johnson 2014); infrastructure (Hildyard 2016), or oil (Labban 2010 2014). This chapter draws from this literature but adopts a narrow definition of financialization that is not entirely shared. This distinguishes it from a related term, commodification, and gives it a meaning at micro level that is not merely consequential or derivative of the macro processes of financialization, which are sometimes rather amorphously viewed as the greater role of finance in economic affairs. Here, commodification refers to where someone takes a part of nature, either in place or extracted and pacified elsewhere, and either alive or dead, frames it as a commodity, and then sells it (see Castree 2003). There has been much specific work on commodification at the intersection of political ecology and economy, on such things as the commodification of water (Bakker 2004), elephants (Moore 2011) and trees (Prudham 2008). However, financialization more specifically, here applies to products which become *interest bearing* as part of their commodity cycle or circuit. In other words, a hectare of forest could generate timber as a commodity or could become a commodity itself as an area of land (and trees, fauna, canopy, insects and so forth) that is bought and sold. It would be financialized if it were, *in addition*, used as a commodity which became interest-bearing. This could happen if it were leased to someone else; if its future expected wood production became tradable; if it became interest-bearing collateral for a loan, or if it were purchased using a mortgage that drew interest or was securitized such that its interest streams could have a different owner than the fixed asset. It could also be financialized if it were reframed as a species bank, habitat bank or biodiversity offset, a carbon sequestration unit under REDD+, or the Clean Development Mechanism (as a certified emissions reduction or CER unit) or another product whose interest stream was detached from the forest as the underlying commodity asset. It could become more than one of these simultaneously.

Historical Roots of Financialization and the Environmental Frontier

Nature has been the source of financialized income for a much longer time than merely in the era of the "new financialization" and its associated neoliberal environmental governance from the 1980s (Smith 2007). Agricultural products and "from-nature" entities – such as wheat, corn, milk, honey, orange juice, oil, gas, sand, concrete and in prior times, bird dung, cowrie shells and so forth – are derived from living and dead organisms, that have been extracted, commodified and pacified. These are the agricultural commodities and "from-nature" entities that have been generated since humans moved from transhumance to agriculture. While these are commodities that first and foremost are traded and then consumed, they have also had secondary markets – futures, spot and insurance markets – for some time. More recently, commodities have been combined into indexes and synthetic indexes (which may also have secondary markets attached) where paper is traded on whether the combined index might rise or fall in price at some future point. Thus "from-nature" entities have first been commodified and then financialized to generate derivative products circulated as securitized paper.

Since the early 1990s, when many authors loosely date the expansion of the role of finance in global economics, these more traditional secondary markets for already pacified nature-based commodities trading in secondary markets and the growth of their derivatives (spot and futures markets) expanded more quickly than any financialization of "new" products (Bryan and Rafferty 2006; Tang and Xiong 2010; UNCTAD 2011). There was a rapid growth in agricultural derivatives markets from 2002 to 2012, generated from traditional nature-based commodities (Clapp and Helleiner 2012: 181). In the US this was accelerated by the removal of position limits which historically restricted speculation, and the sharp rises in commodity prices during the 2000s (Clapp and Helleiner 2012: 186–88). From the early 1990s, the issuing of paper in relation to indexes of stock in commodity-based derivatives was joined by further issues of securities in relation to commodity index funds related to the performance of a bundle of commodities of which agricultural stock typically constituted around a third (US Senate, cited in Clapp and Helleiner 2012: 188). Commodity-linked exchange–traded funds (ETFs) were added in the few years before 2008, with the net effect of a ten-fold increase in commodity index funds between 2003 and mid-2008 from around US$15 billion to US$200 billion (Clapp and Helleiner 2012: 188, citing US Senate 2009: 5). Although complex derivatives trading dropped after the 2008 crash, some novelty innovations common before the crash, such as collateralized debt obligations containing asset-backed securities (ABS-CDOs), have been re-used since as mutations of synthetic index-linked derivatives and bespoke tranche products (Bracking 2016: 30–58). In fact, complex derivatives, based on trading in weather risk and crop insurance, inspired the new insurance products to "assist" Africa with climate change that emerged from the early 2010s within the African Risk Capacity of 2014 and the later InsuResilience fund.

However, much work on the financialization of nature does not distinguish clearly between what can be viewed as a nature-based commodity with a secondary market, and what is a financialized or capitalized asset which is nature-based, that generates an interest or income stream (which may also have a secondary market) (Smith 2007). This latter can be theorized as a frontier product and has encouraged the current debate in political ecology on the financialization of nature which inspired this chapter and its title. Smith first noted this distinction in relation to water purification and carbon sequestration, which generated interest streams in contrast to more traditional extractive resource capitalism or agricultural capital and associated this deepening of the role of finance with a heightened abstraction that allowed exchange values to emerge (Smith 2007). However, Smith's early distinction based in exchange is of limited use, since many new financialized products are not fully exchanged or consumed: people's use of them does not fully consume them. Thus Felli (2014) pointed out that carbon markets do not require carbon as a commodity as such, but instead sell a license to rent the global commons of the atmosphere. Similarly, catastrophe bonds – which are a form of (re)insurance against extreme weather do not trade or exchange the weather, but are interest-bearing and tradable, either linked to a pay-out trigger of volume of claims made by insured entities, or to a synthetic trigger generated by proprietary weather modelling systems and data.

Alongside the growth of traditional secondary markets, new financialized assets from the environmental frontier began to be made from the 1980s. Financialized forest products were created in the public sector in the 1980s as a debt-for-environment swap for highly indebted poor countries by international financial institutions such as the World Bank. The World Bank would lend capital and part of the interest would be denominated in maintaining standing forest in countries such as Brazil. This development was then consolidated by the 1997 Kyoto Protocol, which extended the 1992 United Nations Framework Convention on Climate Change (UNFCCC), to include a market-based system for trading carbon based in units of certified emissions reductions (CERs) generated in Clean Development Mechanism projects and then traded, including in the European Union Exchange and Trading System (EU-ETS). CERs hit their highest prices in the mid-2000s, but values have crashed since. Efforts to spread carbon accounting then moved to mangroves, and to the generalizable aggregate of ecosystem services, and to "reducing emissions from deforestation and forest degradation" (REDD+) forest conservation and biodiversity offsets from the late 1990s. To the extent that the products of these interventions produced tradable carbon the assets on which these were based became financialized, and interest-bearing paper was circulated.

Ecosystem services emerged in the 1990s as the "vanguard of the neoliberalisation of nature" (Dempsey and Robertson 2012: 759). For example, in Costanza et al.'s seminal piece they were valued at $33 trillion for the Earth (1997: 255), a figure which took ecosystem services as a concept from relative obscurity in ecological economics to the popular mainstream. The concept took further momentum from the Millennium Ecosystem Assessment Project (MEA) of 2005 supported by the UNEP and Global Environmental Facility. It was endorsed by the US Environmental Protection Agency (EPA) in 2009, and by the European-funded The Economics of Ecosystems and Biodiversity (TEEB) research from 2008 to 2010. Financialized nature had become framed, abstracted and pacified to provide "services," or even merely experiences or "mitigations," free to circulate as liquid paper (Büscher 2013; Igoe 2013; Sullivan 2013a).

From the 2000s this process was joined by new "green" financial products in capital markets proper, where traders created green themed bonds, lending debt finance to those engaged in activities designated as environmentally beneficial, such as low-carbon transport infrastructure, and renewable energy. Environment theme bonds became a new fixed income asset class, marketed similarly to conventional debt instruments, but with the claimed addition of a de-carbonization effect. Many of the earlier issues were catalysed by public development banks but a more fully private market in green capital has grown. Dividends to investors can be actioned against a wide variety of contracted outcomes, such as the performance of an index of "green companies" or a calculation of achieved emissions reductions. Whereas ecosystem services were largely payments made to custodians against quality control criteria (payments for ecosystem services or PES systems), dividends here are linked to financial performances, with pollution abatement promised as additionality. Thus the "green market" was enabled in green bonds, derivatives, indexes and synthetics from the 2000s onward and grew to include index insurance, risk-based multi-trigger products, and insurance-linked securities from the 2010s indicating a reinsurance regime of tradable derivatives. These new insurance-linked securities are traded in futures markets and involve securitizing the income streams from multiple insurance and bond holders of crop futures.

However, authors have noted that the actual generation of revenue streams from financialized assets has not been as great as either financialization theories, or the range of new products might suggest. For example, Brockington and Duffy (2010) noted their remarkable absence in conservation (see also Dempsey 2017). This might be surprising but is an observation consistent with the narrow definition of financialization used here, as a process generating an interest-bearing commodity or asset which thus produces a contracted derivative income stream (see Lohmann 2016a, 2016b; Hildyard 2016). This is distinct from other writers who might use "financialization" interchangeably with "commodification" or as a broad metaphor for the greater role of finance in "life in general" (see Langley in this volume).

Moving from Commodification to Financialization

To illustrate the complexity of this frontier of financialization, it is useful to discuss further the processes of commodification and financialization theoretically, given that the former is a precursor of the latter. Collard and Dempsey discuss commodification in relation to two types: first, living exotic pets individually sold for companionship and the value humans place on encounters with them (see Haraway (2008: 45) on "encounter value"); and second, the "massified" or aggregated commodification of reproductive life embodied in eco-system services (Collard and Dempsey 2013: 2688). A lively commodity is one whose value derives from its status as a living being, such as a pet, and the commodification process here is conditioned by the hierarchies of species which make some more disposable than others (Collard and Dempsey 2013: 2685). In contrast, in Collard and Dempsey's second example of eco-system services, following Robertson (2012: 386), a "socially necessary abstraction" takes place that transforms the eco system in situ into a carbon credit. The reproductive and generative capacity of the eco-system service is "coproduced through the CDM formulas," becoming a source of exchange value. Castree (2003: 285) referred to this process as "artificially" commodifying a previously non-commodified entity by means of scientific and technical calculation; Historically, this technical work required to secure the translation of ecology into commodity was often left as a black box in work on the economy and nature encounter. However, more recently, the work of Miller (1998, 2002) in economic sociology; Latour (1987) on calculative devices, and Callon (1998, 2007), Çalışkan and Callon (2009, 2010), and Callon and Muniesa (2005) on the performativity of economics (see also MacKenzie 2006, 2009; MacKenzie et al. 2007) and the work done by those studying socio-technical arrangements has spawned a plethora of critical technology studies which analyse the way calculative and market devices contribute to the transformation of nature into value, or the forest, for example, into a carbon credit (see Bracking et al. 2018).

Whether animate or pacified, individual or massified, these commodification processes are a precursor of financialization, in that they create a pacified commodity which is free to be sold, traded and circulated in a market. These processes occur differentially according to species and landscape hierarchies and are contributing to a reordering of ecology and human relationships which aligns and orders the kinds of natures or lives that live or die in relation to those "best able to provide returns" (Dempsey 2013). Heuristically, neoliberal ideas of value have generated the "species must pay to stay" mentality of commodified conservation, whose supporters claim that the revenue generated from commodified species can contribute to financing their survival. Animals to be saved are entrained into surplus value producing assemblages, whereas those to be allowed to die live in a biopolitics of waste and disposability. There is one further step from a commodified animal to its financialization, however, which is that the (abstracted) animal must simultaneously circulate as a financial asset with a derivative income stream generated from it, denominated in an interest-bearing calculation. For example, financialization has occurred when a rhinoceros, for example, becomes the asset underlying a species bond, where the supplier is paid interest by the purchaser, or borrower, on the initial capital exchanged, if the animal remains alive. Here, present day actions and returns are generated from a risk-based orientation to expectations of the future (cf. Johnson 2014).

Recent financialization processes have also produced interest-bearing assets in a range of abstract products which refer to nature, humans and more-than-human contexts modelled in an aggregated or systemic sense – the "massified" commodities that Collard and Dempsey (2013) analyse. The unit in complex products on which a derivative income stream is raised is not a bounded asset or thing, but a complex system, ecology, environment or modelled vulnerability. Johnson (2014: 157) summarized in relation to securitized catastrophe insurance that "place-bound vulnerabilities are rendered into an exploitable, diversifying asset class for financial capital." Catastrophe bonds are a sub-category of the wider asset class called insurance-linked securities (ILS), and represent a convergence of the reinsurance and capital markets begun in the mid-1990s (Culp 2002; World Economic Forum 2008), totalling $40 billion in bonds issued between 1997 and 2011 (Johnson 2014: 157). Trading also occurs in secondary markets for catastrophe bonds that are due to trigger, and which have already done so, which are colloquially referred to as "live" and "dead cat trading" respectively.

Insurance-linked securities, denominated in risk, can correlate together earlier product iterations in the overall arrangement of financialized nature and its governance. In this act of correlation, carbon, natural capital, "green-ness" and multivariate social and ecological outcomes-based accounting systems can all be made commensurate by risk and its modelled pay-out algorithms which form the financial structure of a marketed product. This outcome facilitates further governance of ecology by financiers in that risk is a designation calculated within banks and approved by ratings agencies within a modelled set of financial variables and legal rights of different tiers or tranches of shareholders. When it works, financialization at the environmental frontier works principally for money-holders, whatever its environmental or conservation impact.

But as financialized governance expands, more humans and more-than-human ecologies become entangled by financial calculation and relationships denominated by finance. In specific and discrete places financialized instruments, and the projects and places which underpin them and pay the interest or insurance coupons, involve real people who have only a contingent relationship to the larger political project being pursued by financiers of securing their influence and profits at a global scale. Thus, while the financialized commodity has often been described as abstract and rarefied, or as a "fictive commodity" by those working in the Marxian tradition, its proliferation also conditions and shapes outcomes for different humans and more-than-humans within our everyday lives (see also Langley in this volume). Most obviously, less fortunate species in the species hierarchy are becoming extinct, and vulnerable humans become climate and environmental migrants or mortalities, while the profits from a rarefied and reordered nature are shared differentially according to pre-existing and growing hierarchies of inequality. The practice of financialization also creates new ecological economies, with humans employed, and creating value, as green bond traders, fund managers, carbon accountants and in the white-collar roles of valuation, calculation, and the structuring of financial products. At sites of program and project intervention, where forests, habitats and road and energy infrastructures are being built or maintained, workers are also entrained in new spaces of financialized environment, often on adverse terms. Value is either sourced directly from what is produced or serviced by workers or "project participants," or, as in South African climate change projects, sourced from government sponsoring and liquidating of the capital relation that unfolds (Okem and Bracking 2019). Finance-driven capital has developed a post-2008 "new love affair with real things" (Ouma 2014: 162), but as Ouma asserts, these relations should be read "from below" to understand their socio-technical logics in place. Although environmental stewardship of a financialized asset can create employment and incentives for conservation, this has often been for poor remuneration or reward (Okem and Bracking 2019).

Financialization and the More-Than-Human

Often a new financialized asset is made by the dispossession or abjection of its prior owners or users, whereas sometimes it is conjured from the imagination into virtual form (Igoe 2013). The first process of dispossession has been theorized since Marx as primitive accumulation, or more latterly by Harvey (2003) as accumulation by dispossession. Jason Moore (2010) has also been influential in ecology in his account of the economics of the environmental frontier where accumulation relies on the extraction of the "Four Cheaps" of labour power, food, energy and raw materials. Moore argued that capitalist expansion requires "frontiers of uncapitalised natures" to be constantly expropriated from the "outside" (2014: 36; see also Lohmann 2016a: 44–46).

When a financialized asset is made through dispossession, the vibrant materiality of the more-than-human is often simply made disposable, and death, destruction and extinction ensue. The advance of finance is thus similar in character to its precursor of generalized commodity production and is often experienced by humans and more-than-human species as a brutal and violent encounter. When the encounter does not merely destroy, more-than-human lives become entrained in a space of accumulation that nonetheless defines their possibilities and actions. Financialization continues the capitalist encounter with the more-than-human and coalesces assemblages of things, people, animals and plants into complex value configurations that produce surplus embodied in derivative income streams. The scope and experience of continued more-than-human life becomes conditioned by its co-existence as an interest-bearing asset from which surplus value is extracted.

However, many new financialized environmental assets are a product of both material extraction, and sometimes dispossession of others, and conceptual imagining. Morgan Robertson (2006: 368) analysed how capital had to "see" nature in new ways in order to financialize it. According to Sullivan, this is a process "requiring that the earth-in-crisis is rethought and reworded such that it is brought further into alignment conceptually, semiotically, and materially with capital" (Sullivan 2011: 6). In short, financial logics are applied to ecology to "think" financial products into being in a process that is contested and fluid. For example, Lohmann (2016a, 2016b) describes shifting assemblages of things, people, and more-than-human species where finance encroaches but is then pushed back, only to encroach again, not in a discrete event of border dispossession but in an ever-changing and contested frontier zone.

Resistance and Animism

Commodification and financialization are confounded by two broad types of resistance: first, complexity which derives from the institutional challenges of valuation processes; and second, resistance which also occurs in disparate ways depending on the "nature" of that which is being commodified (Bakker and Bridge 2006). Institutionally, new products are generated as interest bearing assets in valuation processes which entrain, not only other species and plants, but also ideas, expertise, calculative devices and institutions such as banks, multilateral agencies and more bespoke institutions such as the Green Climate Fund, the UNFCCC and so forth. The complexity of financialization, and failure of many experiments, is partly because the successful framing, pacification, commoditization and then financialization of a product requires an institutional arrangement in which ideas, people, institutions and calculation are correlated and work together. But complexity is introduced from competing calculative devices (Latour 1987) within the social articulation of valuation processes, where a calculative device is understood as any procedure, spreadsheet, pro forma, equation, or evaluative practice, which generates an evaluative outcome from assembled inputs and criteria (see Bracking et al. 2018). For example, the calculation of financial return might conflict with the ecological loss account or the accounting for corporate social responsibility. Also, calculations which financialize nature, such as in CERs or REDD+ are ultimately reliant on a government system of reward or subsidy which may or may not materialize. Thus, resistance emerges from the complexity of calculations found in experiments to financialize nature.

Second, further complexity is introduced, which can sometimes dissemble the financialization process, when the animism and agency of the more-than-human itself confounds the production of a financialized unit, such as when a species habitat fails to attract the species required, or when a forest fire destroys a carbon sequestration asset. There is an expansive literature on materiality in geography which theorizes the human and the more-than-human in the natural and social sciences. More recently, this work has tried to engage the natural and social beyond a dualistic model (Braun 2014, 2015; Latour 2013a, 2013b), and includes a large volume of work from feminist scholars and others which re-theorizes agency, animism and lively natures, such as in Jane Bennet's (2005, 2010) idea of "vital materialism." The most recent approaches stress the decentring of the human and an acceptance of the animism of the nonhuman and nature and the relationality of ecology (Ingold 2006, 2011: 67–68), where people and things, other species and nature are in a constant process of becoming (see Massey 2005). Here animism "describes an amodern assumption of the alive sentience of 'other-than-human natures' as animate and relational subjects, rather than inanimate and atomised objects" (Sullivan and Fredriksen 2014: 13). For some prominent ecologists, animism can "resist objectification" (Franke 2012: 4, 7), while multi-species ethnography can decenter human exceptionalism and flatten economic productivist accumulation in favor of the "polyphonic ecologies" of the human and beyond-human future (Sullivan 2018: 69).

If these ideas of vibrant ecology and more-than-human agency have worth, then it is not surprising that many financialization processes become dissembled, since financialized units of nature can only be mechanistically (re)made, tamed, and pacified. A vibrant ecology must be constantly produced and governed by those who would sell it – and is inevitably resistant. As Igoe writes, citing Sullivan, "making nature move [as liquid paper] first required making it sit still as an increasingly deadened object of contemplation," such that "productions of nature for speculation are profoundly anti-ecological…they are made possible by the systematic deadening of animate ecologies and non-capitalist human ontologies" (Igoe, summarizing Sullivan 2013b: 37, 46). Experiments in producing interest-bearing assets from the environmental frontier illustrate these profound contradictions between the ontologies of finance and of animism in understanding the nature of Nature.

Because of the animist nature of the more-than-human, there is also a constant tension between – both theoretically and in practice – nature conceived of as a finite set of resources with limits, or as a vibrant, complex, resilient system which can generate and regenerate surplus (see Nelson 2015). For example, on the one hand there are concepts such as "stranded assets" which are derived from the idea that the atmosphere has limits to its ability to absorb warming gases; on the other hand there are assets being generated, like ecosystem services, within notions of resilience, which suggest that one wetland is exchangeable for another, as if they were infinitely reproducible. Moreover, the contemporary resilience conception seems to also imply that limits can be remade and obviated by technology and science. Financiers, in turn, are adopting one or the other, or a hybrid, of both a "limits conception" and a "generative conception" of ecology without really working through the implications of each.

This economic confusion on how to account for Nature, found in the competing conceptions of the "nature of nature" as finite or flexible, is at the root of many failed experiments in the financialization of Nature. The different conceptions are commensurate with different forms of calculation in economics, namely accounting and index theory and marginal price theory respectively (Dempsey and Robertson 2012: 765–766). For example, Costanza's valuation of total ecosystem services was an aggregated value of everything below the supply curve – an aggregated index value – rather than conforming to marginalist price theory where the value of the next lost or gained unit of services is determined around legible demand and supply curves (Dempsey and Robertson 2012: 766). The categories of "loss and damage," "stranded assets," and valuations of ecosystem services or biodiversity offsets are all examples of aggregated index values. These are needed in a range of government and policy activity (Boyd and Banzhaf 2007), but are not easily translated into decisions over marginal resource use. In fact, modern economics is ill-suited for combining indexical and marginal pricing, exactly the task needed to bring economics to bear on finite resource use. In macro-economics a proxy for the aggregated value of nature-based commodities would be the value of all current nature-based stock, and the marginal price would be indicated by the next public list matched order of a unit of stock about to be sold. However, neither proxy is adequate to account for the intrinsic value of standing nature and other species, since we cannot consume them in order to conserve them. Only that which is consumed is priced by immanent capitalist markets, while loss and damage to the environment remains externalized and largely invisible. In this sense, successful financialization of environmental frontiers must imagine a value that is consumed without compromising the underlying asset.

Conclusion

Historically, financialization processes at environmental frontiers have progressed as dispossessions and imaginings in a series of experiments which have generally been fixed in time and scale and remain relatively rare. For financiers the legally guaranteed contracted income streams and/or rents which can be teased from an environmental fixed asset condition its value, and risk helps aggregate and make calculable those factors which directly affect income. The risk of securing, or not, the derivative income streams from assets is represented directly in the value calculation of a product, which then determines the prices paid for environmental services or bonds. But the context of where surplus value can be found remains within the capital relation *as a whole*, where those with finance capture labor, other species and plants in a variety of exploitive contexts, including in the new green economy (Brockington and Ponte 2015).

However, financiers have experienced profound tensions and contradictions in their experiments to take financialization processes to the environmental frontier of commodified capitalist accumulation, in order to make interest-bearing assets from the more-than-human found there. The institutional arrangements are complex and sometimes fail, while the animism of other species and plants can frustrate calculations. Nonetheless, for those things, people and other species entrained in these experiments the experience can be extremely adverse, and even when life is lost, the rationality and imagination of finance seems to remain potent in capitalist culture and economics. In sum, financialization has failed to meet its marketing promises to assist in the "saving" of Nature, and probably will continue to do so without a broader change in society–ecology relationships.

Bibliography

Bakker, K., 2004. *An Uncooperative Commodity: Privatising Water in England and Wales*. Oxford: Oxford University Press.

Bakker, K. and Bridge, G., 2006. Material worlds? Resource geographies and the "matter of nature". *Progress in Human Geography*, 31, pp. 5–27.

Bennett, J., 2005. *The Enchantment of Modern Life: Attachments, Crossings, and Ethics*. Princeton: Princeton University Press.

Bennet, J., 2010. *Vibrant Matter: A Political Ecology of Things*. Durham: Duke University Press.

Boyd, J. and Banzhaf, S., 2007. What are ecosystem services? The need for standardized environmental accounting units. *Ecological Economics*, 63, pp. 616–626.

Bracking, S., 2016. *Financialisation of Power: How Financiers Rule Africa*. London: Routledge.

Bracking, S., Fredriksen, A., Sullivan, S. and Woodhouse, P. (eds.), 2018. *Valuing Development, Environment and Conservation: Creating Values that Matter*. Abingdon: Routledge.

Braun, B., 2014. The 2013 Antipode RGS-IBG Lecture: New materialisms and neoliberal natures. *Antipode*, 47(1), pp. 1–14.

Braun, B., 2015. Futures: Imagining sociological transformation – An introduction. *Annals of the Association of American Geographers*, 105(2), pp. 239–243.

Brockington, D. and Duffy, R., 2010. Capitalism and conservation: The production and reproduction of biodiversity conservation. *Antipode*, 42(3), pp. 469–484.

Brockington, D. and Ponte S., 2015. The Green Economy in the global South: Experiences, redistributions and resistance. *Third World Quarterly*, 36(12), pp. 2197–2206.

Bryan, D. and Rafferty, M., 2006. *Capitalism with Derivatives*. Basingstoke: Macmillan.

Büscher, B., 2013. Nature on the move: The value and circulation of liquid nature and the emergence of fictitious conservation. *New Proposals: Journal of Marxism and Interdisciplinary Inquiry*, 6(1–2), pp. 20–36.

Calışkan K. and Callon, M., 2009. Economization Part 1: Shifting attention from the economy towards processes of economization. *Economy and Society*, 38, pp. 369–398.

Çalışkan, K. and Callon, M., 2010. Economization Part 2: A research programme for the study of markets. *Economy and Society*, 39, pp. 1–32.

Callon, M., 1998. Introduction: The embeddedness of economic markets in economics. In Callon, M. (ed), *The Laws of the Markets*. Oxford/Malden, MA: Blackwell Publishers/Sociological Review, pp. 1–57.

Callon, M., 2007. What does it mean to say that economics is performative? In MacKenzie, D., Muniesa, F. and Siu, L. (eds.), *Do Economists Make Markets? On the Performativity of Economics*. Princeton, NJ: Princeton University Press.

Callon, M. and Muniesa, F., 2005. Peripheral vision economic markets as calculative collective devices. *Organizational Studies*, 26, pp.1229–1250.

Castree, N., 2003. Environmental issues: Relational ontologies and hybrid politics. *Progress in Human Geography*, 27(2), pp. 203–211.

Clapp, J. and Helleiner, E., 2012. Troubled futures? The global food crisis and the politics of agricultural derivatives regulation. *Review of International Political Economy*, 19(2), pp. 181–207.

Collard, R-C. and Dempsey, J., 2013. Life for sale? The politics of lively commodities. *Environment and Planning A*, 45, pp. 2682–2699.

Cooper, M., 2010. Turbulent worlds: Financial markets and environmental crisis. *Theory, Culture, and Society*, 27(2/3), pp. 167–190.

Costanza, R.d'Arge, R., de Groot, R., Farber, S., Grasso, M., Hannon, B., et al. 1997. The value of the world's ecosystem services and natural capital. *Nature*, 387, pp. 253–260.

Culp, C., 2002. *The Art of Risk Management: Alternative Risk Transfer, Capital Structure, and the Convergence of Insurance and Capital Markets*. New York: John Wiley & Sons.

Dempsey, J., 2013. Biodiversity loss as material risk: Tracking the changing meanings and materialities of biodiversity conservation. *Geoforum*, 45, pp. 41–51.

Dempsey, J., 2017. The Financialization of Nature Conservation? In Christophers, B., Leyshon, A. and Mann, G. (eds.), *Money and Finance after the Crisis*. Chichester: John Wiley & Sons Ltd, pp. 191–216.

Dempsey, J. and Robertson, M., 2012. Ecosystem services: Tensions, impurities, and points of engagement within neoliberalism. *Progress in Human Geography*, 36(6), pp. 758–779.

Felli, R., 2014. On climate rent. *Historical Materialism*, 22(3–4), pp. 251–280.

Franke, A., 2012. Animism: Notes on an exhibition. *e-flux*, 36. Available from https://www.e-flux.com/journal/36/61258/animism-notes-on-an-exhibition/ no. 36

Haraway, D., 2008. *When Species Meet*. Minneapolis, MN: University of Minnesota Press.

Harvey, D., 2003. *The New Imperialism*. Oxford: Oxford University Press.

Hildyard, N., 2016. *Licensed Larceny Infrastructure: Accumulation and the Global South*. Manchester: Manchester University Press.

Igoe, J., 2013. Nature on the move II: Contemplation becomes speculation. *New Proposals: Journal of Marxism and Interdisciplinary Inquiry*, 6(1–2), pp. 37–49.

Ingold, T., 2006. Rethinking the animate, re-animating thought. *Ethnos*, 71(1), pp. 9–20.

Ingold, T., 2011. *Being Alive: Essays on Movement, Knowledge and Description*. London: Routledge.

Johnson, L., 2014. Geographies of securitized catastrophe risk and the implications of climate change. *Economic Geography*, 90(2), pp. 155–185.

Labban, M., 2010. Oil in parallax: Scarcity, markets, and the financialization of accumulation. *Geoforum*, 41(4), pp. 541–552.

Labban, M., 2014. Against value: Accumulation in the oil industry and the biopolitics of labour under finance. *Antipode*, 46(2), pp. 477–496.

Latour, B., 1987. *Science in Action: How to Follow Scientists and Engineers through Society*. Cambridge, MA: Harvard University Press.

Latour, B., 2013a. Telling friends from foes in the time of the Anthropocene. In Hamilton, C., Bonneuil, C. and Gemenne, F. (eds.), *The Anthropocene and the Global Environmental Crisis – Rethinking Modernity in a New Epoch*. London: Routledge, pp. 145–155.

Latour, B., 2013b. Facing Gaia: Six lectures on the political theory of nature. Gifford Lectures on Natural Religion, Edinburgh, February.

Loftus, A. and March, H., 2015. Financialising nature? *Geoforum*, 60, pp. 172–175.

Lohmann, L., 2016a. *Ecosystem Services, Cheap Regulation and the Law of Value*. Mimeo.

Lohmann, L., 2016b. What is the "green" in "green growth"? In Dale, G., Mathai, M.V. and Puppim de Oliveira, J.A. (eds.), *Green Growth: Political Ideology, Political Economy and the Alternatives*. London: Zed Books.

MacKenzie, D., 2006. *An Engine, Not a Camera: How Financial Models Shape Markets*. Cambridge, MA: MIT Press.

MacKenzie, D., 2009. Making things the same: Gases, emission rights and the politics of carbon markets. *Accounting, Organizations and Society*, 34, pp. 440–455.

MacKenzie, D., Muniesa, F., and Siu, L., 2007. *Do Economists Make Markets? On the Performativity of Economics*. Princeton, NJ: Princeton University Press.

Massey, D., 2005. *For Space*. London: Sage.

Miller, D., 1998. A theory of virtualism. In Carrier, J. and Miller, D. (eds.), *A New Political Economy*. Oxford: Berg Publishers.

Miller, D., 2002. Turning Callon the right way up. *Economy and Society*, 31(2), pp. 218–233.

Moore, J., 2010. The end of the road? Agricultural revolutions in the capitalist world-ecology, 1450–2010. *Journal of Agrarian Change*, 10(3), pp. 389–413.

Moore, J., 2014. The end of cheap nature, or how I learned to stop worrying about "the" environment and love the crisis of capitalism. In Suter, C. and Chase-Dunn, C. (eds.), *Structures of the World Political Economy and the Future of Global Conflict and Cooperation*. Berlin: LIT.

Moore, L., 2011. The neoliberal elephant: Exploring the impacts of the trade ban in ivory on the commodification and neoliberalisation of elephants. *Geoforum*, 42, pp. 51–60.

Nelson, S., 2015. Beyond the limits to growth: Ecology and the neoliberal counterrevolution. *Antipode*, 47(2), pp. 461–480.

Okem, A.E. and Bracking, S., 2019. The poverty reduction co-benefits of climate change-related projects in eThekwini Municipality, South Africa. In Cobbinah, P.B. and Addaney, M. (eds.), *The Geography of Climate Change Adaptation in Urban Africa*. Switzerland: Palgrave Macmillan.

Ouma, S., 2014. Situating global finance in the Land Rush Debate: A critical review. *Geoforum*, 57, pp. 162–166.

Prudham, S., 2008. Tall among the trees: Organising against globalist forestry in rural British Columbia. *Journal of Rural Studies*, 24(2), pp. 182–196.

Pryke, M., 2007. Geomoney: An option on frost, going long on clouds. *Geoforum*, 38, pp. 576–588.

Robertson, M.M., 2006. The nature that capital can see: Science, state and market in the commodification of ecosystem services. *Environment and Planning D: Society and Space*, 24, pp. 367–387.

Robertson, M.M., 2012. Measurement and alienation: Making a world of ecosystem services. *Transactions of the Institute of British Geographers*, New Series, 37, pp. 386–401.

Smith, N., 2007. Nature as accumulation strategy. *Socialist Register*, 43, pp. 16–36.

Sullivan, S., 2011. Banking nature? The financialisation of environmental conservation. Working Paper 8, Open Anthropology Cooperative Press, London. Available from http://eprints.bbk.ac.uk/6063/1/Sullivan-Banking-Nature.pdf

Sullivan, S., 2013a. Banking Nature? The spectacular financialisation of environmental conservation. *Antipode*, 45(1), pp. 198–217.

Sullivan, S., 2013b. Nature on the move III: (Re)countenancing an animate nature. *New Proposals*, 6(1/2), pp. 50–71.

Sullivan, S., 2018. On possibilities for salvaged polyphonic ecologies in a ruined world. *Dialogues in Human Geography*, 8(1), pp. 69–72.

Sullivan, S, and Fredriksen, A., 2014. Animism. In Fredriksen, A. et al. (eds.), *A conceptual map for the study of value: An initial mapping of concepts for the project "Human, non-human and environmental value systems: an impossible frontier?"*, pp. 13–16. Available from http://thestudyofvalue.org/publications/#2

Tang, K. and Xiong, W., 2010. Index investment and financialization of commodities (NBER Working Paper 16385). Cambridge, MA: National Bureau of Economic Research.

UNCTAD, 2011. *Price Formation in Financialized Commodity Markets. The Role of Information*. New York and Geneva: United Nations Conference on Trade and Development.

World Economic Forum, 2008. Convergence of insurance and capital markets. WEF Working Papers. Geneva: World Economic Forum.

19

OFFSHORE FINANCE

Rodrigo Fernandez and Reijer Hendrikse

Introduction

Despite increased scrutiny following a streak of data leaks, writing about offshore finance remains a daunting task. Besides the legal complexities that surround offshore finance, powerful interests are dedicated to obscure the workings of tax havens and secrecy jurisdictions, resulting in enduring definitional and statistical limitations, feeding the blatant denial of their very existence. The workings of offshore finance, however, are indispensable to any understanding of financialization, which might be aptly defined as the growing dominance of finance over society at large. Far from being a fringe phenomenon, offshore finance constitutes the nerve center of contemporary capitalism, as the world's dominant capital stocks and flows are today habitually routed and deposited offshore, with global corporations and elite wealth thoroughly interlaced with the offshore world – for reasons of secrecy, tax and related aims to boost asset protection and financial returns. Amongst others, offshore finance is a key driver of mounting inequality, the breakup of social contracts underlying welfare states, ecological disaster, financial crises and rising authoritarianism.

In this chapter, we unpack the mechanisms and players shaping offshore finance. We first detail a number of legal innovations instrumental to the rise of the *global* offshore system. Next, we evaluate different datasets underscoring the weight of offshore capital stocks and flows shaping financialized capitalism. These figures reveal a core geography of offshore financial centers (OFCs) underlying global finance. Although individual OFCs are formally cultivated by governments and sovereign lawmakers, as an integrated system offshore finance is effectively maintained by a handful of global banks, law and accountancy firms. Accordingly, in the concluding section we bring financialization back in and try to come to terms with the sweeping power of offshore finance, which systematically accumulates and assumes, and effectively enjoys and exerts, slivers of state sovereignty anchoring the planetary rule of capital.

A Short History

Although tax avoidance traces a longer history, the global rise of offshore finance coincides with a number of late nineteenth-century legal innovations radically rebooting the geographical makeup of modern capitalism. Notably, the birth of the *private* corporation as "natural person" is traced back to this period: under liberal mythology, leading capitalist states enacted legislation to democratize, or privatize, the right of incorporation hitherto exclusively chartered by sovereign decree (Picciotto 1988). This ignited the rise of large *multi*-national corporations which, in turn, defied the emerging international legal order in which states wielded exclusive territorial power (Picciotto 1999). Although legal "fixes" to accommodate cross-border enterprise existed prior to the twentieth century (Barkan 2013), the paradox between sovereign "enclosure" and capital mobility triggered additional changes.

One innovation was the shell company with little or no material substance. The legal assembly of shell companies opened Pandora's box, as multinationals could henceforth domicile or incorporate themselves in another jurisdiction *without* physically relocating their activities. The right of incorporation, in other words, quickly turned into fictional bookkeeping tools for *non-resident* firms. Another crucial building block was the *bilateral* allocation of tax rights between jurisdictions, anchoring capital mobility in a set of tax treaties devised in the 1920s (Avi-Yonah 2015), distinguishing between "host country" – the jurisdiction of economic activity – and "home country" – the domicile of the owner, investor or corporate headquarters. This arrangement split tax rights between capital importers and exporters, with the United Kingdom (UK) and United States (US) shaping the rules as the world's leading capital exporters. Crucially, these legal principles remain fundamental to today's bilateral web of more than 3,000 tax treaties (McGauran 2013) which, in turn, represents one of the key legal infrastructures upon which the offshore world has matured.

These and other innovations propelled offshore finance forward: the more states "opened up" to cross-border capital via expanding bilateral agreements, the more it made sense to *unilaterally* enact legislation to attract foreign capital, primarily via tax incentives on (fictional) business activities. Decentralized Switzerland and the US played leading roles in the early development of offshore finance, where "ease of incorporation and loose regulation emerged first as a competitive state strategy" (Palan et al. 2010: 110), playing out "locally" between cantons and states *within* sovereign federations. Subsequently, attracting capital rose to prominence *across* the sovereign borders of the international state system, gradually turning offshore finance into a global phenomenon. For example, various states rolled out offshore legislation and strategies to hide industrialist assets during the 1930s (Van Geest et al. 2013), turning them into OFCs.

Resurrecting Global Finance

The postwar era was initially defined by an international regime in which states exerted considerable control over their domestic economies, requiring capital controls which curtailed cross-border finance. Crucially, however, the late 1950s saw the first cracks appear in this order, heralding a key moment in the global ascent of offshore finance: in 1957 the Bank of England decided that *foreign* currency exchange between *non-resident* lenders and borrowers was not subject to any regulation (Burn 1999; Michie 2006; Green 2016). This accounting gimmick heralded the birth of the Eurodollar markets, which made lending US dollars more profitable in the *unregulated* City of London than on Wall Street, seeing banks from the US and across the globe setting up shop in London. The Bank of England aimed to revive the sterling area following Britain's imperial collapse, seeing Britain's crown dependencies and overseas territories transformed into tax havens, with the City at the center of an incipient offshore spider's web spanning the globe (Shaxson 2012; also see Wang in this volume, on the state and financialization)

The growth of the offshore Euromarkets eventually came to undermine the postwar order, which collapsed in the early 1970s (Helleiner 1994). As the US closed the gold window, fixed exchange rates made way for floating rates, introducing novel risks for indebted corporations, governments and households – accelerating the stellar rise in financial derivatives trading in

London, New York and Chicago. Resurgent capital mobility progressively created *transnational* marketplaces, increasingly built via offshore legal entities and financial products, creating difficulties for national regulators. To assess the risk exposures of globalizing banks, for example, the Bank of International Settlements (BIS) created new statistics distinguishing location, domicile and nationality of banking units, confirming the dawn of a new age.

The ascent of neoliberalism – often considered the ideological cover to ignite financialization (Sidaway and Hendrikse 2016) – proved another boost to offshore finance: besides bilateral arrangements, capital mobility became increasingly anchored in *multilateral* frameworks and organizations, seeing offshore finance mushroom and mature, as ever more states deployed unilateral strategies to attract capital. Where the 1980s brought the deregulation of national financial markets, the 1990s shaped the age of financial globalization: national financial centers – traditionally operating as domestic entrepôts connecting borrowings and savings – were at the frontline of these shifts, gradually turning into gateways to London, New York and globalizing OFCs (Bassens and Van Meeteren 2015). Secondary financial centers like Amsterdam, in contrast, steadily lost their monopolies over domestic capital markets (Fernandez 2011). Resultantly, global capital flowing in and out OFCs witnessed spectacular growth over the 1990s – a process that has continued ever since. Recently, however, budding growth rates in foreign direct investment (FDI) into OFCs have stabilized, suggesting that the global shift in capital flows in and out OFCs has normalized. Resultantly, offshore finance is no longer an exotic sideshow alongside regulated "onshore" finance, but instead has become "the new normal."

A Contemporary Picture

Although not wholly unproblematic (see Clark et al. 2015), we advance the term *offshore financial center* (OFC) as principal category for jurisdictions catering for global capital, defined as "a country or jurisdiction that provides financial services to nonresidents on a scale that is incommensurate with the size and the financing of its domestic economy" (Zoromé 2007: 7). Crucially, OFC is a broader term than *tax haven*, as OFCs are also used for "ease of raising funds, speed and lower costs of company formation, and access to reliable legal jurisdictions" (Clark et al. 2015: 238). As such, OFCs are typically subcategorized. For example, the *Tax Justice Network* qualifies OFCs along a spectrum of *secrecy jurisdictions*, viewing this a better term than tax havens (Cobham et al. 2015). Alternatively, Garcia-Bernardo et al. (2017) speak of *conduit* and *sink* jurisdictions, as OFCs function as intermediate or final destinations for mobile capital. Meanwhile, Park (1982) identifies *primary* OFCs like London, supported by *booking, funding* and *collection* centers elsewhere, which overlaps with the hierarchical idea of *first-, second-* and *third-tier* financial centers. As OFCs cultivate niche strategies, subcategorizations become ever more specified, with Palan et al. (2010: 35–38) offering seven typologies, including *incorporation, registration* and *specialist centers*. Distinguishing between on- and offshore components of financial centers, moreover, Clark et al. (2015: 238) speak of "midshore centers," combining offshore facilities with onshore traits. In general, as offshore finance has matured, the authors note that it is "increasingly difficult to distinguish between offshore, midshore, and onshore financial centers" (ibid.). Furthermore, "to name, list and rank tax havens is a political act" (Aalbers 2017: 7), resulting in definitional differences. For example, the European Union (EU) lists 17 non-cooperative tax havens on its blacklist, whereas Palan et al. (2010: 41–44) list 91 OFCs. Notwithstanding these differences, however, what should be remembered is that offshore finance ultimately constitutes *a globally integrated space*: "Supported by their respective states and boasting slightly different packages of legislation, these centres are the physical platforms upon which an integrated offshore finance system has evolved" (Palan 1999: 23).

Key Figures

The apex of global finance – with London and New York as the world's largest financial centers (Z/Yen 2017), not incidentally exhibiting OFC characteristics themselves (Wojcik 2013a) – is thoroughly interwoven with the offshore world. In this section, we distil the core OFCs underlying global finance, building on various datasets. Most approaches utilize macro data, such as foreign direct investment (Haberly and Wojcik 2015a, 2015b), foreign portfolio investment (FPI) (Zoromé 2007), banking statistics (Fichtner 2014), regulation and taxation (Cobham et al. 2015), private wealth (Zucman 2013), corporate profits (Zucman 2014), corporate ownership (Garcia-Bernardo et al. 2017) and trade statistics (Global Financial Integrity 2015) – each of which producing overlapping-yet-distinct OFC geographies. Building on these, we distil an OFC geography instrumental in shaping the global stocks and flows of *corporate financialization* for multinationals (FDI), investment funds (FPI) and banks (relational banking statistics) to assess the size and role of the largest OFCs constituting offshore finance.[1] To enhance the clarity of the data we have condensed our table.[2]

Foreign Direct Investment (FDI)

Inward FDI stock across OFCs (Table 19.1) reveals the dominance of small European countries – The Netherlands, Luxembourg, Ireland, Belgium and Switzerland – alongside the major Asian centers, Hong Kong and Singapore, and Caribbean OFCs: the British Virgin Islands (BVI), Cayman Islands and Bahamas. This geography is confirmed by other FDI studies (Haberly and Wojcik 2015a, 2015b; Fichtner 2014; Fernandez and Hendrikse 2015; Fernandez and Wigger 2017).

Foreign Portfolio Investment (FPI)

Second, Table 19.1 shows the prominence of Luxembourg and the Caymans in portfolio investments, accounting for 40 percent of the total, with the Netherlands and Ireland following at a distance. This corresponds with the existing literature on Luxembourg as leading hub in investment funds (Dörry 2015, 2016). The Caymans are another central node in portfolio flows, acting as the world's largest domicile for hedge funds, and as a stepping stone between US corporations and the wider world (Fichtner 2016). FPI flows are relatively concentrated: the top five OFCs control 75 percent of FPI passing through the broader group of OFCs, compared to 64 percent in banking flows and 63 percent in FDI flows.

Banking Statistics

Table 19.2 zooms in on the flows of banking entities. The international banking statistics (IBS) produced by the BIS are based on two components: locational banking statistics (LBS) and consolidated banking statistics (CBS). These measure different types of cross-border banking flows: the LBS focuses on intragroup flows between related branches and subsidiaries of banks (relational banking), based on the residence of the legal entities. The CBS net out these intragroup positions to chart cross-border risk exposures (and funding) of banks, as well as country risks in which these banks are headquartered. Notwithstanding these differences, both components consistently show the dominance of the Caymans, the Netherlands, Luxembourg and Hong Kong, followed by Switzerland and Singapore. Importantly, data for the BVI are absent.

Table 19.1 FDI and FPI, Nominal and as a Share of Gross Domestic Product (GDP)

	FDI Inward	Ranking Nominal	Ranking/ GDP	FPI Liabilities	Ranking Nominal	Ranking/ GDP
Aruba	37	32	32	431	30	26
Austria	269,683	11	19	367,263	9	15
Bahamas	70,865	18	8	14,531	20	11
Barbados	13,445	24	12	4,244	25	16
Bahrain	3,396	29	28	5,939	23	25
Belgium	616,707	6	17	591,348	6	13
Bermuda	576,832	7	3	552,348	7	3
BVI	1,121,734	4	1	158,089	12	2
Cayman Islands	540,038	8	2	2,574,058	2	1
Curacao	82,529	17	5	114,132	14	5
Cyprus	196,025	12	7	16,068	19	20
Gibraltar	158,650	14	20	912	29	31
Guernsey	33,122	20	20	107,286	15	9
Hong Kong	1,287,566	3	9	455,470	8	12
Ireland	447,358	9	13	1,671,876	4	6
Isle of Man	7,318	28	18	11,521	21	10
Israel	17,777	22	30	101,394	16	24
Jersey	189,115	13	22	261,534	11	19
Kuwait	9,887	26	29	1,599	28	30
Lebanon	7,653	27	26	3,835	26	27
Liechtenstein	10,122	25	14	5,205	24	18
Luxembourg	2,426,033	2	4	2,926,273	1	4
Macao	16,189	23	24	3,249	27	28
Malaysia	97,191	16	25	124,913	13	23
Maldives	88	31	31	1	32	32
Malta	36,529	19	11	7,966	22	21
Mauritius	130,576	15	6	27,427	18	8
Monaco	1,070	30	27	197	31	29
Netherlands	2,960,593	1	10	2,001,555	3	7
Panama	23,547	21	23	38,582	17	22
Singapore	398,834	10	16	277,794	10	17
Switzerland	1,034,279	5	15	897,988	5	14

Table 19.1 is based on 2014 figures in millions US$. Sources: International Monetary Fund (IMF) Coordinated Direct Investment Survey (CDIS) statistics; IMF Coordinated Portfolio Investment Survey (CPIS) statistics; World Bank GDP statistics; United Nations GDP statistics

Table 19.2 Relational Banking Statistics, Nominal and as a Share of GDP

	CBS	Ranking	Ranking/ GDP	LBS	Ranking Nominal	Ranking/ GDP
Aruba	1,544	29	22	1,393	29	23
Austria	230,353	9	21	215,410	9	22
Bahamas	59,695	14	4	126,065	11	4
Barbados	6,901	25	12	31,255	18	5
Bahrain	24,502	18	20	29,249	19	19
Belgium	463,160	5	16	388,073	8	20
Bermuda	86,048	11	2	106,520	12	2
BVI	0	31	31	0	31	31
Cayman Islands	1,217,370	1	1	1,761,747	1	1
Curacao	7,376	24	7	20,822	23	6
Cyprus	33,124	17	9	83,768	15	7
Gibraltar	3,521	28	30	4,339	28	30
Guernsey	39,585	16	19	101,844	13	12
Hong Kong	836,708	2	6	752,580	4	9
Ireland	379,334	7	11	520,629	7	11
Isle of Man	24,115	19	5	25,770	20	8
Israel	21,507	20	29	15,676	25	29
Jersey	80,194	13	26	154,699	10	24
Kuwait	17,430	22	27	21,510	22	27
Lebanon	6,243	26	28	8,747	26	28
Liechtenstein	6,184	27	15	8,154	27	16
Luxembourg	600,709	4	3	1,002,320	3	3
Macao	43,332	15	17	46,733	17	18
Malaysia	167,229	10	23	68,643	16	26
Maldives	940	30	25	886	30	25
Malta	18,843	21	8	23,489	21	10
Mauritius	13,444	23	14	20,289	24	15
Monaco	0	31	31	0	31	31
Netherlands	688,772	3	18	1,026,111	2	17
Panama	83,773	12	10	92,775	14	14
Singapore	410,657	6	13	588,319	6	13
Switzerland	363,273	8	24	598,528	5	21

Table 19.2 is based on 2016 figures in millions of US$. Sources: BIS relational banking statistics; World Bank GDP statistics; United Nations GDP statistics

The OFC Ranking

Table 19.3 details a set of rankings – A (nominal), B (weighted) and C (aggregate) – which function as indicative rankings of a core group of OFCs shaping global financialized capitalism. First, the scores of all nominal indicators from Tables 19.1 and 19.2 are added up, complemented by the scores of outgoing FDI, and LBS liabilities. This results in ranking A, in which the lowest score produces the highest ranking. The Netherlands, for instance, has a score of 14, making it the leading OFC for the variables considered. Secondly, the scores of all weighted indicators (nominal scores adjusted for the size of the domestic economies of the OFCs) from Tables 19.1 and 19.2 are added up, again complemented by the score of the outgoing FDI and LBS liabilities. This produces ranking B. Finally, the combination of rankings A and B result in ranking C.

Ranking A details the absolute size of offshore capital stocks and flows by multinationals, investment funds and banking entities. This ranking is dominated by the Netherlands and Luxembourg, followed by the Cayman Islands, Switzerland and Hong Kong. Crucially, as OFCs are defined as providing financial services "on a scale that is incommensurate with the size and the financing of its domestic economy" (Zoromé 2007: 7), ranking A should be adjusted for the respective size of their gross domestic product (GDP). As a result, ranking B sees the small European countries superseded by micro states and jurisdictions. Although enjoying lawmaking powers of their own, these imperial remnants ultimately fall under the authority of larger states like the US, the UK and the Kingdom of the Netherlands. These small Caribbean islands – the Caymans, Bahamas, Bermuda, Dutch Antilles and BVI – represent the archetypical "fictitious" regulatory spaces (Roberts 1995). Similar jurisdictions in ranking B are Barbados, Cyprus and the Isle of Man. The high position of Luxembourg is remarkable, given the miniature size of the other OFCs. Particularly the territories tied to the UK are noteworthy, as Bermuda, the Caymans, the BVI, Guernsey, Jersey and the Isle of Man fall under the authority of the British Crown.

The combination of both rankings (C) offsets the effects of weighting the scores by the size of GDP. The weighted adjustments for GDP arguably overemphasize micro jurisdictions, conveniently concealing larger OFCs (see Clark et al. 2015). In our final ranking, therefore, *the Caymans, Luxembourg, Bermuda, Hong Kong, the Netherlands, Ireland, the Bahamas, Singapore, Belgium and Switzerland* feature as the ten leading OFCs. To this group we include the *British Virgin Islands*. [3] The exact order within this group depends on the weight given to the nominal ranking and the ranking weighted by GDP – in our case 50/50 – which is open for debate. As a group, however, these OFCs consistently emerge across different rankings and methods. Their global weight in shaping offshore finance is staggering: for example, the group covers 43 percent of the global inward stock of FDI. Together with the US and UK, who take up another 21 percent, *London, New York and our offshore grid capture two thirds of the total global inward stock of FDI.*

Our core group of OFCs covers all major dimensions shaping offshore finance, both functionally and geographically. The group covers the world's major *tax havens*, or *secrecy jurisdictions*, as well as *conduit* and *sink* functions, for *corporate* and *private* purposes, offering minimal regulation, supervision and tax, amidst maximum secrecy and asset protection, whilst being well connected with the rest of the world via extensive bi- and multilateral agreements. The group offers vital incorporation tools, coming with geographical specializations: where Ireland functions as a dedicated platform for head offices, the Netherlands is specialized in facilitating holding companies. Such cross-jurisdictional differences are often in symphony, resulting in popular tax-planning structures such as "the Double Irish with a Dutch sandwich" (Hendrikse 2013). The group is also spread across the world's major markets and time zones: where Hong Kong is the offshore

Table 19.3 OFC Rankings

	Score Nominal	A Ranking Nominal	Score/GDP	B Ranking/GDP	Scores Combined	C FINAL Ranking
Aruba	180	30	149	25	329	30
Austria	60	9	121	21	181	13
Bahamas	92	13	37	5	129	7
Barbados	126	21	56	6	182	14
Bahrain	137	25	133	23	270	25
Belgium	38	6	98	17	136	9
Bermuda	60	9	16	2	76	3
BVI	115	17	97	16	212	20
Cayman Islands	21	3	8	1	29	1
Curacao	115	17	34	4	149	11
Cyprus	91	12	59	7	150	12
Gibraltar	140	27	160	27	300	27
Guernsey	99	15	95	15	194	16
Hong Kong	31	4	61	8	92	4
Ireland	38	6	63	9	101	5
Isle of Man	131	24	64	10	195	17
Israel	126	21	170	31	296	26
Jersey	73	11	142	24	215	21
Kuwait	138	26	167	29	305	28
Lebanon	154	28	164	28	318	29
Liechtenstein	160	29	98	17	258	24
Luxembourg	15	2	22	3	37	2
Macao	122	19	129	22	251	23
Malaysia	92	13	149	25	241	22
Maldives	185	32	170	31	355	32
Malta	129	23	76	12	205	18
Mauritius	123	20	69	11	192	15
Monaco	182	31	169	30	351	31
Netherlands	14	1	87	14	101	5
Panama	100	16	105	19	205	18
Singapore	47	8	86	13	133	8
Switzerland	31	4	110	20	141	10

gateway in and out of China, Ireland and the Netherlands serve US firms in their global operations. Added up, global corporations (Fernandez and Hendrikse 2015), financial institutions and
their complex value and wealth chains (Seabrooke and Wigan 2017) are principally structured
along these OFCs, constituting the nerve center of contemporary capitalism.

Mechanisms and Players

Since the 1990s the offshore world has mushroomed and professionalized, with a growing
number of states offering all kinds of offshore arrangements. As a result, tax-avoidance toolkits
are increasingly peddled to wealthy individuals like holiday packages. Meanwhile, corporations have rolled out elaborate strategies to maximize returns, using a variety of profit-shifting
and transfer-pricing techniques, via cost- or licensing agreements, which relocate profits and
taxes to OFCs. Their funding mechanisms, typically following highly indebted/thin-capitali-
zation strategies, are structured to minimize tax bills. Yet despite massive growth, the basic
mechanisms underlying offshore finance remain the same as a century ago: OFCs essentially
leverage their sovereign capacity to devise and enact law, providing "extraterritorial" spaces
for non-resident capital, and offering legal tools and accounting devices to optimally structure
capital stocks and flows, following a process of *regulatory arbitrage*. In uncoupling real from
legal locations, offshore finance refers to "a set of juridical realms marked by more or less
withdrawal of regulation and taxation on the part of a growing number of states" (Palan 2003:
19, 23), realized through the incessant "unbundling" and "commercialization" of state sovereignty (Hudson 2000; Palan 2002). Crucially, no individual state can singlehandedly exert
meaningful control over the offshore world, as it hinges on fundamental principles of public
international law, i.e. state sovereignty, rendering its regulation extremely difficult (Maurer
2008; Rixen 2013).

Global Intermediaries

Although public actors formally enact offshore legislation, as an *integrated system* the offshore
world is cultivated by professional intermediaries, led by globally operating banks, law and
accountancy firms who are typically overrepresented in OFCs (Murphy and Strausholm 2017)
and enjoy privileged access to lawmakers (Hendrikse 2013), indicative of political capture
(Hampton and Christensen 1999). If "governance fails" in the offshore world (Wojcik 2013b),
it is because too often these intermediary firms effectively appear to govern themselves. The
recent streak of data leaks provides some fascinating insights into the machinery of offshore
finance: where *Swiss Leaks* uncovered a massive tax evasion scheme run by a subsidiary of global
bank HSBC in Switzerland,[4] the *Panama Papers* unveiled the tricks of global law firm Mossack
Fonseca in Panama, who created the shell companies through which HSBC clients evaded their
taxes.[5] *Lux Leaks*, in turn, exposed corporate tax avoidance enabled by the local authorities and
PricewaterhouseCoopers, one of the big four accountancy firms. Through the dedicated
assemblage *hybrid* loans and entities certified by tax rulings (i.e. corporate funding structures that
are fiscally or legally treated differently across jurisdictions, thereby capitalizing on mismatches in
tax codes with government approval), global corporations enjoyed "effective tax rates of less
than 1 percent on the profits they've shuffled into Luxembourg."[6]

> [Appleby] meets with representatives of major clients, many of which are leading
> banks and accounting firms such as KPMG, Ernst & Young and Pricewaterhouse-
> Coopers. In the Cayman Islands, half of Appleby's top 20 clients in 2014 were major

banks and investment firms, including Citigroup, Bank of America, HSBC, Credit
Suisse and Wells Fargo.

(Fitzgibbon 2017)

Referring to the *Paradise Papers*, exposing the endeavours of law firm Appleby, the above quote
reveals that offshore finance is an exclusive world, chiefly anchored in a core group of OFCs
cultivated by a small cabal of intermediaries. These firms assure that their corporate clients
"build, manage and maintain tax haven networks" (Jones et al. 2017). Together with wealthy
families and individuals who own the corporate edifice, "these players have become, as it were,
citizens of a brave new virtual country" (Henry 2012: 11). Again, their makeup is truly global:
from European royals and American *nouveau riche* to the many autocrats currently doubling as
"patriots"; from Chinese princelings and Arab princes to Russian oligarchs and African war-
lords – the global elite has effectively carved out a secretive, tax free and *sovereign* homeland for
itself (also see Harrington in this volume).

Conclusions

Capitalism only triumphs when it becomes identified with the state, when it
becomes the state.

(Braudel 1977: 64)

Although financialization is a contested notion, even skeptics agree that its key themes center
on *shareholder value* orientation, the penetration of *daily life*, and its (historical recurrence as)
accumulation regime (Christophers 2015; also see Fine and Christophers, and Deutschmann in this
volume). In this concluding section, we discuss how offshore finance is entwined with these
aspects defining financialization, and historicize and discuss the current assemblage of sovereignty
anchoring planetary rule of financialized capital.

The offshore world structures and is structured by the financialized mode of capital accumulation, propelled by the logic of shareholder value (Froud et al. 2000). Offshore finance is indispensable to minimize costs, amplify leverage, protect assets, and hence maximize returns – having
transformed global corporations into financialized offshore dwellers. The financial penetration of
non-financial realms, including the larger institutional fabric of the state itself (Hendrikse 2015),
with its invasive calculations shaping daily life (Martin 2002), increasingly encompass value chains
interlaced with the offshore world. Concretely, besides your debts, offshore finance is likely to be
entwined with the clothes you wear, the furniture you sit on, the smartphone you use, the coffee
you sip, and the neighborhood you live in. Although oddly invisible, *offshore finance virtually intersects
with every aspect of onshore life*, rendering the legally crucial term "offshore" increasingly problematic
in practice.

Drawing historical parallels with contemporary offshore finance, Giovanni Arrighi emphasizes
that "the Genoese merchant elite *occupied* places, but was not *defined* by the places it occupied" –
likening this "non-territorial" system to the "Eurodollar market" (1994: 82–83, emphasis original). Building on Braudel (1982[1979]), Arrighi also points to the continued importance of states,
as "capitalism as a world system of accumulation and rule has developed simultaneously in both
spaces" i.e. the *space-of-places* where it became tied to (a) state(s), and the *space-of-flows* encompassing business and financial networks above the control of any state (ibid.: 84). For centuries, the
forces of *coercion and capital* (Tilly 1990) operated together – in harmony, or less so – directing and
shaping one another. For example, both Britain and the Netherlands effectively operated as *company states* (Stern 2011), based on a relative unity of state coercion and corporate capital, using

their quasi-sovereign chartered (East-India) companies to exert vast extraterritorial power in "the pursuit of plenty," making them classic hegemonic states.

Although the state and corporation cannot be viewed separately in any real sense (Barkan 2013; Nitzan and Bichler 2009), ever since hegemonic power started to move from late nineteenth-century Britain to the US, there has been a remarkable shift in the geographical makeup of state sovereignty fueling corporate enterprise: where corporate power has relentlessly commercialized, globalized and intensified since the liberalization of incorporation laws, the sovereignty enabling the subsequent rise of *global* corporations increasingly decomposed and scattered across the globe in the course of the twentieth century. In the words of Arrighi, pointing to the decomposition of territorial sovereignty, which enabled the rise of giant corporations and offshore finance, the "explosive growth of transnational corporations" marked a *decisive new turning point,* which "may well have initiated the withering away of the modern inter-state system as the primary locus of world power" (Arrighi 1994: 73–74; on the political mechanisms of financialization, also see Pagliari and Young in this volume).

To come to terms with the sovereign foundations of offshore financial power, we need to distinguish between formal and effective sovereignty (Agnew 2000), and realize that corporate power is always couched in state power. This puzzle might be compared to Berle and Means' classic account on *The Modern Corporation and Private Property* (2009 [1932]), emphasizing *the divorce of ownership from control* of the modern corporation. In similar fashion, the formal ownership of, and effective control over, state sovereignty appear to have diverged. Specifically, OFCs place financial activities *outside territorial boundaries* but *within the confines of their sovereign will*: although OFC lawmakers are territorially bound, the commercialized sovereignty they offer to non-resident capital is of an *extraterritorial* nature (Palan 2003: 23). Crucially, combined and utilized as a single package by globally operating financial institutions and corporations, the voluminous slivers of commercialized sovereignty readily available across the offshore world effectively fuse and mutate into "a new global form of sovereignty" (Hardt and Negri 2000: xii) – a *commercialized, deterrritorialized* and increasingly *financialized* sovereignty undergirding global corporate capitalism (Picciotto 2011). In other words, if financialization indeed refers to the growing dominance of finance over society at large, then offshore finance might quite literally represent the very crown upon this project.

Notes

1 We foreground 32 established OFCs who jointly cover the principal share of global offshore capital stocks and flows. We have left out the US and the UK from our analysis, as we are interested in unpacking the central offshore grid connecting London and New York with the rest of the world. Most empirical studies focus on FDI. By adding FPI and banking statistics we seek to boost the validity of our study (see Fichtner 2015 for a comparable analysis).

2 For reasons of clarity, Table 19.1 does not show outward FDI data, nor its ranking, and Table 19.2 omits the liabilities of the banking statistics, and its ranking. Both data sources, however, are included in the final OFC ranking in Table 19.3. In all tables, BVI stands for British Virgin Islands, whereas the figures for Curacao include the island of Sint Maarten.

3 As indicated, not all data for the BVI are available, although the BVI represents a key destination for investment funds, FDI flows, hedge funds and shell companies owning real estate worldwide. We therefore believe the BVI belong to our core group of OFCs.

4 See the *Swiss Leaks* dossier compiled by the International Consortium of Investigative Journalists (ICIJ): [https://projects.icij.org/swiss-leaks/].

5 See *Panama Papers* dossier compiled by the ICIJ: [https://panamapapers.icij.org].

6 See the *Lux Leaks* dossier compiled by the ICIJ: [https://www.icij.org/investigations/luxembourg-leaks/].

Bibliography

Aalbers, M., 2017. Financial geography I: Geographies of tax. *Progress in Human Geography*, 42(6), pp. 916–927.

Agnew, J., 2000. Sovereignty regimes: Territoriality and state authority in contemporary world politics. *Annals of the Association of American Geographers*, 95(2), pp. 437–461.

Arrighi, G., 1994. *The Long Twentieth Century: Money, Power, and the Origins of Our Times*. London and New York: Verso.

Avi-Yonah, R.S., 2015. Who invented the single tax principle?: An essay on the history of US treaty policy. *New York Law School Law Review*, 59(2), pp. 305–315.

Bank for International Settlements. *Consolidated Banking Statistics*. Available at https://www.bis.org/statistics/consstats.htm?m=6%7C31%7C70 [Accessed online January 30, 2018].

Barkan, J., 2013. *Corporate Sovereignty: Law and Government under Capitalism*. Minneapolis: University of Minnesota Press.

Bassens, D. and van Meeteren, M., 2015. World cities under conditions of financialized globalization: Towards an augmented world city hypothesis. *Progress in Human Geography*, 39(6), pp. 752–775.

Berle, A.A. and Means, G.C., 2009 [1932]. *The Modern Corporation and Private Property*. New Brunswick, NJ: Transaction Publishers.

Braudel, F., 1977. *Afterthoughts on Material Civilization and Capitalism*. Baltimore, MD: John Hopkins University.

Braudel, F., 1982 [1979]. *The Wheels of Commerce. Civilization and Capitalism: 15th–18th Century. Volume II*. London: William Collins Sons & Co.

Burn, G., 1999. The state, the City and the Euromarkets. *Review of International Political Economy*, 6(2), pp. 225–261.

Christophers, B., 2015. The limits to financialization. *Dialogues in Human Geography*, 5(2), 183–200.

Clark, G.L., Lai, K.P.Y. and Wójcik, D., 2015. Editorial introduction to the special section: Deconstructing offshore finance. *Economic Geography*, 91(3), pp. 237–249.

Cobham, A., Jansky, P. and Meinzer, M., 2015. The financial secrecy index: Shedding new light on the geography of secrecy. *Economic Geography*, 91(3), pp. 281–303.

Dörry, S., 2015. Strategic nodes in investment fund global production networks: The example of the financial centre Luxembourg. *Journal of Economic Geography*, 15(4), pp. 797–814.

Dörry, S., 2016. The role of elites in the co-evolution of international financial markets and financial centres: The case of Luxembourg. *Competition & Change*, 20(1), pp. 21–36.

Fernandez, R., 2011. *Explaining the Decline of the Amsterdam Financial Centre: Globalizing Finance and the Rise of a Hierarchical Inter-City Network*. PhD Thesis, University of Amsterdam.

Fernandez, R. and Hendrikse, R., 2015. *Rich Corporations, Poor Societies: The Financialisation of Apple*. Amsterdam: SOMO. Available at https://www.somo.nl/nl/rich-corporations-poor-societies/ [Accessed online January 20, 2018].

Fernandez, R. and Wigger, A., 2017. Lehman Brothers in the Dutch offshore financial centre: The role of shadow banking in increasing leverage and facilitating debt. *Economy and Society*, 45(3–4), pp. 407–430.

Fichtner, J., 2014. Privateers of the Caribbean: The hedge funds–US–UK–offshore nexus. *Competition and Change*, 18(1), pp. 37–53.

Fichtner, J., 2015. The offshore-intensity ratio: Identifying the strongest magnets for foreign capital. *CITYPREC Working Paper Series* 2015/02. Available at https://papers.ssrn.com/sol3/papers.cfm?abstract_id=2928027 [Accessed online August 20, 2018].

Fichtner, J., 2016. The anatomy of the Cayman Islands offshore financial center: Anglo-America, Japan, and the role of hedge funds. *Review of International Political Economy*, 21(6), pp. 1034–1063.

Fitzgibbon, W. (2017) "Offshore magic circle": Law firm has record of compliance failures. *International Consortium of Investigative Journalists*. Available at https://www.icij.org/investigations/paradise-papers/appleby-offshore-magic-circle-law-firm-record-of-compliance-failures-icij/ [Accessed online January 20, 2018].

Froud, J., Haslam, C. and Johal, S., 2000. Shareholder value and financialization: Consultancy promises, management moves. *Economy and Society*, 29(1), pp. 80–110.

Garcia-Bernardo, J., Fichtner, J., Takes, F.W. and Heemskerk, E.M., 2017. Uncovering offshore financial centers: Conduits and sinks in the global corporate ownership network. *Scientific Reports* 7. Available at https://www.nature.com/articles/s41598-017-06322-9 [Accessed online January 8, 2019].

Global Financial Integrity, 2015. *Financial Flows and Tax Havens: Combining to Limit the Lives of Billions of People*. Washington DC: Global Financial Integrity. Available at https://www.gfintegrity.org/report/

financial-flows-and-tax-havens-combining-to-limit-the-lives-of-billions-of-people/ [Accessed online October 20, 2018].

Green, J., 2016. Anglo-American development, the Euromarkets, and the deeper origins of neoliberal deregulation. *Review of International Studies*, 42(3), pp. 425–449.

Haberly, D. and Wojcik, D., 2015a. Tax havens and the production of offshore FDI: An empirical analysis. *Journal of Economic Geography*, 15(1), pp. 75–101.

Haberly, D. and Wojcik, D., 2015b. Regional blocks and imperial legacies: Mapping the global offshore FDI network. *Economic Geography*, 91(3), pp. 251–280.

Hampton, M.P. and Christensen, J., 1999. A legislature for hire: The capture of the state in Jersey's offshore financial center. In Hampton, M.P. and Abbott, J.P. (eds) *Offshore Finance Centres and Tax Havens: The Rise of Global Capital*. Basingstoke: Palgrave Macmillan, pp. 166–191.

Hardt, M. and Negri, A., 2000. *Empire*. Cambridge, MA: Harvard University Press.

Harrington, B., 2019. Trusts and financialization. In Mader, P., Mertens, D. and Van der Zwan, N. (eds.) *International Handbook of Financialization*, London: Routledge.

Helleiner, E., 1994. *States and the Reemergence of Global Finance: From Bretton Woods to the 1990s*. Ithaca, NY and London: Cornell University Press.

Hendrikse, R., 2013. Entangled geographies of "Irish" finance. *Eurasian Geography and Economics*, 54(2), pp. 182–201.

Hendrikse, R., 2015. *The Long Arm of Finance: Exploring the Financialization of Governments and Public Institutions*. PhD Thesis, University of Amsterdam.

Henry, J.S., 2012. *The Price of Offshore Revisited*. Tax Justice Network. Available online: http://www.taxjustice. net/cms/upload/pdf/Price_of_Offshore_Revisited_120722.pdf [Accessed online January 30, 2018].

Hudson, A., 2000. Offshoreness, globalization and sovereignty: a postmodern geo-political economy? *Transactions of the Institute of British Geographers*, 25(3), pp. 269–283.

International Monetary Fund. *Coordinated Direct Investment Survey (CDIS)*. Available online: http://data.imf. org/?sk=40313609-F037-48C1-84B1-E1F1CE54D6D5&sId=1390030109571 [Accessed online January 30, 2018].

International Monetary Fund. *Coordinated Portfolio Investment Survey (CPIS)*. Available online: http://data. imf.org/?sk=B981B4E3-4E58-467E-9B90-9DE0C3367363 [Accessed online January 30, 2018].

Jones, C., Temouri, Y. and Cobham, A., 2017. Tax haven networks and the role of the Big 4 accountancy firms. *Journal of World Business*, 53(2), pp. 177–193.

Martin, R., 2002. *Financialization of Daily Life*. Philadelphia: Temple University Press.

Maurer, B., 2008. Re-regulating offshore finance? *Geography Compass*, 2(1), pp. 155–175.

McGauran, K., 2013. *Should the Netherlands Sign Tax Treaties with Developing Countries?* Amsterdam: SOMO. Available at https://www.somo.nl/should-the-netherlands-sign-tax-treaties-with-develop ing-countries/ [Accessed online January 30, 2018].

Michie, R., 2006. *The Global Securities Market: A History*. Oxford University Press.

Murphy, R. and Strausholm, S.N., 2017. *The Big Four: A Study of Opacity*. Cambridgeshire: A Report for European United Left/Nordic Green Left (GUE/NGL). Available at http://www.taxresearch.org.uk/ Documents/GUENGLBigFourWeb.pdf [Accessed online January 30, 2018].

Nitzan, J. and Bichler, S., 2009. *Capital as Power: A Study of Order and Creorder*. Abingdon: Routledge.

OECD. 2013. *Addressing Base Erosion and Profit Shifting*. Paris: OECD Publishing. Available at http://dx. doi.org/10.1787/9789264192744-en [accessed online January 8, 2011].

Palan, R., 1999. Offshore and the structural enablement of sovereignty. In Hampton, M.P. and Abbott, J. P. (eds.) *Offshore Finance Centers and Tax Havens: The Rise of Global Capital*, Basingstoke: Macmillan Press, pp. 18–42.

Palan, R., 2002. Tax havens and the commercialization of state sovereignty. *International Organization*, 56 (1), pp. 151–176.

Palan, R., 2003. *The Offshore World. Sovereign Markets, Virtual Places, and Nomad Millionaires*. Ithaca, NY: Cornell University Press.

Palan, R., Murphy, R. and Chavagneux, C., 2010. *Tax Havens: How Globalization Really Works*. Ithaca, NY and London: Cornell University Press.

Park, Y.S., 1982. The economics of offshore financial centers. *Columbia Journal of World Business*, 17(4), pp. 31–35.

Picciotto, S., 1988. The control of transnational capital and the democratisation of the international state. *Journal of Law and Society*, 15(1), pp. 58–76.

Picciotto, S., 1999. Offshore: The state as legal fiction. In Hampton, M.P. and Abbott, J. (eds.) *Offshore Finance Centres and Tax Havens: The Rise of Global Capital*. Basingstoke: Palgrave Macmillan, pp. 43–79.

Picciotto, S., 2011. *Regulating Global Corporate Capitalism*. Cambridge: Cambridge University Press.

Rixen, T., 2013. Why reregulation after the crisis is feeble: Shadow banking, offshore financial centers, and jurisdictional competition. *Regulation & Governance*, 7(4), pp. 435–459.

Roberts, S., 1995. Small place, big money: The Cayman Islands and the international financial system. *Economic Geography*, 71(3), pp. 237–256.

Seabrooke, L. and Wigan, D., 2017. The governance of global wealth chains. *Review of International Political Economy*, 24(1), pp. 1–29.

Shaxson, N., 2012. *Treasure Islands: Tax Havens and the Men Who Stole the World*. London: Vintage.

Sidaway, J.D. and Hendrikse, R., 2016. Neoliberalism version 3+. In Springer, S., Birch, K. and MacLeavy, J. (eds.) *The Handbook of Neoliberalism*. New York and London: Routledge, 574–582.

Stern, P., 2011. *The Company-State: Corporate Sovereignty and the Early Modern Foundations of the British Empire in India*. Oxford: Oxford University Press.

Tilly, C., 1990. *Coercion, Capital, and European States: AD 990–1992*, Cambridge, MA: Blackwell Publishers.

Van Geest, M., Van Kleef, J., Smits, H.W., 2013. *Het Belastingparadijs: Waarom niemand hier belasting betaalt – behalve u*. Amsterdam/Antwerpen: Business Contact.

Wojcik, D., 2013a. The dark side of NY-LON: Financial centres and the global financial crisis. *Urban Studies*, 50(13), pp. 2736–2752.

Wojcik, D., 2013b. Where governance fails: Advanced business services and the offshore world. *Progress in Human Geography*, 37(3), pp. 330–347.

Z/Yen. 2017. *The Global Financial Centres Index 22, September 2017*. London: Z/Yen and Shenzhen: China Development Institute. Available online http://www.longfinance.net/images/GFCI22_Report.pdf [Accessed online January 20, 2018].

Zoromé, A., 2007. *Concept of Offshore Financial Centers: In Search of an Operational Definition*. Washington DC: IMF. Working Paper 07/87. Available at https://www.imf.org/external/pubs/ft/wp/2007/wp 0787.pdf [Accessed online January 8, 2018].

Zucman, G., 2013. The missing wealth of nations: Are Europe and the U.S. net debtors or net creditors? *The Quarterly Journal of Economics*, 128(3), pp. 1321–1364.

Zucman, G., 2014. Taxing across borders: Tracking personal wealth and corporate profits. *Journal of Economic Perspectives*, 28(4), pp. 121–148.

PART D

Actors, Agency and Politics of Financialization

20

CENTRAL BANKING, SHADOW BANKING, AND INFRASTRUCTURAL POWER[1]

Benjamin Braun and Daniela Gabor

Introduction

The global expansion of the financial sector has transformed capitalism, with significant consequences for the distribution of income, wealth, and power. While the earlier financialization literature often focused on the behavior of shareholders and corporate management, political economists have increasingly zeroed in on dynamics taking place at the core of the financial system, namely the rise of shadow banking, and of market-based finance more generally (Godechot 2016; Maxfield, Winecoff and Young 2017; Thiemann 2018). The new frontier for this research agenda, we argue, is the question of how power operates at the hybrid, public–private core of the monetary system, where banks transact with the central bank (Braun 2018b).

This chapter is concerned with the economic and political connections between the institutionalization of central bank dominance and the rise and resilience of shadow banking. In a nutshell, we argue that shadow money markets have come to serve as the governance infrastructure for central banks. This *infrastructural entanglement* has increased central banks' dependence on market-based finance, and thus the infrastructural power financial actors are able to exercise in the political process.

Political scientists and sociologists have tended to shy away from this question. Monetary and financial power operates not only "beneath open and immediate political conflict" (Pierson 2016: 129), but also beneath layers of technical complexity that are difficult to peel away. In recent years, important progress has been made in the study of the instrumental and structural power of the financial sector (Culpepper 2015; Pagliari and Young 2016; Woll 2016; Pagliari and Young, this volume). For the most part, however, this research has focused on state-finance interactions that take place on the turf and according to the rules of the political rule-making process. What this literature tends to overlook is a crucial set of interactions between private financial actors and public agencies that take place "beneath open and immediate political conflict," on the turf and according to the rules of financial markets.

The paradigmatic example is modern central banking. The key features of modern central banks are their independence and their (mandated) focus on price stability. This institutional arrangement, which generally prioritizes low inflation over full employment, both stems from and entrenches unequal power between capital and labor in a low-salience, technocratic policy area. Political scientists, sociologists, and economists have thoroughly studied the *political and macroeconomic consequences* of central bank independence (McNamara 2002; Polillo and Guillién 2005). By contrast, little is known about the *financial consequences* of modern central banking. More generally, there is a lack not only of empirical studies, but also of theoretical reflection about how power operates at the intersection of public monetary authority and private banking and financial markets.

In this chapter, we argue that central banks have acted as decisive catalysts for the crucial development at the heart of financialization: the rise of shadow money and shadow banking. While most accounts explain the rise and resilience of shadow banking as the outcome of market-led financial innovation aided by regulatory capture, we advance a view that places greater emphasis on the role of state actors: shadow money and shadow banking have co-evolved with the elephant in the room of financialization, namely central banking.

Monetary policy represents a peculiar form of economic state power in that it works in and through financial markets (Krippner 2011; Braun 2018a, 2018b; Walter and Wansleben 2019). Its reach and effectiveness depend directly "on the structure of financial markets and on the economic characteristics of market participants" (ECB 2000: 47). While the quote illustrates that technocrats were aware of this central bank–finance nexus, the tranquillity of the "Great Moderation" – a two-decade period starting in the late 1980 characterized by low inflation and stable growth rates – was such that (political) economists largely ignored this nexus. Crucially, however, this period of calm and institutionalized central bank dominance coincided with the transformation of traditional banking into "securitized" (Gorton and Metrick 2012) or "market-based" banking (Hardie et al. 2013), and with the growth of the broader shadow banking system (Lysandrou and Nesvetailova 2015; Gabor 2018; Thiemann 2018). The hallmark of that system is the securitization of both sides of banks' balance sheets – market-based funding via the repo market on the liability side and market-based lending via asset-backed securities (ABSs) on the asset side. These markets were at the heart of the global financial crisis of 2008, which abruptly ended the "Great Moderation" and forced central banks to intervene on an unprecedented scale to stabilize the shadow banking system (Mehrling 2010; Gabor and Ban 2016; Jacobs and King 2016; Murau 2017).

The global shift towards inflation targeting in the 1990s placed the burden of macroeconomic governance squarely onto the shoulders of central banks. The policy tools of the latter, however, were not necessarily up to the task, and monetary policymakers sought ways to translate their (indirect) control over the interbank money market into control over macroeconomic aggregates (Braun 2018a). In the process, they shaped "the structure of financial markets" (ECB 2000: 47) in ways that would support monetary governability. Those ways, it turned out, also boosted the private creation of shadow money.

The remainder of the chapter will develop our argument in three steps. The first section reviews the growing, interdisciplinary literature on the public–private hybridity of money and finance. Understanding that hybridity is key to understanding what is special about central banking as a form of state agency. As explained in the second section, central bank agency is not primarily administrative, but market-based. Its reach and scope, therefore, is closely intertwined with the reach and scope of those financial markets that constitute the infrastructure for monetary governance. The flipside of that infrastructural entanglement is infrastructural power enjoyed by financial market actors. The third section shows how infrastructural entanglement and power played out in the US and in the euro area. The US Federal Reserve and the European Central Bank both advocated and actively promoted, for monetary policy purposes, the development of shadow money. The conclusion discusses the applicability of our approach to other instances of infrastructural entanglement at the state–finance nexus, and for the study of power in the process of financialization more generally.

The Essential Hybridity of Money and Finance

The literature on the history of money and finance shows that financial innovation is often driven by the interaction between banking and central banking (Konings 2011; Knafo 2013). When it comes to the more recent rise of shadow banking, however, awareness for the reciprocal nature of this interaction has been less pronounced. The political economy literatures on banking and central banking have largely remained separate. On one hand, comparative political economists have added depth and detail to Zysman's (1983) classic distinction between bank-based and market-based financial systems (Hardie et al. 2013). The crucial question of how "the structure of finance contributes to the state's capacity to act in the economy" (Zysman 1983: 298), which students of earlier historical periods have discussed (Konings 2011; Krippner 2011), has somewhat been lost in the market-based finance literature. On the other hand, the political-economy literature on central banks has tended to abstract from the operational details of central banking. Whether they focus on international monetary arrangements or on social groups' preferences for inflation, employment or exchange rates, these studies have largely bracketed the question of exactly *how* central banks establish and maintain control over their domestic economies, let alone how they project power in global financial markets (Frieden 1991; Bernhard Broz and Clark 2003).

What has been missing from these two literatures, thereby preventing their rapprochement, is an awareness of the essential hybridity of money and finance. This is despite a long, interdisciplinary tradition of scholars whose thinking revolved explicitly around hybridity (Innes 1914; Keynes 1930; Schumpeter 1954). For a number of reasons, however, these authors' insights got lost between the cracks of academic disciplines – economists focusing on private actors and markets, sociologists and political scientists focusing on public actors and institutions. The global financial crisis, however, renewed scholarly interest in the hybridity of money and finance, including in economics (Mehrling 2010, 2013), law (Pistor 2013; Ricks 2016, 2018; Hockett and Omarova 2017), and political economy (Gabor and Ban 2016; Koddenbrock 2017; Murau 2017; Braun 2018b). The two core tenets of this literature are easily stated. First, money is a liability of financial institutions, that is, credit. Ever since the Bank of England first managed to monopolize the issuance of negotiable banknotes in the mid-nineteenth century (Ingham 2004: 135), two main forms of credit-money have coexisted: the liabilities of the central bank (reserves and cash) and the liabilities of commercial banks (deposits). Second, while most of the liabilities that circulate as money are created on the balance sheets of private banks, the moneyness of those liabilities depends ultimately on legal rights granted and financial backing provided by the state (Hockett and Omarova 2017). In technical terms, private-sector liabilities trade at par with public-sector liabilities because the former enjoy special privileges granted by the state, including reserve accounts at the central bank, participation in the payment system, and direct access to lender-of-last-resort liquidity.

What this literature offers is not so much a theory, but a close description of "actually existing" capitalist money. This description has far-reaching implications for the political economy of power and institutional change at the center of the monetary and financial system. The remainder of this chapter discusses these implications for the specific case of shadow money, defined as quasi-monetary liabilities created in the shadow banking system. The argument unfolds in two steps. First, the hybridity view reveals that public actors do not just govern private financial markets through rules and regulations. Instead, they often actively *participate in* those markets, which provide the *governance infrastructure through which public actors seek to govern the economy*. Where state agency is market-based, private financial market actors wield *infrastructural power* vis-à-vis public actors (Braun 2018b). The following section develops this theoretical argument for the infrastructural entanglement between central banks and the shadow banking system.

Second, when private financial actors innovate, they create "shadow money" – financial liabilities that fulfill quasi-monetary functions within the financial system, but without (ex ante) state support (Gabor and Vestergaard 2016; Murau 2017). There is nothing new to this – Henry Simons worried about central banks giving private finance "too much freedom [...] in directing changes in the quantity of money and money-substitutes" in 1936 (Simons 1936: 3). While shadow money greases the wheels of credit creation and securities trading during good times, liquidity tends to evaporate at times of financial stress (Gorton and Metrick 2012). Classic examples are the repo market at the domestic level, and the Eurodollar market at the international level (Altamura 2017; Gabor 2016a; Green 2016). What the hybridity view reveals is that shadow money does not, as a rule, evolve in a purely private realm. Focusing on the US and Europe, the third section of this chapter shows that central banks can drive private monetary innovation, encouraging finance to monetize new forms of credit.

In Search of Monetary Governability: Market-based Agency and Infrastructural Entanglement

Since the onset of modern central banking in the late nineteenth century, the share of the burden of macroeconomic stabilization carried by monetary policy has greatly increased. In relation to the weight of that burden, monetary policy must be seen as a *weak* instrument of macroeconomic governance. Compared to fiscal policy, the link between monetary policy and macroeconomic outcomes is indirect and prone to disruption. Establishing and maintaining monetary governability therefore requires purposeful action – discursive and institutional – by central bankers (Krippner 2011; Braun 2015 2018a; Dutta 2018; Wansleben 2018; Walter 2019). In abstract terms, the segment of the economy the central bank controls – the interbank money market – is small and insignificant relative to the economy as a whole. More specifically, central bankers, regardless of the monetary-policy regime they operate under, face two challenges. First, the central bank has direct control only over the *policy* interest rate at which it lends reserves to private financial institutions, whereas the *market* rates at which the latter lend to each other are beyond direct central bank control. This disconnect gives rise to the challenge of monetary policy *implementation* – the challenge of how to deploy the limited instruments of monetary policy to steer short-term interest rates. Second, the challenge of monetary policy *transmission* arises from the gap between this short-term interest rate and the rates of employment, growth, and inflation, which constitute the ultimate targets of most central banks.

In order to tackle these challenges, central banks have historically relied on two types of agency. Like other government bodies, central banks hold and exert *administrative authority*, "setting, interpreting and applying statutory rules" (Hellwig 2014: 5–6). Most importantly, central banks have a statutory monopoly to create central bank money, which takes the form of cash (notes and coins) and reserves. The latter are deposits held by commercial banks, and sometimes other financial institutions, in accounts at the central bank. Banks need reserves to settle debts among each other, and to make payments to the government. Central banks also have the authority to impose reserve requirements on banks, usually set at a small percentage of (certain) liabilities. Together, banks' dependence on reserves and central banks' monopoly on their creation gives central banks significant control over the price of money in the interbank money market. In addition to this core monetary power, the statutory rights of central banks often include far-reaching administrative powers in policy areas such as the payment system, foreign exchange transactions, and banking regulation and supervision. In short, central banks, in pursuit of their policy goals, act on the financial system through administrative authority.

In addition to administrative authority, however, central banks also rely on *market-based agency*. Central banks implement monetary policy by transacting with other (commercial) banks. These are transactions "on a *quid-pro-quo* basis, such as taking deposits from banks, granting loans to banks, or buying and selling assets in open markets" (Hellwig 2014: 5–6, original emphasis). While other government bodies also engage in market transactions, these transactions are not a policy instrument to move market prices but instead serve a specific purpose (i.e., purchasing land to build a road). For central banks, by contrast, market transactions are the main policy instrument. This market-based agency thus distinguishes central banks from most other government bodies. Whereas the latter act on the economy by setting and enforcing rules, central bank control over economic conditions rests not only on administrative authority, but also on market transactions into which private actors enter at their own discretion.

Central banks shape the structure of the financial system both through administrative authority and through market-based agency (see Thiemann in this volume). While both types of agency are geared towards monetary governability, they follow different logics and affect the financial system in different ways. Historically, administrative authority has often been geared towards imposing *limits* on private financial transactions for the purpose of enhancing the central bank control over financial conditions. The effectiveness of market-based agency, by contrast, tends to depend on *deep and liquid markets* for money and securities.

The use of administrative authority for monetary governability purposes has a long tradition, ranging from nineteenth-century Britain (Knafo 2013: 7, 15) to Regulation Q, through which the Federal Bank (Fed) expanded its direct control over interest rates from the interbank money market to the retail deposit market (Krippner 2011). Other central banks, too, used "direct" instruments, such as interest rate ceilings and credit controls, to control conditions in credit markets for monetary policy purposes (Baliño and Zamalloa 1997). While many central banks gradually abandoned such direct monetary policy instruments from the 1980s onwards (see p. 00), some countries have continued to rely on them. Most importantly, the People's Bank of China (PBOC) has resorted to a mix of interest rate ceilings and capital controls in order to square large-scale foreign-exchange interventions with low domestic inflation (Gruin 2013). More recently, the post-2008 expansion of central bank mandates to include macroprudential responsibilities means that even the most invasive deployment of administrative authority is under consideration by policymakers, including structural reforms that would change the legal, organizational, and economic structure of banks (Omarova 2018; Thiemann 2018).

The continued relevance of administrative authority notwithstanding, in the context of the financial liberalization policies of the 1980s, central banks took a decisive turn from "direct" to "indirect" policy instruments (Baliño and Zamalloa 1997). Since then, most central banks have sought to steer the market interest rate in the interbank market – the "operational target" of monetary policy – by deploying the trinity of reserve requirements, open market operations, and standing facilities (Bindseil 2004: 9). This indirect approach has increased the infrastructural entanglement between central banks and those parts of the financial system in which they conduct their open market operations.

Michael Mann developed the concept of infrastructural power to distinguish modern forms of state power from the "despotic power" pre-modern, absolutist rulers had relied on to govern their subjects (Mann 1993). By contrast, bureaucratic-democratic states developed the capacity to control their territory and population, and thus to "penetrate civil society, and to implement logistically political decisions" (Mann 1984: 189). While Mann theorized the power of the state, he did acknowledge that infrastructural power was "a two-way street" (Mann 1993: 59). A state that governs through civil society infrastructures at the same time becomes dependent. Civil-society structures that serve as conduits for governance are empowered vis-à-vis the state.

Today, the financial system is arguably the governance infrastructure *par excellence* (see also Woll 2017; Ricks 2018). This allows us to reverse Mann's theoretical perspective to focus on the infrastructural power of *private actors* over public actors (Braun 2018b). It should be noted that the mechanism here is different from either instrumental power, which is based on the lobbying capacity of finance (see Epstein in this volume), or from structural power, which is based on the ability of finance (and business more generally) to threaten an investment strike. Of course, not all parts of the state rely on financial markets as governance infrastructures in equal measure. Rather, specific parts of the financial system exercise infrastructural power vis-à-vis specific parts of the state. While therefore not universally applicable, the infrastructural power approach offers "a higher-resolution view of the policymaking apparatus, and thus a more nuanced theory of the scope and reach of the political power of finance" (Braun 2018b: 7).

In the following section, we will zoom in on the most consequential instance of infrastructural entanglement and power in the contemporary financial system – that between central banking and shadow banking. Decisions by most leading central banks to conduct their open market operations in the form of (reverse) repurchase transactions, or repos, made them particularly dependent on deep, liquid and, in the case of the euro area, transnationally integrated, repo markets.

Shadow Money in the US and in the Euro Area

Monetary theorists and historians conceptualize the process through which new monies are developed as an eminently private endeavour. For Hyman Minsky (1986: 228), "everyone can create money; the problem is to get it accepted". Charles Kindleberger (1978) argued that private finance fuels the flames of financial instability by creating close money substitutes that monetize credit. Monetary history provides a long list of such experiments, some of which have crossed over into "proper," means of settlement: "money." In both accounts, and in the large scholarship these have influenced, central banks are silent, and rather helpless, witnesses. The case for controlling the supply of money rests on the ability to correctly identify which new monies matter for creating additional demand pressures. Central banks have suffered so many defeats at the hand of Goodhart's law – "any observed statistical regularity will tend to collapse once pressure is placed upon it for control purposes" (Goodhart 2006: 757) – that there are few left who make a serious case for targeting the supply of money. The age of inflation targeting promised a new scientific paradigm for central banks that did not require them to closely monitor *how* credit is monetized, since *the pace* of monetization would be set by the interest rate policy of the central bank. A closer look at the historical evolution of shadow money, however, challenges this view.

Shadow Money: A Very Short Introduction

The Financial Stability Board defined shadow banking as the "system of credit intermediation that involves entities and activities outside the regular banking system" (FSB 2011: 3). Shadow money, a recent addition to the monetary vocabulary, conceptualizes promises to pay created by banks and shadow banks – such as money market funds or hedge funds – in the process of lending through capital markets (Pozsar 2014; Gabor and Vestergaard 2016; Murau 2017). It is the money of (globalized) financial systems organized around securities markets. These promises to pay backed by tradable collateral are known as repos or securities financing transactions. Repos derive their moneyness, understood as their capacity to preserve parity to settlement money, from legal and risk practices of collateral valuation. When a bank creates shadow money, it creates a promise to pay backed by tradable collateral, usually government-issued or private-sector-issued bonds. The holder of shadow money cannot rely on traditional guarantees of banks' promises to pay, namely deposit guarantees and central bank support, but instead relies on collateral. Legally, collateral belongs to the holder because shadow money creation is structured as a sale and repurchase of collateral that belongs to the shadow money issuer. Economically, collateral belongs to the shadow money creator, who assumes the risks and reaps the rewards of securities it deploys as collateral. Put differently, shadow money funds the securities used as collateral. But legal ownership is not sufficient to preserve convertibility at par between shadow and bank money. Rather, collateral is marked to market on a daily basis, to ensure full parity between the market value of collateral posted and the shadow money IOU. Divergences (fall in market price of collateral) are settled by (more) collateral or cash posted by the shadow money creator. In sum, the term shadow money refers to securities that fulfil the same functions, but do not enjoy the same government guarantees, as money "proper."

Since the late 1970s, shadow money has been an attractive method to monetize credit created through securities markets (Ban and Gabor 2016; Gabor 2016a). Most notoriously, both Bear Stearns and Lehman Brothers created shadow money to fund their rapidly expanding balance sheets, and both fell because the private mechanism for preserving moneyness – the daily valuation of collateral – proved eminently fragile in moments of crisis. When private collateral valuation broke down, central banks reacted with a mixture of surprise and disbelief. Ben Bernanke confessed that he had viewed overnight shadow money as the safest funding for (shadow) banks. The ECB wondered how it could have lost sight of an activity that had grown systemic, albeit in the shadows (Gabor and Ban 2016).

The US Federal Reserve and Shadow Money

Central banks may not have thought in terms of shadow money, but they were familiar and closely engaged with repo markets. In late 1990s, the US Federal Reserve was confronted with a peculiar predicament. While the world was celebrating central bank independence as a mark of "scientific" economic governance after the populist era of monetizing government bonds, the US Federal Reserve worried about projections that the US government would pay down all its debt by 2012. A world without US government debt, they worried, was a world filled with monetary dangers. Market participants would not have a safe, liquid asset to turn to in times of distress.

The US Fed dismissed proposals that the government put its securities-creating powers in the service of capital markets, issuing debt divorced from its fiscal needs. This raised complex questions of what to do with the cash raised, questions that neither the Fed nor the US Treasury thought could be addressed without fundamentally involving the state in the process of private resource allocation. Instead, the Fed embraced a market-solution that put shadow money creation at its core. It proposed to use shadow money creation in order to create private substitutes for US Treasuries. Shadow money would liquefy collateral securities such as mortgage-backed securities and asset backed securities.

Rather than seeking to limit shadow money supply, the Fed actively encouraged its expansion, seeking market solutions to political problems. It lobbied Congress to ensure that holders of shadow money backed by private (securitized) collateral had the same legal rights to collateral as those holding shadow money issued against US government debt. The Fed also changed its lending practices. In the early 2000s, banks could issue shadow money backed by private collateral to borrow from the Fed. These concrete steps contrast starkly with the picture of central banks watching passively from the margins, as financial institutions find new ways to monetize credit and circumvent rules (Gabor 2016a).

The European Central Bank and Shadow Money

The European Central Bank (ECB) provides a similar challenge to the received wisdom that innovation occurs in the market and is followed by adaptation in policymaking. In its early days, the ECB actively shaped the creation of shadow euros, that is, of shadow money created against euro-area securities collateral. For the ECB, it wasn't so much financial stability that was at stake in its active encouragement of financial innovation, since the institution only had a mandate for price stability, as the effectiveness of monetary policy. The designers of the ECB were well aware of Minsky's insight that evolutionary changes in finance can pose significant challenges for monetary policy making, and identified those evolutionary changes in the increasing importance of securities markets. But larger securities markets sharpened the contradictions of a single currency with many sovereign bond markets. The ECB worried that the transmission mechanism of monetary policy would be impaired because of the differences in liquidity and yield across the public debt markets of the countries participating in the euro project.

The ECB found itself in a predicament similar to that confronting the US Fed at the time. The solution to its diagnosed problem was political: pulling together sovereign debt issuance into Eurobonds. Since this political solution turned out to be impossible to deliver, the ECB turned to shadow euros. It decided that it would organize the implementation of monetary policy via shadow euros that treated all euro area government bonds as equal collateral. Put simply, the ECB would not follow the traditional approach to open market operations, that involved outright buying (and selling) government bonds from (to) banks. Rather, it would lend to banks via repo transactions, with the collateral framework organized so that the nationality of government bonds did not matter. A Greek bank could borrow from the Eurosystem – by issuing repos (shadow money) to the ECB – on the same collateral terms if it used Greek government debt or German Bunds as collateral.

In doing so, the ECB stressed that it hoped to set an example that private finance would follow. Shadow euros offered a vehicle for the ECB to incentivize the private sector to integrate government bond markets, liquefying those public securities that did not benefit from the size of the Italian bond market or the fiscal reputation of the German Bund. This turned out to be a strikingly, albeit temporarily, successful experiment. By the time of the collapse of Lehman, private shadow euro creation had risen to around EUR 7 trillion, of which EUR 6 trillion were backed by sovereign collateral.

Shadow Money and Infrastructural Power

The growing importance of shadow dollars and shadow euros simultaneously reflects an evolutionary shift in credit creation via securities markets and deliberate state policy to solve intractable political problems posed by the rise of market-based finance. If shadow money is a mark of the growing infrastructural power of private finance, then the crisis of shadow money in both Europe and the US provides several insights into the limits and potentialities of that infrastructural power. Historically, shadow money is not exceptional in that its privately produced moneyness could not withstand the pressures of a financial crisis. The crisis of shadow money, conceived as a run on US repo markets (Gorton and Metrick 2012) and a run on periphery sovereign collateral in the euro area (Gabor and Ban 2016) suggests that infrastructural entanglement, no matter how deep, cannot generate the immediate state responses that would preserve shadow moneyness. It took the Federal Reserve several months, and the collapse of Bear Sterns and Lehman Brothers, to introduce measures that safeguarded shadow dollar moneyness, notably the term securities lending facility and the primary dealer credit facility (Gabor 2016a; Murau 2017). More strikingly, it took the European Central Bank three long years to negotiate a political compromise that allowed it to stabilize shadow euros through the Outright Monetary Transactions program (Gabor and Ban 2016). Put differently, private finance's ability to put infrastructural power in the service of its survival, threatened by the crisis, is not automatic.

Paradoxically, the limits to infrastructural power *during* the financial crisis translate into opportunities in the *post*-crisis environment. Here, the interests of the shadow banking sector have proven enormously resilient, in spite of the fact that academics, regulators, and politicians had singled out shadow banking as the key culprit of the crisis. Various recent studies have shown that those interests found their way into the political process via the alliance between central banking and shadow banking. Thus, the ECB played a crucial role in fending off an aggressive proposal by the European Commission for a financial transaction tax that would have taxed repo transactions (Gabor 2016b; Kalaitzake 2017). Similarly, the ECB went out of its way to protect the securitization market. It provided collateral easing and quantitative easing, and successfully lobbied the European Commission and national governments for regulatory easing (Braun 2018b). In both cases, the ECB cited concerns over the potential negative consequences for monetary governability. This is the transmission mechanism of the infrastructural power of shadow banking: the ECB's readiness to throw around its weight in Brussels to protect the financial infrastructure through which it governs the economy.

Conclusion

Financialization is a process of enormous complexity. Determining where power and agency reside, and if and how they drive financialization, poses difficult analytical challenges. Private financial innovation, the instrumental power of financial actors to influence political decision-makers through lobbying – these are sources of power that have helped the rise and resilience of shadow banking. They cannot explain, however, why financial innovation in this area has partly been state-led, with central banks actively promoting the development of deep, liquid, and transnationally integrated repo markets. They also cannot explain why, in the global financial crisis, central banks backstopped some forms of shadow banking but not others. When secur-itization markets were threatened by market turmoil or by regulatory action, the Fed and the ECB came to their rescue. This chapter has argued that an important source of power for shadow banks is their infrastructural entanglement with central banks. Central banks depend on shadow bank activities for the implementation and transmission of monetary policy. Herein lies the infrastructural power of the issuers of shadow money.

Across the world, policy implementation by central banks has come to rely on open market operations in domestic repo markets. This marketization of monetary policy has seen a new twist with the widespread adoption, in the aftermath of the global financial crisis, of "unconventional" monetary policy measures, notably quantitative easing. Here, different types of purchase programs imply entanglement with different segments of the financial system. Thus, the ECB bought mostly government bonds and corporate bonds, whereas the Fed bought large quantities of mortgage-backed securities. The Bank of Japan and the Swiss National Bank, by contrast, purchased large quantities of domestic (BoJ) and foreign (SNB) equities, thus giving rise to infrastructural entanglement with a different financial market segment.

Finally, infrastructural entanglement and power are not limited to monetary policy, but are increasingly important features of financial systems around the world. At the national level, the marketization of sovereign debt management practices has certainly increased infrastructural entanglement between treasuries and capital markets (Lemoine 2016; Fastenrath, Schwan and Trampusch 2017; Wang in this volume). At the European level, the European Commission's

Capital Markets Union is best understood as an experiment in "governing through financial markets" (Braun, Gabor and Hübner 2018). In alliance with the member states and the ECB, the Commission seeks to boost investment, stability, and cross-border risk sharing by expanding cross-border capital markets and securitization. Nor is infrastructural entanglement between the state and financial markets limited to the Western world. The Chinese state in particular has used the financial system to project power and to accelerate economic development (Gruin 2013; Wang 2015). And while concerns over the sustainability of the growth of shadow money in China have grown, the government has been hesitant to reign in the shadow banking sector (Gabor 2018). Disentangling finance and the state, and thus curbing the infrastructural power of the former is not, it appears, on the agenda of the Communist Party.

Note

1 We would like to thank Sahil Dutta, Rodrigo Fernandez, Philip Mader, and Daniel Mertens for their comments on earlier versions of this chapter.

Bibliography

Altamura, C.E., 2017. *European Banks and the Rise of International Finance: The Post-Bretton Woods Era.* Routledge.
Baliño, T.J.T. and Zamalloa, L.M. (eds.), 1997. *Instruments of Monetary Management: Issues and Country Experiences.* Washington, D.C.: International Monetary Fund.
Ban, C. and Gabor, D., 2016. The political economy of shadow banking. *Review of International Political Economy*, 23(6), pp. 901–914.
Bernhard, W., Broz, J.L. and Clark, W.R. (eds.), 2003. *The Political Economy of Monetary Institutions.* Cambridge, MA: MIT Press.
Bindseil, U., 2004. *The Operational Target of Monetary Policy and the Rise and Fall of Reserve Position Doctrine.* ECB Working Paper no. 372. Frankfurt: European Central Bank.
Braun, B., 2015. Governing the future: The European Central Bank's expectation management during the Great Moderation. *Economy and Society*, 44(3), pp. 367–391.
Braun, B., 2018a. Central bank planning? Unconventional monetary policy and the price of bending the yield curve. In Beckert, J. and Bronk, R. (eds.), *Uncertain Futures: Imaginaries, Narratives, and Calculation in the Economy.* Oxford: Oxford University Press, pp. 194–216.
Braun, B., 2018b. Central banking and the infrastructural power of finance: The case of ECB support for repo and securitization markets. *Socio-Economic Review*, Epub ahead of print.
Braun, B., Gabor, D. and Hübner, M., 2018. Governing through financial markets: Towards a critical political economy of Capital Markets Union. *Competition & Change*, 22(2), pp. 101–116.
Culpepper, P.D., 2015. Structural power and political science in the post-crisis era. *Business and Politics*, 17(3), pp. 391–409.
Dutta, S.J., 2018. *Depoliticising Money? The Transformation from Keynesian to Neoliberal Monetary Governance in Britain.* Presented to "Financialisation and the Future of Money" workshop, Brighton, 16–18 May.
ECB, 2000. *Monetary Policy Transmission in the Euro Area.* Monthly Bulletin July 2000.
Fastenrath, F., Schwan, M. and Trampusch, C., 2017. Where states and markets meet: The financialisation of sovereign debt management. *New Political Economy*, 22(3), pp. 273–293.
Frieden, J.A., 1991. Invested interests: The politics of national economic policies in a world of global finance. *International Organization*, 45(4), pp. 425–451.
FSB, 2011. *Shadow Banking: Strengthening Oversight and Regulation.* Financial Stability Board. Available at http://www.fsb.org/wp-content/uploads/r_111027a.pdf [Accessed March 1, 2019].
Gabor, D., 2016a. The (impossible) repo trinity: The political economy of repo markets. *Review of International Political Economy*, 23(6), pp. 967–1000.
Gabor, D., 2016b. A step too far? The European Financial Transactions Tax on shadow banking. *Journal of European Public Policy*, 23(6), pp. 925–945.
Gabor, D., 2018. Goodbye (Chinese) shadow banking, hello market-based finance. *Development and Change*, Epub ahead of print.

Gabor, D. and Ban, C., 2016. Banking on bonds: The new links between states and markets. *Journal of Common Market Studies*, 54(3), pp. 617–635.

Gabor, D. and Vestergaard, J., 2016. *Towards a Theory of Shadow Money*. INET Working Paper. London: Institute for New Economic Thinking.

Godechot, O., 2016. Financialization is marketization! A study of the respective impacts of various dimensions of financialization on the increase in global inequality. *Sociological Science*, 3, pp. 495–519.

Goodhart, C., 2006. The ECB and the conduct of monetary policy: Goodhart's Law and lessons from the euro area. *JCMS: Journal of Common Market Studies*, 44(4), pp. 757–778.

Gorton, G. and Metrick, A., 2012. Securitized banking and the run on repo. *Journal of Financial Economics*, 104(3), pp. 425–451.

Green, J., 2016. Anglo-American development, the Euromarkets, and the deeper origins of neoliberal deregulation. *Review of International Studies*, 42(3), pp. 425–449.

Gruin, J., 2013. Asset or liability? The role of the financial system in the political economy of China's rebalancing. *Journal of Current Chinese Affairs*, 42(4), pp. 73–104.

Hardie, I. et al., 2013. Banks and the false dichotomy in the comparative political economy of finance. *World Politics*, 65(4), pp. 691–728.

Hellwig, M., 2014. *Financial Stability, Monetary Policy, Banking Supervision, and Central Banking*. Paper presented at the First ECB Forum, Sintra, 25 May 2014. Preprints of the Max Planck Institute for Research on Collective Goods, 2014/9.

Hockett, R.C. and Omarova, S.T., 2017. The finance franchise. *Cornell Law Review*, 102, pp. 1143–1218.

Ingham, G., 2004. *The Nature of Money*. Cambridge: Polity.

Innes, M.A., 1914. The credit theory of money. *Banking Law Journal*, 31, pp. 151–168.

Jacobs, L. and King, D., 2016. *Fed Power: How Finance Wins*. Oxford: Oxford University Press.

Kalaitzake, M., 2017. Death by a thousand cuts? Financial political power and the case of the European Financial Transaction Tax. *New Political Economy*, 22(6), pp. 709–726.

Keynes, J.M., 1930. *A Treatise on Money*. New York: Harcourt, Brace.

Kindleberger, C.P., 1978. *Manias, Panics, and Crashes: A History of Financial Crises*. New York: John Wiley & Sons.

Knafo, S., 2013. *The Making of Modern Finance: Liberal Governance and the Gold Standard*. Abingdon: Routledge.

Koddenbrock, K., 2017. *What Money Does: An Inquiry into the Backbone of Capitalist Political Economy*. Cologne: Max Planck Institute for the Study of Societies.

Konings, M., 2011. *The Development of American Finance*. Cambridge: Cambridge University Press.

Krippner, G.R., 2011. *Capitalizing on Crisis. The Political Origins of the Rise of Finance*. Cambridge, MA: Harvard University Press.

Lemoine, B., 2016. *L'ordre de la dette: Enquête sur les infortunes de l'État et la prospérité du marché*. La Découverte.

Lysandrou, P. and Nesvetailova, A., 2015. The role of shadow banking entities in the financial crisis: A disaggregated view. *Review of International Political Economy*, 22(2), pp. 257–279.

Mann, M., 1984. The autonomous power of the state: Its origins, mechanisms and results. *European Journal of Sociology*, 25(2), pp. 185–213.

Mann, M., 1993. *The Sources of Social Power. Vol. II: The Rise of Classes and Nation-states, 1760–1914*. Cambridge: Cambridge University Press.

Maxfield, S., Winecoff, W.K. and Young, K.L., 2017. An empirical investigation of the financialization convergence hypothesis. *Review of International Political Economy*, 24(6), pp. 1004–1029.

McNamara, K., 2002. Rational fictions: Central bank independence and the social logic of delegation. *West European Politics*, 25(1), pp. 47–76.

Mehrling, P., 2010. *The New Lombard Street: How the Fed Became the Dealer of Last Resort*. Princeton, NJ: Princeton University Press.

Mehrling, P., 2013. Essential hybridity: A money view of FX. *Journal of Comparative Economics*, 41(2), pp. 355–363.

Minsky, H.P., 1986. *Stabilizing an Unstable Economy*. New Haven: Yale University Press.

Murau, S., 2017. Shadow money and the public money supply: The impact of the 2007–2009 financial crisis on the monetary system. *Review of International Political Economy*, 24(5), pp. 802–838.

Omarova, S.T., 2018. *Central Banks, Systemic Risk and Financial Sector Structural Reform*. Ithaca, NY: Cornell University.

Pagliari, S. and Young, K., 2016. The interest ecology of financial regulation: Interest group plurality in the design of financial regulatory policies. *Socio-Economic Review*, 14(2), pp. 309–337.

Pierson, P., 2016. Power in historical institutionalism. In Fioretos, O., Falleti, T.G. and Sheingate, A. (eds.), *The Oxford Handbook of Historical Institutionalism*. Oxford: Oxford University Press, pp. 124–141.

Pistor, K., 2013. A legal theory of finance. *Journal of Comparative Economics*, 41(2), pp. 315–330.

Polillo, S. and Guillién, M.F., 2005. Globalization pressures and the state: The worldwide spread of central bank independence. *American Journal of Sociology*, 110(6), pp. 1764–1802.

Pozsar, Z., 2014. *Shadow Banking: The Money View*. OFR Working Paper 14–04. Office of Financial Research.

Ricks, M., 2016. *The Money Problem: Rethinking Financial Regulation*. Chicago, IL: University of Chicago Press.

Ricks, M., 2018. Money as infrastructure. *Columbia Business Law Review*, 3, pp. 757–851.

Schumpeter, J.A., 1954. *History of Economic Analysis*. London: Allen & Unwin.

Simons, H.C., 1936. Rules versus authorities in monetary policy. *Journal of Political Economy*, 44(1), pp. 1–30.

Thiemann, M., 2018. *The Growth of Shadow Banking: A Comparative Institutional Analysis*. Cambridge: Cambridge University Press.

Walter, T., 2019. Formalizing the future: How central banks set out to govern expectations but ended up (en-)trapped in indicators. *Historical Social Research, 44(2)*, pp. 103-130.

Walter, T. and Wansleben, L., 2019. How central bankers learned to love financialization: The Fed, the Bank, and the enlisting of unfettered markets in the conduct of monetary policy. *Socio-Economic Review*, Epub ahead of print.

Wang, Y., 2015. The rise of the "shareholding state': financialization of economic management in China. *Socio-Economic Review*, 13(3), pp. 603–625.

Wansleben, L., 2018. How expectations became governable: Institutional change and the performative power of central banks. *Theory and Society*, 47(6), pp. 773–803.

Woll, C., 2016. Politics in the interest of capital: A not-so-organized combat. *Politics & Society*, 44(3), pp. 373–391.

Woll, C., 2017. State action in financial times. In King, D. and Le Galès, P. (eds.), *Reconfiguring European States in Crisis*. Oxford: Oxford University Press, pp. 201–214.

Zysman, J., 1983. *Governments, Markets, and Growth: Financial Systems and the Politics of Industrial Change*. Ithaca, NY: Cornell University Press.

21

SECURITIES EXCHANGES

Subjects and Agents of Financialization

Johannes Petry

Introduction

Securities exchanges are core institutions of modern capitalism, almost metonymic with capital markets and their development. But how have these institutions contributed to financialization? In vernacular language, the terms stock exchange and stock market are often used interchangeably. Exchanges are depicted as neutral spaces; they themselves are not perceived as actors in their own right. However, as this chapter argues, this is an outdated understanding of exchanges as these have transformed fundamentally and in so doing have become important agents of and key actors in financialization – both promoting financialization and acting as infrastructures within financialization processes.

Similar to other financial institutions, since the 1980s, marketization, internationalization, and digitization have fundamentally transformed exchanges and their role in capital markets. From being mere *marketplaces* – national, member-controlled, non-profit organizations and physical trading locations with little agency – exchanges have transformed into what can be called *market actors*: autonomous and profit-driven actors who sell their markets, technologies, products and services to investors, and who actively create, regulate and shape (electronic) markets around the world and across asset classes. Thereby, exchanges were both shaped by financialization but also became key actors in financialization processes themselves. To explore this issue, this chapter discusses three interrelated questions: What is an exchange? How (and why) have they changed? And why does this matter for financialization?

Next to secondary literature, the chapter draws on financial news coverage, financial market databases, an analysis of 312 annual reports from exchanges,[1] and 59 expert interviews conducted with exchanges, brokers and other market participants in London, Frankfurt, Hong Kong, Shanghai and Singapore between May 2017 and September 2018. The rest of this chapter is structured as follows. The first section provides an overview of the existing literature on financialization and exchanges. The second section analyses the transformation of exchanges from marketplaces to market actors by highlighting how and why they changed through marketization, internationalization and digitization. The third section discusses exchanges after this transformation. The fourth section outlines why this matters for the study of financialization, focusing on how exchanges shape the workings of capital markets, financial globalization and the spread of disintermediated financial practices, as well as changing power dynamics in global finance. The fifth section concludes.

Exchanges in the Financialization Literature

Capital markets stand at the heart of and are a precondition for most of the phenomena associated with financialization (see Mader et al., this volume). But as this book section emphasizes, financialization is not only an external, structural force. It is enacted by and through certain agents. Surprisingly, exchanges – those actors who organize capital markets – have received relatively little attention in the financialization literature. In fact, exchanges are mostly viewed as neutral marketplaces with little or no agency.

Next to historical accounts of individual exchanges (e.g. Michie 1999), political economists have rather focused on the impact that financial liberalization had on exchanges' members (Cerny 1989; Moran 1990), the electronification of exchange markets (Zaloom 2006; Gorham and Singh 2009), the politics of establishing certain exchanges (Lütz 1998; Lavelle 2004; Posner 2009) or their role as policy actors (Mügge 2011). Their own role as actors in capital markets has been analyzed only partially (Wójcik 2012; Botzem and Dahl 2014), focusing for instance on them creating financial products (Millo 2007), facilitating high frequency trading (HFT) (MacKenzie et al. 2012), and the fragmentation of equity markets (Castelle et al. 2016). But these accounts have not linked exchanges and their activities to broader processes of financialization. However, as the next sections demonstrate, exchanges have both been impacted by financialization themselves and have over time become crucial agents for capital market development and the politics of financialization.

What is an Exchange?

In its beginnings, the exchange was solely a marketplace, a physical location (e.g. a coffee house) where merchants met to negotiate business deals and eventually agreed to jointly finance enterprises. Pre-modern forms of exchanges have existed at least since the fourteenth century in Venice, Florence and Genoa. This was followed by the founding of the Amsterdam Stock Exchange through the Dutch East India Company in 1602 which – while not the first exchange as such – was the first embodiment of what we perceive as modern stock markets. As Braudel (1983: 101) noted, "what was new in Amsterdam was the volume, the fluidity of the market and publicity it received, and the speculative freedom of transactions." Thus, the modern exchange was born. And from their inception until the 1980s, exchanges did not change much. For sure, the advent of pre-modern information technologies such as the telegraph led to changes in trading practices, a consolidation and establishment of national-level exchanges, regulation changed with recurring market crashes, existing markets matured, and new markets for products such as futures emerged (see Engel 2013). But little about the basic principles of what exchanges were and how they functioned changed.

Historically, (almost) all securities exchanges were member-owned. The members held all the power, the exchange was a non-profit organization and did not have much agency. As Weitzman (2011: 184) stated about the historic development of Chicago's commodity exchanges, "member control was reflected in their attitude to even the most senior exchange employees, who the traders regarded as their employees." The function of exchanges was that of marketplaces where members could trade securities, commodities or other assets. Such trading took place on a trading floor, pit or ring, where only physically present members could trade a small range of products, limited both by national boundaries and asset classes, for instance stocks of one countries' companies or certain commodities (e.g. base metals). This hardly changed over the centuries. As a special issue on exchanges in *The Banker* (Skeete 2008) stated, "[u]ntil the 1980s, exchanges would, in their essentials, have been recognizable to a merchant who was trading in the 14th century – the time of their inception."

However, in the 1980s and 1990s, exchanges themselves became subject to three interlinked, mutually reinforcing processes which overhauled their role in capital markets. First, while exchanges gained more agency, as market actors they also became themselves subjected to competitive pressures from other exchanges (marketization). Second, from a mostly national focus their business activities became international, leading to consolidation and cooperation between exchanges (internationalization). Third, they turned from physical trading locations into financial technology companies (digitization). While these macro-processes (which are closely linked with financialization themselves) impacted all aspects and elements of financial markets, in the next section their impact on exchanges is analysed before turning to how these transformed exchanges subsequently contributed to financialization processes.

Marketization: Ownership, Agency and Competition

Marketization does not only encompass shifting ownership structures, it also works at a deeper level, and is best understood as the facilitation of "policies and processes oriented towards continuing the diffusion of market discipline" (Carroll and Jarvis 2014: 1). Likewise, the marketization of exchanges is characterized by both changes in ownership structures as well as the introduction of competitive dynamics.

The marketization of exchanges is strongly linked to neoliberal economic reforms and restructuring which placed a greater emphasis on privatization and financial market deregulation in the 1980s and 1990s. Financial liberalization reforms such as May Day in the US (1975), the Big Bang in the UK (1986) or the EU Investment Services Directive (1993) allowed brokers to charge varying commission rates, enabled foreign participation in previously national stock markets and abolished rules requiring orders to be executed solely on exchanges, introducing a great deal of competition into the exchange industry. Exchanges were now suddenly in a marketplace for marketplaces (Castelle et al. 2016). In the face of such pressures, exchanges needed to modernize, become more efficient and customer focused, which is why many demutualized and went public, becoming traded on capital markets themselves. While the first member-owned exchange only demutualized in 1993, 50% of the world's largest exchanges had demutualized by 2002 and by 2010 they were all demutualized (with the notable exception of the state-owned Chinese exchanges). Further, many of these exchanges self-listed and 69% had become publicly traded companies by 2018 (see Figure 21.1).

While older scholarly accounts of how exchanges work stressed the role of the exchange's members (see Baker 1984; Abolafia, 1996), through demutualization a lot of the power to organize the marketplace shifted towards exchanges themselves, whose role became much more architectural in that sense. As one interviewee told me:

> I think, demutualization is probably the most striking [change] in the fact that the exchanges are now fully in charge of their own destiny. They can decide what they want to compete on, decide what they want to launch, what areas of business they want to expand or attract from, whereas before they were looking after their own membership. [...] So, I think it's really taking charge of their corporate direction... [that] is probably the biggest single change.[2]

However, while exchanges gained more agency, they now had to generate profits and maximize shareholder value in a completely different environment. As Lee (2002: 1) noted, at the end of this process, "exchanges now have customers, not members". Exchanges now also had to compete with their former members and owners (e.g. banks, brokers) – who tried to side-step

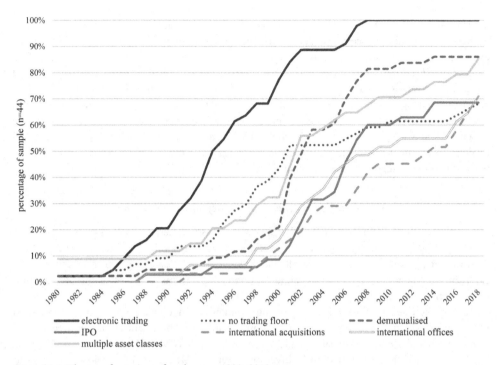

Figure 21.1 The transformation of exchanges, 1980–2018
Sample of 44 largest exchanges globally; author's calculation, based on corporate reports, exchange website information and financial news.

exchanges by setting up or backing non-exchange trading platforms such as alternative trading systems (ATS), inter-dealer crossing networks or dark pools – and with one another, for listings, customers, order flow and market share as they needed to generate profits. This process was intensified by regulations such as Regulation ATS (1998) in the US or MiFID (2005) in Europe which facilitated this competition. By 2010, European exchanges had lost more than 20% of the trading on stock markets and between 2005 and 2009 NYSE's US-market share decreased from 79.1% to 27.4% (Lannoo and Valiante 2010).

The rapid development of over-the-counter (OTC) derivative markets also pressured futures exchanges, as emphasized by former Chicago Mercantile Exchange (CME) chairman Leo Melamed who stated that: "it is no secret that the combined onslaught of globalization, OTC competition, and technological advancement, have put enormous pressure on traditional futures exchanges. Indeed, in some quarters, there is a growing belief that the good days for traditional exchanges is behind them" (cited in Nystedt 2004: 4). The looming internationalization of exchanges only intensified these dynamics.

Internationalization: Expansion, Consolidation and Cooperation

From being institutions mainly focused on their respective national markets shielded from the outside world, increasing cross-border integration from the 1980s onwards exposed exchanges to global markets themselves which both increased competitive pressures on exchanges but also created possibilities to scale up their business, to exploit or create new markets. Liquidity attracts liquidity – size matters, and in a global world, their national markets had become too small: in order to survive, exchanges had to gain in size and had to venture into global markets.

As erstwhile national institutions – in the words of former NYSE CEO John Thain "every country has an army, a flag and an exchange" (Biglari 2007) –, exchanges started to form huge organizations spanning the globe. While the first international mergers and acquisitions (M&A) between exchanges only occurred in the early 1990s, 71% of the largest exchanges had engaged in international M&A activities by 2018 (see Figure 21.1). As a result of a series of mergers in the 1990s and 2000s, previously "individual" marketplaces such as the NYSE, Chicago Mercantile Exchange or Nasdaq became (acquired by) globally active exchange groups such as ICE Group, CME Group or Nasdaq OMX that now controlled markets all around the world.[3] Exchanges also started to acquire many of their non-exchange competitors, literally buying back some of the market share they had lost a few years earlier.[4] Futures exchanges also started buying stock exchanges and vice versa, as well as trading venues for bonds, foreign exchange, carbon emissions, commodity and financial derivatives – with 85% of the largest exchanges now offering trading in multiple asset classes (see Figure 21.1). However, mergers between exchanges have political limitations as exchanges are still understood as quasi-public, quasi-national institutions with a strategic importance for their respective economies, as demonstrated by many failed high-profile mergers between exchanges.[5] Less liberal countries such as Taiwan or Korea do not even allow foreigners to own a majority of their exchanges or exchanges are completely state-owned as in China.

Next to consolidation within their own industry, exchanges started buying other financial services providers such as index and data providers or clearing houses – all leading to a diversification of exchanges' business models. Further, exchanges started to form alliances, create joint ventures, cross-list and jointly develop products or create connectivities between markets by linking their trading platforms and facilitating the development of HFT infrastructures (MacKenzie et al. 2012; Wójcik 2012). From the 1990s onwards, exchanges also started to internationalize their operations, opening offices around the world to gain access to local financial communities; these offices are usually staffed with sales and business development personnel whose job is to onboard new clients and open up new markets. While CME was the first exchange to open an international office in 1987, in 2002 the then top-20 exchanges had already established 48 offices, and in 2017 the top-20 exchanges had 181 offices.[6] Overall, internationalization amplified the competitive pressures that exchanges had been subjected to but also opened up opportunities for consolidation, an expansion of their business models, new forms of inter-exchange cooperation and for them to venture into new markets.

Digitization: Electronic Trading, Data and Technology

Despite powerful images such as commemorating Initial Public Offerings (IPOs), the ceremonial ringing of the bell, or hectic activity on open out-cry trading floors, after the late 1990s traditional face-to-face trading was gradually superseded by electronic markets (Gorham and Singh 2009). Already launched as fully electronic marketplaces, newcomer exchanges such as OM, Nasdaq, ICE or Eurex soon acquired vast market shares across asset classes, forcing incumbent floor-based exchanges such as NYMEX or LIFFE to their knees in breath taking market showdowns. The future of trading was bound to become electronic. By 2008, all major exchanges had adopted electronic trading. By 2018, 68% had closed their physical trading floors (see Figure 21.1) – often only retaining them to "keep up appearances" for the spectacle, ceremonial events and news reporting. However, digitization also fundamentally changed the workings of exchanges.

On one side, electronic trading facilitated the marketization and internationalization of exchanges. Digitization further curtailed the power of the exchange's members who long tried to resist electronification. Instead of members physically making markets and prices in the trading pits, rings and floors via open-outcry (see Zaloom 2006), the shift from floor-based to electronic trading transferred a lot of their power to the exchanges themselves. By running electronic matching engines, exchanges were able to replace the price-making function originally performed by floor-trading members which enabled them to facilitate financial trading on their terms. Digitization also increased competition as now everyone with some venture capital and a few lines of code was able to create a new trading platform. As already discussed, these platforms massively drove down the price of trading, partially because they did not have the huge overhead of traditional exchanges.[7] On the other side, the proliferation of data and computing capacity opened up completely new business fields for them. As exchanges were hard pressed to find new sources of revenue, they realized that the electronification of markets and the rapid development of information technology created many opportunities for them to capitalize upon. As Wójcik (2012: 131) noted, "while in the mid-1980s it was an achievement for SEAQ in London to execute up to 10 trades per second [...], in 2010 computers [could] generate thousands of orders per second each."

Digitization had fundamentally changed the game. Market data became a resource that could be utilized by exchanges who realized that they sat on a gold mine. Not only could they sell market data, they could also use it to create new services and products, such as analytical tools, indices, reporting, post-trade services such as central clearing or settlement or sell their technology – often enforcing the exclusivity of their products through a vertical silo business model. Consequently, exchanges started investing heavily into market data, data analytics, and indices, which facilitated the expansion of new asset classes such as financial derivatives based on continuous streams of market data (Millo 2007). As a result, exchanges have increasingly become "content providers" (Lee 2002), selling market data, technology and other services to their clients.

Digitization also facilitated the internationalization of exchanges. Instead of requiring access to a physical trading floor in one specific location, everyone with the necessary hard- and software could participate in these markets, as long as regulatory and organizational obstacles had been resolved. Digitization overhauled traditional trading technologies (open-outcry floor trading) tied to their traditional corporate governance form (mutuality), reinforced marketization and internationalization pressures, and simultaneously opened up a whole new range of business opportunities for exchanges.

The Exchange as Market Actor

Despite these processes of marketization, internationalization and digitization, the public perception of exchanges is still nostalgically clinging to their historic form, taking little account of the fact that between the 1980s and today, exchanges have changed beyond recognition. First, while exchanges have become actors in their own right, they have also become subject to competition, forcing them to innovate, generate profits and diversify their business model. Second, exchanges have become more global and complex institutions. Third, exchanges have become electronic markets and financial technology companies. From being mere *marketplaces* – national, member-controlled, non-profit organizations and physical trading locations with little agency – exchanges have transformed into what can be called *market actors*: autonomous and profit-driven actors who sell their markets, technologies, products and services to investors, and who actively create, regulate and shape (electronic) markets around the world and across asset classes. Figure 21.1 summarizes this transformation of exchanges.

Once "traditional" stock exchanges today only make between 5–20% of their profits through the listing and trading of stocks – which is their original function for facilitating corporate finance (Zysman 1983). Exchanges have diversified their business horizontally – by adding new asset classes to their portfolio – and vertically, by offering various other products and services. You can now buy proprietary market data and data analytic tools from exchanges, license their indices, use their benchmarks as reference prices, trade various financial products and asset classes on their different trading platforms – not only equities but also bonds, currencies, commodities or derivatives –, co-locate your servers next to theirs, and use their clearing house, settlement, collateral management, custodian services and regulatory reporting tools. Through this consolidation, exchanges gained control over large parts of capital market trading infrastructures – a business that turned out to be hugely profitable.

An analysis of exchanges' business segment revenue reporting illustrates these changes. At London Stock Exchange (LSE) Group, stock trading revenues declined to 8.40%, while its index business FTSE Russell (37.65%) and post-trading/clearing business LCH.Clearnet (36.72%) became much more prominent (LSE 2017). ICE Group who runs the NYSE, the world's largest stock market, as well as dozens of other marketplaces such as LIFFE or NYBOT, has over the years heavily invested into data, analytics and indices, now generating 54% of its revenue with this business segment (ICE 2017). In 2017, stock trading revenues at Nasdaq – the company that, next to the iconic Nasdaq market, also runs ten markets in Northern Europe – were at only 11% while its corporate services (27.89%), market data (23.72%) and technology (12.08%) segments all became more important (Nasdaq 2017). Over time, stock trading revenue at Deutsche Börse Group decreased from 35.35% in 2000 to 7.17% in 2017 while derivatives and clearing increased to 40.70% and its post-trade business to 36.02% (DBG 2017). This development is similar for most global exchanges. While stock trading has become less important, exchanges today mostly generate their rising revenues through derivatives, post-trading services, indices and market data.

While traditionally every country had an exchange of varying size, a new global hierarchy between exchanges has emerged. An enormous concentration of marketplaces, liquidity and power has taken place, and a majority of markets are now controlled by a few global exchange groups (CME Group, ICE Group, Nasdaq, Deutsche Börse Group, LSE Group and Cboe). These global exchange groups are complemented by a few regional players (HKEx, SGX, Euronext) and some larger national exchanges (Japanese JPX, Brazilian B3, Canadian TMX, Indian and Chinese exchanges). These global exchange groups run the largest, most prestigious markets, dominate discussions within the industry, own important technological know-how, indices and products as well as large parts of global market infrastructures. Within a context of asset management capitalism, exchange-traded funds (ETFs) and a rise of passive investment (see Fichtner, this volume), exchanges have only gained additional power to shape markets. Today, a small number of global exchanges holds significant power over the governance, development and organization of global capital markets.

How Exchanges Shape Financialization

As the contributions to this part of the handbook highlight, financialization is not only an external, structural force, it is enacted by and through certain agents. While exchanges have themselves been influenced by processes of financialization they are also crucial actors in and agents of financialization processes. First, as market organizers, exchanges shape capital market dynamics, facilitating volatility and speculation. Second, exchanges are crucial facilitators of capital market development globally. Third, power dynamics within capital markets have shifted with exchanges becoming more powerful actors vis-à-vis both other market actors as well as states.

Shaping Capital Markets: Financialized Trading, Volatility and Speculation

By creating, organizing and enabling capital markets in the first place, exchanges are able to shape their form, content and dynamics. Rather than investors who are active within a market, exchanges play a much more architectural role for markets as they control and create the infrastructural arrangements that are necessary for their functioning in the first place. As organizers of markets, exchanges provide a public good and should be concerned with the long-term stability of markets, but they are also profit-driven businesses in need of creating shareholder value. This is an important contradiction at the heart of exchanges because in their roles as market organizers and marketplayers they have contradictory incentives. As the NYSE (cited in Macey and O'Hara 2005: 572) stated in a 2003 white paper (while still mutually owned), "the [cooperative ownership] structure [of the NYSE] seeks to maximize the efficiency, reliability and integrity of the market, rather than to maximize profit as in the public company model." Not only have exchanges' business models become more short-term-oriented, but this also has effects on the markets they organize.

As exchanges' revenues depend on investors trading in their markets, they have an incentive to develop these markets in a way that trading activity (and thereby speculation and volatility) increases. Exchanges for instance provide the necessary infrastructures (i.e. co-location, direct market access), trading rules (new order types, e.g. flash orders) and products (data analytic tools, real-time market data) that enable HFT in the first place. While proponents of HFT argue that it increases market liquidity, its opponents argue that it actually sucks up liquidity, severely threatens market stability, and that HFT trading is usually to the detriment of less technologically sophisticated traders (MacKenzie et al. 2012: 288–290). Exchanges also facilitate the increased trading of derivatives for instance by creating these financial products in the first place (Millo 2007) as well as encouraging larger trading volumes through market maker schemes or fee rebates for those investors who trade large volumes of these contracts. By facilitating high trading volumes and by reinforcing corporate governance standards, exchanges also facilitate shareholder value orientation in listed companies (Erturk, this volume).

More than mere bystanders, exchanges are gatekeepers of capital markets, deciding who gets in, what is traded and how trading is conducted, as investor strategies are influenced by trading regulations and the products they can use – they are agents of financialization as they engage in financial structuring and liquidity provision (see Chiapello, this volume). While deregulation was meant to facilitate market processes, control over marketplaces has since concentrated in the hands of a few global exchanges who are now crucial in enabling financialized corporate practices and speculative trading which leads to volatility in markets, potentially impacting financial stability.

Financial Globalization: Spreading Capital Markets around the World

From 1980 to 2005, the number of countries with stock exchanges increased from 59 to 117 (Weber et al. 2009). By connecting evermore investors, providing them with more investment opportunities and internationalizing financial products and markets, exchanges also facilitate the globalization of capital markets. Cross-border market integration is not a given, but only possible through institutional changes such as widespread regulatory harmonization (e.g. MiFID), the formation of global marketplaces through exchanges (e.g. through trading hour extensions), or the creation of links between markets (e.g. cross listings). While the role of the state and international financial institutions (Lavelle 2004), domestic political coalitions (Zhang 2009) and pressures from global markets (Cerny 1989) have been highlighted as push factors for capital market development, the role of exchanges in these processes is less well understood (but see Botzem and Dahl 2014).

Where does the knowledge of how to create capital markets come from? In fact, global exchange groups have been crucial in training regulators, investors and "local" exchange operators in how advanced financial markets work. Further, they have been exporting their financial technologies and infrastructures to underdeveloped markets, helped to develop these in the first place and sometimes even run these smaller markets, promising to create growth by capitalizing on their economies of scale and help create new financial products and services. In return, the global exchanges earn fees, buy (a stake in) those (much) smaller exchanges and have preferential access to their market data and products. While primarily commercially driven, there is also an almost missionary element to these activities as these global exchanges see it as their task to spread the gospel of efficient markets across the globe (Weitzman 2011).

This role of exchanges can for instance be observed in how capital markets developed in East Asia. Nasdaq for instance "provides technology to more or less all the exchanges in Asia-Pacific,"[8] thereby helping them to develop these capital markets. CME Group also has multiple cooperations and ownership stakes with Asian exchanges helping to develop financial products or enable their trading on CME's 24h-trading platform Globex.[9] Next to cross-listings with Korean (KRX) and Taiwanese (TAIFEX) exchanges, Deutsche Börse formed a joint venture with the Shanghai Stock Exchange and the China Financial Futures Exchange (CFFEX), the China Europe International Exchange (CEINEX), whose aim is to facilitate China's capital market development abroad. The Japanese (JPX) and Korean (KRX) exchanges meanwhile have heavily invested in South East Asian markets, partially owning and establishing new exchanges in Myanmar, Laos and Cambodia, while as part of the Belt and Road Initiative Chinese exchanges have partially acquired exchanges in Pakistan, Kazakhstan or Bangladesh. Countless similar arrangements exist or have already been conducted. Exchanges have turned into agents of financial globalization, spreading the development of capital markets globally, thereby immensely facilitating financialization processes.

The Politics of Financialization: Shifting Dynamics of Power and Governance in Finance

Through consolidations in the exchange industry, global giants like CME, ICE or Nasdaq have emerged as actors with tremendous political and economic power, directly influencing power dynamics within global finance and the politics of financialization. While banks were once their owners/members, this relationship has changed completely as they have become clients and competitors of now demutualized, profit-driven global exchanges. While for a long time banks had the upper hand, trying to circumvent paying exchange fees by backing ATS or by threatening to move their derivatives business OTC,[10] post-global financial crisis, these dynamics have reversed. Banks have been increasingly constrained by regulations, while exchanges have consistently gained business from them: by facilitating central clearing on (exchange-owned) clearing houses, by trying to get OTC derivatives trading onto exchanges (futurization) and by lobbying regulations such as MiFID II, EMIR and Dodd-Frank (see for instance Ferrarini and Moloney 2012; Helleiner et al. 2018). While the power of banks has somewhat decreased since the global financial crisis, the centrality of exchanges in global finance has increased significantly.

Next to their increased power within finance, power dynamics towards states have also changed (see also Wang, this volume). This is especially important in light of the historically close relationship between states and exchanges, with the perception of exchanges as national icons with a quasi-public task of running capital markets, thereby conducting many monitoring, regulatory and supervisory functions. By occupying these roles, exchanges had a privileged position in policy processes or preferential access to policy makers. As for instance one former exchange representative noted:

So, we would have for example a monthly meeting with the Bank of England. One month they would host lunch, next month we would host lunch. It was because the government through the Bank would like to have a finger at the pulse of what was happening. [...] So, that gave us some leverage in the corridors of power... with the government, the Treasury and across the political hue. [...] Exchanges had an important role to play.[11]

While exchanges are no longer quasi-public national institutions but rather profit-oriented global corporations, close relationships between exchanges and states still persist today, which raises questions over whether their influence might have become too big. In contrast to banks, trust in exchanges and their actions remains relatively unquestioned post-crisis – also because they facilitate a neutral image of themselves. As Botzem and Dahl (2014: 78) emphasize, "rather than highlighting their own actorhood, they depict themselves as a marketplace [...] which leads to a vast underrating of their impact on processes of economic and institutional change."

But their actions are anything but neutral. As index providers, exchanges for instance decide about countries' inclusions or exclusions into their indices, yielding considerable power over investment flows (Alloway et al. 2017), whereas by enabling hedging and exit possibilities (Hardie 2012) or by deciding on clearing house collateral frameworks they can have a significant impact on countries' refinancing operations (Genito 2019) – in both instances constraining governments' behaviors and nudging them towards conforming with a neoliberal rulebook of disintermediated, "free" capital markets that exchanges organize (see for instance, Doll 2019). Overall, exchanges have been central in the politics of financialization and financial regulation.

Conclusion

While exchanges represent one of the institutional foundations of modern capitalism, since the late-1980s, exchanges have undergone a major transformation, being impacted by financialization processes themselves. From solely being marketplaces, marketization, internationalization and digitization led to a transformation of exchanges and overhauled their role in capital markets. First, from having little agency, demutualization turned exchanges into actors in their own right but also subjected them to market dynamics and competitive pressures. Second, from a mainly national focus their business became increasingly international and they diversified their geographical and business scope enormously. Third, due to digitization they turned from being physical trading locations to running electronic markets and becoming financial technology companies. Today, exchanges are global corporations with a wide variety of business activities, both acting within and organizing, governing, shaping capital markets – in that sense they have turned from marketplaces to market actors.

Thereby, exchanges have become both important agents of and key actors in financialization. First, by organizing markets exchanges decide what can be traded and by whom. However, their transformation has created incentives for them to create market structures that facilitate more volatility and speculation, thereby contributing to financialized trading and corporate governance practices. Second, through selling and exporting their financial technologies and expertise, exchanges have been important actors in the development of capital markets and spreading market-based financial practices globally. Third, exchanges have emerged as powerful players within global finance, both vis-à-vis banks but also with regard to regulators and states, influencing financial regulation and the politics of financialization. By raising questions about the changed role of exchanges in capital markets, this chapter highlights the role of exchanges as important actors in and agents of financialization. Capital markets do not emerge out of a vacuum, but actors propel their development. Exchanges are one of these important actors.

While this chapter has provided an overview of exchanges, their transformation and how they contribute to financialization processes, obviously exchanges are not uniform and there are significant differences between them. State-owned exchanges in China for instance certainly play a different role in markets than global exchanges. A future avenue of research could therefore be a more detailed, comparative analysis of the (possibly diverging) roles that exchanges perform in capital markets and financialization processes. It also remains unclear how exchanges relate to other market actors in a changing post-crisis global financial ecosystem, for instance to banks, high frequency traders, index providers or asset managers. And, especially when it comes to derivative markets, exchanges are still dwarfed by OTC trading. How do these different markets interact and what does it entail for the power of exchanges? In a changing post-financial crisis world, addressing these questions could offer important insights for our understanding of current transformations of global finance and its role in financialized capitalism.

Notes

1 This sample (n=44) is comprised of the largest stock and derivatives exchanges globally as well as the largest exchanges for each world region (e.g. Johannesburg Stock Exchange for Africa).
2 Interview with business development unit of global exchange in London (11 October 2017).
3 *Wall Street Journal*, 3 March 2016, p.17; see also: https://tinyurl.com/y54zs6jh (last accessed: 10 September 2018).
4 Nasdaq acquired BRUT in 2004 and Inet in 2006, NYSE bought Archipelago/ArcaEx in 2006, LSE acquired a majority in Turquoise in 2009, and in 2017 Cboe acquired BATS Global Markets.
5 Such as attempted takeover of LSE by Nasdaq in 2006, TMX Group by LSE in 2011, or mergers between the Australian and Singaporean exchanges in 2011, NYSE Euronext and Deutsche Börse in 2012, and between Deutsche Börse and LSE in 2017.
6 Data obtained from exchanges' annual reports (2002 and 2017).
7 Interview with CEO of alternative trading system in London (11 October 2017).
8 Interview with general manager of global exchange in Hong Kong (5 July 2017).
9 See: http://www.cmegroup.com/international/ (last accessed: 22 June 2018).
10 Interviews with business development units of global exchanges in London and Frankfurt (11 October and 2 November 2017).
11 Interview with former CEO of exchange in London (8 January 2018).

Bibliography

Abolafia, M.Y., 1996. *Making Markets: Opportunism and Restraint on Wall Street*. Cambridge, MA: Harvard University Press.

Alloway, T., Burger, D. & Evans, R., 2017. Index providers rule the world—For now, at least. *Bloomberg*, 27 November.

Baker, W.E., 1984. The Social structure of a national securities market. *American Journal of Sociology*, 89(4), pp. 775–811.

Biglari, H., 2007. Strategic view: Exchanges seek a new model. *Financial Times*, 16 November.

Botzem, S. & Dahl, M., 2014. Trust in transparency: Value dynamics and the reorganization of the Baltic financial markets. In Alexius, S. & Hallström, K.T. (eds.) *Configuring Value Conflicts in Markets*. Cheltenham: Edward Elgar, pp. 63–81.

Braudel, F., 1983. *Civilization and Capitalism, 15th–18th Century: The Wheels of Commerce*. New York: Harper & Row.

Carroll, T. & Jarvis, D.S.L. (eds.), 2014. *The Politics of Marketising Asia*. Basingstoke: Palgrave Macmillan.

Castelle, M., Millo, Y., Beunza, D. & Lubin, D.C., 2016. Where do electronic markets come from? Regulation and the transformation of financial exchanges. *Economy and Society*, 45(2), pp. 166–200.

Cerny, P.G., 1989. The 'Little Big Bang' in Paris: Financial market deregulation in a dirigiste system. *European Journal of Political Research*, 17(2), pp. 169–192.

DBG, 2017. *Financial Report*. Frankfurt: Deutsche Börse Group.

Doll, I.O., 2019. Argentina wants MSCI to upgrade local shares to emerging status. *Bloomberg*, 7 January.

Engel, A., 2013. Futures and risk: The rise and demise of the hedger-speculator dichotomy. *Socio-Economic Review*, 11(3), pp. 553–576.

Ferrarini, G. & Moloney, N., 2012. Reshaping order execution in the EU and the role of interest groups: From MiFID I to MiFID II. *European Business Organization Law Review*, 13(4), pp. 557–597.

Genito, L., 2019. *What Markets Fear: Understanding the European Sovereign Debt Crisis Through the Lens of Repo Market Liquidity*. PhD Thesis, University of Warwick.

Gorham, M. & Singh, N., 2009. *Electronic Exchanges: The Global Transformation from Pits to Bits*. Burlington, MA: Elsevier.

Hardie, I., 2012. *Financialization and Government Borrowing Capacity in Emerging Markets*. Basingstoke: Palgrave Macmillan.

Helleiner, E., Pagliari, S. & Spagna, I. (eds.), 2018. *Governing the World's Biggest Market: The Politics of Derivatives Regulation After the 2008 Crisis*. Oxford: Oxford University Press.

ICE, 2017. *Annual Report*. Altanta: Intercontinental Exchange Group.

Lannoo, K. & Valiante, D., 2010. The MiFID Metamorphosis. *European Capital Markets Institute*, ECMI Policy Brief No. 16/October 2010.

Lavelle, K.C., 2004. *The Politics of Equity Finance in Emerging Markets*. Oxford: Oxford University Press.

Lee, R., 2002. The future of securities exchanges. *The Wharton Financial Institutions Center*, Working Paper 02–14.

LSE, 2017. *Annual Report*. London: London Stock Exchange Group.

Lütz, S., 1998. The revival of the nation-state? Stock exchange regulation in an era of globalized financial markets. *Journal of European Public Policy*, 5(1), pp. 153–168.

Macey, J.R. & O'Hara, M., 2005. From markets to venues: Securities regulation in an evolving world. *Stanford Law Review*, 58(2), pp. 563–616.

MacKenzie, D., Beunza, D., Millo, Y. & Pardo-Guerra, J.P., 2012. Drilling through the Allegheny Mountains. Liquidity, materiality and high-frequency trading. *Journal of Cultural Economy*, 5(3), pp. 279–296.

Michie, R., 1999. *The London Stock Exchange: A History*. Oxford: Oxford University Press.

Millo, Y., 2007. Making things deliverable: The origins of index-based derivatives. *The Sociological Review*, 55(2), pp. 196–214.

Moran, M., 1990. *The Politics of the Financial Services Revolution: The USA, UK and Japan*. Basingstoke: Palgrave Macmillan.

Mügge, D., 2011. *Widen the Market, Narrow the Competition: Banker Interests and the Making of a European Capital Market*. Colchester: ECPR Press.

Muniesa, F., 2014. *The Provoked Economy: Economic Reality and the Performative Turn*. London: Routledge.

Nasdaq, 2017. *Annual Report (Form 10-K)*. New York: Nasdaq Group.

Nystedt, J., 2004. Derivative market competition: OTC markets versus organized derivative exchanges. *International Monetary Fund*, IMF Working Paper WP/04/61.

Posner, E., 2009. *The Origins of Europe's New Stock Markets*. Cambridge, MA: Harvard University Press.

Skeete, H., 2008. A new breed of exchange. *The Banker*, 5 May.

Weber, K., Davis, G.F. & Lounsbury, M., 2009. Policy as myth and ceremony? The global spread of stock exchanges, 1980–2005. *Academy of Management Journal*, 52(6), pp. 1319–1347.

Weitzman, H., 2011. Chicago's decade of innovation: 1972–1982. In: Harris, L. (ed.), *Regulated Exchanges: Dynamic Agents of Economic Growth*. Oxford: Oxford University Press, pp. 174–201.

Wójcik, D., 2012. *The Global Stock Market: Issuers, Investors, and Intermediaries in an Uneven World*. Oxford: Oxford University Press.

Zaloom, C., 2006. *Out of the Pits: Traders and Technology from Chicago to London*. Chicago, IL: University Chicago Press.

Zhang, X., 2009. From banks to markets: Malaysian and Taiwanese finance in transition. *Review of International Political Economy*, 16(3), pp. 382–408.

Zysman, J., 1983. *Government, markets and growth: Financial systems and the politics of industrial change*. Ithaca, NY: Cornell University Press.

22

THE RISE OF INSTITUTIONAL INVESTORS

Jan Fichtner

Introduction

Since the 1980s, institutional investors have increased their assets under management enormously. This trend has been driven both by rapidly growing equity markets and by the fact that households increasingly shifted from direct stock ownership to holdings via asset managers. Moreover, institutional investors benefited from the development that many countries changed their pension systems from "defined benefit" to "defined contribution" schemes that involve investment via asset managers (Rutterford and Hannah 2016). Through these developments, institutional investors have become large owners of publicly listed corporations in virtually all countries that have developed equity markets. This chapter focuses on how institutional investors have shaped and driven the financialization of listed companies and the financial sector itself, primarily by demanding the maximization of short-term shareholder value. The main measures to increase shareholder value have included share buybacks and special dividends as well as mergers. Additionally, many institutional investors have pushed for an alignment of (short-term) interests between managers and shareholders through stock-based forms of remuneration, thus reinforcing the financialization of listed corporations.

In this chapter, we understand the financialization of listed corporations as a process in which companies increasingly focus their strategic thinking exclusively on financial matters, such as the short-term maximization of profits and techniques of financial engineering which help in reaching that goal (see also Erturk in this volume). Such finance-driven firm strategies necessarily are often detrimental to the interests of stakeholders such as workers and suppliers, and may increase the risks for the economy at large through higher corporate debt loads. Potential consequences that the financialization of listed companies may entail include reduced investment in long-term research and development, reduced competition between firms in concentrated markets, extremely elevated levels of executive compensation, and thus increased economic inequality and lower economic growth (Horn 2017). This chapter seeks to contribute to exposing the (frequently hidden) power relations that underlie and drive the process of corporate financialization in many countries, and show how these relations have changed over time. Therefore, this chapter begins with a brief overview of the emergence of institutional investors and of equity markets in general as the former are inextricably linked to the latter. This is followed by a characterization of the specific roles that private equity funds, hedge funds, and mutual funds have played in corporate financialization. Hedge funds and private equity funds can be classified as the high fee segment of the asset management industry, while mutual funds arguably constitute the medium fee segment. Subsequently, the focus shifts on the rapidly growing low fee segment, which consists of passive index funds. In contrast to the fragmented mutual fund and hedge fund industries, the burgeoning index fund industry is heavily concentrated in the hands of what Fichtner Heemskerk and Garcia-Bernardo (2017) call the "Big Three." BlackRock, Vanguard and State Street form this small group of giant US passive asset managers, which is rapidly becoming a pivotal force for corporate control in many countries. Therefore, the "Big Three" represent a crucial factor for the financialization (but potentially also the de-financialization) of listed corporations.

Emergence and Overview of Institutional Investors

Many precursors of modern financial markets were developed in the Netherlands. In the seventeenth century, the Dutch East India Company became the first company to list shares on a public stock market. Such a public listing on the stock market enabled the corporation to raise capital from many different private investors, which could subsequently be utilized to finance risky but also very lucrative business endeavors overseas. Besides being arguably the first major transnational corporation in history, the Dutch East India Company pioneered modern corporate governance. In 1622, there was even the first case of what might today be called "shareholder activism" when one investor voiced his discontent about how the company was run (De Jongh 2011). The development of public stock markets enabled companies to raise capital on a large scale through the issuance of shares and thus created an additional instrument to corporate bonds. Thus, since that time the primary beneficial function of stock markets for the economy as a whole was to channel money from investors to companies that used it to fund their activities.

Arguably the first modern mutual funds were created in the late 1920s in Boston when companies such as State Street and Wellington offered open-end funds that for the first time enabled the continuous issuance and redemption of shares. This made them accessible to a much wider range of investors. These actively managed mutual funds could invest both in stocks and bonds. The United States enacted key pieces of regulation for mutual funds and other investment instruments during the 1930s and 1940s, which inter alia created the Securities and Exchange Commission (SEC). These measures subsequently enabled the emergence of institutional investors during the 1950s and 1960s, when also both private equity and hedge funds began to emerge in embryonic form. In the 1970s, Vanguard created the first index fund, a new concept where the fund manager is not actively selecting different stocks in order to maximize returns. Instead, the fund simply replicates established stock indices, such as the S&P 500 (which comprises the largest listed US corporations), and keeps costs low. The aim of this original index fund was to enable retail investors for the first time to achieve a diversified yet also cost-efficient investment in equities (Bogle 2016). Thus, by the late 1970s almost all major kinds of contemporary institutional investors had been developed.

Institutional investors can have different legal forms and follow diverse investment strategies, what they have in common is that they are "intermediary investors" – they are institutions that manage *other people's money* (Kay 2016). During the 1970s, institutional investors were still quite small in absolute and relative terms. For example, institutional investors only held less than 20 percent of total outstanding stock by listed companies in the United States in the early 1970s (Useem 1996). It was during the 1980s and 1990s when financial markets started to grow enormously in many countries and transnational financial flows developed rapidly that institutional investors began their real rise to become the pivotal financial actors they are today.

In 2016, the top 500 global asset managers together had US$81.2 trillion in assets under management, which is slightly more than global GDP. The top 20 asset managers account for over 42 percent of this enormous figure. Asset managers from the United States dominate the top 500 and manage over 53 percent of total global assets. The second largest country is the UK with British asset managers accounting for almost 8 percent of global assets, while France on place three accounts for about 7 percent. Germany and Canada complete the top five, accounting for six, respectively five percent of total assets (WillisTowersWatson 2017).

For the purposes of this chapter, it is instructive to analytically separate the asset management industry into three different segments of institutional investors: a high fee segment consisting of private equity and hedge funds, a medium fee segment comprised of traditional actively managed mutual funds, and the relatively new burgeoning segment of passive index funds. The institutional investors of each segment play different roles for the financialization of publicly listed corporations, thus it makes sense to discuss them separately. The medium fee segment comes first, because for many decades mutual funds had been by far the most dominant form of institutional investor. Therefore they are often referred to as "traditional" asset managers, whereas hedge funds and private equity funds, which grew later, are frequently labeled "alternative" asset managers.

The Medium Fee Segment: Actively Managed Mutual Funds

As mentioned above, mutual funds first developed in the 1920s in the United States. The main reason why they became so successful was that private individuals could for the first time invest with ease even relatively small amounts of money in a diversified portfolio of stocks (and/or bonds). Mutual funds have grown significantly from the 1950s to the 1970s, albeit from a small base. Their real take-off happened during the 1970s and 1980s. One crucial development was the introduction of so-called "401(k)" pension plans in the United States in the early 1980s, through which individuals could invest a part of their salary in a very tax-efficient way. Mutual funds were the main recipients of these investments (often via pension funds). The rise of defined contribution pension plans, therefore, fueled the growth of actively managed mutual funds.

Concurrently to this beginning boost of mutual funds, the SEC instituted a new rule in 1982, which enabled the development of a major mechanism for the financialization of listed corporations – share buybacks, which before had been considered as market manipulation. The deregulation-minded President Reagan had appointed the first Wall Street executive as head of the SEC since the 1930s, John Shad. Shad reportedly believed that allowing share buybacks would lead to increases in stock prices, and thus be beneficial to shareholders (Lazonick 2015). The main intended effect of share buybacks is that they reduce the number of outstanding (i.e. publicly traded) shares. This improves a range of financial firm ratios that have been advocated by proponents of shareholder value maximization, such as earnings per share (EPS). Repurchased shares are either canceled or kept as treasury shares (with the main aim to use them for mergers and acquisitions and/or for stock-based executive remuneration).

As such, share-buybacks constitute pure short-term financial engineering to increase the share price; they have no effect on revenues or total profits. However, they reduce the amount of funds that are available for long-term research and development and other kinds of investment. Moreover, a problematic aspect is that coupled with stock options, which became more widely used during the 1960s and 1970s, share buybacks can cause management to pursue purely financial aims at the expense of prioritizing long-term strategies including research and development. When the exercise of stock options is tied to the attainment of specific EPS values, this clearly can be seen as a financialized moral hazard problem for management.

Lazonick has convincingly argued that the rise of the "maximizing shareholder value" ideology in the mid-1980s has led to a paradigm shift of publicly listed corporations from a model of "retain-and-reinvest" to "downsize-and-distribute" (Lazonick 2015; see also Lazonick and O'Sullivan 2000). In the retain-and-reinvest model, corporations seek to retain earnings and reinvest them in productive capacities. Corporations adhering to the downsize-and-distribute paradigm primarily distribute corporate cash to shareholders while cutting expenses for investment and labor. According to Lazonick, the ascent of the "buyback corporation" is mainly responsible for many of the negative effects often ascribed to financialization, such as drastically increased income inequity, heightened employment instability, and reduced innovative capabilities of many firms (see also Davis 2008).

The volume of buybacks in the United States alone is staggering. From 2004 to end-2015, the companies of the S&P 500 have spent more than US$4.5 trillion for repurchasing their own shares.[1] This has led to the situation that the US stock market has completely changed its function during the last three decades, turning from an institution that brings capital from investors to firms that use it for investment into a mechanism that channels funds out of listed firms to investors. Remarkably, from 2000 to 2017 the US stock market facilitated *negative* net equity issuance of almost US$5.4 trillion![2] In other words, the US stock market has been utilized to channel capital out of corporations on an unprecedented scale. We know that the top one percent in the United States own approximately 40 percent of total stock market wealth – while the top ten percent even own about 80 percent (Wolff 2014; see also Godechot in this volume). Hence, we can conclude that the American stock market has become a giant device that extracts capital from listed corporations to distribute it to capital-owners. Mutual funds have been generally supportive of the increased use of share buybacks and the growing trend of mergers and acquisitions, which actually often diminish the value of the amalgamated corporation, inter alia due to high fees paid to investment banks and law firms.

Writing in the mid-1990s, Michael Useem coined the term "investor capitalism" to characterize the ascent of institutional investors that happened in the previous decades. The prior period, which he calls "managerial capitalism" was marked by the dominance of management, as the ownership of most listed US corporations was dispersed – the famous separation of ownership and control described by Berle and Means in 1932. According to Useem (1996: 207), the rise of institutional investors led to a rebalancing of power between shareholders and management – "negotiated relations between co-equals."

A decade later, Davis (2008) introduced the term "new finance capitalism." Davis found that by 2005 mutual funds had accumulated five percent blockholdings in hundreds of US companies. Being the single largest shareholder gave the biggest mutual funds – such as his running example Fidelity – power over the corporate governance of these companies by means of dominating corporate elections. However, he found that the large mutual fund groups preferred to sell their shares ("exit") rather than to exert direct influence ("voice") over the corporate governance of their investee firms. Thus, Davis (2008: 13) concluded that "networks of concentrated yet liquid ownership without control seem to be the distinctive feature of the new finance capitalism." During the 2000s, it became more common to refer to mutual funds as "traditional" asset managers. In contrast to this supposedly conventional way of asset management, private equity and hedge funds portrayed themselves as "alternative" investors.

The High Fee Segment: Private Equity and Hedge Funds

Alfred W. Jones created the first "hedged fund" in 1949 in the United States. His idea was to create an investment fund whose performance was protected (or hedged) against the general movement of the market (Lhabitant 2007). Jones combined "long" positions (i.e. buying stocks with the expectation that their value will increase) in supposedly undervalued stocks with short-selling stocks believed to be overvalued. Additionally, he borrowed funds to amplify returns – a method widely practiced by hedge funds today, known as leverage. The fee model of hedge funds was also novel; most managers took 20 percent of the realized profits, combined with a management fee of 2 percent (known as "2-and-20"), which is still the prevalent structure today.

During the 1940s, however, most people on Wall Street saw leverage and short-selling as "too racy for professionals entrusted with other people's savings" (Mallaby 2010: 23). Thus, it is not surprising that between the 1950s and the 1990s hedge funds were largely unknown to the general public and the assets these funds had under management amounted to only a tiny fraction of the overall financial markets. They were just too small to matter – for business and for academia. To date, no universally accepted definition of hedge funds exists. In general, hedge funds are private and largely unregulated investment vehicles that primarily cater to wealthy individuals and institutional investors and are able to employ any investment strategy (Fichtner 2013a).

During the 1980s, many hedge funds changed their investment strategies. Whereas before most actually tried to limit risks by diversifying and hedging their investments, now – after the end of Bretton Woods – many employed quite risky and speculative concentrated bets using the plethora of new financial markets and instruments, such as foreign currencies and deriva-tives. Hence, the term "hedge" funds increasingly became a misnomer – perhaps a more apt term since then would be "wager" or "speculation" funds (although some funds still hedge in the traditional sense). In the 1990s and 2000s, hedge funds enjoyed phenomenal growth, largely driven by an influx of capital from high net-worth individuals (ibid.). In 1990, there were about 500 hedge funds with assets of about US$40 billion. By late 2007, this number had skyrocketed to a pre-crisis peak of about 10,000 funds managing close to US$2,000 billion. In 2017, approximately 8,300 hedge funds had about US$3,200 billion in assets under management.

The hedge fund industry is dispersed; there are many small funds and only few large ones. Arguably, this is because there are no significant economies of scale. Many funds even seek to limit their size, because they want to avoid that their trades affect market prices. However, at the same time the global hedge fund industry is a uniquely concentrated financial industry geo-graphically. Hedge fund managers are almost exclusively based in New York and London, while most funds have their legal domicile in the Cayman Islands and Delaware (Fichtner 2016).

Private equity funds are also often legally based in Delaware and other tax havens. Moreover, private equity funds are similar to hedge funds in the respect that they charge high fees. The major difference is that – as their name suggests – private equity funds mainly acquire listed corporations and take them off the public stock markets through so-called leveraged buy-outs (Appelbaum and Batt 2014). Usually the debt load of the target firm is then increased sub-stantially while dividends are paid out to the private equity fund. Froud and Williams (2007) have called this business model "value extraction" through financial engineering. Hence, the short-term financial interests of the private equity fund often dominate over the medium and long-term interests of employees, suppliers and other stakeholders in the firm. This is the way in which private equity funds contribute to the financialization of (listed) corporations.

Hedge funds and private equity funds still only represent a small proportion of the entire global financial stock – below 3 percent each. However, because of leverage and their unique ability to concentrate assets in a few investments, hedge funds have an impact that is several times greater than this small proportion would suggest. In other words, their high agility and their capacity to place large concentrated bets enable hedge funds to influence markets much more than other investors are able to. Hedge funds are also very active investors, representing high shares of the trading in many segments of financial markets. Hence, hedge funds have become influential actors in many markets (Fichtner 2013a).

Some hedge funds played an important role in the pumping up of the US real estate bubble that eventually triggered the global financial crisis and others initiated the bursting of that bubble. The hedge funds Magnetar and Paulson & Co cooperated with investment banks such as Goldman Sachs to create large quantities of highly complex collateralized debt obligations (CDOs) which could be sold to unsophisticated investors that did not fully understand these opaque (and ultimately toxic) financial products. Subsequently, Magnetar and other hedge funds wagered against the very same CDOs they helped to create using another arcane financial instrument – credit default swaps (CDS) (Eisinger and Bernstein 2010). In what has been dubbed "the greatest trade ever" Paulson & Co made a stunning profit of about US$15 billion in 2007 with bets on the crash of the real-estate market in the United States (Zuckerman 2009).

One subgroup of the hedge fund industry that is crucial for the financialization of listed corporations are so-called "activist" hedge funds, which have three main features. First, activist hedge funds try to increase the market value of the targeted company. Second, they try to benefit from perceived market imbalances, such as undervalued firms. Third, in many instances activist hedge funds benefit from asset transfers at the expense of other stakeholders in the firm such as workers, suppliers or creditors (Fichtner 2013b). Activist hedge funds typically acquire stakes of between 5 and 10 percent of the outstanding shares of a listed corporation. Then they call for measures to increase short-term shareholder value: the payment of special dividends, the launch of share buyback programs or the sale of divisions that are not judged part of the "core competency" of the company. Sometimes funds team up and form "wolf packs" to amplify their impact on target firms (Briggs 2006).

Some large deals set important precedents and thus demonstrated the potential power of activist hedge funds over listed corporations, for example the "Deutsche Börse affair" (Watson 2005). In this episode, a group of hedge funds bought a large stake in the leading German stock exchange operator. Subsequently they forced the firm to abandon the proposed takeover of the London Stock Exchange and instead to pay out "surplus" cash to shareholders. Another case was the two activist funds TCI and Atticus pushing for the record-breaking takeover of the Dutch bank ABN Amro by Royal Bank of Scotland, Fortis and Banco Santander in 2007. This risky deal later turned out to be catastrophic for Fortis and Royal Bank of Scotland as it was done completely in cash, which these banks had borrowed, rather than being financed by the issuance of new shares. It left them with large amounts of debt, and both banks subsequently had to be bailed out by their home countries. Activist hedge funds see companies predominantly as bundles of financial assets that can be dismembered, traded and recombined rather than as sources of production and employment, and thus have driven particularly intense forms of corporate financialization. Though still quite a small subgroup of the whole hedge fund industry, activist funds have reached a new all-time high in assets under management in 2017 (*Financial Times* 2017a). Likewise, private equity funds have record levels of capital at their disposal (*Financial Times* 2017b).

Hedge funds and private equity funds exert kinds of disciplinary power of listed corporations that do not have "protective" blockholders, i.e. large permanent shareholders that support long-term strategies of their investee companies (Fichtner 2015). Because if they do not have such suppliers of "patient" capital, it would be rational for listed firms to implement some of the typical demands to maximize shareholder value in order not to become viable targets. Of course, such effects are mediated by the institutional configurations of political economies, such as ownership structures. Ownership of listed companies is different in Germany and Japan, where patient capital in the form of domestic blockholders still exists, compared to the United

Institutional Investors

Kingdom and United States, which are normally seen as dominated by impatient capital. The United Kingdom and the United States are traditionally portrayed as political economies in which few listed firms have large blockholders. Instead, most firms are assumed to have dispersed ownership structures with many different institutional and private investors (the famous separation of ownership and control). However, since the global financial crisis there is a powerful ongoing trend that is fundamentally changing the ownership structures of listed firms in the United States and elsewhere – the rise of passive index funds.

The Low Fee Segment: Passive Index Funds

The basic premise of index funds is that historically the vast majority of actively managed mutual funds have not been able to "beat" (financially outperform) broad-based stock market indices, such as the S&P 500 (Bogle 2016). Yet they charge considerable fees. Hence in 1976, Vanguard created the first index mutual fund that replicated the S&P 500 and kept costs for investors low. Index funds replicate stock indices by buying shares of the member firms of the particular index and then hold them "forever" (unless the composition of the index changes). At that time, the concept was being attacked by many on Wall Street as "un-American" because there was no attempt to beat the market. And, in fact, index funds remained a small niche for almost three decades. In the early 1990s, State Street introduced exchange traded funds (ETFs), which have in common with index mutual funds that they track stock indices and keep costs low. The main difference is that ETFs trade continuously the entire trading day, which makes them much more liquid and thus more attractive for institutional investors such as hedge funds. Index funds are much cheaper than active mutual funds, with fees of around 0.1 percent. Lauded by some as the "democratization" of investing, these low fees have driven the enormous increase in assets under management in recent years (Novick 2017).

During the last decade, investors have shifted capital from expensive actively managed mutual funds to cheap index mutual funds and ETFs on a massive scale. Between 2008 and 2017 investors sold holdings of active US equity mutual funds worth roughly US$1,300 billion, while buying passively managed US equity funds to the tune of approximately US$1,600 billion – a historically unprecedented money mass-migration within one decade of about US$3,000 billion in the United States alone (see Figure 22.1).

In contrast to the fragmented mutual fund industry (big players such as Fidelity notwithstanding), the large and rapidly growing index funds industry is dominated by just three American asset management firms: BlackRock, Vanguard, and State Street, which Fichtner Heemskerk and Garcia-Bernardo (2017) consequently call the "Big Three." Together, they have well over US$13 trillion in assets under management, and control 80–90 percent of all assets in passive index funds (ibid.; WillisTowersWatson 2017). First mover advantage and powerful economies of scale facilitate high concentration in the index fund industry and make it difficult for new competitors to take business from the incumbents. These centripetal forces make the structurally oligopolistic index fund industry markedly different from the rather centrifugally structured hedge fund and active mutual fund industries in which thousands of funds compete. Due to the enormous inflows of capital in recent years the Big Three have acquired significant shareholdings in thousands of listed corporations both in the United States and internationally. In 2015, the Big Three, seen together (as one investor block), would have been the largest single shareholder in 88 percent of all S&P 500 firms, with a mean combined ownership of almost 18 percent (Fichtner Heemskerk and Garcia-Bernardo 2017). Thus, the rise of passive index funds is leading to a concentration of corporate ownership in the hands of the Big Three.

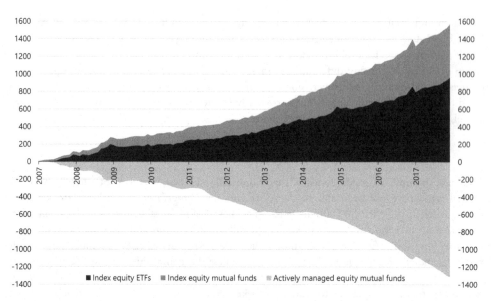

Figure 22.1 Cumulative flows Into Index Funds and Out of Actively Managed Funds (bn US$)

The exact effects of the Big Three on listed corporations are yet under-researched, however. Moreover, BlackRock, Vanguard and State Street are still in the process of adapting to their new role as the "de facto permanent governing board" of most US listed firms (Haberly and Wójcik 2016). On the one hand, passive investors have little incentives to be concerned with firm-level governance performance, because they simply aim to replicate the performance of a group of firms while minimizing costs. On the other hand, the re-concentration of corporate ownership in the hands of the Big Three may imply a re-concentration of corporate control, since passive asset managers have the ability to exercise the voting rights of the stocks owned by their funds. Research by Fichtner Heemskerk and Garcia-Bernardo (2017) has found that the Big Three pursue coordinated voting strategies across all of their many individual funds, which is a key precondition for effectively exerting shareholder power. Their analysis has also shown that generally BlackRock, Vanguard and State Street vote in favor of management (rather than taking activist decisions against managements) at annual general meetings.

In addition to corporate control via voting, the Big Three may exert power via two channels that are far less visible. First, they pursue private engagements with the management of companies in which they own shares to discuss issues deemed important for the particular corporation. BlackRock, for example, had almost 1,500 such private engagements from mid-2015 to mid-2016 and 1,300 the year later (BlackRock 2017). Secondly, due to the large combined ownership position of the Big Three in many listed firms, it is possible that executives of these companies would "internalize" their known objectives. This is plausible because the management of all large corporations is well-informed about who the largest shareholders are and they also know the objectives of the Big Three. Moreover, management depends on the enormous voting power of BlackRock, Vanguard and State Street in proxy fights with activist investors or other shareholder conflicts. There is an emerging academic debate whether such "common ownership" (which can also involve large non-index investors) is causing affected firms active in concentrated markets, such as airlines or banks in the United States, to compete less fiercely, which could result in higher prices for consumers (Azar Schmalz and Tecu 2018; Schmalz 2018). The hypothesized reason is that large common owners have the interest that all their portfolio firms maximize profits. If one of these firms lowers prices significantly to win business from its competitors, this arguably lowers profits for all of them, which would be detrimental to the interests of a common owner.

Braun (2016) has rightly argued that index funds may, in principle, act as "patient" capital that could facilitate long-term strategies of listed companies. In fact, index funds are invested "forever" in the firms that are members of a particular index and thus are in a position to potentially focus on the long-term well-being of their investee companies. For now, however, the actual voting behavior of BlackRock is not supporting the claim that the asset manager acts as a champion of long-termism. As argued above, two cogent proxies for short-termist and financialized behavior of listed corporations are share-buybacks as well as mergers and acquisitions. According to data from ProxyInsight for the period 2011–2017, the Big Three voted in favor of these two measures in the vast majority of cases at annual general meetings of listed firms from the United States, the United Kingdom, Japan, France and Germany. This does not necessarily mean, however, that it is impossible for the Big Three to become agents for corporate de-financialization. All three giant asset managers are currently undergoing significant transformations as they adjust to their almost public utility-like role as the dominant common owners of a continually increasing number of listed companies.

Conclusion

During the last hundred years, institutional investors have risen from being niche players to becoming large owners of an increasing number of listed corporations in many countries – partly driven by the shift from "defined benefit" to "defined contribution" pension schemes. During the 1970s, individuals still held roughly 80 percent of listed corporations in the United States, while institutional investors only held 20 percent. Since then the positions have turned, individual investors now hold less than 20 percent. Different kinds of institutional investors have played key roles in different phases of their development and growth. Actively managed mutual funds (the "medium fee" segment) developed as early as the 1920s and have remained the largest kind of institutional investor until today (measured by assets under management). Private equity and hedge funds (the "high fee" segment) grew rapidly in the 1990s and 2000s but nonetheless both are significantly smaller than mutual funds.

Arguably, private equity and (activist) hedge funds have driven the financialization of listed companies by demanding the maximization of short-term shareholder value, inter alia through special dividends and share buybacks, and more generally evaluating corporations as bundles of assets that should be split and recombined to maximize financial returns. The mantra of "downsize-and-distribute" that emerged in the 1980s has by now largely displaced the old "retain-and-reinvest" model, at least in the United States. According to Lazonick, this shift is largely responsible for many of the negative effects of financialization such as increased inequality and lower economic growth. In fact, the function of public stock markets has been completely reversed during the rise of financialization. Whereas corporations once used them to issue equity to fund investment, now the opposite happens. Since 2000, US equity markets have facilitated an extraction of capital from listed corporations to investors (i.e. primarily the top 1–10 percent) of over US$5 trillion, thanks to share buybacks.

This chapter also discussed an ongoing momentous development within the institutional investment fund space – the rise of index funds. The burgeoning index fund industry is dominated by just three large US asset managers. Collectively, BlackRock, Vanguard and State Street are rapidly becoming the new dominant owners of most US listed corporations – and are expanding their reach in other countries too. Together, BlackRock, Vanguard and State Street now have assets under management that are four times as large as the entire hedge fund industry, which includes over 8,000 funds. As index fund managers the "Big Three" are invested permanently in their thousands of portfolio companies.

Therefore, in contrast to most active institutional investors that buy and sell companies frequently, they have the clear potential to become agents of corporate de-financialization and long-termism. On the one hand, the extremely broad ownership in thousands of firms means that the Big Three arguably do not have firm-specific interests but rather industry- or economy-wide interests. On the other hand, being index investors means that too risky firm behavior or very short-term strategies will eventually impact the portfolios of their retail investors in a negative way. BlackRock already claims to be a champion of long-termism. For now, their actual voting behavior is not supporting that claim, however.

Due to their enormous size and broad corporate ownership, the Big Three perform an almost public utility-like role in the United States and increasingly in other countries as well. Hence, in the next years, the public, regulators and investors of the Big Three might press for a voting behavior that is more congruent with their proclaimed long-term or "patient" corporate governance strategies. Such a transformation of the Big Three into "agents of corporate de-financialization" is far from certain, of course, as they face conflicting interests between maximizing investor inflows while minimizing costs and exposure to (new) regulation. However, what is certain is that from all the institutional investors discussed in this chapter, the Big Three index investors have by far the highest potential to stop and potentially reverse the financialization of listed corporations.

Notes

1 Calculations by the author based on Lazonick (2015) and FactSet (2016).
2 Gross equity issuance minus retirements (stock repurchases as well as mergers and acquisitions); author's calculations based on Federal Reserve (2017).

Bibliography

Appelbaum, E. and Batt, R., 2014. *Private Equity at Work: When Wall Street Manages Main Street*. New York: Russell Sage Foundation.

Azar, J., Schmalz, M. and Tecu, I., 2018. Anti-Competitive Effects of Common Ownership. *Journal of Finance*, 73(4), pp. 1513–1565.

Berle, A. and Means, G.C., 1932. *The Modern Corporation and Private Property*. New York: Macmillan.

BlackRock, 2017. *Investment Stewardship Priorities 2017–2018*. Available at https://tinyurl.com/y8bgda2v [Accessed November 23, 2018].

Bogle, J.C., 2016. The Index Mutual Fund: 40 Years of Growth, Change, and Challenge. *Financial Analysts Journal*, January/February. Available at http://www.cfapubs.org/doi/pdf/10.2469/faj.v72.n1.5 [Accessed November 23, 2018].

Braun, B., 2016. From Performativity to Political Economy: Index Investing, ETFs and Asset Manager Capitalism. *New Political Economy*, 21(3), pp. 257–273.

Briggs, T.W., 2006. Corporate Governance and the New Hedge Fund Activism: An Empirical Analysis. *Journal of Corporation Law*, 32(4), pp. 681–738.

Davis, G.F., 2008. A New Finance Capitalism? Mutual Funds and Ownership Re-concentration in the United States. *European Management Review*, 5(1), pp. 11–21.

De Jongh, M., 2011. Shareholder Activists Avant la Lettre: The "Complaining Participants" in the Dutch East India Company. In Koppell, J., (ed.), *Origins of Shareholder Advocacy*. London: Palgrave Macmillan, pp. 1622–1625.

Eisinger, J. and Bernstein, J., 2010. *The Magnetar Trade: How One Hedge Fund Helped Keep the Bubble Going*. Available at https://tinyurl.com/yacdnkb2 [Accessed November 23, 2018].

FactSet, 2016. *Buyback Quarterly Q4–15.* Available at https://www.factset.com/websitefiles/PDFs/buyback/buyback_3.17.16/view [Accessed November 23, 2018].

Federal Reserve, 2017. *Quarterly Issuance and Retirement.* Available at https://www.federalreserve.gov/releases/efa/equity-issuance-retirement-quarterly.htm [Accessed November 23, 2018].

Fichtner, J., 2013a. The Rise of Hedge Funds: A Story of Inequality. *Momentum Quarterly,* 2(1), pp. 3–20.

Fichtner, J., 2013b. Hedge Funds: Agents of Change for Financialization. *Critical Perspectives on International Business,* 9(4), pp. 358–376.

Fichtner, J., 2015. Rhenish Capitalism Meets Activist Hedge Funds: Blockholders and the Impact of Impatient Capital. *Competition & Change,* 19(4), pp. 336–352.

Fichtner, J., 2016. The Anatomy of the Cayman Islands Offshore Financial Center: Anglo-America, Japan, and the Role of Hedge Funds. *Review of International Political Economy,* 23(6), pp. 1034–1063.

Fichtner, J., Heemskerk, E.M. and Garcia-Bernardo, J., 2017. Hidden Power of the Big Three? Passive Index Funds, Re-concentration of Corporate Ownership, and New Financial Risk. *Business and Politics,* 19(2), pp. 298–326.

Financial Times, 2017a. Activists Have Boardrooms Singing to a New Tune. 23 December, p.13.

Financial Times, 2017b. Private Equity Fundraising Hits Post-Crisis High. Available at https://www.ft.com/content/906b2b86-828c-11e7-94e2-c5b903247afd [Accessed November 23, 2018].

Froud, J. and Williams, K., 2007. Private Equity and the Culture of Value Extraction. *New Political Economy,* 12(3), pp. 405–420.

Haberly, D. and Wójcik, D., 2016. Earth Incorporated: Centralization and Variegation in the Global Company Network. *Economic Geography,* 93(3), pp. 241–266.

Horn, L., 2017. The Financialization of the Corporation. In Baars, G. and Spicer, A. (eds.), *The Corporation: A Critical, Multi-Disciplinary Handbook.* Cambridge: Cambridge University Press, pp. 281–290.

Kay, J., 2016. *Other People's Money: Masters of the Universe or Servants to the People?* London: Profile Books.

Lazonick, W. and O'Sullivan, M., 2000. Maximizing Shareholder Value: A New Ideology for Corporate Governance. *Economy & Society,* 29(1), pp. 13–35.

Lazonick, W., 2015. *Stock Buybacks: From Retain-and-reinvest to Downsize-and-distribute.* Brookings. Available at https://www.brookings.edu/wp-content/uploads/2016/06/lazonick.pdf [Accessed November 23, 2018].

Lhabitant, F.-S., 2007. *Handbook of Hedge Funds.* Chichester: Wiley.

Mallaby, S., 2010. *More Money than God: Hedge Funds and the Making of a New Elite.* London: Bloomsbury.

Novick, B., 2017. How Index Funds Democratize Investing. *The Wall Street Journal.* Available at https://tinyurl.com/y73fyl39 [Accessed November 23, 2018].

Rutterford, J. and Hannah, L., 2016. The Rise of Institutional Investors. In Chambers, D. and Dimson, E., (eds.), *Financial Market History: Reflections on the Past for Investors Today.* New York: CFA Institute Research Foundation, pp. 242–263.

Schmalz, M.C., 2018. Common-Ownership Concentration and Corporate Conduct. *Annual Review of Financial Economics,* 10(1), pp. 413–448.

Useem, M., 1996. *Investor Capitalism: How Money Managers are changing the Face of Corporate America.* New York: BasicBooks.

Watson, M., 2005. Hedge Funds, the Deutsche Börse Affair and Predatory Anglo-American Capitalism. *The Political Quarterly,* 76(4), pp. 516–528.

WillisTowersWatson, 2017. The World's 500 Largest Asset Managers – Year End 2016. Available at https://tinyurl.com/ycketcgk [Accessed November 23, 2018].

Wolff, E.N., 2014. Household Wealth Trends in the United States, 1962–2013: What Happened over the Great Recession? *NBER Working Paper.* No. 20733.

Zuckerman, G., 2009. *The Greatest Trade Ever: The Behind-the-Scenes Story of How John Paulson Defied Wall Street and Made Financial History.* New York: Broadway Books.

23

TRUSTS AND FINANCIALIZATION[1]

Brooke Harrington

> The trust is an effort to escape from the ever-deepening and ever-recurrent crises in capitalism. It is the confession of the upper middle class – the class that has most used the trust – that the contradictions in capitalism cannot be resolved.
>
> *(Franklin 1933: 475)*

Introduction

Just as financialization has been identified as a response to recurring crises in capitalism (Arrighi 1994; Krippner 2011), so has the trust. Though Franklin's observations in the epigraph above were made in the context of the Great Depression, they refer to a long-standing pattern of wealth accumulation being wiped out by recurrent economic contractions. The trust, as a legal structure for holding assets, has proven to be a useful tool for protecting wealth from these crises, and for allowing capital to grow in spite of them (Harrington 2016). Trusts are often used to structure international finance (Langbein 1995) as well as private wealth, although they have been overlooked in the financialization literature in favor of corporations (Krippner 2011).

Trusts are a type of asset-holding structure that facilitate the profit maximization and international capital mobility characteristic of financialization (Krippner 2005: 203). Although trusts originated in medieval England (Harrington 2012b), their exceptional "generality and elasticity" (Maitland 1936: 129) has allowed them to survive the transition from feudalism to capitalism, contributing and adapting to the global spread of financialization. As Krippner (2011) has documented, economies that once were grounded in making and selling things have shifted from creating to distributing wealth: what another scholar of financialization calls "mov[ing] wealth from one hand to another" (Mukunda 2014). This shift, which took hold in the US and other major world economies in the last quarter of the twentieth century (Krippner 2005), demanded tools to shift wealth across borders with minimal cost and effort. Trusts offered a ready-made legal structure to achieve these ends (Beaverstock et al. 2013). Their distinctive characteristics permit the nearly frictionless global movement of capital, maximizing profits by minimizing compliance costs and tax obligations, as well as by sheltering assets from tax authorities and creditors.

For both private individuals and firms, the freedom from taxation and many forms of regulation make trusts a "privileged site of accumulation" (Krippner 2005: 181) – a position in the economy that facilitates the ease and speed of amassing capital. As a result, trusts expanded from their historical uses in the service of high-net-worth individuals, to application in large international financial transactions among corporations (Parkinson 2008). By examining trusts' role in private and corporate finance, this chapter will argue that they contribute to financialization in three significant ways: by consolidating the power of the investor as the central figure in the global economy; by facilitating the dominance of Anglo-American finance; and by increasing the autonomy of finance from the nation-state system.

Toward a Sociology of Trusts

Trusts are asset-holding structures that maximize capital mobility and profits through what one scholar calls a set of "tricks" for "manipulating facets of ownership" (Moffat 2009: 5). Trusts acquire this power as a result of two defining features: the birfurcation of ownership, and a distinctive legal status. A trust is created when one person (known as the trustee) accepts assets from a second person (the settlor), for the benefit of a third person (the beneficiary).[2] In this arrangement, legal ownership and responsibility for the assets pass from the settlor to the trustee, but the use and enjoyment of the assets go the beneficiaries. Thus, ownership is split into two components: legal and beneficial. The trustee has special obligations, including the requirement to act as a "fiduciary," meaning to own and manage the trust assets in the best interests of the beneficiaries, rather than for personal gain (Langbein 1995).[3]

In addition to divided ownership, the other conceptually distinctive aspect of trusts is their status and treatment in law. Unlike other asset-holding structures, such as foundations or corporations, trusts are not separate legal entities. Instead, trusts are private relationships – recognized by the laws of many countries, but not possessed of a "legal personality" in their own right. This has a number of consequences; for example, a trust cannot be sued or go bankrupt, as legal entities like corporations can.

These characteristics have made trusts key elements in contemporary global finance – characterized as a global "shell game" (Fitch 2003), in which lawyers and finance professionals orchestrate trans-national capital movements "in a fashion that operates within the letter but against the spirit of the law" (Moffat 2009: 113). Because trusts are not publicly registered and are subject to very few legal controls, they make it possible to move large sums of capital around the world at very low cost compared to more highly regulated structures, such as corporations. This means fewer transaction and compliance costs attach to assets held in trust, which contributes to profit maximization – another key feature of financialization (Krippner 2005: 200).

The distinctive way that trusts organize asset ownership has made them useful not only for wealthy individuals, but for corporations (Langbein 1997). For example, trusts commonly function as containers for corporate shares; this has been the organizational structure underlying mutual funds since their inception in the late 1700s (Reid 2006). Trusts have also become a tool of structured finance for corporations, underlying bond issues and making asset securitization possible (Langbein 1995). On a global scale, "trusts, and especially purpose trusts, play an increasingly important part in international financial transactions" (Parkinson 2005: 335).

Offshore financial centers play a particularly important role in linking trusts to financialization. The laws of many such jurisdictions have been tailored specifically to maximize the financial benefits that trusts can provide to firms and individuals. In particular, the split-ownership concept underlying trusts has been magnified in economic significance through the use of offshore legislation. A common strategy is to give legal ownership of assets to trustees based in offshore locales where tax and regulatory expenses are negligible to non-existent. As a matter of international law, trust assets are only subject to regulation and taxation in the jurisdiction where the legal owner lives. So trustees strategically base themselves in countries that offer the lowest compliance costs and tax rates. Jurisdictions all over the world compete to offer the most attractive regimes (*Economist* 2013), but historically the dominant player has been the UK, along with its territories and former colonies.

Using trusts in this way, a Russian national living in London can benefit from a multi-million-dollar portfolio of US stocks held in a Cayman Islands trust without paying tax on the profits, because he is not the legal owner of the assets.[4] The trustee is the only one liable for any legal obligations associated with the portfolio, and since the Caymans imposes no tax on capital gains or income, profits can flow unimpeded to the beneficial owner in London. For the same reason – divided ownership – the trust assets are untouchable by the Russian's creditors, legal heirs and divorcing spouses (Parkinson 2005; Harrington 2016). Finally, should that Cayman Islands trust be threatened by an unwanted obligation, or if a more attractive taxation or regulatory regime becomes available elsewhere, the trust form makes it easy to move the assets with minimal cost from one jurisdiction to another.[5] The following sections elaborate on these and other features of the trust that hold particular interest for sociologists.

Comparing Trusts and Corporations as Privileged Sites of Accumulation

As instruments for accumulating and growing capital, trusts predate the better-known corporate form of organization. In fact, before the corporate form became widely available in the mid-nineteenth century, many industrial and commercial enterprises during the previous 100 years were organized through trusts; these were known as "deed of settlement" firms (Moffat 2009). By the twentieth century, corporations became the dominant form of business organization by offering limited liability and the convenience of a separate "legal personality," which could enter into contracts and obtain loans. But trusts have remained the preferred vehicle for collective investment, as well as estate planning and private asset protection.

The light regulatory burden imposed on trusts has been key to their ongoing appeal compared to corporations. These qualities make trusts highly adaptable instruments for transferring capital, particularly on an international scale. Since so few rules apply to them, trusts can be tailored to a wide variety of private and commercial purposes. In contrast, corporations have historically attracted considerable regulatory attention due to their long-standing connection with fraud and economic crises (Chancellor 1999; Harrington 2012a). Regulation of firms has increased during the era of financialization due in part to the greater frequency of such crises (Krippner 2011). But trusts largely avoided such regulatory scrutiny by virtue of their status as private relationships; unlike corporations, regulating trusts was not seen as a matter of public interest.[6] Thus, while corporations are "encumbered with restrictions of a regulatory character, designed to protect creditors and shareholders…the commercial trust continues to offer the transaction planner nearly unlimited flexibility in design" (Langbein 1997: 184–185).

Of course, these qualities of elasticity, generality and design flexibility are only realized through the intervention of social agents – in particular, the financial and legal professionals who deploy trusts as part of their everyday practices. These professionals take on the duties of trustees, and strategize with clients to determine what assets should be held in trust, and under what country's laws a trust should be placed. This points up an important distinction: trusts did not create financialization. Rather, experts found in trusts a ready-made tool to accomplish some of the tasks financialization requires, such as maximization of capital mobility and profits with minimum regulatory friction. This use of trusts thrives and depends on the gaps and conflicts among national legal systems, creating strategic disarray rather than convergence (Harrington 2016).

Thus, trusts are in many ways an example *par excellence* of what Krippner calls a "privileged site of accumulation" (2005: 181). Specifically, trusts provide four unique advantages in the accrual of economic and political power. First, compared to firms, trusts are exempt from an entire level or realm of taxation: while corporate income is taxed twice – first at the corporation level, and then again when distributed to shareholders – trust assets are only taxed once, when distributed to beneficiaries (and even that may be avoidable).[7] In addition to this privileged tax status, assets held in trust enjoy a degree of protection from legal judgements and other claims that corporations do not; thus, corporations can go bankrupt, but trusts cannot. Third, since trusts are far more lightly regulated than corporations, they incur much lower compliance costs. These lower costs may be one reason that the fortunes of the wealthy, who are the primary users of private trusts, grow at a faster rate than average (Wolff 2012).

These three factors contribute to economic privilege by allowing assets in trust to accumulate more quickly, and with fewer threats than assets held in a corporate structure. Add to this the fourth and final distinction that gives trusts an edge over corporations as a site of privileged accumulation: privacy. While corporations must be publicly registered, disclosing the names of their directors – and often those of their shareholders – trusts are completely unregistered entities in all but a few countries; furthermore, the identities of beneficial owners are everywhere treated as closely guarded secrets (Conn 2015). This provides both economic and political privileges. Economically, privacy increases freedom from the rule of law: when the true beneficial owners of assets cannot be identified, they cannot be taxed or regulated (Shaxson 2011). Politically, the privacy surrounding trusts provides protection from public accountability, allowing individuals to accumulate not just wealth but power through means such as contributions to political campaigns and lobbying activities – all anonymously, using the trust structure to shield their identities.

Quantifying What is Known about Trusts

The lack of regulation and registration of trusts makes it impossible to know the total number of trusts worldwide, or the value of the assets they contain (Chester 1982; Sharman 2006). This is part of a more general problem associated with research on elites: the wealthy are almost totally excluded from publicly available datasets (Kopczuk and Saez 2004). Surveys "systematically underrepresent the rich and do not reflect the holdings of the super-rich" (Davies et al. 2008: 17). Indeed, the members of the Forbes 400 are explicitly excluded even from datasets that oversample on wealth, such as the Survey of Consumer Finances (Budría et al. 2002). Some individuals even pay to be left off of the Forbes 400 list, in order to protect their privacy even further (Demick 1990; Kolhatkar 2006).

Such individuals – along with a growing number of firms – value trusts all the more highly as the secrecy and light regulation trusts afford become increasingly rare. In other domains of finance, transparency is becoming the norm (Seabrooke 2011); the trust is very much an outlier in this regard. But the same features that make trusts so attractive for users also make them very difficult to study. With few exceptions, data that would allow us to quantify trusts' significance in the international political economy are carefully protected behind legal barriers.

Recent interest in stratification has brought to light how the "politically dangerous" information needed to estimate the extent of trust assets and other sources of wealth inequality has been obscured (Pinçon and Pinçon-Charlot 1998: 8). For example, professional trustees can face civil or criminal penalties for divulging information about trust assets or beneficiaries. Even if they believe the trusts they manage are linked to illegal activities, trustees are subject to "strict confidentiality statutes, which not only ensure that the disclosure of client information to third parties is actionable in a civil court, but also render the offending professional liable to a fine and/or imprisonment for a criminal offense" (Parkinson 2004: 9).

The data that occasionally do come to light on trusts generally emerge from two sources. The first is lawsuits, which usually generate public trial records in which the magnitude and structure of wealth held in trust can be exposed. Examples include the Pritzker family of Chicago: a suit launched by a beneficiary accusing the trustees of apportioning trust assets unfairly laid out for public view the family's $15 billion fortune, which was held in 60 companies and 2,500 trusts (Jaffe and Lane 2004). In the corporate arena, a prosecution by the US Securities and Exchange Commission brought to light a "maze" of dozens of offshore trusts, located primarily in the Cayman Islands and the Isle of Man, used by brothers Sam and Charles Wyly to hide $1 billion worth of stocks in their family firm; this structure enabled the brothers to evade regulations against insider trading and pocket $550 million in capital gains, tax free (Guinto 2013; Savchuck 2014).

The second major data source on trusts is theft. In recent years, there have been a few high-profile cases of employees from offshore banks and other wealth management firms stealing and selling databases of trust beneficiaries to governments and journalists. This includes private account information stolen from organizations in Panama, Liechtenstein, Luxembourg and parts of the Caribbean (Gauthier-Villars and Ball 2010; Bowers 2014; Harrington 2016). This suggests the problem with trust data gleaned from leaks and lawsuits: they are often anecdotal and unsystematic. Scholarly research can use them only as illustrations.

Notable exceptions to this pattern of data unavailability on trusts come from the painstaking calculations of a handful of economists. In particular, Edward Wolff (2012) and Gabriel Zucman (2015) have found ingenious ways to estimate portions of the information that would allow an educated guess about the extent of assets held in trust, at least within the US. Recent work by Saez and Zucman (2016) suggests that private trust assets average $5.2 million for American households in the top 1% by wealth; according to Wolff (2012), the next 9% of households hold trust assets averaging $949,800 in value. Compare this to Sitkoff and Schanzenbach's (2005) estimate of $1 million as the average value of a domestic private trust account.

Since the top 10% of households own more than 90% of all private trust wealth in the US (Wolff 2012), we can use data from this group to make a rough estimate of the asset value these trusts represent. By combining the findings from Saez and Zucman (2016) with those of Wolff (2012), it appears that Americans' private trust wealth amounts to just over $16 trillion.[8] This is roughly equivalent to the GDP of the US – a relationship between household wealth and GDP consistent with trends going back decades (Piketty and Zucman 2014). While this figure for the US is speculative, it is the best available for now, and seems to square with other information we have on the broader parameters of private wealth. For example, recent estimates suggest that there is $46 trillion in private wealth in the US (Boston Consulting Group 2013); the calculation proposed in this article suggests that about 35 percent of that is held in trust.

However, at least two key questions remain unanswered about the position of trusts in the global economy. First, the kinds of estimates provided by Wolff (2012), as well as by Saez and Zucman (2016), are unique to the US: there are no equivalent data for other countries as yet. This work is very much on the cutting edge of research in economics and finance. Second, it is unclear how much *corporate* wealth is held in trust. Experts in corporate uses of trusts claim that "The aggregate assets of these commercial trusts now dwarf the assets held in personal trusts by a ratio of something like 20-to-1" (Langbein 2004: 57). However, this seems unlikely, since it implies a total value of at least $320 trillion for commercial trusts, which exceeds by a wide margin estimates of the $225 trillion total value of corporate wealth worldwide (Lund et al. 2013).

As a result, it is difficult to put a precise quantity on trusts' significance within a financialized economy. The best data available for now suggest that the aggregate of private and corporate wealth held in trusts runs into the tens of trillions of dollars and exceeds the GDPs of the world's largest economies. Until better data are available, this study must restrict itself to non-quantitative means of suggesting the role trusts play in the world economy.

Trusts and Financialization

Building on the conceptualization of trusts offered in the previous section, this paper will argue that these structures contribute to financialization in three significant ways: by consolidating the power of the investor as the central figure in the global economy; by maintaining and enlarging the Anglo-American character of finance worldwide; and by increasing the autonomy of finance from the nation-state system.

In the first instance, trusts consolidate the power of investors by making certain kinds of large-scale investment legally and economically feasible. Thus, they are the preferred organizational form for mutual funds, pension funds and other forms of institutional investment. Both corporate and individual investors reap distinctive profit-making opportunities and protections by using trusts, as opposed to alternative structures.

In the second case, trusts are linked inextricably to the ways in which the Anglo-American approach has left its mark on financialization (Van der Zwan 2014). We see this in two ways. As part of British imperial expansion, the Common Law framework was imposed on the colonies; the trust concept was among the most "distinctive" (Maitland 2011 [1909]) elements of that transplanted legal system. The trust remains as a legacy in the modern law of almost all the former colonies, including the major tax havens of the world. Even in countries that were never British colonies, and never adopted the Common Law tradition, there is increasing recognition and even legal adoption of trusts; this has been driven by pressure in those countries to integrate with a global financial system dominated by the Anglo-American approach. In other words, trusts are both an expression and a facilitator of the essentially Anglo-American character of financialization.

In the third case, trusts loosen the constraints of the law on assets and their owners. The privacy provided by trusts and the light regulatory burden they enjoy allow assets to move largely unimpeded from jurisdiction to jurisdiction; owners (beneficial or legal) are free to "shop" for the most hospitable legal regime for those assets. Thus, the trust has enabled finance itself to become hyper-mobile, enjoying a large measure of autonomy from the laws of any particular nation-state.

Economic Dominance of Investors.

A defining characteristic of financialization is the placement of investors, rather than producers, at the center of the world economy (Van der Zwan 2014). In past decades, roughly coinciding with the rise of financialization, the trust's relative freedom from regulatory oversight has made it a very attractive vehicle for large-scale investing, such as bond issues, mutual funds, pension funds and hedge funds. While all of those investments can be organized through other structures, trusts are preferred for several reasons, including reduced transaction costs and flexibility concerning matters such as how creditors are to be repaid (Moffat 2009).

As a result, trusts permit investing to occur on a scale that would not otherwise be practical, streamlining investments and payouts better than the corporate form, and doing so with less regulatory friction. This has facilitated the growth of key areas of finance, such as the mutual fund industry. As Malkiel (2013) has pointed out, mutual funds in the US managed less than $26 billion in assets as of 1980; by 2010, the total value of assets in mutual funds had grown to $3.5 trillion, representing 135-fold increase.

While a number of forces drove the influx of capital, it is not often acknowledged how the trust structure made this growth possible, as well as profitable. By reducing transaction costs, the trust made collective investing a lucrative domain of finance; organizationally, it provided the tools that enabled millions of Americans to participate in the financial markets. This mass inflow of new investors was a crucial step in the financialization of the US economy: individuals who might not be able to afford more than a handful of stocks (at an average cost of $35 per share) could suddenly invest across a broad spectrum of industries through the mechanism of mutual funds (Harrington 2008). Trusts are thus implicated in "the shift from passive savers to active investors [which is] associated with financialization" (Beaverstock et al. 2013: 843).

The power that trusts give to investors in the contemporary financialized economy can be illustrated in part by the subprime mortgage crisis that underpinned the 2008 crash. The comparatively light regulation to which trusts are subject makes them convenient for use in high-risk, high-profit investments. Thus, when banks went in search of new ways to attract capital, they turned to the trust structure, using them to bundle assets like mortgages and resell them as investment vehicles (Langbein 1995). Millions of individual mortgage obligations were poured into trusts, like ingredients into a casserole dish; the contents were then sliced into "tranches" and sold to investors around the world.

This scheme, on which the whole subprime mortgage crisis was based, hinged on the divided-ownership concept that distinguishes the trust: while the trust owned all the mortgages as a group, the right to collect the mortgage payments could be parceled out to thousands of investors as "beneficiaries" of the trust. This divided-ownership structure dramatically increased the profit potential of these securities by broadening the range of individuals and entities who could invest in them (Winnett 2008). Unfortunately, this broad range, combined with the riskiness of the underlying securities, proved to be the undoing of the world financial system: the result was a "contagion" of losses that spread as if transmitted by "contaminated food" (Dodd and Mills 2008: 14). Without trusts, there might have been no subprime mortgage crisis; because of trusts, the crisis spread globally. This underscores the trust's power to put investors at the center of the economy, albeit in a negative way.

Global Spread of the Anglo-American Approach to Finance.

Financialization has been portrayed in the scholarly literature as "a decidedly Anglo-American phenomenon" (Van der Zwan 2014: 114–115; see also Deeg and O'Sullivan 2009: 738). As this phenomenon has propagated worldwide, trusts have formed an inextricable part of the package. The stage was set by the global reach of British colonialism, which imposed the Common Law tradition on each imperial territory. This meant that the trust diffused with the rest of the Common Law framework into every corner of the Empire. The remnants of that legacy can still be observed in today's leading offshore financial centers, most of which are current or former British territories, including Singapore, Hong Kong, the Channel Islands, Bermuda, the Cayman Islands, and the British Virgin Islands. These jurisdictions are now where many trusts are domiciled, and where most of the innovations in the law and design of trusts are taking place (Parkinson 2004).

Onshore, many of the world's great financial powers – such as the US and other former British colonies – have also enshrined the trust as part of their own adaptations of the Common Law tradition. As one scholar put it nearly a century ago, in a review of British imperial power,

> Wherever the Common Law penetrates, it carries with it its younger sister Equity along with the whole apparatus of Trusts and the distinction of legal and equitable ownership...
>
> *(Lee 1915: 99–100)*

The spread of the trust has created an efficient system of capital transfers for both individuals and corporations, realizing the project of global financial coordination begun by the British in the eighteenth and nineteenth centuries. But rather than state-led coordination, the system is tied together by "globalized localisms" (Jensen and Santos 2000) like the Anglo-American trust.

It is particularly noteworthy that in the past few decades – coinciding with the rise of financialization – the trust has been formally recognized and even adopted into law by countries that were never part of the British Empire. The recognition of trusts by states that have not adopted the Common Law regime has been driven by the pressure of private and corporate capital seeking "new global circuits of accumulation" (Robinson 2001: 173). Though most new wealth is being generated outside of Europe and North America, much of it returns to trusts based in the UK and the former territories of the British Empire: "Eastern Europe, the Middle East, North Africa and Russia are all areas of political instability and/or high liquidity...they are therefore key markets for wealth-management services...whichever market we're talking about, there's invariably a London connection" (Marr 2014: 75; see also White 2014). In other words, most of the world's wealth passes through London at some point to benefit from wealth management services, in which the creation and management of trusts play a significant role (Harrington 2016). In this sense, trusts have been instrumental in driving the financialization of the British economy, as well as disseminating the Anglo-American model of finance worldwide.

Autonomy of Finance from the Nation-state.

As Van der Zwan (2014: 100) has observed, financialization is characterized in part by the increasing autonomy of finance from the political economy of nation-states. If state power consists in its ability to tax effectively (Goldstone 1991; Li 2002), then trusts have long posed a significant threat to that power, enabling wealth to transcend the nation-state system entirely. This has occurred via two key mechanisms: fortifying the "shroud of secrecy" (Shaxson 2011: 42) surrounding trusts, and creating hypermobility for trusts and the capital they contain (Beaverstock et al. 2004). Through these two means, trusts have been used to advance a far more ambitious agenda than tax avoidance (Harrington 2016). In effect, they have enabled finance practitioners and capital to escape the "sovereign national cage" (Palan 2002: 168).

Concurrent with the rise of financialization, the late twentieth century "saw a flowering in discretionary trusts intended to make the beneficial owners of trusts unidentifiable, so that no-one will owe taxes on those assets and no-one's creditors will be able to collect their debts therefrom" (Hofri 2015: 43). These structures – also known as asset protection trusts – make it difficult, if not impossible, to subject trusts or their beneficiaries to state power: that is, to enforce tax obligations or accountability to creditors, heirs and litigants. Trusts explicitly designed to thwart such obligations were pioneered by the Cook Islands, a remote jurisdiction in the South Pacific, in their 1989 International Trusts Act. Among other things, this Act states that assets held in Cook Islands trusts will not be subject to any judgment by a foreign court, and cannot be accessed for punitive damages or payments to creditors. In effect, this puts such trusts "outside the rule of law" (Wayne 2013a).

These trusts are designed not just for tax avoidance, but for *law* avoidance in general. Providing firms and wealthy individuals with freedom from state power has proved to be a highly successful (and highly lucrative) strategy. To date, no effort to break a Cook Islands trust – despite numerous attempts by the US government, among other powerful states – has been successful. Meanwhile, the six registered trust companies in the Cook Islands generate 8 percent of the island's $300 million GDP, after tourism and ahead of fishing (Wayne 2013b). To compete for their own share of these fees, at least 25 other countries have followed the Cook Islands in creating asset protection trust legislation of their own.

As this example suggests, the laws pertaining to trusts serve mainly to protect the structures and their beneficiaries. In contrast, few laws – if any – exist to protect the public interest from the use of trusts, even when it comes to preventing them from being used to facilitate money laundering and corruption (Hofri 2015). Trusts' increasingly global recognition allows capital to move quickly and conveniently across borders; so while the law may have a long arm, trusts can easily slip through its fingers. The modern instantiation of the trust for asset protection is thus "an innovation that allows actors to greatly minimize, if not fully escape, centralized country laws, in favor of alternative legal systems" (Quack 2007: 643).

This increasing autonomy of capital relative to the law exemplifies the "declining ability of the national state to intervene in the process of capital accumulation...[and] the newfound power that transnational capital acquired over nation-states" (Robinson 2001: 169). This chapter extends that insight by specifying the trust as a means by which capital becomes transnational and financialization expands globally. While those who downplay the rise of finance worldwide often point to the lack of formal coordination among states, or what Krippner diplomatically terms "the rather limited extent to which international economic integration is in evidence" (2005: 202). But exploitation of this fragmented system is crucial to the growing power of financialization. This suggests that those who doubt the ascendancy of global finance vis-à-vis states (Krippner calls them "globalization skeptics") may be looking in the wrong place for the "new world order." It has not taken the form of an international "super state" to govern global finance, but of a set of practices – such as the private and corporate use of trusts – that exploit and thrive on the divisions in the old Westphalian order.

Discussion

Trusts provide a legal structure enabling financialization to spread and consolidate power globally. Unlike corporations, trusts are private arrangements: as a result, they are free from public registration and most of the regulatory burden imposed on firms. In a political economy characterized by growing market regulation (Seabrooke 2011), trusts inhabit a distinctive space that resists transparency and governance. Although they have been largely overlooked in the scholarly literature, trusts offer unusual benefits in terms of secrecy, flexibility, profit maximization, and ease of international mobility.

Over centuries, trusts have evolved to meet the changing demands of private and corporate capital. Indeed, what Braudel once observed of capitalism – that it persists due to "its unlimited flexibility, its capacity for change and *adaptation*" (1992: 433, emphasis in original) – could equally well be said of the trust structure. It has mutated from its origins as a device for holding title to landed wealth to become a vehicle for active investment in securities, making it a mainstay of contemporary asset protection and structured finance (Langbein 1995).

However, one distinctive feature of trusts has remained unchanged over 700 years: the concept of divided ownership. The notion of detaching the benefits from the responsibilities of owning property makes possible many of the trust's legal "tricks" (Moffat 2009). It also provided a ready-made tool to serve the interests of financialization: when capital mobility was on the rise (Arrighi 1994), trusts were there to facilitate nearly frictionless international asset transfers; when new sources of profit maximization were sought (Krippner 2011) trusts offered a distinctive way to cut tax and regulatory compliance costs. Trusts did not create financialization, but rather coincided with it, accelerating its spread as a global phenomenon.

It achieved this in three ways: by contributing to the economic centrality of investors; by representing and facilitating the imprint of the Anglo-American tradition on finance; and by providing financial actors and assets with greater autonomy from the nation-state system. As detailed in the previous sections, these consequences stemmed from an iterative series of modifications in international law and the trust structure itself, in response to the demands of capital. These modifications began soon after the rise of financialization in the late 1970s, and continue to the present day, exemplifying the "great elasticity and generality" (Maitland 1936: 129) that allowed trusts to endure long past their origins in the Middle Ages (Harrington 2012b, 2016).

Notes

1 This chapter is an abridged version of an article originally published under the same title in *Socio-Economic Review* 15 (1).
2 Here, "person" can refer either to a natural person (a human being) or a legal person, such as a corporation.
3 A body of law has arisen to protect the interest of beneficiaries to trusts. Trustees are legally bound to manage the assets in the best interests of the beneficiaries, and to distribute any proceeds of those assets according to the instructions set out when the trust was founded. Trustees are forbidden from using or benefitting from the assets in any way.
4 Beneficiaries *are* liable to pay tax on the distributions they receive from trusts, but there are many ways to make those distributions tax-free – for example, by labelling them as "loan repayments" to the beneficiaries.
5 This power to move the *situs* of the trust must be specifically stated in the trust instrument – the document that sets out the blueprint for the trust. This power, known as a "flee clause," is commonly included in contemporary trust instruments, particularly for offshore use.
6 Those familiar with American history may find this confusing, since in the late nineteenth and early twentieth centuries, much public policy was focused on "trust busting." However, this term was a misnomer in that it actually referred to corporate monopolies, some of which – like Standard Oil – used trusts as part of their structure. Despite the terminology, the policy agenda was not set against trusts *per se*, but rather against the monopolies (Dudden 1957).
7 See note 3.
8 Specifically, this involves using Wolff's (2012) findings on the percentage of assets held in trust by the top 10 percent of US households, then combining them with estimates from Saez and Zucman (2016) on the total number of those households in the top 10 percent, and the average wealth of those households, excluding their primary residences (this is standard for estimations of net worth). Saez and Zucman draw from the same data source as Wolff (the US Survey of Consumer Finances), but add data from the Forbes 400 survey of America's wealthiest families. Since the Survey of Consumer Finances is known to under-represent those wealthy families (Kennickell 2009), this additional dataset enables Saez and Zucman to create a more accurate estimate of household wealth at the top of the spectrum. However, their findings must still be combined with those of Wolff in order to estimate the total amount of private wealth held in trust by Americans, since only Wolff calculates the percentage of household wealth that is actually held in trust. While Saez and Zucman acknowledge the significance of trusts as a source of wealth, they do not split out household assets in sufficient detail to estimate what percentage of that wealth is held in trust.

Bibliography

Arrighi, G., 1994. *The Long Twentieth Century*. London: Verso.
Beaverstock, J., Hall, S. and Wainwright, T., 2013. Servicing the Super-Rich: New Financial Elites and the Rise of the Private Wealth Management Retail Ecology. *Regional Studies*, 47, pp. 843–849.
Beaverstock, J., Hubbard, P. and Short, J., 2004. Getting Away with It? Exposing the Geographies of the Super-Rich. *Geoforum*, 35, pp. 401–407.
Boston Consulting Group, 2013. *Global Wealth 2014: Riding a Wave of Growth*. Boston: BCG.
Bowers, S., 2014. Luxembourg Tax Whistleblower Says He Acted Out of Conviction. *The Guardian*, 15 December. Accessed August 28, 2015: http://www.theguardian.com/world/2014/dec/15/luxembourg-tax-avoidance-whistleblower-conviction
Braudel, F., 1992. *Civilization and Capitalism, 15th–18th Century, Vol. II: The Wheels of Commerce*. Berkeley: University of California Press.
Budría, S., Díaz-Giménez, J., Ríos-Rull, J.-V. and Quadrini, V., 2002. Updated Facts on the US Distributions of Earnings, Income, and Wealth. *Federal Reserve Bank of Minneapolis Quarterly Review*, 26, pp. 2–35.

Chancellor, E., 1999. *Devil Take the Hindmost: A History of Financial Speculation*. New York: Farrar, Straus and Giroux.

Chester, R., 1982. *Inheritance, Wealth and Society*. Bloomington, IN: Indiana University Press.

Conn, P., 2015. *Transparency of Share Ownership, Shareholder Communications, and Voting in Global Capital Markets*. Melbourne, Australia: Computershare/Georgeson.

Davies, J., Sandström, S., Shorrocks, A. and Wolff, E., 2008. The World Distribution of Household Wealth. World Institute for Development Economics Research, Discussion Paper 2008/03. Helsinki, UNI-WIDER.

Deeg, R. and O'Sullivan, M., 2009. The Political Economy of Global Finance Capital. *World Politics*, 61, pp. 731–763.

Demick, B., 1990. The 400 Richest: Many Folks Try to Stay Off List. *Philadelphia Inquirer*, 7 October.

Dodd, R. and Mills, P., 2008. Outbreak: U.S. Subprime Contagion. *Finance & Development*, June, pp. 14–18.

Dudden, A., 1957. Men Against Monopoly: The Prelude to Trust-Busting. *Journal of the History of Ideas*, 18, 587–593.

Economist, 2013. Trawling for Business: The Gambia Looks to Join a Beleaguered Club. *Economist*, August 24. Accessed December 10, 2014: http://www.economist.com/news/finance-and-economics/21584019-gambia-looks-join-beleaguered-club-trawling-business

Fitch, S., 2003. Pritzker vs. Pritzker. *Forbes*, November 24.

Franklin, M., 1933. Administrative Law in the United States. *Tulane Law Review*, 19, pp. 473–506.

Gauthier-Villars, D. and Ball, D., 2010. Mass Leak of Client Data Rattles Swiss Banking. *Wall Street Journal*, 8 July. Accessed August 28, 2015: http://www.wsj.com/articles/SB10001424052748704629804575324510662164360.

Goldstone, J., 1991. *Revolution and Rebellion in the Early Modern World*. Berkeley: University of California Press.

Guinto, J., 2013. Sam Wyly's $550 Million Problem. *D Magazine*, February. Accessed July 14, 2014: http://www.dmagazine.com/publications/d-magazine/2013/february/sam-wyly-fight-to-keep-family-fortune?single=1.

Harrington, B., 2008 *Pop Finance: Investment Clubs and Stock Market Populism*. Princeton, NJ: Princeton University Press.

Harrington, B., 2012a. The Sociology of Financial Fraud. In Knorr-Cetina, K. and Preda, A. (eds.), *The Oxford Handbook of the Sociology of Finance*. New York: Oxford University Press, pp. 393–410.

Harrington, B., 2012b. From Trustees to Wealth Managers. In Erreygers, G. and Cunliffe, J. (eds.), *Inherited Wealth, Justice, and Equality*. London: Routledge, pp. 190–209.

Harrington, B., 2016. *Capital without Borders: Wealth Management and the One Percent*. Cambridge, MA: Harvard University Press.

Hall, P., 1973. *Family Structure and Class Consolidation Among the Boston Brahmins*. Ph.D. diss., State University of New York, Stony Brook.

Hofri, A., 2015. The Stripping of the Trust: A Study in Legal Evolution. *University of Toronto Law Journal*, 65, pp. 1–47.

Jaffe, D. and Lane, S., 2004. Sustaining a Family Dynasty: Key Issues Facing Multi-Generational Business- and Investment-Owning Families. *Family Business Review*, 17, pp. 5–18.

Jenson, J. and Santos, B., 2000. Introduction: Case Studies and Common Trends in Globalizations. In J. Jenson and B. Santos (eds.), *Globalizing Institutions: Case Studies in Regulation and Innovation*. Aldershot, UK: Ashgate, pp. 9–26.

Kennickell, A., 2009. Ponds and Streams: Wealth and Income in the US, 1989 to 2007. Federal Reserve Board Finance and Economics Discussion Series, Washington, DC: Federal Reserve Board. Accessed April 12, 2012: http://www.federalreserve.gov/pubs/feds/2009/200913/200913pap.pdf.

Kolhatkar, S., 2006. Inside the Billionaire Service Industry. *The Atlantic*, September 2006.

Kopczuk, W. and Saez, E., 2004. Top Wealth Shares in the United States, 1916–2000: Evidence from Estate Tax Returns. *National Tax Journal*, 57, pp. 445–487.

Krippner, G., 2005. The Financialization of the American Economy. *Socio-Economic Review*, 3, pp. 173–208.

Krippner, G., 2011. *Capitalizing on Crisis: The Political Origins of the Rise of Finance*. Cambridge, MA: Harvard University Press.

Langbein, J., 1995. The Contractarian Basis of the Law of Trusts. *Yale Law Journal*, 105, pp. 625–675.

Langbein, J., 1997. The Secret Life of the Trust: The Trust as an Instrument of Commerce. *Yale Law Review*, 107, pp. 165–189.

Langbein, J., 2004. Rise of the Management Trust. *Trusts & Estates*, 142, pp. 52–57.

Lee, R., 1915. The Civil Law and the Common Law: A World Survey. *Michigan Law Review*, 14, 89–101.

Li, R., 2002. Alternative Routes to State Breakdown: Toward an Integrated Model of Territorial Disintegration. *Sociological Theory*, 20, pp. 1–23.

Lund, S., Daruvala, T., Dobbs, R., Härle, P., Kwek, J.-H. and Falcón, R., 2013. *Financial Globalization: Retreat or Reset?* London: McKinsey & Company.

Maitland, F., 2011 [1909]. *Equity: A Course of Lectures.* Cambridge: Cambridge University Press.

Maitland, F., 1936. *Selected Essays.* Cambridge: Cambridge University Press.

Malkiel, B., 2013. Asset Management Fees and the Growth of Finance. *Journal of Economic Perspectives*, 27, pp. 97–108.

Marr, R., 2014. Jersey: Riding the Tides of Change. *STEP Journal*, p. 75.

Moffat, G., 2009. *Trust Law: Text and Materials.* Cambridge, UK: Cambridge University Press.

Mukunda, G., 2014. The Price of Wall Street's Power. *Harvard Business Review.* Accessed January 16, 2015: https://hbr.org/2014/06/the-price-of-wall-streets-power

Palan, R., 2002. Tax Havens and the Commercialization of State Sovereignty. *International Organization*, 56, pp. 151–176.

Parkinson, M., 2004. *Certificate in International Trust Management.* Birmingham: Central Law Training.

Parkinson, M., 2005. *Diploma in International Trust Management: Trust Creation: Law and Practice, 3rd Edition.* Birmingham: Central Law Training.

Parkinson, M., 2008. *Trustee Investment and Financial Appraisal, 4th Edition.* Birmingham: Central Law Training.

Piketty, T. and Zucman, G., 2014. Capital Is Back: Wealth-Income Ratios in Rich Countries, 1700–2010. *Quarterly Journal of Economics*, 129, pp. 1255–1310.

Pinçon, M. and Pinçon-Charlot, M., 1998. *Grand Fortunes: Dynasties of Wealth in France.* New York: Algora Publishing.

Quack, S., 2007. Legal Professionals and Trans-National Law Making: A Case of Distributed Agency. *Organization*, 14, pp. 643–666.

Reid, B., 2006. *ICI Fact Book, 46th Edition.* Washington, DC: Investment Company Institute.

Robinson, W., 2001. Social Theory and Globalization: The Rise of a Transnational State. *Theory and Society*, 30, pp. 157–200.

Saez, E. and Zucman, G., 2016. Wealth Inequality in the United States since 1913: Evidence from Capitalized Income Tax Data. *Quarterly Journal of Economics*, 131, pp. 519–578.

Savchuk, K., 2014. Jury Finds Wyly Brothers Engaged in Fraud by Hiding Trades in Offshore Trusts. *Forbes*, 5 August. Accessed July 14, 2014: http://www.forbes.com/sites/katiasavchuk/2014/05/08/jurors-weigh-fraud-charges-against-wyly-brothers-accused-of-13-year-scheme-of-secrecy/.

Sayer, A., 2015. *Why We Can't Afford the Rich.* Bristol: Policy Press.

Seabrooke, L., 2011. Crisis of Confidence: International Organizations and Learning after the Financial Meltdown. *Socio-Economic Review*, 9, pp. 574–579.

Sharman, J., 2006. *Havens in a Storm: The Struggle for Global Tax Regulation.* Ithaca, NY: Cornell University Press.

Shaxson, N., 2011. *Treasure Islands: Tax Havens and the Men Who Stole the World.* London: Random House.

Sitkoff, R. and Schanzenbach, M., 2005. Jurisdictional Competition for Trust Funds: An Empirical Analysis of Perpetuities and Taxes. *Yale Law Journal*, 115, pp. 356–437.

Van der Zwan, N., 2014. Making Sense of Financialization. *Socio-Economic Review*, 12(1), pp. 99–129.

Wayne, L., 2013. Cook Islands, a Paradise of Untouchable Assets. *New York Times.* Accessed December 10, 2014: http://www.nytimes.com/2013/12/15/business/international/paradise-of-untouchable-assets.html?pagewanted=3&_r=1&pagewanted=print.

Wayne, L., 2013. Unlocking the Secrets of the Cook Islands. *International Consortium of Investigative Journalists.* Accessed December 10, 2014: http://www.icij.org/blog/2013/12/unlocking-secrets-cook-islands

White, A., 2014. Is the Luxury London Housing Bubble About to Burst? *The Telegraph.* Accessed January 19, 2015: http://www.telegraph.co.uk/finance/personalfinance/houseprices/11199948/Has-London s-luxury-housing-market-hit-its-peak.html.

Winnett, R., 2008. Northern Rock in £3bn Bailout from Taxpayer. *The Telegraph.* Accessed December 1, 2014: http://www.telegraph.co.uk/finance/newsbysector/banksandfinance/2794277/Northern-Rock-in-3bn-bail-out-from-taxpayer.html.

Wolff, E., 2012. The Asset Price Meltdown and the Wealth of the Middle Class. Working Paper 18559, National Bureau of Economic Research.

Zucman, G., 2015. *The Hidden Wealth of Nations.* Chicago, IL: University of Chicago Press.

24

IMPACT INVESTING, SOCIAL ENTERPRISE AND GLOBAL DEVELOPMENT

Dennis Stolz and Karen P.Y. Lai

Introduction

Those who partake in philanthropic activities today make use of financial means to transform traditional ways of grant-making into a profit-oriented investment process called "impact investing." Initially coming from the sphere of US philanthropy, impact investing developed into a vibrant financial market of global scale (Mudaliar, Bass, & Dithrich 2017). Over the last decade, the gradual shift of elite philanthropy into an immediate tool for profit-making had crucial consequences in practice: what was formerly a donation- or grant-based transfer of funds between a benefactor and a recipient now becomes an investment targeted at a problem. Resulting funds leverage upon what is called "social entrepreneurship."

Under social entrepreneurship, innovative and profitable business models are seen as enabling entrepreneurs to tackle social problems and generate collective public benefits. As the financial driver of this process, impact investing facilitates the production of tangible goods and services for local communities that were previously marginalized in terms of infrastructure or social service provision, in areas such as rural energy, water and sanitation, education, healthcare and social housing. Along these lines, impact investments mostly flow into for-profit ventures that supply underserved markets in remote areas. For elite philanthropists, this creates a powerful development narrative of "serving the underserved," which they employ in public communication strategies. Moreover, it induces private foundations to collaborate with development banks, agencies and regulatory authorities, especially in the Global South. The global scale of their activities requires a reliable market infrastructure and globally networked financial industry to facilitate corresponding investments in "sustainable" economic activity and "inclusive development." These proceedings coincide with the emergence of an institutional nexus, which we call the *philanthropy–finance–development complex.* [1] Among others, it includes private foundations, foreign aid and financial institutions. Together, this nexus represents a proliferating multi-billion-dollar industry (Mawdsley 2015; Gabor & Brooks 2017). In 2017, investors worldwide managed at least USD 228 billion in impact investment assets. Some 54 percent of those asset values refer to projects in the Global South, with concentrations in Oceania (3 percent), Latin America (16 percent), Africa (17 percent) and Asia (18 percent) (Mudaliar, Bass, & Dithrich 2017).

Spurred by the intensifying globalization of capital, philanthropy has gradually become ever more subjugated to "financial motives, financial markets, financial actors and financial institutions" (Epstein 2005: 3). In line with Fine's (2010) definition of financialization, we argue that "[philanthropic] activity in general has become subject to the logics and imperatives of interest-bearing capital" (p. 99). This transformation of philanthropy under financialized logics is defined as a spatial process of capital accumulation subjected to the imperatives of interest-bearing capital, in accordance with specific ideologies of development. The rest of this chapter elucidates the logics, institutional arrangements and rationales behind this transformation process, the key actors and institutions involved, and the corresponding geographical landscape produced.[2]

Spatial Dynamics of Philanthropy: From Local to Global

Philanthropy as a concept and philosophy has sparked a myriad of meanings and practices in many different geographical contexts and at different points of time. These spatially confined approaches are likewise grounded in contextually different trajectories of class building. Some trace the concept of capitalist philanthropy from proto-capitalist Italy, others date it back to seventeenth-century Europe, where wealthy aristocrats set up mutual aid societies. Thereafter, Western philanthropy gradually moved away from aristocratic *noblesse oblige* to contemporary forms of "giving" practised by the super-rich – led by people like Bill Gates or Mark Zuckerberg (Hay & Mueller 2013).

However, philanthropic giving is also deeply rooted in non-capitalist mercantile systems and religious beliefs outside the Western world. For hundreds of years, Arabic-speaking elites, for example, pursued their own version of charity and alms-giving within their local communities. Those practices are called *sadaqa* and work along archaic traditions and deep-seated beliefs. Analogous to the concept of Western charitable foundations and aid societies, Muslims created institutions like the *awqaf*, alongside specific vehicles for "doing good" called *zakat* (al-Qaradawi 1999; Carnie 2017). These practices continued to influence contemporary Islamic banking and financial products.[3] Similarly, Asian societies had designed their own rationales for philanthropic practices. In China, for instance, bridges, temples, hospitals and especially schools (due to Confucian emphasis on education, and service to family and community) were frequently built on charitable land or with the help of cash endowments set up by local elites (including nobility and business magnates). Village social welfare, such as clinics, refugee shelters or soup kitchens, was regularly paid for and administered by prominent resident households (Fuller 2010). Given these geographical variations of charity and alms-giving, and their distinct historical trajectories, it would be simplistic to assume a globally homogenized investment space of private charity in general. Established regional practices of philanthropy continue to exist, including their cultural variations. Rather, impact investing adds another intersecting global layer to those more traditional approaches, which requires mediation by international financial markets.

Both concepts, impact investing and social entrepreneurship, are American by origin and initially nurtured by the neo-liberal turn, unleashed by the Reagan administration. In the 1980s, based on the ideology that competition for private investments resulted in greater efficiency of service provision, the US government started to contract commercial non-governmental actors for providing public services. These new for-profit service providers were the first social enterprises. Henceforth, social enterprises were heralded for providing market-based opportunities for their "beneficiaries," who were otherwise excluded or disadvantaged from economic activities (Barman 2016). Spearheaded by the Rockefeller Foundation and "a group of leaders from philanthropy, finance and development" in 2007 (Rockefeller Foundation 2012: x), financing social enterprises became a global approach to facilitate a more inclusive capitalism. Praised as a potentially new "asset class" (JP Morgan 2010), impact investments flow only into those ventures that promise the production of surplus-value. Therefore, it needs the labor of real people who build, create and run hospitals, power plants and many other civil infrastructures or social services. Apart from their supposedly positive social impact those projects generate cash flows resulting from electricity bills, school fees, housing rents or medical charges – the basis for profit of enterprise and return on investment, which generates margins comparable to conventional venture capital (Brest & Born 2013).

In more general terms, the field of philanthropy cannot be grasped in isolation from the broader trends and principles that constantly re-configure the capitalist space-economy. With the intense expansion of capital and wage labor relations across the globe, philanthropy has likewise become increasingly global in scale – at least for the specific segment of the super-rich. In this context, Rothkopf (2008) proclaims the global regime of a superclass that share common values and practices while using their global linkages and monetary power to assert leverage on socio-political processes according to their wishes. Philanthropy exists as a popular device in their toolkit to create a common framework for the capitalist way of life around the world. In this vein, Warren Buffet proclaims: "There's class warfare, all right, but it's my class, the rich class, that's making war, and we're winning" (Stein 2006). Buffet put several billion dollars of his personal wealth into the Bill and Melinda Gates Foundation, while also serving as the organization's trustee. Among others, Gates and Buffet represent the apex of a group of super-rich trying to make impact investing a truly global movement (McGoey 2015). Reports such as the one in the *New York Times* fit into this picture: "Warren Buffett and Bill Gates are visiting China this week to coax commitments to charity out of their Chinese counterparts. The Americans will be in China to 'spread the word that it's good to give'" (Fuller 2010). Along these lines, the impact investing discourse speaks to a global public while seeking to "expand ethicalised finance capital into a broader social power to make subprime citizens more valuable and reconcile present risks with more desirable futures" (Kish & Leroy 2015: 635). Since the collapse of Lehman Brothers in 2008, this new form of philanthropy has become a thriving business to "reinvigorate capitalism itself" at a global scale (Porter & Kramer 2011).

Along similar lines, Short (2013) speaks about the inception of a "Second Gilded Age," as the contemporary period resembles the extreme concentration of wealth and power that was held amongst American elite clans like the Carnegies, Morgans or Vanderbilts at the turn of the twentieth century. Short's historical reference is significant since the corresponding "First Gilded Age" has had significant influence on the formation of a highly institutionalized philanthropic sector in the Western hemisphere with lasting legacy. In fact, Arrighi (1994) documents charitable activities mobilized by the *House of Medici* that trace back to the days of the fifteenth century. Similarly, Engels (1845) explains, while writing about *The Condition of the Working Class in England*:

> The English bourgeoisie is charitable out of self-interest; it gives nothing outright, but regards its gifts as a business matter, makes a bargain with the poor, saying: "If I spend this much upon benevolent institutions, I thereby purchase the right not to be troubled any further, and you are bound thereby to stay in your dusky holes and not to irritate my tender nerves by exposing your misery".
>
> *(p. 222)*

While the relationship between philanthropy and the general accumulation process has always been symbiotic, it is the subsequent degree of institutionalization and the growth of private mammoth foundations in late nineteenth-century America that gives the field a new and extremely powerful drive (McGoey 2015; Barker 2017). The most powerful private and liberal foundations in the US that emerged at that time still call the shots within the field of global philanthropy today. The basis of their power is historically grounded but correlates at the same time with both their immense financial clout and connectivity to other institutions (Harvey 2013). The New York-based Rockefeller Foundation, for example, works very closely with the bankers of JP Morgan to structure specific financial products and strategies – impact investments can include a complex mix of debt and equity (Šoštarić 2015; Encourage Capital 2017). The logic of interest-bearing capital requires distinct financial expertise to channel investments across the globe. The role of state actors is also important in shaping the philanthropy–finance–development complex. For instance, the National Bank of Cambodia recently declared to support microfinance institutions (MFI) "by offering cheap loans, lowering license fees or delaying the imposition of reserve requirements. [...] the central bank could give loans at 3 to 4 percent interest to MFIs as long as they leave a deposit in U.S. dollars or provide a guarantor" (\o "Posts by Hang Sokunthea" Sokunthea 2017).

However, seeing the market for impact investing as a monolithic field with a single power center would be misleading. Despite historical power structures dominated by US foundations, which surely play a significant role in shaping discourses about elite philanthropy, impact investing of the super-rich is highly globalized. Ultra-wealthy elites residing in Asia – such as Hong Kong, Singapore and India – are catching up in aligning their philanthropic giving with the new financialized paradigm (Šoštarić 2015). While super-rich outside the US are not able to mobilize capital for impact investments through foundations and family offices, due to regulatory constraints, they invest through their wealth management and associated private equity funds (Lombard Odier 2017). There is a developing consciousness for a new "way of giving" among the super-rich, especially amongst younger generations. One empirical example derived from a fieldwork interview in 2016 (with a financial advisor who works with Asian philanthropists) is the Yet-Sen Chen family. The industrial clan based in Hong Kong was long led by the late Robert Yet-Sen Chen, who had founded a small manufacturing empire in the 1960s (the Wahum Group). When his son James took over the business operations and opened a family foundation in the early 2000s

> he also looked on the history of the family's philanthropy. In the first two generations the wealth had gone back into China: in the building of schools and hospitals in the place where his grandfather had come from. And that is a very typical Chinese way of viewing philanthropy. It is all going back to the place of the ancestors and the founders of the company. And still that continues, today. But James, being American educated, became exposed to global philanthropy. He wanted to see that the family's philanthropy would not only continue a kind of historical track but could also find a new modern meaning. And, he set up an investment company for the family's philanthropy which could also be used to make impact investing.
> *(Interview with private impact fund manager, Singapore, January 2017)*

Although culturally diverse and spatially dissociated forms of philanthropy have existed at different points in time, different forms of philanthropy or gift-exchange have always been a vehicle controlled by ruling social elites to hold class antagonisms in check, even if the concept of "class" had developed different meanings in diverse geographical contexts (Mauss 1997). Regarding philanthropic practices, this core similarity makes it easier for the globally linked *nouveaux riches* today to create common beliefs and rationales, and to defend their class interests across borders. Thereby, their common denominator becomes the language of finance, which again correlates with the *zeitgeist*.

Impact Investing in the Era of Financialization: Social Entrepreneurship and Impact Investing

Founded in the Indian province of Bihar, the start-up company and so-called social enterprise Husk Power Systems (HPS) have installed 84 mini-power plants since 2012. The internationally trained engineers and founders of Husk – Charles Ransler and Gyanesh Pandey – had developed a proprietary engine running on a methane-like gas released by heating rice husks. While villagers traditionally have used agricultural waste for heating in the past, it has not been common for electricity generation. Initially, they planned to construct a small number of generators for providing electricity to a few villages. However, the technology offered their company immense growth potential, as such husks – a waste product of rice milling – are plentiful in those villages. Today, HPS uses their incinerators to provide energy to more than 200,000 people spread across 300 townships. By 2020, Husk seeks to supply electricity to more than 10 million villagers all over rural India. Beyond selling the use value of electricity, the company plans to generate further profits in the global market for carbon credits (i.e. earnings from emission savings) by selling credit surplus (Revkin 2008). The latter phenomenon points to the intersection with financialized global climate policies and nature conservation approaches (Dempsey & Suarez 2016).

Such social enterprises purportedly create a significant positive social impact for their employees and local communities, as proclaimed by Husk Power Systems (2015) on their corporate website:

> Each plant serves around 400 households, saving approximately 42,000 litres of kerosene and 18,000 litres of diesel per year, significantly reducing indoor air pollution and improving health conditions [...] HPS promotes economic development by enabling businesses to stay open after dark and allowing children to study at night. [...] Additionally, it creates employment through its livelihood programme [...] which largely employs women. This enables sustainable development within the communities HPS serves.

Impact investing's underlying concept of reconciliation between market and morals is powerful, but not entirely new, as it conveys a post-modernized interpretation of Adam Smith's invisible hand vis-à-vis the moral sentiments of market exchange (Smith 2002 [1790]). It seems that for new philanthropists, "the market and social responsibility are not opposites, but can be reunited for mutual benefit [...] their goal is not to earn money, but to change the world (and as a by-product, make even more money)" (Zizek 2006).

In public, tech-billionaires like Bill Gates appear as leaders for the impact investment movement and the global financial industry arising from it. They make use of their private foundations and family offices, but also operate through specialized fund vehicles affiliated to private wealth managements of major investment banks. Unlike traditional foundations of the late nineteenth century which pursued a practice of pure grant-making, today's super-rich see themselves as social financiers, or more technically speaking, as *impact investors*. By harnessing the logic of capital, they transform the act of philanthropic giving into a profit-oriented investment process. The projected surge of impact investment assets would offer potential profits between USD 183 and 667 billion (JP Morgan 2010) as successful social enterprises easily achieve between 20–30 percent return on investment. Husk is an attractive example for these growth fantasies: between 2008 and 2011, the London-based Shell Foundation provided four rounds of seed-funding for research and development, pilot projects, expansion and worker's training. Furthermore, several specialized funds – like Acumen (New York) or LGT Venture

Philanthropy (Zurich and Singapore) – added loan capital that totalled USD 1.65 million. In 2010, Husk raised a further USD 1.25 million from the International Financial Corporation (IFC), followed by another USD 5 million fund from different other investment vehicles in 2012. Such growth projections even prompted Husk's management to aspire towards a listing on the Indian stock exchange (Brest & Born 2013).

A Global Institutional Landscape: The Philanthropy–Finance–Development Complex

The orchestration of hegemonic ideas among capitalist elites unfolds not as free-floating but requires mediating institutions. In the field of impact investing, these key actors include private foundations, development agencies, private investment and development banks, incubators and fund vehicles. Such institutions operate on various scales and are organized territorially, while their actions correspondingly define a specific sphere of political influence. Banks like JP Morgan and development agencies like USAID, for instance, operate at a global scale, which require them to establish office locations in metropolitan cores all around the globe – in New York, Singapore or New Delhi.

Private foundations and philanthropists, such as Rockefeller, then co-operate with those global actors forming what we call a "philanthropy–finance–development complex" (Gabor & Brooks 2017). The global governance of impact investments implies a dense web of institutions producing a distinctive geographical landscape and corporatist forms of organization, alongside entrepreneurial and financialized modes of action (Harvey 2001). While traditional philanthropy was exclusively based on money from foundations and other forms of charity, impact investments get leverage from two further groups of financiers: firstly, so-called Development Finance Institititions (DFIs), especially from Europe (KfW, Norfund, SIFEM); and secondly, a group of commercial private equity financiers (ResponsAbility, Sequoia Capital etc.) who receive the lion's share of their funding from private wealth managers working for the private banking industry (e.g. BNP Parisbas, Development Bank Singapore, Lombard Odier, UBS etc.). The latter tap into the savings of other high net worth clients (see Harrington in this volume) around the globe, which is why impact investing becomes also popular among the super-rich in Asia, Europe and Latin America. The corresponding diversity of funding streams adds institutional complexity to the field. At once, financial complexity goes hand in hand with *geographical* intricacy which makes impact investing a truly global movement.

This coalition of financial and development institutions spreads impact investments, as well as associated ideas and rationales, globally. In this vein, they create the new "asset class": to deliver investment support to small firms in developing countries as a new financial instrument, which in their eyes provides an "optimal solution to social problems through the construction of a new organisational field" (Barman 2016: 198). A telling statement from Judith Rodin, who was until recently the long-standing president of the Rockefeller Foundation, emphasises these global ambitions. Rodin herself deeply embodies the nexus between US finance and philanthropy. Before working for Rockefeller, she served on the board of directors for Citibank and Blackrock:

> We recognised, if you put a price tag on all the social and environmental needs around the world, it is in the trillions. All of the philanthropy in the world is only $590 billion. So, the needs far exceed the resources. The one place where there are hundreds of trillions of dollars is in the private capital markets.
>
> *(Rodin, cited in Kozlowski 2012)*

In concrete terms, these institutional networks define a set of universal practices, principles and norms (such as social entrepreneurship or social impact) which thereafter guide their actions and communication with each other. It is through this institutional perspective that one can fully grasp how impact investments link small farmers in rural India to the boardrooms of corporate foundations in New York, the corridors of the World Economic Forum at Davos and business incubators in Mumbai.

The execution of those ideas and their usage towards the actual production of space are operationalized though particular actors – the bureaucrats, development aides, bankers etc. The combined action of multiple human microforces and their social interaction through forms of exchange create systemic institutional power, correlating spatial effects and symbolic meaning (Kohn 2003). In times of financialization, these concrete actions are increasingly framed and driven by financial motives and rationales. At once, one cannot isolate the horizontal field of social interaction from more vertical institutional structures and overarching discourses, which create a transcending space of common beliefs and values. A key example for this process in the field is the popularization of the "social enterprise" concept. Around the same time when neoliberalism became popular as a political project, the social enterprise concept was created by William "Bill" Drayton in 1980. Drayton was a political advisor to US president Carter and a great advocate of market-based governance. He founded Ashoka, a non-profit think-tank headquartered in Washington, which became a very influential global networking platform promoting social entrepreneurship by affiliating social entrepreneurs to the Ashoka organization. One of the most prominent Ashoka fellows is Nobel Prize Laureate and microfinance-pioneer Muhammad Yunus. The microfinance industry has played a crucial role in the advancement towards impact investing in developing countries in recent years, particularly since the first of those investments had financial inclusion as a central theme (Roy 2010). Following Drayton, the social enterprise approach became further popularized by Klaus Schwab, a pioneer of the World Economic Forum, while over time philanthropists started gradually diversifying their portfolios beyond microfinance and into other sectors.

Another key group of actors are elite executives associated with the financial boom of venture capital. Their experiences significantly shaped the newly emerging model for philanthropy which has gained steam since the 1990s. Coming from their venture capital world, super-rich from finance and tech companies initially found it difficult to do philanthropy. They could not understand it through the habitual framework of doing business; as a result, they were trying to interpret philanthropy through their venture capital model. Their involvement in philanthropic activities led to a process model that looks like a conventional venture capital investment which creates powerful debt-relationships between investors and investees (Figure 24.1). They create specialized funds to channel money into social enterprises, help them grow, and then sell those companies while making a return to the investors and themselves. The underlying investment cycle splits up technically into two major processes: an early stage seed-funding and incubation phase (termed "venture philanthropy") and a growth investment, which strives to scale up and is branded with the more popular term "impact investing."

In concrete social practice, this model unfolds and translates into a specific investment process, with different institutions clustering around it, demonstrating how the philanthropy–finance–development complex works on the ground. At the beginning of the cycle, foundations like Rockefeller or Gates consult their bank managers, like those of JP Morgan. The bank selects a fund product for the investor, while the fund vehicle itself collects the money from the investor via the bank and channels it – as interest-bearing capital – into a peculiar portfolio of social enterprises. The investors can thereby choose among different sectors, regions and rates of profitability. In this way, they create a specific balance between "social impact" and financial returns.

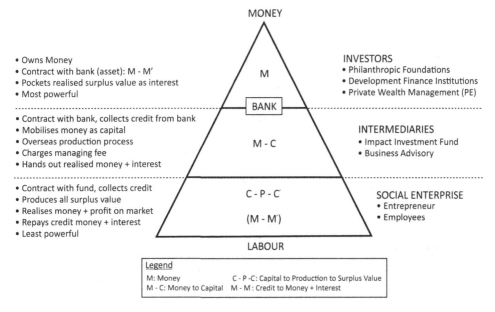

Figure 24.1 Impact Investing in Practice – An Institutional Model
Source: The authors

On the ground, business intelligence agencies or advisors serve as business consultants to social enterprises. Those advisors are important middlemen in the field. They speak the language of finance of investors and fund managers, and also understand the concerns of laboring social entrepreneurs and their employees, so they can translate between both parties. These business intelligence advisors open bank accounts, file relevant paper work, deal with courts and civil administrations, oversee the money flows between funds and enterprises, and give concrete advice to business activities – all in close dialogue with the fund management to assure returns on investment.

Private foundations play another important role in the field. Apart from being major investors themselves, the most powerful among them also invest into the institutional infrastructure of the market, especially into fund vehicles and network platforms. One such example is the Impact Investment Exchange (IIX) based in Singapore. This organization is officially funded by the Bangladeshi Durreen Shahnaz, one of many investment-banker-turned-social-entrepreneurs from New York (John et al. 2013: 119). However, half of the IIX operational costs are covered by the Rockefeller Foundation and other Wall Street organizations. Among a whole range of structured instruments to finance social enterprises, IIX is developing a so-called Impact Exchange. Like a conventional stock exchange, this platform is supposed to provide liquidity for investors through the listing, trading, clearing and settlement of "impact securities" (ibid.). Today, IIX is one of the most important fund vehicles facilitating impact investments in Southeast Asia. Figure 24.2 shows how the interest-bearing capital of investors (such as foundations or development banks) flows into fund vehicles, which are supported by business intelligence (such as incubators and consultancy firms), to feed into the formation and operations of social enterprises on the ground.

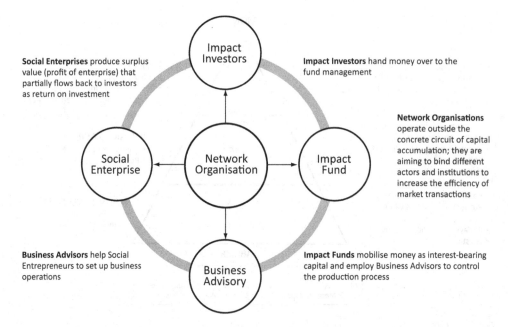

Figure 24.2 The Investment Process
Source: The authors

Impact Investing and the Tale of Global Development

Under the mask of global philanthropy, there is capital's powerful drive to create another "world after its own image" (Marx & Engels 1969 [1848]: 16). In the words of Bill Gates:

> [C]orporations have the skills to make technological innovations work for the poor [...] We need a more creative capitalism: an attempt to stretch the reach of market forces so that more companies can benefit from doing work that makes more people better off. We need new ways to bring far more people into the system – capitalism –that has done so much good in the world.
>
> *(cited in Roy 2010: 25–26)*

As one of the world's leading western philanthropists, Gates' remarks are a homage to the power and functionality of capital. For impact investors, the employment of finance capital creates the only effective opportunity to free people at the bottom of the pyramid from their assumed impoverishment and misery. Emanating from their own style and standard of living, impact investors claim that their funds facilitate the repeal of social inequality by stimulating entrepreneurial activity of social enterprise across the globe, while creating opportunities of wage labor and livelihood development for related communities of local consumers (JP Morgan 2010; Bugg-Levine & Emerson 2011; Rockefeller Foundation 2012). In this vein, the investor defines what poverty and development are.

This capitalist idea of development implies that notions like (women's) empowerment, poverty, and sustainability are always associated with the possession and profit-seeking usage of money. They are thus relentlessly drenched with the idea of capitalism as the only viable and desirable way of life.

This is also reflected in the way "social impact" is ultimately measured and quantified by specialized data providers who report to fund managers and investors.

> What is the change created in their lives, how many of them got jobs later, how much did their income increase, were they able to save money? [...] So that in the end of the day you can tell every investor, for every dollar you invest you are making, let's say 5 dollars of social impact. Out of these 5 dollars there are many ways to cut that and to understand. You can say 3 dollars go towards impacting women and 2 towards men.
> *(Personal interview with business intelligence firm, Singapore, June 2016)*

In this view, "underdevelopment" – especially in the Global South – accordingly stems from an insufficient integration into the world market and money-based systems of production and consumption. From the subaltern perspective, however, local communities in rural or "less integrated" geographies of the Global South had always lived their autonomous methods of "development," which are nonetheless often vanquished by capitalism. Along these lines, local communities have usually endured hundreds of years of other forms of exploitation, extraction and colonial rule. However, at least for very remote places money had no or only little use value for the people populating them. Or, to recall another intriguing statement from an interviewee in India:

> Many of the rural and informal economies in India, they are not run by cash, they have barter systems. So, everyone from outside thinks they will die – but nobody dies.
> *(Personal interview with social business advisor, Mumbai, February 2017)*

By employing the imperial force of money as capital, impact investments create an uneven power relationship between investors, investees and broader local communities. Once in operation, the monetary social bond, woven by processes of market exchange, gives investors the ability to control. This capacity emerges from the growing significance of (relational) value for those societies and their social reproduction process. When money further penetrates the social fabric of these concrete communities, it ultimately starts to shape their inner social relations.[4] As such, investors hold monopolized control over the "thing" now driving the reproduction process – money – which creates a new form of dependency (see also Bateman 2010; Mader 2015). Henceforth, social entrepreneurs and their employees need to offer their labor power in exchange for money to survive. In turn, their labor must yield a profit for the investor.

> Once you are supported by an investor-backed fund, you are not working anymore for yourself. Because frankly speaking, my quality of life was better five years ago [before the investor came in]. Now I am always scared: "what if you only grow by 10 to 15 percent?" When an investor is sitting there, then you must grow and spend money also. If you do not spend money you might not grow. It is a risk. But that is the reason. Because you are loaded up with so much risk. Either you go up or you crash. [...] My quality of life was better before [laughing loudly] and I had much less risk. I never mortgaged my house. Now I mortgaged my house twice!
> *(Personal interview with social entrepreneur, New Delhi, December 2016)*

Conclusion

Impact investing originates from the United States of America and could only emerge from a specific historical and regulatory context. Since the 1980s, financial expansion on a world scale has coincided with the trans-nationalization of Western capital and power networks under US control (Arrighi 1994; Van der Pijl 1984). The mindset and practice of US foundations to use their philanthropic monies in a profitable way on a global scale – especially regarding strata of the super-rich – is part of this general development. Philanthropy has always been "an appendage" of the general accumulation process. Only those who accumulated significant amounts of wealth in the past, can afford to spend it on "gifts for public benefit" in the future. However, the increasing influence of financialization upon the formation of social relations across time and space has had huge consequences for the elite discourse about "giving" and charity as well. By law, public and private foundations in the US are required to direct only 5 percent of their financial endowments to their charitable mission. The remaining 95 percent is usually invested in conventional financial markets to accrue high financial returns. Impact investing should eventually enable foundations to switch from using this 95 percent in regular stock markets, towards profit-orientated investments in enterprises and projects that create positive social and environmental impacts (Barman 2016; Hummels & de Leede 2014).

Today, more and more super-rich US philanthropists believe that impact investing – the profit-seeking allocation of their endowments – caters a growing recognition that "existing resources are insufficient to address severe poverty, inequality, environmental destruction and other complex, *global issues*" (Rockefeller Foundation 2012, emphasis added). The Global South thus became a major target for impact investors across the world. In their efforts to spur positive socio-economic change and development around the globe, those philanthropists are supported by development finance institutions and private equity funds. The latter tap into the wealth of other super-rich in Asia, Europe and Latin America, which makes impact investing a truly global movement. All those different funding streams flow into specialized "impact funds" whose managers operationalize the actual impact investment process by communicating and surveiling the labor process of social entepreneurs. Together, all these institutions have built the *philanthropy–finance–development* complex.

Today, the global governance of impact investments form a dense web of institutional layers producing a distinctive geographical landscape and corporatist forms of institutional organization, alongside entrepreneurial and financialized modes of action. This form of philanthropic giving has major political-economic impact; in many countries the Gates Foundation is among the biggest economic forces with incredible power to leverage the policy of the nation-state – inevitably towards deeper integration into global financial networks and financial logics. Freeing "the poor" from their impoverishment and developing their livelihoods towards the world of capital creates new financial logics, relationships and structures. Such financialized modes of "giving" emphasise individual enterprise and freedom (especially in terms of economic and social impacts) but conceal the inherent inequalities of such arrangements. "A world of individuality and freedom on the surface conceals a world of conformity and coercion underneath" (Harvey 1985: 2). Along these lines, impact investing is about to create a "world after its own image" – as another world of structural dependency develops between rich and poor vis-à-vis capital and labor.

Notes

1 Our terminology is inspired by Gabor & Brooks (2017), but while they refer to a "fintech–philanthropy–development complex" and focus on a technological aspect of impact investing, we refer to philanthropy–finance–development complex as an institutional frame.
2 Our analysis is based on 30 in-depth qualitative interviews with elite practitioners (such as social entrepreneurs, consultants, impact fund managers, and impact investors) in New York, Singapore, Mumbai and New Delhi conducted in 2016 and 2017.

3   Although the intersections of Islamic banking and finance with Western neoliberal market structures are creating more complex product characteristics and market features (see Pollard & Samers 2007; Lai & Samers 2017).

4   The subsequent scale of social change is dependent on specific historical trajectories, which define how new monetary activities are negotiated and hybridize with already existing cultural practices and traditional values.

Bibliography

al-Qaradawi, Y., 1999. *Fiqh az-zakat: A Comparative Study: The Rules, Regulations and Philosophy of Zakat in the Light of the Qur'an and Sunna*. London: Dar Al Taqwa.

Arrighi, G., 1994. *The Long Twentieth Century: Money, Power, and the Origins of Our Times*. London: Verso.

Barker, M., 2017. *Under the Mask of Philanthropy*. Leicester: Hextail Press.

Barman, E., 2016. *Caring Capitalism. The Meaning and Measure of Social Value*. Boston: Cambridge University Press.

Bateman, M., 2010. *Why Doesn't Microfinance Work?: The Destructive Rise of Local Neoliberalism*. London: Zed.

Birla, R., 2009. *Stages of Capital: Law, Culture, and Market Governance in Late Colonial India*. Durham: Duke University Press.

Bishop, M. and Green, M., 2008. *Philanthrocapitalism. How Giving Can Save The World*. London: Bloomsbury Press.

Brest, P. and Born, K., 2013. *Unpacking the Impact in Impact Investing*. Available at https://tinyurl.com/yc5kldyp [Accessed February 2, 2019].

Bugg-Levine, A. and Emerson, J., 2011. *Impact Investing. Transforming How We Make Money While Making a Difference*. New Jersey: Wiley.

Callahan, D., 2017. *The Givers. Wealth, Power, and Philanthropy in a New Gilded Age*. New York: Alfred A. Knopf.

Carnie, C., 2017. *How Philanthropy Is Changing in Europe*. Chicago: University of Chicago Press.

Dempsey, J. and Suarez, D.C., 2016. Arrested development? The promises and paradoxes of "selling nature to save it", *Annals of the American Association of Geographers*, 106(3), pp. 653–671.

Encourage Capital, 2017. *Investing for Sustainable Global Fisheries*. New York: Encourage Capital.

Engels, F., 1845. *Condition of the Working Class in England*. Leipzig: Otto Wigand.

Epstein, G., 2005. Introduction: Financialization and the world economy. In G. Epstein (ed.). *Financialization and the World Economy*. Cheltenham: Edward Elgar, pp. 3–16.

Fine, B., 2010. Locating financialization. *Historical Materialism*, 18(2), pp. 97–116.

Fuller, P., 2010. China's charitable past. *The New York Times*. Available at https://tinyurl.com/2b9urc6 [Accessed February 2, 2019].

Gabor, D. and Brooks, S., 2017. The digital revolution in financial inclusion: International development in the fintech era. *New Political Econony*, 22(4), pp. 423–436.

Harvey, D., 1985. *Consciousness and the Urban Experience*. Oxford: Basil Blackwell.

Harvey, D., 2001. *Spaces to Capital: Towards a Critical Geography*. New York: Routledge.

Harvey, D., 2006 [1982]. *Limits to Capital*. London: Verso.

Harvey, D., 2013. *A Companion to Marx's Capital. Volume 2*. London: Verso.

Hay, I. and Mueller, S., 2013. Questioning generosity in the golden age of philanthropy: Towards critical geographies of super-philanthropy. *Progress in Human Geography*, 38(5), pp. 635–653.

Hummels, H. and de Leede, M., 2014. The emergence of impact investments: The case of microfinance. In C. Louche and T. Hebb (eds.), *Socially Responsible Investment in the 21st Century: Does it Make a Difference for Society?*Bingley: Emerald Group Publishing Limited, pp. 91–115.

Husk Power Systems, 2015. Community impact. Available at https://tinyurl.com/y9s49ng8 [Accessed February 2, 2019].

John, R., Chia, A. and Ito, K., 2013. *Corporate Philanthropy in Asia. Innovations that Unlock the Resources of Business for the Common Good*. Singapore: Asia Centre for Social Entrepreneurship & Philanthropy.

JP Morgan, 2010. *Impact Investments. An Emerging Asset Class*. New York: JP Morgan Global Research and The Rockefeller Foundation.

Kish, Z. and Leroy, J., 2015. Bonded life. *Cultural Studies*, 29(5–6), pp. 530–551.

Kohn, M., 2003. *Radical Space. Building the House of the People*. London: Cornell University Press.

Kozlowski, L., 2012. Impact investing: The power of two bottom lines. [Online] Available at: https://www.forbes.com/sites/lorikozlowski/2012/10/02/impact-investing-the-power-of-two-bottom-lines/#3b8fec061edc [Accessed April 9, 2018].

Lai, K. and Samers, M., 2017. Conceptualising Islamic Banking and Finance: A comparison of its development and governance in Malaysia and Singapore. *The Pacific Review*, 30(4), pp. 405–424.

Lombard Odier, 2017. *Next Gen Impact Investing Survey*. Hongkong and Singapore: Lombard Odier.

Mader, P., 2015. *The Political Economy of Microfinance: Financializing Poverty*. Basingstoke: Palgrave MacMillan.

Marx, K., 2009 [1867]. *Das Kapital. Kritik der Politischen Ökonomie*. Cologne: Anaconda.

Marx, K. and Engels, F., 1969 [1848]. The Communist Manifesto. In F. Engels, *Marx/Engels Selected Works*. Moscow: Progress Publishers, pp. 98–137.

Mauss, M., 1997. *The Gift. The Form and Reason for Exchange in Archaic Societies*. London: Routledge.

Mawdsley, E., 2015. DFID, the private sector and the re-centring of an economic growth agenda in international development. *Gobal Society*, 29(3), pp. 339–358.

McGoey, L., 2015. *No Such Thing as a Free Gift*. London: Verso.

Mudaliar, A., Bass, R. and Dithrich, H., 2017. *Annual Impact Investor Survey 2018*. New York: GIIN.

Pollard, J. and Samers, M., 2007. Islamic banking and finance: Postcolonial political economy and the decentering of economic geography. *Transactions of the Institute of British Geographers*, 32(3), pp. 313–330. doi:10.1111/j.1475-5661.2007.00255.x.

Porter, M.E., and Kramer, M.R., 2011. Creating shared value. *Harvard Business Review*, 89(1/2), pp. 62–77.

Revkin, A., 2008. Husk Power for India . *The New York Times*. Available at https://tinyurl.com/ydbmq5lv [Accessed February 2, 2019].

Rockefeller Foundation, 2012. Accelerating impact. Achievements, challenges and what's next in building the impact investing industry. Available at https://tinyurl.com/y8635ojx [Accessed February 2, 2019].

Rothkopf, D., 2008. *Superclass: The Global Power Elite and the World They Are Making*. New York: Farrar, Straus and Giroux.

Roy, A., 2010. *Poverty Capital. Microfinance and the Making of Development*. New York: Routledge.

Short, J., 2013. Economic wealth and political power in the second Gilded Age. Establishing geographies of the super-rich: Axes for analysis of abundance. In I. Hay (ed.), *Geographies of the Super-Rich*. Cheltenham: Edward Elgar, pp. 26–42.

Smith, A., 2002 [1790]. *The Theory of Modern Sentiment*. Cambridge: Cambridge University Press.

Sokunthea, H., 2017. Central Bank agrees to help microfinance institutions, MFIs say. *The Cambodia Daily*. Available at https://tinyurl.com/yddgu9gx [Accessed February 2, 2019].

Šoštarić, M., 2015. *Singapore, the Impact Investing Hub of Asia. A Comparison with Hong Kong*. Singapore: Lien Centre for Social Innovation.

Stein, B., 2006. In class warfare, guess which class is winning. *The New York Times*. Available at https://www.nytimes.com/2006/11/26/business/yourmoney/26every.html [Accessed September 13, 2019].

Van der Pijl, K., 1984. *The Making of an Atlantic Ruling Class*. London: Verso.

Zizek, S., 2006. The Liberal Communists of Porto Davos. *The Times*. Available at https://tinyurl.com/y9bpcq2c [Accessed February 2, 2019].

25

MICRO-CREDIT AND THE FINANCIALIZATION OF LOW-INCOME HOUSEHOLDS

Felipe González

Introduction

Households came to participate in the financialization of the economy and society by increasingly relying on all sorts of financial instruments to carry their material and cultural reproduction. Mortgages, student loans, credit cards, consumer loans, insurances, and the like, became part of the everyday life of ordinary citizens, in a way that scholars described as the "democratization of finance" (Erturk, Froud, Johal, Leaver and Williams 2007). This chapter deals with a specific aspect of the financialization of households worldwide: the extension of multiple forms of micro-credits to low-income populations.

This financialization of households came about from a restructuration of the political economies in both the advanced and developing economies (Bonizzi 2013). Corporations developed skills to raise capital without relying on banks through the retention of own profits, pushing banks towards households and individuals as sources of profits (Lapavitsas 2011). Workers' revenues thus became the new focus of banks by expanding financial assets such as mortgages, consumer credit, insurances and pensions. This meant that households' consumption came to be mediated by financial institutions that extract value directly from wages, instead of surplus production (Lapavitsas 2011). Thus, financialization entails the rise of financial profits and incomes from households, as much as it brings about higher levels of household debt.

Governments played an important role in fostering the financialization of households worldwide. In some countries, governments encouraged the creation of markets for consumer credit and mortgages by deregulating interest rates, creating financial infrastructures and in some cases directly lending money to their citizens (Quinn 2010; Trumbull 2014). In parallel, the embracing of neoliberal policies set the stage for the retrenchment of the welfare state, pushing households to rely more heavily on credit as a way of compensating for cuts in social benefits (Crouch 2011; Montgomerie 2013). In this sense, household debt has been driven by a set of interrelated phenomena, such as higher income volatility (Duménil and Lévy 2008; Iacoviello 2008; Kumhof Rancière and Winant 2015), lack of safety net (Montgomerie 2013) and rising income inequality (Charles and Lundy 2013; Coibion Gorodnichenko Kudlyak and Mondragon 2014; Alvarez-Cuadrado and Japaridze 2017). For this reason, social spending correlates negatively with increasing levels of household debt across nations (Prasad 2012; Kus 2013).

The "democratization of credit" over the last decades has resulted in higher levels of house-hold debt in both advanced and developing economies. Even though comparative research shows a considerable variation in levels of household debt across cases, depending on institu-tional arrangements, credit supply and cultural factors (Gordon 2012; Kus 2013; Róna-Tas and Guseva 2014; Trumbull 2014), evidence shows that during the last two or three decades there has been a consistent trend towards the growth of household debt levels (Lewin-Epstein and Semyonov 2016). Among advanced economies, generally, mortgages account for a high share of household debt, which explains why household debt levels are considerably high. For instance, according to the OECD Economic Outlook (OECD 2017), household debt ranges between 80% and 100% of GDP in some developed countries (United States, United Kingdom, Sweden, New Zealand), while in others it rocketed to more than 120% of the GDP (Australia, Switzerland, Denmark).

Household debt has also increased in developing economies, even though total levels of debt remain considerably lower than in most advanced economies. Altogether, data from the Bank for International Settlements (BIS) shows that household debt in emerging markets rose from 19.5% of the GDP in 2008 to almost 40% in 2017. In Turkey, for example, household debt rose from around 7% of the GDP in 2002 to 29% in 2007 (Bonizzi 2013), whereas in Chile, it grew from 35% of the GDP in 2000 to 63.5% in 2016 (González 2018). By the same token, according to the BIS, household debt in Greece and Colombia rose from 13.9% of the GDP in 2008 to 57% in 2017, and from 9.7% to 25.9%, respectively.

To some extent, lower household debt levels among developing countries reflect the increasing availability of different sorts of consumer credit, which includes consumer bank loans, revolving credit and micro-credit, rather than mortgages. In countries like Slovakia, Malaysia, Brazil and South Africa, for example, consumer credit was pivotal in the expansion of the demand for goods and services among middle and low-income households, precluding the transition towards mass-consumption societies (Rethel 2010; Bonizzi 2013; James 2014; Lavinas 2017). Similarly in post-communist countries in Eastern Europe and Asia, markets for credit cards have expanded explosively since the 2000s (Róna-Tas and Guseva 2014). Nowadays, international comparisons show that household debt among European emerging economies, such as Poland, the Czech Republic and Hungary, average around 30% of GDP, whereas household debt levels among emerging Asian economies tend to average around 60%.

Nonetheless, the financialization of households is not a new phenomenon. The extension of modern forms of credit to individuals can be traced back to the first credit cards issued by French retailers in the late nineteenth century (Ossandón 2013; Trumbull 2014); the consumer loans issued by manufacturers trying to sell durable goods such as home appliances and cars in the early twentieth century (Calder 1999; Carruthers and Ariovich 2010; Gordon 2012); or loan sharks lending money to the new working classes (Hyman 2013). Nevertheless, a dis-tinctive feature of the financialization of households is its scope, which expanded its frontiers towards populations and regions that have been historically excluded from traditional circuits of finance, most notably from the banking system. In this sense, the extension of micro-credit is one of the defining features of the financialization of households in the twenty-first century.

Micro-credit and the Financialization of Low-income Households

Micro-credit has been pivotal to the financialization of households, alongside the extension of sub-prime mortgages, health insurances, retirement plans, investment devices and student loans, among others. I consider micro-credits as small amounts of unsecured debt devised to target populations traditionally excluded from the banking system and for which there is no available information. Micro-credit is thus one of the most important instruments through which finan-cialization reaches low-income households. Lenders providing them have different organiza-tional structures and follow varied business models. These include payday lending, small consumer loans from specialized agencies, door-to-door moneylenders, private micro-credit institutions, state-owned banks and retailers.

Despite the wide variety of organizational and regional differences among micro-credit institutions, as well as the purposes for which people acquire these loans, they have distinctive features that make them empirically and theoretically relevant. To begin with, these credits articulate new geographies of financialization whereby poorer households come to participate in broader circuits of financial accumulation (Mader 2015). Micro-credits expanded the frontiers of financialization both within the city and in rural areas. Largely, said expansion is part of a major move towards financial inclusion marketed by international agencies – the G20, the IMF and the World Bank – NGOs and states, which conceive finance as a key policy instrument to overcome poverty and tackle public problems (Lavinas 2017). In some cases, governments have sought to fund, subsidize and promote the inclusion of poorer households in marginalized areas, while in others it is private lenders who have sought to take advantage of lax regulatory envir-onments and of new risk management techniques to expand their business model. Indeed, in many cases outside the developed world, different forms of micro-credit proliferate among populations that still do not have access to the mortgage market and, by extension, to any sources of wealth that could serve as collateral.

Micro-credit also presents great variation. On the supply side, lenders differ in the way they frame prospective borrowers and issue credits. Some lenders have embraced techniques that rely on rational calculations that aim at extending credit to large segments of the population in more or less automatized ways, while others still rely on face-to-face relations to assess prospective borrowers. On the demand side, micro-credit became part of the repertoire of economic practices, creating and/or overlapping with existing circuits of debt and local cultures of debt, risk and discipline. In regions such as Latin America, informal forms of credit have a long tra-dition in both rural and urban areas, and the new circuits of commerce were embedded in existing networks of cooperation and political patronage (Villareal 2000). Similarly, micro-credit institutions in Islamic countries re-framed their business model according to the sharia principles that set different moral and economic standards, embedding credit relations in existing values and normative conceptions about risk and debt (Karim Tarazi and Reille 2008; Masih 2017).

Key Actors in Micro-credit Expansion

Door to Door and Payday Lenders

In most advanced economies, retail banking has played a crucial role in financializing house-holds through different investment vehicles and forms of credit (Erturk et al. 2007; Lapavitsas 2011). However, when it comes to understanding the financialization of the "unbanked," new lenders have come to play a prominent role within landscape of retail finance, among which *door-to-door* and *payday moneylenders* are protagonists (Datta and Guermond, this volume).

The so called "home-collected credit industry" is a characteristic feature of poor inner-city, public-sector housing estates and peripheral areas within the UK, where mainstream financial providers are averse to do business (Leyshon, Signoretta, Knights, Alferoff and Burton 2006). This industry is also known as door-to-door moneylending. Door-to-door moneylenders sell their products on the doorstep, based on the work of self-employed agents that make a living out of their weekly collections. In this way, these lenders have a distinctive way of issuing credit and producing information about their prospective borrowers, which relies on street agents rather than branches or at-a-distance means of communication. Like department stores, these companies invest in potential trustworthy customers by lending small amounts of money and registering their behavior. Unlike retail lenders, however, home-collected credit companies do not rely on credit scoring systems and information about customers is not used to predict the behavior of new clients. As Leyshon et al. (2006) describe it, some of the information provided by customers is used to verify the existence of judgements and, alongside weekly income statements, some companies only ask for the address to collect payment, while others use paper recording methods and visits from agents. In this way, a distinctive feature of this industry is that, to the extent that loans are collected on a weekly basis, the relationship between the agent and the customer is crucial to build up personal knowledge to continually asses both the ability and the willingness of customers to pay.

A different type of non-traditional actor driving the financialization of low-income households is *payday lending*. Payday lending consists in the issuance of unsecured short-term loans that are usually extended for a two-week period of time. Due to its short-time horizon, payday lending is by definition a means for the poorer to cope with emergencies at a high price, which may sum up to 400% annualized interest rate (Aitken 2013b). Nowadays, payday lending is one of the most important industries financializing the "unbanked" in countries such as the US, Australia, Canada, and more recently Mexico and Eastern European countries (Aitken 2013b). The first payday lender was opened in the early 1990s in the US, and in the aftermath of the 2008 financial crisis there were tens of thousands. In the last decade, payday lenders in the US have expanded their business model to Mexico successfully, while one of the largest payday lender in the domestic British credit market (*International Personal Finance*) expanded its network to South Africa and Eastern European countries such as Poland, Hungary, Czech Republic and Rumania (Aitken 2013b).

Due to its high interest rates, payday lending's predatory practices proliferate in lax regulatory environments. In Anglo-American societies, for instance, the payday loan industry has received fierce opposition led by consumers' advocates and regulatory agencies that have sought to regulate maximum annual interest rates (Aitken 2013b). Moreover, payday lending tends to consistently concentrate in economically distressed communities, particularly in minority, moderately poor and military neighborhoods (Gallmeyer and Roberts 2009). As Gallmeyer and Roberts (2009: 532) show, "Payday lenders are more likely to be present in communities characterized by higher percentages of race/ethnic minorities, foreign born, young adults, senior citizens, and military personnel."

Consistent with the stratification of payday lending, Rowlingson, Appleyard, and Gardner (2016) argue that the underlying forces driving the expansion of payday lending are the confluence of income-insecurity and cuts in welfare provision. This is supported by households' surveys that show that most customers of payday lending consume credit to cope with unexpected increases in expenses or due to income shocks (Rowlingson et al. 2016). However, an interesting finding drawn from qualitative research on the payday lending industry is that, even though interest rates are high, consumers deemed positive the ease of access and the possibility of maintaining dignity and privacy, especially with regards to online application processes (Rowlingson et al. 2016).

Microfinance Institutions

Microfinance institutions represent a critical actor in the expansion of micro-credit to the unbanked across the globe. Microfinance organizations initially arose as a solution to poverty in underdeveloped countries and they became popular in the 1990s under the umbrella of international organizations promoting access to financial services (Aitken 2013a; Mader 2014, 2015). Switching afterwards to the rhetoric of "financial inclusion," micro-credit became a profitable business for new lenders that sought to make profits by turning the social ties of the poor into a stream of financial assets (Byström 2008).[1] In this way, this type of credit falls under the category of "social finance," which may be understood, following Paul Langley (2018: 3) as a way of "marketization that makes possible the capitalization of the social economy to address collective social problems."

There are three distinctive features that define these lending organizations. Firstly, the business model of microfinance has travelled all around the world and it is geographically based in third world countries and in most cases in rural areas (Shakya and Rankin (2008) counted more than 132 countries in 2008). Worldwide, these organizations issue small loans that have investment purposes, though evidence shows that a great deal of borrowers use them for multiple purposes. Secondly, maybe the most distinctive feature of microfinance organizations is the fact that their business model relies on a very different set of practices that come to shape the way in which poor households come to participate in financial circuits. Most fundamentally, the social-organization of microfinance differs from the department-store credit card and payday lenders in that microfinance institutions do not rely on financial information in order to frame prospective customers but on a different "innovation": the "social collateral."

Following Grameen Bank's innovation in Bangladesh in the 1970s, many international organizations, local NGOs and governments have pursued the financialization of mostly-rural communities by implementing a "collective-loan" methodology (also known as "communal bank"). According to this method, a group of – poor – women take a loan with the micro-lending institution and distribute it into small loans (Maclean 2013). The idea is that the group administrates the loan through peer pressure and the system is thus based in a "social collateral" that substitutes other types of wealth (Angulo Salazar 2014). Thus, credit not only relies on lenders' ability to assess the trustworthiness of individuals, but in the organizational capabilities of borrowers to become group members – such as "committees of women entrepreneurs" (Schuster 2014). As a consequence, an interesting feature of this industry is that micro-credit has the ability to shape the sociality and circuits of obligations among its users. Finally, it is worth noticing that micro-credit is highly gendered. As Schuster (2014: 564) puts it, a "key aspect of micro-credit is the pervasive assumption that women are more responsible borrowers than men and also that they are more likely to pass along their gains to their children and families." This is common to the microfinance industry more broadly. In rural Mexico, as in other countries in Latin America and Asia, for instance, microfinance is mostly offered to women in solidarity groups.

Department Stores

A key actor driving the financialization of households in developing economies are department stores, which rely on modern and impersonal risk-management techniques to massively financialize households at the low end of the social ladder. The department store is a site where financial innovations have taken place historically. It was present in the expansion of instalment credit throughout the first half of the twentieth century in several regions of the world. Sellers of durable goods such as sewing machines in Japan (Gordon 2012), cars and home appliances in the US (Calder 1999), and clothing and footwear in the first department stores in France (Trumbull 2014), systematically issued instalment credit as a way of selling their own goods.

The novelty of contemporary department stores, however, is that they rely on modern risk-based pricing techniques to financialize low-income consumers, which places them in a particular position in relation to other lenders. Department store credit cards are now common in several countries. Already in the early 1960s, almost 90 percent of department stores in the US had their own credit card (Trumbull 2014). While in many countries bank cards have since then become the most important mediator between consumers and merchants (Guseva 2005), this has not happened in Latin American countries, where the large majority of the population does not have access to the banking system. Here, department stores became the most important source of credit for households. In this sense, department stores in Chile represent a critical case to characterize this peculiar *financial ecology*, as this is the most financialized country in the region and the business model of department stores is exported to neighbor countries such as Argentina, Peru, Colombia and Brazil (Ossandón 2013; Wilkis 2014).

In Chile, department stores consolidated in the 1980s. Nowadays, they are modern companies that operate as conglomerates of companies that own banks, supermarkets, insurance companies, travel agencies and home improvement stores. This business model is known as "multi-channel retailing." As Ossandón's research shows, department stores have successfully invested in expanding the market to low-income populations through the embrace of a particular risk-management technique known as "sowing" (Ossandón 2013). "Sowing" consists of creating consumers by progressively lending very small amounts of money to unknown customers in order to engage people in credit relations and produce financial information. As the metaphor suggests, some of these consumers will pay their debts and a long-lasting credit relation will flourish (and information is created), while others will perish without generating great losses. Thus, with the help of a black list credit bureau, department stores systematically improved their predicting ability, refined their credit assessment policies and targeted new populations.

"Sowing" allowed department stores to innovate and expand the business to new financial profiles that represent important segments of the middle-low income groups: housewives, youth, retired or seasonal workers, among others. This is, for example, how they went on differentiating their lending policies for workers and pensioners. As most lenders at the bottom end of financialization, department stores have less restrictive lending policies, especially with regard to income requirements. A normal department store, for instance, requires a minimum income of USD 200–300 for workers, while only USD 120 for pensioners. In general, such requirements relate to the fact that, unlike banks that differentiate their products according to the profile of their customers, department stores marketize credit cards as a very homogeneous product where the main difference is not the interest rates charged, but the available "room" on their credit card balance sheet.

Finally, there are two further features that differentiate Chilean department stores from their counterparts in other parts of the world. On the one hand, this sort of credit works as *earmarked money* (Zelizer 2002): most transactions with department store credit cards are attached to within store purchases. This means that the department store credit card does not necessarily work as substitute for social spending, but as a permanent extension of consumers' incomes to acquire home appliances, clothing and footwear. On the other hand, a great difference these organizations present alongside other lenders is that most of them operate mainly in shopping malls. These have proliferated in both urban and suburban areas, which contradicts the conventional idea among financialization scholars that low-income finance represents a separate *financial ecology*.

Micro-credit and Household Debt in Local Contexts

Micro-credit embeds in local circuits of commerce and exchanges, as well as existing conceptions about debt. In many rural areas of Latin America, new monetarized forms of debt such as bank or cooperative loans, coexist with an extended network of formal and informal lenders that have been around since colonial times. For instance, characterizing the "financial ecology" of three towns in rural areas of West Mexico, Villareal (2000) distinguishes at least four coexisting forms of debt. The "loan" or *préstamo* traditionally issued by landowners used to be one of the most common forms of lending, and it was normally quantified in spices and working hours rather than in monetary terms. By the same token, debts to relatives and friends have also been a crucial source of credit in rural areas, especially under the moral imperative of assisting the ones in need of financial aid. In a similar vein, as Villareal and others document (Villareal 2008; Zanotelli 2014), monetarized forms of credit have characterized the extension of loans in rural areas of México in the last decades, mainly driven by two types of lenders. Firstly, government sponsored loans that target farmers in need of implements and agricultural supplies. And secondly, the credit system of local shops that have traditionally implemented the so-called "deferred payment" or *fiado*, normally used by workers to buy their living expenses while they wait for their salary.[2] All these forms of debt not only represent different rationalities and modes of calculation, but also they are framed in different ways. While *préstamos* is a common word used to refer to both formal and informal loans, "credit" is used to talk about formal debts with banks or financial institutions, as well as the potential to acquire debt.

Thus, the multiple network of lenders creates a complex system of exchanges in which equivalences between monetary and non-monetary debts are established. These systems of exchange include farmers paying with crops, landowners lending money, local retailers lending through deferred payment, relatives sending remittances and neighbors doing favors. Local retail lenders may even be aware of these intricate relations and rely on a mixed strategy to frame prospective borrowers. As Angulo Salazar (2014) documents, microfinance institutions in Mexico manage their loan portfolio with the help of risk pricing techniques alongside peer pressure and co-signers (known as debtors in solidarity).

To the extent that households are entangled in a network of financial obligations that include exchanges with microfinance institutions and individual networks, formal and informal sources of credit are different expressions of the same debt. People juggling with department store credit cards, for example, acquire informal loans with relatives to serve a formal debt (Gonzalez 2015). In rural areas of Madagascar, informal credit institutions (such as *varo-maitso*) and cash advances from rice traders coexist with microfinance sources of credit that are often used as substitution strategies (Wampfler, Bouquet and Ralison 2014). In a similar vein, in Noapara Village, Bangladesh, informal credit characterized by idiosyncratic credit limits and family and friend credit that is interest free (due to Islamic principles) is preferred over formalized application and repayment procedures of banks (Fenton, Paavola and Tallontire 2017).

Probably, one of the most notable intersections of micro-credit and local cultures is to be found in Islamic finance. Micro-credit takes a different form in Muslim countries, where Islamic principles provide the social and economic template upon which finance may be organized. Currently, there are more than 650 million individuals living with less than two USD a day in Islamic countries, becoming an important target for governments and international organizations promoting access to micro-credit (Zulkhibri 2016). According to Islamic principles, there are at least three strategic factors that demarcate the limits of financial contracts: the prohibition of charging interest without means of sharing risk between lender and borrower (*Riba*); the principle of avoiding uncertainty and lack of clarity (*Gharar*); and the prohibition of gambling (Miah and Suzuki 2015; Masih 2017). To the extent that risk is not dealt with individually but collectively, and that loans are conceived for productive purposes, said principles cohere with the solidary approach of micro-credit. Furthermore, Islamic microfinance operates under the assumption that credit is issued to alleviate the situation of poor people with unknown credit records.

Given the complexity of financial circuits among the poor, it is not surprising that empirical research has revealed the existence of a complex set of financial practices and skills (Villareal 2008; Guérin, Morvant-Roux and Villarreal 2014). Following this line of reasoning, an important insight from these ethnographical approaches is that existing cultures of debt can collide with contemporary cultures of financialization (see also Weiss in this volume). Villareal (2008), for example, shows that financial calculations are carried through parameters that are not necessarily monetary, but also socially and culturally bounded. Saving, investing and getting indebted are embedded in locally situated moral codes and traditions, as well as rules of reciprocity, whereby local "financial cultures" can in many cases enter into contradiction with the "economistic" frameworks or circuits of valuation that formal finances tend to demand from their users. Similarly, Maclean (2013) shows for rural credit programs in Bolivia that the whole industry is based on gendered and colonial constructions of risk and responsibility that clash with the understandings of the beneficiaries. In this line, it has been proven that socially controlled micro-credit tends to tension the relationship between reciprocity and solidarity among microfinance users (Shakya and Rankin 2008).

Conclusion

This chapter has provided an overview of the different *articulations* that one might find when assessing the financialization of low-income consumers across different regions. The overview here sketched is far from being exhaustive. New lenders and financial industries emerge constantly and in unexpected ways. Some of these may articulate circuits of financial exchanges with the poor through the utilization of new payment structures, such as mobile phones. In any case, the picture that emerges is one in which the social geography at the low end of financialization is in many cases associated by the emergence of predatory industries in economically and socially distressed communities (Gallmeyer and Roberts 2009). This is why a key feature of the financialization of households has been its distinctive relation with vulnerable populations, as this process is subjected to racialized, gendered and stratified extension of credit (Maclean 2013; Rankin 2013; James 2014). In other words, certain populations have become specific targets of lenders among low-income households, which implies that the impacts of financialization are unevenly distributed among them.

The financialization of the poorer segments of the population via micro-credit is not only an economic phenomenon. To the extent that credit has become part of the economic toolkit of middle and low-income households worldwide, the financialization of poor households is also a cultural transformation whereby people internalize calculative frames, time horizons and rationalities. By the same token, the literature here surveyed suggests that the financialization of households is also embedded in local conceptions of debt that may facilitate or obstruct the expansion of micro-finance.

The expansion of micro-credit has also a political dimension. Even though the motives driving households to consume micro-credit are diverse, studies targeting the poor indeed tend to affirm the idea that the financialization at the bottom of the pyramid is driven by necessity. As shown, vulnerable borrowers use these credits for different purposes: to cope with instability (Angulo Salazar 2014), natural disasters (Fenton et al. 2017) or as a way of capitalizing the gap between incomes and necessities (Servet and Saiag 2014). Thus, the expansion of micro-credit may have distributive outcomes – such as income inequality and lack of opportunities – less salient issues, at the same time it may produce new patterns of exploitation, exclusion and social control. Research needs to move on to characterize these patterns in a way that calls into question the dominant discourse through which "finance for the poor" is marketized among international agencies and states. The financial industries here surveyed – payday money lenders, door-to-door money lenders, micro-finance institutions and department stores – certainly suggest a less optimistic view of micro-credit as a solution to public problems.

Notes

1 *Compartamos Banco* in Mexico, for example, began as an NGO following charitable principles, but became one of the most profitable banks in the country (Hummel 2014).
2 The *fiado* is not openly offered to customers, but rather a selective strategy used by small merchants that relies on a social framing of customers that includes economic and moral reputation.

Bibliography

Aitken, R., 2013a. The financialization of micro-credit. *Development and Change*, 44(3), pp. 473–499.

Aitken, R., 2013b. Finding the edges of payday lending. *Perspectives on Global Development and Technology*, 12(3), pp. 377–409.

Alvarez-Cuadrado, F. and Japaridze, I., 2017. Trickle-down consumption, financial deregulation, inequality, and indebtedness. *Journal of Economic Behavior & Organization*, 134, pp. 1–26.

Angulo Salazar, L., 2014. The social costs of microfinance and over-indebtedness for women. In Guérin, I., Morvant-Roux, S. and Magdalena, V. (eds.), *Microfinance, Debt and Over-Indebtedness*, first edition. London: Routledge, pp. 232–252.

Bonizzi, B., 2013. Financialization in developing and emerging countries. *International Journal of Political Economy*, 42(4), pp. 83–107.

Byström, H.N.E., 2008. The microfinance collateralized debt obligation: A modern Robin Hood? *World Development*, 36(11), pp. 2109–2126.

Calder, L., 1999. *Financing the American Dream: A Cultural History of Consumer Credit*. Princeton, NJ: Princeton University Press.

Carruthers, B.G. and Ariovich, L., 2010. *Money and Credit: A Sociological Approach*. Cambridge: Polity Press.

Charles, M. and Lundy, J.D., 2013. The Local Joneses: Household Consumption and Income Inequality in Large Metropolitan Areas. *Research in Social Stratification and Mobility*, 34, pp. 14–29.

Coibion, O., Gorodnichenko, Y., Kudlyak, M. and Mondragon, J., 2014. Does greater inequality lead to more household borrowing? New evidence from household data. *NBER Working Paper No. 19850*. Cambridge, MA: National Bureau of Economic Research.

Crouch, C., 2011. *The Strange Non-Death of Neoliberalism*. Cambridge: Polity Press.

Duménil, G. and Lévy, D., 2008. Financialization, neoliberalism and income inequality in the USA. In Erturk, I., Froud, J., Johal, S., Leaver, A. and Williams, K. (eds.), *Financialization at Work*. London: Routledge, pp. 223–237.

Erturk, I., Froud, J., Johal, S., Leaver, A., and Williams, K., 2007. The Democratization Of Finance? Promises, outcomes and conditions. *Review of International Political Economy*, 14(4), pp. 553–575.

Fenton, A., Paavola, J. and Tallontire, A., 2017. The role of microfinance in household livelihood adaptation in Satkhira District, Southwest Bangladesh. *World Development*, 92, pp. 192–202.

Gallmeyer, A. and Roberts, W.T., 2009. Payday lenders and economically distressed communities: A spatial analysis of financial predation. *The Social Science Journal*, 46(3), pp. 521–538.

Gonzalez, F., 2015. Where are the consumers? *Cultural Studies*, 29(5–6), pp. 1–26.

González, F., 2018. Crédito, deuda y gubernamentalidad financiera en Chile. *Revista Mexicana de Sociología*, 80(4), pp. 881–908.

Gordon, A., 2012. Credit in a nation of savers: The growth of consumer borrowing in Japan. In Logemann, J. (ed.), *The Development of Consumer Credit in Global Perspective: Business, Regulation and Culture*. New York: Palgrave Macmillan, pp. 63–81.

Guérin, I., Morvant-Roux, S. and Villarreal, M., 2014. Introduction: Microfinance, debt and over-indebtedness. In Guérin, I., Morvant-Roux, S. and Villarreal, M. (eds.), *Microfinance, Debt and Over-Indebtedness*, first edition. London: Routledge, pp. 1–23.

Guseva, A., 2005. Building new markets: A comparison of the Russian and American credit card markets. *Socio-Economic Review*, 3(3), pp. 437–466.

Hummel, A., 2014. The commercialization of microcredits and local consumerism: Examples of over-indebtedness from indigenous Mexico. In Guérin, I., Morvant-Roux, S. and Magdalena, V. (eds.), *Microfinance, Debt and Over-Indebtedness*, first edition. London: Routledge, pp. 253–271.

Hyman, L., 2013. *Debtor Nation: The History of America in Red Ink*. Princeton, NJ: Princeton University Press.

Iacoviello, M., 2008. Household debt and income inequality, 1963–2003. *Journal of Money, Credit and Banking*, 40(5), pp. 929–965.

James, D., 2014. "Deeper into a hole?" Borrowing and lending in South Africa. *Current Anthropology*, 55 (9), pp. 17–29.

Karim, N., Tarazi, M. and Reille, X., 2008. Islamic microfinance: An emerging market niche. *Consultative Group to Assist the Poor*, 49.

Kumhof, M., Rancière, R. and Winant, P., 2015. Inequality, leverage, and crises. *American Economic Review*, 105(3), pp. 1217–1245.

Kus, B., 2013. Credit, consumption, and debt: Comparative perspectives. *International Journal of Comparative Sociology*, 54(3), pp. 183–186.

Langley, P., 2018. The folds of social finance: Making markets, remaking the social. *Environment and Planning A: Economy and Space*, advance online, pp. 1–18. doi:10.1177/0308518x17752682

Lapavitsas, C., 2011. Theorizing financialization. *Work, Employment & Society*, 25(4), pp. 611–626.

Lavinas, L., 2017. *The Takeover of Social Policy by Financialization*. New York: Palgrave Macmillan.

Lewin-Epstein, N. and Semyonov, M., 2016. Household debt in midlife and old age: A multinational study. *International Journal of Comparative Sociology*, 57(3), pp. 151–172.

Leyshon, A., Signoretta, P., Knights, D., Alferoff, C. and Burton, D., 2006. Walking with moneylenders: The ecology of the UK home-collected credit industry. *Urban Studies*, 43(1), pp. 161–186.

Maclean, K., 2013. Gender, risk and micro-financial subjectivities. *Antipode*, 45(2), pp. 455–473.

Mader, P., 2014. Financialisation through microfinance: Civil society and market-building in India. *Asian Studies Review*, 38(4), pp. 601–619.

Mader, P., 2015. *The Political Economy of Microfinance: Financializing Poverty*. Houndmills: Palgrave Macmillan.

Masih, M., 2017. Islamic finance and banking. *Emerging Markets Finance and Trade*, 53(7), pp. 1455–1457.

Miah, M.D., and Suzuki, Y., 2015. Transcending the trend of financialization: The heterodox vs. Islamic economics view. *Journal of Economic and Social Thought*, 2(4), pp. 226–241.

Montgomerie, J., 2013. America's debt safety-net. *Public Administration*, 91(4), pp. 871–888.

OECD, 2017. Resilience in a time of high debt. *OECD Economic Outlook*, 2. https://doi.org/10.1787/eco_outlook-v2017-2-3-en

Ossandón, J., 2013. Sowing consumers in the garden of mass retailing in Chile. *Consumption Markets & Culture*, 17(5), pp. 429–447.

Prasad, M., 2012. *The Land of Too Much: American Abundance and the Paradox of Poverty*. Cambridge, MA: Harvard University Press.

Quinn, S.L., 2010. *Government Policy, Housing, and the Origins of Securitization, 1780–1968*. PhD Thesis, University of California.

Rankin, K.N., 2013. A critical geography of poverty finance. *Third World Quarterly*, 34(4), pp. 547–568.

Rethel, L., 2010. Financialisation and the Malaysian political economy. *Globalizations*, 7(4), pp. 489–506.

Róna-Tas, Á. and Guseva, A., 2014. *Plastic Money: Constructing Markets for Credit Cards in Eight Post-communist Countries*. Stanford, CA: Stanford Univ. Press.

Rowlingson, K., Appleyard, L. and Gardner, J., 2016. Payday lending in the UK: The regul(aris)ation of a necessary evil? *Journal of Social Policy*, 45(3), pp. 527–543.

Schuster, C.E., 2014. The social unit of debt: Gender and creditworthiness in Paraguayan microfinance. *American Ethnologist*, 41(3), pp. 563–578.

Servet, J.-M. and Saiag, H., 2014. Household over-indebtedness in northern and southern countries: A macro-perspective. In Guérin, I., Morvant-Roux, S. and Magdalena, V. (eds.), *Microfinance, Debt and Over-Indebtedness*, first edition. London: Routledge, pp. 24–45.

Shakya, Y.B. and Rankin, K.N., 2008. The politics of subversion in development practice: An exploration of microfinance in Nepal and Vietnam. *The Journal of Development Studies*, 44(8), pp. 1214–1235.

Trumbull, G., 2014. *Consumer Lending in France and America: Credit and Welfare*. Cambridge: Cambridge University Press.

Villarreal, M., 2000. Deudas, drogas, fiado y prestado en las tiendas de abarrotes rurales. *Desacatos*, 3, pp. 69–88.

Villarreal, M., 2008. Sacando cuentas: Prácticas financieras y marcos de calculabilidad en el México rural. *Revista Crítica en Desarrollo*, 2, pp. 131–149.

Wampfler, B., Bouquet, E. and Ralison, E., 2014. Does juggling mean struggling? Insights into the financial practices of rural households in Madagascar. In Guérin, I., Morvant-Roux, S. and Magdalena, V. (eds.), *Microfinance, Debt and Over-Indebtedness*, first edition. London: Routledge, pp. 211–231.

Wilkis, A., 2014. Sociología del crédito y economía de las clases populares. *Revista Mexicana de Sociología*, 76(2), pp. 225–252.

Zanotelli, F., 2014. Multiplying debt and dependence: Gender strategies and the social risks of financial inclusion in Western Mexico. In Guérin, I., Morvant-Roux, S. and Magdalena, V. (eds.), *Microfinance, Debt and Over-Indebtedness*, first edition. London: Routledge, pp. 192–210.

Zelizer, V.A., 2002. The social meaning of money. In Biggart, N.W. (ed.), *Readings in Economic Sociology*. Oxford: Blackwell, pp. 315–330.

Zulkhibri, M., 2016. Financial inclusion, financial inclusion policy and Islamic finance. *Macroeconomics and Finance in Emerging Market Economies*, 9(3), pp. 303–320.

26

THE COLLATERALIZATION OF SOCIAL POLICY BY FINANCIAL MARKETS IN THE GLOBAL SOUTH[1]

Lena Lavinas

Introduction

Under the aegis of financialization, the forms, content, and objectives of social policy have been reshaped, and so has social policy's complementarity with the accumulation regime now dominated by finance.

Fine (2014) remarks that financialization has exerted a profound influence on social policy, especially as it has subverted and inserted itself into public forms of economic and social welfare provision. As a consequence, consumption patterns have been radically reframed in favor of market forms of provision. Schelkle goes a step further, arguing that "the market-creating role of social policy goes beyond the exclusive identification with social policy with redistribution of risks or resources" (2012: 5). Social policy may underpin and even create financial markets, particularly mass markets for consumer credit, mortgages and pensions. In examining how financial markets have dramatically altered the conventional landscape of derivatives and securitization directly affecting households, henceforth seen as the asset base of globally traded asset-based securities, Bryan and Rafferty conclude that "increasingly, the search for yield may come to drive social policy" (2014: 898).

Along the same lines, Leyshon and Thrift (2007: 98) had already warned that the dynamics of the securitization process tend to "identify almost anything that might provide a stable source of income," underscoring the link between stable income sources and financial speculation. As they note, the financial system, to survive, "must continuously prospect for new asset seams that can be turned into collateral" through novel strategies of capitalization.

The transformation of social policy into collateral reflects the breadth logic of financialized capitalism, which converts cash transfers, pensions, and other monetary schemes – sources of regular income streams, that is – into assets placed at the disposal of the financial sector. They are then used to service debt and generate new income streams.

In this process, modern finance has upended the logic of access to rights. Social policy in the form of entitlements – originally conceived of as a mechanism for decommodification – has been increasingly called upon to serve as collateral to access financial markets. This same process ultimately takes entitlements and transforms them from rights into assets. It follows, then, that reforming social policy is at the center of the work of finance in this moment. I argue that through certain social policies – especially cash transfers paid by the state – the financial sector no longer has to rely on the requirement of liquid assets to make offers to low-income groups and the poor. In this workaround, the state both exempts cash transfer recipients from posting collateral and provides the very collateral that is a precondition for the expansion of financial markets.

This chapter will address how the Global South, with its dearth of strong social policy institutions, has been drawn into this process, with a special focus on Brazil and South Africa.

Taking Brazil and South Africa as examples, this chapter analyzes how various forms of cash transfers are used to expand consumer credit and other lines of credit. Society's most vulnerable are made into sources of profit as a result, reinforcing the so-called welfare-credit link. The result is a phenomenon of unprecedented scope in the developing world, the process by which low-income households have accrued astonishing levels of debt, alongside the constant uptick in sources of welfare provided through multiple links to the financial sector.

The Context and the Facts

What do Brazil, South Africa, Argentina, Tanzania, Mexico, Burkina Faso, and several countries of the Middle East and South Asia have in common, out of all those that make up what is now labeled the Global South? All of them, in recent years, have adopted anti-poverty cash transfer programs. In many cases, those programs became the backbone of incipient, fragile social protection mechanisms in places where such systems were either deficient or nonexistent.

A recent World Bank report on the topic – *The State of Social Safety Nets 2018* – can give a sense of the swift advance of the various forms of welfare transfers in the 2000s and the coverage they attained as they became flagship programs. Under the category of welfare transfers, the World Bank includes two forms of support: conditional and non-conditional monetary transfers and social pensions fall under one set, while another includes some in-kind transfers such as food and school feeding schemes, along with fee waivers and targeted subsidies (World Bank 2018a: 6). This being said, the bulk of these welfare transfers is monetary and does not go toward providing for social services. Likewise, the World Bank uses two methodologies to calculate spending on cash transfers: one of them considers spending as a whole (including all of the forms mentioned above), while another calculates a subset "without health fee waivers." In this chapter, when spending is referred to, it is without health fee waivers. According to the report, developing countries[2] spend, on average, 1.5% of their GDP on these programs whereas OECD countries spend 2.7%. The percentage evidently varies considerably from country to country and across regions, from 7% of GDP in Georgia to 3.5% in Chile and under 1% in countless poorer countries.

Even so, it is notable that certain regions such as Latin America and the Caribbean[3] and Europe and Central Asia have seen a substantive rise in spending on cash-transfer assistance programs. In Latin America and the Caribbean, spending tripled in just over ten years, going from 0.43% of GDP to 1.26% in 2015. Europe and Central Asia saw more modest but still noteworthy growth, from 1.26% in 2003 to 1.63% of GDP in 2014. And across all the regions of the Global South, with the exception of the Middle East and North Africa (45%), monetary transfers make up over 50% of welfare spending. In three regions – Europe and Central Asia, Latin America and the Caribbean, and East Asia and the Pacific – more than half of the population receives some sort of monetary benefit. In the poorest quintile of the distribution, that ratio rises to at least two-thirds. This means that today only a minority (33%) of the world poor live without a monetary safety net.

The average household benefit amount also differs significantly across countries, from PPP US$ 106 received per month in upper-middle income countries to PPP US$ 27 in low-income countries (World Bank 2018a: 25). Low-value benefits may help to mitigate the destitution of the neediest, but are not likely to lift them out of poverty. In any event, whatever the amount of the benefit, the volume of monetary transfers within assistance policies is noteworthy.

The report estimates that 2.5 billion people (one-third of the world's population) are covered by safety net programs in developing and transitional countries. The extent of the group covered by these social minimums, which is poised to grow even further, indicates that we are past the time when poverty was a mark of exclusion. Today, in a globalized, finance-dominated economy, poverty is expressed through specific forms of inclusion.

In order to cope with the effects of the economic crisis in the aftermath of the Great Financial Crisis, the ILO, alongside 19 other multilateral organizations, the World Bank, and the IMF, took the lead in supporting a new format for social protection systems, one that clearly considers the rule of fiscal austerity, for it significantly reduces public spending. The Social Protection Floor for a Fair and Inclusive Globalization (2011) has two well-defined pillars. On one hand, it proposes the adoption of various social transfers (in cash or in kind), such as pensions for the elderly and persons with disabilities, child benefits, income support benefits for the unemployed, single mothers or the working poor, aimed at ensuring basic income security. On the other, it advocates for the universal – albeit bare-bones – provision of essential services in sectors such as healthcare, education, housing, and water and sanitation, among others, in keeping with each nation's priorities. These floors are not specified, nor is it argued that they should be provided publicly and free of charge. However, their very definition questions the idea of universality, since minimum floors in healthcare and education are unlikely to constitute adequate coverage.

In this new world, the social protection floors paradigm fits like a glove for it offers a conceptual framework that legitimates, guides, and enforces adhesion to a model that permanently reinforces dynamics of social inclusion. Even as it adjusts its own definition of what it means to be universal – no longer working towards the same standards for all, as were once put forth in the 1950 *The Quest for Universality*[4] – the ILO affirms that "the floor's income-led approach can contribute to combating imbalances in the global economy by inducing reductions in precautionary savings and increases in the purchasing power of emerging consumer classes in developing countries, thereby strengthening the national markets" (2011: XXV).

One might ask whether benefits of such low value, however regular, could sufficiently drive the expansion of domestic markets. What is clear is that they fuel the forced march of monetization across the developing world. In regions where income insecurity is chronic, labor precarious, informality pervasive, and income deficits a permanent feature of life for the majority, welfare programs turn out to be more than just a safety net: they are a constant link to the market. In such regions, where the degree of monetization for the poorest is intermittent at best, social policy in the form of cash transfers seeks to prevent a return to a subsistence economy and ensure the permanence and growth of cash flows. That growth is magnified through access to new digital technologies that are facilitating and expanding the practice of carrying out financial transfers and transactions on cell phones. There is no longer any need for the massive investments in infrastructure that characterized the era of industrial capitalism in Western economies – and which made it possible for social policy to provide broad horizontal access to housing, adequate sanitation, transportation, etc.

This brings us to another point in common amongst Global South countries in this new millennium. Despite their immense cultural, economic, social and ethnic heterogeneity, which is also expressed in the ways in which each inserts itself into the global economy, the countries of peripheral capitalism also have something else in common in the age of mass financialization (Becker et al. 2010; Lavinas Araújo and Bruno 2019): they have been targeted by ambitious, well-orchestrated programs of financial inclusion underwritten by the state.

With financial deregulation running wild despite the Basel Accords (see also Thiemann in this volume) and with the financialization of the global economy having found nothing to halt its progress for all the harm caused to the real economy, a new arsenal of rules and norms is coming into place to make financial inclusion an instrument that seeks to serve social justice, well-being and economic development. Thus, in the wake of the Great Financial Crisis of 2008, we are witness to yet another coordinated assault led by the G20 with the voluntary and immediate adhesion of non-G20 countries, representatives of private banks, financial institutions and other organizations, all bent on redefining the aims of international cooperation towards democratizing finance (Erturk 2007) by way of "universal access to and use of financial services" (Global Partnership for Financial Inclusion 2011: 1). The taskforce also includes multilateral bodies such as the International Monetary Fund and the World Bank, and key institutions, such as the Alliance for Financial Inclusion (AFI), the Consultative Group to Assist the Poor (CGAP), and the International Finance Corporation (IFC). This complex network of institutions under the Global Partnership for Financial Inclusion, with direct participation from the Central Banks of each member country, has met annually since 2011. Its objective is to incentivize, ease the implementation of and refine strategies for financial inclusion, seeking to accelerate the process and closely monitoring the results.

And those results are already tangible. According to a World Bank survey (2018b), the adoption of national strategies of financial inclusion is already a reality throughout the Global South. Across all developing regions surveyed, more than three-quarters of countries declared that, as of 2017, they were either in the process of implementing a number of initiatives along these lines or had already done so. The survey also indicated that among the mechanisms that drove the financial inclusion of low-income households, a state-led strategy prevailed. Encouraging or mandating recipients of government transfers to open a bank account was reported to be the most effective lever by far, kick-starting an integrated strategy between the state and the financial sector. Yet again across all regions, no less than 60% of countries reported having privileged this pathway for banking the "unbanked."

State-encouraged bankarization[5] appears as a powerful mechanism in the constitution of "inclusive financial systems," that mantra of the new millennium. From 2011 to 2017, the share of formal account holders among the poorest 40% increased by half, from 41.3% to 60.5% worldwide (World Bank 2018b).

It would be foolhardy to ignore the obvious correlation between the trend towards the universalization of money transfers, that has come to constitute the bulk of social policy in the developing world, and the sea change in mounting levels of financial inclusion, especially among those who were known as the "unbanked" not so long ago. The universalization of financial inclusion (Soederberg 2014) is an integrated process that runs alongside the universalization of cash transfers, and has become a touchstone of social policy in the age of financialization.

Bridging the Gap: Collateral for Debt

Of the factors inhibiting the process of financial inclusion, poverty – that is, a persistent lack of income – emerges as a decisive element, though it does not stand alone.

In analyzing the effects of one such strategy to boost financial inclusion – in this case, incentivizing people to open savings accounts at private banks in Chile, Malawi, and Uganda – Dupas et al. (2016) arrive at two separate conclusions. In the two African nations, neither countless financial incentives nor technical assistance during the account opening process was enough to see a marked rise in account rates among the target groups (mostly the rural poor). "The illiquidity of the bank account was a deterrent" (ibid.: 19), given the predominance of subsistence production, underdeveloped monetary circuits, and hence high income volatility.

The results should not come as much of a surprise, given that holding a savings account correlates positively with income. Malawi and Uganda are extremely poor countries whose absolute annual spending on social safety nets per capita ranks among the lowest in the world, close to the median value for the Sub-Saharan region (World Bank 2018b: 25). Moreover, these government transfers are wholly (Malawi) or nearly entirely (Uganda) donor-funded (ibid.: 18), which suggests that it would be difficult to increase their size. This is to say that the sum provided for safety nets is insufficient to incentivize bankarization because it fails to satisfactorily reduce income gaps, nor does it adequately mitigate the extreme privation suffered by the beneficiary population. The article by Dupas and al. does not say, however, if these beneficiary families were establishing other connections to the financial sector through microinsurance or some form of microcredit, which seems quite likely.

In the case of Chile, meanwhile, where bank account ownership is much more widely spread, the authors attributed low adhesion to savings accounts among lower income brackets to the fact that the state's social policy provided monetary benefits such as family subsidies or social pensions, relieving users from the need to save and, likewise, facilitating access to other financial products, such as consumer credit. That is to say, the state ensured liquidity and a regular income stream through social policy, making it possible for government transfer recipients with no savings or other assets to enjoy wide and easy access to credit lines. The authors acknowledged that taking out loans, using credit cards or buying on instalment payments compensates for the lack of savings amidst Chilean low-income beneficiaries of cash transfers. However, this is only possible, in my opinion, because these groups' incorporation into the market is not only permanent but also underwritten by a considerable regular benefit – 770 \$PPP per annum, on average (World Bank 2018a) – that comes to serve as collateral. While far above the global average (66 \$PPP per annum), these government transfers still do not meet all the basic needs of those living in poverty in middle-income Chile, which means that they must turn to the financial system in order to improve their consumption patterns.

And so it has been that in recent years, in step with models recommended by multilateral agencies, the Global South has seen the spread of a great variety of mechanisms for guaranteeing monetary income (conditional cash transfers; unconditional cash transfers, social pensions; child grants; family subsidies, etc.), provided and administered by the State, where the common denominator is the goal of ensuring regular income streams. These mechanisms have had the effect of reconfiguring social policy, giving it a new scope and an unprecedented function: to serve as collateral (Lavinas 2018) to the use of the financial sector.

The definition of collateral is straightforward enough, and doesn't seem controversial. Collateral is a security pledged for the payment of a loan so as to decrease the risk of default, making the loan less risky. Now, in these times of financialization, its use is broadening in order to enhance financial markets associated to novel financial products (Riles 2011).

When lending to low-income groups whose creditworthiness cannot be assessed directly, financial institutions face an adverse selection problem. To address it they can either apply higher interest rates, which may render the loan unattractive or even prohibitive for the borrower, or require sufficient collateral as appropriate insurance against the high risk-borrower.[6] Neither option is viable for low-income or poor borrowers: they cannot afford paying high interest rates, nor do they have any kind of physical or financial assets to secure a loan.

It is precisely in these contexts – in which credit rationing and lack of creditworthiness hinder one another's expansion – that social policy comes to serve as collateral,[7] reducing risks for both borrowers and lenders. Credit rationing is a situation in which lending institutions are unwilling to advance additional funds to borrowers at the prevailing market interest rate, even if the latter are willing to pay higher interest rates.

Generally, collateral can be "used as a screening device" (Sena 2008: 17) only if potential borrowers are wealthy enough to fully guarantee the loan. In the absence of any assets, and given the personal profile of these new potential borrowers and consumers of financial products, social policy will function as the "screening device." Cash transfers underwritten by the state and now enshrined as the blueprint for social policy in the Global South (Lavinas 2013) have come to fulfill collateral requirements, beyond their more conventional role of mitigating poverty.

The role of the state is also altered. Since creditors rely on connections (recurring information-gathering so as to estimate the risk of default) and collaterals (to cut losses in case of default), to encourage mass inclusion into the financial system, as noted by Krippner (2017), it falls to the state to strengthen the twin strategies upon which the expansion of financial markets rests: the creation of collateral on one hand, and the systematizing of information about the "unbanked" and undocumented on the other.

The implementation of income transfer programs has meant providing potential beneficiaries with documents to facilitate the targeting process that is inherent to poverty-fighting programs, as well as creating detailed records that are to be periodically updated. Seen in the context of potential loans, these make up for the lack of a credit track record, which might otherwise constrain users' access to financial resources by increasing the cost of borrowing.

When financial inclusion policies are adopted with the aim of expanding the existing array of financial products, credit in particular, it is common for public databases containing the records of cash-transfer beneficiaries to be shared with local financial institutions. This serves to cut costs when drawing up clients' credit scores.

The state is also committed, through its Central Bank and other public authorities, to improving financial literacy among income transfer recipients as an antidote to over-indebtedness and default (Lavinas 2018). While income transfer programs once called for mandatory school attendance and regular visits to health care centers, when available, now they require adults to attend financial education courses and have made the topic mandatory course content in primary and secondary schools, as well as in textbooks (see also Lazarus in this volume). According to the *Global Financial Inclusion and Consumer Protection Survey* (2017), half of the countries in Latin America and the Caribbean have adopted financial education as a component of public cash transfer programs, under the supervision of Central Banks. In two other regions, Sub-Saharan Africa and East Asia and the Pacific, a third of programs follow the same lines, the most immediate result of which has been to facilitate the development of an investor mentality among low-income and poor households and intertwine poverty and finance.

Nevertheless, the State's most important role is still to consolidate novel social schemes, lauded as innovative (Lavinas 2013) for being market-inclusive and cheap, and to provide new regulations so as to invigorate consumption and what was once known as social protection through access to financial devices. Regular income streams, even at very low levels, are key to smoothing and accelerating the process of market incorporation in regions where the shift to a salaried society never materialized. By the same token, they boost dynamics of financialization more broadly (securitization process, derivative markets) and free financial markets.

One of the most startling consequences has been the exponential growth of household debt and debt ratios, phenomena now characteristic of the start of this century. Brazil and South Africa may serve as examples in this respect.

Brazil and South Africa: Similar Paths of Collateralization

Indeed, Brazil and South Africa have much in common. Over the course of the 1990s, as they went through processes of redemocratization, both nations turned to a varied array of social policies, designed to address levels of poverty and inequality so high that the two seemed to be fighting for the top spot. In the mid-1990s, Brazil and South Africa's Gini coefficients were above 0.6. In both countries, social spending comes largely in the form of cash transfers, whether retirement or welfare benefits, with the latter becoming increasingly important as a potent mechanism for incorporating large, previously excluded contingents into mass consumer markets (Lavinas 2013). Two-thirds of Brazilian social spending has taken the form of monetary transfers, to the detriment of decommodified forms of direct provision (Lavinas 2017). This share is even higher for South Africa.

As in Brazil, financialization is far advanced in South Africa (James 2015). It was helped along by the liberalization and financial deregulation of the late 1980s, which ran in parallel with the democratic transition and which served to rid the financial markets of checks on their expansion. "The quite extraordinary liberalizing of credit provision," as James refers to it (2012: 24), marked the onset of the new millennium in both countries. By way of example: the share of domestic credit to the private sector as a percentage of GDP rose from 27.7% in 2003 to 66.8% in 2015 in Brazil, whereas in South Africa it went from 115.9% to 147.7% over the same period. Credit growth continued to abound through the 2000s.

In both South Africa (Marais 2011; James 2014) and Brazil (Bruno 2011; Feijó et al. 2016), the financialization of the economy did not translate into an increase in productive investment that might promote structural changes in the pattern of accumulation and growth. Rather, it facilitated the unprecedented phenomenon of mass financialization (Becker et al. 2010; Lavinas Araújo and Bruno 2019). The swift paring away of credit constraints, or what South Africans referred to as "credit apartheid," led to the financial inclusion of broad swathes of the poor and working classes in both countries, beyond welfare recipients, taking in those seeking the kind of living conditions and opportunities they had been led to expect with the consolidation of democracy. The flipside of the coin is that Brazil and South Africa now display worrisome levels of household indebtedness and default rates.

In South Africa, the post-apartheid period has been marked by institutional innovations on the score of social policy, with the introduction of countless cash transfer mechanisms such as the old age grant and child support grant, among other social assistance benefits. In 2018, the number of social grant recipients stood at 17.4 million, up from 2 million in 1994. More than 12 million children receive an income support of 32 US$ on a monthly basis (Blackmore 2018). It has been estimated that a third of the South African population receives welfare grants, with spending equivalent to 3.4% of GDP in 2015 (South Africa National Treasury 2015). These social grants constitute the most important element of the social wage, a four-pillar means-tested social policy targeting the poor.

With the expansion of safety net coverage deepening the monetization of the poorest sectors of society, a wave of financial inclusion was made possible as grants were deposited directly into the individual accounts of beneficiaries (opened for this very purpose). In South Africa, the company designated to make these payments, Cash Payment Services, and its ancillary firms have taken to using the data of millions of welfare recipients to "cross sell" funeral policies, micro-loans, micro-insurances and other financial products to them. Payments are automatically deducted from the secure monthly flows of welfare payments. As Neves and James note, "the profits from these sales exceed the fee CPS receives from the government to distribute the grants" (2017: 2). This is not an isolated case: the largest private insurers in South Africa did the same with social grants paid to children, although the practice was subsequently outlawed. These should not be seen as wrongdoings but rather practices that are inherent to financialization.

The capture of welfare benefits by rentier logic has not spared other groups, whose regular income streams, including retirement benefits and public-sector salaries, are also paid by the state. More research from James (2018) shows how these new lending practices in South Africa have spread in particular to new civil servants in the post-apartheid era. Lacking in fixed assets that might serve as collateral, but with a regular, albeit modest, salary, they become the ideal prey for a financial system hungry for income streams to be converted into financial assets, which may in turn generate new streams of income. This continuous, growing path to debt explains why debt as a percentage of household income has passed the 70% mark in South Africa (South African Reserve Bank 2017), a high one by any standard.[8]

Brazil's recent trajectory has much in common with South Africa's in terms of the use of social policy as a mechanism to secure credit, consumer credit in particular. The now world-famous Bolsa Família program, created in 2004 along with social pensions for the disabled and the elderly poor, reaches approximately 50 million people, but accounts for just 1.5% of the country's GDP (Lavinas 2017). Monthly benefits vary from 10 US$ (for the child benefit under Bolsa Família) to a minimum wage (for social pensions), the equivalent of around 270 US$. Payments are made into fee-free individual accounts which are opened once the benefit is approved. Just as in South Africa, this formal link between welfare payments and an individual bank account paves the way for the acquisition of a growing number of financial products tailored to the needy, including funeral insurance, consumer loans, as well as new methods of payments for different kinds of goods or services, such as instalment payments.

Similarly, the 27.5 million people who receive retirement benefits from the public system, two-thirds of which are equal to a monthly minimum wage, and the country's 12 million civil servants, are eligible for a special form of credit known as consigned credit (*crédito consignado*), created in 2003 under the Workers' Party's first administration. This is a loan where instalments are deducted automatically from civil servants' paychecks or from public retirement plans or death pensions. On entering into a loan or financing agreement, or beginning to use a credit card conceded by financial institutions, the borrowers issue irrevocable authorization for the instalments to be taken out of their paychecks. The cap on these payments is set at 35% of net pay. They enjoy more favorable loan conditions and lower interest rates as compared to non-consigned loans, because the state is the guarantor of their salaries and their pensions. Even so, net interest rates remain extremely high. In 2016, for instance, they ranged from 27% to 49% per year on average (Lavinas 2017). Borrowers are also on the hook for default insurance, making it significantly harder to keep up with payments (mandatory insurance to prevent default increases the cost of the loan).

Within financial institutions, consigned credit has thus inaugurated the practice of engaging in an "active search" for retirees, which may even be carried out by correspondent banks, as well as competition for state and municipal payrolls, indicating the central clienteles for this sort of credit and thus excluding risks of moral hazard.

It is indisputable that people's ability to borrow was considerably increased by these new credit lines; but their ability to pay back loans did not keep pace. In 2014, debt–income ratio for overall borrowers hit an average of 64%. For the lowest-income borrowers, those earning up to three minimum wages (approximately 810 US$ per month), the debt-to-income ratio stood at 73% (Brazilian Central Bank 2014). Recent figures are even more troubling, showing that in the thick of a severe economic recession, which has lingered from 2015–2017, a record-breaking 60 million adults are now in default (SPC-CNDL 2017), 90% of them from the lower middle classes and below the poverty line. Expenses on clothing and food account for the vast majority of these unpaid debts.

Not even the poorest of the poor have been spared from the debt spiral. A growing number of Bolsa Família recipients are indebted – 1.4 million households have taken out loans, on average, ten times greater than their monthly stipend – and in default. According to the Brazilian Central Bank (2018), for this group, the default rate – the definition of default being a payment delay of 90 days or more – is three times higher than the rate for similar low-income groups that have not benefited by the poverty-fighting program. Because of their poverty, they pay interest rates higher than what is already a high average: an indication that, indeed, discriminatory practices do persist.

In Conclusion

In the developing world, a wide array of financial institutional arrangements targeting the less fortunate and the poor has surfaced since the 1980s in the wake of neoliberalism's rise (Bateman 2017). These programs have swept across countries lacking in social policies, hawking the idea that the less fortunate might escape poverty by dint of personal effort and discipline, coupled with expanded access to financial devices. Support for the microfinance model grew massively in the 1990s and became the backbone of strategies put forth by international agencies and designed to tackle new social risks and underdevelopment. And yet microcredit experiments, beyond expanding the reach of financial markets and financializing poverty (Duvendack and Mader 2017), never proved effective in reducing poverty, nor did they advance local economic development.

The great financial crises of 2008 gave way to the restructuring of global finance, a process that led to more effective coordination among actors in the financial system, international agencies, and national authorities in the common task of broadening the scale and scope of access to credit and other financial products. Financial markets were moving forward at a still-sluggish pace across the Global South, revealing potential left untapped because of barriers to the spread of financialization.

The state, by using social policy schemes, is key in eliminating those barriers.

First, the state grants the needy the right to a monetary transfer by virtue of their poverty. In so doing, under financialized capitalism, the state also enables welfare recipients to become potential borrowers. By the same token, the latter are relieved from posting collateral: the regular stipend they receive from the state serves as collateral. In other words, being entitled to safety net coverage takes the place of having to provide liquid assets. Nevertheless, the logic of collateralizing financial transactions is preserved and extended, which is imperative for financial markets.

Secondly, the state pays the benefit through deposits or into individual accounts not always subject to fees or other regular requirements. In this case, data on these special bank holders are provided by the state, in charge of maintaining and updating databases in order to hone its targeting welfare system and avoid misuses of the benefits. These databases (sometimes fingerprint-driven like in South Africa) are then shared with the financial sector, reducing their costs and risks by providing them with information about the lives of welfare recipients so that they might identify the product or form of financial transaction best suited to each, establishing a more lasting, trusting relationship with these new consumers.

The state is also the source for financial and economic education strategies designed to shape the connections between the newly banked and the financial sector, as well as educating a generation of finance consumers through financial-inclusion programs implemented in schools and universities, justified by the argument that they strengthen individual economic rights. It is the direct participation of the state, through myriad practices and instruments that ultimately allows the financial sector to adapt procedures and requirements on the way to making financialization a massive, global and irreversible phenomenon.

Finally, the state is crucial in stimulating the creation of liabilities that are nothing but a way of generating, on the other end, financial wealth. Along with the public sector debt, the indebtedness of households, amplified by the proliferation of income transfers underwritten by the state, constitute an essential pillar to the process of financialization. In both cases, the state stands out either by coordinating mechanisms which produce debt or by being directly involved in producing debt (public debt).

This is how financialization, working through the state, has engendered new forms of expropriation and control, subsuming and instrumentalizing social policy. Conceived in the second half of the twentieth century as a path towards freedom from the market, social policy has now become a source of dependence upon the market and even disenfranchisement through the market.

The collateralization of social policy reflects this trend and challenges the so-called novel dynamics of social inclusion in which entitlements are made to play the role of assets. We are driven to examine the logic that precedes and informs the expansion of an array of social rights in the developing world, and how this threatens to undermine rather than consolidate citizenship as we know it today. Rights are divorcing from genuinely emancipatory trajectories to service debt and boost the development of financial markets across the Global South.

Notes

1 I am thankful to Alfredo Saad Filho and Deborah James for their critical comments on a previous draft.
2 A total of 124 countries are in the sample.
3 Estimated data for seven countries that account for 75% of the region's population.
4 For more information on the so called "Golden Age" of the fight for universality, refer to *The International Labour Organization and the Quest for Social Justice, 1919–2009.* Gerry Rodgers, Eddy Lee, Lee Swepston and Jasmien Van Daele (eds.). International Labour Office. – Geneva: ILO, 2009.
5 Bankarization here is understood as "the establishment of stable and broad relationships between financial institutions and their users as regards a range of available services" (Morales and Yañez 2006).
6 As underlined by Sena (2008: 18), under full information about the borrower, financial institutions prefer not to secure a loan with collateral for "collateral is costly to liquidate in case of default."
7 Ever since microcredit and microfinance have become the spearhead of the neoliberal onslaught (Bateman 2017), as an alternative to social policies, a lack of physical collateral has produced new collateral schemes, such as social collateral, especially in asset-poor areas. A borrowing group acts as a guarantor for each other member's loans, screening and monitoring each other and ensuring that the loan is used in income-generating activities and will be repaid in order to avoid penalties for the group (see also Postelnicu, Hermes and Szafarz 2013). According to Duvendack and Mader (2017: 43), social collateral is the most disciplining device whose power "lies not so much in [its] capacity to punish as in [its] normalizing of individuals' behavior." Shiller (2012) emphasizes that a variety of collateral agreements, allied with information technology, constitute financial innovations that facilitate access to financial markets.
8 According to the US Federal Reserve, the debt-to-income ratio with regard to consumer loans (no ties attached) should not exceed 30%.

Bibliography

Barr, N., 2004. *Economics of the Welfare State.* Oxford: Oxford University Press, 4th edition.
Bateman, M., 2017. The Political Economy of Microfinance. In Bateman, M. and Maclean, K. (eds.), *Seduced and Betrayed. Exposing the Contemporary Microfinance Phenomenon.* Santa Fe: School for Advanced Research Press, pp. 17–31.
Becker, J., Jäger, J., Leubolt, B. and Weissenbacher, R., 2010. Peripheral Financialization and Vulnerability to Crisis: A Regulationist Perspective. *Competition and Change*, 14(3–4), pp. 225–247.
Blackmore, S.M., 2018. Oral Presentation, International Seminar on Redistributive Tax Systems, São Paulo, June 4–6, Panel 3: Bric's Tax Systems.
Brazilian Central Bank, 2014. *Relatório de Inclusão Financeira.* Brasília DF.

Brazilian Central Bank, 2018. *Relatório de Economia Bancária*. Brasília DF.

Bruno, M., 2011. Financerização e crescimento econômico: o caso do Brasil. *Revista Com Ciência*, 28, Campinas: SBPC.

Bryan, D. and Rafferty, M., 2014. Financial Derivatives as Social Policy beyond Crisis. *Sociology*, 48 (5), pp. 887–903.

Dupas, P., Karlan, D., Robinson, J. and Ubfal, D., 2016. Banking the Unbanked? Evidence from Three Countries. *Working Paper*440. Washington, DC: Center for Global Development.

Duvendack, M. and Mader, P., 2017. Poverty Reduction or the Financialization of Poverty. In Bateman, M. and Maclean, K. (eds.), *Seduced and Betrayed. Exposing the Contemporary Microfinance Phenomenon*. Santa Fe: School for Advanced Research Press, pp. 33–46.

Erturk, I., Froud, J., Johal, S., Leaver, A. and Williams, K., 2007. The Democratization of Finance? Promises, Outcomes and Conditions. *Review of International Political Economy*, 14(4), pp. 553–575.

Feijó, C., Lamônica, M.T. and Lima, S.S., 2016. *Financialization and Structural Change: The Brazilian Case in the 2000s*. CEDE – Centro de Estudos sobre Desigualdade e Desenvolvimento, UFF. Texto para Discussão n. 118, outubro de 2016.

Fine, B., 2014. The Continuing Enigmas of Social Policy. *UNRISD Working Paper* 2014/10. Geneva: UNRISD.

Global Partnership for Financial Inclusion, 2011. *The First G20 Global Partnership for Financial Inclusion*. Forum Report.

ILO, 2011. *The Social Protection Floor for a Fair and Inclusive Globalization*. Report of the Social Protection Floor Advisory Group. Geneva: ILO.

James, D., 2012. Money-go-round: Personal Economies of Wealth, Aspiration and Indebtedness. *Africa: The Journal of the International African Institute*, 82(1), pp. 20–40.

James, D., 2014. Deeper into a Hole? Borrowing and Lending in South Africa. *Current Anthropology*, 55(9), pp. 517–529.

James, D., 2015. *Money From Nothing. Indebtedness and Aspiration in South Africa*. Stanford, CA: Stanford University Press.

James, D., 2018. Mediating Indebtedness in South Africa. *Ethnos: Journal of Anthropology*, 83(5), pp. 814–831. doi:10.1080/00141844.2017.1362450

Krippner, G.R., 2017. Democracy of Credit: Ownership and the Politics of Credit Access in Late Twentieth-Century America. *American Journal of Sociology*, 123(1), pp. 1–47.

Lavinas, L., 2013. 21st Century Welfare. *New Left Review*, 84, November–December 2013, pp. 5–40.

Lavinas, L., 2017. *The Takeover of Social Policy by Financialization. The Brazilian Paradox*. New York: Palgrave Macmillan.

Lavinas, L., 2018. The Collateralization of Social Policy under Financialized Capitalism. *Development and Change*, 49(2), pp. 502–517.

Lavinas, L., Araújo, E. and Bruno, M., 2019. Brazil: From Eliticized to Mass-based Financialization. *Revue de la Régulation*, 25, 1st Semester, Spring.

Leyshon, A. and Thrift, N., 2007. The Capitalization of Almost Everything. The Future of Finance and Capitalism. *Theory, Culture & Society*, 24(7–8), pp. 97–115.

Mader, P., 2015. *The Political Economy of Microfinance. Financializing Poverty*. London: Palgrave Macmillan.

Marais, H., 2011. *South Africa Pushed to the Limit: The Political Economy of Change*. London: Zed Books.

Morales, L. and Yañez, A., 2006. *La Bancarización en Chile, Concepto y Medición*. Série Técnica de Estudios de la Superintendencia de Bancos e Instituciones Financieras. Santiago, Chile.

Neves, D. and James, D., 2017. South Africa's Social Grants: Busting the Myth about Financial Inclusion. *The Conversation*. https://theconversation.com/south-africas-social-grants-busting-the-myth-about-financial-inclusion-74776. Version of Record Online April 15 2018.

Postelnicu, L., Hermes, N. and Szafarz, A., 2013. Defining Social Collateral in Microfinance Group Lending. *CEB Working Paper* No. 13/050. Centre Emile Berheim, Research Institute in Management Sciences.

Riles, A., 2011. *Collateral Knowledge. Legal Reasoning in the Global Financial Markets*. Chicago, IL: The University of Chicago Press.

Roa, M.J., 2015. Financial Inclusion in Latin America and the Caribbean: Access, Usage and Quality. *CEMLA Research Papers* 19. Mexico D.F: Center for Latin American Monetary Studies.

Schelkle, W., 2012. In the Spotlight of Crisis: How Social Policies Create, Correct, and Compensate Financial Markets. *Politics & Society*, 40(1), pp. 3–8.

Shiller, R., 2012. *Finance and the Good Society*. Princeton: Princeton University Press.

Sena, V., 2008. *Credit and Collateral*. London and New York: Routledge.

SPC-CNDL, 2017. *Pesquisa sobre Inadimplência*. Rio de Janeiro.

Soederberg, S., 2014. *Debtfare States and the Poverty Industry. Money, Discipline and the Surplus Population*. London and New York: Routledge.

South Africa National Treasury, 2015. Database.

South African Reserve Bank, 2017. *Financial Stability Review*. 2nd edition. Pretoria.

Stockhammer, E., 2004. Financialisation and the Slowdown of Accumulation. *Cambridge Journal of Economics*, 28(5), pp. 719–741.

Sweezy, P., 1994. The Triumph of Financial Capital. *The Monthly Review*, 46(2).

UNCTAD, 2017. *Beyond Austerity: Towards a Global New Deal*. Trade and Development Report 2017. New York and Geneva.

World Bank, 2018a. *The State of Social Safety Nets 2018*. Washington, DC: World Bank.

World Bank, 2018b. *Global Financial Inclusion and Consumer Protection (FICP) Survey*. 2017 Report. Swiss Confederation.

27A

ESSAY FORUM: LABOR IN FINANCIALIZATION

Value Logics and Labor: Collateral Damage or Central Focus?

Paul Thompson and Jean Cushen

Contributors to this discussion were asked to consider the extent to which the financialization discourse addresses labor issues and the short answer has to be "not very much or very well." Whilst a good case can be made for a variety of topics covered (Van der Zwan 2014), the weight of research and analysis falls on macro-economic issues that explore the destabilizing impact of financialization on economic growth. Political economy literatures do not completely ignore impacts on labor, but issues of risk and instability are framed as secondary effects of macro regime-level changes. Where effects on labor appear, these are largely as collateral damage; from depressed wages or rising indebtedness, lacklustre innovation, vulnerability to crises and skewed distributional outcomes. The goal of this section of the Handbook is to explore the ways in which labor has entered the picture and to make a specific case that the business models and financial mechanisms of non-financial corporations work through as well as impact on labor. It is also important to recognize that financialization research on firms and labor already poses a massive challenge to the previously dominant human capital and knowledge economy narratives whose causal chain starts in labor or product markets (Dundon and Rafferty 2018). This challenge is finally being recognized in policy debates within human resource professional circles (see Findlay et al. 2018).

We begin by depicting in Figure 27.1 how financialization is linked with labor. This figure presents "themes" of financialization which impact labor as well as the three "territories" in which labor both effects and is affected. Both are further addressed in contributions to this Forum section of the Handbook.

The common themes chart how a financialized trajectory of accumulation destabilizes labor across various dimensions of production and reproduction. Accumulation, through ongoing short-term speculation and asset restructuring reflects and shapes the competing claims of agents within industrial and financial circuits of capital (Stockhammer 2008; Müller 2013; Stockhammer and Köhler in this volume). For capital and corporate executives, the terms and conditions under which labor is provided within industrial and productive circuits have become negotiable absorbers of risk; labor is a source from which value can be routinely extracted to heighten gains and mitigate losses within the financial circuit. (Lapavitsas 2011; Lazonick and Mazzucato 2013; Erturk

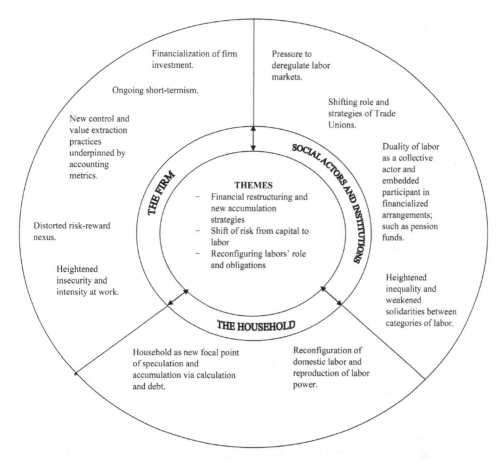

Figure 27.1 Financialization and Labor: Themes and Territories of Impact

in this volume). Consequently, under financialization, labor's role and value obligations have expanded. While not uniform in its effects and room for maneuver, labor must frequently absorb financialized restructuring and risks whilst engaging in calculative financial activities to mitigate losses within personal terms and conditions.

Some of the emphases in Figure 27.1 reflect different research questions and dimensions of labor. McCarthy (2014, and in this volume) focuses on ways in which, at the institutional level, financialization imposes a shareholder value logic that disrupts institutional arrangements – in this case workers' assets in pensions funds – identified by comparative political economy literatures. This logic is reinforced by political decisions to deregulate and decollectivize the employment relationship (Rubery 2015: 634). The literatures, while avoiding assertions of convergence, show how financialization weakens institutions that legitimize labors' value claims. The deregulation of labor markets, whilst not only attributable to financialization, is apparent across a range of OECD countries and shows capital has reasserted its power over organized labor and labor markets in the US, UK and Western Europe.

While unions seek strategies to secure their position, financialization introduces new barriers to labor building labor solidarity; for example, competition between labor for financial investment and the pressure for concession bargaining hampers unions' perceived utility (Grady and Simms

2018). Solidarities are also constrained by increasingly polarized labor markets arising in part from the transfer of risk to migrant and often outsourced labor in financialized business models of some sectors (Datta and Guermond in this volume). Institutional logics at national or sectoral level can create practical and reputational counter-pressures to financialization. Exposure to capital markets can be offset by accessing finance in national or regional banks, corporate governance require-ments or even different reporting rules. There is evidence that national private equity firms are less detrimental to labor than foreign equivalents (Stevenot et al. 2017). However, the rise of global finance and value chains diminishes traditional distinctions between liberal and coordinated market economies and national institutions do not wholly deflect novel financialized pressures. Research on EU information and consultation legislation shows it is largely evaded by managers of multinational companies, who cite stock market regulation and reporting requirements as the primary driver (Pulignano and Waddington 2019).

The erosion of state protections and the social wage in many contexts may be a factor in labor seeking financial stability outside the workplace, prompting explorations of the financia-lization of the household and everyday life (Van der Zwan 2014; Grady and Simms 2018; Adkins in this volume; Montgomerie in this volume). This trend, however, also has to be linked to the broader shifts in the circuits of capital, the search for new sources of profits and the commodification (framed as "democratization") of finance (Bryan et al. 2009; Lapavitsas 2011; McCarthy in this volume). Other household-focused scholars see financialized accumulation leading to a reconfiguration of the home as an object of calculation and the inclusion of women and unpaid domestic labor within circuits of capital (Adkins and Deyer 2016). The expansion of the commodity form and the role of the household in restructuring of risk, debt and labor are important developments. However, a focus on value extraction beyond the labor process has too often led to a displacement perspective and a paucity of research on the relations between financialization and the point of production.

The stream of labor-focused research draws largely from our own work (Thompson 2003, 2013; Cushen and Thompson 2016), but also from Clark (2009, 2011), Appelbaum Batt and Clark (2013), Appelbaum and Batt (2014) and Gospel et al. (2014). Such contributions examine how financialization affects and is experienced by waged labor within production, uncovering the new, often concurrent, dynamics of value creation and extraction at firm and value chain level. However, to examine and explain primary impacts on and involvement of labor, it has been necessary to confront perceptions that financialization has marginalized labor as a source of value due to the proportionate size and influence of the financial sector and financial engineering.

To explain why the "displacement of labor in production" arguments are mistaken, we have to consider how non-financial corporations are highly financialized. Large firms are not only increasingly subject to shareholder value pressures through capital markets, growth strategies indicate firms are also active players in those processes through markets for corporate control and leveraging value from financial assets (Lazonick and O'Sullivan 2000; Dore 2008; Erturk in this volume). As firm assets become more disposable, a recurring outcome is perpetual restructuring, whether that is through delayering, divestment, disaggregation or downsizing. Through such initiatives, laborers are not passive side-line actors, but are active participants in delivering value.

An early and widely referenced observation of these trends came through Thompson's (2003) disconnected capitalism thesis (DCT). Financialization drove a wedge (or exacerbated the gap) between managerial objectives in the sphere of work (discretionary effort, investment of human capital) and employed people (disposability, shift of risk), thus undermining the stability and reciprocity necessary for local high performance work system "bargains." The DCT influenced other workplace research, particularly case studies that charted the constraints on mutual gains practices and negative consequences for employee attitudes and behaviors (see Thompson 2013, for a summary). Our own evidence from an ethnography of a leading IT company ("Avatar") is used to show how an award-winning HR department and its "employment deal" crashed and burned as its rhetoric and practices collided with corporate-level financial strictures (Cushen and Thompson 2012).

Other accounts of impacts on labor, particularly with the involvement of new investment funds, show a mixed cross-national picture (Bacon et al. 2010; Gospel et al. 2014). Gospel et al. (2014) nevertheless share largely pessimistic conclusions about the effects of mechanisms such as shorter time horizons and changes in the balance of power in corporate governance, but argue that "downstream" labor impacts are largely indirect and difficult to detect. It is certainly true that shareholder value pressures are often difficult to disentangle in their effects on issues such as job insecurity and work intensification from other medium-term trends such as systemic rationalization.

However, in our recent analytical work (Cushen and Thompson 2016, and see also Baud and Durand 2012), we have attempted to more carefully specify how "upstream" pressures are "translated" by meso-level mechanisms into workplace (or downstream) outcomes. This has primarily involved the identification of how novel accounting techniques, metrics and budgeting processes play a key role in embedding broader financialized objectives in labor-centered value extraction and creation (Chiapello in this volume). They work both through metrics to meet expectations of future performance (profit financialization) and those geared towards squeezing operational expenditures and costs (control financialization) (see Clark and Macey 2015, on these terms). Gleadle and Haslam (2010) document how within bio-pharma firms medical scientists "pitch" internally for capital investment through connecting their research to future income. The firms subsequently report on R&D progress via investor specified milestones to boost firm valuation. This denotes a progression in management control techniques whereby the onus is on employees to quantify their value creation at the point of production.

Localized accounting processes are molded to replicate firm valuation metrics and, in this way, investor preferences are ratcheted downwards to shape working life. For example, within Avatar, group headquarters routinely passed down cost cutting measures to meet such metrics that could only be met by reducing operational expenditures that had adverse effects on employee rewards (such as annual bonuses) and job security (for example through downsizing, centralization and outsourcing). The scope for investment in human and physical capital is reduced and these are, in part, measured through their ability to squeeze labor costs and create value at the same time. Following a private equity takeover of the Automobile Association in the UK, pressures to service the debt and dividend payments led to a target of "managing out of the business" 3,400 employees (Clark 2011).

Such mechanisms are not uniform, mediated as they are by national and sectoral institutional practices. Another key point of variation is the form of agency at firm level. Research on the private equity business model is instructive (Clark 2009, 2011; Appelbaum et al. 2013; Appelbaum and Batt 2014). Although these authors have emphasized that "breaches of trust" and value extraction are spread across a variety of stakeholders, it is also clear from their own case evidence that labor is particularly vulnerable to managerial requirements to service debt, interest payments and higher than average returns over a short time period. That vulnerability can be expressed through additional risks of job destruction, value transfers from worker wages, pensions and benefits, and work intensification.

Taken as a whole, new research has challenged mainstream financialization scholarship to make better connections to varieties of labor. Although this strand of research has made considerable strides in recent years, there are many things we do not know or know well enough. Some labor issues are best addressed at level of the value chain or production network and a recent wave of studies is filling a gap (Milburg 2008; Baud and Durand 2012; Montalban and Sakinç 2013; Parker et al. 2018). However, more work exploring the relationship and tensions between concurrent organizational value extraction and value creation strategies delivered by employees at the heart of the labor process is required. We also call for research into the connection between the terrains of labour and financialization identified in Figure 27.1. Such accounts are essential to understanding the daily experience behind aggregate trends of worsening terms and conditions, as well as compounding impacts across the terrains of financialization.

Bibliography

Adkins L. and Dever M., 2016. The financialisation of social reproduction: Domestic labor and promissory value. In Adkins L. and Dever M. (eds.), *The Post-Fordist Sexual Contract*. London: Palgrave Macmillan.

Appelbaum, E. and Batt, R., 2014. *Private Equity at Work: When Wall Street Manages Main Street*. New York: Russell Sage Foundation.

Appelbaum, E., Batt, R. and Clark, I., 2013. Implications of financial capitalism for employment relations research: Evidence from breach of trust and implicit contracts in private equity buyouts. *British Journal of Industrial Relations*, 51(3), pp. 498–518.

Bacon, N., Wright, M., Scholes, L. and Meuleman, M., 2010. Assessing the impact of private equity on industrial relations in Europe. *Human Relations*, 63(9), pp. 1343–1370.

Baud C. and Durand C., 2012. Financialization, globalization and the making of profits by leading retailers. *Socio-Economic Review*, 10(2), pp. 241–266.

Bryan D., Martin R. and Rafferty M. (2009) Financialization and Marx: Giving labor and capital a financial makeover. *Review of Radical Political Economics*, 41(4), pp. 458–472.

Clark I., 2009. Owners and managers: Disconnecting managerial capitalism? Understanding the private-equity business model. *Work, Employment and Society*, 23(4), pp. 775–786.

Clark, I., 2011. Private equity, "union recognition" and value-extraction at the Automobile Association: The GMB as an emergency service? *Industrial Relations Journal*, 42(1), pp. 36–50.

Clark, I. and Macey, R., 2015. How is financialization contagious? How do HR practices help capture workplace outcomes in financialized firms? In: *Conference Proceedings*. Presented at the 33rd International Labor Process Conference, Athens.

Cushen, J. and Thompson, P., 2012. Doing the right thing? HRM and the angry knowledge worker. *New Technology, Work and Employment*, 27(2), pp. 79–92.

Cushen, J. and Thompson, P., 2016. Financialization and value: Why labor and the labor process still matter. *Work, Employment and Society*, 30(2), pp. 352–365.

Dore, R., 2008. Financialization of the global economy. *Industrial and Corporate Change*, 17(6), pp. 1097–1112.

Dundon, T. and Rafferty, A., 2018. The (potential) demise of HRM? *Human Resource Management Journal*, 28(3), pp. 377–391.

Findlay, P., Thompson, P., Cooper, C. and Pascoe-Deslauriers, R., 2018. Creating and capturing value at work: Who benefits? *Chartered Institute of Personnel and Development, Research Report Parts 1 & 2*, London: CIPD, January.

Gleadle, P. and Haslam, C., 2010. An exploratory study of an early stage R&D-intensive firm under financialization. *Accounting Forum*, 34(1), pp. 54–65.

Gospel, H., Pendleton, A. and Vitols, S., 2014. *Financialization, New Investment Funds and Labor: An International Comparison*. Oxford: Oxford University Press.

Grady, J. and Simms, M., 2018. Trade unions and the challenge of fostering solidarities in an era of financialisation. *Economic and Industrial Democracy*, https://doi.org/10.1177/0143831X18759792.

Lapavitsas, C., 2011. Theorizing financialization. *Work, Employment and Society*, 25(4), pp. 611–626.

Lazonick, W. and O'Sullivan M., 2000. Maximizing shareholder value: A new ideology for corporate governance. *Economy and Society*, 29(1), pp.13–35.

Lazonick, W. and Mazzucato, M., 2013. The risk-reward nexus in the innovation-inequality relationship: who takes the risks? Who gets the rewards? *Industrial and Corporate Change*, 22(4), pp. 1093–1128.

McCarthy, M.A., (2014). Turning labor into capital: Pension funds and the corporate control of finance. *Politics & Society*, 42(4), pp. 455–487.

Meyer, B., 2017. Financialization, technological change, and trade union decline. *Socio-Economic Review*https://doi.org/10.1093/ser/mwx022

Milburg W., 2008. Shifting sources and uses of profits: Sustaining US financialization with global value chains. *Economy and Society*, 37(3), pp. 420–451.

Montalban, M., and Sakinç, M.E., 2013. Financialization and productive models in the pharmaceutical industry. *Industrial and Corporate Change*, 22(4), pp. 981–1030.

Müller, J., 2013. *Theses on Financialisation and the Ambivalence of Capitalist Growth*. DFG-Kollegforscher-gruppe Postwachstumsgesellschaften, Working Paper.

Parker, R., Cox, S. and Thompson, P., 2018. Financialization and value-based control: Lessons from the Australian mining supply chain. *Economic Geography*, 94(1), pp. 49–67.

Pulignano, V. and Waddington, J., 2019. Management, European Works Councils and institutional malleability. *European Journal of Industrial Relations*. https://doi.org/10.1177/0959680118824512

Rubery, J., 2015. Change at work: Feminisation, flexibilisation, fragmentation and financialisation. *Employee Relations*, 37(6), pp. 633–644.

Stevenot, A., Guery, L., Wood, G. and Brewster, C., 2017. Country of origin effects and new financial actors: Private equity investment and work and employment practices of French firms. *British Journal of Industrial Relations*, 56(4), pp. 859–881.

Stockhammer, E., 2008. Some stylized facts on the finance-dominated accumulation regime. *Competition & Change*, 12(2), pp. 184–202.

Thompson, P., 2003. Disconnected capitalism: Or why employers can't keep their side of the bargain. *Work, Employment and Society*, 17(2), pp. 359–378.

Thompson, P., 2013. Financialization and the workplace: Extending and applying the disconnected capitalism thesis. *Work, Employment and Society*, 27(3), pp. 472–478.

Van der Zwan, N., 2014. Making sense of financialization. *Socio-Economic Review*, 12(1), pp. 99–129.

27B

ESSAY FORUM: LABOR IN FINANCIALIZATION

Financialization and/of Migrant Labor

Kavita Datta and Vincent Guermond

Migrant labor is a significant presence in contemporary economies with over 64% of 872 million migrants worldwide moving to work (ILO 2018). Credited for being a source of "fresh skills" responding to labor shortages in host economies, migrant workers are valued as "development agents" by home nations where they augment private household income by sending remittances. Yet research documents the extensive abuse of this labor force, capturing everyday experiences of wage suppression, poor working conditions and exploitative recruitment practices (Davies 2018). Not surprisingly, the protection of migrant workers' rights features prominently in international agendas including the ILO's (2015) Decent Work commitment and Global Compact on Migration.

Migrant labor does not feature significantly in emerging research on the financialization–labor nexus which notes the broader erosion of labor value as capital has become less reliant upon labor quality, intensity and cooperation (see also Horton 2017). In light of this lacuna, we advance three observations in this chapter. First, we elaborate upon financialization and migrant labor high-lighting that migrants are pivotal in financialized economies as both low and highly skilled workers. Our second observation pertains to a critical exposition of the foundations upon which the financialization of remittances as a set of "development" initiatives is built. In turn, the co-option of migrant workers into financialization projects is the focus of our third reflection.

Financialization and Migrant Labor

Structural shifts in the global political economy brought on by neoliberal reform and the increased prominence of finance over the last 40 years have intensified historic processes of the subordination of migrant labor (Datta 2012). Spatially and temporally variegated, in advanced economies this period is associated with rapid de-industrialization and the shift to a service economy in which subcontracting and outsourcing are the norm (Wills et al. 2010). Meanwhile, poorer countries in the global economy have undergone significant neoliberal economic reform, instituted through the imposition of Structural Adjustment Programs. Laying the conditions for the "coerced mass movement of peoples," millions of men and women have moved to find work locally, regionally and increasingly internationally, in response to widespread dispossession including the destruction of entire employment sectors, the stagnation and/or depression of wages and commodification of land (Ferguson and McNally 2015: 8; also Datta 2012).

In turn, the nexus of financialized neoliberalism, restrictive immigration regimes and discriminatory welfare policies have cheapened low-skilled migrant labor. In London, for instance, a "migrant division of labor" is evidenced in the dominance of migrants in low paid work where immigration status intersects with gendered and racial cleavages to produce a hierarchy of descending political and socio-economic rights, terms and conditions of work (Wills et al. 2010). Comprising a "hyper-precarious section of the working class," migrant workers' particular vulnerabilities were exposed in the 2007 financial crisis with widespread retrenchments partly attributable to their concentration in volatile sectors such as construction and hospitality (Ferguson and McNally 2015: 5; Buckley 2012). In turn, the return migration of heavily indebted migrants to countries which historically dealt with structural labor market problems through labor export strategies has had devastating consequences on households and local economies.

If low paid migrant workers are one side of the financialization–migrant labor story, their highly skilled counterparts are the other. Their significance as key architects of financialization (particularly in relation to "innovations" such as securities, hedge funds and private equity markets), illustrate that finance has not disempowered all workers equally and that class is an enduring labor market differentiator. Indeed, this global "talent" valued for both its technical and tacit embodied skills, is widely regarded as underpinning the City of London's position as a key financial center, with approximately 25% of City jobs occupied by workers from the USA and Europe as well as BRIC economies, particularly India and China (Beaverstock and Hall 2012; Hall 2018).

The Financialization of Remittances

Our second observation relates to the financialization of remittances – the "fruit" of migrant labor – which underpin transnational social reproduction (Datta 2016). Global remittances amounted to US$ 689 billion in 2018, with US$ 528 billion sent to poorer countries where they are predominantly invested in food, education and health (World Bank and KNOMAD 2018). Yet, a "remittance-to-development" agenda advocates the leveraging of remittances to promote economic growth, alleviate poverty, facilitate individuals/households' access to formal financial services and institutions, as well as countries' access to capital markets (Hudson 2008; Datta 2012; Bakker 2015).

These initiatives promote the use of formal remittance transfer channels, remittance-linked financial services (interest-bearing mobile wallets, insurance, credit, mortgages) and assets (shares and government-issued bonds), and using remittances as collateral to issue new debt via securitization. Collectively they constitute "the expansion of the frontier of financial accumulation" (Mader 2014: 606; also Kunz 2011; Cross 2015; Datta 2016; Guermond and Sylla 2018). The financializing of remittances encourages migrant workers and their families to dedicate an ever-increasing fraction of their wage remittances to the management of formal financial debts and assets (thus exposing them as Adkins (in this volume) argues to the "ups and downs of speculative markets") in order to secure their future. In contrast, in global development and financial inclusion discourses, the provision of social reproductive services either by the state or existing "informal" arrangements such as Rotating Savings and Credit Associations (ROSCAs) are deemed inefficient, and even backwards, and in need of formalization and market restructuring.

It is undeniable that the extension of finance to new territories broadens the possibilities for financial capital to extract profit from wages. However, both proponents and critics of these "development" projects overlook the foundations upon which they are built. Drawing upon our first observation on the organized cheapening of particular segments of migrant labor, we argue that a critical understanding of the genealogies and the outcomes of the financialization of migrants' wage remittances requires locating transnational families' livelihood strategies within international migration regimes that create conditions of oppression, exploitation and inequality (Cole 2012). The adoption of a transnational lens brings into view relations between cross-border movements of capital, labor and wages in the context of the social reproduction of class relations at a global scale and the central roles of racism and imperialism in the (re)production of these social relations (Grosfoguel et al. 2014; Ferguson and McNally 2015).

In effect, the two-way movement of workers and (a fraction of) their wages benefit capital in two ways. First, it provides a precarious cheap source of labor in global North countries. Second, it displaces the cost of producing the next generation of workers to the global South where living costs are lower and to which global North states do not contribute. Thus, despite constituting collective cross-border livelihood strategies, transnational families and the under-lying social practices of money remitting/receiving play an essential part in "perpetuating the cheap social reproduction of the current and future working class" (Ferguson and McNally 2015: 13). They are, therefore, part and parcel of the *modus operandi* of global capitalism, and development initiatives aimed at leveraging the financial potential of remittances further accentuate such processes.

The Financialization of Migrant Workers

Our final observation relates to the financialization *of* migrant workers, drawing upon research on everyday, mundane and banal financializations, which nudge individuals and households to both take risks and assume responsibility for their present and future financial well-being (Langley in this volume). In an era in which (young) men and women aspire to be *migrants*, increasingly restrictive and commodified immigration landscapes necessitate risk taking such as an insertion into local and global debt markets in order to facilitate mobility (Baey and Yeoh 2018; Datta and Aznar 2018). In turn, narratives of responsibilization and the ascription of particular identities and agential capacities onto migrants – such as the "hard working migrant" and "national heroes" – underpin the migration–development nexus which demands that migrants maintain active meaningful and developmental relationships with the places from which they came. Efforts to change or improve the financial behavior of migrants is implicit in financial inclusion initiatives, which encourage migrants to save, invest and borrow rather than share and give.

This individualization of financial matters and the belief that people's choices can be shaped to lift them out of poverty are linked to the behavioral approaches to poverty alleviation (Berndt 2015; Gabor and Brooks 2017). While grounded analysis of the ways in which these nudge processes take place is limited, recent research on the financialization of the migration–development agenda, such as the failed attempts of the Colombian state to promote remittances-for-housing programs has shown that the everyday construction of finan-cialized subjects is not a straightforward process that can be generalized across place and space (Zapata 2013, 2018). Further research is needed on how the structural forces of financialization shape – and are shaped by – the financial behaviors, practices and expectations of migrant workers and their families.

In this chapter, we propose that scholars critically interrogate the co-constitution of financializa-tion and migrant labor. In so doing we must be attentive to the genealogies and ramifications of financialization processes among people, places and spaces which are often regarded as peripheral *and* the ways in which race, racism, (neo)colonialism and coloniality complicate how financialization processes unfold in, and between, countries of the global North and South.

Bibliography

Baey, G. and Yeoh, B., 2018. "The lottery of my life": Migration trajectories and the production of precarity among Bangladeshi migrant workers in Singapore's construction industry. *Asian and Pacific Migration Journal,* 27(3), pp. 249–272.

Bakker, M., 2015. Discursive representations and policy mobility: How migrant remittances became a "development tool." *Global Networks*, 15(1), pp. 21–42.

Beaverstock, J. and Hall, S., 2012. Competing for talent: Global mobility, immigration and the City of London's labor market. *Cambridge Journal of Regions, Economy and Society*, 5, pp. 27–287.

Berndt, C., 2015. Behavioural economics, experimentalism and the marketization of development. *Economy and Society*, 44(4), pp. 567–591.

Buckley, M., 2012. From Kerala to Dubai and back again: Construction migrants and the global economic crisis. *Geoforum*, 43, pp. 250–259.

Cole, P., 2012. The ethics of open borders. Talk delivered for the Conway Hall Ethical Society Sunday Morning Lecture Series, London, 9 December, Available at https://www.academia.edu/2283956/The_Ethics_of_Open_Borders [Accessed January 2019].

Cross, H., 2015. Finance, development, and remittances: Extending the Scale Of Accumulation In Migrant Labor Regimes. *Globalizations*, 12(3), pp. 305–321.

Datta, K., 2016. "Mainstreaming" the "alternative'? The financialization of transnational migrant remittances. In Pollard, J. and Martin, R. (eds.), *Handbook on the Geographies of Money and Finance*. Cheltenham: Edward Elgar, pp. 539–561.

Datta, K., 2012. *Migrants and their Money: Surviving Financial Exclusion in London*. Bristol: Policy Press.

Datta, K. and Aznar, C., 2018. The space-times of migration and debt: Re-positioning migrants' debt and credit practices and institutions in, and through, London. *Geoforum*, 98(January), pp. 300–308.

Davies, J., 2018. From severe to routine labor exploitation: The case of migrant workers in the UK food industry. *Criminology and Criminal Justice*. https://doi.org/10.1177/1748895818762264

Ferguson, S. and McNally, D., 2015. Precarious migrants: Gender, race and the social reproduction of a global working class. *Socialist Register*, 51, pp. 1–23.

Gabor, D. and Brooks, S., 2017. The digital revolution in financial inclusion: International development in the fintech era. *New Political Economy*, 22(4), pp. 423–436.

Guermond, V. and Sylla, S.N., 2018. When monetary coloniality meets 21st century finance: Development in the franc zone. *Discover Society*, 60. Available at https://discoversociety.org/2018/09/04/when-monetary-coloniality-meets-21st-century-finance-development-in-the-franc-zone/ [Accessed October 2018].

Grosfoguel, R., Oso, L. and Christou, A., 2014. Racism, intersectionality and migration studies: Framing some theoretical reflections. *Identities: Global Studies in Culture and Power*, 22(6), pp. 635–652.

Hall, S., 2018. Reframing labour market mobility in global finance: Chinese elites in London's financial district. *Urban Geography*. https://doi.org/10.1080/02723638.2018.1472442

Horton, A., 2017. Financialization of care: Investment and organising in the UK and US. PhD thesis submitted to the School of Geography, Queen Mary University of London.

Hudson, D., 2008. Developing geographies of financialization: Banking the poor and remittance securitization. *Contemporary Politics*, 14(3), pp. 315–333.

Kunz, R., 2011. *The Political Economy of Global Remittances: Gender, Governmentality and Neoliberalism*. New York: Routledge.

ILO, 2015. *Promoting Decent Work for Migrant Workers*. Available at www.un.org/en/development/desa/population/migration/events/coordination/13/documents/backgrounddocs/GFMD_ILO_Discussion%20Paper_Promoting%20Decent%20Work%20for%20MWs.pdf [Accessed June 2018].

ILO, 2018. *World Employment and Social Outlook: Trends 2018*. Available at https://www.ilo.org/global/research/global-reports/weso/2018/WCMS_615594/lang–en/index.htm [Accessed June 2018].

Mader, P., 2014. Financialisation through microfinance: Civil society and market-building in India. *Asian Studies Review*, 38(4), pp. 601–619.

Wills, J., Datta, K., Evans, Y., Herbert, J., May, J. and McIlwaine, C., 2010. *Global Cities at Work: New Migrant Divisions of Labor*. London: Pluto Press.

World Bank and KNOMAD, 2018. Migration and remittances: Recent developments and outlooks: Transit migration. Available at http://www.knomad.org/publicatiom/migration-and-developm ent-brief-29 [Accessed August 2018].

Zapata, G., 2013. The migration–development nexus: Rendering migrants as transnational financial subjects through housing. *Geoforum*, 47, pp. 93–102.

Zapata, G., 2018. Transnational migration, remittances and the financialization of housing in Colombia. *Housing Studies*, 33(3), pp. 343–360.

27C

ESSAY FORUM: LABOR IN FINANCIALIZATION

Labor in the Financial Era: Assets, Debt and the Speculative Worker

Lisa Adkins

In this short essay I outline how the wage labor relation is restructuring in the context of financial expansion. Within the extant literature on financialization attention to such restructuring has been limited, if recognized at all. In large part, this is because of the operation of a general assumption (found especially in a particular strand of post-Marxist thinking) that the expansion of finance from the 1970s onwards has amounted to a process of the real subsumption of labor to finance capital (see e.g. Bryan, Rafferty and Jefferis 2015). This subsumption is expressed in how the whole of the lives of workers as well as the lives of potential workers – from places of dwelling through healthcare to education – are incorporated into and dependent upon the operations of finance capital, not least via the necessity of securitized mortgages, credit, and loans to support life. Alongside asset inflation, and especially asset inflation in regard to housing, one particularly powerful mechanism of this entanglement of labor with finance capital is wage stagnation. At play across advanced liberal societies from the mid-1970s onwards, wage repression is one critical feature of the financial era (Stockhammer 2013; Wisman 2013). Operating in concert with ongoing welfare reform, including the emergence of asset-based welfare, the outcome of long-term and now thoroughly embedded wage repression is that wages are now both stagnant and highly contingent with many workers – even when engaged in full-time waged work – not earning enough to meet the costs of life.[1] As a consequence, and supported by changes to the operations of consumer credit markets (Aalbers 2016), workers are compelled to fund their lives and life-times via consumer credit, loans and mortgages, that is, to substitute wages for debt (Barba and Pivetti 2009). Wage stagnation operates, then, as a powerful mechanism of the enrolment of labor into the architectures of finance, with the outcome that workers must become experts at juggling repressed and often volatile incomes and managing their contracted financial commitments (Adkins 2018).

Despite the important observation that stagnant wages entangle workers in the architectures of finance there are, as Cooper (2015) has noted, surprisingly few analyses which directly consider either the relationship between stagnant wages and financial expansion or, more broadly, the relationship between the restructuring of labor and such expansion. This is the case despite the fact that wage stagnation and financial expansion are historically coterminous. It is also the case notwithstanding recent excellent analyses of the rise of precarious and insecure forms of work (see e.g. Standing 2011; Peck and Theodore 2012; Lorey 2015).[2] This problem, I would suggest, is the outcome of two widespread and related assumptions prevalent in analyses of the growth of finance. The first – found, for instance, at the core of Streeck's (2014a) analysis of contemporary capitalism – is that the growth of finance, and especially the generation of wealth from finance, proceeds separately from and is not dependent upon wage labor. The second is that the value of finance is immaterial, fictitious and unstable and parasitic on the value that labor creates, indeed that any value created by finance is not "real" value (see e.g. Chesnais 2014).

These assumptions tend to bracket the entanglement of wage laborers with finance. Lapavitsas (2009, 2011), for example, has considered how financial expansion has opened out specific opportunities for finance capital (banks and financial institutions) to mine the wages of workers for profit, indeed, to profit from the wages and salaries of workers beyond the surplus already extracted from labor power in the labor process, that is, beyond the exploitation of labor power. This takes place, he suggests, via the extraction of profit in the form of interest accruing on various forms of securitized credit debt. Lapavitsas observes further that this form of profit extraction presupposes the involvement of workers in the mechanisms of finance "in order to meet elementary needs, such as housing, education, [and] health" (Lapavitsas 2009: 129). It is only under such conditions, he suggests, that financial institutions can extract profits from wages. The subsumption of labor to capital has, in other words, afforded systemic opportunities for finance capital to open out new forms of extraction vis-à-vis wage laborers, and especially in situations where workers do not earn enough to live and must turn to debt to address this gap.

While the observation that the expansion of finance has opened out new opportunities for the extraction of profit by financial capital from wages is accurate, a focus on this form of extraction does not come to grips with (or indeed explain) how wages have become repressed and stagnant in the financial era. It overlooks how the process of the exchange of labor power for money has been substantially rewritten in the context of financial expansion. And here it is worth recalling that in the Keynesian era, for male workers in particular, wages were typically set via compacts (or contracts) between organized labor, employers and the state. Through such compacts, and via indexation to inflation rates and the costs of living, wages were set at rates which covered the reproduction of labor and life and especially the costs of the heteronormative household, a household which, via the unpaid labor of women, reproduced and maintained labor power on a daily basis. While operating as a mechanism to distribute welfare for male wage-earners, many workers were, then, excluded from national wage setting agreements, with the "family wage" negotiated between organized labor, employers and the state forming a central pillar in the operations of the racial and sexual contracts of Keynesianism (Cooper 2012). Thus, characteristically, it was organized white male workers who were the recipients and beneficiaries of the Keynesian or Fordist family wage.

One strong assumption in accounts of the financial era is that financial expansion has gone hand in hand with a dismantling of the wage setting contracts or compacts typical of Keynesianism, a dismantling that has taken place via institutional (especially by legal and policy) means (see e.g. Harvey 2010; Streeck 2014b). Despite the existence of this narrative, and notwithstanding processes of the decentralization of wage bargaining, it must be recognized that within the financial era wages are *as* organized as they were within the Keynesian era. Post-financial crisis austerity measures, for example, which have fixed and capped wage rates as part of a broader pursuit of reductions to price, have been orchestrated and synchronized by the state in concert with employers. But it is not simply that this kind of institutional wage repression must be recognized to be taking place within the financial era. For also at issue are new forms of the indexation of wages. This latter is explicitly on view in Finland. While Finland's ongoing tripartism (that is, economic corporatism) might, at first sight, suggest that it may not serve as a particularly interesting site or case to track such developments, through the forging of a new social contract between the state, employers and unions, a devaluation of the price of labor has been orchestrated. This devaluation has been explicitly designed to address state spending deficits in the context of the operations of European Monetary Union public expenditure rules. Indeed, through the new social contract wages have been indexed to measures of national debt (Adkins et al. 2019). What is imperative about this indexing is how it attests to how the price of labor has become critical to the fiscal stability of nations. Indeed, it points to how in the financial era, the labor force operates as a form of risk-absorbing collateral for the state (Tadiar 2013). If, then, in the Keynesian era the state provided certain guarantees to workers, and especially to male workers, with labor power and its daily reproduction driving capitalist growth, in the financial era labor itself underwrites the state, fuelling its fiscal stability, credit ratings and sustainability.

What is of significance in regard to the Finnish case is not only how it makes explicit this underwriting, but also how it draws attention to the significance of corporatist structures within the process of the organized devaluation of the price of labor. The enduring significance of such structures in the financial era has also been made unequivocal by Humphrys and Cahill (2017) in their analysis of the agreement (or social contract) made between organized labor and the state in Australia in the 1980s (an agreement formally known as *The Accord*). Focusing on wages, working conditions and living standards, the reforms associated with *The Accord* are usually considered as progressive and as a repudiation of the kinds reforms taking place contemporaneously in the UK and US, not least because they gave workers access to a range of provisions such as healthcare. Nonetheless, this set of policy measures forged agreement between the state and organized labor for all workers to compensate static real wage growth with extended access to superannuation schemes (that is, access to financial assets comprising of different combinations of asset classes).

Thus while the Keynesian or Fordist worker exchanged their labor power for wages, in the financial era employment for the worker (or at least for some workers) is compensated not so much by wages (which are paid at rates which do not necessarily cover the costs of life) but by access to financial assets, and especially access to the future income generating potential of such assets; a potential which is promised but far from guaranteed. Through agreements such as *The Accord*, in the financial era wages have then, become assetized, that is, have taken on the characteristics of income generating assets, with the worker becoming less of a seller of their labor power and more a manager of their assets (including not only employment related assets such as superannuation but also housing) and with it, a manager of their own fates (Adkins 2015, 2018). Indeed, this process of assetization should be understood as part of the broader trend mapped by Piketty (2014) whereby asset ownership is replacing the wage as the key distributor of life chances. As I have stressed here, however, understanding this process requires going beyond the broad idea that labor has simply been subsumed by financial capital and/or that financial expansion has opened out new opportunities for the expropriation of profits from workers. It also requires revision of the idea that labor in the financial era is deregulated and disorganized and/or has simply been quashed by capital in a ceaseless drive for reductions to the price of labor. Instead, understanding this process requires careful examination of how, in the period of financial expansion, the wage labor relationship is being rewritten and restructured. In this short essay I have outlined three such forms of restructuring: first, the rewriting of labor as guarantor of the financial stability of the state in the context of sovereign indebtedness; second, the assetization of wages; and third, the emergence of a worker for whom employment is an access point to the potentialities of financial assets.

One especially pressing set of questions about this worker and the speculative order in which survival must now be realized concerns how this order is linked to shifting dynamics of class, race and gender. Many of the dynamics I have described in this essay have been central to the winding back of the gendered, classed and racialized dynamics of the Keynesian order. The expansion of finance has, for example, been coterminous with the pouring of women into labor markets on a global scale, while shifts in the operations of credit markets have meant that many of the gendered and racialized exclusions previously operating in those markets have abated. This ostensive inclusion, however, can easily obscure how in the speculative order exposure to financial risk is borne more heavily by women and racial minorities than by many men since the former typically rely more heavily on credit to survive (Adkins 2018). It also obscures how the expansion of finance has gone hand in hand with a wholesale reinstitutionalization of the heteronormative family and family values, not least through the reinvention of the tradition of private family responsibility (Cooper 2017). The speculative order is then not simply a financial and monetary order but must be recognized to concern a wholesale set of social relations.

Notes

1 This has been made especially clear in regard to housing in Anglo-Saxon economies where house price and rent to income ratios have risen dramatically. This has created an affordability crisis with specific generational dynamics (Ryan-Collins 2018).
2 While such analyses show how the rise of precarity is linked to changing class formations, they tend not to consider how the transformations to work and labor that they describe may relate to the expansion of finance.

Bibliography

Aalbers, M., 2016. *The Financialization of Housing: A Political Economy Approach.* London: Routledge.
Adkins, L., 2015. What are post-Fordist wages? Simmel, labor money and the problem of value. *South Atlantic Quarterly*, 114(2), pp. 331–353.
Adkins, L., 2018. *The Time of Money.* Stanford, CA: Stanford University Press.
Adkins, L., Kortesoja, M., Mannevuo, M. and Ylöstalo, H., 2019. Experimenting with price: Crafting the new social contract in Finland. *Critical Sociology*, 45(4-5), pp. 683–696.
Barba, A. and Pivetti, M., 2009. Rising household debt, its causes and macroeconomic implications: A long-period analysis. *Cambridge Journal of Economics*, 33(1), pp. 113–137.
Bryan, D., Rafferty, M. and Jefferis, C., 2015. Risk and value: Finance, labor and production. *South Atlantic Quarterly*, 114(2), pp. 307–330.
Cooper, M., 2012. Workfare, familyfare, Godfare: Transforming contingency into necessity. *South Atlantic Quarterly*, 111(4), pp. 643–661.
Cooper, M., 2015. Shadow money and the shadow workforce: Rethinking labor and liquidity. *South Atlantic Quarterly*, 114(2), pp. 395–423.
Cooper, M., 2017. *Family Values: Between Neoliberalism and the New Social Conservatism.* New York, NY: Zed Press.
Chesnais, F., 2014. Fictitious capital in the context of global over-accumulation and changing international economic power relationships. In Bellofiore, R. and Vertova, G. (eds.), *The Great Recession and the Contradictions of Contemporary Capitalism.* Cheltenham, UK: Edward Elgar, pp. 65–82.
Harvey, D., 2010. *The Enigma of Capital and the Crises of Capitalism.* London: Profile Books.
Humphrys, E. and Cahill, D., 2017. How labour made neoliberalism. *Critical Sociology*, 43(4–5), pp. 669–684.
Lapavitsas, C., 2009. Financialized capitalism: Crisis and financial expropriation. *Historical Materialism*, 17(2), pp. 117–148.
Lapavitsas, C., 2011. Theorizing financialization. *Work, Employment and Society*, 25(4), pp. 611–626.
Lorey, I., 2015. *State of Insecurity: Government of the Precarious.* London: Verso.
Peck, J. and Theodore, N., 2012. Politicizing contingent labor: Countering neoliberal labor market regulation … from the bottom up? *South Atlantic Quarterly*, 111(4), pp. 741–761.
Piketty, T., 2014. *Capital in the Twenty-First Century.* Cambridge, MA: Harvard University Press.
Ryan-Collins, J., 2018. *Why Can't you Afford a Home?* Cambridge: Polity.
Standing, G., 2011. *The Precariat: The New Dangerous Class.* London: Bloomsbury.

Stockhammer, E., 2013. *Why Have Wage Shares Fallen? A Panel Analysis of the Determinants of Functional Income Distribution*. Geneva: International Labour Office.

Streeck, W., 2014a. How will capitalism end? *New Left Review*, 87, pp. 35–64.

Streeck, W., 2014b. *Buying Time: The Delayed Crisis of Democratic Capitalism*. London: Verso.

Tadiar, N., 2013. Life times of disposability within neoliberalism. *Social Text*, 35(1), pp. 19–48.

Wisman, J., (2013) Wage stagnation, rising inequality and the financial crisis of 2008. *Cambridge Journal of Economics*, 37(4), pp. 921–945.

27D

ESSAY FORUM: LABOR IN FINANCIALIZATION

A Dual Democratization of Finance? Labor's Political Question after Financialization

Michael A. McCarthy

Workers have long been subject to relations of debt and credit. But since the mid-twentieth century, through their pension funds or 401(k) plans, mutual funds, and mortgages, workers have become increasingly submerged in financial markets for the provisioning of their everyday needs. And as Adkins notes in the previous essay, this might be both caused by and a cause of wage stagnation in distinct ways. Consider the fact that the proportion of households in the US invested in the stock market has increased from 20% in 1983 to 52% in 2001 (Davis 2009: 213). And across both wealthy and non-wealthy households, the proportion of financial assets owned relative to non-financial assets owned has grown (Keister 2005). This democratization of finance on the basis of its allocation has penetrated into people's lives, generating both a new financial culture that has increased tolerance for financial risk and policy preferences that are more consistent with the interests of finance capital (Fligstein and Goldstein 2015; Pagliari et al. 2018; see Pagliari and Young in this volume).

For organized labor in the US, involvement in financial investment and speculation preceded the onset of financialization itself by at least two decades (see Krippner 2011). In the US, pension funds were installed on a widespread basis after World War II through collective bargaining agreements. Even with the turn toward fringe benefits during the war to subvert wartime wage controls, before the war's end most American employees with a pension tended to be wealthier salaried employees, often in more professional fields or in management. That quickly changed in the postwar era because of worker organizing for fringe benefits, like health care and retirement plans. Unions organized for employer-sponsored retirement plans as an alternative to expanded public provisioning of retirement income and health benefits, which they were unable to obtain through their political coalitions. By 1957, over 50 percent of all unionized workers in the US had a pension plan; 10 million of the total 17 million American workers with a pension were themselves unionized (US Bureau of Labor Statistics 1957). These funds grew rapidly. Pension fund holdings increased from $26 billion in 1952 to $10.8 trillion on the eve of the Great Recession in 2007 (Board of Governors 2010). But this was not a uniquely American phenomena, employer-based pension plans were increasingly adopted in other parts of the advanced capitalist world as well.

In many rich democracies, countries like Italy, France, Austria, Greece, Portugal, and Germany, large earnings-related public retirement programs account for much of workers retirement income. In countries with multi-pillar systems however, like the US, the UK, Switzerland, Denmark and the Netherlands, workers' savings are also tied up in occupational funds. On the one hand, these funds are massive – accounting for about 25 percent of GDP in Jamaica, 38 percent in Hong Kong, 48 percent in Denmark, 55 percent in Israel, 56 percent in South Africa, 60 percent in Chile, 80 percent of GDP in the US, 85 percent in Canada, 95 percent in the UK, 121 percent in Australia, 127 percent in Switzerland, and 180 percent in the Netherlands (OECD 2018). On the other hand, workers' finance has turned toward investment strategies that are inextricably tied up with speculative financial markets – in the US, for instance, by the mid-1970s occupational pension funds controlled nearly 25 percent of all American corporate equity (Board of Governors 2010). Indeed, with this democratization of finance, modern capitalism in liberal economies has been described as "pension fund capitalism." It is no surprise that the countries with the most financialized pension systems, with their workers' funds tied up in international financial markets, saw the greatest losses during the 2008 downturn. Pension investment returns were -38 percent in Ireland, -27 percent in Australia, and -26 percent in the US (OECD 2009).

The democratization of finance has not just exposed working-class people to the ups and downs of speculative markets – part and parcel of this process has been a shift of workers toward borrowing that saddles families with greater amounts of debt (see also Adkins in this volume). Unique forces at both ends of the labor market have pushed poor and middle-class workers into new financialized schemes of survival, often heavily reliant on borrowing. For the poor at the bottom of the labor market, especially in the UK and US, welfare state retrenchment removed existing sources of stability and security. Financial intermediaries and financial companies in the private market have been the primary beneficiaries as poor people have been forced into new strategies for survival (Cutler and Waine 2001), a process that has been highly profitable for financial companies (Soederberg 2014). In the move away from public support in the US in particular, payday loan and check cashing outlets have flourished in poor neighborhoods, their extraordinarily high rates of interest deepening both the debt and the poverty experienced by those who are forced to use them (Caskey 1994; Rivlin 2010; Baradaran 2015; Gonzalez in this volume). For middle-class workers, wage stagnation has failed to keep their lifestyle affordable due to rising costs of living. The result has been a turn to larger amounts of credit card debt and home mortgage debt to finance household consumption. Household debt for the American middle class has dramatically risen as a result. The proportion of debt to income lurched from 0.14 in 1983 to 0.61 in 2008 (Dynan 2009). This debt has become a source of deep new financial angst and anxiety for working-class people. As Dienst notes, "debts are the means by which misery becomes socialized" (2011: 150).

But a crucial second question remains. Access to financial assets has been democratized, but to what extent has the control over those financial assets itself been democratized? And, normatively, should it be? Democracy can be limited in both the scope of issues that are decided on collectively and the process through which those things are decided on collectively. For the most part, control of workers' finance lays outside of the scope of democracy, with governance either left to corporate boards, fiduciaries or the decisions of individual workers. Yet the social importance of labor's capital has long been acknowledged and explored by analysts. Because of its importance and sheer size in capitalist economies, scholars and activists regularly return to the question of popular uses of workers' capital (Rifkin and Barber 1978; Ghilarducci 2000; Fung et al. 2001; McCarthy 2014; Croft and Malhotra 2016; Webber 2018).

Historically, workers and their organizations in some political economies have made significant efforts at collective control of finance, but with only limited success. In the US, in 1923 the

Amalgamated Clothing Workers of America founded the Amalgamated Bank of New York. Two years later, Samuel Gompers, the President of the American Federation of Labor, founded the Union Labor Life Insurance Company, to offer financial products to workers. American unions have retained this interest. The AFL-CIO established the Capital Stewardship Program in 1997, which has worked with Change to Win's Office of Investment to issue shareholder proxy voting guidelines and shareholder voting initiatives (Croft and Malhotra 2016: 36). In Quebec, the Fédération des trailailleurs et traivailleuses du Québec (FTQ) established the Solidarity Fund in 1983, which ever since has repatriated workers' investment into the province. On probably the largest scale attempted, Rudolph Meidner, one of the key architects of the Swedish welfare state, proposed and nearly achieved a corporate-asset levy on new profits that would be run in a worker-controlled fund (Meidner 1978; Pontusson 1994). These efforts have had very mixed results. Even in the case of the Swedish wage-earner funds, what was once a socialist strategy turned out to usher in a complex and contradictory form of neoliberalization since the 1990s (Belfrage and Ryner 2009).

Similarly, in most countries with developed occupational pension systems, workers and their organizations have made attempts to democratically decide how to allocate their retirement investment, again with only very limited success (see Skerrett et al. 2017). In the US, there is a long history, dating back to the postwar period in which these funds were installed, of unions attempting to control the allocation of the finance in their collectively bargained funds. Yet, this effort was met with significant counter organizing by corporate elites and American policymakers. Legislation such as the Taft-Hartley Act of 1947 and the Employee Retirement Income Security Act of 1974 stripped workers of any ability to control their financial assets collectively (McCarthy 2017). Understanding why the state has done this is worth the scholarly investigation. But more broadly, moving the scholarship on labor and financialization forward, one line of thought for scholars might focus on the potential for a "second democratization" of finance.

Normatively, current social dilemmas related to austerity, inequality, and wage stagnation make questions related to how workers might democratically decide how toallocate their financial assets pressing for researchers. Even in countries where labor representatives do have a greater say in pension investment, such as in several European welfare states, there remains important work to be done on how workers might overcome their perceived lack of expertise to help direct the flow of funds in ways that serve the social good. In case studies of financial democratization across time, researchers might ask: how have workers and their organizations tried? To paraphrase Piven and Cloward (1977), how have they succeeded – and why have they failed? Developing this research requires a comparative dimension – which takes into account the experience of workers' finance in the global south and developing world without just focusing on advanced political economies (Harris 2017; Lavinas this volume). In exploring these issues, researchers might consider how this financial democratization has brought workers together across borders and political boundaries or how it might. Furthermore, how has workers' finance been used strategically in labor management disputes or to reshape corporate governance, in the form of shareholder proxy voting? Has workers' finance changed labor subjectivities or modified its repertoire of social movement tactics at all? Many more research questions could be posed. Asking about, and pushing for, a second democratization of finance offers an empirically and theoretically rich research path for scholars in financialization studies – and one with deep normative implications about how finance *should* operate.

Bibliography

Baradaran, M., 2015. *How the Other Half Banks: Exclusion, Exploitation, and the Threat to Democracy*. Cambridge, MA: Harvard University Press.

Belfrage, C. and Ryner, M., 2009. Renegotiating the Swedish social democratic settlement: From pension fund socialism to neoliberalization. *Politics & Society*, 37(2), pp. 257–288.

Board of Governors, 2010. Federal Reserve Statistical Release, Z.1, Flow of Funds Accounts of the United States. http://www.federalreserve.gov/releases/z1/20100311

Caskey, J.P., 1994. *Fringe Banking: Check-Cashing Outlets, Pawnshops, and the Poor.* Russell Sage Foundation.

Cutler, T. and Waine, B., 2001. Social insecurity and the retreat from social democracy: Occupational welfare in the long boom and financialization. *Review of International Political Economy*, 8, pp. 96–117.

Croft, T. and Malhotra, A., 2016. *The Responsible Investor Handbook: Mobilizing Workers' Capital for a Sustainable World.* Sheffield: Greenleaf Publishing.

Davis, G., 2009. *Managed by the Markets: How Financed Re-Shaped America.* New York: Oxford University Press.

Dienst, R., 2011. *The Bonds of Debt: Borrowing Against the Common Good.* London: Verso Books.

Dynan, K.E., 2009. Changing household financial opportunities and economic security. *Journal of Economic Perspectives*, 23, pp. 49–68.

Fligstein, N. and Goldstein, A., 2015. The emergence of finance culture in American households, 1989–2007. *Socio-Economic Review*, 13(3), pp. 575–601.

Fung, A., Hebb, T. and Rogers, J. (eds.), 2001. *Working Capital: The Power of Labor's Pensions.* Ithaca: Cornell University Press.

Ghilarducci, T., 2000. *Labor's Capital: The Economics and Politics of Private Pensions.* Boston: MIT Press.

Harris, K., 2017. *A Social Revolution: Politics and the Welfare State in Iran.* Berkeley: University of California Press.

Keister, L.A., 2005. *Getting Rich: America's New Rich and How They Got That Way.* New York: Cambridge University Press.

Krippner, G., 2011. *Capitalizing on Crisis.* Boston: Harvard University Press.

McCarthy, M., 2014. Turning labor into capital: Pension funds and the corporate control of finance. *Politics & Society*, 42(4), pp. 455–487.

McCarthy, M., 2017. *Dismantling Solidarity: Capitalist Politics and American Pensions since the New Deal.* Ithaca: Cornell University Press.

Meidner, R., 1978. *Employee Investment Funds: An Approach to Collective Capital Formation.* London: George Allen & Unwin.

OECD, 2009. *Pensions and the Crisis: How Should Retirement-Income Systems Respond to Financial and Economic Pressures?* Paris: OECD.

OECD, 2018. *Pension Funds' Assets (Indicator).* doi:10.1787/d66f4f9f-en (Accessed September 2018).

Piven, F.F. and Cloward, R., 1977. *Poor People's Movements: Why They Succeed, How They Fail.* New York: Pantheon Books.

Pagliari, S., Phillips, L.M. and Young, K.L., 2018. The financialization of policy preferences: Financial asset ownership, regulation and crisis management. *Socio-Economic Review*, https://doi.org/10.1093/ser/mwy027.

Pontusson, J., 1994. *The Limits of Social Democracy.* Ithaca: Cornell University Press.

Rifkin, J. and Barber, R., 1978. *The North Will Rise Again.* Boston: Beacon Press.

Rivlin, G., 2010. *Broke, USA: From Pawnshops to Poverty, Inc. – How the Working Poor Became Big Business.* New York: Harper Collins.

Skerrett, K., Weststar, J., Archer, S. and Roberts, C. (eds.), 2017. *The Contradictions of Pension Fund Capitalism.* Ithaca, NY: Cornell University Press.

Soederberg, S., 2014. *Debtfare States and the Poverty Industry: Money, Discipline, and the Surplus Population.* London: Routledge.

US Bureau of Labor Statistics, 1957. Digest of one-hundred selected pension plans under collective bargaining. *Bulletin No. 1232.*

Webber, D., 2018. *The Rise of the Working-Class Shareholder: Labor's Last Best Weapon.* Cambridge: Harvard University Press.

PART E

Techniques, Technologies and Cultures of Financialization

28

CULTURE AND FINANCIALIZATION

Four Approaches

Max Haiven

Introduction

The difficulty of the task of providing an overview of the relationship between culture and financialization stems not only from the fact that both terms are hotly debated and seek to identify complex phenomena. It also stems from the fact that the spheres one is seeking to describe (culture and finance) are, today, substantially transforming one another. For noted cultural theorist Frederic Jameson (1998a: 60), what we typically identify as post-Bretton Woods financialization coincides with and, indeed, is part and parcel of "the becoming economic of the cultural and the becoming cultural of the economic." What are we, for instance, to make of a moment when central bank governors, investment bank CEOs and other major financial luminaries must carefully script and stage their public announcements to forestall (or, occasionally, foment) seismic market movements? Or what of the way institutions and practitioners of the arts, now recast as spheres of "cultural production" or the "creative economy," seem to have embraced many of the logics, priorities, dispositions and practices from the financial world (Haiven 2014b; Vishmidt 2015)? It is not only that culture, today, is big business, hence of interest to financial speculators. Nor is it simply that activities in the financial sector are deeply shaped by "cultural" factors like aesthetics, belief, language games, representation, spectacle and performance (MacKenzie 2006; Marazzi 2008; Knorr-Cetina 2011; Davis 2018). It is, more broadly, that in some ways culture and finance name one another's horizon of disappearance in a neoliberal, globalized world (Jameson 1998b; Martin 2015).

This chapter briefly examines the relationship between culture and financialization from four inter-related angles. First, we explore *finance culture*. Here I mean culture in the more anthropological sense of the term and intend to outline some of the notable scholarship on the institutional codes, value systems, representational schemas, quotidian practices and structures of feeling that circulate in and hold together corporations and institutions in the financial sector. Here we will take the example of the institutional culture of Wall Street investment banks.

Second, I want to outline some dimensions of the *cultures of financialization*, by which I mean the way the logics, codes, value paradigms, speculative ethos, measurements and metaphors of the financial sector have filtered into other (non-financial) economic and social spheres, offering a set of techniques or *dispositifs* for the recalibration of institutional priorities towards an alignment with financialization. Here, we will examine the financialization of Anglo-American universities.

Third, I want to dwell on the *financialization of cultural production,* by which I mean two things: (a) the increased influence of the financial sector on creative industries and creative workers, and (b) the role of film, fiction, art and other creative media in exploring and critiquing financialization. I take up the example of the financialization of the (visual) art world.

Fourth, I turn to the quandaries of *cultural production about financialization,* discussing how producers might adequately represent and respond to financialization, contrasting several recent Hollywood films with John Lanchester's novel *Capital.*

Approaching Financialization and Culture

All too often the cultural dimensions of financialization are sidelined in favor of what can appear to be more substantial and material discussions of its economic, political, geographic and sociological aspects. Yet a number of authors have noted the importance of paying close attention to culture in the study of financialization, for a diversity of reasons.

Jameson's work since the 1980s has been singularly influential in investigating not only the impact of financialization on culture, but the integration of the two. Jameson follows on and develops the bridging of two notions of culture first theorized by members of the Birmingham School credited with pioneering the field of cultural studies: on the one hand, culture as the realm of creative production, on the other culture in the anthropological sense of a complex lifeworld, a society's remit of beliefs, rituals, social institutions and practices (McRobbie 2005). Jameson theorized postmodernism as the "cultural logic of late capitalism," the way the rise of speculative capital shaped and was shaped by both notions of culture (Jameson 1991). Hence Jameson encourages a reading of literature, film, architecture and contemporary art as, on the one hand, symptomatic of deeper political-economic shifts and, on the other, in some ways constitutive of those shifts. Jameson has sought to maintain a deep connection between political economy and culture without falling prey to the trap of economic determinism.

Another important theorist who has sought to bridge this gap is anthropologist Arjun Appadurai, whose work has stressed the "grassroots" development of financial ideas, cultures and structures of feeling, both within the financial realm itself and also in the wider world (Appadurai 2016). For Appadurai, institutional and corporate ecosystems and the realm of daily praxis are spaces where cultures of valuation are produced in dialogue with the overarching economic system. This is as true in the offices of Goldman Sachs as it is in the slums of Mumbai. His work sensitizes us to the way that "the economy" which is being "financialized" is made up of social actors whose actions, relationships, identities and practices are, in sum, "cultural." But, by the same token, that zones of "culture" are inexorably influenced and shaped by "the economy."

These themes are addressed quite directly in the pioneering work of Paul du Gay and Michael Pryke, culminating in their edited collection of 2002 *Cultural Economy* which set forth some key terms for an exploration of (a) how "culture" (both in terms of expressive and creative works and in terms of a fabric of social life) is produced within economic fields of value and power and (b) how the realm that we understand as "the economic" is produced in substantial ways *through* culture (see also Thrift 2000). Such an approach necessarily puts both concepts under critical scrutiny as in some ways arbitrary or at least flexible markers of two territories which, while conventionally imagined to be very distant to one another, overlap in complex ways (see Best and Paterson 2010). This work, and that of others, has led to a thriving interdisciplinary field, notably represented in the last decade in the pages of the *Journal of Cultural Economy* and other periodicals.

In this vein, my definition of financialization as a cultural phenomenon implies more than simply the subordination of a distinct and discrete arena of "culture" to economic pressures. Rather, I am seeking to outline the ethos germane to and in part constitutive of the historical moment and socio-economic processes of financialization. This is an ethos where the techniques, metaphors, dispositions, narratives, ideas, ideologies and relational practices we associate with high finance come to have purchase over a wide diversity of other fields of practice, social life and imaginative expression (Haiven 2014a; McClanahan 2016). This ethos is characterized, in general terms, by the imperative towards speculation, monetary measurement, individualistic competition in which anything and everything of material or immaterial value is transformed into an asset to be leveraged. Importantly, as Randy Martin (2002, 2007, 2015) argues, financialization is distinguished from commodification and monetization by the way it demands a transformation of the imagination towards a mapping of future potentials, the calculative activities of risk management and notions of hedging, leveraging and securitization. Financialization here appears as a habit of the imagination that reorients individuals, institutions and society at large towards the conscription of the future itself, with each actor competing to better anticipate and thereby profit from potential trajectories of present-day activities (Haiven 2014a; Ascher 2016). The financialization of culture also names the way these tendencies are expressed not only in fields that come under the direct subordination of money (e.g. firms, public institutions, personal finances), but also in the fields of practice defined by other forms of value, such as cultural capital, social capital or subcultural capital.

Finance Culture

This brings us to our first approach to the question of culture and financialization: the institutional cultures of the production of financial wealth, by which I mean those of the financial sector, including the many "cultures" of investment banks, hedge funds, private equity firms, central banks, public and private financial governance and oversight organizations, bond-rating agencies, accountancy firms and more. This work has been undertaken by a wide range of sociologists and anthropologists focused on a vast diversity of issues (Zaloom 2006; Finel-Honigman 2009; see also Weiss in this volume).

One of the most revealing ethnographies of financial cultures is detailed in Karen Ho's 2009 book *Liquidated*. Identifying herself as a "downsized anthropologist," Ho worked for years in the back offices of Wall Street investment banks, gaining vital data through participant observation and detailed interviews. Her observations paint a vivid picture of an institutional culture that has a momentous influence on the rest of the world. For one, she confirmed the image of a highly competitive, ruthless and macho world hyperbolized for mass audiences in films like Oliver Stone's *Wall Street* or Martin Scorsese's *The Wolf of Wall Street* (see also McDowell 1997). She explains that many of the executives and aspiring executives of such firms are gleaned from extremely pricy Ivy League universities, and how it is expected that they will endure gruelling hours and maltreatment as a rite of passage within the firm. Indeed, careers in finance are typically short but intense and institutions churn through and dispose of young talent at a vertiginous rate. It is a culture that prizes swiftness, daring and cunning, held in place in part by an occult system of annual bonuses to reward success and punish anything less than excelsior performance.

Importantly, Ho notes that this institutional culture rewards its participants with the idea that they are the best of the best, the most intelligent and competent people in society. This, then, justifies the incredible power the financial sector wields over the economy, over other firms, over society at large: indeed, the investment bankers Ho interviewed generally thought of themselves as serving a beneficial social role by acting as agents of the infallible market, as what I have called "angels of creative destruction" (Haiven 2014b). Ho notes that the effect is the redrafting of the economy and society in finance's own image.

Ho's fascinating ethnographic research reveals how, for all its mystique of sanguine calculative reason, the financial sector is held together by the common dramas of culture that animate all societies, communities and social institutions. Indeed, her research and that of others shows us that the cultivation and sustenance of such institutional cultures is vital to the sustainability and competitiveness of financial firms. It also explains how these firms exist within a broader network of mutually reinforcing institutions, including other companies, educational institutions, parafinancial zones of confluence and sociality (strip clubs, the art world, corporate boards). But even more importantly, her research shows us that the culture of the financial firm has impacts beyond its own corridors: the culture of finance as exhibited in these firms has a massive influence on the culture and the political-economic reality of actors and institutions throughout the capitalist economy that these firms superintend.

Cultures of Financialization

This leads us to our second valence of the intersection of culture and financialization, which names the diverse and deeply disturbing ways the processes of financialization have come to shape and recalibrate institutional governance, social priorities and the general ethos of public and private sector organizations who, at least on the surface, appear to have little or nothing to do with the financial sector. Much work has been done in the field of political economy to seek to understand how, in the post-Bretton Woods moment, the governance of all manner of capitalist firms shifts towards the maximization of "shareholder value," typically at the expense of long-term strategy or economic sustainability, to say nothing of the workers, environments and communities sacrificed on the altar of ever greater quarterly stock performance (see Erturk in this volume). Likewise, there has been a fair amount of attention paid to the disciplinary use of debt, whereby private firms and also whole national governments and public institutions are brought to heel by the expectations or demands of creditors (Ross 2014; Lazzarato 2015; Vogl 2017).

But underneath this political-economic phenomena is a broader cultural shift of which the financialization of Anglo-American post-secondary education is a good bellwether. Here, the introduction or escalation in tuition fees has been accompanied by a state-backed expansion of access to credit, ensuring that the first truly adult experience of many citizens is consigning oneself to post-graduation financial obligations that typically constitute several times the average annual income (McGettigan 2013; Ross 2014). Yet these economic and policy shifts are both the cause and the consequence of a cultural transformation where education, once widely imagined as a public good and the responsibility of society at large, is recast as an individualized commodity. Each individual is now responsible for "investing" in their "human capital" by enrolling in post-secondary education or other forms of training at their own expense (see Brown 2015).

This is a key example of the way financialization encourages the conditions for intensified privatization, individualization, neoliberal restructuring and free-market solutions, while at the same time presenting individualized solutions to these transformations. Young people, from one perspective abandoned by their society, are now recast as savvy, empowered "investors." And as "investors" they come to demand an ever-more financialized model of education: one that promises results when it comes time to try one's luck on the increasingly uncertain job markets. Financialization in this sense is not experienced as a dystopian imposition from above, but a transformation in the nature of agency and empowerment (see Haiven 2014a).

Meanwhile, within universities themselves, financialization has also led to a recalibration of institutional cultures to better align with the overarching financialized paradigm. For one, the hierarchies and governance of such institutions increasingly comes to mirror the pattern in high finance, with a highly paid executive branch commanding an ever-increasing share of both budgets and institutional power (Martin 2011). Universities, which often also control considerable endowments, are increasingly concerned with managing their own financial investments in profitable ways (Eaton et al. 2016; de Angelis and Harvie 2009). Universities in major urban centers have begun to recraft themselves as major players in speculative real-estate markets, leveraging their public or not-for profit status and residual credibility as beneficial social institutions (Goddard, Coombes, Kempton and Vallance 2014; Valverde and Briggs 2015). Funding for the professoriate is increasingly tied to the speculative value of research outcomes, especially to the extent these can be either supported or validated by outside public or private bodies, notably corporations (Newfield 2011; Martin 2011). Out of a desire to open new revenue streams, many prestigious universities have leveraged their academic reputations into global brands, sometimes partnering with private interests to invest in speculative overseas satellite campuses in "emerging economies" (Edu-factory Collective 2009). This is to say nothing of the way predatory firms have manipulated universities (as they have cities and whole nations) into dubious if not outright usurious debt relationships (Russel, Sloan and Smith 2016; Eaton et al. 2016).

The example of the financialization of the university is a good illustration of the cultural impacts of financialization for a few reasons. First, universities are allegedly the custodians of culture. While one should not participate in any mythology that imagines that the Anglo-American university was ever free of political or economic influence, the recalibration of this influence towards financialization offers a useful index of profound intertwined cultural and economic trends and tendencies. Second, the Anglo-American university's residual guild-like structure has been at times replaced by, at times leveraged into, a financial logic, which tells us something about how financialization spreads through social institutions not only through directly hegemonic economic impositions, but also *culturally*, which is to say by a subtle influence over ideas, priorities and patterns. Third and related, the fact that the university remains by and large a public or at least not-for-profit institution means that its financialization can indicate the degree to which that process more generally represents a deep shift on the level of relationships, expectations, notions of value and social hierarchies (Newfield 2011; McGettigan 2013).

The Financialization of Cultural Production

The third layer of the relationship of culture and financialization we will explore here is the reciprocal influence of financialization on cultural production, and of cultural production on finance. Cultural production here refers to a wide range of market-mediated expressive or communicative activities, including the spheres of film and television, digital media, print and literature, music, the performing arts and, the focus of this section, visual art.

In general terms, studies and critiques of the influence of the capitalist market on cultural expression have a long pedigree, especially in the tradition of thinkers associated with the Frankfurt School and the Birmingham School. More recently, many scholars have shifted their focus towards the conditions of cultural and creative labor, especially in light of the pivot of many post-industrial nations and cities towards identifying "culture" and "creativity" as economic catalysts (Banks, Gill and Taylor 2013). Meanwhile, of course, cultural production and distribution have become global corporate concerns, with film, music and print production being increasingly dominated by financialized global empires (Mosco 2010), many of them tied to high tech and web-oriented firms like Apple, Alphabet (parent company of Google and YouTube), Amazon, Netflix and Spotify (Fuchs 2015).

The rise of these conditions and platforms has encouraged cultural producers, from novelists to film-makers to musicians to artists, to imagine and advance themselves in a financialized and entrepreneurial register. While the commodification of culture is nothing new, increasingly cultural producers today are recognizing that success demands not only technical and artistic excellence (indeed, sometimes this can be a liability) but also a virtuosity in self-promotion, networking and hype (Kozłowski, Kurant, Sowa, Szadkowski and Szreder 2015; McRobbie 2015). As early as the turn of the millennium cultural studies scholar Angela McRobbie (2004) wryly identified artists as the "pioneers of the new economy," the model workers for a post-Fordist capitalism no longer interested in compliant and machine-like industrial workers but, rather, in self-activating, imaginative, free-wheeling "entrepreneurs of the self," to borrow Foucault's (2008: 226) turn of phrase (see also Rose 1990).

Although the example of the market for fine art may at first appear marginal to financialized capitalism, I join others in thinking it has great deal to teach us about the relationship of financialization to cultural production today(Malik and Phillips 2012; Vishmidt 2015; Haiven 2018). Perhaps most notoriously, this relationship has recently (since roughly 1990) been marked by the astronomically high prices achieved at auction by contemporary artworks, largely thanks to the competitive bidding power of an ascendant subclass euphemized as "high net worth individuals" (Adam 2017). This has led to a massive boom in the sales and prices of contemporary and post-war artworks, in part because of the influx of new global players eager to obtain unique and esteemed luxury items, in part because many antiquities and works by old masters and impressionists are now in permanent collections and so removed from the market (Horowitz 2011). This condition has led critics like Marc C. Taylor (2011) to decry the "financialization of art": the orientation of many artists, as well as dealers, gallerists, auction houses and other intermediaries, to cater to the whims of the financial elite. This is emblematized for Taylor in the work of superstar artists like Damien Hirst, Takashi Murakami and Jeff Koons, all of whom employ legions of (typically precariously employed) assistants to churn out charismatic, recognizable and extremely expensive "baubles for billionaires."

Beyond the depraved circus of glitzy auctions and art-world badboys, the broader financialization of art has a great deal to teach us about how something as obstreperous and often explicitly anti-capitalist as contemporary art is folded into the machinations of financialization (Gielen 2010). First, as the hunger for contemporary art has deepened, it has given rise to a panoply of institutions, start-ups and ventures aimed at providing liquidity to what is otherwise a notoriously opaque and cryptic art market. These include art investment funds (which allow investors to pool money to collectively buy artworks for speculative purposes), deluxe "freeport" facilities to store the accumulated loot, and online platforms that purport to use algorithms to detect and advise on the "next big thing" (the hot art trend whose assets can be bought cheap now and soon sold dear) (Steyerl 2017; Haiven 2018). Art has long been considered an "alternative asset class" for the wealthy, and has also long been a vehicle through which the super-wealthy avoid taxes (Cabra and Hudson 2013). It has also, as Pierre Bourdieu (1984) and others have shown, long been an essential tool by which the financial elite have sought to secure their own class reproduction, offering a means towards esteem, cultural capital and the social capital that can come with the connections and relationships art collecting can provide (Velthuis 2007). But the financialization of art today demonstrates the degree to which, under financialization, seemingly anything can and does become a speculative asset through a complex set of institutional and, importantly, cultural transformations (Malik and Phillips 2012; Deloitte 2016).

While it may seem that the art market is a provincial example of the financialization of culture it offers us a useful example of the complex ways that financialization's influence percolates throughout even so ideosyncratic a field. As the artist and writer Andrea Fraser (2012) points out, it is not simply that the money of high finance trickles down through the hierarchies of the art world to reach, ultimately, even the most radical and independent institutions. It is also that the logics of financialization come to structure the whole field of cultural production (see also

Stakemeier and Vishmidt 2016). Public museums and galleries are often overseen by boards of directors made up of financiers and collectors, eager to leverage their influence to have the institution invest in the work of artists also in their own portfolios, thereby raising their market prices (Thompson 2010; Thornton 2008). Cuts to public funding for the arts has meant that, increasingly, art institutions, art schools and artists themselves cater to the whims of collectors and market intermediaries, whims that are ever fickle and volatile, meaning that throughout the art world there is a fair degree of speculative activity ongoing to produce the "next big thing." Even those artists and institutions who seek to explicitly reject the pressure and largesse of finance end up speculating on how to avoid its shadow, maneuvers which, ironically, might well be the most successful at producing the "next big thing." Even when public galleries or museums are not compelled to seek out self-serving donors, there often remains the imperative to maximize a return on a public "investment," with institutions orienting themselves to attracting larger and "more engaged" audiences and offering programming that can prove some sort of measurable "impact" on society or culture at large (Bishop 2012).

The structure of the art market, when taken as a whole industry, is an expressive, at times hyperbolic portrait of the future of all labour markets under financialization: a vast pool of unpaid or underpaid workers (would-be artists) investing in themselves and producing work in order that they might compete for recognition and thereby stand a chance of being elevated to the tiny fraction of 1% of such workers who manage to even earn a sustainable living at their vocation (see Adkins et al., this volume).

In this sense, the financialization of visual art represents a case study of the ways that financialization saturates and reshapes a sphere of cultural production. But it also offers us a window into some of the ways various fields of cultural production are enfolded into the circuits of financial accumulation, even (perhaps even especially) when the content of that cultural production might critique financialization or its influence.

Cultural Production about Financialization

This brief sketch of the financialized art market reveals the contours of financialization in one of the places we presume it least likely to manifest: the allegedly almost autonomous realm of creativity and imagination. Unlike the heavy-handed influence of the wealthy and powerful in times gone by, which demanded that artists create portraits and monumental works to glorify or ornament the ruling class, the influence of financialization on the production of art is more subtle, but arguably more insidious. It implies a radical transformation of the economic, institutional and social ecology within which culture is produced, while at the same time preserving (if not propagandizing) the sacrosanct creative freedom of the individual artist. As Martin (2015) explains, today's moment of financialization arises as a means by which capitalism can reorganize itself to preserve and profit from autonomous, experimental, renegade and self-actualizing actors throughout society (see also Boltanski & Chiapello 2005). Because it is vested in transforming all social actors into vehicles for and innovators of further financialization (often driven precisely by the material pressures of financialization itself), this system is not averse to critique, provocation, resistance and individual rebellion. Indeed, it thrives in part because of these, so long as they are manifested in individualized and financialized ways. We should not see this "cultural" tendency as somehow tangential to, contingent to or simply symptomatic of financialized capitalism; it is structural (see Langley in this volume).

What, then, of cultural production that would seek to reveal, challenge or critique financialization? Is it all doomed to reincorporation or, worse, inadvertently becoming the prompt for the system's next stage of evolution?

It can be tempting to mobilize the moral authority, aesthetic charm and communicative flexibility of cultural forms like film, visual art, performance or literature to reveal the "truth" of the otherwise hidden financial world. Recent Hollywood films like *The Big Short, Inside Job, The Wolf of Wall Street, Wall Street: Money Never Sleeps, Margin Call* and *Equity*, as well as the TV series *Billions* have sought to leverage the notoriety of post-2008 Wall Street as a means to, themselves, rake in returns for the movie studios and investors, posing themselves as cautionary tales or pedagogical vehicles (Parvulescu 2017). One of the long-standing virtues of the financial sector within capitalism is that it presents a villainous face of the system, but also one that is largely resilient to public outrage. The sector can well afford to be represented as the source of economic inequality and corruption because it has little to fear. Workers can strike in factories, riot and loot retailers and blockade ports, but rarely have targeted financiers or their infrastructure, which in any case today are distributed in highly secured offices around the world (Clover 2016). For this reason, too, cultural representations of finance have tended to cause us to imagine arcane, mysterious, shadowy and conspiratorial scenes (see Crosthwaite, Knight and Marsh 2014).

But beyond simply trying to vivify the machinations of the financial sector (as important as that work is) there is the broader question of how critical cultural producers might represent *financialization*, which is to say the broader economic, political, sociological and cultural transformation that is the subject of this book. This represents a profound challenge precisely because it is so multidimensional.

One example of such an attempt from the realm of literature is John Lanchester's 2012 novel *Capital*, set prior to and during the 2008 financial crisis. While one of the book's many characters is indeed a City of London financial executive, the focus of the book is a mundane South London street where a whole cast of characters live out loosely interconnected lives. The novel seeks to map out many of the complex and subtle dimensions of financialization through the fates of its characters, in the process revealing that, though they are all grappling with conditions of precarity and "risk-management," they are still divided by deep(ening) inequalities based on class, gender, age, citizenship status and more. What emerges from the novel, which Lanchester wrote at the same time as he was preparing a highly successful non-fiction account of the financial crisis (Lanchester 2010), is a tableau of subjective shadows cast by the stark and withering light of unleashed finance capital. Financialization itself is only elliptically referred to in the novel's title, an allusion both to money, to the notion of London as a capital city, and, of course, to Marx's famous trilogy (though Lanchester's approach is decidedly not Marxian) (see Shaw 2015).

The absent presence (or present absence) of financialization in Lanchester's work is, in a sense, symptomatic of the fundamental challenge for representing financialization, which is itself, in part, a system for representing the world in a speculative fashion. As Leigh Claire La Berge (2015) persuasively shows in the case of literature, financialization itself marks a transformation in the structure of capitalist totality such that residual forms and methods for representation are riven, and as such fiction about finance and financialization offer us a vantage from which to think through both the changing nature of capitalism and culture together.

Conclusion

In each of these approaches, financialization is revealed to be a profound shaper of cultural production, whether or not the content of the resultant cultural text explicitly or intentionally references it. The readings of structural and systemic powers into or onto literature and other cultural production is by now an accepted and very fruitful methodology (see Jameson 1981; Eagleton 2000). But something more is at stake.

Even as we focus on its cultural dimensions, we should never forget that financialization names a material process or part of a suite of material processes that are arguably fundamentally recalibrating the fabric of social life. Martin (2015) suggests that the "order of the derivative" (the financial instrument which he sees as instrumental and paradigmatic) has drastically and irrevocably ushered in a new moment of both fragmentation and interconnectivity as people, populations and economies are transformed by the combined force of money and technology. Alberto Toscano and Jeff Kinkle (2015) echo Frederic Jameson's (1998b) observation that these shifts in the very nature of social life under late capitalism, though they may appear in the form of post-modern aesthetics and cultural habits, signal a transformed landscape of cognition, one where the ability to "cognitively map" the social totality is sundered.

If this is indeed true, then we may no longer find the term "culture" useful, nor the term "economy" for that matter: if the realms they described ever were truly distinct (which is in fact doubtful), today they are certainly not. Studying the intersection of culture and financialization, then, profoundly challenges us to think anew about both.

Bibliography

Adam, G., 2017. *Dark Side of the Boom: The Excesses of the Art Market in the 21st Century.* Farnham, Surrey; Burlington, Lund Humphries.

Appadurai, A., 2016. *Banking on Words: The Failure of Language in the Age of Derivative Finance.* Chicago, IL, London: The University of Chicago Press.

Ascher, I., 2016. *Portfolio Society: On the Capitalist Mode of Prediction.* New York, NY: Zone Books.

Banks, M., Gill, R. and Taylor, S. (eds.), 2013. *Theorizing Cultural Work: Labour, Continuity and Change in the Creative Industries.* London and New York: Routledge.

Berardi, F., 2009. *Precarious Rhapsody: Semiocapitalism and the Pathologies of the Post-alpha Generation.* New York: Autonomedia.

Best, J. and Paterson, M. (eds.), 2010. *Cultural Political Economy.* London and New York: Routledge.

Bishop, C., 2012. *Artificial Hells: Participatory Art and the Politics of Spectatorship.* London and New York: Verso.

Boltanski, L. and Chiapello, E., 2005. *The New Spirit of Capitalism.* London and New York: Verso.

Bourdieu, P., 1984. *Distinction: A Social Critique of the Judgement of Taste.* Cambridge, MA: Harvard University Press.

Bourdieu, P., 1993. *The Field of Cultural Production: Essays on Art and Literature.* New York: Columbia University Press.

Brown, W., 2015. *Undoing the Demos: Neoliberalism's Stealth Revolution.* New York: Zone.

Cabra, M. and Hudson, M., 2013, April 23. Mega-rich use tax havens to buy and sell masterpieces. Available at https://www.icij.org/offshore/mega-rich-use-tax-havens-buy-and-sell-masterpieces [Accessed February 27, 2017].

Clover, J., 2016. *Riot. Strike. Riot: The New Era of Uprisings.* London and New York: Verso.

Crosthwaite, P., Knight, P. and Marsh, N. (eds.), 2014. *Show Me the Money: The Image of Finance, 1700 to the Present.* Manchester: Manchester University Press.

Davis, A., 2018. Defining speculative value in the age of financialized capitalism. *The Sociological Review,* 66 (1), pp. 3–19.

De Angelis, M. and Harvie, D., 2009. "Cognitive capitalism" and the rat-race: How capital measures immaterial labour in British universities. *Historical Materialism,* 17(3), pp. 3–30.

Deloitte. (2016). *Art and Finance Report 2016.* Luxembourg. Available at https://www2.deloitte.com/content/dam/Deloitte/lu/Documents/financial-services/artandfinance/lu-en-artandfinancereport-08092014.pdf.

Du Gay, P. and Pryke, M. (eds.), 2002. *Cultural Economy: Cultural Analysis and Commercial Life.* London, Thousand Oaks, CA and New Delhi: SAGE.

Du Gay, P., Millo, Y. and Tuck, P., 2012. Making government liquid: Shifts in governance using financialisation as a political device. *Environment and Planning D: Society and Space,* 30(6), pp. 1083–1099.

Eagleton, T., 2000. *The Idea of Culture.* Oxford and Malden MA: Blackwell.

Eaton, C., Habinek, J., Goldstein, A., Dioun, C., Santibáñez Godoy, D.G. and Osley-Thomas, R., 2016. The financialization of US higher education. *Socio-Economic Review,* 14(3), pp. 507–535.

The Edu-factory Collective, (ed.), 2009. *Toward a Global Autonomous University: Cognitive Labor, the Production of Knowledge, and Exodus from the Education Factory.* New York: Autonomedia.

Finel-Honigman, I., 2009. *A Cultural History of Finance*. London and New York: Routledge.

Foucault, M., 2008. *The Birth of Biopolitics*. London and New York: Palgrave Macmillan.

Fraser, A., 2012. There's no place like home / L'1% c'est moi. *Continent*, 2(3), pp. 186–201.

Fuchs, C., 2015. *Culture and Economy in the Age of Social Media*. New York: Routledge.

Gielen, P., 2010. *The Murmuring of the Artistic Multitude: Global Art, Memory and Post-Fordism*. Amsterdam: Valiz.

Goddard, J., Coombes, M., Kempton, L. and Vallance, P., 2014. Universities as anchor institutions in cities in a turbulent funding environment: Vulnerable institutions and vulnerable places in England. *Cambridge Journal of Regions, Economy and Society*, 7(2), pp. 307–325.

Haiven, M., 2014a. *Cultures of Financialization: Fictitious Capital in Popular Culture and Everyday Life*. London and New York: Palgrave Macmillan.

Haiven, M., 2014b. The creative and the derivative: Historicizing creativity under post- Bretton Woods financialization. *Radical History Review*, 118, pp. 113–138.

Haiven, M., 2015. Art and money: Three aesthetic strategies in an age of financialisation. *Finance and Society*, 1(1), pp. 38–60.

Haiven, M., 2018. *Art after Money, Money after Art: Creative Strategies Against Financialization*. London: Pluto.

Harvey, D., 2006. *The Limits to Capital*. 2nd ed. London and New York: Verso.

Harvey, D., 2014. *Seventeen Contradictions and the End of Capitalism*. Oxford and New York: Oxford University Press.

Hilferding, R., 1981. *Finance Capital. A Study of the Latest Phase of Capitalist Development*. London: Routledge & Kegan Paul.

Ho, K., 2009. *Liquidated: An Ethnography of Wall Street*. Durham, NC and London: Duke University Press.

Holmes, B., 2007. The speculative performance: Art's financial futures. *Transversal*. Available at http://eip cp.net/transversal/0507/holmes/en

Horowitz, N., 2011. *Art of the Deal: Contemporary Art in a Global Financial Market*. Princeton, NJ and London: Princeton University Press.

Jameson, F., 1981. *The Political Unconscious*. Ithica, NY: Cornell University Press.

Jameson, F., 1991. *Postmodernism, or the Cultural Logic of Late Capitalism*. Durham, NC and London: Duke University Press.

Jameson, F., 1998a. Notes on globalization as a philosophical issue. In F. Jameson and M. Miyoshi (eds.), *The Cultures of Globalization*. Durham, NC: Duke University Press, pp. 54–77.

Jameson, F., 1998b. *The Cultural Turn : Selected Writings on the Postmodern, 1983–1998*. London and New York: Verso.

Knorr-Cetina, K., 2011. The market spectacle. *Rethinking Capitalism*, 2, 1–4.

Kozłowski, M., Kurant, A., Sowa, J., Szadkowski, K. and Szreder, J. (eds.), 2015. *A Joy Forever: The Political Economy of Social Creativity*. London: Mayfly.

La Berge, L.C., 2015. *Scandals and Abstraction: Financial Fiction of the Long 1980s*. New York: Oxford University Press.

Lanchester, J., 2010. *I.O.U: Why Everyone Owes Everyone and No One Can Pay*. New York: Simon & Schuster.

Lanchester, J., 2012. *Capital*. New York: Norton.

Lapavitsas, C., 2013. *Profiting Without Producing: How Finance Exploits Us All*. London and New York: Verso.

Lazzarato, M., 2015. *Governing by Debt*. South Pasadena, CA: Semiotext(e).

Lenin, V.I., 1948. *Imperialism, the Highest Stage of Capitalism; A Popular Outline*. Revised translation. London: Lawrence & Wishart.

Levitt, K., 2013. *From the Great Transformation to the Great Financialization: On Karl Polanyi and Other Essays*. Halifax and Winnipeg: Fernwood.

Luxemburg, R., 2003. *The Accumulation of Capital*. London and New York: Routledge.

MacKenzie, D., 2006. *An Engine, not a Camera : How Financial Models Shape Markets*. Cambridge, MA: MIT Press.

Malik, S. and Phillips, A., 2012. Tainted love: Art's ethos and capitalization. In M. Lind and O. Velthuis (eds.), *Contemporary Art and its Commercial Markets. A Report on Current Conditions and Future Scenarios*. Berlin: Sternberg, pp. 209–240.

Marazzi, C., 2008. *Capital and Language: From the New Economy to the War Economy*. New York: Semiotext(e).

Martin, R., 2002. *Financialization of Daily Life*. Philadelphia, PA: Temple University Press.

Martin, R., 2007. *An Empire of Indifference: American War and the Financial Logic of Risk Management*. Durham NC and London: Duke University Press.

Martin, R., 2011. *Under New Management Universities, Administrative Labor, and the Professional Turn*. Philadelphia: Temple University Press.

Martin, R., 2015. *Knowledge LTD: Towards a Social Logic of the Derivative*. Philadelphia: Temple University Press.

McClanahan, A., 2016. *Dead Pledges: Debt, Crisis, and Twenty-first-century Culture*. Stanford, CA and London: Stanford University Press.

McDowell, L., 1997. *Capital Culture: Gender at Work in the City*. Oxford and Malden MA: Blackwell.

McGettigan, A., 2013. *The Great University Gamble: Money, Markets and the Future of Higher Education*. London and New York: Pluto.

McRobbie, A., 2004. "Everyone is creative": Artists as pioneers of the new economy? In T. Bennett and E.B. Silva (eds.), *Contemporary Culture and Everyday Life*. London: British Sociological Association, pp. 186–202.

McRobbie, A., 2005. *The Uses of Cultural Studies*. London: Sage.

McRobbie, A., 2015. *Be Creative: Making a Living in the New Culture Industries*. Cambridge, UK and Malden, MA: Polity Press.

Mosco, V., 2010. *The Political Economy of Communication*. Los Angeles, CA: SAGE.

Neff, G., 2012. *Venture Labor: Work and the Burden of Risk in Innovative Industries*. Cambridge, MA: MIT Press.

Nelson, A., 1999. *Marx's Concept of Money: The God of Commodities*. London and New York: Routledge.

Newfield, C., 2011. *Unmaking the Public University: The Forty-Year Assault on the Middle Class*. Cambridge, MA: Harvard University Press.

O'Neil, C., 2016. *Weapons of Math Destruction: How Big Data Increases Inequality and Threatens Democracy*. New York: Penguin.

Parvulescu, C. (ed.), 2017. *Global Finance On Screen: From Wall Street to Side Street*. London and New York: Routledge.

Pasquale, F., 2015. *The Black Box Society: The Secret Algorithms that Control Money and Information*. Cambridge: Harvard University Press.

Passquinelli, M., 2006. Immaterial civil war: Prototypes of conflict within cognitive capitalism. Available at http://www.rekombinant.org/ImmCivilWar.pdf.

Perelman, M., 1987. *Marx's Crisis Theory: Scarcity, Labour and Finance*. New York and London: Praeger.

Pryke, M. and du Gay, P., 2007. Take an issue: Cultural economy and finance. *Economy and Society* 36(3), pp. 339–354.

Rose, N., 1990. *Governing the Soul: The Shaping of the Private Self*. London: Routledge.

Ross, A., 2014. *Creditocracy*. New York: OR Books.

Russel, D., Sloan, C. and Smith, A., 2016. *The Financialization of Higher Education: What Swaps Cost our Schools and Students*. New York: The Roosevet Institute. Available at http://rooseveltinstitute.org/financialization-higher-education/.

Shaw, K., 2015. *Crunch Lit*. London: Bloomsbury.

Stakemeier, K. and Vishmidt, M., 2016. *Reproducing Autonomy: Work, Money, Crisis and Contemporary Art*. London: Mute.

Steyerl, H., 2017. *Duty Free Art: Art in the Age of Planetary Civil War*. London and New York: Verso.

Taylor, M.C., 2011. Financialization of art. *Capitalism and Society*, 6(2), pp. 1–19.

Thompson, D., 2010. *The $12 Million Stuffed Shark: The Curious Economics of Contemporary Art*. London and New York: Palgrave Macmillan.

Thornton, S., 2008. *Seven Days in the Art World*. New York: WW Norton.

Thrift, N., 2000. Performing cultures in the new economy. *Annals of the American Association of Geographers*, 90(4), pp. 674–692.

Toscano, A., and Kinkle, J., 2015. *Cartographies of the Absolute*. Winchester: Zero Books.

Valverde, M. and Briggs, J., 2015. *The University as Urban Developer: A Research Report*. Toronto: Centre for Criminology & Sociolegal Studies, University of Toronto. Available at https://utopenletter.files.wordpress.com/2015/11/university-as-developer-2015.pdf.

Velthuis, O., 2007. *Talking Prices: Symbolic Meanings of Prices on the Market for Contemporary Art*. Princeton, NJ: Princeton University Press.

Vercellone, C., 2007. From formal subsumption to general intellect: Elements for a Marxist reading of the thesis of cognitive capitalism. *Historical Materialism*, 15(1), pp. 13–36.

Vishmidt, M., 2015. Notes on speculation as a mode of production in art and capital. In M. Kozłowski, A. Kurant, J. Sowa, K. Szadkowski and J. Szreder (eds.), *Joy Forever: The Political Economy of Social Creativity*. London: Mayfly, pp. 47–64.

Vogl, J., 2017. *The Ascendancy of Finance*. Cambridge and Malden, MA: Polity Press.

Zaloom, C., 2006. *Out of the Pits: Traders and Technology from Chicago to London*. Chicago, IL: University of Chicago Press.

29

FINANCIALIZATION AS MATHEMATIZATION

The Calculative and Regulatory Consequences of Risk Management

Nathan Coombs and Arjen van der Heide

Introduction

That financial markets play an increasingly important role in capitalist economies is beyond doubt. Today large firms often turn to bond markets rather than banks to finance their operations; and many banks focus on securitizing assets instead of investing in the traditional sense. Over recent decades the notion of financialization has been adopted by critically minded scholars seeking to relate these trends to problems such as declining economic productivity, rising inequality and heightened financial fragility (Stockhammer 2004; Alvarez 2015; Tridico and Pariboni 2018). While rival explanatory lenses have also been proposed (most notably, globalization and neoliberalism), financialization scholars see these problems as predictable symptoms of the increasing share of global economic income ending up in the pockets of financial actors since the 1970s.

What enabled the financialization process? There are a diverse range of explanations provided in the current volume, but this chapter contributes to an emerging literature which focuses specifically on the mathematization of valuation practices within finance. We argue that the financialization of the banking sector was not just the result of intensified quantification (as in Chiapello's (2015) framing of the issue); contingent regulatory decisions played an equally essential role. And we demonstrate that this is the case through a historical overview of the rise of risk management in the banking sector, focusing on key "moments" in the story. In particular, we identify the Black–Scholes–Merton (BSM) formula, Value-at-Risk (VaR) modelling and Collateralized Debt Obligation (CDO) valuation as three cumulative developments in financial modelling which allowed risk to be moved off-balance-sheet and regulatory capital minimized. We also draw attention to how regulators played an active role in pushing market actors towards adopting the risk management strategies pioneered and promoted by leading firms.

The discussion begins by situating work on calculative practices in the wider literature on financialization. The following section provides a historical overview of the rise of risk management. The next section addresses how the Basel Committee on Banking Supervision enthusiastically embraced the new science of financial risk management in the 1990s. The story is then completed in the final section which turns to how securitization, particularly CDOs, provided banks with an opportunity to move risk off their balance sheets and reduce their regulatory capital. The conclusion reflects on the ambiguous fate of risk management in the aftermath of the global financial crisis. On the one hand, very little has changed: derivatives continue to circulate in large volumes, securitization quickly recovered in the United States, and the use of VaR-like techniques for calculating firms' regulatory capital remains firmly entrenched. On the other hand, public authorities are subjecting these techniques to greater oversight and beginning to develop their own models for controlling the complex financial system they helped bring into being. We thus conclude that while significant attempts at regulatory reform have been made, the calculative and regulatory infrastructures set in place by the banking sector's financialization remain mostly unperturbed.

Calculative Engines of Financialization

To speak of "financialization" is to describe a process whereby the financial sector has grown in size and assumed an increasingly central role in the economy. It is also to pose the question of how this happened. Most of the answers focusing on the historical period from the 1970s to the present focus on the extra-financial reasons that enabled the transformation, whether that is the shareholder value revolution in corporate management or the economic policy shifts often identified with "neoliberalism." However, inspired in part by the social studies of finance (SSF), a new literature is turning its attention to the mathematization of financial valuation practices.

The most expansive attempt is Chiapello (2015, see also in this volume). Chiapello argues that the spread of economizing quantifications generally takes the form of financialized valuation practices which have "colonized" domains as varied as investment valuation, accounting standards, and banking supervision. Carruthers (2015) and Besedovsky (2017) understand the changing function of credit ratings similarly. While initially introduced as a commensuration tool to establish a descriptive *ordinal* ranking of the creditworthiness of corporations and states, the introduction of securitization in the 1970s drove the credit-rating agencies to hire a raft of "quants" whose probabilistic methods imbued the ratings with *cardinal* significance. The result was that market actors began to interpret the ratings as carrying implied probabilities of default, allowing the construction of instruments based on levels of risk adjusted yield (with results, in the case of mortgage-backed securities, which we discuss below. Lengwiler (2016) follows a parallel set of developments in the insurance industry, where the increasing prominence of financial mathematics in the 1990s helped to push debates away from a focus on the challenges of state provision to the needs of profit-oriented investors. In sum, what these studies show is the importance of the epistemic shift brought about by the application of financial mathematics, changing fundamentally what finance does and what it is for.

This chapter contributes to this literature, but with the crucial difference that it understands financialization not simply as an effect of these transformations on the "real" economy but as a process which has transformed the banking sector itself. Although that might seem a needlessly provocative move, it is not without precedent. For example, it follows a similar path to Hardie's (2011) definition of financialization as the tradability of risk. In coining the definition, Hardie's aim is to furnish a metric that allows him to compare the borrowing capacity of emerging markets vis-à-vis the financialization of their government bond markets. Financial mechanisms can, on this understanding, be more or less financialized. Crucially, this approach involves breaking away from a monolithic image of "finance." If SSF has contributed a vital methodological insight to the broader field of finance studies, it is that finance is composed of a myriad of different evaluation cultures and institutional norms that do not cohere into a unified whole.

When we talk of the banking sector becoming financialized we are thus referring to a particular set of evaluation practices which have since the 1970s come to capture its imagination and that of the regulators which oversee it. In the language of the sector itself, these evaluation practices are called "risk management."

As we shall see over the coming pages, understanding risk management techniques as a driver of financialization involves highlighting risk management's double-sided nature. The rise of risk management is not, as the words might suggest, indicative of the financial sector becoming chronically risk-averse – the expansion of the use of derivatives from the early 1980s was as much about enabling new strategies for market speculation as it was about employing hedging strategies in portfolio management (Field 2003). As a result, following the thread linking together BSM, VaR and CDO valuation shows how considering these techniques as just quantifying economizations glosses over a crucial dimension of the story with implications for the political economy of finance (cf. Chiapello 2015). Our history shows that the aim of risk management techniques to place risk into circulation was equally about removing it off-balance-sheet for the purpose of minimizing regulatory capital. We also draw attention to the contingency of the regulatory decisions which entrenched these practices. The developments described did not need to take this direction; and could indeed still take another route. Against this measure we are thus able to conclude with a judicious evaluation of whether post-crisis regulatory reforms have done anything to reverse, hinder or redirect the banking sector's financialization.

A History of Risk Management

The conceptual foundations of risk management can be traced to modern portfolio theory (Field 2003). Portfolio theory became a topic of scientific investigation in the 1950s and 1960s, around the same time that risk emerged as an object of analysis throughout society (Power 2007: 12). The work of Harry Markowitz (1952) and others (Treynor 1961; Sharpe 1964; Lintner 1965) established the idea that there is a trade-off between the risk and return of an investment that can be optimized through the construction of an efficient portfolio. The capital asset pricing model (CAPM) provides the theoretical rationale. It distinguishes between two aspects of financial risk: asset-specific risk which can be mitigated by subsuming the asset in a diversified portfolio (and should therefore not be priced), and non-diversifiable risk or "market risk," for which investors should be compensated with a risk premium (Treynor 1961).

The notion of a risk-return trade-off was developed further with the publication of the Black-Scholes (1973) and Merton (1973) options pricing formula (henceforth, BSM). Albeit at much lower volumes, derivative contracts had been traded for centuries using rule of thumb heuristics. Yet, the BSM model greatly facilitated the proliferation of derivatives by providing a scientific approach to pricing derivatives that distinguished the practice from reckless gambling (MacKenzie and Millo 2003).

At the model's heart is the idea of a "replicating portfolio." It was possible, BSM suggested, to construct a continuously adjusted portfolio containing the underlying asset and "risk-free" assets such as a cash deposit or treasury bonds that would replicate the pay-offs of the option contract itself. On the basis of the "no-arbitrage" principle, which builds on the efficient market hypothesis (Fama 1970) – no opportunity for riskless profit should exist since it would immediately be exploited and disappear – it follows that the price of the option must be equal to the cost of the replicating portfolio. The model therefore put the relative pricing of risk central in the valuation of financial assets (MacKenzie 2006).

An initial application of BSM was on the trading floors of the Chicago Board Options Exchange, where after entering the trading floor in 1975 and gradually becoming incorporated in trading strategies, market prices and those predicted by the model gradually converged until the stock market crash in 1987 (MacKenzie 2006: 174–177). Another important use of BSM in the period before the crash was portfolio insurance. In the late 1970s, firms realized that it could be used to create "synthetic put option" for market portfolios, setting a floor to how far the value of such a portfolio could drop (Leland and Rubinstein 1988; MacKenzie 2006: 180). However, when in October 1987 there was an unprecedented 22.6% "nosedive" in market prices, analyses concluded that markets did not only react to external events, but had acquired their own "irrational" internal dynamic caused, *inter-alia*, by strategies such as portfolio insurance and derivatives (Brady Commission 1988). Yet the crash did not lead to the demise of risk management; it was a catalyst for its further development (Field 2003).

In the years which followed, banks continued to invest in novel risk-management techniques. New metrics emerged that sought to turn risk into a manageable object, such as "risk-adjusted return-on-capital" (James 1996). Perhaps the most significant of these was Value-at-Risk (VaR), which in its simplest form is a representation of the distribution of expected returns of an investment and can therefore be considered a "natural progression" from the mean-variance method of modern portfolio theory (Dowd 1998: 19; Holton 2002). While the metric remained impracticable for a long time due to the demanding computations, by the late 1980s, once computer power had increased sufficiently, VaR eventually became the de facto standard for measuring risk in major banks and hedge funds. VaR allows various forms of risk to be represented, compared and aggregated in a single metric that can be understood intuitively (Kavanagh 2003). With the introduction of VaR, capital allocation became a central problem of risk management: by establishing a connection between the riskiness of a portfolio and its rate of return, banks' management could compare the economic capital required for certain activities, allowing them to funnel funds into those activities with the best risk-return trade-off (Holton 2002; Kavanagh 2003; Rosen 2003).

Initially, quantitative risk management dealt primarily with market risk. However, during the 1990s other types of risk increasingly started to be analysed with methods consistent with BSM. Arbitrage-free pricing frameworks were developed for instruments such as credit and interest rate derivatives (Huault and Rainelli-Le Montagner 2009; Spears 2014). Robert Merton (1974) had shown how you could analyse credit risk in corporate debt by modelling equity as a call option on a firm's assets. Similarly, interest rate modelling took off from the late-1980s onwards and culminated in the publication of the Heath–Jarrow–Morton (1992) framework, which provided a general no-arbitrage framework for modelling interest rate risk (Spears 2014). Though some risks proved difficult to quantify, such as liquidity and operational risk, the Black–Scholes paradigm provided an intellectual resource that showed practitioners how various forms of uncertainty could be abstracted from financial markets and the economy more generally, and be turned into a "manageable" and tradable object.

The Basel Accords: From Ignorance to Enthusiasm

In the early 1990s, regulators became increasingly conscious of banks' own risk management systems. While regulators were initially reluctant to rely on these systems to determine banks' capital adequacy, they eventually started to perceive these techniques as superior. The first international capital accord, Basel I, was agreed in 1988 and was the result of a long and difficult political process. As Charles Goodhart (2011) describes, the Basel Committee on Banking Supervision (BCBS) was tasked with creating an international capital standard without having an effective internal mechanism to "impose its will on a recalcitrant member" (Goodhart 2011: 548). Although national representatives recognized the importance of a shared standard, and indeed agreed that the capital adequacy ratio should to some extent reflect the riskiness of banks' activities, agreeing on appropriate risk weightings proved difficult. Ultimately, the Basel Committee agreed on a standard that required banks to hold a minimum of 8% of capital against risk-weighted assets; assets were classified in one of five "buckets" each of which was attributed a different weight. For example, while OECD sovereign bonds were assigned a 0% risk weighting, riskier assets such as corporate bonds and equities were weighted at 100% (BCBS 1988).

Basel I was considered an intermediate step towards a full capital standard regime, as it accounted only for credit risk. The text of the agreement contained an announcement that the Committee would also investigate possible methods for setting capital standards for interest rate and investment risk, an investigation that began in the mid-1980s (BCBS 1988: 2). Eventually the BCBS published a proposed bucket-like methodology for the assessment of market risk in 1993, to which banks replied disapprovingly, claiming that the risk management systems they used internally to manage their trading book were more sophisticated (Goodhart 2011: 247). As Goodhart notes, when possibilities for using these methods for regulatory capital were explored, BCBS working groups increasingly "found the work of the major international banks in assessing their own market risk to be impressive" (Goodhart 2011: 249). The 1996 "Market Amendment" to the Basel I regime allowed banks to use their internal models to assess market risk. It used the VaR measure produced by these models as a basis for calculating capital requirements, which also included a factor to account for the quality of the models to encourage firms to improve them – an element that was enthusiastically supported by Robert Merton (Goodhart 2011: 256).

The approach to regulatory capital adopted in the 1996 Market Risk Amendment was further elaborated in the 2004 Basel II regime. Though Basel I had broadly achieved many of its initial aims, it also contained significant weaknesses (Kern 2015), especially the treatment of credit risk. The risk buckets were regarded as "ad hoc and broad-brush, based on subjective (and political) judgment," and would lead to "serious distortions in bank asset portfolios" (Goodhart 2011: 195). To remedy these shortcomings, Basel II allowed banks to use internal models to also calculate credit risk. Banks could now use their own estimates of parameters such as the probability of default and the loss-given-default to derive a distribution of "default VaR" (a weighted distribution of value at risk due to credit exposure). In doing so, banks would build on Merton's (1974) framework to treat the possibility of default as an option that could be valued using option pricing techniques. Moreover, the Basel accords sought actively to motivate banks to improve their internal methodology, promising reductions in regulatory capital (BCBS 2001).

From Basel I to Basel II, supervisors thus changed from being sceptical about the usefulness of internal models to becoming risk-management enthusiasts, who actively sought to improve banks' risk management systems by offering them rewards in the form of capital reductions for doing so. This was reflected in a broader ideological shift that took root in banking supervision. Chairman of the Fed at the time, Alan Greenspan, for instance, famously embraced risk management as a win–win solution allowing supervisors and firms to work together in enhancing the resilience of the financial system. It seemed to provide an opportunity to develop a seemingly rational, objective and scientific approach for determining capital adequacy standards that would "depoliticize" capital regulation and establish greater trust in supervisor–industry relations.

Securitization as Risk Management

The embedding of risk-capital techniques in regulation provided an impetus for the development of additional risk management techniques. On the one hand, regulators came to see risk management as a useful tool to "stabilize" financial markets. On the other, banks sought to develop increasingly complex risk-management constructions to reduce their regulatory capital, while at the same time retaining the profits arising from the new activities. Securitization offered the means to achieve both goals.

The modern practice of securitization began in the 1970s with the US government-sponsored enterprises (GSEs), Freddie Mac and Fannie Mae, in an effort to expand credit in mortgage markets. House ownership has long been an important feature of the American economy and its realization unified both sides of the American political spectrum. In the 1960s, the Johnson administration perceived the traditional model of mortgage provision to be inadequate to cater to the housing needs of the baby boomer generation and to expand house ownership amongst lower income households. Mortgage-Backed Securities (MBSs) – a type of securitization that would later become part of a larger class of Asset-Backed Securities (ABSs) including, among other things, the income streams of automobile loans and credit cards – provided a technique to expand mortgage credit without needing to increase government expenditure or to keep the mortgages on the books of the GSEs (Fligstein and Goldstein 2012).

In an ABS transaction, a bank moves assets from its balance sheet into a special purpose vehicle, which is then sliced into different tranches each bearing different levels of credit risk. The more "senior" and "safest" tranches of ABSs are typically funded by issuing bonds to investors; the junior tranche or tranches are typically funded by equity from the originating bank to provide an incentive for the bank to maintain adequate credit standards for the assets included in the ABS (Donnelly and Embrechts 2010; MacKenzie 2011). Issuing ABSs allows a bank to pass off at least part of its credit risk onto investors who are rewarded, in turn, with a risk premium. Moreover, the ABS transaction frees up capital on the bank's balance sheet, allowing it to take on new credit risk by underwriting new loans. Through this mechanism, the creation of MBSs was considered a useful tool for aggregating and diffusing geographically concentrated risk and to free up the balance sheet of banks to enhance their ability to under-write new mortgages (Aalbers 2008; Aalbers, Fernandez and Wijburg in this volume; Poon 2009; MacKenzie 2011; Fligstein & Goldstein 2012).

Credit risk evaluation played a crucial role in the construction and management of ABSs. The modelling of credit risk, in which rating agencies such as Standard & Poor's and Moody's took a leading role, is necessary so that buyers of ABSs can judge whether the size of the "risk premium" makes it worthwhile to engage in a transaction. The importance of credit ratings meant that the securities and "knowledge of the securities" were "coproduced": the ABS tranches were designed specifically to achieve certain ratings (MacKenzie 2011: 1795). The evaluation of an ABS requires credit rating agencies and banks to estimate the probability of default, and, in the case of a MBS, the risk of prepayment of individual loans in the pool as well as the correlation of risks across different assets – a complicated problem that in the case of early ABSs was dealt with implicitly and procedurally rather than mathematically (MacKenzie 2011: 1796–97, 1802–04). For example, credit rating agencies would apply penalties to a security's rating if they thought that the included mortgages were too geographically concentrated.

From the 1990s onwards, securitization became an important activity of banks' derivatives departments, who sought to construct Collateralized Debt Obligations (CDOs) from corporate debt (MacKenzie 2011: 1803–1804). Similar to ABSs, the main purpose for banks to construct big balance-sheet CDOs was "to shed credit risk from their portfolios of loans to corporations and to reduce the capital reserves that regulators insisted they hold in respect to that lending" (MacKenzie 2011: 1800). National regulatory bodies were aware of banks moving assets off balance sheet towards unregulated entities, but allowed them to do so at the perceived benefit of domestic banks' international competitive position (Thiemann 2014; in this volume).

The shifting organizational locus of securitization that came with CDOs, however, would have important implications for how these assets were evaluated. Professionals at banks' derivatives departments had a proclivity for adopting mathematical solutions rather than procedural ones (MacKenzie and Spears 2014). Hence, banks adopted the Gaussian copula family of models to quantify the correlation between the probabilities of default on pools of assets in a manner loosely analogous to a Black–Scholes approach to pricing and measuring risk. The use of Gaussian copula models became widespread with the publication of JP Morgan's CreditMetrics risk management software in 1997, and would in subsequent years also be adopted by credit rating agencies (Donnelly and Embrechts 2010; MacKenzie 2011; MacKenzie and Spears 2014).

Similar to ABSs, CDOs not only allowed banks to move their assets off balance sheet, but also provided a profitable arbitrage opportunity. The risk premium demanded by investors to share their credit risk burden was often sufficiently low to boost banks' profits without taking on additional risk. Annual issuance of CDOs grew explosively from less than $70bn in 2000 to more than $500bn at the market's peak year in 2006 (SIFMA 2016). Not only the amount, but also the structure of CDOs changed rapidly. In the years leading up to the global financial crisis, more than half of the debt underpinning CDOs did not consist of corporate bonds but rather of repackaged ABSs. Differences between how ABSs were valued and the quantitative approaches to the valuation of CDOs had led to a "fatally attractive arbitrage opportunity," on which banks sought to capitalize by constructing ABS-CDOs (MacKenzie 2011: 1778). Thus, the use of quantitative risk management techniques enabled banks to profit from various forms of arbitrage. It also facilitated large-scale removal of various forms of consumer and corporate credit from banks' balance sheets, where they were subject to capital regulation, to off-balance-sheet entities, where they were not. In combination with derivatives-enabled portfolio management and internal VaR models for calculating regulatory capital, securitization brought to completion the financialization of the banking sector – a system of baroque complexity grounded in decades of developments in mathematical financial theory.

However, the 2007–2009 crisis revealed the fragility of this system. In late 2006 and continuing in 2007, US house prices began to fall. Two large subprime mortgage originators declared bankruptcy and credit rating agencies downgraded MBSs. In August, these downgrades triggered the first interbank panic. Concerns about the solvency of counterparties and the liquidity of bonds led to increasing collateral demands in short-term debt markets, eroding banks' equity capital buffers (Gorton and Metrick 2012).

The problem was compounded by special purpose vehicles incurring heavy losses. When Lehman Brothers filed for bankruptcy in September 2008, US authorities, fearing the collapse of the entire financial system, made unprecedented interventions to keep it afloat (see Epstein in this volume). The GSEs were brought into the conservatorship of the federal government. The Federal Reserve also lent $85 billion to the insurer AIG, who had been prolific in writing credit default swaps on now failing securitized products. Yet those interventions would pale in comparison to the Troubled Asset Relief Program, which authorized US authorities to spend up to $700 billion purchasing predominantly securitized assets. And so the story goes on, morphing from a banking crisis into a potentially catastrophic sovereign debt crisis until the announcement of the Outright Monetary Transactions program by the European Central Bank in August 2012 (Braun 2015: 420).

The quantitative techniques traced out in this chapter contributed to the crisis in three main ways. First, derivatives pricing through BSM, VaR modelling of market and credit risk, and mathematical CDO valuation, rest with the idea that risk is a manageable object that can be sliced, diced, and traded with precision. When markets began to behave in unexpected ways, the promise of taming uncertainty and converting it into measurable risk proved illusory. Second, these techniques, once credited with distributing risk safely throughout the financial system, had the unintended consequence of making it hard for practitioners to know where risks were concentrated in the event of a crisis. Since firms did not know who among their counterparties was potentially insolvent, and fearing precipitous declines in the value of their collateral, liquidity dried up and a damaging credit crunch ensued. It is these opaque circulations of risk which have come to be distilled into the rubrics of "systemic risk" and "interconnectedness" prevalent after the crisis. Third, from its inception risk management was motivated at least in part by economizing on regulatory capital. The risk-sensitive VaR metric allowed banks to reduce their capital buffers and increase their leverage. Basel II pivoted on the assumption of an incentive alignment between the stability-seeking objectives of public authorities and the profit-maximizing objectives of private actors. That was reflected in failures of bank supervisors to sufficiently monitor how banks' internal models were being used to calculate their regulatory capital. Finally, the use of off-balance-sheet special purpose entities to conduct securitization and manufacture CDOs, while not grounded in financial theory, drew support from these techniques' affinities to established risk management practices.

Conclusion: Post-crisis Denouement

This chapter has argued that the financialization of the banking sector involved cumulative developments in quantitative risk management techniques. Although contributing to a new literature focused on the role of calculative practices in the financialization process, we have emphasised the contingent regulatory decisions which contributed to the shift. It is possible that many of the techniques would still have been employed in the absence of the regulatory seal of approval provided by the Basel Committee on Banking Supervision. But it is unlikely that the banking sector would have been so profoundly transformed, or financial stability risks so amplified.

Of course, when the house of cards came tumbling down during the financial crisis many of the assumptions of risk management were called into question, at least for a time. Among the most authoritative accounts are by the US Financial Crisis Inquiry Commission (FCIC 2011) and the UK's Turner Review (FSA 2009). Both see derivatives, VaR modelling, and securitization as transforming finance from the 1970s onwards into a newly complex and unstable form. The Turner Review goes so far as to identify the model of securitized credit intermediation as having an "inherent" tendency to promote systemic risk (FSA 2009: 43).

It is therefore surprising that so little seems to have changed in the years since. Some figures are instructive. According to data by the Bank for International Settlements, although there has been a marked shift from over-the-counter to exchange-traded derivatives in the post-crisis era, there has been no overall reduction in the notional market value of derivatives since 2009 (BIS 2017). There are similar continuities with securitization. While issuance in Europe never recovered to its pre-crisis peak, in the United States securitization issuance stood at $1.4 trillion in 2009 and by 2016 increased to $1.8 trillion (AFME 2017: 6).

At the same time, if the financialized banking sector is understood as an amalgam of calculative practices and regulatory rules, then characterizing the post-crisis period is more difficult. The big idea for responding to this new financial world is of course macroprudential regulation: an acknowledgement that neither the incentives of financial institutions nor a regulatory focus on individual firms are sufficient to prevent another crisis (Baker 2013). Instead, it would be necessary to empower regulators with the means to know and control the financial system *as a whole* and implement counter-cyclical policies to lean against the growth of credit and bolster the resilience of the system. Before and immediately after the crisis, the tools that would allow regulators to pursue these goals simply did not exist. Yet in the years since, the development of metrics for measuring systemic risk and agent-based modelling techniques have taken regulators ever further away from standard neoclassical theories in the area of financial stability (Bookstaber

2017). Some scholars have gone so far as to portray macroprudential policies as a bold challenge to neoliberalism (Baker & Widmaier 2015). More recently, however, a sober, even sombre, appraisal of the achievements of the policy-shift has emerged. As mooted interventionist policies to smooth the credit cycle have given way to simply improving bank capitalization, commentators once enthused by regulators' counter-cyclical ambitions have found fault in practically the entire sweep of post-crisis regulation (Underhill 2015).

Nevertheless, the extent to which post-crisis regulation has deviated from its pre-crisis trajectory remains an open question. Part of the difficulty is that the answer depends in large part on which aspect of regulation is focused on and one's evaluative standard. Those hoping to see a radical departure from the status quo ante will inevitably be disappointed, whereas those attuned to incremental advances are likely to see a somewhat more promising picture. What is clear is that on the terms proposed in this chapter there has been no clear reversal of the banking sector's financialization. There has been no retreat from mathematized risk management as the overarching paradigm of financial practices and their supervision.

Bibliography

Aalbers, M.B., 2008. The financialization of home and the mortgage market crisis. *Competition & Change*, 12(2), pp. 148–166.

AFME (Association of Financial Markets in Europe), 2017. *Securitisation Data Report: European Structured Finance: Q1: 2017*. London.

Alvarez, I., 2015. Financialization, non-financial corporations and income inequality: The case of France. *Socio-Economic Review*, 13(3), pp. 449–475.

Baker, A., 2013. The new political economy of the macroprudential ideational shift. *New Political Economy*, 18(1), pp.112–139.

Baker, A. and Widmaier, W., 2015. Macroprudential ideas and contested social purpose: A response to Terrence Casey. *The British Journal of Politics & International Relations*, 17(2), pp. 371–380.

BCBS (Basel Committee on Banking Supervision), 1988. *International Convergence of Capital Measurement and Capital Standards*. Basel: Basel Committee on Banking Supervision.

BCBS (Basel Committee on Banking Supervision), 2001. *The Internal Ratings-Based Approach*. Basel: Basel Committee on Banking Supervision.

Besedovsky, N., 2017. Financialization as calculative practice: The rise of structured finance and the cultural and calculative transformation of credit rating agencies. *Socio-Economic Review*, 16(1), pp.61–84.

BIS (Bank for International Settlements), 2017. *Statistical Release: OTC Derivatives Statistics at End-June 2017*. Basel: Basel Committee on Banking Supervision.

Black, F. and Scholes, M., 1973. The pricing of options and corporate liabilities. *Journal of Political Economy*, 81(3), pp. 637–654.

Bookstaber, R., 2017. *The End of Theory: Financial Crises, the Failure of Economics, and the Sweep of Human Interaction*. Princeton, NJ: Princeton University Press.

Brady Commission, 1988. *Report of the Presidential Task Force on Market Mechanisms*. Washington, DC.

Braun, B., 2015. Preparedness, crisis management and policy change: The Euro area at the critical juncture of 2008–2013. *The British Journal of Politics and International Relations*, 17(3), pp. 419–441.

Carruthers, B.G., 2015. Financialization and the institutional foundations of the new capitalism. *Socio-Economic Review*, 13(2), pp. 379–398.

Chiapello, E., 2015. Financialisation of valuation. *Human Studies*, 38(1), pp. 13–35.

Donnelly, C. and Embrechts, P., 2010. The devil is in the tails: Actuarial mathematics and the subprime mortgage crisis. *ASTIN Bulletin*, 40(1), pp. 1–33.

Dowd, K., 1998. *Beyond Value at Risk: The New Science of Risk Management*. Chichester: John Wiley & Sons.

Fama, E.F., 1970. Efficient capital markets: A review of theory and empirical work. *Journal of Finance*, 25 (2), pp. 383–417.

FCIC, 2011. *Financial Crisis Inquiry Report: Final Report of the National Commission on the Causes of the Financial and Economic Crisis in the United States*. Washington, DC.

Field, P., 2003. *Modern Risk Management: A History*. London: Risk Books.

Fligstein, N. and Goldstein, A., 2012. A long strange trip: The state and mortgage securitization, 1968–2010. In Knorr Cetina, K. and Preda, A. (eds.), *The Oxford Handbook of the Sociology of Finance*, first edition. Oxford: Oxford University Press, pp. 339–356.

FSA (Financial Services Authority), 2009. *The Turner Review: A Regulatory Response to the Global Banking Crisis*. London.

Goodhart, C., 2011. *The Basel Committee on Banking Supervision: A History of the Early Years 1974–1997*. Cambridge: Cambridge University Press.

Gorton, G. and Metrick, A., 2012. Securitized banking and the run on repo. *Journal of Financial Economics*, 104(3), pp.425–451.

Hardie, I., 2011. How much can governments borrow? Financialization and emerging markets government borrowing capacity. *Review of International Political Economy*, 18(2), pp. 141–167.

Heath, B.Y.D., Jarrow, R. and Morton, A., 1992. Bond pricing and the term structure of interest rates: A new methodology for contingent claims valuation. *Econometrica*, 60(1), pp. 77–105.

Holton, G.A., 2002. History of value-at-risk: 1922–1998. Working Paper, 25 July.

Huault, I. and Rainelli-Le Montagner, H., 2009. Market shaping as an answer to ambiguities: The case of credit derivatives. *Organization Studies*, 30(5), pp. 549–575.

James, C., 1996. *RAROC Based Capital Budgeting and Performance Evaluation: A Case Study of Bank Capital Allocation*. Paper presented at the Wharton Financial Institutions Center. Available at: https://papers.ssrn.com/sol3/papers.cfm?abstract_id=1000.

Kavanagh, B., 2003. A retrospective look at market risk. In Field, P. (ed.), *Modern Risk Management: A History*. London: Risk Books, pp. 251–260.

Kern, A., 2015. *The Role of Capital in Supporting Banking Stability*. In Maloney, N., Ferran, E. and Payne, J. (eds.), *Oxford Handbook of Financial Regulation*. Oxford: Oxford University Press, pp. 335–363.

Leland, H. and Rubinstein, M., 1988. The evolution of portfolio insurance. In Luskin, D. (ed.), *Dynamic Hedging: A Guide to Portfolio Insurance*. Chichester, NY: John Wiley & Sons.

Lengwiler, M., 2016. Risky calculations: Financial mathematics and securitization since the 1970s. *Historical Social Research*, 41(2), pp. 258–279.

Lintner, J., 1965. Security prices, risk, and maximal gains from diversification. *The Journal of Finance*, 20(4), pp. 587–615.

MacKenzie, D.A., 2006. *An Engine, Not a Camera: How Financial Models Shape Markets*. Cambridge, MA: MIT Press.

MacKenzie, D.A., 2011. The credit crisis as a problem in the sociology of knowledge. *American Journal of Sociology*, 116(6), pp. 1778–1841.

MacKenzie, D.A. and Millo, Y., 2003. Constructing a market, performing theory: The historical sociology of a financial derivatives exchange. *American Journal of Sociology*, 109(1), pp. 107–145.

MacKenzie, D.A. and Spears, T., 2014. "The formula that killed Wall Street": The Gaussian copula and modelling practices in investment banking. *Social Studies of Science*, 44(3), pp. 393–417.

Markowitz, H., 1952. Portfolio selection. *The Journal of Finance*, 7(1), pp. 77–91.

Merton, R.C., 1973. Theory of rational option pricing. *The Bell Journal of Economics and Management Science*, 4 (1), pp. 141–183.

Merton, R.C., 1974. On the pricing of corporate debt: The risk structure of interest rates. *The Journal of Finance*, 29(2), pp. 449–470.

Poon, M., 2009. From new deal institutions to capital markets: Commercial consumer risk scores and the making of subprime mortgage finance. *Accounting, Organizations and Society*, 34(5), pp. 654–674.

Power, M., 2007. *Organized Uncertainty: Designing a World of Risk Management*. Oxford: Oxford University Press.

Rosen, D., 2003. The development of risk management software. In Field, P. (ed.), *Modern Risk Management: A History*. London: Risk Books, pp. 135–150.

SIFMA. 2016. Global CDO Issuance. *Statistical Bulletin*. Available at: https://www.sifma.org/.

Sharpe, W.F., 1964. Capital asset prices: A theory of market equilibrium under conditions of risk. *The Journal of Finance*, 19(3), pp. 425–442.

Spears, T., 2014. *Engineering Value, Engineering Risk: What Derivatives Quants Know and What Their Models Do*. PhD thesis, University of Edinburgh.

Stockhammer, E., 2004. Financialisation and the slowdown of accumulation. *Cambridge Journal of Economics*, 28 (5), pp. 719–741.

Thiemann, M., 2014. In the shadow of Basel: How competitive politics bred the crisis. *Review of International Political Economy*, 21(6), pp. 1203–1239.

Treynor, J.L. (1961). Toward a theory of market value of risky assets. Unpublished Manuscript.

Tridico, P. and Pariboni, R., 2018. Inequality, financialization, and economic decline. *Journal of Post Keynesian Economics*, 41(2), pp. 236–259.

Underhill, G.R.D., 2015. The emerging post-crisis financial architecture: The Path-dependency of ideational adverse selection. *The British Journal of Politics and International Relations*, 17(3), pp. 461–493.

30

"A MACHINE FOR LIVING"

The Cultural Economy of Financial Subjectivity

Rob Aitken

Financialization occupies a space at the very heart of how we understand our globalized present and its relation to a range of possible futures. As this volume indicates, this concept refers to the diverse ways in which finance is now at the center of our social and economic lives: "The machinery for measuring, modelling, managing, predicting, commoditizing, and exploiting risk," argues Arjun Appadurai (2016: 44), "has become the central diacritic of modern capitalism." As the late Randy Martin (2016) has implored, however, financialization is not merely an economic form, but a *cultural* practice, a set of scripts about how we are supposed to live our everyday lives (see Hiss 2013). Broadly, the wide extension of finance as a powerful force has resulted in a culture criss-crossed by the language and practice of calculation as a dominant vector of social life, what Max Haiven (2014: 4) refers to as the "financialized imagination": "the rhizomatic and diffuse appearance of financial metaphors, practices, narratives, ideals, measurements, ideologies and identities throughout the social fabric" (see also Davis and Walsh 2016).

If financialization is understood in cultural tones, what kind of culture does it constitute? What is at stake in referring to finance as a kind of culture? In this chapter, I argue that the work on the culture of finance (what we often refer to as the *cultural economy* of finance) is crucial because it raises the issue of financial subjectivity as a central concern. If finance pervades the social fabric it must, by extension, confront the worlds of everyday practice and identity.[1] As Martin noted, financialization as culture provokes questions about how we define our sense of self and citizenship, framing our subjectivity and moral compass. Financialization redefines what it means to govern ourselves and becomes what Martin describes as a "machine for living" (Martin 2002, 2013, 2016). Following Martin's lead, there is now an important stream of research on financialization that emphasizes the "making up" of financial subjects, especially in everyday life. Those of us who have not often imagined our lives in relation to the world of high finance are now increasingly asked to make connections to finance, to rework ourselves as investors in our own lives, and to adopt risk-taking and risk pricing behaviors. Research on this aspect of financialization attends to the ways in which everyday actors are assembled as financial agents, not as passive or malleable objects of financial impositions, but as *subjects* navigating liberalized global financial networks. This research focuses on the complex ways in which ever-widening populations are constituted as the risk-bearing, investing or indebted subjects that are amenable to finance and the constraints and opportunities it generates.

In punctuating the impact of this work, I point in this chapter to two broad conceptual contributions developed in the literature on everyday cultures and financial subjectivity. First, I note the importance of what I refer to, borrowing from Muniesa et al. (2017), as a *logic of configuration* – the processes by which objects, practices and bodies are constituted as financial categories in the first place. Configuration directs attention to the broad ways in which everyday actors are asked to bear risk, assume debt, or invest in the spaces of global finance. Configuration suggests that the way we become financial actors – the way we come to identify as savers or investors or debtors – is not automatic or straightforward but requires work and efforts of all sorts and neither is it guaranteed in advance to work.

Second, I point to a *logic of selection*. Selection refers to the social sorting by which those capable of autonomy in global financial networks are differentiated from those constituted as incapable of it. Put a bit differently, not all populations are asked to enter into financial practices in uniform fashion. Some populations are included in financial services in coercive or very costly ways, and some are not afforded the opportunity to access financial services such as credit or basic banking accounts in any meaningful fashion at all – the fate of the large numbers of globally unbanked. Financial institutions are now preoccupied with finely determined gradations, often informed by "big data," which sort populations into diverse categories of risk each attached to different levels of access to (and barriers to) financial services. Financialization, I argue, entails both the constitution of financial, investing or risk-bearing subjects absorbed into mainstream financial networks, as well as the delineation of those whose relationship to finance is limited, differentiated or constrained. I conclude by speculating about the political possibilities in an era of financialization.

Configuration

To take seriously financialization as culture invokes the analytical weight of cultural economy as a way of understanding finance, not as a unitary and coherent culture in itself, but as a set of practices which are particular, historical and contingent. Making finance visible in terms of *cultural analysis* entails attention to the ways in which "economic" spaces or practices are constituted in the first place. Cultural economy, argue du Gay and Pryke (see also Aitken 2007: 47) places analytical attention onto

> the practical ways in which "economically relevant activity" is performed and enacted […] the ways in which the "making up" or "construction" of economic realities is undertaken and achieved; how those activities, objects and persons we categorize as "economic" are built up or assembled from a number of parts.
>
> *(du Gay and Pryke 2002: 5)*

This offers a specific way of understanding markets as spaces assembled through the "socio-technical and embodied processes that assemble calculative exchange" (Langley forthcoming: 6). Viewed through this lens, financial practices are not already given categories but devices assembled from diverse parts.

Cultural economy implies that we are required to examine the way in which everyday cultures which anchor finance as a way of thinking and living our lives actually emerge. The prominence of finance in our lives, and the conversion of our everyday lives into forms governed in financial language and practices (as forms of "investments," "human capital" and "risk") are not simply given or automatic conditions but the result of ongoing work and effort. This suggests, by extension, a certain inflection of the conception of financialization in relation to what Muniesa et al. (2017) refer to as a practice of *configuration* (see also Aitken 2017a: 278). They suggest that financialization is the process through which objects are framed as assets capable of carrying financial value and generating a return on investment. Finance capital "is best understood as a process…not a thing in itself…but rather a form of action, a method of control, an act of configuration, an *operation*" (Muniesa et al. 2017: 14, emphasis in original). Financialization is the process by which objects become associated with the world of finance, become legible and governed as financial assets (Muniesa et al. 2017). Put a bit differently, before anything – ranging from subprime mortgage payments to the very way we imagine our own individual futures – can be understood as a financial object, as something understood and governed as something with financial value, it must first be framed, made visible and *configured* as such.

The very basis or beginning of this process of configuration is the search for raw assets in new and often unexpected places and the conversion of those assets into income streams that can be inserted into financial instruments (Aitken 2017a: 278). In Leyshon and Thrift's important formulation, financial value is built, first and foremost, from the incessant but mundane prospecting for new assets "which then – and only then – allows speculation to take place" (Leyshon and Thrift 2007: 98; see also Pani 2014: 216–217). In this process inert objects, some of them far removed from the world of finance, are captured and reworked as the basis of financial instruments (see also Montgomerie 2008: 245). Far from dramatic or tumultuous, financialization, for Leyshon and Thrift (2007: 98), is the mundane "impulse to identify almost anything that might provide a stable source of income, on which more speculation might be built." This precedes financial accumulation and corporate governance orientation with a prior moment in which objects practices and spaces, often distant from the mainstreams of finance, are converted into financialized assets in the first place (Aitken 2017a: 270).

Our era of intense financialization has sent financial institutions exploring for income streams – for example from student loans, shifts in agricultural commodity prices, or rental housing receipts and from much else besides – that could be inserted and *configured* into new kinds of financial instruments, repackaged and sold as financial assets in their own right to investors. The process of financialization is ambitious and entails the configuration not only of new assets in financial markets but also ever-widening kinds of populations that could understand themselves as risk-bearing, investing or indebted subjects capable of navigating those markets. As financial markets have become increasingly fitted into the fabric of everyday life (see Langley in this volume), there has been a parallel process by which new middle-class, working-class and poor populations, some of which have not had much contact with "high finance," have been asked to enter those markets as investors, savers or subjects capable of bearing risk and credit. Finance, Lazzarato notes (2012: 49–50), requires "the production of subjectivity…the injunction to become an economic 'subject'." Just as new objects need to be constituted as assets before they can circulate through financial markets, and before they can generate and carry financial value, so too must new populations be constituted as "financial subjects," as actors with certain kinds of agency, before they can enter financial markets (see Aitken 2015: 166–168; see also Hall 2012).

Configuring new kinds of financial markets implies a relationship between financialization and "subjectivity"; the ways in which we are not just objects of but subjects capable of some degree of autonomy and capacity in financial markets. Key to these new forms of financial subjectivity are neoliberal commitments: a self that is governed in the name of its own choice and security, an entrepreneurial practice of "investment" as long-term work on the self, and an ongoing openness to risk as a key to active citizenship. As Foucault has noted, neoliberalism is concerned with "affording everyone a sort of economic space within which they can take on and confront risks" (Foucault 2008: 144). The language and practice of finance is key to and consistent with neoliberal subjectivity; a place, as Martin describes (2002: 8–9), where we can exercise "self-mastery that channels doubt over uncertain identity into fruitful activity" (see also Langley 2008: 135). The world of personal finance entails practical sites – everyday borrowing arrangements, investment/saving mechanisms – in which everyday actors are asked to exhibit responsibility and calculation. As "techniques of the self," these practices of everyday finance encourage us to experiment in self fashioning in ways that echo "a particular configuration of the ideas of risk, responsibility and autonomy that is associated with advanced modernity...[and which] encourages subjects to take on responsibility for social risks and their own welfare in the market" (Maclean 2013: 458). The cultures of everyday finance are increasingly bound up in neoliberalism as a process in which "individuals are made responsible for 'managing' their own financial subjectivities" (Hall and Appleyard 2012: 460). Research enumerates the diverse attempts to enrol subjects into forms of financialized saving, investing, insuring, borrowing and banking (see Langley and Leaver 2012).

In my own work (Aitken 2007), I have argued that American financial institutions have often, throughout the twentieth century, encouraged working-class populations to find their own security in private investment plans. This attempt to create what I describe as a culture of "popular finance" has taken a range of different forms: programs of "mass investment" pursued in the mid-century campaigns of the New York Stock Exchange; efforts of financial advertisers to address an emergent middle class; and more recent practices of "asset-based social policy" and "ethical investing." In these instances, "capital" is not external to (or determinant of) everyday culture, but itself made in those everyday places. "Capital," I argue (Aitken 2007: 10), has "existed as much 'inside' the mundane world of everyday culture as it has been strangely external to it."

The efforts to prospect for new financial assets, and to carve out new forms of financial subjectivity around them, are experienced with a particular intensity at the edges of the global financial system. There are now profitable and organized attempts to enrol those outside of or on the margins of the mainstream financial system into formalized financial services. These practices, including payday lending, micro-insurance and micro-credit seek to incorporate those without access to credit, basic bank accounts, savings/investing mechanisms or insurance options into formalized financial markets (see Aitken 2015; Gonzalez this volume). In doing so, these mechanisms find financial value at the very edges of the financial system by designing financial services specifically designed for the "financially excluded." As I have argued (Aitken 2015: 8), these practices seek "the transformation of...particular kinds of human bodies...into objects capable of generating financialized income streams." Previously unbanked populations are converted into both sources of financial value and financial subjects capable of carrying themselves, in one way or another, in the spaces of global financial markets.

These diverse attempts at mobilizing new forms of financial subjectivity among everyday populations are linked to forms of financial market liberalization of the past several decades. Nonetheless these forms of everyday financial subjectivity also have much longer and complicated histories (Aitken 2017b). The practices of tax-deferral, for example, are key to neoliberal financial subjectivity but also emblematic of these longer trajectories. Tax-deferral mechanisms allow savers/investors to defer tax payments for income that is placed in some form of registered saving or investing mechanism often oriented to retirement saving. Although important to the "retirement investor" subjectivity that Langley and Learner (2012) describe, tax deferral has both a longer and more diverse political history than is often acknowledged. Introduced in the United Kingdom and Canada in the 1950s, tax deferral draws upon even longer attempts by state policymakers to shape everyday financial conduct through various government annuities and savings schemes. These mechanisms, which foster personal financial conduct as a kind of "technique of the self," have been mobilized, not only to support neoliberal conceptions of enterprising citizenship but also for nationalist and politically conservative political visions that predate neoliberalism (Aitken 2017b; see also Riles 2011; Brasset and Clark 2012).

This complexity echoes and implies the importance of what commentators have described as the "uneven" or "variegated" processes with which the financialization of everyday life has been shaped. Langley (2007: 80), for example, reminds us that everyday actors "cannot identify with the subject position of the investor to which they are summoned in an unambiguous manner, and therefore negotiate and contest disciplinary power relations in important ways." On one hand, everyday actors are often asked to treat financial practices as "techniques of the self," what Foucault describes as mechanisms which allow individuals to mount "operations on their own bodies [...] conduct and way of being" (Foucault 1988: 16–49). On the other hand, individuals often face cross-pressures that prevent them from assuming the financial identities that planners, advertisers or advisors suggest. Financial subjects, notes Langley (2007: 80), are not only investors but also consumers, workers and other economic or social identities that they cannot always reconcile. Individuals do not seamlessly "identify" with the categories they are asked to assume. Rather, they mediate, refuse, navigate, refract and rework the categories they are summoned to carry. This results in what Appleyard et al. (2016a, 2016b) refer to as the "variegated" relationships that prevail in credit networks for low-income groups (see also Langley and Leaver 2012). We need to pay particular attention to the "heterogeneous and variegated qualities of markets 'on the ground,'" and the uneven forms of financial subjectivity and identification those qualities enact (Langley forthcoming: 7). Powerful private and public actors – government officials, investment houses, financial exchanges, actuarial scientists, personal finance advisors, pension managers, credit counsellors – have attempted to constitute everyday actors as entrepreneurial-financial subjects. Yet, the manners with which those populations have identified with these attempts have been uneven, contested and contradictory. The unevenness of financial subjectivity arises from the ways in which different populations are called distinctively into markets and the differential terms and conditions imposed upon them once they arrive – a set of conditions shaped by the logics of *selection*.

Selection

The attempt to *configure* everyday populations as subjects who could carry value or risk in financial markets is deeply conditioned by another way in which everyday financial identities are shaped; a logic of *selection*. Philip Ashton has described selection in relation to "financial exception," a set of emergency responses by the state to financial crises preoccupied with the isolation of "problematic financial assets whose losses and capacity for contagion threatened the broader norms of risk-taking within financial markets" (Ashton 2011: 1801; Ashton 2012). To contain crises, policymakers and bankers frequently select "toxic" or "distressed" assets and remove them from circulation. "The chaos of financial panic" argues Ashton, "involves a characteristic logic of selection, requiring situation-specific determinations of which assets or risks need to be expulsed or removed from circulation" (Ashton 2011: 1797; see also Ashton 2012: 787). Here, I want to adapt the term in order to describe a key element of financialization. If financialization concerns the configuration of financial assets and subjects, it also, at the same time, involves the *selection* of risk. Risk entails the formatting of some uncertainties as fungible commodities that can be priced and traded. Financial exchange, however, implies selection, the delineation of uncertainties that can be commodified as risks from those that cannot. Before anything can be governed and traded as a risk, it must first be separated from uncertainties that are financially irredeemable, forms of *bare danger*. [2]

Selection is at the heart of experiments in everyday financial subjectivity. It is implicated, for example in the "financial exclusion" of those who cannot access basic financial services. The World Bank reports that at least two billion of the global poor remain starkly unbanked without access to financial accounts (Demirguc-Kunt et al. 2014; see also Aitken 2015). This sits alongside specific histories of financial exclusion such as "redlining" by the Home Owners' Loan Corporation that created colour-coded maps for American cities between 1935 and 1940 indicating risk-levels for real estate investment. These maps isolated certain neighborhoods excluded from credit by dint of their racial and ethnic composition (Hillier 2005). Early histories of constructing everyday financial subjectivity in life insurance networks are similarly riddled with changing frameworks of selection in which particular populations are discovered as risks that could be predicted and managed, while other populations are conceived as too risky or dangerous to be profitably insured. Over the course of 100 years beginning in 1850, actuarial scientists debated and assembled detailed knowledge of the uncertainties and inherent riskiness entailed in the lives of various "suspect" populations – women, African-Americans, immigrants, "natives" – that were rendered "uninsurable" (see, for example, Levy 2012). Racist formulations were often invoked to systematically exclude populations from insurance practices (see for example Hoffman 1896).

Notwithstanding the immense weight of these forms of exclusion, the selection common to contemporary forms of financialization often invokes more complicated designations and sortings of everyday financial subjects. The distinction between inclusion and exclusion is sometimes overdrawn in contrast to more complicated matrices of risk (Langley 2008; see also Appleyard et al. 2016a, 2016b). Many of the pressures that culminated in the financial spasms of 2007/2008 were fuelled, for example, not by strictly exclusionary practices but by greater gradations of differentiated risk categories attached to highly stratified conditions and costs. For Poon (2009), this shift to more complicated gradations of risk was key to making subprime mortgages attractive to global pools of investors. FICO[3] scoring became increasingly deployed in the scoring of subprime mortgage categories not simply to determine which cases could be removed or screened-out but to place cases within a vast range of finely graded categories of risk. This created a new space of calculative possibility "extended to the exploitation of stabilized grades of credit quality accessed through scores to create multiple borrowing options tailored to accommodate varying levels of risk" (Poon 2009: 7). Langley's discussion of the "contemporary assemblage of consumer credit" reveals a similar process in which borrowers are increasingly subjected to financialized risk assessment that places them within larger pools of everyday borrowers. Increasingly called to take on consumer credit, ever-widening populations of potential borrowers are addressed through the techniques of formal credit scoring. As Langley suggests (2014: 451), "credit history and scoring techniques make it possible for lenders to differentiate, sort, target and price customers in terms of risk…and the risk-based prices they pay" (Langley 2014: 451). These techniques constitute categories of differentiated credit risk attached to "risk-based prices," which impose differential costs.

This complex selection is also key to the practices by which those outside of and "invisible" to lenders and formalized financial institutions are addressed as potential financial subjects. On the one hand, the number of people without any credit history or the ability to enter into mainstream credit networks marks one of the most striking forms of global financial "expulsion"; what Sassen (2014: 1) describes as intractable bodies "expelled from the core social and economic orders of our time." The Center for Financial Services Innovation, for example (2013), reports that at least 68 million Americans are invisible to existing credit reporting mechanisms, a figure deeply stratified by race and gender (see Predmore this volume). On the other hand, there is now a proliferation of innovative attempts to incorporate the "credit invisible" into credit reporting practices. Some mechanisms use non-financial payment streams for rental, utilities or other regular payments, or other data from consumption patterns or public information generated in legal proceedings such as bankruptcy, traffic violations, delinquency or tenant–landlord disputes, to generate algorithmic assessments of creditworthiness for those without formal credit histories. There have also been attempts to use data from mobile phone usage, digital or online footprints as proxies for assessments of credit risk (Schenker 2015; see also Aitken 2017a: 283). Finally, there is now widespread use of psychometric testing to determine creditworthiness for the unbanked, premised on the assumption that borrowers "have certain types of personal attributes that can…predict their future willingness to pay off debts" (Finberg 2016).

These techniques of scoring the unbanked embody a complicated logic of selection. At one level, the efforts to score the unbanked can often harden the line between those included in and those excluded from formalized credit markets. Because some of the alternative data used to make the unbanked "credit-visible" are based on deeply racialized processes – as in some landlord–tenant dispute proceedings – the scores generated can often "confirm" or entrench particular bodies as irredeemable credit risks. As Wu (2015) puts it "while credit invisibility poses real and significant problems…in some areas, no credit history is better than a bad one" (see also Yu and McLaughlin 2014: 27; Aitken 2017a: 290). Yet, for those who receive positive credit assessments through alternative scoring techniques, "inclusion" is a strikingly complicated status. Newly visible credit consumers are not incorporated into prime credit markets but into highly segmented credit categories subjected to stricter terms and higher costs, often for those least able to afford them. Alternative scoring is not a tool of "inclusion" but a "skimming" mechanism that locates individuals along complex risk matrices, all of which entail higher costs than prime credit markets. The Entrepreneurial Finance Lab at Harvard (EFL), for example, describes its assessment technology as allowing for "risk sorting on difficult to evaluate segments – unbanked, independent workers…thin file borrowers" (EFL 2013: 6). Selection entails both a hardening of the line between those allowed to enter and those denied access to formal credit markets, but also a greater segmentation for those "included" (see also Fourcade and Healy 2017).

Finally, insurance is key among financial sorting practices. Both historical and contemporary forms of insurance have been deeply implicated in the construction and extension of new kinds of financial subjectivity among those who have largely been outside the purview of formalized risk management mechanisms. Contemporary experiments in micro-insurance as well as historical forms of industrial insurance have contributed to what French and Kneale (2009) refer to as the constitution of the "insurantial subject" among working-class and popular sectors. Life insurance, in particular, has been preoccupied with the ways in which insurable and uninsurable lives might be selected and the kinds of risk pools that selected lives might constitute. The "insurantial subject" has consequently been a diverse and ever-changing form of identity. A key example relates to a debate in life insurance circles during the late nineteenth and early twentieth centuries regarding the selection of "tropical" risks. Insurers became preoccupied with the ways in which insurable lives were to be selected in the tropical and colonial worlds. They debated not only which "settler" and "native" lives could be insured, but also about how to price those lives – decisions that were deeply informed by dubious assumptions related to race and imperialism (see Congrès International d'Actuaries 1901).

At the heart of everyday financial subjectivity, then, is not only the configuration of everyday populations as financial agents, but also the selection that delineates, in the first place, which bodies are capable of these forms of subjectivity and in what degrees. The selected are incorporated as finely segmented gradations, each carrying differentiated forms of access at highly uneven costs. In these terms, financialization entails a constant adjustment of which bodies are inside and outside of finance, and what kinds of differentiation impinge on these bodies – conditions, in turn, that mark the complex political opportunities and limits of our "financialized imagination."

Conclusion: Where are the Politics of Financialization Located?

To live as a financial subject and "act as one's own capital" (Martin 2009: 347) complicates the political possibilities of everyday life. The positions that financial subjects occupy are often not readable as locations easily placed "inside" or "outside" of finance. There certainly are bodies "cast out" of finance or whose "incorporation" into the financial realm is through a newly minted (negative) credit score that entrenches obstacles to formal credit; "newly-born 'at risk' populations for whom risks prove unbearable" (Martin 2009; 348). Yet, financial subjects increasingly take up a range of heterogeneous positions within financial markets. They are not "included" in any simple fashion, but as "uncertain" or "variegated" agents, they are exposed to deeply stratified conditions and costs.

The politics that can be exercised through forms of financial subjectivity sketch, therefore, a complex topology. Although some activists do invoke a strictly oppositional kind of politics to finance based on an "inside/outside" logic – a push against finance from some location ostensibly outside of its reach (see Neocleous and Rigakos 2011; see Laskaridis et al. in this volume, on struggles against "illegitimate" debt) – the politics of finance are now often posed in more complicated terms. The political questions associated with financial subjectivity – what are the limits of an everyday life increasingly subject to the logic of finance? How might the cultures of finance be reworked? What are the possibilities for *other* kinds of calculations in the moment of financialization? – are now often framed in *relational* terms. These terms help us think the politics of finance not as emanating from outside of it, but from our complex, differentiated and uneven *relation* to finance. The question is how we might refashion our relations to the world of finance and its configurations; a world whose interior we incompletely inhabit.[4]

This is not to suggest that there is no space for opposition from outside of finance, but rather, that there is now a great deal of political action exploiting the ambiguities of our financial subjectivity. Our political impulses, in this context, are negotiations with the logic of finance in the "cramped spaces" of everyday life. This implies more than the recognition that we occupy uncertain and uneven financial subjectivities, and thereby complicate and diversify the political implications of those subjectivities in our financial practices. Tooker and Clarke (2018) make the case for a series of relational financial practices, existing in a liminal space, which bring financial and "social" calculation into uneasy confrontation. In some forms of micro-credit or "peer to peer" lending, for example, we are both asset-building subjects and actors with other political or social intentions. "'Calculative' and 'caring' relations commingle," they argue, "as people exercise agency in their financial interactions with others. Attending to relational work allows us to discern ethical and political possibilities in quotidian practices within markets, rather than premising change on some external 'great refusal'" (Tooker and Clarke 2018: 5).

Financialization research has begun to reframe subjectivity as a site with relatively undetermined political implications, limits and possibilities. Because recent forms of financialized subjectivity involve redrawing the borders between capital and a range of populations not often connected to the world of "high finance," those borders are not lines of "zero width" (Walker 2010) but sites of intense but ambiguous political practice. Because forms of financial subjectivity position us more closely within the rational-calculative world of finance, they often limit political possibility; subsuming forms of "social" action within the need to "become an asset" and seek return on investment. Yet, these spaces are not predetermined but subject to negotiation that might allow us to rework the metaphors of finance in unique and creative ways. Although the "financialized imagination" that pervades our everyday lives is often calculative and instrumental, the complexity of financial subjectivity implies more possibilities than normally suggested. with finance as well as its possible refashionings.

Notes

1 "Everyday" is a slippery category. In this chapter, I do not want to invoke any predetermined or fixed sense of what constitutes the "everyday" but I use the term in a nominal sense to refer to the diverse array of attempts by financial institutions, experts, professionals and advisors to appeal to those populations they conceive as outside or not sufficiently engaged by private financial markets and arrangements (see Aitken 2007; also Langley 2008).

2 My reference here to "bare danger" is a refraction of Agamben's notion of bare life (see Agamben 2005). Maintaining circulation in global finance entails "the 'sifting' of the 'good form the bad, ensuring that things are always in movement, constantly moving around, continually going from one point to another" (Foucault 2007: 65, quoted in Langley 2014; 62; Langley 2013: 109).

3 FICO is Fair Isaac and Company, a key global financial data analysis firm.

4 This inverts a language common to the critical political economy tradition which conceives of critique as a practice that consists of "standing back" from the world in order to inquire into the ways in which that world is historically constituted (see, for example, Cox 1981).

Bibliography

Agamben, G., 2005. *State of Exception*. Chicago, IL: University of Chicago Press.

Aitken, R., 2007. *Performing Capital: Toward a Cultural Economy of Popular and Global Finance*. New York: Palgrave.

Aitken, R., 2015. *Fringe Finance: Crossing and Contesting the Borders of Global Finance*. London: Routledge/ RIPE Series in Global Political Economy.

Aitken, R., 2017a. "All Data is Credit Data": Constituting the Unbanked. *Competition and Change*, 21(4), pp. 274–300.

Aitken, R., 2017b. "An Economics of Capital": Genealogies of Everyday Financial Conduct. *Journal of Historical Sociology*, pp. 1–23.

Appadurai, A., 2016. *Banking on Words: The Failure of Language in the Age of Derivative Finance*. Chicago, IL: Chicago University Press.

Appleyard, L., Rowlingson, K. and Gardner, J., 2016a. Payday Lending in the UK: The Regul(aris)ation of a Necessary Evil? *Journal of Social Policy*, 45(3), pp. 527–543.

Appleyard, L., Rowlingson, K. and Gardner, J. 2016b. The Variegated Financialization of Sub-Prime Credit Markets. *Competition and Change*, 20(5), pp. 297–313.

Ashton, P., 2011. The Financial Exception and the Reconfiguration of Credit Risk in US Mortgage Markets. *Environment and Planning A*, 43(8), pp. 1796–1812.

Ashton, P., 2012. "Troubled Assets": The Financial Emergency and Racialized Risk. *International Journal of Urban and Regional Research*, 36(4), pp. 773–790.

Brassett, J. and Clarke, C., 2012. Performing the Sub-Prime Crisis: Trauma and the Financial Event. *International Political Sociology*, 6(4), pp. 4–20.

Center for Financial Services Innovation, 2013. *Uncovering Opportunity: The True Potential of the Underserved Market*. Chicago, IL: Centre for Financial Services Innovation.

Congrès International d'Actuaries, 1901. *Transactions: Trosième Congrès International d'Actuaries*. Paris: Librarie des Assurances.

Cox, R.W., 1981. Social Forces, States and World Orders: Beyond International Relations Theory. *Millennium: Journal of International Relations*, 10(2), pp. 126–155.

Davis, A. and Walsh, C., 2016. The Role of the State in the Financialization of the UK Economy. *Political Studies*, 64(3), pp. 666–682.

Demirguc-Kunt, A., Klapper, L., Singer, D. and Van Oudheusden, P., 2014. The Global Findex Database 2014: Measuring Financial Inclusion Around the World. World Bank Policy Research Working Paper 7255.

EFL. 2013. *Credit Bureau Data Reliable Scoring Presentation*. Cambridge: EFL Global Ltd.

Finberg, R., 2016. Fintech Spotlight: Data vs. data – The Battle to Understand Online Lending Borrowers. *Finance Magnates*, 3 March.

Du Gay, P. and Pryke, M. (eds.), 2002. *Cultural Economy: Cultural Analysis and Commercial Life*. London: Sage.

Foucault, M., 1988. *Technologies of the Self*. Amherst: University of Massachusetts Press.

Rob Aitken

Foucault, M., 2007. *Security, Territory, Population: Lectures at the College de France, 1977, 1978*. Basingstoke: Palgrave Macmillan.

Foucault, M., 2008. *The Birth of Biopolitics*. New York: Palgrave Macmillan.

Fourcade, M. and Healy, K., 2017. Seeing Like a Market. *Socio-Economic Review*, 15(1), pp. 9–29.

French, S. and Kneale, J., 2009. Excessive Financialization: Insuring Lifestyles, Envlivening Subjects, and Everyday Spaces of Biosocial Excess. *Environment and Planning D*, 27(6), pp. 1030–1053.

Hall, S., 2012. Geographies of Money and Finance II: Financailization and Financial Subjects. *Progress in Human Geography*, 36(3): 403–411.

Hall, S. and Appleyard, L., 2012. Financial Business Education and the Remaking of Gendered Investment Banking Subjects in the (post-crisis) City of London. *Journal of Cultural Economy*, 5(4), pp. 457–472.

Havien, M., 2014. *Cultures of Financialization: Fictitious Capital in Popular Culture and Everyday Life*. New York: Palgrave Macmillan.

Hillier, A.E., 2005. Residential Security Maps and Neighbourhood Appraisals: The Home Owners' Loan Corporation and the Case of Philadelphia. *Social Science History*, 29(2), pp. 207–233.

Hiss, S., 2013. The Politics of the Financialization of Sustainability. *Competition and Change*, 17(3), pp. 234–247.

Hoffman, F.L., 1896. *Race Traits and Tendencies of the American Negro*. New York: The Lawbook Exchange Ltd.

Langley, P., 2007. Uncertain Subjects of Anglo-American Financialization. *Cultural Critique*, 65, pp. 66–91.

Langley, P., 2008. *The Everyday Life of Global Finance: Saving and Borrowing in Anglo-America*. Oxford: Oxford University Press.

Langley, P., 2013. Toxic Assets: Turbulence and Biopolitical Security: Governing the Crisis of Global Financial Circulation. *Security Dialogue*, 44, pp. 111–126.

Langley, P., 2014. Equipping Entrepreneurs: Consuming Credit and Credit Scores. *Consumption Markets and Culture*, 17(4), pp. 448–467.

Langley, P., Forthcoming. The Folds of Social Finance: Making Markets, Remaking the Social. *Environment and Planning A*, pp. 1–18.

Langley, P. and Leaver, A., 2012. Remaking Retirement Investors: Behavioural Economics and Defined-Contribution Occupational Pensions. *Journal of Cultural Economy*, 5(4), pp. 473–488.

Lazzarato, M., 2012. *The Making of Indebted Man: An Essay on the Neoliberal Condition*. Paris: Semiotex(te).

Leyshon, A. and Thrift, N., 2007. The Capitalization of Almost Everything: The Future of Finance and Capitalism. *Theory, Culture and Society*, 24(7–8), pp. 97–115.

Levy, J., 2012. *Freaks of Fortune: The Emerging World of Capitalism and Risk in America*. Cambridge, MA: Harvard University Press.

Maclean, K., 2013. Gender, Risk and Micro-Financial Subjectivities. *Antipode*, 45(2), pp. 455–473.

Martin, R., 2002. *Financialization of Daily Life*. Philadelphia, PA: Temple University Press.

Martin, R., 2009. Whose Crisis is that: Thinking Finance Otherwise. *Ephemera: Theory and Politics in Organization*, 9(4), pp. 344–349.

Martin, R., 2013. After Economy? Social Logics of the Derivative. *Social Text*, 21(1), pp. 83–106.

Martin, R., 2016. From the Critique of Political Economy to the Critique of Finance. In Lee, B. and Martin, R. (eds.). *Derivatives and the Wealth of Societies*. Chicago, IL: University of Chicago Press: 174–196.

Montgomerie, J., 2008. Bridging the Critical Divide: Global Finance, Financialization, and Contemporary Capitalism. *Contemporary Politics*, 14(3), pp. 233–253.

Muniesa, F., Doganova, L., Ortiz, H., Pina-Stranger, A., Paterson, F., Bourgoin, A., Ehrenstein, V., Juven, P., Pontille, D., Sarac-Lesavre, B. and Yon, G., 2017. *Capitalization: A Cultural Guide*. Paris: Presses des Mines.

Neocleous, M. and Rigakos, G. (eds.), 2011. *Anti-Security*. Ottawa: Red Quill Books.

Pani, R., 2014. A Fetish and Fiction of Finance: Unraveling the Subprime Crisis. *Economic Geography*, 90 (2), pp. 213–235.

Poon, M., 2009. From New Deal Institutions to Capital Markets: Commercial Consumer Risk Scores and the Making of Subprime Mortgage Finance. Paris: Centre de Sociologie de L'Innovation/Mines Paris Tech, CSI Working Paper No. 014.

Riles, A., 2011. *Collateral Knowledge: Legal Reasoning in the Global Financial Markets*. Chicago, IL: University of Chicago Press.

Sassen, S., 2014. *Expulsions: Brutality and Complexity in the Global Economy*. Cambridge, MA: Harvard University Press.

Schenker, J., 2015. Fintech Start-Ups Need not be a Threat. *Informilo Magazine*, 12 October.

Tooker, L. and Clarke, C., 2018. Experiments in Relational Finance: Harnessing the Social in Everyday Debt and Credit. *Theory, Culture and Society*, 35(3), pp. 1–20.

Walker, R.B.J., 2010. *After the Globe, Before the World*. London: Routledge.

Wark, M., 2017. After Capitalism, the Derivative. *Public Seminar*, 9 April 2017.

Wu, C., 2015. Proceed with Caution on Credit Scoring with Alternative Data. *American Banker*, 11 June.

Yu, P. and McLaughlin, J., 2014. *Big Data: A Big Disappointment for Scoring Consumer Credit Risk*. Boston, MA: National Consumer Law Centre.

31

INDEBTEDNESS AND FINANCIALIZATION IN EVERYDAY LIFE

Johnna Montgomerie

Introduction

This chapter offers a novel reading of the political economy and cultural economy literature on financialization and debt as it coalesces around understandings of "indebtedness." This is refracted through the conceptual lens of the "household" to make visible key sites, or socio-spatial scales, where indebtedness precariously integrates financialization into everyday life. The aim is to provide a comprehensive account of how indebtedness is driving, sustaining and reproducing financialization, but in ways that also make financialization vulnerable and fragile. This is achieved, first, by "reading together" the political economy and cultural economy literatures which although theoretically very different, substantively both seek to understand the transformative dynamics of financialization and debt in the present-day. In practice, this means imposing a basic conceptual frame of the household balance sheet, both assets and liabilities, because both political and cultural economy approaches share this basic framework when they account for how financialization unfolds at the scale of the household. What becomes apparent is that "indebtedness" is a dynamic transformative force in which debt reconfigures how individuals, households, communities, national economies and global financial markets are connected to each other. From this vantage point, the significance of indebtedness is reinterpreted using the household as a conceptual lens, which means not simply treating the household as a black box and assuming it simply responds to economic stimuli in a predictable way (to, for example, low interest rates). Instead, the household becomes a conceptual lens that makes visible how the mundane everyday activities of households (their actions, reactions, inactions) expose the vulnerabilities of financialization.

Political Economy and Cultural Economy Perspectives on Financialization and Debt

Financialization became a commonly used term to explain what is different about the present-day economy; in particular, compared to the previous postwar Keynesian economy but in relation to contemporary neoliberalism (Froud 2002; Krippner 2005). The growing ubiquity of the term financialization is used "to describe a host of structural changes in the advanced political economies," which share a common evaluation of how global finance has altered the underlying logics of economic activity as well as the workings of democratic society (Van der Zwan 2014: 99). For Van der Zwan (2014), the literature on financialization is divided into three main streams of inquiry each using the term financialization to characterize transformations leading to: (a) the emergence of a new regime of accumulation; (b) the ascendency of the shareholder value orientation; (c) the financialization of everyday life (100). From this substantive view of change, the study of financialization consists of two distinct methodological approaches: political economy and cultural economy, which analyse the same substantive processes of financialization but diverge in their methodological approach. In other words, to investigate how these approaches apply the "interface between ontology (how the world is), epistemology (how the world can be known), substantive theory (how the world is understood) and method (how the world is examined)" (Montgomerie 2017: 4). One the one hand, the political economy approach makes connections between the structures and institutions to explain the patterns of change in the regime of accumulation, the firm, and the demand-side of the economy (Boyer 2000; Crouch 2009; Froud et al. 2010; Hay 2013). On the other hand, a cultural economy approach to financialization explains how the calculative practices of risk management work within the entrepreneurial discourses of neoliberalism, which creates the capillary power of finance in the mundane routines of the everyday and corporate governance practices of firm managers to the de-centered networks of global financial markets (De Goede 2004; Martin 2007; Langley 2008a).

Importantly, both political and cultural economy recognize the centrality of debt – as a social, legal and material relation – in the advent of financialization. The political economy reading of debt connects the everyday to the regime of accumulation by explaining that individuals are dependent on wages and salaries for their income, which have remained stagnant for many or declined in real terms, which has created demand for debt to plug the gap (Montgomerie 2009; Boyer 2012; Gamble 2014). Especially in the Anglo-American economies, the mutual dependence on finance-led and consumption-dependent growth fosters a recognizable form of dependence on debt in everyday life. Cultural economy approaches focus on the socio-cultural processes of inter-subjective meaning-making about debt in everyday life; from which emergent subjectivities are treated as indicative of the transformations that make financialization (Haiven 2014; Stanley et al. 2016). This reading of financial transformation explains how new financial identities tied to liberal notions of self-disciplines make sense of the many new forms of borrowing available to individuals (as a result of financial deregulation and financialization). For example, residential mortgages and homeownership, and whether one is a buy-to-let landlord, owner-occupier or subprime borrower reveals the normative hierarchy of individuals' relationship to decentered global financial markets (Leyshon and French 2009; Soaita and Searle 2016). Here, debt shapes the formation of financial subjectivities, which incorporate a specific sensitivity to the lived experience and emotive elements of individual financial practices and how they integrate with the organizational dimensions of firms and the political economy of finance-led growth (Deville 2015; Davey 2017; Lai 2017).

Taken together, the political economy and cultural economy understandings of the connections between debt and financialization create a robust understanding of indebtedness as a transformative force (not simply a social relation, or a contract between borrower and lender). As such, the power of finance in everyday life is mediated through cultural conversations that give finance meaning, but also financial power amasses in the macroeconomic structures that are dependent on debt to produce financialized growth. Thus, debt exists as a material contract between borrower and lender, but this is situated within a much larger socio-cultural context of collective meaning-making that sets the parameters in which individuals access debt to participate in the economy. In other words, the macroeconomic structural dependence on debt is mirrored in the cultural articulations of the necessities of debt within financialized societies.

Indebtedness connects the overlapping logics of financialization as they materialize in everyday life, from the changing dynamics between individuals and household to how financial flows shape national economies and global markets.

What draws together the political and cultural economy approaches is their inquiry into the scale of the everyday as a means of understanding indebtedness as constitutive of the causes and consequences of financialization. Initially, the methodological divide was between cultural economy of Foucauldian governmentality (Aitken 2008; Langley 2008b) and the political economy of Weberian agent-centric preferences (Broome 2009; Seabrooke 2010). Juanita Elias and Adrienne Roberts' (2016) decisive intervention up-ended this framing by pointing out the extensive feminist literature using the concept of the everyday as a gender lens to connect the mundane practices and minutiae of everyday life – such as the affective and embodied experiences of work and employment, consumption and spending habits, householding practices, and localized or individualized forms of resistance – to large-scale movements of financialization, crisis and austerity (see also Predmore in this volume). As such, it is from the feminist intervention that we see a new avenue for meaningful dialogue between political and cultural economy interrogations of the everyday (Hozic and True 2016; Tepe-Belfrage and Montgomerie 2016). Thus feminist interventions into the study of financialization and the everyday crucially recognize the deeply gendered subjectivities that emerge at the scale of the individual and express prevailing power of large-scale de-centered networks of the global economy (Hall 2012; Pollard 2013). Indebtedness shapes financialized subjects in ways that deliberately fragment the economistic idea of a coherent unitary individual rational actor and foregrounds gendered power relations as the embodiment of debt's power in contemporary financialized capitalism (Roberts 2015). Thus, the long-standing feminist intervention of understanding the household brings a new conceptual clarity to how financialization occurs at the scale of the everyday, which is largely obscured by the bifurcated political and cultural economy accounts.

Using the Household as a Lens to Analyse Financialization and Indebtedness

The feminist literature on "the household" is extensive, and cannot be fully developed in this short chapter, but includes feminist economists' engagement with women's unpaid (and uncounted) work in the home and low-paid work in labor markets (Waring 1989; Elson and Cagatay 2000; Himmelweit 2002), Feminist Political Economy's articulation of the unvalued labor of social reproduction (Bakker 2007; Steans and Tepe 2010; Elias and Rai 2018), feminist geographers' conceptualization of the unseen power relations in the political construction of scale/space where the household is the sphere of social reproduction and consumption (Katz 2001; Marston 2008; Massey 2013); as well as Feminist International Relations' articulation of the household as a site of normalizing gendered violence and poverty (Peterson 2010; True 2012; Runyan 2018). Building on these feminist insights, this chapter proceeds by offering a novel analysis of household indebtedness that draws together an understanding of everyday financialization from both sides of the socially constructed household balance sheet. This balance sheet framework draws inspiration from Miranda Joseph's (2014) *Debt to Society*, which interrogates how modes of accounting create, sustain, or transform the social relations of debt by producing recognizable structures that foster specific types of indebtedness in everyday life. From this framing we can see the connections between indebtedness and changes in the household balance sheet; but the significance of the balance sheet is as a common register for conceptualizing the economic activity taking place at the scale of the household. Thus, reinterpreting indebtedness through the lens of the household balance sheet makes visible three key processes driving, sustaining, and reproducing financialization. First, financialization of the household led to a transition from interest-bearing savings to retail investment products; second, and relatedly, financialization transformed homeownership into a highly leveraged savings vehicle; thirdly, debt is increasingly a necessity to participate in the economy.

Evaluating financialization through the lens of the household makes visible the daily life in constituting what we observe as a macroeconomic phenomenon of financialization as well as how socio-cultural dynamics shape the ways in which the different groups within society can participate in and benefit from financialization. In other words, how the political economy of stagnating incomes and easy access to debt, as a result of financialization, works together with the cultural economy of entrepreneurial forms of citizenship which condition how individuals participate, or are valued as participants, in a financialized economy. Indeed, the moral framing of debt in a financialized society becomes important here. According to Lazzarato (2012), debt under financialization uses the moral economy of guilt to inflict economic punishment on the indebted. This moral framing of guilt about debts has become pervasive in shaping contemporary social relations that animate neoliberal politics and economics. In other words, the macroeconomic structural dependence on debt is mirrored in the cultural articulations of the value of indebtedness within financialized societies. For example, when debt is for investment in housing or higher education it is "good"; while borrowing for consumerism or any reason that results in an inability to manage debt is "bad." However, a feminist moral economy of debt goes further by interrogating the increasingly intimate relationship between financialization, indebtedness and social reproduction at the scale of the household that relies heavily on the unpaid work within the home to "care for debts" (Montgomerie and Tepe-Belfrage 2016).

From Small Savers to Small Investors

The first route through which the household is integrated into financialization through the routines of everyday life is by switching savings flows from interest-bearing accounts to retail financial products (in turn, invested in a portfolio of financial products). This transition is visible in both political and cultural economy accounts of financialization in Anglo-America (Toporowski 2000; Langley 2004), but when reinterpreted through the lens of the household we see significant tensions and vulnerabilities that are not widely recognized. In the Anglo-American context households began switching to private pension savings in the 1980s and increasingly so as interest rates began to fall steadily after the mid-1990s (Harmes 2001). The standard political economy interpretation is that lower interest rate yields on liquid savings push households to higher-risk retail investment products because they can deliver capital gains (Froud et al. 2001; Hay 2011). The structural push of low interest rates is matched by the pull of public policy. Specifically, the introduction of asset-based welfare in Anglo-America encouraged individual citizens to think of their asset purchases as investments that they might cash in to fuel their consumption at some time in the future (Finlayson 2009; Prabhakar 2013).

Cultural Economy understands this shift discursively, in which individuals (not households) understand their relationship to financial products (for example using different savings products or types of pension investments) as an opportunity to take on more risk in the hope of generating more wealth gains. By doing so, these individuals enact an entrepreneurial subjectivity, seeking to manage their household balance sheet as a firm would by managing the risk profile of their asset portfolio to generate profit. "[T]he fashioning of financial identities and everyday consumption practices in arenas that are cultural as much as they are economic" (Allon and Redden 2012: 376). The emphasis is on the formation and/or complexities of financial subjects seeking security from private wealth accumulation, which according to Allon and Redden, is increasingly dependent on debt and underpinned by greater levels of risk and insecurity.

Using the household as a lens makes visible the interplay between culture and materiality in a way that does not reduce culture to "another sphere" in which market transformation takes place. Rather, the household lens shows the ways in which financialization is uniquely vulnerable to small-scale shocks. If we consider that less than half of households are "small savers/investors," under financialization this sub-group of households has become the feedstock of the institutional investor sector. Put simply, when households regularly remit present-day income into financial markets, via pension funds and other forms of retail portfolio investments, they do so whether markets are high or low and provide financial markets with a steady flow of revenue (see Fichtner this volume). This is a lucrative revenue stream for the financial sector, as financialization makes global markets more vulnerable the losses incurred from flash-crashes, downturns, corporate scandals, market crisis and systemic crisis are simply "downloaded" on to the average retail investor, or the household (Bryan 2010; Engelen et al. 2011). Since 2008, in particular as a result of Quantitative Easing (QE), this problem has only amplified. This point is made most elegantly in Green and Lavery's (2015) analysis of how the QE monetary policy framework drives up asset-price inflation in general, but this only translates into wealth gains for the top five percent of households. This trend reveals an important limitation to financialization: the capacity of most households to use financial markets for wealth-gains has become increasingly constrained under financialization. Initially, interest-bearing savings accounts were decimated by low interest rates (cutting off a source of risk-free liquid savings for households). Now, QE ensures the declining long-term profitability of portfolio investments (because QE keeps yields on government debt low). Thus, most households are made worse-off by financialization, despite the common-sense consensus that access to financial gains has been "democratized." In other words, the global financial system can no longer offer households a meaningful form of low-risk long-term cash savings because of financialization.

Homeownership is a Highly Leveraged Investment Savings Vehicle

The second, and arguably most significant, route through which the household is integrated into financialization is residential mortgages, in which "the home" represents both the political economy of housing and the cultural economy of homeownership (Langley 2006; Cook, Smith, and Searle 2009; French, Leyshon, and Wainwright 2011). Residential housing is a central configuration of financialized growth in Anglo-America. When banks developed their "originate and distribute" business model, residential mortgages became the main way to create money and generate interest revenue for lenders. Residential mortgage markets are a means to create substantial amounts of new debt deposits, which can be easily bundled together and re-sold multiple times across global financial markets (McLeay et al. 2014; Pettifor 2017). The advantage for lenders to create debt deposits secured against residential property, is that it is encouraged by government policies supporting homeownership and the interest revenue can be securitized to generate short-term revenue streams from long-term debts (Bryan and Rafferty 2014; Aalbers 2016). Additionally, as the 2008 global financial crisis made clear, losses on residential mortgages incurred as a result of the property bubble (fuelled by cheap mortgage loans) are downloaded on to the mortgage borrower (Mian and Sufi 2014). In other words, households must absorb the losses of speculative lending in residential mortgage markets, but banks are given a bailout for the losses they incur as a result of their over-lending. More to the point, households have become highly leveraged investors (Watson 2010; Lowe et al. 2012); and, thus, more vulnerable to small shocks in property and mortgage markets.

Credit-fuelled asset appreciation in residential housing is a driving force of financialization that maps closely on to households' desire for secure shelter and a long-term savings vehicles. However, while residential mortgages bolster aggregate demand as house prices increase, homeowners use mortgages to convert equity into cash to fuel additional consumption. The rapid uptake in home-equity loans (HELs) shows the degree to which many see their house not only as a source of long-term savings ("my house is my pension") but also as a source of cash that serves to shore-up aggregate demand (Doling and Ronald 2010b). As such, property prices become the bellwether of personal/household financial prosperity and national economic vitality. Put simply, an increased uptake of home equity loans means that even those households with asset holdings – those considered more financially secure than households without any assets – are more vulnerable to income shocks, like all overleveraged investors are. The mutual dependence of people to secure housing and shelter, of banks to secure profit by issuing mortgage loans, and of the national government to privatize welfare costs has created a situation where indebtedness is the root of savings, investment and growth, connecting the aggregate to the everyday level. However, financialization is also made vulnerable because mortgage risks, or the losses incurred when prices do not rapidly increase year on year or when interest rates go up, are just passed on to households. Put simply, financialization has meant that wealth losses from a downswing in the housing market are downloaded onto households. Stagnant wage-growth in Anglo-America means that households have many claims on their present-day incomes. Even if most households can continue to service the existing mortgage stock, at some point affordability or house price decline will inhibit the use of residential property as a source of cheap credit. As yet, the inequalities between homeowners that are asset-rich and those with leveraged homes remain unseen, the exception being a recognition in the central role of financialized housing in intergenerational inequality (Fuller et al. 2019). Still it is apparent that indebtedness is linked to homeownership, and this is making many households more vulnerable to every manner of financial market or economic shock, as all over-leveraged investors are.

Small Debts and the Normalization of Indebtedness

The third route through which households integrate into financialization is consumer debts, which here encompasses an array of retail debt products (see also Gonzalez in this volume). On the one hand, non-mortgage loans represent a very small proportion of overall stock of household debt, which is fragmented across many different types of loans; on the other hand, these small loans charge much higher interest rates and, thus, are profitable for lenders. Put simply, consumer credit is a small but lucrative retail debt market. Typically, each retail loan product is evaluated in relation to its function: to get a university degree, purchase a car, or to fund consumption. This contractual perspective on consumer debt, in which the type of loan is equated directly with the function of the debt itself is misleading because it narrows the understanding of consumer debt to nothing more than a function or consequence of hyper-consumerism (Calder 1999; Klein 1999). In this reading, it is the culture of consumerism that necessitates debt, as income cannot keep up with the wants of Anglo-American consumers (Burton 2008; Montgomerie 2009). Therefore, financialization successfully grafted onto the socio-cultural dynamics of consumerism, yet this ignores the important ways in which consumer finance has become an economy in and of itself, as Langley (2014) articulates the relevance of "the consumption of consumer credit" (418). However, cultural economy readings of consumerism curiously ignore the important way in which consumption, as part of social reproduction, is already deeply rooted in affect and relationality. Indeed, cultural economy may recognize that consumption is not functional but mediated and made, nor an indulgence of wants or desire for luxury; however, consumption is not simply an outcome of markets, social reproduction casts consumption as a significant part of meeting basic human needs that demands direct participation in the everyday economy (McFall 2002; Zwick and Dholakia 2006; Carruthers and Ariovich 2010).

For this reason, using the household as a lens to reinterpret the interplay between financialization and indebtedness makes possible a more in-depth consideration of gendered dynamics. In other words, the household can reveal how consumer debt produces or amplifies financial inequalities. As households take on many other types of debts (besides mortgages) this growing stock of high cost consumer debt (such as overdrafts, credit cards, car loans, lines of credit and student loans) cumulatively act as pre-emptory legal claims against present-day income. Taken as a whole, these debts can cost as much as 20 percent of take-home income to service (Bryan et al. 2011; European Commission 2008). Regardless of the type of loan, when contextualized as part of the household balance sheet, all small and high-cost consumer loans are an item of "debt servicing" expenditure that drains monthly cash flow. From this vantage point we can see how consumer credit integrates another segment of households directly into financialization, namely households that are not portfolio investors or homeowners, extending the financialization of everyday life into the middle- and low-income households. Moreover, we can recognize that households' lower down the income distribution use of small-scale consumer debts shows the ways in which financialization conditions participation in economic life (Montgomerie 2009; Gibbons 2014). More troublesome is how consumer debt, under conditions of financialization, acts as a form of social protection, or safety-net (Montgomerie 2013; Soederberg 2014). Whether it is to pay bills during unemployment, to cover emergencies and unforeseen events (like car accidents or illness), or to fund health related expenses, debt acts as a safety-net for many households, which means that indebtedness is a necessity, not an option.

Conclusion

This chapter provided a joined-up reading of the political economy and cultural economy literature on financialization and indebtedness in order to understand how financialization manifests in everyday life. It does so through the novel use of the "household" as a conceptual lens to make visible key sites, or socio-spatial scales, where indebtedness precariously integrates financialization into everyday life. Using the simple framework of the household balance sheet this chapter looked at the three important ways financialization integrates into the everyday life of households, and how these coalesce in ways that ensure indebtedness is driving, sustaining and reproducing financialization. On the asset side, financialization of everyday life has made the relatively small number of households with asset-holdings more integrated into volatile market downswings. In a different way, homeownership under conditions of financialization has transformed the home from a "safe" asset that acts as a long-term savings vehicle ("my house is my pension") into a highly leveraged asset (via home-equity loans and house-price inflation) in which the household acts as the shock-absorber for property market swings caused by the intensification of financialization. Residential housing illustrates the elaborate material, regulatory, cultural, political dynamics that transform "the home" into both asset and liability that requires the wider household to care for not only to meet debt obligations but also to survive and reproduce itself. Finally, this chapter explained how small-scale consumer debts integrate a large segment of households lower down the income distribution scale into the financialization of everyday life by making debt a necessity for economic participation and also a safety-net in times of need.

Using the household as a conceptual lens to make visible the mundane everyday activities of households, creates a new intellectual space for analysing the inequalities and power hierarchies at play in the unfolding of financialization. This means foregrounding how the household, in its members' actions, reactions, inactions, seeks to manage the vulnerabilities of financialization. This is particularly relevant since the 2008 global financial crisis and the on-set of austerity in Anglo-America. Seen through the lens of the household we can demystify debt-driven austerity by disrupting the discourses of complexity that hide the politics and power relations that make austerity possible (Christophers 2015). Indeed, the household provides a fruitful means of connecting the everyday experiences of financialization to austerity: "to more fully consider the ways in which austerity can be encountered at and across a range of social spaces, with growing interest in how austerity politics play out in everyday personal lives" (Hall 2018: 1). Debt continues to play a central role within austerity, in which the overlapping dependence on debt (after the 2008 financial crisis) of national governments, central banks, financial institutions, and households underwrites the continued financialization of the economy and society in precarious and fragile ways.

Bibliography

Aalbers, M.B., 2016. *The Financialization of Housing: A Political Economy Approach.* London and New York: Routledge.

Aitken, R., 2008. *Performing Capital: Toward a Cultural Economy of Popular and Global Finance.* Basingstoke: Palgrave MacMillan.

Allon, F. and Redden, G., 2012. The Global Financial Crisis and the Culture of Continual Growth. *Journal of Cultural Economy,* 5(4), pp. 375–390.

Bakker, I., 2007. Social Reproduction and the Constitution of a Gendered Political Economy. *New Political Economy,* 12(4), pp. 541–556.

Boyer, R., 2012. The Four Fallacies of Contemporary Austerity Policies: The Lost Keynesian Legacy. *Cambridge Journal Economics,* 36(1), pp. 283–312.

Boyer, R., 2000. Is a Finance-Led Growth Regime a Viable Alternative to Fordism? A Preliminary Analysis. *Economy and Society,* 29(1), pp. 111–145.

Broome, A., 2009. Money for Nothing: Everyday Actors and Monetary Crises. *Journal of International Relations and Development,* 12(1), pp. 3–30.

Bryan, D., 2010. The Duality of Labour and the Financial Crisis. *The Economic and Labour Relations Review,* 20(2), pp. 49–59.

Bryan, D. and Rafferty, M., 2014. Political Economy and Housing in the Twenty-first Century – From Mobile Homes to Liquid Housing? *Housing, Theory and Society,* 31(4), pp. 404–412.

Bryan, M., Taylor, M. and Veliziotis, M., 2011. *Over-indebtedness in Great Britain: An Analysis Using the Wealth and Assets Survey and Household Annual Debtors Survey.* Report to the Department for Business, Innovation and Skills. Available at https://tinyurl.com/y4xuvpta [Accessed February 21, 2019].

Burton, D., 2008. *Credit and Consumer Society.* London: Routledge.

Calder, L.G., 1999. *Financing the American Dream: A Cultural History of Consumer Credit.* Princeton, NJ: Princeton University Press.

Carruthers, B.G. and Ariovich, L., 2010. *Money and Credit: A Sociological Approach.* Cambridge: Polity.

Christophers, B., 2015. The Limits to Financialization. *Dialogues in Human Geography,* 5(2), pp. 183–200.

Cook, N., Smith, S.J. and Searle, B.A., 2009. Mortgage Markets and Cultures of Consumption. *Consumption Markets & Culture,* 12(2), pp. 133–154.

Crouch, C., 2009. Privatised Keynesianism: An Unacknowledged Policy Regime. *British Journal of Politics and International Relations,* 11(3), pp. 382–399.

Davey, R., 2017. Polluter Pays? Understanding Austerity through Debt Advice in the UK. *Anthropology Today,* 33(5), pp. 8–11.

de Goede, M., 2004. Repoliticizing Financial Risk. *Economy and Society,* 33(2), pp. 197–217.

Deville, J., 2015. *Lived Economies of Default: Consumer Credit, Debt Collection and the Capture of Affect.* London and New York: Routledge.

Doling, J. and Ronald, R., 2010a. Home Ownership and Asset-based Welfare. *Journal of Housing and the Built Environment,* 25, pp. 165–173.

Doling, J., Ronald, R., 2010b. Property-based Welfare and European Homeowners: How Would Housing Perform as a Pension? *Journal of Housing and the Built Environment,* 25(2), pp. 227–241.

Elias, J. and Rai, S.M., 2018. Feminist Everyday Political Economy: Space, Time, and Violence. *Review of International Studies,* online first, pp. 1–20.

Elias, J. and Roberts, A., 2016. Feminist Global Political Economies of the Everyday: From Bananas to Bingo. *Globalizations,* 13(6), pp. 787–800.

Elson, D. and Cagatay, N., 2000. The Social Content of Macroeconomic Policies. *World Development*, 28 (7), pp. 1347–1364.

Engelen, E., Ertürk, I., Froud, J., Johal, S., Leaver, A., Moran, M., Nilsson, A. and Williams, K., 2011. *After the Great Complacence: Financial Crisis and the Politics of Reform*. Oxford: Oxford University Press.

European Commission, 2008. *Towards a Common Operational European Definition of Over-Indebtedness*.

Finlayson, A., 2009. Financialisation, Financial Literacy and Asset-Based Welfare. *British Journal of Politics & International Relations*, 11(3), pp. 400–421.

French, S., Leyshon, A. and Wainwright, T., 2011. Financializing Space, Spacing Financialization. *Progress in Human Geography*, 35(6), pp. 798–819.

Froud, J., Johal, S. and Williams, K., 2002. Financialisation and the Coupon Pool. *Capital and Class*, 26(3), pp. 119–151.

Froud, J., Johal, S., Haslam, C. and Williams, K., 2001. Accumulation under Conditions of Inequality. *Review of International Political Economy*, 8(1), pp. 66–95.

Froud, J., Johal, S., Montgomerie, J. and Williams, K., 2010. Escaping the Tyranny of Earned Income? The Failure of Finance as Social Innovation. *New Political Economy*, 15(1), pp. 147–164.

Fuller, G.W., Johnston, A. and Regan, A., 2019. Housing Prices and Wealth Inequality in Western Europe. *West European Politics*, 1–24.

Gamble, A., 2014. *Crisis Without End? The Unravelling of Western Prosperity*. Basingstoke: Palgrave Macmillan.

Gibbons, D., 2014. *Solving Britain's Personal Debt Crisis*. London: Searching Finance.

Green, J. and Lavery, S., 2015. The Regressive Recovery: Distribution, Inequality and State Power in Britain's Post-Crisis Political Economy. *New Political Economy*, 20(6), pp. 894–923.

Haiven, M., 2014. *Cultures of Financialization: Fictitious Capital in Popular Culture and Everyday Life*. Springer.

Hall, S., 2012. Geographies of Money and Finance II: Financialization and Financial Subjects. *Progress in Human Geography*, 36(3), pp. 403–411.

Hall, S.M., 2018. The Personal is Political: Feminist Geographies of/in Austerity. *Geoforum*, online first. Available at https://doi.org/10.1016/j.geoforum.2018.04.010.

Harmes, A., 2001. Mass Investment Culture. *New Left Review*, 9, pp. 103–124.

Hay, C., 2013. *The Failure of Anglo-liberal Capitalism*. Basingstoke: Palgrave Macmillan.

Hay, C., 2011. Pathology Without Crisis? The Strange Demise of the Anglo-Liberal Growth Model. *Government and Opposition*, 46(1), pp. 1–31.

Himmelweit, S., 2002. Making Visible the Hidden Economy: The Case for Gender-Impact Analysis of Economic Policy. *Feminist Economics*, 8(1), pp. 49–70.

Joseph, M., 2014. *Debt to Society: Accounting for Life under Capitalism*. Minneapolis: University Of Minnesota Press.

Katz, C., 2001. Vagabond Capitalism and the Necessity of Social Reproduction. *Antipode*, 33(4), pp. 709–728.

Klein, L., 1999. *It's in the Cards: Consumer Credit and the American Experience*. Westport: Praeger Publishers.

Krippner, G., 2005. Financialization and the American Economy. *Socio-Economic Review*, 3(2), pp. 173–208.

Lai, K.P., 2017. Unpacking Financial Subjectivities: Intimacies, Governance and Socioeconomic Practices in Financialisation. *Environment and Planning D*, 35(5), pp. 913–932.

Langley, P., 2004. In the Eye of the "Perfect Storm": The Final Salary Pensions Crisis and Financialisation of Anglo-American Capitalism. *New Political Economy*, 9(4), pp. 539–558.

Langley, P., 2006. Securitising Suburbia: The Transformation of Anglo-American Mortgage Finance. *Competition & Change*, 10(3), pp. 283–299.

Langley, P., 2008a. Financialization and Consumer Credit Boom. *Competition & Change*, 12(2), pp. 133–147.

Langley, P., 2008b. *The Everyday Life of Global Finance: Saving and Borrowing in America*. Oxford: Oxford University Press.

Langley, P., 2014. Consuming Credit. *Consumption Markets & Culture*, 17(5), pp. 417–428.

Lazzarato, M., 2012. *The Making of the Indebted Man*. Los Angeles: Semiotext(e).

Leyshon, A. and French, S., 2009. "We All Live in a Robbie Fowler House": The Geographies of the Buy to Let Market in the UK. *The British Journal of Politics & International Relations*, 11(3), pp. 438–460.

Lowe, S.G., Searle, B.A. and Smith, S.J., 2012. From Housing Wealth to Mortgage Debt: The Emergence of Britain's Asset-Shaped Welfare State. *Social Policy and Society*, 11(1), pp. 105–116.

Marston, S.A., 2008. A Long Way from Home: Domesticating the Social Production of Scale. In Sheppard, E. and McMaster, R.B. (eds.), *Scale and Geographic Inquiry: Nature, Society, and Method*. New York: John Wiley & Sons, pp. 170–191.

Martin, R., 2007. *An Empire of Indifference: American War and the Financial Logic of Risk Management*. Durham and London: Duke University Press.

Massey, D., 2013. *Space, Place and Gender*. New York: John Wiley & Sons.

McFall, L., 2002. Advertising, Persuasion and the Culture/Economy Dualism. In du Gay, P. and Pryke, M. (eds.), *Cultural Economy: Cultural Analysis and Commercial Life*. London: Sage, pp. 148–165.

McLeay, M., Radia, A. and Thomas, R., 2014. *Money in the Modern Economy* (No. Q1), Quarterly Bulletin. Bank of England, London.

Mian, A. and Sufi, A., 2014. *House of Debt: How They (and You) Caused the Great Recession, and How We Can Prevent It from Happening Again*. Chicago: University of Chicago Press.

Montgomerie, J., 2013. America's Debt Safety-net. *Public Administration*, 91(4), pp. 871–888.

Montgomerie, J., 2009. The Pursuit of (Past) Happiness? Middle-class Indebtedness and Anglo-American Financialisation. *New Political Economy*, 14(1), pp. 1–24.

Montgomerie, J. (ed.), 2017. *Critical Methods in Political and Cultural Economy*. London: Routledge.

Montgomerie, J. and Tepe-Belfrage, D., 2016. Caring for Debts: How the Household Economy Exposes the Limits of Financialisation. *Critical Sociology*, 43(4–5), pp. 653–668.

Peterson, V.S., 2010. Global Householding amid Global Crises. *Politics & Gender*, 6(2), pp. 271–281.

Pettifor, A., 2017. *The Production of Money: How to Break the Power of the Banks*. London: Verso.

Pollard, J., 2013. Gendering Capital: Financial Crisis, Financialization and (an Agenda for) Economic Geography. *Progress in Human Geography*, 37(3), pp. 403–423.

Prabhakar, R., 2013. Asset-based Welfare: Financialization or Financial Inclusion? *Critical Social Policy*, 33 (4), pp. 658–678.

Roberts, A., 2015. Gender, Financial Deepening and the Production of Embodied Finance: Towards a Critical Feminist Analysis. *Global Society*, 29(1), pp. 107–127.

Runyan, A.S., 2018. *Global Gender Issues in the New Millennium*. London: Routledge.

Schwartz, H., 2009. *Subprime Nation: American Power, Global Capital, and the Housing Bubble*. Ithaca: Cornell University Press.

Seabrooke, L., 2010. What Do I Get? The Everyday Politics of Expectations and the Subprime Crisis. *New Political Economy*, 15(1), pp. 51–70.

Soaita, A.M. and Searle, B.A., 2016. Debt Amnesia: Homeowners' Discourses on the Financial Costs and Gains of Homebuying. *Environment and Planning A*, 48(6), pp. 1087–1106.

Soederberg, S., 2014. *Debtfare States and the Poverty Industry: Money, Discipline and the Surplus Population*. London and New York: Routledge.

Stanley, L., Deville, J. and Montgomerie, J., 2016. Digital Debt Management: The Everyday Life of Austerity. *New Formations*, 87, pp. 64–82.

Steans, J. and Tepe, D., 2010. Social Reproduction in International Political Economy: Theoretical Insights and International, Transnational and Local Sitings. *Review of International Political Economy*, 17(5), pp. 807–815.

Tepe-Belfrage, D. and Montgomerie, J., 2016. Broken Britain: Post-Crisis Austerity and the Trouble with the Troubled Families Programme. In Hozic, A.A. and True, J. (eds.), *Scandalous Economics: Gender and the Politics of Financial Crises*. Oxford: Oxford University Press, pp. 79–91.

Toporowski, J., 2000. *The End of Finance: The Theory of Capital Market Inflation, Financial Derivatives, and Pension Fund Capitalism*. London: Routledge.

Hozic, A.A. and True, J. (eds.), 2016. *Scandalous Economics: Gender and the Politics of Financial Crises*. Oxford: Oxford University Press.

True, J., 2012. *The Political Economy of Violence Against Women*. Oxford: Oxford University Press.

Van der Zwan, N., 2014. Making Sense of Financialization. *Socio-Economic Review*, 12(1), pp. 99–129.

Waring, M., 1989. *If Women Counted: A New Feminist Economics*. London: Macmillan.

Watson, M., 2010. House Price Keynesianism and the Contradictions of the Modern Investor Subject. *Housing Studies*, 25(3), pp. 413–426.

Zwick, D. and Dholakia, N., 2006. The Epistemic Consumption Object and Postsocial Consumption: Expanding Consumer-Object Theory in Consumer Research. *Consumption Markets & Culture*, 9(1), pp. 17–43.

32

FINANCIAL LITERACY EDUCATION

A Questionable Answer to the Financialization of Everyday Life

Jeanne Lazarus

Introduction

Since the end of the 1990s, the idea that all responsible governments must promote financial education policies has been spreading, nationally and internationally. This need is backed up by a repetitive narrative: because of economic instability, the increased role of financial markets in household finances, and the withdrawal of the welfare state, individuals face increasing risks. To address these risks, they must improve their financial literacy, in order to make the most informed choices and transform their behavior. Individuals therefore seem to stand alone against financial risks, with states, backed by financial companies and non-profit organizations, providing them merely with informational tools. In 2015, the OECD counted 59 countries that had implemented national strategies to enhance financial literacy (OECD 2016). The rise of financial literacy is a successful example of the construction of a public problem, carried out by political entrepreneurs using cognitive and semantic strategies.

Financial Literacy Education is a heuristic object for scholars interested in the financialization process, because it connects financial institutions, public policies and everyday life. It is both a result and an instrument of the "financialization of everyday life" (Langley in this volume). Many scholars have shown that Financial Literacy Education (FLE) aims at creating self-governing individuals (Marron 2014; Clarke 2015). It is a major tool in the making of the "financial subject," whose subjectivity is adapted to the newly financialized world (Langley and Leyshon 2012). The financial education project has developed hand in hand with a specific knowledge, originated from behavioral economics. It also carries a normative dimension: in the realm of FLE, household finances and their inherent risks are the sole responsibility of individuals, in line with the idea of a "risk shift" (Hacker 2006). Planning ahead, practicing thrift and savvy investing, i.e., adopting a morally appropriate behavior, is the good way to face risks in the world of FLE.

As this chapter will show, financial literacy education's main success is not the improvement of consumers' knowledge and know-how but the displacement of the way public policies identify the source of individual's financial problems, such that these seem to stem neither from financial products, nor from social structures and inequalities, but from individuals' behaviors.

This chapter proceeds in two parts: the first focuses on the building of a new political issue; the second discusses the political implication of the spread of financial literacy education.

The Framing of a Political Issue

The OECD has played a crucial role in the construction of financial literacy as a public issue, and has also designed the framework to address it. In 2003, the OECD launched a financial education project that responded to growing demands from member countries. In 2005, it published a report entitled *Improving Financial Literacy, Analysis of Issues and Policies* which was presented as "the first major international study on financial education" and aimed at showing why governments should take this issue into account and listing existing good practices (OECD 2005). This report is invariably quoted as a reference for defining the problem of populations' financial literacy and as an initial step in constructing the problem.

OECD's concerns with financial literacy started with pensions. Financial literacy is a subject for the OECD department of financial market, insurance and pensions. It raised the alarm at the beginning of the 2000s, because of a major change in private pensions systems: the shift from Defined Benefit (DB) to Defined Contributions (DC) plans. This shift emanated from a consensus for the privatization of pension systems, notably within the World Bank (Holzmann and Jorgensen 1999). In the "DC world" (Langley and Leaver 2012), it is not only that risks are higher – pensioners do not have any guarantee of the amount they will have – but every wage earner has to develop high cognitive skills. They must evaluate how much they will save (their *defined* contribution), and choose their pension plan accordingly. According to the OECD (2005), these two individual choices will have a huge impact on individual and collective well-being. The organization also stresses that individuals do not save enough money, ultimately condemning them to be poor in their old age and creating a burden for public solidarity.

Two other subjects were bundled with the initial pension issue: the 2005 report discusses overindebtedness and banking exclusion – the fact that people are "unbanked" or "under-banked" in rich and poor countries. After the subprime crisis, the problem with borrowers' lack of financial literacy gained further importance and expanded to household budget management. The narrative shifted: the subprime crisis provided evidence for the need for financial literacy. It was especially true in the USA where government, bankers and scholars explained that the crisis could have been avoided if people had been more financially literate (Pinto 2013). Economists measured correlation between low mathematical skills and mortgage (Gerardi et al. 2013) or credit card defaults (Agarwal and Mazumder 2013). Critics of predatory lenders were used to fuel a narrative of blaming the victims, suggesting that people should be more financially literate in order to avoid signing contracts without understanding their contents.

Taking a leading role, the OECD also frames the problematics of financial education issues. The organization disseminates definitions and "guidelines" for developing and evaluating programs. A major tool is the international network it has built up: the INFE (International Network on Financial Education), which brings together *circa* 70 countries. In addition, it regularly organizes conferences throughout the world: central bankers, leaders of the big private banks, non-profit organizations, scientific experts and involved public actors meet to share their experiences, and strengthen a common language and problematization. Usual participants include high-level members of the ministry of economics, regulators, central banks and when they exist, financial literacy public bodies. The host country's minister of Finance will often open the conference with a speech promoting financial literacy.

The OECD's cognitive framework is deeply influenced by behavioral economics, which is the discipline of most of its financial literacy experts (Agarwal and Mazumder 2013). This leads to an emphasis on individual behavior: governments have to develop people's awareness of financial risks, but the final responsibility of one's financial situation is individual. The international organization imposes "Financial Literacy" as a term encompassing both "financial education" and "financial capability." Financial literacy has become the ultimate goal: educated, consumers will be more "financially literate." The IMF, the World Bank and the G20[1] play a similar dual role of accumulating knowledge and setting up international policies.

While the notion of financial literacy comes from non-academic spaces, its development relies on academic legitimacy: research on the subject is increasing, with researchers who are situated at the interface between public policy and scientific research, multiplying publications on the one hand, and interventions with governments on the other hand. They seek to provide evidence of the need for financial education (Mitchell and Lusardi 2011). A few international experts have a key role in establishing a common knowledge through important surveys and providing states with survey grids. For example, France commissioned a study on the level of financial literacy by adapting the 2010 OECD survey and using many of its questions (CCSF 2015).

The implementation of financial literacy programs occurs at the national level. The English-speaking countries (UK, USA, Australia and New Zealand) were the first to develop financial education policies, even before the OECD began to show concern for the subject. The financial literacy framework has therefore been mostly designed to echo the consumer financial landscape of these countries, characterized by individualized financial protections and a strong welfare state retrenchment (Pierson 1994). The British case is emblematic: financial literacy has been a political solution to the serious challenges of the 1986 Social Security Act (Zokaityte 2017). The 1986 Act transformed the British social security by rendering optional the affiliation to an occupational pension scheme. Instead, it created a "privatized system of pension provision." This individualization was accompanied by the implementation of a "self-regulation" of the UK financial system. At least 1.5 million people were "advised" by financial counsellors to opt out from their generous occupational plans to subscribe to personal pensions, more expensive and more risky. This led to a national mis-selling scandal. At the time, regulators did not focus on the liberalization of the pension system, but on consumers' competencies. In the 1980s, consumers were presented as "choosers." The 1990s showed that dishonest sellers could take advantage of financial consumers' lack of knowledge. Financial education appeared as a perfect solution to meet regulation and political goals (the New Labour and its "third way" social policy): it was a way to take public action and to protect individuals without hurting the market, since governments target individual behaviors. The correlation between the launch of financial education policies and pensions reforms can be found in many countries. New Zealand, for instance, launched these policies in 1993 (Cameron and Wood 2016), but also in Israel (Maman and Rosenhek 2019) or in Eastern Europe (Lazarus 2016).

Elsewhere, and especially in the Global South, the narrative of the need for the financial education of the population is based on the recent spread of financial products and credits. This is the case in South Africa, which has developed major financial education projects, as well as in Latin American and Asian countries. The programs are designed to make people adopt the money management methods promoted in rich countries: using banking supports, borrowing by measuring monthly repayment capacities, saving regularly by using financial products, and overall, break with the so-called informal economy (Lundberg and Mulaj 2014). Micro-credits play a key role here: they enjoy a strong legitimacy, being framed as an anti-poverty and benevolent tool, reinforced by Muhammad Yunus' Nobel Peace Prize in 2006. Nonetheless, the 2010 Indian "micro-credit crisis" – after the 2008–2009 Nicaragua, Morocco, Pakistan and Bosnia crises – shed light on the financial distress of many borrowers and the exploitative practices of many companies (Servet 2011). Here again, financial literacy has been presented as a solution, ironically, to be provided by micro-loan companies (Guérin 2012).

Despite these differences across geographies, policymakers everywhere describe the implementation of financial literacy education as a means to protect citizens from the liberalization of financial markets and more broadly from the financialization of the domestic sphere, processes which are thus taken for granted. As financialization scholars have suggested, FLE is made to adapt practices, but above all the individual's subjectivity to this new world (Langley and Leaver 2012; Clarke 2015). It participates in the large movement of naturalizing the introduction of financial tools in households (Langley 2008): debts, investment plans, insurance are inevitable and one needs to learn how to manage them in order to be a respectable citizen (Arthur 2014).

What? For Whom? By Whom?

What are the contents of these programs? Synthetically, they fall under three types. First are pension funds, retirement preparation and the choice of investment products. According to these programs, being financially literate means being an autonomous consumer, able to compare investment products. Financial literacy education thus intends to provide information and tools to compare and choose, but also to make people aware of the necessity to care about their own financial protection. For example, countries like the UK that have implemented drastic reforms of their pension system, may develop financial literacy in order to inform citizens that they won't get as much money as they expected from the previous system. Companies helping their employees choose their pension fund can also contribute to this kind of program.

The second category of financial education programs focuses on budgeting and using bank accounts and means of payment: people must learn how to spend, save and borrow in what financial educators judge to be the appropriate way. They aim to make people "see" where their money goes, using budget grids, account books or apps, but also equip them with tools to manage their future. These tools are called "what ifs" in OECD conferences: what if I save 100 dollars every month? What if I raise my monthly credit repayment? Etc. This kind of financial education aims at transforming people's behaviors, in a quite ambiguous way: it could be seen as the promotion of thrifty money management, but it can also be perceived as a way to help individuals participate in the market. Being aware of what they spend and the way banks operate, individuals thus become empowered.

This financial literacy can be transmitted through websites or applications, but also through training for pupils or adults. An ethnographic observation of financial literacy programs in France showed that the main "tool" used is to teach participants how to sort their money. Money management can then be described as "tidying one's room and seeking shelter" (Lazarus 2016). The South African financial literacy body delivered its message via a popular soap opera: one of the main characters had debt issues, and got advice from another character. The effect on the financial behavior of viewers was measured by comparing it with that of people who had not watched the show. The operation has proven its impact (Berg and Zia 2013).

The third mode is individual support, provided by social workers or non-profit organizations. It targets deprived or over-indebted people, sometimes during a single meeting, sometimes throughout a longer relationship. When these supports are not public, states or foundations may subsidize them; while others fall into the "social business" category, such as the UK for-profit debt management companies or the micro-credit companies which provide financial education classes. Some of these organizations provide debt mediation services, as in Belgium. In the USA, since the 2005 Bankruptcy Abuse Prevention and Consumer Protection Act (BAPCPA), financial advice is compulsory when citizens go bankrupt. They must meet with a counselor before choosing the kind of bankruptcy they will file for before receiving budget advices. Law scholar Michael Sousa (Sousa 2013) has interviewed people who met with counselors and describes their lack of interest: most of them consider their problems not as the result of a bad money management, but as the result of a difficulty they met or a general lack of money.

The various financial literacy programs target different audiences. Advice on savings and investments is designed for middle-class wage earners, in order to help them to cope with the risk shift, and stabilize their way of life in the midst of the financialization of daily life, for example to finance children's education. For deprived people, financial education programs are focused on budgeting: sorting money, using technical devices like credit cards, bank account, remittances transactions, etc. This somehow follows the distinction made by Randy Martin (2007) between valorized "risk-takers," who must be encouraged, and the people "at risk," who have failed to reach autonomy and are a burden for the societies.

Specific groups are particularly targeted: women (Bucher-Koenen et al. 2016) and poor families. In the USA, some programs are specially designed for troops and veterans, for whom a dedicated legislation was even put in place in 2007 to protect them from loan sharks near barracks (Goulet 2007). Financial literacy educators are also concerned with young people: whether they are children in school or young employees who must be made aware of the financial risks they incur and the need to insure against them. However, some promoters of financial literacy emphasize that students have time to forget what they learned in school before time comes to use this knowledge. Therefore, they argue for "teachable moments": a house move, a first job, a real estate purchase, marriage, birth of a child, etc. (Kaiser and Menkhoff 2017).

Three categories of actors provide financial literacy education tools: public organizations, charities and financial institutions, often working in partnership. Banks and lenders deeply influence the framing of financial education. All OECD summits on financial literacy invite bank representatives who present their initiatives (e.g. HSBC, Visa, Citigroup, ING, etc). Some financial institutions are directly involved, such as Visa, which has developed many financial literacy initiatives around the world, participated in OECD discussions, even funded surveys (OECD 2016). Other banks fund foundations, but also non-profits or government programs. When they do not finance them directly, they participate on their boards. This cognitive domination of banks leads to the assimilation of alternative ways of counting and managing money as being irrational or ignorant. For example, they define a specific way of money circulation and specific means of calculation, such as the monthly cycles of money that individuals have to deal with, even if their own cash flows are not on a monthly rhythm.

Despite the growth of financial literacy programs, two blind spots remain. First, their contents are barely discussed by international organizations or governments. The promotion of education seems to be a goal *per se*, as if any training had the same utility. Financial literacy appears to be more of a political tool rather than a true pedagogical concern. The second blind spot is that of evaluation. Financial literacy promoters are inspired by an economic approach to public policies, implying evidence-based evaluation. Thus, OECD provides multiple guidelines on evaluation, and many seminars are devoted to evaluation. A part of the *Handbook of Financial Literacy* is dedicated to assessment, discussing the best evaluation practices (Aprea et al. 2016). However, the very evaluation of the effectiveness of existing programs remains scarce, if not non-existent. To date, there is nothing in the literature that demonstrates a long-term usefulness. Some experiments with directly evaluable utility have been made, as for example Duflo and Saez's survey (Duflo and Saez 2002) on a training for retirement savings plans in a company, which showed its effectiveness on those who had followed it. However, there is no training with students and the general public which has ever led to convincing results (Mandell and Klein 2009).

Here is the real puzzle: financial literacy policy has never been proven effective. Nonetheless, it has reached the status of an indispensable policy for populations' well-being. It is promoted by international organizations, it is financed by states which are otherwise cutting expenditures, and big companies, which are supposed to act rationally. How can this be explained? What if these programs were not primarily crafted to provide technical tools to make people make better financial decisions? What if, instead, their main utility is to offer a simple answer to issues that are recognized by policymakers as extremely complicated? In doing so, they transmit a particular normativity, defining the right way for individuals to cope with the financialization of their domestic finances. They also avoid questioning financial institutions' practices, since the responsibility is mainly viewed on the consumer's side.

Critical Analysis of Financial Literacy

A Political Answer

The promotion of financial education is a political response to the challenges posed by economic liberalization. This is assumed by its promoters, but it is also the target of significant criticism.

Elizabeth Pinto applied a "narrative policy analysis" to financial literacy education in Canada (Pinto 2013). She highlights a "dominant" narrative and a scarcer "counter-narrative." Both acknowledge the need for financial education for Canadians who have to fight against personal economic instability. Nevertheless, the advocates of the dominant narrative (on the side of the state and economic institutions) consider that this education must be built hand-in-hand with banks, since the main issue is consumers' lack of knowledge; the champions of the second narrative blame the banks for using the dominant narrative to pursue their dishonest business practices. They ask for more regulation to protect financial consumers (Willis 2008; 2011).

One approach "blames" the consumer, the other one blames banks, but both consider that pragmatically speaking financial education empowers consumers. For example, in the French financial education experiments, banks and charities work together because they agree to the usefulness of financial education (Lazarus 2013). However, some people, like Lauren Willis, a US law professor, radically challenge the need for financial education. Willis (2008, 2011) argues that massive funding would be necessary to obtain the results promised by financial education, while US citizens do not even agree to pay for basic public education. From her point of view, the financial industry supports financial education to avoid regulation – the microfinance industry does the same (Mader 2017).

Two conceptions of governmental citizen-consumer protection are opposed here. On the one side, Willis and opponents of financial education consider that states must prevent certain markets from developing, ensure the protection of household finances by public services (particularly, health and education) and provide collective insurance through the welfare state. This conception underlies the creation of the US Consumer Financial Protection Bureau (CFPB), a federal agency implemented by the Dodd-Frank Act in 2010 (Kastner 2016). On the other side, proponents of financial education believe that the market can better protect citizens than the state, through private insurance and competition. The market is ideologically considered as more efficient than any public organization. This is in line with replacing pay-as-you-go pension schemes by pension funds, but also with replacing DB pensions with DC pension schemes.

However, Jacob Hacker (2006) described the "risk shift" in the USA and the transfer of risks previously faced collectively onto the households; in order to denounce it and show its harmful effects, but also to show that it resulted from political choices that could possibly be reversed in the future. FLE proponents tend to naturalize this risk shift: in their rhetoric, like natural events, the Welfare State is inexorably withdrawing, the labor market is naturally unstable and finance has irreversibly expanded (OECD 2005). Thus, citizens, responsible and accountable, must cope with this new situation, with the benevolent help of states through financial education.

Inequalities or social and economic power struggle are not part of the picture. Governing becomes a government of conduct (Dubuisson-Quellier 2016) and the political intervention is essentially intended to change individual behavior, not socio-economic structures.

Measuring and Defining

The financial education project is intrinsically linked to a particular vision of politics, public policies and the relationship between citizens, states and the market. It carries a normative dimension that has been the subject of many social scientific studies. First, FLE defines the rules for good money management. It is obvious in the surveys designed to measure the latter. Whether OECD surveys (the last major one dates from 2016 (OECD 2016), the OECD having compiled data from 30 countries), US FINRA surveys (which partly overlap), three elements are always measured: knowledge, attitudes and behaviors. The measurement of knowledge leads to the recurrent denunciation of people's ignorance: only a tiny part of the population succeeds in financial calculations that are considered "simple" by the authors of these surveys (in particular the calculation of compound interest). But normativity is mainly to be found in the analysis of answers to questions measuring attitudes and behaviors. For example, respondents are asked to say whether they more or less agree with the following sentences: "I tend to live for today and let tomorrow take care of itself" (Atkinson and Messy 2012). The right attitude is to plan rather than live from day to day. Good behavior is being both a prudent manager and an informed consumer: paying bills, monitoring accounts, comparing financial products and avoiding exorbitant bank or credit card fees.

These surveys produce a conception of good self-management that relates to an economically stable middle-class lifestyle, using banking services and means of payment, but also mathematical methods of calculation. The literature on poor people's budget management suggests that most of their practices do not require calculation. Since Hoggart's (1957) work, at least, it has been established that money shortage translates into day-to-day survival strategies that can lead to exceptional spending when money is there. The careful planning proposed by financial educators is not compatible with instable cash flows. Many commentators underline the irony of financial literacy for poor people focusing on individual behaviors (and on what behavioral economics call "bias") rather than on their low incomes. A controversy about McDonalds' financial literacy program provides a shining example of the fact that monetary resources are at least as important as good money behavior: a target budget grid was provided to employees to guide them in their expenses. Not only the grid was unrealistic (i.e., the health insurance cost $20) but more importantly, in the "resources" columns, employees had to work two jobs in order to make ends meet (Haiven 2017).

A Normative Project

The financialization scholarship has been very much interested in financial education to understand how it transforms subjectivities and creates "financial subjects" (Langley in this volume). Inspired by Michel Foucault's work on governmentality, these works show how the use of financial tools creates constraints that people have interiorized, they feel that it is their own responsibility to fulfill the behavior that is wanted from them to maintain and reinforce the social structure of capitalism. Donncha Marron (2014), for instance, describes financial literacy education as "a form of advanced liberal governmentality." He considers it another tool of neo-liberalism that presents itself as depoliticized, coercing individuals and dissocializing societies. In this vein, Johnna Montgomerie and Daniela Tepe-Belfrage (2016) stress the link between austerity policies, the "responsabilization" discourse and the stigmatization of the poor. By focusing on "literacy," public policies tend to explain poverty as coming from a lack of knowledge, but also from lacking moral norms: "Behavioural economic frames of 'debt denial' (...) pathologises debt as a psychological deficiency; while high-cost lenders are not subjected to similar forms of analysis" (ibid.: 893). Chris Clarke (2015) argues that financial literacy education's main purpose is to constitute resilient participants to the market: financial market crises are presented as natural disasters that individuals must prepare to face.

Financial literacy has changed the narratives and the distribution of responsibilities between creditors and debtors (Ramsay 2017). For example, in France, the overindebtedness procedure has long been organized by distinguishing between active and passive debtors (who have faced "life accidents"). Since 2014 and a survey on the debtors' trajectory, the narrative is more individualized: some people in the same financial situation are able to make ends meet, while others are not. In these circumstances, financial literacy education should be the answer to their difficulties. Ramsay highlights the fact that not only is morality embedded in law, but moral discourse may actually transform the law. This is very clear in the US case: from the 1980s on, the consumer credit industry has called for a harsher bankruptcy law, using the narrative "must pay/should pay." It argued that people are not incentivized to pay back their loan since they can easily have their debts written off. President Bush Jr. went in this direction, when implementing the "Bankruptcy Abuse Prevention and Consumer Protection Act" in 2005. When signing the act, Bush praised "a nation of personal responsibility" (ibid.).

Many researchers consider that FLE "tends to reinforce and reify conventional, neoliberal approaches, attitudes, and ideologies toward debt, credit, finance, and money" (Haiven 2017: 349; in this volume). Chris Arthur (2014), for instance, analyzed Canadian TV reality shows, where indebted participants are taught "good" financial behaviors. Instead of financial pedagogy, these initiatives create more insecurity through depoliticization: they naturalize a life of debt and inequalities. Poor people are responsible for their situation, since the shows' message is that a good financial behavior may resolve any difficult situation (ibid.). For these reasons, scholars have proposed to create a Critical Financial Literacy (Hütten et al. 2018) that does not focus on individual behavior, but will empower citizens to understand the role of finance in society and to fight for financial regulation.

Conclusion

One objective of financial literacy education has certainly achieved: raising awareness on the issue, on the policy-makers' side. Financial literacy promoters have convinced many officials that financial education can protect individuals and societies. Yet, how people's behavior is actually transformed is not measured. The few serious evaluations that exist raise serious doubts as to whether behaviors actually change, let alone whether individuals truly benefit from any such change. Nonetheless, it is interesting to note that policy-makers, often far from offering practical training, are mainly interested in awareness raising, to which they ascribe almost magical powers in response to macroeconomic problems. The actors working closest to the subjects of financial education have much more modest ambitions: they just hope to provide an umbrella to people, knowing that many hazards may overwhelm all the good practices they could teach. This is a crucial battle for future political decisions on social protection. If households are able to protect their own finances by developing wise behaviors, is the welfare state still necessary? Conversely, if money management is as simple as money educators pretend it is – comparable to good housekeeping –, why should it need public policies? It is important to sort out here what financial literacy can and cannot do: can it replace the regulation of financial products as a way of protecting individuals? Can it replace risk pooling? Finally, can it offset the stagnation of labor income and the decline in purchasing power? Focusing attention on the practices of individuals has certainly a strong political interest, and can genuinely help people, in particular by protecting them from costly fees. This, however, is insufficient to carry out a real public policy of protection of household resources.

Critical social sciences do not decry financial education *per se* but the way it is framed: the institutions that deliver it, the kind of knowledge on which it is built, its intertwining with a decrease in the regulation of consumer finance. They all suggest that financial education is a tool to depoliticize financial issues, reducing education to a pragmatic issue while forgetting that education is normative by definition. Financialization studies can deconstruct this apparent neutrality, by showing the ideology it carries and by unveiling the choices underlying the framing of FLE.

Note

1 Since 2011, the improvement of financial literacy is one of the G20 "High-level principles."

Bibliography

Agarwal, S. and Mazumder, B., 2013. Cognitive Abilities and Household Financial Decision Making. *American Economic Journal: Applied Economics*, 5(1), pp. 193–207.

Aprea, C., Wuttke, E., Breuer, K., Koh, N.K., Davies, P., Greimel-Fuhrmann, B. and Lopus, J.S. (eds.), 2016. *International Handbook of Financial Literacy*. Singapore: Springer.

Arthur, C., 2014. Financial Literacy Education as Public Pedagogy for the Capitalist Debt Economy. *TOPIA: Canadian Journal of Cultural Studies*, 30, pp. 147–164.

Atkinson, A. and Messy, F.-A., 2012. Measuring Financial Literacy. *OECD Working Papers on Finance, Insurance and Private Pensions*. Paris: Organisation for Economic Co-operation and Development.

Berg, G. and Zia, B., 2013. *Harnessing Emotional Connections to Improve Financial Decisions*. World Bank, No. 6407.

Bucher-Koenen, T., Lusardi, A., Alessie, R.J.M. and Van Rooij, M.C.J., 2016. *How Financially Literate are Women? An Overview and New Insights*. Global Financial Literacy Excellence Center, No. WP 2016–2011.

Cameron, M.P. and Wood, P., 2016. The Policy Context for Financial Education in New Zealand. In Aprea, C., Wuttke, E., Breuer, K., Koh, N.K., Davies, P., Greimel-Fuhrmann, B. and Lopus, J.S. (eds.), *International Handbook of Financial Literacy*. Singapore: Springer, pp. 179–192.

CCSF, 2015. *La définition et la mise en oeuvre d'une stratégie nationale en matière d'éducation financière*. Paris.

Clarke, C., 2015. Learning to Fail: Resilience and the Empty Promise of Financial Literacy Education. *Consumption Markets & Culture*, 18(3), pp. 257–276.

Dubuisson-Quellier, S., 2016. *Gouverner les conduites*. Paris: Presses de Sciences Po.

Duflo, E. and Saez, E., 2002. Participation and Investment Decisions in a Retirement Plan: The Influence of Colleagues' Choices. *Journal of Public Economics*, 85(1), pp. 121–148.

Gerardi, K., Goette, L. and Meier, S., 2013. Numerical Ability Predicts Mortgage Default. *Proceedings of the National Academy of Sciences*, 110(28), pp. 11267–11271.

Goulet, D., 2007. Protecting our Protectors: The Defense Department's New Rules to Prevent Predatory Lending to Military Personnel. *Loyola Consumer Law Review*, 20(1), pp. 81–99.

Guérin, I., 2012. Households' Over-indebtedness and the Fallacy of Financial Education: Insights from Economic Anthropology. *Microfinance in Crisis Working Paper Series* 2012–2011.

Hacker, J.S., 2006. *The Great Risk Shift: The New Economic Insecurity and the Decline of the American Dream*. New York: Oxford University Press.

Haiven, M., 2017. The Uses of Financial Literacy. *Cultural Politics*, 13(3), pp. 348–369.

Hoggart, R., 1957. *The Uses of Literacy: Aspects of Working-Class Life*. London: Chatto and Windus.

Holzmann, R. and Jorgensen, S., 1999. Social Protection as Social Risk Management: Conceptual Underpinnings for the Social Protection Sector Strategy Paper. *Journal of International Development*, 11(7), pp. 1005–1027.

Hütten, M., Maman, D., Rosenhek, Z. and Thiemann, M., 2018. Critical Financial Literacy: An Agenda. *International Journal of Pluralism and Economics Education*, 9(3), pp. 274–291.

Kaiser, T. and Menkhoff, L., 2017. Does Financial Education Impact Financial Literacy and Financial Behavior, and If So, When? *World Bank Economic Review*, 31(3), pp. 611–630.

Kastner, L., 2016. *The Power of Weak Interests in Financial Reforms. Explaining the Creation of a US Consumer Agency*. Maxpo Discussion Paper No. 16/1.

Langley, P., 2008. *The Everyday Life of Global Finance: Saving And Borrowing in Anglo-America*. Oxford: Oxford University Press.

Langley, P. and Leaver, A., 2012. Remaking Retirement Investors. *Journal of Cultural Economy*, 5(4), pp. 473–488.

Langley, P. and Leyshon, A., 2012. Guest Editors' Introduction. *Journal of Cultural Economy*, 5(4), pp. 369–373.

Lazarus, J., 2013. De l'aide à la responsabilisation. *Genèses*, 93(4), pp. 76–97.

Lazarus, J., 2016. Gouverner les conduites par l'éducation financière: l'ascension de la financial literacy. In Dubuisson-Quellier, S. (ed.), *Gouverner les conduites*. Paris: Presses de Sciences Po, pp. 93–125.

Lundberg, M. and Mulaj, F. (eds.), 2014. *Enhancing Financial Capability and Behavior in Low and Middle-income Countries*. Washington DC: World Bank.

Mader, P., 2017. How Much Voice for Borrowers? Restricted Feedback and Recursivity in Microfinance. *Global Policy*, 8(4), pp. 540–552.

Maman, D. and Rosenhek, Z., 2019. Responsibility, Planning and Risk Management: Moralizing Everyday Finance through Financial Education. *The British Journal of Sociology*, 8(1). https://doi.org/10.1111/1468-4446.12698

Mandell, L. and Klein, L., 2009. The Impact of Financial Literacy Education on Subsequent Financial Behavior. *Journal of Financial Counseling and Planning*, 20(1), pp. 15–24.

Marron, D., 2014. "Informed, Educated and more Confident": Financial Capability and the Problematization of Personal Finance Consumption. *Consumption Markets & Culture*, 17(5), pp. 491–511.

Martin, R., 2007. *An Empire of Indifference: American War and the Financial Logic of Risk Management*. Durham, NC: Duke University Press.

Mitchell, O.S. and Lusardi, A. (eds.), 2011. *Financial Literacy: Implications for Retirement Security and the Financial Marketplace*. Oxford, New York: Oxford University Press.

Montgomerie, J. and Tepe-Belfrage, D., 2016. A Feminist Moral-Political Economy of Uneven Reform in Austerity Britain: Fostering Financial and Parental Literacy. *Globalizations*, 13(6), pp. 890–905.

OECD, 2005. *Improving Financial Literacy. Analysis of Issues and Policies*. Paris: OECD.

OECD, 2016. *OECD/INFE International Survey of Adult Financial Literacy Competencies*. Paris: OECD.

Pierson, P., 1994. *Dismantling the Welfare State?: Reagan, Thatcher and the Politics of Retrenchment*. Cambridge: Cambridge University Press.

Pinto, L.E., 2013. When Politics Trump Evidence: Financial Literacy Education Narratives following the Global Financial Crisis. *Journal of Education Policy*, 28(1), pp. 95–120.

Ramsay, I., 2017. *Personal Insolvency in the 21st Century: A Comparative Analysis of the US and Europe*. Oxford: Hart Publishing.

Servet, J.-M., 2011. La crise du microcrédit en Andhra Pradesh (Inde). *Revue Tiers Monde*, (207), pp. 43–59.

Sousa, M., 2013. Just Punch My Bankruptcy Ticket: A Qualitative Study of Mandatory Debtor Financial Education. *Marquette Law Review*, 97(2), pp. 391–467.

Willis, L.E., 2008. Against Financial Literacy Education. *Iowa Law Review*, 94, 8–10.

Willis, L.E., 2011. The Financial Education Fallacy. *The American Economic Review*, 101(3), pp. 429–434.

Wolf, M., 2018. Ain't Misbehaving: Behavioral Economics and the Making of Financial Literacy. *Economic Sociology: The European Electronic Newsletter*, 19(2), pp. 10–18.

Zokaityte, A., 2017. *Financial Literacy Education. Edu-Regulating our Saving and Spending Habits*. Basingstoke: Palgrave Macmillan.

33

CULTURES OF DEBT MANAGEMENT ENTER CITY HALL

Laura Deruytter and Sebastian Möller

Introduction: Financial Culture and City Hall

The impressive ascent of finance and its entry into ostensibly non-economic domains of life does not only yield institutional and cultural change in upper levels of the state and the everyday life of its citizens but also significantly influences local governments. In this chapter, we argue that financialization changes the way public administrators and local policy-makers in city hall think, behave, and relate to the financial sector. One particularly vivid impression from field research illustrates this ongoing transformation nicely. It comes from a German city where the head of the treasury department was interviewed about municipal borrowing practices. His office, situated in a venerable building representing the local government's authority, radiates the spirit of past decades with its dark wood paneling, chunky furniture, and vintage paintings on the wall. You can sense that the city which currently finds itself in a rather strained financial position must have seen times of prosperity in the past. The treasurer himself has the appearance and habitus of a rather typical representative of a senior civil servant. His white hair indicates that he must have done this job for some time. So far, everything seems to fit the general perception of local government.

What was striking, however, was the treasurer's palpable enthusiasm for financial markets and innovation. This did not only come out of the conversation and the stock exchange motifs of the paintings in his office but rather from the fact that the wooden desk was dominated by two computer screens, one displaying the user interface of a portfolio management software used by the treasury to perform their financial operations (i.e. borrowing money, loan repayments, cash flow management, derivatives and investment administration) and the other showing current market developments provided by Reuters. During the interview, it became clear that both the pace of financial markets and portfolio theory shape the mundane practices of this treasurer. For instance, the timing of loan tendering is determined by a close monitoring of capital markets and the debt stock is managed as a portfolio that needs to fulfill certain financial ratios. Accordingly, the treasurer perceived himself as a sophisticated market participant and talked about financial practices including the conclusion of interest rate swaps and daily contacts to international banks in an astonishingly normalized manner.

This internalization and normalization of financial market logics in local state administrations presents an example of what Chiapello has called "the gradual colonization by specific financialised techniques and calculation methods" (Chiapello 2015: 15; Chiapello, this volume). Accordingly, this chapter focuses on the everyday life of financial administration of European local authorities prior to and after the financial crisis. Not only German cities have deepened their connection to global finance, examples are found in other countries as well. In the 2000s, Italian and French municipalities invested heavily in interest rate swaps, while Norwegian municipalities tried to profit from speculation with US mortgage backed securities. Since the crisis, the connection with financial investors and advisors has not weakened, yet rather morphed into new forms, often under conditions of austerity, economic recession and strict balanced budget requirements. These observations raise fundamental questions on financialized practices of subnational governments addressed in this chapter: What has changed in the way local authorities organize, perform and perceive their financial activities? Can we find traces of a financialized culture within the local state and if so, how did it enter the realm of local government?

Studying Municipal Debt Management as a Socially Constructed, Multi-Layered Process

As the financialization of European local governments is a recent phenomenon, gaining momentum only in the early 2000s, the literature is relatively limited and focuses mostly on specific single cases. Political economists have discussed country-specific cases of (mis)selling of derivatives and the entangling of local politics with global finance (Pacewicz 2013; Hendrikse and Sidaway 2014; Lagna 2015), while geographers have examined the impact of new financial products on urban development (Rutland 2010; Weber 2010). Changes to local governance further link with critical accountancy and public management studies (Luby 2012), state rescaling (Brenner 1999) and broader discussions on public debt (Streeck 2013) and state financialization (Wang, this volume).

To this literature, we aim to add a sociologically informed perspective. New financial practices of local authorities as illustrated are often presented as rational and purely technical innovations by both public management scholars and practitioners from the field. However, we argue that they are context-specific, socially constructed, contested and variegated in nature (see also Engelen et al. 2010). We apply a narrow focus to the notion of local authority, focusing on the city treasury as an arena of institutional and cultural change impacting the core of the local state. Using the concept of culture stresses the socially constructed nature of how local administrations "do" public finance. By focusing on cultural shifts within local public administrations, we follow Chiapello's internalist approach of interpreting financialization as "the diffusion of financialised conventions" (Chiapello 2015: 14; Chiapello, this volume). We are particularly interested in how traditional cultures of risk aversion in city hall are gradually infused by novel practices of active risk management that prevail in the corporate and financial sectors. We analyze and illustrate this transformation on a micro-, meso- and macro-level, thereby situating everyday municipal debt management against more general conditions of financial market dynamics and policy paradigms.

On the micro-level, the main transformation of city hall's finances concerns the very invention of local authority debt (or treasury) management. Today, debt management is presented by actors in the field as an almost natural way of doing public finance. Traditionally however, municipal debt was not actively managed. Rather, the city treasury would usually take on long-term loans from their local principal banks (in some countries these include publicly owned banks such as savings banks or Landesbanken) or, in the case of the UK, from a specialized state agency. Moreover, the main point of reference were single loans (as opposed to the whole debt portfolio) and city treasurers, in general, had a rather risk-averse mindset. Risk, however, was perceived differently by city treasurers according to their respective administrative culture as indicated by diverging preferences for fixed or floating rate loans in different countries. The new debt management approach pushing forward both financialization and harmonization of municipal practices had to be established first by actors with vested interests. How did that happen? In the discussion below, we distinguish between *rationalities* and *technologies*. For us, rationalities are the concrete translations of broader ideologies to make sense and take decisions in day-to-day debt management, for example, fiscal prudence. The normalization and materialization of rationalities went hand in hand with the diffusion of new technologies offered by the financial sector, such as municipal bonds, accounting systems and portfolio management software. In the words of Peck and Whiteside (2016: 21) financial technologies serve as "carriers for financial rationalities and imperatives," deepening the relation between local governments and financial markets. Analyzing the entry of financial rationalities and technologies thus helps us answer the question: *Why* did city treasurers believe a novel, active form of debt management was necessary (rationalities), and *how* did they implement this (technologies)?

The shift from risk aversiveness to active debt management did not occur in a singular, idiosyncratic way. Novel financial practices were only used because conditions on a meso- and macro-level created the needs and possibilities for them. On the meso-level, we discuss immediate, conjunctural conditions that are caused by financial market dynamics, such as the changing relation between banks as suppliers of financial products and local governments as their customers. Here, we zoom in on the difference between the pre-crisis and post-crisis conjuncture, as each period requires the management of particular risks and opportunities. For example, in the pre-crisis episode of volatile interest rates, banks – driven by competitive pressure and in search for new income – sold interest rate swaps to local governments. Now, in a low interest-rate environment, as we shall see, other products are being developed.

On the macro-scale, we consider long-term, structural conditions that underwrite processes of state- and market-restructuring across several decades. We discuss three important changes: The ascent of New Public Management (NPM), the impact of state rescaling and fiscal retrenchment under austerity regimes. As a policy paradigm, New Public Management introduced private sector standards of efficiency into public administration (Pollitt and Bouckaert 2011; Sanderson 2001) and promoted outsourcing of state functions to a newly emerging public services industry (Froud et al. 2017). Over several decades, the NPM ideology has been adopted and modified by policy makers, and it continues to remain highly influential. This is visible in for example in the promotion of debt management by consultancy services, and performance ratios in everyday accounting by city treasurers.

Micro-level: City Hall's New Financial Practices

Rationalities: The Invention of Municipal Debt Management

The adoption of a financialized culture in city hall manifests itself, firstly, in changing rationalities. The main difference to pre-financialized rationalities of public finance lies in the changing self- and market-perceptions by public administrators. Municipal treasurers increasingly have turned into semi-professional market observers and analysts trying to capitalize on all sorts of new market opportunities and financial engineering. This comes with a perception of risk as calculable and profitable (Petzold 2014: 63–64) and the internalization of mainstream financial economic ideas like portfolio theory and yield curve models. The introduction of corporate treasury procedures and models to local government mirrors institutional and ideational change on the national level, where policies of sovereign debt management have been introduced in the late 1990s and early 2000s (Trampusch 2015; Livne and Yonay 2016; Preunkert 2017). Under the new approach, the occasional duty of taking on and servicing loans turns into a daily business of managing a city's debt portfolio. The portfolio approach gradually supersedes traditional thinking in single loans. This integrated view creates continuous incentives to optimize the portfolio with new financial products, and adopt core parameters to try to beat the market or hedge against potential risks.

This, however, requires a different mindset and expertise than traditionally prevalent in local public administrations. Therefore, the invention and dissemination of municipal debt management created new demands for external advice and regular training of the administrative staff, reinforcing and diffusing this newly financialized rationality. However, the imbalance of financial expertise between local government and the financial sector is not significantly reduced due to the lack of in-house monitoring capacities, constant financial innovation, the opacity of market information and the advanced knowledge of banks and brokers. As we already know from the realm of private households, policies of financial literacy education are often targeted at encouraging sophisticated investment practices rather than pure consumer protection (Wolf 2018; Lazarus, this volume). Accordingly, financial literate public administrators may actually fall in the trap of over-confidentiality or at least will be even more susceptible to further financialization. Furthermore, in many cases, debt management has been outsourced to the public services industry as a result of staff cuts in local government, further undermining the creation of a level playing field.

Active debt management has emerged as a new requirement for local authorities in many European countries from the early 2000s onwards and was pushed for by a coalition of banks, financial service providers, municipal and professional associations, policy-makers from higher-level government, and, in some cases, individual treasurers and councilors with a professional background and public management academics. Apparently, storytelling and the mobilization of economic expectations was crucial for the diffusion of debt management and financial innovation (Fastenrath et al. 2017).

Although debt management practices usually are not subject to controversies among political parties, somewhat counterintuitively, social-democratic city governments appear more receptive to these rationalities. This can be explained by their ambition to maintain a certain level of welfarism in spite of fiscal consolidation and structural change. The cities of Manchester (UK) and Linz (Austria) are good examples for this for they have been early adopters of debt management while being governed by the political left (Möller 2016). The strategic move by many banks and service firms to advocate debt management as potential profit center, i.e. a way to not only reduce interest payments but also generate additional revenues, matches this municipal demand for innovative solutions in a tougher fiscal environment. On the other hand, debt management can also be interpreted as an evasive move by city governments to circumvent budget constraints and to postpone ramifications of the consolidation state (Streeck 2013), yet through financial means. Lagna (2015: 284) for example describes how Italian municipalities used interest rate swaps to circumvent limits on expenditures, in his view a "political-strategic move" of accountancy deception to challenge supranational and national neoliberal austerity regimes. This creates an interesting and problematic double-dynamic of contesting austerity while normalizing financial market rationalities.

Technologies: Derivatives and Accounting

While some financial products, such as municipal bonds, have a much longer history, the diversity and scale of their adoption has strongly widened since the late 1990s. While in the US, bonds have traditionally been a means of municipal finance, in the European context their emergence marks a change in the traditionally bank-based financing of the local state.

Municipal bonds are debt securities issued by a municipality or one of its agencies, in order to collect money for investment in large-scale public projects, but sometimes also to balance the budget. The bonds can be supported by the credit and taxing abilities of the municipality (general obligation), or revenues from a public project, for example a water utility (revenue bonds). Munibonds are more than a technical alternative to traditional loans. They create new "bonds" between cities and investors and open up opportunities of financializing the local state. For instance, interests of potential investors might be prioritized over needs of the constituency and cities have to appear attractive to potential investors (Petzold 2014: 47–48). This paves the way for the adoption of financial performance measurements and increases the pressure towards external evaluation by credit rating agencies (Omstedt, 2019). Issuing a municipal bond is also a much more complex process than taking on a loan, as it comes with new administrative costs and often requires the services of additional financial firms. Many city treasurers expect to attract new investors and internalize financial market logics in order to do so. In Europe, the size of subnational governments and their fiscal autonomy plays a role in the adoption of municipal bonds, and as a consequence, federalized countries such as Germany and Spain are leading the market (Vetter et al. 2014). Yet, also in centralized countries, there is a growing interest. In 2014, the UK government established a municipal bond agency with the aim to build a deep and liquid munibond market, and an alternative for loans from a centrally funded Public Works Loan Board (PWLB). Likewise in France in 2013, the Agence France Local was created to increase capital markets' funding for municipalities. In Belgium, smaller municipalities co-operated to issue a bond collectively for the first time in 2013.

Interest rate derivatives constitute another type of financial products that have entered city hall recently. Derivatives are complex financial products that derive their value from the development of underlying products or indicators, for instance commodity prices, interest rates or stock market values. Put bluntly, they are financial markets' solutions to problems often created by the very same financial markets. One particular feature of the derivatives market is that most contracts are agreed on without any third party, over the counter (OTC). Therefore, OTC derivative transactions are in general far less regulated than other financial market activities.

In municipal debt management, interest rate derivatives are used for hedging or optimizing the portfolio by turning floating rate loans into fixed rate loans or vice versa. They add another layer to the original creditor–debtor relation. Often (but not necessarily), derivative and credit are congruent in amount, currency and maturity. After the financial crisis of 2008/9, this became a regulatory requirement in many jurisdictions in order to curb speculation and to contain risk. In general, derivatives introduce more actors, more cash flows and more complexity to an existing credit relation and, often, ironically, even more uncertainty. The most common derivative in municipal debt management is the interest swap that comes in many different forms and degrees of complexity ranging from plain "vanilla" (simple) to "spread-ladder" (complex). Prior to the crisis, a particular form of embedded municipal derivatives had emerged in the UK as reaction to stronger regulation after the famous Hammersmith & Fulham swap disaster in the 1990s (Tickell 1998), namely so-called LOBO loans (Möller 2017). The emergence of this product is particularly remarkable since British local authorities have access to publicly provided loans at rather low rates.

Another technology concerns the accounting system of local governments. How municipalities report on their debt as well as the ratios used by supervising authorities to monitor financial health represent a particular manifestation of NPM, with quantitative performance metrics playing a central role. For example, the European Union's Fiscal Compact of 2012 stipulates new budgeting rules, requiring more details on local governments' debt and translating austerity measurements into concrete ratios. While budgeting systems can be interpreted as a technology to discipline governments, there are also cases in which municipalities do the opposite and "play the books" to circumvent budget constraints, for example when derivatives are used because they do not have to be reported to supervising authorities. The "off-balancing" of municipal debt and investment to governmental "satellites" that do not appear on the local budget is another example for this type of creative budgeting that actually increases the financial and political leeway of municipal governments (Deruytter and Bassens, 2017; Beswick and Penny, 2018).

Finally, devices such as portfolio management software have changed the way public administrators manage public finances and perceive themselves and markets. For instance, banks have designed computer programs for municipal debt management that allow for analyzing the impact of market changes for the entire debt portfolio. Moreover, in a press article about sky-rocketing loans of the city of Essen, denominated in Swiss Franc, the city treasurer was reported to constantly check the foreign currency app on his smartphone displaying in real time the fluctuation of the municipal debt (Hecking 2015). This shows how financialization comes with digitalization and datafication, in the realm of local governments and elsewhere. These technologies – financial products, accounting systems and devices – exemplify elements that are changing the everyday practice of debt management. Having discussed these "mundane" aspects of public management, we now connect them to facilitating market configurations.

Meso-level: Pre- and Post-crisis Market Dynamics

Differentiating between a pre- and post-crisis conjuncture, the period leading up to the crisis (2001–2008) was marked by the globalization of banks, some of whom developed new financial products aimed at local governments in particular. This development is most outspoken in Europe, as until the late 1990s, municipal finance was a fairly closed market: most debt consisted of long-term loans issued by local, regional or house banks (Canuto and Liu 2010). The creation of the Eurozone in 1999 opened the domestic markets and increased competition, leading to an influx of British, American and even Japanese banks, who exported their foreign experience with derivatives and new forms of credit. At that time, the US municipal bond market was already developed to a much deeper extent: US municipalities had started to rely on bonds heavily from the 1980s onwards, with new products, such as revenue bonds, swaps and options, appearing in the 1990s (Peck and Whiteside 2016).

A second factor is the consolidation of the European banking market after 1999, as "home-grown" banks embarked on cross-border mergers and acquisitions, creating a receptive environment for the diffusion of financial products. For example, in the 1990s, Dexia – originally a cooperative bank owned by Belgian municipalities – grew exponentially into an international conglomerate specialized in the financing of governments, merging with Credit Local de France and acquiring amongst others the Spanish Banco Credito Local, the German Rekord Holding and the American Financial Security Assurance (FSA). Dexia would later sell complex derivatives to local governments, some of them turning extremely toxic during the financial crisis (for a notorious example, see the French city of Saint-Etienne). In Germany, the acquisition of Morgan Grenfell (1992) and Bankers Trust (1999) by Deutsche Bank were game changers since new expertise became available for targeting local governments in the following years.

In other cases, takeovers by Anglo-American financial institutions introduced new products and business models, like the Austrian bank BAWAG.PSK that was formerly owned by trade unions and became involved in a highly controversial derivative deal with the city of Linz (Möller 2016). Meanwhile, its competitor Bank Austria was acquired by the Italian UniCredit Group and also became active in the municipal derivatives sector. Furthermore, public or cooperative banks such as the German WestLB and several Raiffeisenbanken engaged in this new market.

Another important pre-crisis market condition was the relatively high interest rate volatility. Financial institutions, sometimes local banks, offered municipalities solutions to manage interest rate fluctuations on long-term debt, as a way to save money. For example, municipalities were convinced to issue floating-rate bonds instead of fixed-rate bonds, and to subsequently turn floating-rate into a "synthetic" fixed-rate by using an interest rate swap (Dodd 2010). This allegedly "prudent" practice of saving money married nicely with calls by NPM-advocates, such as consultancy firms providing public budget management services (e.g. Deloitte, Capita), supposedly to improve on financial ratios. As Hurl (2017: 64) notes, those service firms are engaged in "reducing the normative to the normal" and thereby not only normalizing new practices and management cultures within the state but also its very contraction.

This was accompanied by financial market euphoria among citizens and, to a growing extent, city treasurers, senior level civil servants, and city councilors. The *zeitgeist* had turned against traditional forms of risk-averse public debt administration that increasingly had been perceived as conservative, boring and missed opportunity. If everyone else was benefitting from financial innovation, why should cash-strapped cities not do so as well? This cultural shift is nicely illustrated by the conviction held by many municipal finance officers that not embracing financial innovation would actually constitute an irresponsible handling of taxpayer's money. The financial crisis however exposed that market risks can be hard to manage. When interest rates became extremely volatile between 2008 and 2009, several derivative deals for European municipalities went awry. The German city of Pforzheim, for example, faced a loss of €57 million on a swap agreement with JP Morgan that was meant to mitigate costs of an earlier deal with Deutsche Bank (Hendrikse and Sidaway 2014). As these deals previously had largely remained under the radar of supervising authorities and the broader public, the crisis was also an "eye-opener" on the regulatory, political and academic front.

Following the crisis, market configurations changed in at least two ways. First, with regard to the supply-side of municipal finance, banks became more strictly regulated under the Basel III regime, making long-term loans to municipalities more expensive for banks to hold and less profitable, as interest rates had dropped significantly. In search for new income, banks developed short-term bonds or commercial paper, increasingly used in countries such as Belgium (Gilot 2014), which connect governments and investors directly. Banks, servicing the deal, do not take any debt on their account, but transfer credit risks to investors and earn on fees. Moreover, the banking sector has experienced significant consolidation processes with many players exiting the municipal finance market or vanishing altogether, like WestLB. A series of court proceedings and reputational damages also rendered municipal derivatives less attractive for most banks. In this environment, the first fintech firms emerged with new services, like Loanbox and Finance Active, who offer governments digital tools for portfolio management, information on potential investors and respective platforms for lending customized for public sector clients.

Second, with regard to the demand-side, municipalities' access to financial markets transformed as well. During the crisis, shortages of credit increased the competition between cities to attract funding, while some of the "losers" of the crisis – for example, poorer Belgian municipalities who had invested heavily in Dexia derivatives – were punished for being now less "bankable" (*Le Soir* 2011). In the post-crisis period, the economic recession and austerity measurements made governments consider innovative financial instruments to manage their tightening fiscal revenues. In the UK for example, where cuts in public spending impacted local budgets heavily, Tax Increment Financing (TIF) – already in use in the US – was introduced; allowing municipalities to mobilize future tax revenues to borrow against in the present (Weber 2010; Strickland 2013). In that way, even in the current low-interest rate environment, structured financial products did not disappear from municipal debt management. Once introduced and internalized, debt management instruments and ideologies continue to have a strong impact. In particular, city treasurers are now looking for instruments to safeguard current interest rate levels for the uncertain future and reduce interest payments on existing loans with interest rates that seem far too high given the current market environment. Especially highly indebted municipalities will continue to be open for creative solutions and will be targeted by banks, financial advisors and fintech firms respectively.

Macro-level: New Public Management, State Rescaling and Austerity

To understand the deeper roots and impact of this new debt management on society in the long-term, we connect it to political, social and economic changes on other scales, which contribute to a more systemic regime of financialization. Amongst these changes, the restructuring of the local state can be understood as the precursor of its financialization. Against the background of economic crisis, rising unemployment and public debt, NPM theorists proposed a more "flexible" government, focused on the three Es of public services: economy, efficiency and effectiveness (Hood 1991). NPM reforms introduced private sector management methods to local government including contracting-out, performance management and service orientation (Sanderson 2001; Martin 2002). In the analysis of Rhodes (1996), the entry of third-party actors such as private operators, auditors and arms-length public agencies led to a wider shift from government to governance. After its establishment in the US and the UK, NPM gradually also transformed local government in continental Europe. For example, inspired by private sector standards of performance measurement and financial legibility, governments have been pushed to adopt new ways of budgeting and accounting. In the EU, the European System of Accounts specifies budgetary rules and austerity goals arising from the Fiscal Compact of 2012. As a result, stricter balanced budget ratios and limits to debt exposure are being implemented. This impacts the perception of financial "health" of local governments as well as political decisions regarding investments in public services.

Secondly, there has also been a considerable (yet variegated) process of state rescaling (Brenner 1999). In the wake of globalization and the transformation of the state, political authority has been significantly restructured including the upscaling (centralization and internationalization) and downscaling (decentralization and devolution) of legal powers and material capacities. This has led to a transfer of responsibilities within (and partly above) the state. As a result, local authorities often ended up with more competences but fewer capacities under a tightened regime of supervision and performance management. State restructuring impacts the ability and necessity to turn to financial markets. For example, Lagna (2015) describes how in Italy in the early 2000s fiscal and administrative devolution in conjunction with declining central state transfers were crucial conditions for municipal engagement with derivatives.

Finally, neoliberal policies promoted a fiscal retrenchment of the state. Since the 1980s, austerity is becoming a dominant and increasingly institutionalized policy paradigm, changing the very nature of the state (Streeck 2013). While under Keynesian policies governments relied on revenues through tax in order to invest and stimulate their economy (tax state), stagnating economic returns and deregulation of financial markets incentivized governments to borrow money in order to postpone economic crisises (debt state). More recently, the state takes the form of a consolidation state that radically cuts public expenditures, prioritizing debt repayment and balanced budgets over social policy goals (Streeck 2013). Fiscal retrenchment during the last decades can be witnessed in several countries. In the US, federal cutbacks in local state funding from 1981 onwards were an important driver for municipalities to search for new income through financial means, such as municipal bonds (Peck and Whiteside 2016). In the UK, post-crisis austerity politics evoked large cuts in public services on the local level, with councils increasingly outsourcing government functions in response (Crewe 2016; Froud et al. 2017).

These conditions have put local governments under rising financial pressures, increased competition for funds, and motivated the turn towards debt management in order to realize urgently needed savings. In that sense, the financialization of local governments can be partly considered as an instance of "constraint-driven financialization" (Aalbers et al. 2017: 585), as municipalities use financial innovation in an attempt to cope with economic, political and budgetary constraints. These changes were accompanied by a steady growth of financial markets boosted by deregulation and liberalization policies including the privatization and commercialization of public banks. With this, state-related sectors, such as water or transport companies, have been perceived increasingly as attractive investment opportunities by banks and investment funds (Pike et al., 2019). Consequently, the involvement of the local state in financial markets not only changes in quantitative terms (intensity), but also in regard to quality.

Conclusion

Financialization changes how public administrators and local policy-makers in city hall think, behave, and relate to the financial sector. Traditionally mostly risk-averse and conservative financial administration turned into active debt management, triggering a quantitatively and qualitatively transformed financial market involvement. Rationalities and technologies have normalized this new financial culture, implemented through derivative products and new budgetary systems, and normalized by consultancies and professional associations. While conjunctural market conditions such as interest rate environments underwrote a particular demand for these practices, broader conditions of austerity regimes and changing policy paradigms facilitated an institutional and ideational shift at the local level.

Much can be learned from our cases for other instances of financializing public institutions and for financialization as cultural change. Firstly, financialization often takes the form of a self-reinforcing process. However, it cannot be fully understood without analyzing related but separate dynamics at the meso- and macro-level that pave its way by generating opportunities and constraints that facilitate financialization. Secondly, since financialization is a socially constructed and variegated process, a sociologically informed study can provide enriching insights to existing political economy, economic geography and political science accounts. Business strategies, coalitional dynamics as well as sensemaking and narratives are key to understand why financialization unfolds in a particular manner. Finally, despite efforts of actors with vested interests to present new forms of financial management as a technical and rational change, the entry of financialized cultures in public institutions is a deeply political process since it affects the distribution of power and resources, transforms the character of statehood and legitimizes financialization on a broader scale. Moreover, under financialization, financial market actors emerge as a new constituency of local policymaking, challenging its democratic character and potentially decreasing political leeway (Pagliari and Young, this volume). Still, local state financialization seems to be less prone to contestation and politicization. There have been some examples of contestation from outside local government like the #NoLobo campaign run by Debt Resistance UK or citizen debt audits in Spain, Italy and France (Toussaint et al., this volume). Whether such politicization can set processes of definancialization in motion remains to be seen. Likewise, contestation and frictions within public institutions under financializing pressures merit further academic attention.

Regarding avenues for further research, comparative case studies on municipal debt management can advance our understanding of mechanisms of local state financialization, and transnational links between seemingly local instances of institutional and ideational change. Pushing forward the focus on financialized administrative culture, further studies should aim at mapping and analyzing distinct narratives and discourses around public finance, for story-telling and the promotion of certain ideas appear crucial drivers and stabilizers of financialization. More-over, ethnographic studies could contribute to a more fine-grained understanding of the the ascent of active debt mangement within the state. In order to fully grasp this transformation, however, further research should avoid exclusively focusing on the administrative process in city hall and idiosyncratic context conditions, a shortcoming of much of the previous NPM and local govern-ment scholarship.

A final interesting question for further research concerns the distinction of exogenous and endogenous financialization: Where can we actually locate agency in the process of local state financialization? Is this a top-down process of financial contamination or can we also find instances of active restructuring and experimenting by state actors themselves? Arguably, the latter would constitute an even stronger indication of normalization of financialized culture and raise funda-mental concerns about the reversibility of the rise of financial market logics. As Peck and Whiteside (2016: 242) have argued, "[C]ity governments have become 'active agents' in the process of municipal financialization (...), although hardly under circumstances of their own choosing." These circumstances have been heavily shaped by the central state, international organizations and supra-national policies. After all, the state is both object and agent of financialization (Pike et al. 2019). This intriguing double-character merits much more academic attention, especially if we want to identify potentials for definancialization.

Bibliography

Aalbers, M., Van Loon, J. and Fernandez, R., 2017. The financialization of a social housing provider. *International Journal of Urban and Regional Research*, 41(4), pp. 572–587.

Beswick, J., Penny, J., 2018. Demolishing the present to sell off the future? The emergence of 'financia-lized municipal entrepreneurialism' in London. *International Journal of Urban and Regional Research*, 42(4), pp. 612–632.

Brenner, N., 1999. Globalisation as reterritorialisation: The re-scaling of urban governance in the European Union. *Urban Studies*, 36(3), pp. 431–451.

Canuto, O. and Liu, L., 2010. Subnational debt and the global financial crisis. *World Bank Economic Premise* 12/2010.

Chiapello, E., 2015. Financialisation of valuation. *Human Studies*, 38(1), pp. 13–35.

Crewe, T., 2016. The strange death of municipal England. *London Review of Books*, 38(24), pp. 6–10.

Dodd, R., 2010. Municipal bombs. *Finance & Development*, June, pp. 33–35.

Deruytter, L., and Bassens, D., 2017. The Financialization of the Belgian Local State: Intermunicipal Companies as Shadow Banks. *Paper presented at Annual Meeting of the Association of American Geographers* (Boston, 5–9 April 2017)

Engelen, E., Erturk, I., Froud, J., Leaver, A. and Williams, K., 2010. Reconceptualizing financial innovation: Frame, conjucture and bricolage. *Economy and Society*, 39(1), pp. 33–63.

Fastenrath, F., Orban, A. and Trampusch, C., 2017. From economic gains to social losses. How stories shape expectations in the case of German municipal finance. *MPIfG Discussion Paper* 17/20. Cologne: MPIfG.

Froud, J., Johal, S., Moran, M. and Williams, K., 2017. Outsourcing the state: New sources of elite power. *Theory, Culture & Society*, 34(5–6), pp. 77–101.

Froud, J. and Williams, K., 2007. Private equity and the culture of value extraction. *New Political Economy*, 12(3), pp. 405–420.

Gilot, B., 2014. Gemeenten gaan de kapitaalmarkt op. VVSG, *Lokaal*, June, pp. 8–9.

Hecking, C., 2015. Essen gehört den Banken. *Die Zeit* 04/2015.

Hendrikse, R. and Sidaway, J., 2014. Financial wizardry and the Golden City: Tracking the financial crisis through Pforzheim, Germany. *Transactions*, 39(2), pp. 195–208.

Hood, C., 1991. A public management for all seasons? *Public Administration*, 69(1), pp. 3–19.

Hurl, C., 2017. Operationalizing austerity: The role of transnational professional service firms in local government restructuring. *Innovation: The European Journal of Social Science Research*, 31(1), pp. 55–67.

Lagna, A., 2015. Italian municipalities and the politics of financial derivatives: Rethinking the Foucauldian perspective. *Competition & Change*, 19(4), pp. 283–300.

Le Soir, 2011. Ce que va coûter Dexia à chaque Bruxellois. 17 November 2011.

Livne, R. and Yonay, Y., 2016. Performing neoliberal governmentality: An ethnography of financialized sovereign debt management practices. *Socio-Economic Review*, 14(2), pp. 339–362.

Luby, M.L., 2012. The use of financial derivatives in state and local government bond refinancings: Playing with fire or prudent debt management? *Journal of Public Budgeting, Accounting & Financial Management*, 24(1), pp. 1–31.

Martin, S., 2002. The modernization of UK local government. Markets, managers, monitors and mixed fortunes. *Public Management Review*, 4(3), pp. 291–307.

Möller, S., 2016. When global finance knocks at city hall's door: Derivatives and municipal debt management. Paper presented at Workshop Interdisciplinary Perspectives on Global Finance (Bremen, 21–23 September 2016).

Möller, S., 2017. From Hammersmith to Newham: Austerity, local authority debt & financial markets. *Discover Society*, 47, August.

Omstedt, M., 2019. Reading risk: The practices, limits and politics of municipal bond rating. *Environment and Planning A: Economy and Space*, https://doi.org/10.1177/0308518X19880903

Pacewicz, J., 2013. Tax increment financing, economic development professionals and the financialization of urban politics. *Socio-Economic Review*, 11(3), pp. 413–440.

Peck, J., and Whiteside, H., 2016. Financializing Detroit. *Economic Geography*, 92(3), pp. 235–268.

Petzold, C., 2014. Kommunale Finanzgeschäfte. Die Auswirkung der Finanzialisierung auf die lokale Demokratie. *Forum Humangeographie 11.* Frankfurt: Goethe University.

Pike, A., O'Brien, P., Strickland, T., Thrower, G. and Tomaney, J., 2019. *Financialising City Statecraft and infrastructure*. Cheltenham: Edward Elgar.

Pollitt, C. and Bouckaert, G., 2011. *Public Management Reform: A Comparative Analysis. New Public Management, Governance, and the Neo-Weberian State* (3rd ed.). New York: Oxford University Press.

Preunkert, J., 2017. Financialization of government debt? European government debt management approaches 1980–2007. *Competition & Change*, 21(1), pp. 27–44.

Rhodes, R., 1996. The new governance: Governing without government. *Political Studies*, 44(4), pp. 652–667.

Rutland, T., 2010. The financialization of urban redevelopment. *Geography Compass*, 4(8), pp. 1167–1178.

Sanderson, I., 2001. Performance management, evaluation and learning in modern local government. *Public Administration*, 79(2), pp. 297–313.

Streeck, W., 2013. *Buying Time. The Delayed Crisis of Democratic Capitalism*. London: Verso.

Strickland, T., 2013. The financialisation of urban development: Tax Increment Financing in Newcastle upon Tyne. *Local Economy*, 28(4), pp. 384–398.

Tickell, A., 1998. Creative finance and the local state: The Hammersmith and Fulham swaps affair. *Political Geography*, 17(7), pp. 865–881.

Trampusch, C., 2015. The financialisation of sovereign debt: An institutional analysis of the reforms in German public debt management. *German Politics*, 24(2), pp. 119–319.

Vetter, S., Zipfel, F. and Fritsche, J., 2014. Small is beautiful? Capital market funding for sub-sovereign authorities on the rise. *Deutsche Bank, EU Monitor*.

Weber, R., 2010. Selling city futures: The financialization of urban redevelopment policy. *Economic Geography*, 86(3), pp. 251–274.

Wolf, M., 2018. Ain't misbehaving: Behavioral economics and the making of financial literacy. *Economic Sociology. The European Electronic Newsletter*, 19(2), pp. 10–18.

PART F

Instabilities, Insecurities and the Discontents of Financialization

34

FINANCIALIZATION AND THE INCREASE IN INEQUALITY[1]

Olivier Godechot

Two major evolutions of capitalism marked the two decades preceding the global financial crisis: financialization and a severe increase of inequalities. On the one hand, finance has a growing hold on economic activity, both directly, as shown by near doubling of its share of GDP (moving hence from 5 to 8% in the United States between 1980 and 2007), and indirectly by transforming the management of firms and the savings of households. On the other hand, inequalities in income, wealth and even more wages increased sharply in developed countries, with the top 0.1% of the highest paid workers in the United States tripling their share of wages, from 1.6% in 1980 to 5% in 2007.

The temporal coincidence of these two transformations did not go unnoticed. On the one hand, social movements such as Occupy Wall Street accused finance of being the main vector for increasing inequality. On the other hand, some have also argued that rising inequality was at the root of the 2008 financial crisis: faced with the obvious enrichment of the elite, modest US households reportedly tried to maintain their position by resorting massively to debt. Does this temporal coincidence imply correlation? Does correlation imply causality? And, if there is a causal link between the two trends, what is its direction?

This chapter summarizes recent literature that has studied the link between finance and inequality. It will provide substantial evidence that the growth of financial activity led to more inequality in market societies in recent decades. The most obvious channel is that financial market activity, fuelled by an ongoing process of financial deregulation, created niches with very high wages for some of its professionals. Indeed, in those niches, financiers acquire a "hold-up power" over their firm: they appropriate key assets (knowledge, teams, and clients) and can move them or efficiently threaten to move them to a competitor. This enhanced bargaining power increased the finance wage premium and can already produce on its own a substantial increase in inequality. Other channels, more indirect, also count. The growing submission of non-financial firms to "shareholder value" imperatives increases within-firm inequality. Households' investments in financial securities and, moreover, their growing indebtedness have contrasting effects: the development of credit cards and subprime mortgages enabled lower-income households to access credit. However, this access comes with higher risks of over-indebtedness and higher financial costs than for higher-income households. Finally, it can be seen that inequality conversely contributed (albeit modestly) to financialization, through increased securitization as well as growing indebtedness via "keeping up with the Joneses" mechanisms.

More Finance, More Inequality

Cross-country Evidence

The growth of finance and the growth of inequality are clearly correlated in developed countries. Many studies have documented this phenomenon for OECD countries with various aggregate measures of national inequality and of financial activities, such as volume of stocks traded, bank profitability, and securities under bank assets (Kus 2012), capitalization and financial incomes of non-financial firms (Dünhaupt 2014), credit intermediation and capitalization (Denk and Cournède 2015), capitalization and finance's operating surplus (Flaherty 2015), and size of the FIRE sector and of its labor force (Roberts and Kwon 2017). In my own research (Godechot 2016), which I will summarize below, I offer a systematic comparison of the relative impact of a set of measures of financial activities on a set of measures of inequality. My study focuses on 18 OECD countries for which I have measures of both inequality and financialization.[2]

As dependent variables I used the OECD income inequality decile ratios such as the ratio of the median to the bottom 10% threshold (i.e. D5/D1), the ratio of the top 10% threshold to the bottom 10% threshold (i.e. D9/D1) and the ratio of the top 10% threshold to the median (i.e. D9/D5), and from the World Top Income Database the top 10%, 1%, 0.1% and 0.01% of income shares.[3] The increase in inequality over my sample has been general and obvious from 1980 to 2007: the ratio D9/D1 multiplied by 1.1, moving from 2.9 to 3.2, the top 1% income share multiplied by 1.6, moving from 6.5% to 10.2% and that of the top 0.01% multiplied by 2.7, moving from 0.5% to 1.4%.

As a first proxy, financialization can be measured using the evolution of the share of the financial sector (comprising both finance and insurance) in economic activity (i.e. GDP), as reported in industry national accounts gathered and standardized by the OECD. Three arguments support this approximation. First, the most iconic financial transformations of financialization (like the financial markets boom) occurred precisely in the finance sector. Second, most financial transformations taking place outside the financial sector also translate into financial transactions and therefore contribute to the value added of this sector. Third, the finance and insurance sectors have the advantage of being more precise than the often used "FIRE" sector – finance, real estate and service to business – (Krippner 2005; Flaherty 2015; Roberts and Kwon 2017) which also includes many subsectors unrelated to finance.

Looking across the 18 countries, financialization has no effect on inequality at the bottom of the income hierarchy (i.e. D5/D1 ratio) but it drives inequality at the top: an increase in the share of finance in GDP by one standard deviation increases the top 10% share by 0.12 standard deviation, the top 1% share by 0.23, the top 0.1% share by 0.28 and the top 0.01% share by 0.41. To put this another way, if one focuses on the 1980–2007 sequence of rising inequality, based on my regressions, one can estimate that one fifth of the increase of the incomes of the top 1%, one quarter of that of the top 0.1% and fully two fifths of that of the top 0.01% share can be attributed to the increase in the size of the financial sector (Table 34.1). These first results show that the impact of the size of finance on inequality grows stronger as one moves up the income distribution scale. It increases the income gap between the top and the very top much more than the gap between the middle and the bottom strata.

Generally, other studies (Kus 2012; Dünhaupt 2014; Denk and Cournède 2015; Flaherty 2015; Roberts and Kwon 2017) find similar results. The intensity of the correlation varies with the inequality measure, the variable proxying financialization, and the type of model. Only Huber, Huo and Stephens (2017) claim that they find no impact of financialization when they

Table 34.1 Contribution of Financialization to the 1980–2007 Period of Increasing Inequality in 18 OECD Countries

	1980	2007	Counterfactual 2007 level in the absence of financialization	Contribution of financialization to the increase in inequality
Finance/GDP	4.66	6.59		
D5/D1	1.65	1.66	.	.
D9/D5	1.71	1.89	1.87	15%
D9/D1	2.83	3.17	3.10	20%
Top 10% share	28.96	34.48	33.81	12%
Top 1% share	6.46	10.23	9.47	20%
Top 0.1% share	1.61	3.62	3.07	27%
Top 0.01% share	0.50	1.37	1.01	41%

Note: I use the aforementioned regression parameters to calculate the average evolution of inequality for 18 countries (17 for the top 0.1% and 12 for the top 0.01%) that would have prevailed in the absence of financialization between 1980 and 2007. Between 1980 and 2007, the top 1% share increased from 6.5% of income to 10.2%. If finance's share of GDP had remained constant, the counterfactual share of finance would have been 9.5% according to my model. Financialization therefore accounts for 20% of the evolution of this inequality measure.

introduce the share of finance in the GDP in their regressions modelling the top 1% share. However, they already control for capitalization to GDP, highly significant in all models, which is also a good proxy of financialization.

Growth in financial activity indicators is thus positively tied to growth in income inequality. Can we interpret this correlation causally as the impact of financialization on inequality, or could it be due to reverse causal effect of inequality on financialization? Thanks to "dynamic panel regressions," most aforementioned studies also account for possible reverse causality mechanisms and still find a positive contribution of finance on inequality. Hence, we may conclude that more finance leads to more inequality.

Scholars diverge, however, on the causal mechanism through which financialization impacts inequality. Some insist on the institutional impact of financialization, such as its interaction with the weakening of labor institutions like unions and work councils (Darcillon 2015 and 2016; Flaherty 2015; see also McCarthy in this volume), and their combination with varieties of capitalism. Others highlight the emergence of a new ideological regime, for instance with ideologies of shareholder value (Lazonick and O'Sullivan 2000) having changed the conduct of non-financial firms (Lin and Tomaskovic-Devey 2013; Dünhaupt 2014; see Erturk in this volume). However one of the most robust drivers of inequality, especially when approached with the notion of top income shares, are indicators of stock market activity such as capitalization to GDP (Kus 2012; Dünhaupt 2014), or stock trading volume to GDP (Godechot 2016).

While the institutional factors that a political economy approach pinpoints may also matter, the importance of stock market activity that the statistical relationships above highlighted should lead us to focus on more direct mechanisms. In fact, behind stock market activity, there is a community of financiers that make a living out of it. The financial labor market (Zaloom 2006; Ho 2009; Ortiz 2014; Godechot 2017), with its high wages and its flamboyant bonus culture, is the elephant in the room that many institutional studies ignore.

Isolating the Role of the Financial Labor Market

Micro data on individual income and wages can help to make clearer the link between finance and inequality, simply by enabling to measure the contribution of financial workers to the growth of inequality. Between 1989 and 2006, the average bonus on Wall Street increased 8.9 times, rising from 25,000 dollars to 225,000 dollars (Godechot 2017). In France, the income of the 100 highest paid finance managers increased nine-fold between 1996 and 2007, from 535,000 to 4.7 million euros. Meanwhile the remuneration of the 100 highest paid CEOs increased threefold over the same period (Godechot 2012).

The existence of a financial wage premium is now well documented. Philippon and Reshef (2012) show, controlling for skills, how finance in the United States paid its workers more than other sectors throughout the twentieth century. The wage premium peaked in the early 1930s at 40%, declined to 0% from 1945 to 1980, and increased tremendously reaching +50% in the mid-2000s. Similarly, Denk (2015) finds that the financial wage premium in 2010 averaged at 28% in European countries. Based on US Current Population Survey data, Lin (2015) studies more in depth the heterogeneity of the wage gap and its evolution between finance and other sectors: at the bottom of the wage hierarchy workers in finance were substantially better paid in the 1970s than in other industries but they lost their advantages in the 2000s. Conversely, top earners were not better paid in finance than elsewhere in the 1970s but they widened considerably the gap during the last 30 years. Consequently, the financial wage premium which used to be important for female and minority workers now peaks for white male top earners (Lin and Neely 2017). This confirms, on a larger scale, earlier results from Roth (2006), which compared the wages in finance in the 1990s of males and females coming from the same business school and found that the gender gap amounted to 40%, surpassing the gap in other sectors.

This high wage gap is not without distributional consequences. Decomposition exercises show that 70% of the rise of top 1% wage share in United Kingdom between 1998 and 2008 benefited those working in finance (Bell and Van Reenen 2014). Bakija Cole and Heim (2012) calculated that finance's contribution to the increase in top income shares was of 32% in the United States between 1997 and 2005.

I investigated in detail financiers' contribution to inequality in France thanks to French Social Security DADS (*Déclaration Annuelle de Données Sociales*) dataset (Godechot 2012).[4] Contrary to the view put forward by many social scientists, who generally consider France to be a good example of stability in terms of maintaining lower levels of inequality during the last 30 years – as shown by the declining D9/D1 ratio –, the DADS data show a sharp surge at the very top of the wage distribution in the mid-1990s. Hence, the top 0.1% increased its share of the total wage bill by 0.85 percentage points, moving up from 1.1% in 1996 to 1.95% in 2007. Half of this increase accrued to finance, whereas service to business and other sectors each contributed nearly 23%, and entertainment to 8% of the rise (Figure 34.1). When moving into the top 0.01%, I find that incomes earned in the financial industry made a contribution of 57% to the increase in the share of the working rich. The impact of finance on the increase of the top 1%'s share was also high, with a contribution of around 40%.

The French case (where finance contributes to half of the increase in inequality), which stands between UK (finance contributing to two-thirds) and US (one third), is all the more interesting as it is not in line with classical analysis of French political economy. Here, despite a strong state, coordinating the economy with unions and firms, in a way that is generally viewed as limiting inequality, finance served as a disruptive force challenging the otherwise more equalitarian norms in pay.

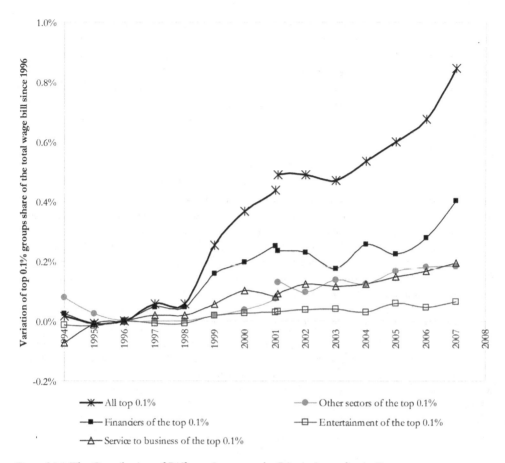

Figure 34.1 The Contribution of Different Sectors to the Rise in Inequality in France

Understanding the Financial Wage Gap

The investigation of the links between finance and national income inequality lead us therefore to isolate the surge in financial wages as one of the main driving mechanisms. This invites us to explore the underlying reasons of such a surge. Several factors, reviewed hereafter, were put forward in order to account for the financial wage gap: deregulation, talent, and hold-ups.

Deregulation

Many researches stress the crucial importance of deregulation. States deliberately promoted financial markets as a means of overcoming the breakdown of the Bretton Woods international monetary order, as well as for addressing the demands of minority or consumerist social movements, and compensating for the growing ineffectiveness of interventionist economic policies and the high cost of welfare state systems (Krippner 2011 for the USA; Lagneau-Ymonet and Riva 2015 for France).

Hence, Philippon and Reshef (2012) found that the financial wage premium was notably higher in the US during two periods of financial deregulation: the interwar period and the last three decades. Consequently, they estimate that deregulation alone explains 23% of the gap. Boustanifar,

Grant and Reshef (2018) confirm a similar result for OECD countries: one standard deviation of their deregulation index increases the wage gap between finance and non-finance by 0.2 to 0.3 standard deviations. Flaherty (2015) shows consequently that financial deregulation also contributed to inequality in OECD countries through an increase in the share of the top 1%.

The mechanisms that drive the positive impact of financial deregulation on inequality still need to be understood. If deregulation leads to more market competition, it should diminish the banks' revenues resulting from a monopolistic position, which would be shared out between workers and shareholders. For instance, the US airline deregulation in the 1980s decreased airline employees' high wages. Moreover, not all forms of financial deregulation go in the same direction. Previous work showed for instance that, in the US, the progressive removal of restrictions on intrastate branching for retail banks in the 1980s diminished bankers' pay by 4% and overall inequality also by 4% (Beck, Levine and Levkov 2010). However, the financial deregulation typical of financialization is more one that enables finance to develop new products and new markets rather than one that enhances competition in existing markets.

Philippon and Reshef (2012) consider here that this type of deregulation ought to enhance workers' creativity in the design of new financial products and intensify employers' competition for this type of "talent." However, in reality the financial sector is far from truly competitive. For instance, Goldstein and Fligstein (2017) discovered that the concentration of the subprime market among very few Mortgage Backed Securities issuers and originators was very high, and that it intensified in the years preceding the financial crisis. The dismantlement of the Glass-Steagall act in the 1990s, and the relaxing of anti-trust regulations did not enhance competition, but on the contrary enabled a growing vertical integration. Financial market deregulation therefore worked to create lucrative financial niches that financial players managed to protect with multiple barriers to entry, such as vertical integration and the increasing complexity of products.

Human Capital

Human capital is a second factor often put forward for explaining increasing inequality. Modern growth is often said to be skill-biased: demand for skills increases faster than the supply of those skills, leading to a growing wage gap between skilled and unskilled workers. This argument has also been made for finance. This sector went through an important revolution in the 1980s, with the mathematization of portfolio management, following the Black and Scholes formula, and its computerization (Coombs and Van der Heide in this volume). This led to the recruitment of very skilled workers (including rocket scientists) coming from mathematics, physics, economics and computer science (Godechot 2001; Zaloom 2006; Ho 2009). Indeed, the share of high-skilled workers in the financial sector increased tremendously (Philippon and Reshef 2012; Boustanifar Grant and Reshef 2018). Célérier and Vallée (2017) try to demonstrate that high wages in finance are only due to "talent" – for which they use the rankings of French engineering schools as a proxy. It is true that the return to "talent" is much higher in Finance than in other sectors. However, they overlook the financial wage premium itself, and the fact that less "talented" workers, according to their proxy measure, still earn much higher wages in the financial sector than more "talented" workers working outside finance. This simple phenomenon remains difficult to reconcile with their suggestion of a "competitive market framework" explaining earnings differentials. The much better careers obtained by students from elite schools who entered the job market during times of financial boom, compared with those who entered during times of financial crisis, also offer quasi-experimental proof of the rent component of financial wages (Oyer 2008).

Superstars

A sophisticated variant of the human capital argument has been proposed with the "superstar" mechanism (Rosen 1981; Gabaix and Landier 2008; Célérier and Vallée 2017). The size of financial activities could multiply the productive impact of talent. Finance is a sector characterized by scalability. If a financial operator can obtain a return on a portfolio that is a fraction higher than that of her colleague, then it is profitable to allocate a larger portfolio to the former, and she can claim additional remuneration from this fraction multiplied by the size of the portfolio she manages. This market theory might well explain local earnings' hierarchies within trading rooms. However, it rests on unrealistic assumptions, such as a perfect matching between "innate" talent hierarchies and portfolio sizes. It also fails to explain the difference of wages between sectors for people of similar talent, without referring to some form of market imperfection.

Hold-up

The concept of "hold-up" was introduced by neo-institutionalist economics in order to characterize post-contractual renegotiation between two actors where one can opportunistically leverage threats of ending the collaboration and consequently devaluating the partner's investments (Klein Crawford and Alchian 1978; Williamson 1985). More than elsewhere, some financial workers, for instance traders, can appropriate the financial firms' key assets, especially the immaterial assets that the firm cannot fully protect, such as human capital (knowledge, know-how, etc.) and social capital (clients, teams). Financiers can move these assets or efficiently threaten to move them to a competitor offering higher wages. Hence, I described how, in a 2001 wage renegotiation, the head of a trading room and his deputy were granted 10 and 7 million euros, respectively, by effectively threatening to move their whole teams, and therefore the core of the firm's financial activity, to a competitor (Godechot 2017). Therefore, the "hold-up" mechanism offers a more realistic explanation for some very high salaries. It differs from the idea of superstars capturing all the gains, by extending the notion of "talent" not only to "innate" talent (or talent acquired during education), but also to "talent" acquired on the job and more generally to all the resources accumulated in the financial enterprise. Employees who can transport profit-making financial activity with them can bargain to receive considerable remuneration.

This hold-up mechanism accounts for the capture and distribution of the income from financial activity and makes it possible to understand why, at "market equilibrium," the remuneration of this sector is higher than elsewhere. It helps to understand how the ordinary functioning of the financial labor market can contribute to global inequality.

Financialization Beyond the Financial Sector

However, finance is not just a specific niche labor market. By organizing the match between financial needs and financial supply, it plays a special role vis-à-vis other institutional sectors such as non-financial firms or households. Providing credit to firms and households, organizing and reorganizing ownership, is not without distributional consequences. Therefore, beyond the labor market of stock exchange professionals, we find also other channels of lesser quantitative importance, through which financialization fuels the increase in inequality.

Financialization of Non-financial Firms

Looking beyond the financial sector itself, non-financial firms have been deeply transformed by the managerial doctrine of shareholder value (Lazonick and O'Sullivan 2000). This doctrine was promoted not so much by shareholders per se but rather by a set of actors working in financial or consulting firms and speaking in the name of shareholders, including corporate raiders in the early 1980s (Heilbron, Verheul and Quak 2014), consultants (Froud et al. 2000), financial analysts (Zuckerman 1999), and institutional investors (Jung and Dobbin 2016; Erturk in this volume). These actors contributed to the "performance" of Jensen and Meckling's (1976) theory of the firm as an organization devoted uniquely to maximize the return to its owners, the shareholders. They implemented, if not all the recommendations, at least those that would match their personal interests in their professional position (Jung and Dobbin 2016).

Among the recommendations, the shareholder value doctrine prioritizes the remuneration of shareholders over all other ways in which corporate earnings could be used, such as for self-financing investment. It also encourages corporations to take on more debt (as a source of financing and as a disciplining mechanism) and argues for incentive plans for executives, often in the form of stock options. It pushes firms to de-diversify, restructure themselves around core activities, and outsource and downsize all activities which are non-central.

In addition to the application of the canon of shareholder value, non-financial companies also have come to devote a significant portion of their activities to financial operations (Krippner 2005; Lin and Tomaskovic-Devey 2013). They thus acquire large portfolios of securities and combine the sale of goods and services with the sale of consumer credit, as, for instance in the case of the automobile industry.

One of the most striking results of financialization is the increase in executive pay, which contradicts the anti-managerialist early spirit of shareholder value (Goldstein 2012). Firms which engage the most in downsizing, merger and acquisitions (Goldstein 2012), or industries relying the most on financial incomes (Lin and Tomaskovic-Devey 2013) pay higher wages to their executives. Firms, especially those owned mostly by institutional investors and where CEOs are highly incentivized to maximize through short-term profit thanks to stock options, also put pressure on the salaries of the middle or of the bottom of the wage hierarchy through downsizing (Jung 2016).

Financialization of Households

Many scholars of financialization have also emphasized changes to households, particularly in how they increasingly engage in financial modes of calculation. The promotion of "popular capitalism" in the 1980s by political leaders like Margaret Thatcher and even more so of households' participation in private pension funds (Montagne 2006) increasingly reoriented household savings towards the purchase of financial securities (Fligstein and Goldstein 2015). Moreover, in a context of low interest rates, banks redeployed their mortgage and consumer credit activity towards the households with the most modest means –including "sub-prime" borrowers– from whom higher interest rates could be charged, at limited risk – as was then thought – thanks to securitization.

Poor households, unlike rich households, cannot access the most lucrative and diversified financial products for their savings (Piketty 2014; see also Gonzalez in this volume). When there is a boom, they often enter the stock or the real estate market later, and suffer relatively more from the following crash (Kus 2012). When they borrow, they do so under very unfavorable conditions and expose themselves to over-indebtedness and the subsequent risk of eviction from their homes. This classic mechanism of cumulative inequality exacerbates an already skewed distribution of wealth (Piketty 2014).

Assessing the specific contribution of the household credit boom to inequality is nevertheless difficult. Easing access to credit has long been a policy for building a more inclusive society, especially in countries where social welfare is underdeveloped (Prasad 2012). In the United

States, in the 1970s, feminist and minority groups mobilized to ban the use of ethnic and gender categories in the scoring methods used by banks in order to grant credits (Krippner 2017). Those mobilizations combined with fragmented retail banks favored the adoption of the Fair and Isaac credit score, which scores people on the basis only of their credit history (Poon 2009).

This new way of setting equivalences changed not so much the level of inequality in access to credit as its structure, and its set of winners and losers (Fourcade and Healy 2013). Banks now assign their customers the average risk profile of persons with a similar credit history instead of assigning the average risk profile of persons with the same ethnic and gender categories. The development of new credit products, especially the subprime loans after the 2000s, probably enabled some parts of the population that had traditionally been excluded from formal loans to gain access to credit and enter the real estate market or start a business, thus diminishing income and wealth inequality at the state level in the United States (Beck, Levine and Levkov 2010). However, with the crisis, many faced very high interest rates, suffered credit repayment incidents and finally lost their house, thus increasing inequality (Fligstein and Rucks-Ahidiana 2015).

We still need a global assessment of the impact of the differences in access to and payments for credit on inequality, combining both pre-crisis and post-crisis periods. OECD cross section data show that mortgage growth is tied to increased gaps between upper-middle class households (the top decile) and the rest of the population. However, this mechanism has little to say about the even greater distortion at the very top of the income hierarchy. Moreover, the contribution of mortgage lending to inequality disappears once we control for stock market activity, suggesting that mortgage lending's impact on inequality in fact results from securitization and the resultant gains for those who earn their incomes working in the financial industry (Godechot 2016).

Does Inequality Cause Financialization?

What about the reverse causality? One obvious effect of growing inequality is the constitution of a class of increasingly wealthy households which, unlike the middle classes, whose wealth is primarily held in real estate, save primarily in the form of financial securities (Piketty 2014). This fuels demand for financial services. The richest households can hire wealth managers who select the most favorable financial arrangements, often located in tax havens, to protect wealth not only from taxation but also from socio-political risks, family disputes and even creditors (Harrington 2016; Alstadsæter, Johannesen and Zucman 2017).

The hypothesis of a reverse effect of inequalities on financialization was formulated mainly to account for the 2008 financial crisis and the strong growth in debt that preceded it. Indebtedness can be viewed as a way of resolving or managing distributional conflicts between rich and poor (Streeck 2014), especially when no redistributive welfare state is ready to step in (Prasad 2012). The suggestion is that modestly situated households, faced with stagnant or even falling incomes, were nevertheless dragged into status competition with richer strata, and reacted to the increase in inequalities by increasing their indebtedness, particularly in relation to real estate. This would have fuelled the household over-indebtedness that ultimately provoked the financial crisis.

This mechanism of "keeping up with the Joneses" has often been formulated theoretically (Kumhof, Rancière and Winant 2015) but empirically often remains unverified (for an exception, see Gonzalez in this volume). Some research confirms it, but also nuances claims about its magnitude. The most unequal urban areas are those where concerns about the quality and size of housing matter most and where debt is growing most strongly (Fligstein, Hastings and Goldstein 2017). But it is above all the upper middle classes (the 80–98% fractiles) that have engaged in such strategies, notably via home equity loans, in order not to be left behind by the real elites (Fligstein and Goldstein 2015); less the working classes, who are confined to subprime loans. Therefore, rising inequalities contributed also to the growth of debt, and consequently to securitization and therefore to financialization, but probably in proportions that remain quite modest.

Conclusion

Financialization and growing inequality are thus linked through multiple channels that fuel a cumulative dynamic. The financial labor market, particularly between 1995 and 2007, is undeniably a main source.

Despite the cumulative and convergent results of recent literature in this area, many questions remain open on the link between finance and inequality. More precision is still needed particularly on the global impact on inequality of non-financial firms' financialization or households' investment in pension funds or increased access to credit. Building bridges with literature on the role of finance in developing countries could also help to measure the threshold where finance starts becoming a curse (see Karwowski in this volume).

Finally, the impact of the 2007–2008 global financial crisis still needs to be assessed. The crisis reduced both the size of the financial sector and the scale of inequality (especially measured as top income shares). Has the finance-inequality link remained unchanged despite the downturn? Or does the resilience of financial wages in times of crisis also prevent any return of inequality to the pre-financial boom levels?

Notes

1 I would like to thank Philip Mader, Natascha van der Zwan and Allison Rovny for their useful comments, advices and corrections which helped me to considerably improve this chapter. Remaining errors and limitations are mine.
2 I used the following countries: Australia, Canada, Denmark, Finland, France, Germany, Ireland, Italy, Japan, the Netherlands, New Zealand, Norway, Portugal, Spain, Sweden, Switzerland, the United Kingdom, and the United States. The top 0.1% share is not defined for Finland, nor is the top 0.01% share for Finland, Ireland, New Zealand or Norway.
3 Cf. http://topincomes.parisschoolofeconomics.eu/
4 Access to the DADS data was obtained through the CASD (*Centre d'Accès Sécurisé aux Données*) dedicated to researchers authorized by the French *Comité du secret statistique*.

Bibliography

Alstadsæter, A., Johannesen, N. and Zucman, G., 2017. *Who Owns the Wealth in Tax Havens? Macro Evidence and Implications for Global Inequality.* NBER Working Paper 23805.
Bakija, J., Cole, A. and Heim, B., 2012. *Jobs and Income Growth of Top Earners and the Causes of Changing Income Inequality: Evidence from US Tax Return Data.* Working Paper. Available at https://tinyurl.com/y9adfeyt [Accessed April 1, 2018].
Beck, T., Levine, R. and Levkov, A., 2010. Big bad banks? The winners and losers from bank deregulation in the United States. *Journal of Finance*, 65(5), pp. 1637–1667.
Bell, B. and Van Reenen, J., 2014. Bankers and their bonuses. *Economic Journal*, 124(574), pp. F1–F21.
Boustanifar, H., Grant, E. and Reshef, A., 2018. Wages and human capital in finance: International evidence, 1970–2011. *Review of Finance*, 22(2), pp. 699–745.
Célérier, C. and Vallée, B., 2017. *Returns to Talent and the Finance Wage Premium*, Working Paper. Available at https://tinyurl.com/y9adfeyt [Accessed April 1, 2018].
Darcillon, T., 2015. How does finance affect labor market institutions? An empirical analysis in 16 OECD countries. *Socio-Economic Review*, 13(3), pp. 477–504.
Darcillon, T., 2016. Do interactions between finance and labour market institutions affect the income distribution? *Labour*, 30(3), pp. 235–257.

Denk, O., 2015. *Financial Sector Pay and Labour Income Inequality: Evidence from Europe*. OECD Economic Department Working Papers n°1225.

Denk, O. and Cournède, B., 2015. *Finance and Income Inequality in OECD Countries*. OECD Economics Department Working Papers n°1224, OECD Publishing.

Dünhaupt, P., 2014. *An Empirical Assessment of the Contribution of Financialization and Corporate Governance to the Rise in Income Inequality*. Working Paper n°41/2014, Institute for International Political Economy Berlin. Available at https://tinyurl.com/ya2uamtk [Accessed April 1, 2018]

Flaherty, E., 2015. Top incomes under finance-driven capitalism, 1990–2010: Power resources and regulatory orders. *Socio-Economic Review*, 13(3): pp. 417–447.

Fligstein, N. and Goldstein, A., 2015. The emergence of a finance culture in American households, 1989–2007. *Socio-Economic Review*, 13(3), pp. 575–601.

Fligstein, N. and Rucks-Ahidiana, Z., 2015. The rich stay richer: The effects on the 2007–2009 financial crisis on household welfare. *Research in the Sociology of Organization*, 28, pp. 155–185.

Fligstein, N., Hastings, O. and Goldstein, A., 2017. Keeping up with the Joneses: How households fared in the era of high income inequality and the housing price bubble, 1999–2007. *Socius*, 3: 2378023117722330.

Fourcade, M. and Healy, K., 2013. Classification situations: Life-chances in the neoliberal era. *Accounting, Organizations and Society*, 38(8), pp. 559–572.

Froud, J., Haslam, C., Johal, S. and Williams, K., 2000. Shareholder value and financialization: Consultancy promises, management moves. *Economy and Society*, 29(1), pp. 80–110.

Gabaix, X. and Landier, A., 2008. Why has CEO pay increased so much? *The Quarterly Journal of Economics*, 123(1), pp. 49–100.

Godechot, O., 2001. *Les traders. Essai de sociologie des marchés financiers*. Paris: La Découverte.

Godechot, O., 2012. Is finance responsible for the rise in wage inequality in France? *Socio-Economic Review*, 10(2), pp. 1–24.

Godechot, O., 2013. Financialization and sociospatial divides. *L'Année sociologique* (English edition), 63(1), pp. 17–50.

Godechot, O., 2016. Financialization is marketization! A study on the respective impact of various dimensions of financialization on the increase in global inequality. *Sociological Science*, 3, pp. 495–519.

Godechot, O., 2017. *Wages, Bonuses and Appropriation of Profit in the Financial Industry*. London: Routledge.

Goldstein, A., 2012. Revenge of the managers: Labor cost-cutting and the paradoxical resurgence of managerialism in the shareholder value era, 1984 to 2001. *American Sociological Review*, 77(2), pp. 268–294.

Goldstein, A. and Fligstein, N., 2017. Financial markets as production markets: The industrial roots of the mortgage meltdown. *Socio-Economic Review*, 15(3), pp. 483–510.

Heilbron, J., Verheul, J. and Quak, S., 2014. The origins and early diffusion of shareholder value in the United States. *Theory and Society*, 43(1), pp. 1–22.

Harrington, B., 2016. *Capital without Borders*. Harvard University Press.

Ho, K., 2009. *Liquidated: An Ethnography of Wall Street*. Duke University Press.

Huber, E., Huo, J. and Stephens, J., 2017. Power, policy, and top income shares. *Socio-Economic Review*, mwx027.

Jensen, M. and Meckling, W., 1976. Theory of the firm: Managerial behavior, agency costs and ownership structure. *Journal of Financial Economics*, 3(4), pp. 305–360.

Jung, J. and Dobbin, F., 2016. Agency theory as prophecy: How boards, analysts, and fund managers perform their roles. *Seattle University Law Review*, 39: 291–320.

Jung, J., 2016. Through the contested terrain: Implementation of downsizing announcements by large US firms, 1984 to 2005. *American Sociological Review*, 81(2), pp. 347–373.

Klein, B., Crawford, R. and Alchian, A., 1978. Vertical integration, appropriable rents, and the competitive contracting process. *The Journal of Law and Economics*, 21(2), pp. 297–326.

Krippner, G., 2005. The financialization of the American economy. *Socio-economic Review*, 3(2), pp. 173–208.

Krippner, G., 2011. *Capitalizing on Crisis*. Cambridge (MA): Harvard University Press.

Krippner, G., 2017. Democracy of credit: Ownership and the politics of credit access in late twentieth-century America. *American Journal of Sociology*, 123(1), pp. 1–47.

Kus, B., 2012. Financialization and income inequality in OECD nations: 1995–2007. *The Economic and Social Review*, 43(4), pp. 477–495.

Kumhof, M., Rancière, R. and Winant, P., 2015. Inequality, leverage, and crises. *American Economic Review*, 105(3), pp. 1217–1245.

Lazonick, W. and O'Sullivan, M., 2000. Maximizing shareholder value: A new ideology for corporate governance. *Economy and Society*, 29(1), pp. 13–35.

Lagneau-Ymonet, P. and Riva, A., 2015. *Histoire de la Bourse*. Paris: La Découverte.

Lin, K.-H. and Tomaskovic-Devey, D., 2013. Financialization and US income inequality, 1970–2008. *American Journal of Sociology*, 118(5), pp. 1284–1329.

Lin, K.-H., 2015. The financial premium in the US labor market: A distributional analysis. *Social Forces*, 94(1), pp. 1–30.

Lin, K.-H. and Neely, M., (2017) Gender, parental status, and the wage premium in finance. *Social Currents*, 4(6), pp. 535–555.

Montagne, S., 2006. *Les fonds de pension: Entre protection sociale et spéculation financière*. Paris: Odile Jacob.

Ortiz, H., 2014. *Valeur financière et vérité: enquête d'anthropologie politique sur l'évaluation des entreprises cotées en bourse*. Paris: Presses de Sciences Po.

Oyer, P., 2008. The making of an investment banker: Stock market shocks, career choice, and lifetime income. *Journal of Finance*, 63(6), pp. 2601–2628.

Prasad, M., 2012. *The Land of Too Much: American Abundance and the Paradox of Poverty*. Cambridge, MA: Harvard University Press.

Poon, M., 2009. From new deal institutions to capital markets: Commercial consumer risk scores and the making of subprime mortgage finance. *Accounting, Organizations and Society*, 34(5), pp. 654–674.

Piketty, T., 2014. *Capital in the XXIst Century*, Cambridge, MA: Harvard University Press.

Philippon, T. and Reshef, A., 2012. Wages and human capital in the US finance industry: 1909–2006. *Quarterly Journal of Economics*, 127(4): pp. 1551–1609.

Roberts, A. and Kwon, R., 2017. Finance, inequality and the varieties of capitalism in post-industrial democracies. *Socio-Economic Review*, 15(3), pp. 511–538.

Rosen, S., 1981. The economics of superstars. *American Economic Review*, 71(5), pp. 845–858.

Roth, L.-M., 2006. *Selling Women Short: Gender and Money on Wall Street*. Princeton, NJ: Princeton University Press.

Streeck, W., 2014. *Buying Time: The Delayed Crisis of Democratic Capitalism*. London: Verso Books.

Williamson, O., 1985. *The Economic Institutions of Capitalism: Firms, Markets, Relational Contracting*. New York: Free Press.

Zaloom, C., 2006. *Out of the Pits: Traders and Technology from Chicago to London*. Chicago, IL: University of Chicago Press.

Zuckerman, E., 1999. The categorical imperative: Securities analysts and the illegitimacy discount. *American Journal of Sociology*, 104(5), pp. 1398–1438.

35

FINANCIALIZATION AND THE CRISIS OF DEMOCRACY

Andreas Nölke

Introduction[1]

The financialization of the world economy poses a major challenge for democratic legitimacy. Given the increased importance and instability of financial markets, democratic decision-making is regularly subjected to considerable pressure due to short-term decision-making, for example, with regard to rescue packages for banks. Such a process leads to a shrinking of the policy space, a shift in decision-making power from elected to non-elected actors, and, finally, to outcomes that are considered inadequate by the electorate at large. These problems, though well known in the public debate after the global financial crisis (GFC) of 2008, have hardly been analyzed in a systematic manner. Moreover, we neither know whether financialization is compatible at all with the perspective of a legitimate and well-working democratic system, nor how we could reduce the problematic aspects of financialization on democratic legitimacy. Similarly, we do not know how political systems should be restructured in order to regain their legitimacy in the face of financialized economies.

This contribution explores the structural influence of financialization – operationalized with respect to the size, network character and complexity of the financial sector – on the character of democracy. It does not ask the reverse causal question, namely the influence of democratic decision-making on the financial system and the expansion of financialization (Krippner 2011; Lipscy 2011). It will also exclude questions about the often problematical "democratization of finance" (financial inclusion), i.e. the increased access of broad societal strata to financial services in both industrialized and developing countries (Ertürk et al. 2008; Krippner 2011; Block 2014; Mader 2018).

Based on the conceptual framework developed by Fritz Scharpf (1999), democracy is defined in this contribution as the participation of citizens in decision-making using democratic processes (input legitimacy) and the opportunity of an effective implementation of these decisions in order to solve important social problems (output legitimacy). The focus of this contribution is on conventional parliamentary democracy at the national level (for finance and democracy on the European level see Mügge 2011) and it assumes national democracy is not severely limited by strong hierarchies between states. It neither addresses radical aspects of democracy, e.g. with regard to the debate around the democratization of economic life through, e.g., co-determination or worker co-operatives (Malleson 2014), nor considers democracy as a weapon to stabilize the economy or to limit the influence of certain economic actors from the financial sector (Weber 2018).

First I will examine the hypothesis that financialization has led to a decrease of both input and output legitimacy in Western democracies. For this purpose, I will identify a number of causal channels on how financialization negatively affects democracy. Based on these results, I will subsequently discuss policy options for political systems and civil society. However, before we can embark on this endeavor we need to clarify what is meant by financialization for the purposes of this contribution, and how the contribution relates to existing research.

Financialization and Democracy: The State of the Debate

The last decade has witnessed the emergence of a comprehensive literature on financialization. In this context, financialization has pointed towards a process of deep structural change within the economies of Western countries and some emerging markets. For the purpose of this contribution financialization will be operationalized using (a) the increasing size of the financial sector and its companies (e.g. share of financial sector profits within total domestic profits, degree of concentration in the financial sector), (b) the increasing density of networks within the sector (e.g. based on the dissolution of restrictions for international capital mobility and (c) its increasing technical complexity (e.g. in terms of the spread of new financial instruments such as derivatives and structured products). Although I will try to disentangle these three aspects of financialization as clearly as possible, they nevertheless feed on each other and are therefore inherently entwined. Moreover, my focus is on the conventional understanding of financialization that has evolved over the last two decades and is widely shared in the literature (see Mader et al. in this volume). It does not include the more recent debate on financialization as money creation though private (shadow) banks and the important role of repo markets (see Braun and Gabor in this volume), although I will return to this topic in the conclusion.

The literature on financialization has demonstrated the influence of the financial sector on very different spheres of society, economy and ecology (Heires and Nölke 2014; van der Zwan 2014). However, only during the last years publications have analyzed the relationship between financialization and democracy. Most of these studies focus on the lobbying activity of the financial sector in the UK and the US and the related political influence of the financial sector (Beetham 2011; Ertürk et al. 2011; Davis and Williams 2017; see Pagliari and Young in this volume). For the UK, e. g., these studies have demonstrated that the City of London developed a "distributional coalition in the financial sector" during the 2000s that has been able to block reforms that would have tried to limit innovations in the sector (Froud et al. 2011: 116). Based on this observation it is claimed that reformers were unable to exercise democratic control over the financial sector, even after the GFC. Similar studies for the US focus on the successful lobbying of the financial industry before and after the crisis, including the support of the financial industry by other societal forces (Hacker and Pierson 2010: 152–204; Johnson and Kwak 2010; Scherrer 2011.)

However, all of these studies lack a sound grounding in theories of democratic legitimacy as well as a comprehensive picture of the potential causal linkages between financialization and limitations of democracy. Although it is intuitively plausible that a high degree of financialization is a challenge for democracy, the specific causal channels have not been discussed in a systematic way. In the following, I will try to address these shortcomings.

How Does Financialization Negatively Affect Democracy?

Over the last centuries, political theory has developed several normative traditions of thinking about democracy. To put it in a very rough and simple way, the most important distinction is between the liberal and the republican traditions (Bellamy 2007), with deliberative theories as a more recent third version. Republican theories, going back to thinkers like Aristotle, highlight the importance of the common good and, following Rousseau, of equal participation in majority choices to attain this common good. Liberal theories, going back to Hobbes and Locke, highlight the importance of the individual and of non-majoritarian institutions that are protecting the rights of the latter, such as constitutional courts (and a system of checks and balances more generally). Deliberative theories of democracy have been developed in the late twentieth century by philosophers such as Rawls and Habermas. They claim that democratic decision-making mainly depends on authentic deliberation, not mainly on voting. In the following I will base my argument on Republican concepts, based on the assumption that most contemporary citizens associate democracy primarily with majority voting and the pursuit of the common good, less with the protection of individual rights or the quality of discourses.

Arguably the most important operationalization of Republican thoughts on contemporary democratic practices has been as developed by Fritz Scharpf (1999, 2003). According to Scharpf, democracy can be operationalized in terms of the concepts of input and output legitimacy. Legitimate democracy according to this concept either requires input *or* output legitimacy, thereby following the two main traditions of Republican thought (input: Rousseau, output: Aristotle). Input legitimacy implies that citizens are central to decision-making using democratic procedures. Output legitimacy is given if governing leads to effective problem-solving in the perspective of the governed. For the purposes of this chapter I will combine both concepts and will speak of legitimate democratic rule – in a slightly modified version of Scharpf's concept – if the decisions made in democratic procedures are *also* implemented. Output legitimacy also implies that the democratically legitimized decision-makers have functional alternatives at their disposal; otherwise, decision-making is meaningless. According to this concept, we can talk of legitimate parliamentary democracy at the national level if democratic procedures on this level are working well *and* national decision-makers enjoy the autonomy (or sovereignty) to implement the decisions that were taken with democratic procedures, and to solve the related problems.

In order to systematically study the causal channels through which financialization negatively effects the input and output legitimacy of Western democracies, we can distinguish between (a) the size of the financial sector and its institutions, (b) its highly networked character and (c) its technical complexity. These three features will structure the subsequent discussion. Generally, we can identify two central and mutually interlinked dynamics in this regard. First, the dominance of financial interests and logics constrains feasible political options on the output side. Second, financialization leads to a shift of decision-making power from elected to non-elected actors on the input side. Moreover, both dynamics share structural and discursive aspects: both the size and the complexity of the financial sector share a clear material basis but are also discursively represented.

The negative repercussions of financialization on democratic legitimacy are fundamentally based on typical features of the financial sector that cannot be found in other economic sectors. The process of financialization further intensifies these specific features. At the core of the program is the fundamental instability of the financial sector in comparison to other economic sectors: "instability [is] written into its DNA" (Engelen 2012: 360–382, 361). On the one hand, this instability is based on the fact that banks (and other financial institutions) are fundamentally fragile institutions due to the possibility of credit defaults and bankruptcies. On the other hand, compared to other economic sectors, financial markets are governed by rather short-term dynamics, particularly in the context of boom and bust cycles. Financialization has increased this traditional problem of the financial sector. Financialization goes hand in hand with credit growth and strongly increased interactions between transnational financial markets. Furthermore, increased securitization makes it difficult to identify non-performing loans. In a crisis situation, banks stop credit provision to other banks, which leads to domino effects triggering a crisis of the whole system, as has become obvious during the Irish case (Kelly 2009: 4).

427

This basic mechanism has been further strengthened through the processes of concentration and an increasing networking process within the financial sectors. Even middle-sized banks are today considered too big to fail, or at least too interconnected to fail (Financial Stability Board 2013). The corresponding expectation of government bail-outs further increases the tendency of banks to undertake increased risks. Furthermore, this problematic mechanism is reinforced through inappropriate public interventions, as a consequence of the complexity of the financial sector and its instruments. In the following, I will take a closer look at the three issues of size, networked character and technical complexity.

The Size of the Financial Sector and its Institutions

The GFC has made more than obvious how the growing size of financial markets is challenging democracy, in particular through substantial financial sector rescue packages. These packages are remarkable in view of their size, but they also pose a tremendous challenge to democratic rule that is supposed to be based on the will of the electorate. Using the argument that "There is no alternative" these rescue packages were very often implemented against the clear majority of public opinion. A typical example is the $ 700 billion funding authorization of the so-called "Troubled Asset Relief Programmes" in the US in October 2008. Although the program clearly had little support in either society or Congress, it was still implemented to prevent the financial crisis from deepening (Scherrer 2011: 219–247).

However, the limitations of democratic decision-making not only became obvious in directly addressing the GFC, but also during subsequent regulatory efforts. Public opinion after the crisis in the US and Europe was clearly in favor of a much stricter regulation of financial markets and in favor of a reduction of its importance for the economy at large. Yet regulations that were enacted fell short of expectations (Admati and Hellwig 2013; Moschella and Tsingou 2013; Helleiner 2014). In particular in countries where the financial sector is associated with a very high contribution to GDP such as the United Kingdom, regulators shied away from a more severe regulation.

The GFC has demonstrated that the size of the financial sector poses a massive challenge for democracy, especially if financial institutions are considered too big to fail. Therefore, rescue operations become unavoidable in the perception of most observers (for a dissenting perspective see Dorn 2015). Banks were rescued despite public opinion, and taxpayers had to bear the expenses for these rescue operations. From such a perspective, "too big to fail" arguments mean that certain policy options are unavailable, or impossible. Thus, the policy space of democratically legitimated institutions is severely constrained (output legitimacy).

The size of the financial sector and of individual institutions can also lead to problems for democracy on the input side. This is particularly relevant where financial institutions are so large that they are able to strongly influence political decision-making to the disadvantage of other actors due to their resources. We do not necessarily have to follow the thesis of a "Wall Street-Treasury Complex" (Bhagwati 1998: 7–11) in order to worry about the role of campaign financing by finance institutions in the US elections, or the general clout of the financial sector in debates about the future of the US economic model (Gilens 2014). Similarly, the lobbying power of the financial sector in Brussels dwarfs those of civil society groups such as Finance Watch (Ford and Philipponnat 2013). According to calculations by Corporate Europe Observatory and Austrian unions, the financial industry tries to influence EU decision-making with five times more entities and seven times more encounters with the EU institutions than NGOs, trade unions and consumer organizations combined (CEO/Arbeiterkammer/ÖBG 2014: 11).

To wrap up, the large size of the financial sector under conditions of financialization negatively affects input legitimacy based on its massive lobbying clout. At the same time, it severely constrains ouput legitimacy because of the (perceived) need to undertake big financial sector rescue packages and because of its importance to GDP, with the latter leading to finance-friendly regulation.

The Networked Character of the Financial Sector

Not only the growing size of the financial sector, but also its increasingly networked character leads to specific problems for democratic legitimacy. These challenges stem from the problems of control of a densely networked financial sector; from the growing risk of contagion spreading through companies within the network; and the specific relocation options for companies within a densely networked financial sector. The networked character of the financial sectors thus depicts two phenomena, on the one side its interconnectedness in daily operations and on the other side its power concentration through interest organization. The first relates to power via the exit option, the second via the voice option, to put it in the classical terminology of Albert O. Hirschman (1970).

In the network of global capital flows between multinational companies, financial sector companies form a particularly dense network center that can be perceived as a "super-entity" of global corporate control and thereby one that limits opportunities for national regulation (Vitali, Glattfelder and Battiston 2011). Similarly, inter-bank trade and high degrees of similarities with regard to investment portfolios contribute to the densely networked character of financial sector companies. This highly networked character adds to the systemic risk of the sector that limits the democratic policy space and may negatively contribute to the assessments of political action (Allen and Gale 2000: 1–33; Jones 2009: 1085–1105; Summer 2013: 277–297). Due to their strongly networked character, financial companies can easily exploit regulatory arbitrage and can threaten to relocate assets and staff, also in comparison to companies in the production sector (Young et al. 2018).

The densely networked character of the financial sector not only limits democratic policy options and therefore output legitimacy; it also contributes to the political weight of the financial sector and, therefore, poses problems for input legitimacy (see Epstein this volume). The dense network of institutions of the financial sector – e.g. in the context of the Institute for International Finance or the G30 – eases considerably the organization of its lobbying power vis-à-vis the regulation of the sector, as can also be seen with respect to the spatial concentration in the City of London (Ertürk et al. 2011). Particularly problematic is the early information access of financial sector experts that very often ensure that regulation proposals in favor of the financial sector are very difficult to modify in later (and more public) phases of the democratic decision-making process (Lall 2015: 125–143).

To conclude, the networked character of the financial sector poses a challenge to output legitimacy because the risk of contagion within the sector on the one side and the easy relocation option on the other severely limit the available policy options. At the same time, the network character also becomes problematic with regard to input legitimacy, since it allows for a much easier organization if compared with other social interests.

Technical Complexity of the Financial Sector

Next to the increased instability of the financial sector, financialization also influences democracies through the increased dominance of financial sector interests and logics in society and politics. Irrespective of the possibility of a collapse of individual firms or the sector as a whole, policy options are increasingly evaluated against the background of financial interests or expectations regarding the behavior of investors (Streeck 2014). At the same time, financial market logics are increasingly applied to a wide range of societal sectors in order to model these sectors according to the preferences of the financial sector (see Erturk in this volume). In the context of an increasing dominance of financial sector logics, only those actors who are able to successfully master financial sector discourses are able to influence political decisions.

With regard to the input side of democratic legitimacy, we can observe important dynamics with regard to the allocation of perceived competence and the related access to decision-making bodies. The structural character of the complexity of the financial sector leads to a deflation of expectations with regard to political and administrative competences, while at the same time inflating the importance of financial sector expertise (Fuchs and Graf 2010). During the last decades there has been an increased presence of representatives of the financial sector in national and international advisory and decision-making bodies (Pauly 1997). The prominent role of former Goldman Sachs employees in subsequent US administrations and European governments is only a minor anecdote in this process. The problem of revolving doors between the financial sector and the supervisory organs of the financial sector is particularly well-known (Baker 2010). While career changes between administration and private sector lobbying are not completely unknown in other economic sectors, this problem is particularly acute in the field of financial markets due to its high technical complexity under conditions of financialization.

Not only does the growing importance of financial sector expertise in modern societies pose a problem for effective political regulation, but also the more specific issue of technical, economic and regulatory complexity of many transactions in the sector (Gaffeo and Tamborini 2011: 79–97; Mayntz 2012: 389–400). Here, the complexity of the financial sector influences the input legitimacy of democracy through the reduction and replacement of decision-making competences. Given that many political regulatory bodies have been discredited by and during the GFC, we are witnessing a delegation of regulation to central banks and an increasing participation of representatives of the financial sector in regulatory advisory and decision-making bodies (Weber 2018; see Thiemann in this volume). This reduces the input legitimacy of the political process to a very large extent. Moreover, regulators very often show a considerable cognitive affinity to the regulated which further decreases the democratic control of the financial sector particularly with regard to output legitimacy as certain policy options are conceived of as being completely impossible (Baker 2010).

At the same time, output legitimacy is negatively affected through the limitation of political and regulatory options. A typical aspect of the process of financialization is the ongoing process of innovation with regard to financial products and trade strategies – on a transnational level – that are very difficult to understand for actors who are not part of the financial system (Engelen et al. 2012). Even leading bank managers are regularly not able to judge the effects of certain transactions and dynamics in their own companies (Beunza and Stark 2012: 383–417; Honegger, Neckel and Magnin 2010). Moreover, financial market actors frequently avoid political regulation by relocating activities into the shadow banking sector. Very often new regulations lead to innovations that contradict the original intentions of the regulators.

To sum up, the technical complexity of the financial sector threatens the input legitimacy of our democratic systems because of the inflated importance of financial sector expertise vis-à-vis political decision-making bodies and the corresponding delegation of regulation from parliaments and ministries to independent central banks. It also poses a limit on the policy options available (output legitimacy) because of the opportunity to avoid regulation though the relocation of activities, for example to the shadow banking-sector.

How Can We Reduce the Impact of Financialization on Democratic Legitimacy?

So far, I have demonstrated that financialization poses a massive problem for democratic legitimacy. What can we do about it? Although we have witnessed a steady stream of reforms of financial regulation after the GFC these reforms have not substantially reduced the degree of financialization. Many observers are sceptical of the ability of these reforms to prevent future financial crises (Admati and Hellwig 2013; Moschella and Tsingou 2013; Helleiner 2014). A fundamental reduction of the degree of financialization of our economies, however, is possible in principle. More importantly, this reduction of financialization would need to address the three issues of size, networked character and technical complexity of the financial sector.

The fundamental rule would be to "downsize and simplify finance" (Engelen et al. 2012). More specifically, we would need to reduce the size of banks through a process of de-concentration as implemented during the process of "*trust-busting*" in the US (Bittlingmayer 1993). The powerful instruments of competition policy would be an important lever in this process. Moreover, it would be necessary to prohibit complex financial instruments or increase their transparency in the sector by forcing transactions through clearing houses such as stock exchanges instead of allowing over-the-counter transactions (Engelen et al. 2012). A third important lever would be to democratize financial market supervision in order to decrease the role of technocrats in the supervision process (ibid.). Finally, we can also tackle the problem of the networked character of the financial sector by implementing firewalls between types of financial market activities (ringfencing), or through a "vaccination" of systemically important institutions through extra strong demands for capitalization (Gaffeo and Tamborini 2011; Admati and Hellwig 2013).

However, in order to implement these kinds of drastic measures without massive capital flight, it would be important to "lock in" financial markets first of all, preferably on the national level. There are good arguments for keeping financial sector regulation on the level of the nation state – not only because of the much higher degree of input legitimacy on the national level, but also because a certain degree of diversity of national financial sector regulations would decrease the danger of herd behavior and the related contagion in case of a financial crisis (Dorn 2015). The most important instrument would be capital controls in order to effectively control cross border capital flows (Block 2014; Pettifor 2018). This was the usual practice in the 1950s to 1970s and still is being practiced, more or less, by large emerging markets such as Brazil, China and India (Dierckx 2015). Finally, financial transaction taxes would be important in order to decrease the volume of transactions in the financial sector as well as to limit the dense networking between financial market actors (Engelen et al. 2012; Block 2014; Pettifor 2018).

A de-financialized economy is not a completely utopian idea. It would not necessarily lead to a drastic reduction in other forms of economic globalization such as the trade in goods (Bhagwati 1998: 7–11). In fact, we have witnessed a period of de-financialization – following an earlier financial market excess – before. In the first three decades after the 1940s a drastic curtailing of (cross-border) financial markets went hand in hand with a drastic reduction in the number of financial crises. During this phase of capitalism, transnational financial movements were reduced due to comprehensive capital controls whereby financial markets served as a support for industrialization – not vice versa. Correspondingly, we can decrease the extent of financialization without necessarily curtailing industrial economic activity.

Andreas Nölke

Why the Democratic Challenge is Not Easily Dissolved

Today, steps towards fundamental de-financialization are politically highly unlikely due to the problems outlined. Because of the powerful limits that financialization poses to both input and output legitimacy, there is a high degree of path dependency. Given the lobbying power of the financial sector or the phenomenon of revolving doors, it is highly unlikely that the above measures will be pursued. Another factor that makes a fundamental de-financialization highly improbable stems from the fact that – particularly in the US – the financing of election campaigns strongly depends on contributions from the financial sector. Massive political lobbying by the financial sector can be witnessed not only in the US. For example, we have seen a comprehensive and so far successful campaign of the financial sector in the United Kingdom in order to highlight the contribution of this sector to the gross national product (Ertürk et. al. 2011). These campaigns are flanked by institutional reforms of the standards by which the gross national product is calculated in a way that maximizes the contribution of the latter sector (Nölke 2014).

Moreover, the financial sector can rely on comprehensive societal support, given that the process of financialization has increasingly made inroads into many sectors of society. Financialization also can be considered as a process of a "democratization of finance" by way of allowing larger sections of society access to credit (e.g. for mortgages) and by the establishment of a mass investment culture (Ertürk et al. 2008: 553–575). In particular the evolution of an ownership society has massively contributed to the deepening of the linkage between the financial sector and society at large. Oppositional movements from civil society with regard to financialization are currently quite weak. The US "Occupy Wall Street" campaign was quite short-lived and the highly competent European NGO Finance Watch is constrained with regard to the critical character of its proposals given that the European Union is by far its most important source of funding (Finance Watch 2017).

Large companies from the production sector also are highly unlikely to form a counter-movement to financialization. On the one hand, these companies mobilize an increasing portion of their profits through financial transactions (Krippner 2011). On the other hand, many of these companies seem to depend on the existence of big global banking corporations in order to operate successfully under conditions of globalization. Actually, financial industry groups are extremely successful in leveraging their influence by tying in their interests with those of other economic sectors that are indirectly affected by the regulation in question (see Pagliari and Young in this volume; Young et al. 2018).

Finally, the increasingly networked character of financial markets under conditions of financialization poses a major problem for its democratic re-regulation. An effective regulation of financial markets on the international level is very unlikely since states have very different interests with regard to this regulation. Particularly the US and the UK will not agree to a thorough regulation of transnational financial flows (e.g. capital controls, transaction tax) because they have focused their economies quite strongly on the management of financialization (Kalinowski 2013: 471–496). Given all of these factors, it does not seem very likely that we can master the democracy problem posed by financialization any time soon.

Conclusion

I have demonstrated that the financialization of capitalism over the last three decades poses a massive challenge for legitimate democratic rule. Arguably, this challenge is way more important for democratic legitimacy than other economic phenomena under globalization. In order to demonstrate this challenge I have focused on the size, the networked character and the technical complexity of the financial sector. Financialization both poses challenges for input and output legitimacy, even if we limit ourthelves to the classical debates on the expansion of the financial sector. Additional challenges for democratic legitimacy are posed by the fact that private banks play a central role with regard to the creation of money, as highlighted by a debate that is just starting to unfold (Sahr 2017; Pettifor 2018; Weber 2018).

An improvement of democratic legitimacy through a decrease in financialization is possible in principle, as demonstrated by the decades after the Second World War, but it is highly unlikely under the current circumstances. This is not only due to possible losses of GDP growth but equally due to the powerful political role of the financial sector that still has the resources and will to prevent any substantial de-financialization. A more realistic perspective towards the re-establishment of democratic control over the financial sector is thus the advent of yet another financial crisis. Whether another crisis would lead to a more democratically legitimate rule, however, is not certain. The advent of another massive crisis could well lead to the establishment of (even) more authoritarian models of capitalism.

Finally, the debate on the relationship between financialization and democracy is not exhausted by the issues raised in this contribution. By focusing on the direct effects of financialization on democracy, I have neglected the indirect effects of financialization on democracy. With regard to the latter, two problematic causal channels can be identified. The first refers to increasing inequality following financialization (Dünhaupt 2013a, b; Lin and Tomaskovic-Devey 2013; Godechot in this volume). The latter is, inter alia, based on the very high wages paid in the financial sector and on the increasing returns on capital that have to be contrasted to the downward pressure on wages in the production sector in an era of shareholder value. Increasing inequality, in turn leads to a decreased electoral participation of negatively affected socio-economic groups and, therefore, to a negative impact on the legitimacy of our current democratic systems (Merkel and Petring 2011: 109–128; Schäfer 2010: 131–156; Streeck and Mertens 2010).

The second causal channel refers to indirect effects of financialization on democracy caused by the GFC and the Eurozone crisis. Arguably, their devastating effects were only possible due to a high degree of financialization (Heires and Nölke 2011; Nölke 2018). Moreover, the GFC as well as the Eurozone crisis have led to a massive loss of trust in our democratic political systems, as exemplified in the rise of right-wing neo-populist parties. More specifically, we can identify two ways in which major economic crises negatively affect democracy. On the macro level, a general degradation of economic circumstances leads to a loss of trust in democracy and its institutions. On the micro level, the personal experience of joblessness leads to a general political alienation (Gangl and Giustozzi 2018). If we add these two causal channels to the ones discussed in this chapter, the challenge that financialization poses for democracy becomes nearly insurmountable.

Note

1 This chapter is a revised version of Nölke 2016. For highly useful comments on a previous version I'm heavily indebted to Daniel Mertens, Natascha van der Zwan and Reijer Hendrikse.

Bibliography

Admati, A. and Hellwig, M., 2013. *The Bankers' New Clothes: What's Wrong with Banking and What to Do about it*. Princeton, NJ: Princeton University Press.

Allen, F. and Gale D., 2000. Financial Contagion. *Journal of Political Economy*, 108(1), pp. 1–33.

Baker, A., 2010. Restraining Regulatory Capture? Anglo-America, Crisis Politics and Trajectories of Change in Global Financial Governance. *International Affairs*, 86(3), pp. 647–663.

Andreas Nölke

Bellamy, R., 2007. *Political Constitutionalism: A Republican Defence of the Constitutionality of Democracy.* Cambridge: Cambridge University Press.

Bhagwati, J., 1998. The Capital Myth: The Difference between Trade in Widgets and Dollars. *Foreign Affairs*, 77(3), pp. 7–11.

Bittlingmayer, G., 1993. The Stock Market and Early Antitrust Enforcement. *Journal of Law and Economics*, 36(1), pp. 1–32.

Beetham, D., 2011. Unelected Oligarchy. Corporate and Financial Dominance in Britain's Democracy. *Democratic Audit*, online publication.

Beunza, D. and Stark, D., 2012. From Dissonance to Resonance: Cognitive Interdependence in Quantitative Finance. *Economy and Society*, 41(3), pp. 383–417.

Block, F., 2014. Democratizing Finance. *Politics & Society*, 42(1), pp. 3–28.

Braun, B., 2018. Central Banking and the Infrastructural Power of Finance: The Case of ECB Support for Repo and Securitisation. *Socio-Economic Review*, online first: https://doi.org/10.1093/ser/mwy008.

CEO/Arbeiterkammer/ÖGB, 2014. *The Fire Power of the Financial Lobby. A Survey of the Size of the Financial Lobby at the EU Level.* Brussels: Corporate Europe Observatory, The Austrian Federal Chamber of Labour and The Austrian Trade Union Federation.

Davis, A. and Williams, K., 2017. Introduction: Elites and Power after Financialization. *Theory, Culture & Society*, 34(5–6), pp.3–26.

Dierckx, S., 2015. *Capital Controls in China, Brazil and India: Towards the End of the Free Movement of Capital as a Global Norm?* PhD dissertation, Ghent: Ghent University.

Dorn, N., 2015. *Democracy and Diversity in Financial Market Regulation.* London and New York: Routledge.

Dünhaupt, P., 2013a. Financialization and Rentier Income Share: Evidence from the USA and Germany. *IMK Working Paper* 2, Düsseldorf: Institut für Makroökonomie und Konjunkturforschung.

Dünhaupt P., 2013b. The Effect of Financialization on Labor's Share of Income. *IPE Working Paper* 17. Berlin: Hochschule für Wirtschaft und Recht.

Engelen, E., Ertürk, I., Froud, J., Johal, S. and Leaver, A., 2012. Misrule of Experts? The Financial Crisis as Elite Debacle. *Economy and Society*, 41(3), pp. 360–382.

Ertürk, I., Froud, J., Johal, S., Leaver, A., Moran, M. and Williams, K., 2011. City State against National Settlement. UK Economic Policy and Politics after the Financial Crisis. *CRESC Working Paper* 101. Manchester: Centre for Research on Socio-Cultural Change.

Ertürk, I., Froud, J., Johal, S., Leaver, A. and Williams, K., 2008. The Democratization of Finance? Promises, Outcomes and Conditions. *Review of International Political Economy*, 14(4), pp. 553–575.

Finance Watch, 2017. Governance & Funding. Available at http://www.finance-watch.org/about-us/governance-and-funding [Last accessed February 3, 2018].

Financial Stability Board, 2013. Update of Group of Global Systemically Important Banks (G-SIBs). https://www.financialstabilityboard.org/publications/r_131111.htm.

Ford, G. and Philipponnat, T., 2013. The Role of Civil Society in Holding Financial Powers Accountable. *Journal of Civil Society*, 9(2), pp. 178–195.

Froud J., Moran, M., Nilsson, A. and Williams, K., 2011. Opportunity Lost: Mystification, Elite Politics and Financial Reform in the UK. *Socialist Register*, 47, pp. 98–119.

Fuchs, D. and Graf, A., 2010. Bridging Methods. Analysing the Discursive Construction of the Financial Crisis and its Political Responses. *Sustainable Governance Discussion Paper* 02. Münster: Westfälische Wilhelms-Universität.

Gabor, D., 2016. The (Impossible) Repo Trinity: The Political Economy of Repo Markets. *Review of International Political Economy*, 23(6), pp. 967–1000.

Gaffeo E. and Tamborini, P., 2011. If the Financial System Is Complex, How Can We Regulate It? *International Journal of Political Economy*, 40(2), pp. 79–97.

Gangl. M. and Giustozzi, C., 2018. The Erosion of Political Trust in the Great Recession. *CORRODE Working Paper* 5. Frankfurt/Main: Goethe University.

Gilens, M., 2014. *Affluence and Influence: Economic Inequality and Political Power in America.* Princeton: Princeton University Press.

Hacker, J.S. and Pierson, P., 2010. Winner-Take-All Politics: Public Policy, Political Organization, and the Precipitous Rise of Top Incomes in the United States. *Politics & Society*, 38, pp. 152–204.

Heires, M. and Nölke, A., 2011. Finanzkrise und Finanzialisierung. In Kessler, O. (ed.). *Die Internationale Politische Ökonomie der Weltfinanzkrise.* Wiesbaden: Springer VS, pp. 37–52.

Heires, M. and Nölke, A. (eds.), 2014. *Politische Ökonomie der Finanzialisierung.* Wiesbaden: Springer.

434

Helleiner, E., 2014. *The Status Quo Crisis: Global Financial Governance after the 2008 Meltdown*. Oxford: Oxford University Press.

Hirschman, A.O., 1970. *Exit, Voice, and Loyalty: Responses to Decline in Firms, Organizations, and States*. Cambridge: Harvard University Press.

Honegger, C., Neckel, S. and Magnin, C. (eds.), 2010. *Strukturierte Verantwortungslosigkeit: Berichte aus der Bankenwelt*. Berlin: Suhrkamp.

Johnson, S. and Kwak, J., 2010. *13 Bankers: The Wall Street Takeover and the Next Financial Meltdown*. New York: Pantheon Books.

Jones, E., 2009. Output Legitimacy and the Global Financial Crisis: Perceptions Matter. *Journal of Common Market Studies*, 47(5), pp. 1085–1105.

Kalinowski, T., 2013. Regulating International Finance and the Diversity of Capitalism. *Socio-Economic Review*, 11(3), pp. 471–496.

Kelly, M., 2009. The Irish Credit Bubble. *Working Paper Series* 09/32. Dublin: University College Dublin Centre for Economic Research.

Koddenbrock, K., 2017. What Money Does: An Inquiry into the Blackbone of Capitalist Political Economy. *MPIfG Discussion Paper* 17–19. Cologne: Max-Planck-Institute for the Study of Societies.

Krippner, G.R., 2011. *Capitalizing on Crisis: The Political Origins of the Rise of Finance*. Cambridge, MA: Harvard University Press.

Lall, R., 2015. Timing as a Source of Regulatory Influence: A Technical Elite Network Analysis of Global Finance. *Regulation & Governance*, 9(1), pp. 125–143.

Lin, K. and Tomaskovic-Devey, D., 2013. Financialization and US Income Inequality, 1970–2008. *American Journal of Sociology*, 118(5), pp. 1284–1329.

Lipscy, P.Y., 2011. *Democracy and Financial Crisis*. Paper Presented at the Annual Meeting of the International Political Economy Society, November 12, 2011 (E-Publication).

Mader, P., 2018. Contesting Financial Inclusion. *Development and Change*, 49(2), pp. 461–483.

Malleson, Tom, 2014. *After Occupy. Economic Democracy for the 21st Century*. Oxford: Oxford University Press.

Mayntz, R., 2012. Die transnationale Ordnung globalisierter Finanzmärkte. Was lehrt uns die Krise? In: Soeffner, H.-G. (ed.), *Transnationale Vergesellschaftungen*, Bd. 1, Wiesbaden: Springer, pp. 389–400.

Merkel, W. and Petring, A., 2011. Partizipation und Inklusion. In *Demokratie in Deutschland*. Berlin: Friedrich Ebert Stiftung.

Merkel, W., 2014. Is Capitalism Compatible with Democracy? *Zeitschrift für Vergleichende Politikwissenschaft*, 8(2), pp. 109–128.

Moschella, M. and Tsingou, E. (eds.), 2013. *Great Expectations, Slow Transformations: Incremental Change in Financial Governance*. Colchester: ECPR Press.

Mügge, D., 2011. Limits of Legitimacy and the Primacy of Politics in Financial Governance. *Review of International Political Economy*, 18(1), pp. 52–74.

Nölke, A., 2014. Politik der Finanzialisierung: Zum Wohlfahrtsbeitrag des Finanzsektors in Rechnungslegungsstandards und volkswirtschaftlicher Gesamtrechnung. In Heires, M. and Nölke, A. (eds.). *Politische Ökonomie der Finanzialisierung*. Wiesbaden: Springer, pp. 79–96.

Nölke, A., 2016. Finanzialisierung als Herausforderung der Demokratie in westlichen Industriegesellschaften. In Brühlmeier, D. and Mastronardi, P. (eds.), *Demokratie in der Krise: Analysen, Prozesse und Perspektiven*. Zurich: Chronos, pp. 107–118.

Nölke, A., 2018. Finanzialisierung und die Entstehung der Eurokrise: Die Perspektive der Vergleichenden Kapitalismusforschung. *KZfSS Kölner Zeitschrift für Soziologie und Sozialpsychologie*, 70(1), pp. 439–459.

Pauly, L., 1997. *Who Elected the Bankers? Surveillance and Control in the World Economy*. Ithaca, NY: Cornell University Press.

Pettifor, A., 2018. *The Production of Money. How to Break the Power of Bankers*. London: Verso.

Sahr, A., 2017. *Keystroke-Kapitalismus: Ungleichheit auf Knopfdruck*. Hamburg: Hamburger Edition.

Scherrer, C., 2011. Reproducing Hegemony: US Finance Capital and the 2008 Crisis. *Critical Policy Studies*, 5(3), pp. 219–247.

Schäfer, A., 2010. Die Folgen sozialer Ungleichheit für die Demokratie in Westeuropa. *Zeitschrift für vergleichende Politikwissenschaft*, 4(1), pp. 131–156.

Scharpf, F.W., 1999. *Governing in Europe: Effective and Democratic?* Oxford: Oxford University Press.

Scharpf, F.W., 2003. Problem-Solving Effectiveness and Democratic Accountability in the EU. *MPIfG Working Paper* 03–01. Cologne: Max-Planck-Institute for the Study of Societies.

Streeck, W., 2014. The Politics of Public Debt. Neoliberalism, Capitalist Development and the Restructuring of the State. *German Economic Review*, 15(1), pp. 143–165.

Streeck, W. and Mertens, D., 2010. Politik im Defizit. Austerität als fiskalpolitisches Regime. *MPIfG Discussion Paper* 10/5. Cologne: Max-Planck-Institute for the Study of Societies.

Summer, M., 2013. Financial Contagion and Network Analysis. *Annual Review of Financial Economics*, 5, pp. 277–297.

Van der Zwan, N., 2014. Making Sense of Financialization. *Socio-Economic Review*, 12(1), pp. 99–129.

Vitali, S., Glattfelder, J.B. and Battiston, S., 2011. The Network of Global Corporate Control. *PloS one*, 6 (10): e25995.

Weber, B., 2018. *Democratizing Money? Debating Legitimacy in Monetary Reform Proposals*. Cambridge: Cambridge University Press.

Young, K., Banerjee, T. and Schwartz, M., 2018. Capital Strikes as a Corporate Political Strategy: The Structural Power of Business in the Obama Era. *Politics & Society*, 46(1), pp. 3–28.

36

THE BANKERS' CLUB AND THE POWER OF FINANCE

Gerald Epstein

Introduction

The world's bankers brought the global financial and economic system to its knees in 2007–2008. Yet reams of new financial regulations passed by governments on several continents and enormous reform efforts by publicly oriented organizations, some politicians and a number of public servants have, so far, barely made a dent in the problem of finance's disproportionate power. In fact, regulators in the US and elsewhere are back-pedaling on financial regulations put in place after the crisis, despite a lack of evidence that financial institutions are any safer.

This failure to make finance safer and more socially useful is all the more striking given the economic and social costs of the Great Financial Crisis of 2007–2008. In a careful, but conservative estimate of the costs to the US, economists from the Federal Reserve Bank of Dallas find that

> The 2007–2009 financial crisis was associated with a huge loss of economic output and financial wealth, psychological and skill atrophy from extended unemployment, an increase in government intervention and other significant costs…We conservatively estimate that 40 to 90 percent of one year's output ($6 trillion to $14 trillion, the equivalent of $50,000 to $120,000 for every U.S. household) was forgone due to the 2007–2009 recession.
>
> *(Atkinson et al. 2013: 1)*

However, even this estimate might be too low since it does not take into account the long run impacts on productivity and production capacity of the US economy (Ball 2014). Andrew Haldane, Chief Economist of the Bank of England, estimated that the global cost of the crisis could be as much as $200 trillion (Haldane 2010).

In this chapter, I explore why it is that finance has remained so powerful despite the great costs it has imposed on society. We might think of this as an aspect of the *"Political Economy of Financialization."* My explanation is that there is a powerful, multi-layered group of political actors that support and defend finance in the political arena. I call this group *The Bankers' Club*. In this chapter, I describe the role of this *club* in the context of the global financial crisis of 2007 and 2008. To be sure, our experience with banks and bankers during these last several decades has mostly been strongly negative. But we know from economic history and the history of

437

economic thought that an economy needs a financial system that works. In the next section, I discuss positives and negatives of finance through the history of economic thought. I return to the potentially positive side of finance in the conclusion, where I discuss ways to reform and restructure finance. Following the next section, on p. 000, I describe the rise of a highly dangerous and destructive form of finance which I call "Roaring Banking." Next, I describe the "Bankers' Club" to explain why the banks have remained so powerful despite the crisis. I end with a brief illustration of the negative impacts that "Roaring Banking" has had on our economies and a brief summary of the argument.

The Role of Finance in History

The financial system has been analyzed as having a Jekyll and Hyde quality: with one face an essential and highly productive part of the economic system; with another face, a source of stagnation, instability, inequality and crisis.

Some giants of economic thought may help bring clarity. A good place to start is with the famous Austrian economist, Josef Schumpeter, a Harvard Professor and prolific writer. Schumpeter is famous for coining the term *creative destruction – now more commonly called "disruption"-* and for praising the key role of the entrepreneur and innovation in forging economic progress (see also Deutschmann in this volume). Schumpeter (1961) argued in his *Theory of Economic Development* that banking was a key sector that provided entrepreneurs with the resources they need to create new businesses, new technologies, new innovations.

Alexander Gerschenkron, another Harvard economic historian, also cited the key importance of finance in the process of economic development. In his famous article "Economic Backwardness in Historical Perspective," published in 1962, Gerschenkron argued that so-called "late developer" countries often needed to use financial institutions, such as investment banks, and government banks, to amass wealth to invest in capital-intensive advanced industrial production so that these countries could leapfrog ahead of their more mature competitors. This framework helped Gerschenkron explain how France and Germany could catch up with the British economy in the late nineteenth and early twentieth centuries (see Beck and Knafo in this volume). Alice Amsden brought Gerschenkron's story up to date in 2001 by showing the key role played by development banks joined with state-led industrial policy in the success stories of the "late, late developers" of the late twentieth century, such as South Korea, Taiwan and China. These economists saw clearly how finance historically could play a key role in supporting economic growth and transformation.

Moving beyond these great economic thinkers, we find arguments for finance in the real world of politics. In the 1960s and 1970s, political activists and housing advocates in the US highlighted the practice of red-lining, which denied minority households mortgages to buy houses in neighborhoods with high proportions of people of color, and they fought for banks to give more credit for home mortgages in these areas: this is another case where banks were seen as needing to play a bigger role, not a smaller one. And globally, there has recently been a push for "financial inclusion" by the World Bank and other institutions to make it easier for farmers and poor urban dwellers in developing countries to have access to efficient payment mechanisms, bank accounts, and micro credit. Again, these advocates want banks to be more involved in communities, not less (Mader 2018).

On the other side, there are plenty of great economists who have written about the dark side of finance. Take Karl Marx. Marx saw the positive moments that finance could play in capitalism in supporting investment and the "accumulation process." But he was also keenly aware of the "Mr. Hyde" face of finance and how the speculators and financiers in nineteenth-century London could create financial bubbles of dizzying heights, which burst and brought the economy to its knees.

John Maynard Keynes, the great British Economist of the 1920s and 1930s, was deeply ambivalent about finance. Like Gerschenkron, he noted the important role of finance in gathering up funds from many sources to invest in the modern industry. At the same time he was an acute analyst of finance's role in bringing about the Great Depression. Keynes wrote in his famous *General Theory*:

> Speculators may do no harm as bubbles on a steady stream of enterprise. But the position is serious when enterprise becomes the bubble on a whirlpool of speculation. When the capital development of a country becomes a by-product of the activities of a casino, the job is likely to be ill-done.
>
> *(Keynes 1936: 142)*

The late James Tobin, Nobel Laureate, macroeconomist from Yale, though a conventional economist in every way, himself became skeptical about the redeeming features of late twentieth-century finance. Tobin wrote:

> I confess to an uneasy Physiocratic suspicion, perhaps unbecoming in an academic, that we are throwing more and more of our resources, including the cream of our youth, into financial activities remote from the production of goods and services, into activities that generate high private rewards disproportionate to their social productivity. I suspect that the immense power of the computer is being harnessed to this paper economy, not to do the same transactions more economically but to balloon the quantity and variety of financial exchanges…I fear that, as Keynes saw even in his day, the advantages of the liquidity and negotiability of financial instruments come at the cost of facilitating nth-degree speculation which is short-sighted and inefficient.
>
> *(Tobin 1987: 14)*

Hyman Minsky, a follower of Keynes, saw even worse possible outcomes. Minsky was an almost forgotten twentieth-century US economist until the great financial crisis of 2008, when John Cassidy of the *New Yorker* reminded readers that we were living a "Minsky Moment." Minsky had been arguing for years that capitalist financial markets inherently cause great financial instability, even though, despite their destructive moments, they remain an essential part of capitalism. And finally, we have the great MIT economic historian Charles Kindleberger who, in his aptly titled book – *Manias, Panics and Crashes* – showed in meticulous detail how, on a global canvas over five centuries, financial crises have been what he called "a hardy perennial."

Reinhart and Rogoff (2010), illustrated this point by showing the percentage of countries in the world that experienced banking crises in a given year. The data show that financial crises happen every seven years or so, except during one period: the long period between the Second World War and 1980, or so, was characterized by relative tranquility. Some economists have called the period from the end of the Second World War until 1980 or so the *Golden Age of Capitalism*, a period of rapid economic growth, relatively widely shared, in the US, Japan, and many countries in Europe.

I want to emphasize this: a key factor is that during this so-called "Golden Age" in the US, Europe and elsewhere, there was very strong financial regulation in place *and* there was a very strong role of the public sector in the organization of finance. Strong financial regulation and public orientation was ushered in by the New Deal reforms in banking such as the Glass-Steagall act in 1933 that separated commercial banking from more speculative investment banking in the US, and after the war in France with the nationalization of banks, and a strong public role in banking in Germany and Italy.

There are two lessons here for our understanding of finance and what we can do about its failings: First, neither the Jekyll nor the Hyde character of finance is always dominant. One face or the other tends to dominate at different times and places depending on, among other factors, the organization and regulation of finance.

Second, for the good face of finance to dominate, there needs to be both strong financial regulation *and* a greater public orientation of finance itself. This public orientation can take many forms: a large sector of cooperative banks, public banks, or even, in some cases, private banks with a strong public mission. But these need to be a significant part of the financial sector, and vibrant and effective enough to counter-balance the Hyde face of finance.

From Boring Banking to Roaring Banking

What kind of financial system did we have in the tranquil period? Why did Jekyll ultimately give way to Hyde in the 1980s?

Boring Banking

Some economists have called the financial system that was dominant during this "Golden Age," "boring banking" (Krugman 2009). They also call it the era of 3–6–3 banking. Bankers paid depositors 3%, lent out the money at 6%, and arrived at the golf course by 3 in the afternoon. It was boring work (but great golf).

In those days, banks and other financial institutions in the US took in savers' deposits and lent them out to businesses to use to make payroll, build factories, invest in innovations and to help families buy houses. Regulations restricted the risks that banks could take, and the interest rates they could charge. But in return, regulations limited what banks could pay to depositors as interest and what they could earn when they lent money. In the US, they also restricted entry by other banks into their markets. Thus, these rules gave banks local monopolies and limited the amount of competition banks had to face: hence, banking was a relatively easy life (D'Arista 1994; Wolfson and Epstein 2013).

Of course not all was perfect in this world of *Boring Banking*. I already mentioned the scourge of red lining of poor and minority communities in the US. Women could not get loans without the co-signing of their husbands. In addition, banks arguably exercised excessive power over important sectors of society, even then (Kotz 1980; Glasberg 1989). Yet this system was not only relatively tranquil; it was one that for a long time contributed significantly to the growth and development of the US economy. Similar systems with similarly working banking institutions, many of them publicly owned, operated in most European countries with similar effects (Eichengreen 2006).

But this could not last forever. Shifts in the underlying economy, including the large inflation associated with the Vietnam War and OPEC oil price increases, disrupted the constraints imposed by the New Deal regulatory structure – including interest rate ceilings – shaking up the edifice of financial regulation. With the rise of inflation came the rise of interest rates in financial markets in order for lenders to protect their "real value" of their loans. Banks, subject to interest rate ceilings, could not raise their rates on borrowed money or on lending. Thus, the "boring" banks started facing stiff competition from other financial institutions that did not have such strong regulations – institutions such as money market funds, investment banks and foreign banks, largely from the UK and some from the European Continent. The biggest boring banks, such as Citibank, spent millions lobbying politicians to allow them to better compete – to pay higher interest rates for deposits, sell new, fancy financial products, hold less capital as a safety cushion and take on more debt. Investment banks, such as Bear Stearns, Lehman and Goldman Sachs also paid top dollar to avoid restrictions on their behavior (Wall Street Watch 2009; Wilmarth 2013).

The list of legislation, regulatory rulings and judicial decisions is long, but adds up to one thing: in response to the break-down of "boring banking," the banks, with help from their "friends," broke through the barriers that had helped keep them on the golf course but also had become fetters on their ability to thrive in the changing economic environment of the 1980s.

Roaring Banking

Starting in the 2000s, big US and European banks began borrowing huge sums of money on the open market and developing and selling all kinds of risky products. Some of these markets and institutions have been called the "shadow banking system" because they are largely unregulated (see Braun and Gabor in this volume). An interesting question is why they became so aggressive and started to take on so much risk. One answer is simply that they could: with financial de-regulation, there were no external authorities restricting their behavior and, in fact, with "too big to fail" status, they could be assured of being bailed out when things went bust. A second important factor is increased competition. In the US, the financial de-regulation in the 1990s and 2000s meant that banks could become more like "Universal Banks" that existed in Europe and elsewhere. Hence, they attempted to engage in all manner of speculative activity in a variety of areas to win market share from European and Japanese banks – and vice versa. Hence, de-regulation and enhanced competition were the keys to "roaring banking" on both sides of the Atlantic.

The move to complex investments, above all in housing funded by short term wholesale borrowing, was especially true of the largest bank holding companies in the US, who were joined by large banks from Europe. By 2006, Goldman Sachs was making almost 75% of its income from housing-related activities; at Bear Stearns, two-thirds of profits came from such activities; for Lehman Brothers the same (Crotty, Epstein and Levina 2010; see also Aalbers in this volume).

For a long period, Roaring Banking was very good for the banks and the bankers. Banks grew in size, in absolute terms as well as relative to the overall economy. By 2007 the amount of financial assets was almost five times the annual production of goods and services in the US economy. Similar and, in some cases, even greater expansions occurred in European economies as well. This growth allowed the banks and other financial institutions to harvest about 40% of all profits generated in the US economy by 2006, and bankers themselves to earn large bonuses. These large payments (profits and bonuses) help explain how Roaring Banking has been a major engine of social inequality in the US and elsewhere (Godechot in this volume).

The Public Reacts and the Bankers' Club Responds

When the financial crisis hit in September/October of 2008, the public reaction was swift and angry. There were loud calls to end roaring banking and to put the "bankers back in their cages." Presidential candidate Barack Obama gave an eloquent and hard hitting speech in March 2008 at Cooper Union in New York. After the election, Congress initiated a process aiming for re-regulation of finance, which culminated in the Dodd-Frank Act.

Meanwhile, the Federal Reserve under the direction of Ben Bernanke, and the Treasury Department, under the direction of Henry Paulson and later Tim Geithner, ignored the pleas to punish the banks, and they bailed out the banks *and* the bankers. By some estimates, the Treasury Department, the Federal Reserve and other Federal agencies bailed out the banks and other financial institutions to the tune of $20 trillion dollars (Wray 2011) .Similar actions were taken in the UK and Europe. The resuscitated bankers fought to severely weaken the Dodd-Frank Financial Reform Act. When President Trump became president, the US government passed legislation to roll back Dodd-Frank. There has also been strong pressure in Europe to weaken regulatory rules. Their success has been astounding, given the costs and misery that the financial system imposed on the economy.

The Bankers' Club

To understand the resilience of Roaring Banking, we have to examine finance's sources of political strength. This multi-layered support system, which I call "The Bankers' Club," has many members, some better known than others, and some even a bit surprising. Many of these members are individually quite powerful; as a group, they have been, so far, virtually unstoppable.[1]

First, of course, are the bankers themselves. They can lobby politicians, using enormous resources compared to those working on the other side, groups such as the Americans for Financial Reform (AFR) or Better Markets, which are public interest groups, or groups like *Finance Watch* in Europe. AFR and Better Markets have a combined budget of only a few million dollars a year. According to the Center for Responsive Politics, the financial industry and its allies have spent more than eight billion dollars a year in campaign contributions and lobbying, on both Republicans and Democrats over the period 1998–2018.[2]

Economists

A group in the Bankers' Club that is not as obvious as the bankers and the lobbyists are economists. These are academic economists who work for Wall Street on the side. Industry-paid "experts" who work in other fields – climate change, pharmaceuticals and medical devices, health and safety issues with respect to foods or drugs (like cigarettes) – have come under scrutiny in recent decades. But only the Great Financial Crisis brought some scrutiny to economists.

Around the same time as the documentary movie *Inside Job* came out (2010) a paper reporting on 19 prominent academic economists who are specialists in finance and working with two prestigious projects proposing financial reform packages showed that 15 worked with private financial institutions, but only two of them even disclosed (occasionally) these affiliations in articles, speeches, interviews and other public media (see Carrick-Hagenbarth and Epstein 2012). Academic economists who have a reputation for expertise and objectivity can misleadingly buttress the claim that finance is efficient, and that regulation should be mild. This problem of potential undisclosed conflicts of interest among some economists is only the tip of the iceberg when it comes to the roles academic financial economists have played as members of the Bankers' Club. More generally, the mainstream of the economics profession that has focused on financial and macroeconomic economics has, for the most part, given pseudo-scientific support to financial de-regulation, which enabled the massive growth and destructive effects of Roaring Banking. For example, economists were responsible for developing and promoting the so-called "efficient markets' hypothesis that was intended to justify the idea that financial markets were "efficient" and not in need of regulation (Crotty 2009; Crotty 2013).

Non-Financial Corporations

Some of the most powerful, and quite surprising, members of the club are corporations that are not banks at all. These are non-financial corporations, like General Electric, Exxon-Mobil, and Ford Motor Company. In the 1930s many major companies that had been hurt by the Great

Depression blamed the banks for their misfortunes and supported Franklin Delano Roosevelt and the New Deal in bringing finance under control through tough regulations, such as the Glass-Steagall Act. After 2008, it is hard to find a non-financial corporate leader that even raises a finger at finance. Why?

One key explanation is the fact that non-financial corporations themselves now earn more and more of their profits from financial transactions, rather than from the old-fashioned way of making and selling products. This is the one of the key ideas of much work on financialization (Krippner 2011). Another additional explanation is that their CEOs and Boards of Directors often make money through stock options and other financial constructs that often bear little connection to the long-run profitability of their companies. Finally, recent evidence such as the "Panama Papers" and the "Paradise Papers" has demonstrated that some CEOs and others affiliated with non-financial corporations, use financial advisors and other financial institutions to help them hide assets and evade taxes (Shaxson 2011; Harrington 2016).

The Federal Reserve

Perhaps the most import member of the Bankers' Club is the Federal Reserve, the US Central Bank. The Federal Reserve was initially largely set up by bankers; bankers sit on the boards of the regional Federal Reserve Banks; the Fed conducts its policies through the financial markets, and so gets to know these markets and the bankers well; and many Fed officials hope to get good jobs in private finance when their stint of public service is done. To be sure, the Federal Reserve is not simply the "lap dog" of finance. The Fed has bigger responsibilities and has to juggle complex demands. For these and other important historical and structural reasons, the Federal Reserve sees the world through finance colored glasses and often sides against regulation in political fights. This became painfully apparent in the run-up to and aftermath of the financial crisis when the Federal Reserve facilitated the de-regulation that enabled the financial crisis, and then bailed out *the bankers* along with the banks. The Fed is highly dependent on the support of big banks to carry out its monetary policy and to protect its power and independence from the elected government (see Braun and Gabor in this volume).

Assorted Other Members of the Bankers' Club

There are assorted other – and surprising – members of the club. In the run-up to the sub-prime crisis, some community groups, perhaps inadvertently, found themselves supporting loose standards on bank lending in order to support "affordable" housing; worker pension funds' managers are powerful members of the club. In short, the wide membership of the Bankers' Club has made it harder than ever to work against the organized power of finance. But, in identifying these Bankers' Club members, we should not lose sight of probably the biggest political weapon on the side of finance: the threat that if we try to regulate banks, or reduce their size, or refuse to bail them out, they will not provide financial services, or jobs, or will move elsewhere. Are these threats true and credible?

Roaring Banking and the Role of Finance in the Economy

How much has "roaring banking" contributed to our economy? To answer this question, I start simply and ask: what are the roles that finance is supposed to play in our economy? Has Roaring Banking done a good job of playing those roles? A typical text-book will list six important functions the financial sector should play in a modern capitalist economy (see for example, Mishkin 2017).

1. *Channel finance to productive investment:* this is the role emphasized by Schumpeter and Gerschenkron but, in the modern world, we can extend this from corporations to include households, for example for home mortgages, student loans and important durable consumption items like automobiles. In the US, between 1950 and 1990, non-financial corporations, such as those in manufacturing, used funds from the financial markets to finance, on average, 12–15% of their capital expenditures on plant and equipment. After 1990, non-financial corporations relied on financial markets to fund less than 5% of their capital expenditures. This same decline is observable in many other rich countries (see de Souza and Epstein 2014). So finance's Schumpeterian role in funding real investment declined significantly during the period of roaring banking. This happened either because non-financial corporations did not need or want funding from financial markets, or because banks decided they would rather do other things. If finance has been getting more income but providing relatively less credit for investment in plant, equipment and job creation in the "real economy," then what has finance been doing? Banks have been lending an increasing share of their credit not to the non-financial economy, but to one another. They lend to each other as part of an elaborate intermediary chain of bets, counter bets, and speculation (Epstein, Montecino and Levina 2015). The other target was real estate.

2. *Provide efficient mechanisms for families to save for retirement. This includes business sponsored pension funds and personal savings mechanisms.* John C. Bogle, former Chair of Vanguard Investment funds – a highly respected, if not totally neutral, source – argues (and many other experts agree) that the asset management industry by and large over-charges for its services, charging high fees while delivering mediocre returns, compared with simple investment strategies of buying a diversified portfolio and holding onto it for the long term. To illustrate this point, Bogle compared the costs and net returns of actively managed funds – these are funds where investment managers actively pick the stocks and bonds – with index funds, which track a broad basket of stocks, like the S&P 500. The fees paid for actively managed investment funds mostly represent the incomes to those managing the funds. Bogle showed that these costs mean that returns from actively managed funds are more than two percentage points lower than those on index funds. This difference adds up to real money over time. For example, an initial investment of $15,000 held for 40 years at a standard interest rate, will have generated $80,000 more in an index fund compared with a typical actively managed fund. By this measure, roaring banking has done a good job of generating fees for the financial industry, but not so much for households trying to save for retirement (Bogle 2014).

Moreover, this "overcharging" for financial services is not only confined to the asset management industry. It is found in insurance, bank services, and in private equity and hedge funds buying, selling, managing, and sometimes tearing down corporations. There is another lens through which we can look at the impact of roaring banking on the ability of families to save. Most US families' main asset is their home. We saw earlier in this chapter the devastating impact the crisis had on the wealth of many Americans, and especially of Hispanics and African Americans whose wealth was concentrated in their houses (see also Predmore in this volume). The financial system did not help these people and communities save for the future.

3. *Help businesses and households reduce risk. This includes providing house insurance, life insurance, car insurance, and disability insurance.* Some insurance markets work reasonably well, such as car insurance or house insurance, even though they might not always be fairly priced. But Roaring Banking produced new financial products such as credit default swaps (CDS) ostensibly as insurance mechanisms for reducing the overall financial risk in the economy. CDS were supposed to insure banks, pension funds and other financial institutions, which invested in risky mortgage products against the risk that these would drop substantially in value. Instead, these derivatives were bought and sold on secondary markets and themselves became objects of

speculation and generated even more risk and helped spread it to many corners of the financial system.

There were two fundamental flaws in the theory and execution of these products: First, the designers thought that by spreading and insuring risk, risk itself would evaporate or disappear. Second, an important reason why this risk did not just disappear is that these products led bankers to take on more risk, and the products themselves became objects of gambling and speculation. In the end, all this risk did go somewhere: back to the government and taxpayers, who bailed out the banks in 2008–2009.

4. Provide stable and flexible liquidity, so that families and businesses can make investments, but when they need the cash, they can easily and readily sell these assets for cash; and *5. Provide an efficient payment mechanism so that businesses and individuals can buy and sell things easily and at low transaction costs.* "Liquidity" is a slippery concept that economists define in various ways, or often do without a definition of. It basically means the ability to trade (sell) an asset quickly, at low cost, and with little to no loss of value. Money, by definition, is highly liquid. But in financial markets, other assets are also highly liquid, including short term US government securities, like Treasury Bills. Quantitatively speaking, the private banking provision of liquidity is far more important than the Fed's regulation of the money supply. Similarly, the Fed and the private banking system jointly manage the payment system, which allows people to buy goods and services, pay debts and buy and sell financial assets like stocks and bonds.

Has Roaring Banking done a good job of providing liquidity and managing the payments system? The answer is a pretty clear "no" on both counts. Take liquidity first: in the run-up to the financial crisis, the big investment and commercial banks, and mortgage companies provided excessive amounts of liquidity to the housing market, driving up a housing bubble which crashed. When the crash came, these same banks withdrew liquidity, refusing to roll over debts and refusing to provide liquidity to stressed home-owners, forcing financial institutions to sell their assets into a declining market, and driving prices down further. As the panic deepened, the payments mechanism itself began to freeze. Banks around the world did not know which banks were solvent and which were about to go under. The Federal Reserve and other central banks around the world had to massively intervene simply to keep payments for products, salaries, and loans flowing. So, Roaring Banking first fed the bubble and then starved the panicked market, forcing the Federal Reserve to bail out the financial system.

6. Financial innovation: develop new products and processes to make all these activities better, cheaper and more readily available. Financial innovation creates new processes that allow the banks to provide more and better services more cheaply. One of the biggest arguments by the Bankers' Club against regulators and critics is that tough regulation will stifle financial innovation. This was the message that global bankers delivered loudly and clearly to former Federal Reserve Chairman Paul Volcker, who had proposed tougher regulations on risky trading by banks. According to the *Times* of London, at a meeting in London in late 2009, a clearly irritated Mr Volcker said "the biggest innovation you've come up with over the past 20 years has been the ATM machine." He noted that the financial services industry had increased its share of income, but asked: "Is this a reflection of your financial innovation, or just a reflection of what you're paid?" He also said, "I wish someone would give me just one piece of neutral evidence that financial innovation leads to more economic growth!" (*The Times* 2009).

In fact, the key conclusion of a lengthy, comprehensive survey of empirical studies by the American Economic Association's *Journal of Economic Literature* in 2004 found that there is no hard empirical evidence that more financial innovation leads to more economic growth (Frame and White 2004). In a separate study, my colleague James Crotty and I looked at more micro-level studies of financial innovation and found that, at the minimum, 40% of these "innovations" were designed at least in part to avoid taxes and avoid regulations, rather than provide new products or reduce transaction costs or enhance efficiency (Epstein and Crotty 2013).

Conclusion

Since 1980 or so, the financial sector in the US (and elsewhere) has grown out of proportion and taken a growing share of profits and national income. But the services it has provided to the economy and society do not appear to justify this. Using the standard textbook list of the appropriate functions of finance in the economy, it is clear that US banks and other financial institutions since the 1980s have not been effective, and have furthermore acted in destructive ways. Much the same is true of banks and financial institutions in other countries.

Notes

1 There is a wealth of literature on business influence on government and regulatory agencies. Much of this goes under the name of "capture". For a very useful survey of some of this literature, see Carpenter and Moss (2014). In terms of banking specifically in the US, see, for example, Wilmarth 2013.
2 Center for Responsive Politics, OpenSecrets.com. https://www.opensecrets.org/lobby/indus.php?id=F, accessed March 31, 2019.

Bibliography

Atkinson, T., Luttrell, D. and Rosenblum, H., 2013. How Bad Was It? The Costs and Consequences of the 2007-09 Financial Crisis. *Federal Reserve Bank of Dallas, Staff Papers*, No. 20. July.
Ball, L.M., 2014. Long-Term Damage from the Great Recession in OECD Countries. *NBER Working Paper*, 20185, May.
Bettermarkets.com, 2012. [online] Available at https://bettermarkets.com/sites/default/files/Cost%20of%20the%20Crisis%20Fact%20Sheet.pdf [Accessed March 31, 2019].
Bogle, J., 2014. The Arithmetic of "All-In" Investment Expenses. *Financial Analysts Journal*, 70(1), pp.13–21.
Carrick-Hagenbarth, J. and Epstein, G., 2012. Dangerous Interconnectedness: Economists' Conflicts of Interest, Ideology and Financial Crisis. *Cambridge Journal of Economics*, 36(1), pp.43–63.
Carpenter, D. and Moss, D., 2014. *Preventing Regulatory Capture*. New York: Cambridge University Press.
Center for Responsive Politics, OpenSecrets.comhttps://www.opensecrets.org/lobby/indus.php?id=F [Accessed March 31, 2019].
Crotty, J., 2009. Structural Causes of the Global Financial Crisis: A Critical Assessment of the "New Financial Architecture". *Cambridge Journal of Economics*, 33(4), pp.563–580.
Crotty, J., 2013. The Realism of Assumptions Does Matter. In G.A. Epstein and M.H. Wolfson (eds.), *The Handbook of the Political Economy of Financial Crises*. New York: Oxford University Press, pp. 133–158.
Crotty, J., Epstein, G., and Levina, I., 2010. Proprietary Trading is a Bigger Deal than Many Bankers and Pundits Claim. *Economists' Committee for Stable, Accountable, Fair and Efficient Financial Reform Policy Brief* No. 20.
D'Arista, J., 1994. *The Evolution of U.S. Finance: Restructuring Institutions and Markets*. Armonk, New York: M.E. Sharpe.
de Souza, J. and Epstein, G., 2014. Sectoral Net Lending in Six Financial Centers. *PERI Working Paper* No. 346.
Eichengreen, B., 2006. *The European Economy since 1945: Coordinated Capitalism and Beyond*. Princeton, NJ: Princeton University Press.
Epstein, G. and Crotty, J., 2013. How Big is Too Big? On the Social Efficiency of the Financial Sector in the United States. In R. Pollin and J. Wicks-Lim (eds.), *Capitalism on Trial: Explorations in the Tradition of Thomas Weisskopf*. Northampton: Edward Elgar Press, pp. 293–310.
Epstein, G., Montecino, J. and Levina, I., 2015. Long Term Trends in Intra-Financial Sector Lending in the United States, 1950–2012. *Eastern Economic Journal*. Published online, February 23, 2015.
Frame, S. and White, L., 2004. Empirical Studies of Financial Innovation: Lots of Talk, Little Action? *Journal of Economic Literature*, 42(1), pp. 116–144.

Gerschenkron, A., 1962. *Economic Backwardness in Historical Perspective*. Cambridge, MA: Balknap/Harvard University Press.

Glasberg, D., 1989. *The Power of Collective Purse Strings: The Effects of Bank Hegemony on Corporations and the State*. Berkeley: University of California Press.

Haldane, A., 2010. The $100 Billion Question [online]. Bis.org. Available at https://www.bis.org/review/r100406d.pdf [Accessed March 31, 2019].

Harrington, B., 2016. *Capital Without Borders: Wealth Managers and the One Percent*. Harvard University Press.

Jarsulic, M., 2010. *Anatomy of a Financial Crisis*. New York: Palgrave MacMillan.

Keynes, J., 1936. *The General Theory of Employment, Interest and Money*. New York: Harcourt Brace Jovanovic.

Kindleberger, C., 1998. *Manias, Panics and Crashes: A History of Financial Crises*. New York: Basic Books.

Kotz, D., 1980. *Bank Control of Large Corporations in the United States*. Berkeley: University of California Press.

Krippner, G., 2011. *Capitalizing on Crisis: The Political Origins of the Rise of Finance*. Cambridge, MA: Harvard University Press.

Krugman, P., 2009. *Opinion | Making Banking Boring* [online]. Nytimes.com. Available at https://www.nytimes.com/2009/04/10/opinion/10krugman.html [Accessed March 31, 2019].

Mader, P., 2018. Contesting Financial Inclusion. *Development and Change, 49*(2), pp. 461–483.

Mishkin, F., 2017. *The Economics of Money, Banking, and Financial Markets*. 17th ed. Boston: Addison Wesley.

Reinhart, C. and Rogoff, K., 2010. *This Time is Different*. Princeton, NJ: Princeton University Press.

Schumpeter, J., 1961. *The Theory of Economic Development: An Inquiry into Profits, Capital, Credit, Interest and the Business Cycle*. New York: Oxford University Press.

Shaxson, N., 2011. *Treasure Islands: Uncovering the Damage of Offshore Banking and Tax Havens*. New York: St. Martin's Press.

The Times, 2009. "Wake Up, Gentlemen", World's Top Bankers Warned by Former Fed Chairman Volcker," December 9. http://business.timesonline.co.uk/tol/business/industry_sectors/banking_and_finance/article6949387.ece

Tobin, J., 1987. On the Efficiency of the Financial Sector. In P. Jackson (ed.), *Policies for Prosperity; Essays in a Keynesian Mode*. Cambridge, MA: MIT Press.

Wall Street Watch. 2009. "Sold-Out": How Wall Street and Washington Betrayed America. www.wallstreetwatch.org

Wilmarth, A., 2013. Turning a Blind Eye: Why Washington Keeps Giving in to Wall Street. *University of Cincinnati Law Review*, 81(4).

Wolfson, M. and Epstein, G., 2013. *The Handbook of the Political Economy of Financial Crises*. Oxford: Oxford University Press.

Wray, R., 2011. *$29 Trillion: A Detailed Look at the Fed's Bailout of the Financial System* [online]. Levyinstitute.org. Available at http://www.levyinstitute.org/pubs/op_23.pdf [Accessed March 31, 2019].

37

FINANCIALIZATION, SPECULATION AND INSTABILITY

Sunanda Sen

Introduction

Instabilities and inequities, as can be related to the widening spread of financialization in different parts of the world economy, make it relevant to further analyse the origin and implications of the related changes brought in by financialization. The all-encompassing nature of a financialized economy, as described in this volume, is marked by the prevalence of financial assets which offer returns at levels higher than those on similar assets which are backed by real activities. While linked to the risks as perceived, the higher returns on investments in those assets provide an impetus to agents in markets to hold them as a greater proportion of their respective portfolios.

The first section of this chapter outlines the theoretical principles in mainstream economics which have been guiding the official policy prescriptions that are conducive to financialization as well as the resulting micro-level investment strategies. It contrasts assumptions of rationality and calculability with the Keynes–Minsky school of thought that highlights the uncertainty of the future and irrationality of financial markets. The second section examines two particular instances of the greater uncertainty and irrationality of financial markets under financialization, with reference to corporate investments and speculation in commodity markets, in advanced economies as well as emerging economies. The results have been economic stagnation and accumulating instabilities. A brief conclusion reiterates the need to understand financialization as a global driver of instability and uncertainty and the need for policies to hem in deregulated financial markets.

Mainstream Economics and the Question of Rationality versus Uncertainty

Tracing back the origin of financialization, one needs to pay attention to the deregulation of financial markets in different parts of the global economy which started off during the mid-1970s. The added degree of uncertainty, in the new climate of deregulation, contributed much to generate additional risks in the conduct of business in markets. Uncertainty-related risks in deregulated markets generated the need for instruments to manage the unknown prospects related to financial assets. Such situations led to the invention of hedging instruments in the market as covers against enhanced risks. Financial instruments, innovated as derivatives, consisted of forwards, futures, options, swaps, and the likes. All of those were contracted on the basis of what is described as the "underlying," which relied on such financial assets as are originally backed by physical assets, currency, commodities, or even real estates. Instruments as above, clubbed with financial assets which are *not* backed by physical assets, constitute the essential components of the financialization process (examples of financial assets mentioned above include those transacted in the secondary stock markets). Risk-adjusted returns on those financial assets have been usually higher than those backed by physical assets. We recall here that deregulation of the financial markets has generally been responsible for the relatively higher rates of returns on financial assets as compared to those backed up by real assets. With the spread of financialization, there has also emerged in the market professional agents who manage risks to sustain and maximize returns in the face of uncertainty. However, as critics point out, such strategies which try to balance risks with returns do not necessarily materialize.

Investments in both the hedging instruments and in the financial assets transacted in the secondary market tend to rely on the principles underlying mainstream economics which guide investment decisions. The theoretical frame which underlies such prescriptions assumes "rational choice" on the part of economic agents, thus *ruling out uncertainty* in the decision-making process. Agents operating in markets are assumed to rely on an ergodic probability function, in terms of which the future is intractably linked to the past and weights attributed to past events continue to determine the probabilities of outcomes in future (Sen 2018). An essential aspect of models, as above, is the strict assumption that all agents in markets are able to *calculate* probability, which rules out uncertainty. Conclusions derived from such a framework obviously do not stand up to scrutiny to guide investment decisions in the real world as long the latter is assumed to be bereft of uncertainty. Contrary to what is postulated in the rational expectations approach (which underlies the mainstream doctrines advocating financial deregulation), capital markets hardly serve as an informational/signalling agency in the economy (Shackle 1974, cited in Sen 2003: 25). Thus, operating in the free financial markets and relying on instruments like derivatives does not necessarily contribute to efficiency in the financial sector or to material growth in the real economy.

It may be recalled here that the multiplicity of financial investments relying on derivatives, while originating from the same base in terms of specific spheres of real activities (or "underlying" activities), do not expand the base itself. Instead, these amount to a piling up of claims which in turn are linked to the same set of real assets. In terms of the standard convention related to national accounts, capital gains/losses are reckoned as pure transfers which are not included in GDP computations. Finance in its gyration under financialization thus becomes increasingly remote from the real economy; in the meantime, financial innovations and financial assets proliferate within the economy, to hedge and insulate financial assets in the presence of uncertainty.

Limitations of mainstream formulations in framing investment decisions have been evident in the frequent failures of the financialized strategies in achieving their targeted goals of maximizing returns and minimizing risks. Instead, there have been recurrent financial crises which have shaken the basis of the deregulated financial system. A classic example indicating the failures of the financialization process is the subprime crisis of 2008 in the US economy and the effects it had on the world economy as a whole.

Questions have been raised in the literature on the methodology behind mainstream investment decisions, especially on grounds of the limiting assumptions which include the ergodic notion of probability subject to a normal distribution function. It may be mentioned here that the possibility of numerical calculation of probabilities had been subject to criticisms much earlier by Keynes (1921). Attacking the utilitarian and cardinal (or statistical) notions in the frequency theories of probability, Keynes deviated from such quantitative estimations. Instead, the probability

449

relations, as defined in Keynes's *Treatise*, rather spelt out the "*degree*" of belief related to actual observations relying on knowledge (Bateman and Davis 1991).

Keynes's take in the *Treatise* on objective observations was subsequently replaced by Keynes himself with subjective faculties, largely under the influence of Frank Ramsay, a contemporary philosopher-mathematician. With this, decision making by individuals was described in the General Theory (Keynes 1936) as guided by "animal spirits," or a subjective faculty on part of individuals having a "spontaneous urge for actions"; and this was despite the fact that knowledge is never complete about "uncertain" events (Keynes 1937).

Uncertainty-related notions of probability have been further advanced in the post-Keynesian literature as "fundamental uncertainty" which relates to "the un-knowability of the future" (Dunn 2008: 8). As it has been observed, the reason lies in the fact that economic outcomes related to the future may be changed by the current actions on part of individuals, groups and/or governments themselves, with outcomes often out of sight on the part of those responsible for such changes (Davidson 2003; Scazzieri 2011).

Such interpretations of uncertainty and probability relations in a changing world fit in well with Keynes' famous observation "About these matters there is no scientific basis on which to form any calculable probability whatever. We simply do not know" (Keynes 1937: 235–236). It is also relevant in this context that investment decisions by individual agents, influenced by the prevailing business sentiments in the market, are considerably shaped by actions on the part of *others* who operate in a similar manner in the market. The pattern is akin to Keynes' metaphor of a "beauty contest," where opinions are formed on the basis of what other (judges) consider to be most beautiful. Neither rational judgements, nor the probability calculations, as in the prescribed models of investment decisions, are thus tenable in situations as above.

Financialization, Instability and Stagnation

Investment strategies under financialization are subject to strong preferences in markets for short-term financial assets which offer high returns as compensation against the risks. Those assets, however, often fail to achieve the targeted goals. An explanation can be found in the limitations of the investment strategy in terms of the ergodic notion of probability and its numerical assessments as discussed in the previous section. As for the current manifestations of financialization in markets, investment strategies continue to ignore the critiques of the mainstream forecasting models on probability calculations, with much of current-day business practices continuing to rely on models based on a predicted normal distribution function of probability.

With businesses always subject to uncertainties and with hedging devices failing to ensure steady returns on financial assets, it is normal to expect instability in the investment climate generated under financialization. In addition, with speculation providing incentives to hold short-term financial assets, which offer prospects of capital gains as well as higher returns, tendencies are naturally there on the part of agents in the market to allocate a smaller proportion of their portfolio as investments on assets backed by real activities. This clearly signifies possibilities of an impending stagnation to come about in business and tendencies of instabilities therein. A drop in the growth rate, as comes about, would have a negative impact on wages and employment as well.

Financialization helps to raise the share of financial assets in portfolios held by agents in markets. This is because, as pointed out earlier, deregulation usually makes financial assets relatively attractive, with offers of better returns as well as of potential capital gains. As a consequence, financialization is bound to provide incentives to various agents in markets to invest more on financial assets, with a resulting rise in their share relative to the remaining assets in portfolios.

Corporate Behavior

Looking at the related literature in the context of both advanced and the emerging economies one comes across attempts to analyse corporate behavior under financialization (Crotty 1990; Stockhammer 2005–2006; Hein 2012; Sen and Dasgupta 2018). Corporates, while following their primary target of maximizing shareholder value by investing in high-risk short-term financial assets, also pull large financial flows to derivative markets to provide hedges. As it has been pointed out, corporate behavior has been subject to "shareholder value-orientation" (Stockhammer 2005, 2006,), which can be held responsible for a "growth-profit trade off" in business decisions of corporate firms (Crotty 1990). The consequences amount to short-termism at the cost of growth with long-term investments.

We spell out, in the following, the notion of "shareholder value orientation" with a reference to the post-Keynesian theory of firms (Crotty 1990; Stockhammer 2005, 2006, ; Orhangazi 2006; Hein 2012). The latter rests on their institutional setting which includes shareholders, managers and workers. The decision on the part of corporate firms to use a share of their profits on investment depends on the relative weight of the above three major cohorts within firms in shaping such decisions. As for the respective interests, the shareholders remain interested in high profits and rising share prices, the workers in output growth with employment, and managers in high profits and share prices which would add to their performance-related receipts. Dwelling on the sequence as a "shareholder revolution" which lends greater power to shareholders, it is not difficult to explain why firms, led by managers, adopt a business strategy which caters less for long-term investment as compared to those which help share prices and profits in the short term (Stockhammer 2005, 2006, ; see Erturk in this volume).

A pattern as above has been empirically verified in the literature by using data for advanced economies (Stockhammer 2004; Orhangazi 2006; Van Treeck 2008). The statistics reveal a rising share of interests and dividends in profits as distributed by the non-financial corporate firms. This also reflects the on-going tendencies under financialization for corporate capital to hold an increasing share of profits as investments in financial assets. The latter is largely a result of the shareholder–manager alliances which promote short-term profits as against long-term growth in business activities. Treating the rising share of dividends as well as interest in the deployment of corporate income as the indicator of an underlying short-termism in corporate investments, those studies come to the conclusion that such outcomes, largely related to financialization, have been responsible for a simultaneous drop in both investment and accumulation by firms. Observations, as above, point to steady declines in investment out of profits in the major advanced economies. The pattern is similar to a Minskyan paradigm where uncertainty in deregulated capital markets generates short-termism in investments. It is possible to trace the above argument in Minsky's characterization of "money manager capitalism" as the new stage of contemporary capitalism in which "total return on the portfolio is the only criteria used for judging the performance of the managers …. It makes the long view a luxury …. The stated aim of fund managers is to maximize the value of the investments of the holders of its liabilities" (Minsky 1996: 358–359, 363).

With financialization generating the climate for "shareholder value orientation," as described above, it can be a logical corollary that financialization has caused a slowdown in accumulation. Moreover, there emerges a distinct pattern in the distribution of corporate profit income across different stakeholders engaged with the firms, especially with its rising share distributed as dividends and interest payments. A large fraction of profits generated by corporates thus reach out to the "rentiers" who live on the income they earn from past savings.

Developments, as above, provide an indication that preferences for short-term investments, as reflected in the corporate decisions in advanced countries, are negatively associated to real investment (Hein 2012: 125). This counters the view that the rising rentier income-shares in corporate profits earned by corporates may generate a "finance-led-growth" in the real economy, unless of course, the rentiers have a consumption propensity which is higher than that of the national average, which is unlikely (Boyer 2000: 111–115). As already pointed out, in the process, corporate firms invest an increasing portion of the profits earned on short-term financial assets which have no links with the real economy; which include the high-risk financial assets as well as the derivative products for hedging, transacted in secondary stock exchanges (Stockhammer 2005, 2006, : 197).

A similar conclusion has been arrived at in a more recent empirical analysis on US firms between 1970 and 2013 (Davis 2018). The study points at tendencies prevailing among firm managers inhibiting fixed investments, an outcome which results from the shareholder value norms which are closely followed by the large corporates. The study also finds tendencies among the large firms for large-scale repurchasing of their *own* equities, thus contributing further to the respective proportion of financial assets in their portfolios. Attention is also drawn in the paper to the prevalence of leveraged financing on the part of the corporates, thus working further as a deterrent to new investments on fixed capital. As we will point out later, propensities to borrow not only add to further liabilities in future, but also make for Minskyan Ponzi financing when fresh loans are used to service the outstanding debt (see Sotiropoulos and Hillig in this volume).

There exist empirical evidences that financialization has been responsible for a slowdown in accumulations. As pointed out in a study on the distribution of GDP in the OECD from 1960–2000, financialization and shareholder orientation of firms have gone in with the "rising share of interest and dividends in profits of non-financial business," confirming the emergence of rentiers who live on past rather than on current activities (Epstein and Power 2003: 229–248).

Attention paid to the emerging countries reveals similar behavior on the part of corporate firms in India, a major emerging country (Sen and Dasgupta 2018). Decisions about investing large shares of their earnings from profits on short-term financial assets are generally influenced by the growing state of uncertainty, which is the driving force behind speculation under financialization. As with investment patterns in advanced economies, the majority of those short-term assets offer high returns despite being risky. Dwelling on the sequence which lends greater power to shareholders who easily win over the managers, it is not difficult to explain why corporate firms in India, led by managers, usually adopt a business strategy which caters less for long-term investments and more to those which help share prices and profits in the short term. The pattern runs parallel to the statistics in the major advanced economies in terms of the steady decline in the ratio of investment to profits.

Data on corporate investments in India as available from India's central bank (see successive Reserve Bank of India Bulletins between 1990 and 2017) indicates that there has been a steady *rise* in the *share* of financial components in aggregate assets held by the Indian non-financial corporates in the decades preceding 2011–2012. The proportion of securities (financial and industrial) in total assets held by those corporates, as reported by the Reserve Bank of India, has been moving up, from 21.83 percent in 1992–1993 to 46.83 percent in 2010–2011.

Data available on changes in asset shares in India from firm level Prowess data sources of the Centre for Monitoring Indian Economy (CMIE) also indicates a continuous decline in physical assets between 2005 and 2011. The two sources of statistics share a common pattern which reflects the declining share of physical assets in portfolios held by the non-financial corporations (NFCs). Evidently, such changes suggest a pattern where investments in the real economy assume a lower priority for the non-financial corporates in India's private sector.

Data as above can also be explored further to highlight the sources of funds used by the Indian corporate firms. It can be observed that there has been a rising share of funds from sources which are external to firms, consisting of borrowings – from both domestic and overseas sources. Since the onset of the global financial crisis of 2008 there has been a continuous decline in the contribution of equity-finance and of internal reserves as sources of funds to corporate firms. The situation has led firms to resort to additional borrowings. Shares of borrowings in total liabilities of the firms, according to Prowess sources, at respective levels of 35.9 percent in 2008 and 39.6 percent in 2013, have continued to rise since then. The pattern seems to indicate an easier option of financing on the part of the corporates, *which was to meet up liabilities with borrowings*. Moreover, one can notice a drop in domestic as opposed to foreign borrowings, largely facilitated by the liberalized norms for external borrowings (see Sen and Dasgupta 2018. see also Bonizzi et al. in this volume).

It is important to notice here that at the firm-level, the large share of resources procured from borrowings and reserves are effectively in use to manage the "current liabilities" which comprise dividends, interests and related payments. With borrowings contributing further to current liabilities, as above, one here observes a Minskyan Ponzi mode; with fresh borrowings used to meet the current liabilities related to borrowings and the sale of equities in the past (Wray 2011). Such situations will erode the respective asset bases of individual firms as there has been little investment in fixed capital with an accumulation of additional liabilities to meet current liabilities.

As in the advanced economies, corporate non-financial firms in India too seem to be following a path of short-termism in the face of uncertainty under financialization. This considerably dampens the prospects of further investments in physical assets, reflecting a familiar Minskyan situation where uncertainty in deregulated capital markets under financialization generates instability and short termism. To quote Minsky,

> for Ponzi units, the cash flows from operations are not sufficient to fulfil either the repayment of principle or the interest due on outstanding debts by their cash flows from operations. Such units can sell assets or borrow. Borrowing to pay interest or selling assets to pay interest (and even dividends) on common stock lowers the equity of a unit, even as it increases liabilities and the prior commitment of future incomes. A unit that Ponzi finances lowers the margin of safety that it offers the holders of its debts.
>
> *(Minsky 1992: 7; see Sotiropoulos and Hillig in this volume)*

Proclivities, as above, also exist on part of the Indian corporates to invest in short-term financial assets rather than in the long-term physical economy, an aspect which provides the core of the explanation for the stagnation in the non-speculatory real segment of the economy. Instances as above are available in our recent study on corporate investments (Sen and Dasgupta 2018).

Speculation, Derivatives and Commodity Markets

As with the financial markets with trading in equities or currencies, use of derivatives has been common in other markets as well which include those for commodities. The major reason behind the use of the derivative instruments has been the volatility in global commodity prices. Since the beginning of the present century, such prices have been subject to multiple swings, starting with a prolonged boom which pulled up the all-commodity price index from 56 in July 1992 to 219 by July 2008 (with base 1993–1994). The global crisis that followed pushed the index down to 100 by October 2008. Volatility was evident with the quick reversal in prices and the index had peaked again to 210 by April 2011. Commodity prices were subject to sharp downturns within a few years and the index touched 92 by 2016. The recovery that followed led to newer heights of the index around 120 by January 2017.[1] Futures trading as hedging devices was much in use in the context of the volatile commodity prices. As has been claimed, the practice is held responsible for upward pressures as well as instability in those prices (Sen and Paul 2010).

Explanations of the volatilities in global commodity prices, in terms of the tapering of the Quantitative Easing (QE) by the US Federal Reserve as well as the rising import demand from China (UNCTAD 2013: 30–39, 50), need also to recognize the significant presence of financial investors in commodity futures markets. As pointed out in an UNCTAD study,

> A particular feature and a "new twist" to the recent boom is the increasing presence of financial investors in commodity futures markets … during the 2000s, investment in commodity index funds has been heavily concentrated in the buy (long) side of those markets, and such a substantial influx of investment gives rise to futures price bubbles. These, in turn, affect spot prices by altering price expectations and providing incentives to hoard – a phenomenon never evident before.
>
> *(UNCTAD 2013: 30)*

In principle, futures contracts in commodity markets are considered to transfer price risks from market participants of physical commodities in spot markets to agents who are ready to bear risks with speculative interests. Advocacy of future trading is linked to reduction of risks, both for buyers and sellers by minimizing uncertainty and thereby reducing the transaction cost. Also, future trading in commodities is considered to allow risk sharing among various participants like the farmers and the trader. However, it is assumed that the role of the future contracts in "price discovery" can work only with access to full information in the market and with the absence of big players in control of the market (Sen 2013).

With continuing volatility in the global commodity markets, questions have often been raised as to whether commodity futures have been effective in fulfilling their role in terms of "price discovery" and "risk transfers." It has also been pointed out that such claims can be fulfilled provided the participants of the commodity market have access to insider information which usually lies beyond public domain (UNCTAD 2011: 119). It can, however, be pointed out that even then information relating to other asset markets is bound to remain incomplete. Under such circumstances, future trading in commodities would fail to achieve much of the expected results – either in terms of price discovery (e.g., futures prices charting the path for spots) or in terms of risk transfers to those who are willing to bear risks in trading. With interconnected markets in terms of trading as well as investment decisions, more often it is the financial investors who manage multiple markets, not only by virtue of the large positions they usually command but also by managing portfolios across those markets, which include those for equities, currencies and real estates.

Use of futures trading has been quite common both in advanced as well as developing countries. One can here refer to the commodity market in India, a major emerging economy where futures trading has been in practice since a long time. As elsewhere, futures trading has not reduced the volatility in commodity prices in the country. By 2008, the persistent boom in commodity prices, especially related to food grains, led to public concerns and the appointment of an official committee to deliberate on commodity futures trading in the country (A. Sen 2008). Contesting the claim that futures trading has been beneficial for managing risks and discovering prices, the committee set limits in providing hedging facilities universally to all commodities in the market. A genuine case for futures trade, as the committee suggested, needs to rest on providing benefits to farmers who produce the traded commodities. Qualifying the majority report, the chairman of the committee pointed at the rising international commodity prices as a major factor behind the rise in spot market prices for agricultural products, thus dispelling the claim that the futures trade has been a major factor behind price increases in India.

However, as argued in a study on future trading in India's commodity markets (Sen and Paul 2010), while the global stock market downslides were matched by similar downslides in both global equity and commodity prices in 2008, there was not much of a drop in the movements of food prices in India. The reason may be the continuing use of the forward and future contracts as tools for speculation in these items. It can also be related to typical portfolio reshufflings on the part of the financial investors who turned to the commodity markets of India in the wake of the 2008 global financial crisis. Further, the same study also makes the point that futures trading in agricultural goods, especially in food items in India, has neither resulted in price discovery nor less volatility in food prices. Instead, the steep increases in spot prices for the major food items are matched by a granger causal link *from future to spot prices* for commodities on which futures are traded. The sequence disproves the basic idea of having future markets as devices to stabilize movements in spot prices. Moreover, while there have been limited attempts in India to control future trade in some sensitive food items, the continuing rise in prices for essential staple food items like rice, wheat, pulses, and oilseeds has often led to an urgency of deliberating on the related issues (Clapp 2014).

However, the fact remains that with financialization under deregulated markets, little effort is there to regulate the pace of futures trading and the speculation and related hikes in prices that have resulted. As an example, prices of essential food items in India are still within the ambit of futures trading.

Summing up, futures trading in India in agricultural goods, especially in food items, has neither resulted in price discovery nor a reduction of volatility in food prices. Nor are there significant effects in terms of farmers fetching higher prices in the market, as pointed out by the last official committee in India on futures trading. With the opening of cross-border trade, commodity prices in India have been guided by the upward movements in prices in international markets, which again are largely driven by financialized future trading. Instead, futures markets in India seem to have provided new avenues of speculation to traders as well as financiers, as has happened elsewhere. Thus, the use of the derivative instruments under financialization, in the context of global commodity markets seems to have failed to bring in the much acclaimed "market efficiency," for growers as well as consumers in emerging economies like India.

Conclusion

With financialization affecting corporate investments as well as commodity trading, the result is a crippling effect on economies' productive capacity and the availability of resources along with a disproportionate increase in rentier income earned from speculation in the economy. The web of financialized operations also extends further, importing greater uncertainty and speculation into real estate (Aalbers in this volume), currency markets, insurance, and other areas of activity where money circulates through trade in securitized assets. With globalization and the related ease of deregulated financial flows, the patterns of financialized activities, though different in scale, are similar in the advanced economies and the emerging economies like India. The trade in securitized assets even extends to the livelihoods of very poor people, whose income streams, generated in the informal economies of countries like India, have become the basis of the global microfinance industry (Mader 2015).

Concluding, one needs to bring back here the need for regulation, both in the financial market as well as in future markets for commodities and the credit market, to bring back some semblance of a coordination between financial and real activities (see Dow in this volume).

Note

1 https://www.indexmundi.com/commodities, retrieved on June 31, 2018.

Bibliography

Bateman, B.W. and Davis, J.B., 1991. *Keynes's Philosophy: Essays on the Origin of Keynes's Thought*. Basingstoke: Edward Elgar.

Boyer, R., 2000. Is finance-led growth regime a viable alternative to Fordism: A preliminary analysis. *Economy and Society*, 29(1), pp. 111–145.

Clapp, J., 2014. Financialization, distance and global food politics. *The Journal of Peasant Studies*, 41(5), pp. 797–814.

Crotty, J., 1990. Owner–manager conflict and financial theories of investment instability: A critical assessment of Keynes, Tobin and Minsky. *Journal of Post Keynesian Economics*, 12(4), pp. 519–542.

Davidson, P., 2003. The terminology of uncertainty in economics and the philosophy of an active role for government policies. In Runde, J. and Mizuhara, S. (eds.), *The Philosophy of Keynes's Economics: Probability, Uncertainty and Convention*. Oxfordshire: Routledge.

Davis, L.E., 2018. Financialization and the non-financial corporation: An investigation of firm-level investment behavior in the United States. *Metroeconomica*, 69(1), pp. 270–307.

Dunn, S., 2008. *Uncertain Foundations of post-Keynesian Economics: Essays in Explorations*. Oxfordshire: Routledge.

Epstein, G., 2001. *Financialization, Rentier Interests, and Central Bank Policy*. Amherst, MA: Department of Economics, University of Massachusetts (Unpublished manuscript); Available at https://www.peri.uma ss.edu/fileadmin/pdf/financial/fin_Epstein.pdf.

Epstein, G. and Power, D., 2003. Rentier incomes and financial crises: An empirical examination of trends and cycles in some OECD countries. *Canadian Journal of Development Studies*, 24(2), pp. 229–248.

Hein, E., 2012. *The Macro-economics of Finance-dominated Capitalism and its Crisis*. Cheltenham and Northampton: Edward Elgar.

Keynes, J.M., 1921. *A Treatise on Probability*. London: MacMillan.

Keynes, J.M., 1936. *The General Theory of Employment, Output and Money*. London: MacMillan.

Keynes, J.M., 1937. The general theory of employment. *Quarterly Journal of Economics*, 51(2), pp. 209–223.

Mader, P., 2015. *The Political Economy of Microfinance: Financializing Poverty*. London: Palgrave Macmillan.

Minsky, H., 1992. The Financial Instability Hypothesis. *Levy Institute Working Paper* No.74 Annandale-on-Hudson, NY.

Minsky, H., 1996. Uncertainty and the Institutional Structure of Capitalist Economies. *Journal of Economic Issues*, XXX(2), pp. 357–368.

Orhangazi, O., 2006. Financialisation and capital accumulation in the non-financial corporatesector: a theoretical and empirical investigation on the US economy: 1973–2003. *Cambridge Journal of Economics*, 32(6), pp. 863–886.

Palley, T., 2007. Financialisation: What it is and why it matters. Working Paper no. 135, Amherst, MA: Political Economy Research Institute.

Reserve Bank of India Bulletins, Mumbai, various issues.

Scazzieri, R., 2011. A theory of similarity and uncertainty. In Brandolini, S.M.D. and Scazzieri, R. (eds.), *Fundamental Uncertainty: Rationality and Plausible Reasoning*. London: Palgrave Macmillan, pp. 73–103.

Sen, A., 2008. *Report on Commodity Futures Trading*. New Delhi.

Sen, S., 2003. *Global Finance at Risk: On Stagnation and Instability in the Real Economy*. New York: Palgrave-Macmillan.

Sen, S., 2010. Derivatives as risk-management tools. *G-24 Policy Brief* no. 63, December 2.

Sen, S., 2013. Uncertainty and speculation in the Keynesian tradition. In Hirai, T., Marcuzzo, M.C. and Mehrling, P. (eds.), *Keynesian Reflections*. Oxford: Oxford University Press.

Sen, S., 2019. Investment decisions under uncertainty. *Journal of Post Keynesian Economics*. doi:10.1080/01603477.2019.1571927.

Sen, S. and Dasgupta, Z., 2018. Financialisation and corporate investments: The Indian case. *Review of Keynesian Economics*, 6(1), pp. 96–113.

Sen, S. and Paul, M., 2010. Trading in India's commodity future markets . *ISID Working Paper* No. 3. Available at http://www.isid.org.in/pdf/WP1003.PDF.

Shackle, G.L.S., 1974. *Keynesian Kaleidics: The Evolution of General Political Economy*. Edinburgh: Edinburgh University Press.

Stockhammer, E., 2004. Financialisation and the slowdown of accumulation. *Cambridge Journal of Economics*, 28(5), pp. 719–741.

Stockhammer, E., 2005–2006. Shareholder value orientation and the investment-profit puzzle. *Journal of Post-Keynesian Economics*, 28(2), pp. 193–215.

UNCTAD, 2011. *Trade and Development Report*. Genva: United Nations. Available at https://unctad.org/en/Docs/tdr2011_en.pdf

UNCTAD, 2013. *Commodities and Development Report*. Geneva: United Nations. Available at http://unctad.org/en/PublicationsLibrary/suc2011d9_en.pdf.

Van Treeck, T., 2008. Reconsidering the investment-profit nexus in finance-led economies: an ARDL-based approach. *Metroeconomica*, 59(3), pp. 371–404.

Wray, R., 2011. The Minsky Crisis. *Levy Institute of Economics Working Paper* No. 659.

38

REFORMING MONEY TO FIX FINANCIALIZATION?

Beat Weber[1]

Introduction

While the growing role of the financial sector in economic activity has been a long-run object of study in specialized academic analyses of "financialization" (van der Zwan 2014), the Global Financial Crisis has drawn wider attention to the phenomenon and problems associated with it (Greenwood and Scharfstein 2013). Unfortunately, misleading calls for monetary reform have sidelined most other ideas for fundamental economic change in the post-crisis debate.

There is now growing support among both experts and the general public for the view that finance has become "too big" in relation to the non-financial sector (Arcand et al. 2015). The crisis is widely perceived as a result of financial sector excesses: Inflated asset prices, excessive debt, and excessive financial profits. While policy intervention in 2008 prevented financial collapse to avoid a domino effect that would spill over into hurting the non-financial sector, post-crisis policy action focussed on adjusting banking regulation and supervision. Beyond that, bold action to reduce the size of the financial sector, the stock of outstanding claims and associated risks has not come forward so far. Among the many potential policy measures suitable to reduce demand for financial activity, none has managed to become widely adopted: Expanding public housing to reduce demand for credit-financed real estate among low-income households, reducing the unequal accumulation of financial assets over generations by taxing capital income and inheritance more strongly, raising taxes to reduce structural needs for public borrowing, abandoning the favorable tax treatment of debt over equity finance, strengthening pay-as-you-go public pension schemes to reduce the need for private pension insurance, or taxation of various forms of financial activity (IMF 2010; Piketty 2014; Goodhart and Hudson 2018). Instead, expectations for bold policy action to produce fair burden sharing of the cost of crisis and measures to reduce financial fragility have largely been disappointed. This has contributed to the current legitimacy crisis of the political system in many countries (see also Nölke in this volume), and a surge of populism.

In contemporary debates on what to do about financialization, the closest equivalent to a populist rallying cry is the call for monetary reform (Scott 2018). In post-crisis public debate, the view that there is something wrong with money that needs to be fixed is among the most popular ideas for fundamental economic change. An initiative to introduce "Sovereign Money," for instance, has managed to enforce a referendum in Switzerland in 2018. Although

458

rejected at the ballot, it gathered the support of a quarter of those attending the vote. Bitcoin and other "cryptocurrencies" have attracted considerable media attention and speculative activity after 2008. Numerous initiatives to introduce regional currencies have sprung up after the crisis in various countries.

Money and Finance – Time Machines in the Economic System

Money is one among many financial instruments in the economy. It is distinguished from other financial instruments by three functions: 1) it provides a unit of account in an economy – in any currency area, all prices are usually measured in the same currency – serving as a yardstick for the value of assets and liabilities, incomes, taxes, goods and services. Money is also used as 2) a means of payment, facilitating the transfer of ownership of private property (goods, services, assets) and the servicing of debt. And 3) it serves as the most basic means to store value over time.

A key role of money and finance in the economy is to provide tools to deal with the future (Minsky 1986). By incurring debt, economic subjects (firms, individuals, governments) can transfer their own expected future income to the present for immediate spending. By saving, economic subjects can transfer current income to the future. Beyond cash and public sector provision of public goods like social insurance, such transactions with the future in the modern economy are mainly achieved via promises to pay. They are at the heart of financial sector activity (Baecker 1991). Financial markets and institutions revolve around the creation, assessment, acceptance, pricing, trading, and so on, of promises to pay. Promises to pay take various forms, the best known instruments are savings accounts, demand deposits, shares, bonds, and derivatives. All of these instruments are contracts wherein an issuer (e.g. a bank) promises to pay money at some future date under specified conditions. Promises to pay are recorded in balance sheets, where assets must match liabilities. With their balance sheets, financial institutions intermediate among those willing to transfer present income to the future and those willing to transfer expected income from the future to the present. Banks and related financial activities perform the role of time machines for the economy, absorbing the associated risks for their customers.

Key players among financial institutions, banks hold assets (mainly direct credit claims and bonds) that provide temporary finance to debtors. To finance these assets, banks issue liabilities with various characteristics: bank bonds, saving accounts and demand deposits. Bank customers can acquire liabilities of banks suitable to their needs. While all of these liabilities are means to store value, the peculiarity of demand deposits is their liquidity. The financial return of deposits is lower than other savings products, but they can be used to make payments among bank customers just like cash, or they can be exchanged for cash at par value on demand at the bank. When extending credit, banks create a new demand deposit for the debtor, resulting in a swap of claims among contracting parties: Debtors give banks a contract-based promise to repay debt plus interest rate at some future date. In exchange, banks give debtors an immediately exertable claim on the bank in the form of a demand deposit. As soon as the debtor uses the deposit to either withdraw cash or make a payment to someone else's deposit at another bank, the bank must provide cash and replace the resulting gap in its balance sheet by attracting new customers to hold the bank's liabilities.

In offering their own promises to pay as transferable deposits for savers, backed by credit claims on debtors, banks simultaneously offer an alternative to unproductive hoarding of cash for those willing to store or transfer liquid value, and create an important source of finance for the economy. In order to do this, banks must be able to make good on their promises with either cash or deposits issued exclusively by the central bank. By swapping some of their assets against cash with the central bank (or central bank deposits), banks acquire reserves to make payments among each other, to provide for depositors' cash withdrawals, and to fulfill mini-mum reserve requirements. By adjusting the terms of access to its balance sheet (quality requirements for assets received from banks, interest rate charged for credit extended to banks, minimum reserves required from banks), the central bank conducts monetary policy aimed at stabilizing the purchasing power of money (measured in terms of market prices for widely traded goods and services) and other macroeconomic goals depending on its public mandate.

Creditworthiness, i.e. the ability to honor one's promises to pay and service the associated debt, is the key criterion to regulate access to credit. The stock of liabilities and corresponding assets resulting from credit creation flows in the economy is an aggregation of expectations about the future agreed on among contracting parties within a given regulatory framework. As the future is inherently uncertain, creditworthiness can only be assessed by forming expectations. Expectations can change over time. A financial crisis occurs when trust in the future repayment ability under-lying promises to pay is shattered on a large scale. When holding promises to pay appears more risky than initially thought, many asset holders try to obtain money (instead of these promises). As long as the guarantees underpinning money remain intact, money is the riskless asset many holders of risky assets seek to acquire in a crisis. If too many financial asset holders try to sell their assets in order to obtain money, asset prices deteriorate, and those dependent on issuing liabilities for financing their current activity (like corporations, financial institutions, governments) can have difficulty in finding asset holders willing to extend credit to them.

During the Global Financial Crisis, central banks' ability to extend credit to those banks able to provide adequate assets in exchange was used extensively to maintain the ability of key financial institutions to honor their commitments, preventing contagious breakdown of the financial system that would have seen it failing in its role of financing the economy. By catering to the suddenly increased demand for liquidity triggered by a general flight to safety, central banks stabilized the purchasing power of money and general financing conditions, preventing the perceived danger of a return of the Great Depression, in which widespread cash hoarding and investment restraint had resulted in an economy-wide deflation.

The Lure of Monetary Reform

In major currency areas, the Global Financial Crisis has been huge, but it has not been a currency crisis. Money has served as a stable safe haven and monetary policy has contributed to macro-economic stabilization in a period of turmoil. Nevertheless, a number of popular theories presume that money is the key problem behind financialization and financial crisis. Analyzing where they go wrong can be instructive in both understanding the actual operation of current money and finance, and in redirecting attention to the key issues about financialization discussed in more detail in other entries in this handbook (for instance, Dow in this volume; Thiemann in this volume).

There are many ideas for monetary reform. Their point of agreement is that control over money creation is perceived as the key site to gain control over finance and the economy.

Where they differ is on two fundamental questions: First, what is money? Second, who should create money? On the first question, a "commodity view" and a "credit view" of money can be distinguished. On the second question, concepts supporting centralized control of money creation by a state entity can be distinguished from concepts favoring decentralized issuing activity, where various currency issuers either compete with or complement each other. Among answers to the first question regarding the nature of money, each view highlights one dimension of the multi-faceted history of currencies to declare it as money's essence. The "commodity view" focuses on the object dimension of money, tangible cash. The "credit view" focuses on the more abstract dimension of money as a claim, an entry in a balance sheet as the issuer's liability.

Commodity-view Based Monetary Reform Projects: Bitcoin and Sovereign Money

The commodity view of money is strongly rooted in folk theories about money and the economy (Braun 2016). In this perspective, money is expected to be a tangible object that circulates in a stable quantity to facilitate the exchange of what can be expected to be a stable supply of goods and services, resulting in a stable economic system. The economy is assumed to produce a (more or less) constant amount of goods and services each year. Money is primarily seen as a means of payment, a kind of voucher for these goods and services. To be stable, the quantity of money in circulation should be controlled to fit the quantity of goods and services like a glove. In this conception, the scarcity of the money stock in relation to the stock of goods is key to the value of money. Creation of additional money would not result in more goods, but in rising prices for existing goods or assets.

From this perspective, the widespread use of bank-issued promises to pay in retail payments infected a stable economic system with inflation: adding promises to pay to the supply of notes and coins made money fragile and its supply excessive, fuelling speculative asset bubbles, before ending in crisis and government intervention. In this view, a faulty monetary system is the root of financialization. To avoid future excess and fragility, money should cease to be a liability of an issuer and become a pure asset-like object put under strict quantity control to avoid inflation and bubbles. The most popular versions of commodity view-inspired calls for monetary reform are "Sovereign Money" (Jackson and Dyson 2013) and "Bitcoin" (Nakamoto 2008). The first favors centralized control of money creation, the second is based on a decentralized governance mechanism.

Sovereign Money involves reforms of the banking system and the central bank money creation process (see Weber 2018: 160ff.). Demand deposits held by customers would cease to be a claim on the bank protected by deposit insurance, but would be transformed into bank vaults containing central bank cash (or its digital equivalent). Those vaults could be rented by customers for a fee. Saving accounts of customers would be turned into risk bearing claims similar to shares in an investment fund, participating in both profits and losses in banks' credit business.

Among customers, risk-averse savers would be turned into money hoarders, while risk-embracing savers would become something like shareholders. Banks' function to absorb risks on behalf of customers and offering guarantees would be radically reduced. The heart of this reform would be to outlaw banks' ability to offer promises to pay that promise par value to cash and can be used to make payments among customers. Money creation would be centralized in a state-sponsored institution, a kind of reformed central bank. The main aim of "Sovereign Money" is to centralize money issuing powers. Instead of giving access to its balance sheet in exchange against assets received from commercial banks, the primary route for money creation would be for the new money issuing authority to donate money to the government without compensation, but within the limits set by the central bank's money supply goal for the economy. By creating new money for the benefit of government spending without requiring a corresponding asset in exchange, money would be transformed from a liability into an object, in line with the commodity view of money.

By banning commercial banks' ability to fund credit by issuing transferable promises to pay, and centralizing money creation, reformers hope to control the money supply and curb funds for speculative activity. The only source of speculative activity remaining is expected to be savings from risk-tolerant savers that have to bear full risk of their activities. It is assumed that all that is required for such a reform would be a legal act. In 2018, an initiative to introduce Sovereign Money in Switzerland was successful in demanding a plebiscite, but the latter failed to attract sufficient support among voters. Citizen initiatives supporting Sovereign Money are active in a number of other countries, too.

Distrusting centralized governance, by contrast, supporters of crypto coin projects like "Bitcoin" favor market competition among private digital currencies in limited supply. Bitcoin is an open source software-based system that makes available a limited supply of digital objects that supporters call "coins," operating without a responsible legal issuing entity (Nakamoto 2008). It is based on cryptographic mechanisms that attract participants by offering economic incentives to achieve decentralized consensus on governing coin issuance and verification of transactions among coin owners (see Weber 2018: 101ff.). Bitcoin is modeled along a commodity view of money in its most basic form. Here, gold is considered the ideal money: An object of nature in immutable limited supply which does not require trust in the promise of an issuer. Many supporters call Bitcoin and similar schemes "crypto currencies" and expect them to rival existing currencies through decentralized user endorsement. Bitcoin and other coins have started to be traded on private exchanges against official currency, their exchange rate determined by demand and supply and exhibiting strong volatility. In recent years, digital coins have attracted significant speculative activity at times, but failed to establish themselves as rivals to existing currencies.

The popularity of Sovereign Money and Bitcoin is fed by public anger about mismanagement and scandals in the banking sector, and the costs borne by the public for stabilizing the economic and financial system (Epstein in this volume). But they rely on mistaken views about what money and banks actually do, resulting in misleading solutions to problems associated with financializiation. Both are critical of banks' alleged ability to "create money," as if money creation was a scandalous "free lunch" for the issuer, with commercial banks perceived as the main culprit in "Sovereign Money" and central banks cast as lead villains in Bitcoin. In fact, by swapping promises to pay with a debtor,[2] banks incur liabilities and extend guarantees against a fee. Banks' income results from the difference between interest paid on their liabilities and interest received from their assets, compensating the risk absorbed by banks in a credit operation, and other fees for services. This is not an ability to print vouchers for other people's goods at will without having to give anything in return. Banks' income may be regarded as excessive by the public, but given the availability of taxation and bank regulation there is no lack of technical tools to do something about that.

By abolishing the creation of means of payment that are an issuer's liability, both Bitcoin and Sovereign Money hope to turn money into an indestructible, limited stock of objects in line with a commodity view of money. If the stock of money is limited, both conceptions hope that money will function like a stable voucher on the stock of goods. As a result, prices are expected to remain stable and the potential financial instability associated with debt either vanishing or absorbed in bilateral relations between individual debtors and creditors, because credit extension will be limited to lending out cash from the existing stock of money.

This would be a significant break with current arrangements, where a (central) bank issues new means of payment in exchange for claims on future economic activity: By promising to pay back credit out of future income that requires engagement in economic activity to obtain, a debtor receiving new means of payment from the (central) bank makes a binding commitment. In the appropriate circumstances, debtor commitments relate new money to economic activity that results in new goods, services or assets available for money, underpinning money's purchasing power.

Trying to turn money into an object that is issued without creating any obligation for both its creator and its first receiver, Bitcoin and Sovereign Money sever any direct link between money creation and economic production. It is highly questionable whether scarcity of the stock of means of payment alone would be sufficient to keep money users convinced that such a currency is valuable. By imposing stronger constraints on credit – because promises to pay by debtors can be extended only against payments from a limited stock of cash under Bitcoin and Sovereign Money –, the financing of ongoing economic activity might be hurt, resulting in a smaller supply of goods and services. This is because cash owners might not be prepared to incur the risks associated with granting credit if no guarantee by an intermediary (banks etc.) is allowed.

With regard to financialization, limiting the stock of money does not prevent financial bubbles. Cash owners remain free to invest in financial assets. If the return offered by financial assets feeding financial bubbles surpasses those feeding investment in production of non-financial goods and services, speculative activity in the financial sector will remain attractive, and major financial instability will remain a macroeconomic danger that authorities cannot ignore. Reformers supporting Bitcoin or Sovereign Money forget that economic activity does not involve trading a constant stock of goods, but production of a flow of goods, services and assets that requires financing and has no fixed upper or lower limit ex ante. In a decentralized economy, where money circulates according to the spending decisions of its individual owners, there is no automatic link between a limited stock of money on the one hand and a certain stock of goods at stable prices and financial stability on the other. The effects of money on economic activity and money's value depend on its uses. By regulating access to their balance sheets, issuers can create means of payments of stable purchasing power against valuable assets that can finance future economic activity, as long as expectations of contracting parties do not go fatally wrong. Even if issuers of monetary instruments were able to refrain from misinvestment, they are not central planning agencies that control allocation decisions made during the circulation of money in the economy. Limiting the supply of money is not the same thing as directing it towards better uses.

Credit-view Based Monetary Reform Projects: Regional Currencies and MMT

In contrast to the commodity view of money inspiring Bitcoin and Sovereign Money, the double face involved in money issuing – a short-term liability to its issuer, an asset to its holder, created when swapped against a long-term claim on a debtor that is subsequently held on the balance sheet of the issuer – is recognized in credit theories of money (Minsky 1986; Ingham 2004). Whereas in the commodity view of money, the value of money is believed to result from the scarcity of the stock of money in relation to the stock of goods, the main mechanism supporting the value of money according to credit theories lies in the quality of guarantees extended by the issuer. This allows for multiple issuers of monetary instruments to co-exist in a currency area – central bank, commercial banks and similar arrangements. Credit-based money is subject to a permanent flow of money creation and destruction via credit extension and repayment in line with assessments of creditworthiness in view of prospects of the future.

The credit theory of money allows a richer understanding of the current monetary and financial system than most explanations rooted in a commodity view of money. It has also inspired a group of monetary reform ideas. Whereas commodity view-inspired monetary reform concepts try to transform money from a liability into a pure asset-like object that has no backing or counterpart in the issuer's balance sheet, credit view-inspired concepts of money reform affirm money's status as a liability of the issuer. Credit theories stress that economic activity does not consist in trading of a fixed stock of goods against an equivalent stock of money, but that creation of new money can serve as a tool to create additional economic activity. Their focus of reform is to exploit the flexibility associated with credit-based money creation for stimulating additional economic activity in a currency area. The key idea here is that through the assets that serve as counterparts to money creation, additional economic activity can be financed. In this line of thought, problems associated with financialization could be avoided if the issuer took care that money is issued against assets that finance activity outside the financial sector, promoting the production of goods and services instead of financial bubbles. The leading exponents of this credit-view-based approach to monetary reform are concepts for Regional Currencies (Kennedy et al. 2012) and an approach known as "Modern Monetary Theory" (MMT) (Wray 2012).

Key to Regional Currency initiatives is the idea that the financial system drains funds from local economic activity and channels them to financial speculation in financial centers (see Weber 2018: 136ff.). Regional Currency initiatives are an attempt to tackle regional problems of unemployment, lack of competitiveness and drain of local purchasing power by introducing a local currency. The core idea is for local producers and consumers to form a mutual credit network based on an agreement to ascribe creditworthiness to each other. The local currency consists of vouchers that are issued as debt certificates during transactions. When network members engage in a transaction, the seller delivers the goods, and the buyer pays by creating a voucher representing the buyer's debt to the community. The voucher can be used by the seller to buy goods from any other seller in the network. A community association administers the (electronic or paper-based) recording of vouchers, and determines the terms for exchanging vouchers against official national currency.

Modern Monetary Theory (MMT) builds on the observation that in currency areas like the United States, government debt is the key counterpart to money creation accepted by the central bank (see Weber 2018: 193ff.).[3] They conclude that the institutional separation between central banks and governments is misleading – both belong to the public sector. According to MMT, their balance sheets can be consolidated, and any limit on a central bank's acquisition of government bonds that limits government's ability to finance its fiscal policies in line with macroeconomic prosperity goals can be abolished. If government bonds fail to find a market among private market participants due to concerns about the government's continuing ability to service its debt, MMT recommends that the central bank buy any amount of bonds that is needed to fund public policy goals like full employment.

Whereas MMT and Regional Currency both build on credit theories of money, they differ on the appropriate mechanism to govern the issuing of money. MMT favors centralized money creation by the state, whereas Regional Currencies expresses a preference for decentralization, favoring a coexistence of various regional currencies that complement national currencies.

In these two reform ideas, money's status as a liability and its potential role as a productive force are highlighted, but at the price of neglecting quality considerations of assets serving as counterparts to money creation. There is certainly a need to strengthen regulatory and supervisory efforts in the financial sector to foster improved risk assessments in credit creation leading to money creation and reduce waves of euphoria and excessive pessimism. There may be a case for a stronger role of public sector owned banks or tax-financed public investment in influencing resource allocation in the economy. But under any sustainable credit arrangement in the current economic system, creditworthiness will remain the key criterion to guide credit allocation. Making creditworthiness of counterparties a key criterion for allocation of new means of payments establishes an important principle: New money only enters the economy when its initial user has extended a convincing promise to pay it back, or hands over the promise to pay of a third party (i.e. a corporate or government bond). The fact that the issuer demands repayment plus interest requires the debtor to engage in economic activity to obtain the necessary funds. Such contractual commitments of future income support the expectation behind the general acceptance of a currency and money's stable purchasing power that future economic activity will take place resulting in goods and services available for money. If MMT and Regional Currency schemes' main stance against financialization is to create money based on counterpart assets that profit-oriented banks would not accept, this could spell trouble for the currency. If MMT amounts to monetizing non-marketable government debt on a regular basis and Regional Currency schemes provide credit to groups affected by financial exclusion, these schemes impose a burden on their currencies that should actually be borne by tax financed government spending.

There may be some differences in opinion about potential debtors' creditworthiness, but if money issuers' assessments about the quality of assets behind money depart too much from the assessments of currency users, currency users may start to doubt the quality of the currency. There are many currencies in the current world. Currencies must conform to minimum stability requirements in order for users to accept them. User habit and exclusive acceptance of national currency for tax payments by the state may protect existing currencies against competition from other currencies to a certain degree. But as phenomena known as "dollarization" and "euro-ization" in a number of emerging market economies show, there can be circumstances where currency users' disaffection or mistrust become so profound that a collective switch of users to a different currency occurs. Most attempts at implementing Regional Currency schemes have had to learn this. Their main attraction – their geographic boundedness – is also their main quality drawback, often resulting in lack of adoption.

The main point of money in the current economic system is its general acceptance: Unlike other objects of value, money is the most abstract form of value, being exchangeable against any other good or service available. Compared to the universal access granted by official currency to the universe of goods and services, regional currencies give their users access to a much smaller range of goods and services. Any individual offered the choice between a national or a local currency is asked to forgo buying opportunities. Unless there is a strong counterveiling mechanism (e.g. strong peer pressure among local community members in favor of currency acceptance, discounts offered by merchants for those paying in local currency, suppliers who grant exclusive access to attractive goods against local currency, local tax acceptance in local currency), lack of widespread acceptance among locals can be expected. With regard to financialization, credit-view-inspired monetary reform may contribute to shifting allocation towards credit uses outside the financial sector at the point of money creation, but reformed money creation does not avoid the subsequent use of money during its circulation for buying unsound promises to pay that foster financial instability.

Conclusion

Monetary reformers erroneously perceive money creation as the secret control center of the economy that must be fixed in order to tackle problems resulting from financialization. Differences among them result from different views on what money is and who should govern it. In a nutshell, reformers informed by a commodity view of money aim at limiting money creation in order to stop financial asset inflation. Reformers informed by a credit view of money aim at redirecting money creation from fueling financial asset inflation towards financing prosperity within their currency area. Within both camps, supporters differ on whether these goals are best achieved via centralized or decentralized means of governing money.

But efforts to tackle financialization and financial crisis by reforming money are based on conceptual mistakes. In major currency areas, the Global Financial Crisis has not been a currency crisis. Money has retained its purchasing power and central bank intervention has contributed to macroeconomic stabilization in a period of turmoil. Fiscal policy (taxation and public spending), financial regulation and supervision are the main tools to achieve fair burden sharing of crisis costs and to contain the likelihood of major crises in the future resulting from excessive financialization, with properly governed public development banks a potential addition to the public sector toolkit that is still underdeveloped in many countries.

If money embodies economic value in its most abstract form, can we change prevailing moral values in our economic system by changing the values embodied in currency? That is an idea implicit in many ideas for monetary reform. Money must be understood within a system of relations and procedures involving time that conforms to the profit motive driving the economic system in general. While special among credit instruments, money shares many of their characteristics. Credit is based on anticipations of the future. Current debt payments validate past anticipations of the future, and lay the foundation to current anticipations of the future. So what money is ultimately made of is the future. The amount of future is an unknown quantity in the present and can only be an object of expectations. Money's value in terms of purchasing power results not from fixing its supply, but from issuers making it represent assets widely considered valuable (on top of the state's acceptance of a currency for tax payments), and from the conformity of user's acceptance and pricing behavior with the prevailing monetary policy stance. Promises to pay that are created, held and traded in the financial sector are crystallizations of the economy's expectations about the future.

One of the financial sector's main functions is to serve as a time machine for income. In a crisis, banks' expectations about the future may turn out to be incorrect, resulting in a frenzied post-crisis debate about how to improve sound risk management in the sector. But there is no way to *ensure* ex ante that expectations are correct by reforming the governance of money creation – the future is uncertain by nature. As economic activity is fundamentally directed at the future (Beckert 2016), there is no way to clean money and finance from traces of the future and its uncertainty.

Monetary reform is not a silver bullet to de-financialize capitalism and avoid the difficult distributional and allocational questions involved in creating a sustainable economic system.

Notes

1 Views expressed in this text are those of the author and not necessarily those of his employer.
2 The bank receives a long-term credit claim against a debtor. In exchange, the debtor receives a short-term claim on the bank. In line with the credit purpose, the debtor can use this claim on the bank immediately to make payments to other deposit owners or to withdraw cash.
3 In the Euro area for instance, the main counterpart to money creation are claims on the private sector like corporate bonds. In both the US and the Euro area, the central bank is not allowed to buy government bonds directly from government (instead, they must be acquired from private market participants on the secondary market, in order to signal that government finance will not be easily given priority over price stability whenever a conflict between the two arises).

Bibliography

Arcand, J.L., Berkes, E. and Panizza, U., 2015. Too much finance? *Journal of Economic Growth*, 20(2), pp. 105–148.
Baecker, D., 1991. *Womit handeln eigentlich Banken?* Frankfurt: Suhrkamp.
Beckert, J., 2016. *Imagined Futures. Fictional Expectations and Capitalist Dynamics.* Cambridge, MA/London: Harvard University Press.
Braun, B., 2016. Speaking to the people? Money, trust, and central bank legitimacy in the age of Quantitative Easing. *Review of International Political Economy*, 23(6), pp. 1064–1092.
Goodhart, C. and Hudson, M., 2018. Some ways to introduce a modern debt jubilee. Available at https://voxeu.org/article/some-ways-introduce-modern-debt-jubilee
Greenwood, R. and Scharfstein, D., 2013. The growth of finance. *Journal of Economic Perspectives*, 27(2), pp. 3–28.
IMF – International Monetary Fund, 2010. Financial sector taxation. Available at https://www.imf.org/external/np/seminars/eng/2010/paris/pdf/090110.pdf.
Ingham, G., 2004. *The Nature of Money.* Cambridge: Polity Press.
Jackson, A. and Dyson, B., 2013. *Modernising Money. Why our Monetary System is Broken and How it Can be Fixed.* London: Positive Money.
Kennedy, M., Lietaer, B. and Rogers, J., 2012. *People Money. The Promise of Regional Currencies.* Axminster: Triarchy Press.

Minsky, H., 1986. *Stabilizing an Unstable Economy*. New Haven: Yale University Press.
Nakamoto, S., 2008. Bitcoin: A peer-to-peer electronic cash system. Available at http://bitcoin.org/bit coin.pdf
Piketty, T., 2014. *Capital in the 21st Century*. Cambridge, MA and London: Harvard University Press.
Scott, B., 2018. These 5 rebel movements want to change how money works. Available at https://www.huf fingtonpost.com/entry/five-monetary-rebellions-change-money-system_us_5b9a819ae4b0b64a336ca248.
Van der Zwan, N., 2014. State of the art: Making sense of financialization. *Socio-Economic Review*, 12(1), pp. 99–129.
Weber, B., 2018. *Democratizing Money? Debating Legitimacy in Monetary Reform Proposals*. Cambridge: Cambridge University Press.
Wray, L.R., 2012. *Modern Money Theory. A Primer*. New York: Palgrave.

39

MACRO-PRUDENTIAL REGULATION POST-CRISIS AND THE RESILIENCE OF FINANCIALIZATION

Matthias Thiemann

Introduction

How have financial reforms after the 2008 financial crisis transformed the financial system and its impact on capitalist economies? In particular, in how far have post-crisis reforms affected the pro-cyclical character of the system, which has been characterized as a system of compounding bubbles, moving from boom to bust to the next boom (Blyth 2008)? As the frequency and severity of financial booms and busts have increased over the last four decades (Borio 2012) in accord with the secular expansion of financial activities called financialization, few if any questions are more pertinent to our time. The great recession has severely shaken the capacity of democratic societies to deal with any future financial crises stemming from asset price appreciation. At the same time, ongoing processes of asset price appreciation, in particular with respect to real estate breaching pre-crisis levels in the EU (see Figure 39.1), increase inequality (Turner 2015).

In this context, the fate of macro-prudential regulation is of great importance given that it constitutes the technocratic attempt to limit the crisis proneness of the financial system as well as its cyclical character (Crockett 2000). Developing largely outside of the mainstream of Western regulatory thinking before the crisis (Borio 2003), macro-prudential thinking experienced a sudden and unexpected rise after the failure of Lehman and the ensuing recession (Baker 2013a). Rhetorically embraced by the G20 at the 2009 summit as the political answer to the crisis (Lombardi and Moschella 2017), it aims at complementing the focus on individual institutions of the micro-prudential approach. Employing a systemic view, it seeks to increase the resilience of the system as a whole and to lean against the wind as credit booms accelerate (Baker 2013a).

This new approach to regulation, and in particular its anti-cyclical dimension, has been facing severe challenges, both internally in the policy community as well as externally. Internally, institutional capability to limit the financial cycle had to be generated that extended beyond the already given. New policy settings had to be set up against the interests and ideas of entrenched micro-prudential regulators within central banks and financial regulators (Moschella and Tsingou 2013), while new instruments needed to be developed and calibrated. Externally, as Baker points

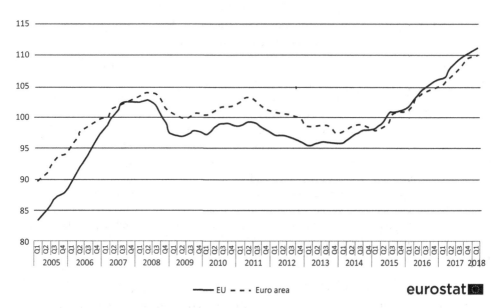

Figure 39.1 House Price Indices Eurostat
Source: Available at http://ec.europa.eu/eurostat/statistics-explained/index.php/Housing_price_statistics_
-_house_price_index. For a similar, albeit less extreme finding on the global level, see http://www.imf.org/
external/research/housing/

out, the political economy of such macro-prudential regulation added further challenges, as constraining the financial cycle in the upswing requires unpopular measures such as credit-rationing
and limiting economic growth (Baker 2015).

These obstacles weigh stronger than attempts of certain central bankers to re-politicize the
issue, who point to the man-made character of the cycle and hence its amenability to change
(cf. Constâncio 2014). As I will argue, central bankers' rhetorical interventions trail off among a
discursive audience that is only too attentive to the political risks such an approach entails. Being
experts, concerns regarding the dangers of anti-cyclical policies for legitimacy of independent
central banks (accountability concerns) outweigh the political desirability one might attach to
these goals. Furthermore, for a policy community that is exclusively focused on processes of social
learning based on evidence, it is very difficult to make progress on the anti-cyclical part of the
macro-prudential agenda due to the rare occurrence of cycles and tail events.[1] For these reasons,
implemented macro-prudential policies seek to stabilize rather than combat the finance-led
growth regime of the economy, its incessant credit growth and asset-price appreciation. Focusing
on system stability rather than changing the characteristics of the system, macroprudential regulation thereby contributes to the limited change that Helleiner calls the "status-quo crisis" (2014).

In order to make the developments leading to the very limited implementation of anti-cyclical
measures intelligible, this chapter proceeds as follows: it first delineates the history of macro-prudential thinking and its ascendance to (rhetorical) prominence, then turns to review the literature's
attempt to explain the limited implementation of anti-cyclical policies, focusing on the external and
internal opposition to them. These explanations will be complemented with work that focuses on
the reputational concerns of central bankers and their related hesitance to undertake anti-cyclical
regulation. The chapter concludes by assessing the implications of these developments for the future
of the financial accumulation regime and possible counter-movements.

Macro-prudential Regulation: The Rise of a New Paradigm as a Consequence of the Crisis

The macro-prudential approach made a first appearance on the international regulatory scene thanks to a speech by the Chairman of the Financial Stability Forum, an international forum established in 1999 after the Asian Financial Crisis to facilitate central bank coordination, only to become the Financial Stability Board after the 2008 crisis. Andrew Crockett in 2000 put macro-prudential regulation on the policy agenda, by spelling out the principles of macro-prudential regulation (Crockett 2000). There, he explicitly introduced the concept of the financial cycle as the focal point of macro-prudential regulatory action. Described as wasteful in the upswing (when surging asset prices feed and are fed by credit expansion) and painful in the downswing, the problem with financial cycles is that they are evident only ex-post to micro-prudential risk management systems of banks (Crockett 2000: 6). Individual market agents, Crockett argued could only evaluate differential, but not overall risks related to the financial cycle. This inability provides the basis for a clear mandate for macro-prudential regulators to mitigate the financial cycle. As Crockett put it:

> In terms of the measurement and mitigation of risk over time, **the key challenge is to take better account of the financial cycle that underlies financial instability**. If risk increases in upswings and materialises in recessions, it stands **to reason that defences should be built up in upswings so as to be relied upon when the rough times arrive**. This would strengthen institutions' ability to weather deteriorating economic conditions, when access to external financing becomes more costly and constrained. **Moreover, by leaning against the wind, it could reduce the amplitude of the financial cycle, thereby limiting the risk of financial distress in the first place**.
>
> *(Crockett 2000: 6, author's emphasis)*

In this quote, the two intermediate objectives of macro-prudential regulation with respect to the financial cycle already come to the fore. On the one hand, its goal is to increase the **resilience** of financial institutions to accumulating risks in the boom. On the other hand, its goal is to temper these risks themselves through anti-cyclical interventions, that is by "leaning against the wind." It is in this context, that the more ambitious part of macro-prudential regulation lies, maybe best formulated by Persaud (2014: 161), "[t]he critical task of the macro-prudential central banker is as a risk manager to the financial system" as a whole. Table 39.1 depicts these two different objectives associated with macro-prudential regulation and the requirements for accurate measurement and swift action they impose.

In the years following the speech by Crockett in 2000, economists at the Bank for International Settlement (BIS) were seeking to measure and operationalize the notion of the financial cycle, suggesting indicators as well as potential mitigating policy tools (Borio and Lowe 2002; Borio 2003). In their quest, they sought to develop an encompassing policy framework to mitigate systemic risks, pointing to interventions both in the cross-sectional dimension of systemic risk and the time dimension. While their advocacy on Basel II remained unheard and their analysis largely ignored, with much of the criticized pro-cyclical reliance on private risk management systems becoming a central part of Basel II, their work helped to build a rather coherent framework that included the development of first indicators of cycles (such as the credit to GDP gap, ibid.).

Hence, when at the height of the crisis, the leaders assembled in the newly founded G20 were looking for a novel policy framework to demonstrate their willingness to act decisively, they could turn to the macro-prudential framework (G-20 2009). The adoption of the macro-prudential

470

Table 39.1 Resiliency vs. Anti-cyclical Measures

Macro-prudential objectives/ characteristics	Resiliency	Anti-cyclical
Concept	Cross-sectional/interconnectedness	Intertemporal/building up of systemic risk over time
Form of regulatory intervention	Time invariant (structural), possibility for due process	Time variant (discretionary), little possibility for due process
Requirement for metrics of systemic risk	Very low, rather theoretically driven than measurement specific, simple over time adjustment (quiet policy learning)	High: need for ex ante warning systems, sufficiently early to allow intervention, sufficiently precise to justify intervention, high likelihood of error
Political exposure of regulator	Limited, in the sense that there is due process and calibration, existence of accepted economic analysis	Very high, no due process, no ex ante calibration, limited scientific knowledge

paradigm, at least its rhetoric was an answer by policy makers to the public outrage generated by the financial crisis (Baker 2013b; Helleiner 2014; Lombardi and Moschella 2017). Yet, looking at the measures introduced to date, only few if any bear a clear anti-cyclical character. The most pertinent global measures introduced in Basel III, such as the designation of Global-Systemically Important Financial Institutions (G-SIFI), the Liquidity Coverage Ratio and the Net Stable Funding Ratio – new measures which are supposed to ensure ongoing funding for large institutions or the systemic risk buffers –, contain no anti-cyclical elements (Claessens and Kodres 2014). Even the most prominent counter-cyclical measure, the Counter-cyclical Capital buffer, has as its prime objective to increase of resilience of the banking system, although it "may also help to lean against the build-up phase of the credit cycle in the first place" (BCBS 2015: 1).

At the national level as well, where most anti-cyclical tools are located, policies to raise the resilience of the system have been much more prominent in the implementation phase than tools to smooth the credit cycle (Barwell 2014; Tucker 2016: 30f; counter-examples include the UK and Sweden, see Belfrage and Kalifatides 2018). Edge and Liang (2017), investigating domestic anti-cyclical capacities of macro-prudential bodies, find that of the 58 countries investigated, only two, the UK and France have macro-prudential governance frameworks which are conducive for the exercise of anti-cyclical policies to reduce credit growth. Hence, the imposition of Loan to Income Ratios or of Loan to Value ratios, measures limiting the provision of mortgages for marginal borrowers or the imposition of higher core capital requirements on mortgages for banks has remained rare, despite recent upswings in the house price cycle (see Figure 39.1). In general, there has been much hesitancy to limit credit growth and intervene in house price appreciation. The debate in Germany on the possible overheating of residential real estate, led since 2015, is a good example (cf. Deutsche Bundesbank 2018). Yet, to date, no measures have been taken.

These lopsided reform efforts – pushing for resilience, but not for the reduction of the cyclical build-up of risks – mean that a central part of the macro-prudential regulatory agenda, deemed crucial by its early advocates, is not implemented. The result is stabilizing the finance-led growth paradigm and its attendant volatility, rather than combatting the ever-continuing expansion of credit in the upswing of the cycle characteristic for the financialization of the economy. How can this policy decision be explained? And what does it mean for the process of financialization? If we want to study why macro-prudential ideas challenging the cyclical character of the financial system have not been implemented, we can draw upon the insights of historical and discursive institutionalism, pointing to the institutional context within which change agents operate as crucial (Moschella and Tsingou 2013). Placed in a technocratic evidence-based institution that favors a depoliticized status, these reform agents had to grapple with the need for international cooperation as well as fears of political exposure.

Explaining the Fate of Macro-prudential Regulation Post-crisis

Accounts focusing on governance issues point to the opposing external interests to macro-prudential regulation as an idea set which challenges the pre-crisis system of market-based governance (Underhill 2015). This challenge, however, remains ineffective because of what is called "ideational adverse selection" (ibid.: 470), where the persistence of private actors' veto capacities within the regulatory community leads to the blocking of macro-prudential policies, such as anti-cyclical regulation deemed as too invasive by powerful private actors (Tsingou 2015).[2] Another governance obstacle for anti-cyclical policies is the fractured policy field. Given that these policies require a large degree of international coordination to avoid circumventions, if any large player, such as the US does not agree to cooperate, anti-cyclical interventions to influence the refinancing of banks, e.g. in repo-markets, become largely futile (Thiemann et al. 2018). The incremental nature of change and the lacking anti-cyclical element can then at least be partially explained by the fact that the shift towards macro-prudential regulation in the US has been characterized as only half-hearted (Persaud 2010; Helleiner 2014), making such international coordination more difficult.

These governance considerations point to the challenges that the macro-prudential ideas faced inside the regulatory community once implementation began, seeking to understand the internal reasons for adoption or rejection of these policies. Here, scholars of financial regulation, basing themselves on the insights of historical institutionalism have identified the potential for fundamental changes in the long run. These reside in the implementation of ambiguous rules and the installation of long-run policy programs that cumulatively could have transformative effects (Baker 2013a, b; Moschella and Tsingou 2013: 205; Langley 2014).

Analyzing regulatory change post-crisis, Baker has pointed out that during the implementation of the macro-prudential agenda in terms of banking regulation, institutional settings as well as interest-based politics have been diluting it, slowing the pace of change (2013b: 52). In addition, macro-prudential regulation has been held back by a lack of data on financial cycles and its crucial drivers, such that change agents often "deliberately decided to embark on a slow moving experimentation with the new regulatory ideas, in order to collect the necessary evidence ... to win the policy debate among technocrats" (Moschella and Tsingou 2013: 204, s. also Thiemann et al 2018a). As such, macro-prudential aims have been mostly achieved through the so-called layering of macro-prudential goals upon existing rules, such as capital requirements (Baker 2013b: 52) or the transformation of regulatory initiatives initially aiming at other goals (Birk and Thiemann 2019).

The problem with these otherwise insightful studies on the implementation of macro-prudential regulation is that there is little attention to the internal strife within the macro-prudential community, that is within the group of macro-prudential policy experts tasked with implementing this new policy program in central banks and financial regulators, over intermediate objectives and tools. This lacuna stems from the perception of the rise of macro-prudential ideas as a third order *Gestalt* flip (Hall 1993). Analyzing the rhetorical shift to macro-prudential regulation, Baker speaks of an ideational paradigm shift, which provides regulators with a new outlook on financial markets; a new lexicon for regulators and a new hierarchy of the policy goals to be pursued, including a strong commitment to reduce the cyclical fluctuations of financialized capitalism (Baker 2014). This, for Baker, allows the macro-prudential regulatory rhetoric to act as a coordinative discourse (ibid.: 176). In this view, macro-prudential regulators as a group are united, and while facing entrenched interests and institutional frictions, could act united as a policy advocacy group (Baker 2013b; see Pagliari and Young in this volume). Baker's claim of a third order change presumes that the problems the new paradigm was supposed to be addressing were rather clear.

However, this was far from the case. As Helleiner has pointed out, the notion of systemic risk and the goals of macro-prudential regulation were vague when the G20 delegated the implementation of such a macro-prudential framework to regulators (Helleiner 2014: 128), leaving the international community of national financial market and banking regulators with the task of operationalizing this new approach largely on their own. This has entailed the challenge for regulators to generate data, identify metrics and trigger points for regulatory action (Bisias et al. 2012), but also to agree on the intermediate objectives that should be pursued (ESRB 2014). For this task, politicians gave little guidance. Beyond the general goals of preserving financial stability and mitigating systemic risks, commonplaces which nowhere found a clear legal definition (Hellwig 2014: 42), there was no specific roadmap or tasks to be pursued. Given this vagueness, the internal expert debate over intermediate objectives, metrics and indicators as well as instruments of macro-prudential regulation was thus of fundamental importance to the final shape of the new policy regime.

According to Helleiner, the vagueness of the mandate has been exploited in the US to install regulatory changes that largely maintain the status quo, which means "enhanced public oversight without constraining private financial activity in significant ways" (Helleiner 2014: 13). To explain these developments, Helleiner points to a generalized national preference regarding limited market intervention (ibid.), which is different from a European, more interventionist stance (Baker 2014). This is rather unsatisfactory, due to its generality and lack of context specificity, in particular its neglect of the organizational/institutional factors which drive this position taking (Hall 1986).

To improve upon these accounts, I analyze these technocratic debates, following the insights of ideational scholarship, which insists that to understand policy paradigm shifts, we need to examine "not only the ideational shift, but the complex processes of discursive interactions" that surround them (Schmidt 2011: 59; see also Schmidt 2008: 310, Thiemann 2019). In the wake of Hall's studies on policy paradigm shifts, which emphasized processes of social learning among policy experts, these authors focus critically on the discursive construction of policy programs in the contestation and debate among technocrats. Authors in this tradition point out that such coordinative discourses among policy experts are driven by an attempt to maintain the depoliticized status of technocrats, seeking to replace political decisions with expertise and the authority of evidence (Strassheim 2015; Wood 2015). In line with these findings, bureaucratic reputation theory has pointed out that agency leaders carefully weigh the implications of newly assigned policy tasks for the independence of their agencies (Carpenter 2010), which in turn might lead to blame avoidance strategies, e.g. the non-implementation of the most contentious issues (Hood 2011). It was these considerations and the desire of central banks to remain apolitical actors which further shaped the timid implementation of anti-cyclical policies and, thus, the regulatory reproduction of financialization.

The Coordinative Discourse Among Policy-makers

Studying the coordinative debate among technocrats charged with implementing macro-prudential policies, the lack of internal unity becomes evident, beginning with the intermediate objectives that

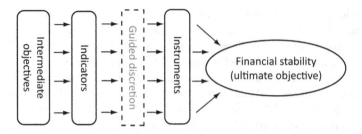

Figure 39.2 Macro-prudential Policy Strategy
Source: ESRB 2014: 8

should be pursued. While defining the intermediate objective is only a first step, it is a crucial one as it drives the measures to be implemented afterwards, as a document of the European Systemic Risk Board (ESRB) in 2014 clarifies.

In this respect, the question of whether macro-prudential regulation should seek to temper the financial cycle or whether it should merely seek to increase the resilience of the system shows both the lack of unity among macro-prudential change agents and the lack of clarity over policy goals. Some have argued that it is a normative necessity to target the financial cycle due to the welfare losses implied by resource misallocation (Persaud 2014; Constâncio 2014, 2016) and the incapacity of monetary policy to affect these issues (Ekholm 2014). For instance, a recent intervention by Karolina Ekholm, Deputy Governor, Sveriges Riksbank clarifies the issues at stake:

> In my view, there is thus an important role for macro-prudential policy in filling a gap created by the difficulties involved in using monetary policy completely symmetrically in upturns and downturns of the financial cycle. According to this view, macro-prudential policy would be the policy area mainly responsible for dampening credit growth and prevent banks from excessive leveraging in an upturn of the financial cycle, while monetary policy would be the policy area mainly responsible for stimulating credit in a downturn.
>
> *(Ekholm 2014: 96)*

As Ekholm's statement clarifies, we live in an era of financial dominance, where central bank intervention is clearly asymmetrical (see also Gabor 2016; Braun and Gabor in this volume). Equipped with little to no capacity to constrain asset price appreciation in the upswing, central banks are forced to intervene in an easing manner in the downswing, thereby adding speculative fuel to future crises.

Others have argued that a global resilience standard is the most realistic goal the policy community can strive for (Cecchetti and Tucker 2016; Tucker 2016). In this line of argument, besides the difficulties of coordinating policy actions around the globe, the attempts to manage the cycle only over-exposes central banks to policy mistakes, putting their legitimacy in peril.[3] Without clear guidelines and metrics for action, policy-makers would be blamed while acting, but also would be blamed when a crisis occurs for non-action. Hence, the difficulties of communicating the reasons for action and the impossibility to subject such action to pre-agreed standardized metrics leads those agents to argue against the "overextension" of central bank mandates (see Tucker 2016; for a counter-argument regarding the capacity to measure and communicate clearly about the cycle, see Aikman et al. 2018).

These different positions in the debate of officials charged with implementing macro-prudential regulation on whether macro-prudential regulation should strive for resilience or for taming the cycle are best exemplified by the positions of the two policy officials leading the task to develop and implement macro-prudential policies at the two most powerful central banks in the Western Hemisphere, Daniel Tarullo at the Federal Reserve Board (2009–2017), and Vitor Constâncio at the European Central Bank (ECB) (2010–2018). Their differences at first glance confirm once more the different macro-prudential stances between the US and Europe noted in the literature, with the US focus on resilience and too big to fail (Persaud 2010; Helleiner 2014) in contrast to the concern regarding the pro-cyclical character of finance as a very European project (Baker 2014: 183). However, reconstructing especially Tarullo's arguments in speeches addressing the macro-prudential community and financial markets will reveal the challenges to legitimate regulatory intervention which the project of anti-cyclical policies poses to regulators, which extends beyond their general ideological and/or cultural preferences.

Constâncio's Position

Since taking up his position in 2010, Vitor Constâncio, Vice-president at the ECB until 2018, has embraced an ambitious macro-prudential policy stance (see e.g. Constâncio 2012, 2014, 2016b). While acknowledging the need to increase the resilience of the system, he has issued passionate pleas that macro-prudential regulation should go beyond that (Constâncio 2016a), stating as the first principle of macro-prudential policy that it should be pre-emptive and strongly counter-cyclical, based upon the concept of the financial cycle. This ambitious policy stance, which requires time-varying interventions by central bankers is concomitant with a rejection of resilience as the sole policy goal. He rejects the attempts to merely increase resilience and claims that, while much easier to achieve (raise bank capital to 25% capital, add a good resolution regime and mop up the mess afterwards), it would be completely unacceptable from a welfare perspective to observe a housing bubble and asset price growth and not to intervene (Constâncio 2014: 17).

Constâncio's language is clearly a politicizing one (Wood 2015: 13) that emphasizes the contingent character of the financial cycle which is amenable to intervention by the public. Quoting the metaphor of King Canute, equating the building of dykes with measures for increasing resilience, he points out that "we have no hope of taming the tide" (Constâncio 2014: 17). However, as he points out himself, the analogy is slightly misleading, "because financial instability is something man-made, and not an unassailable fact of nature" (ibid.: 18). In this quote, Constâncio points to the man-made nature of the financial cycle and hence the capacity of human agents to change it. He goes on to point to the welfare losses incurred due to the cycle and the dangers of simply seeking to raise the resilience as nobody can predict the exact place or the intensity of the next crisis. In this sense, Constâncio's position takes a critical perspective on house price appreciation, a central feature of financialization and its implied wastefulness, making it a moral imperative for central banks to act against it.

Yet, Constâncio's politicizing speeches in which people are asked to take their fate into their own hands are voiced not in the political communicative discourse, addressing the masses suffering from house price appreciation, but within the coordinative discourse among central bankers. Here, these ideas/this discourse have/has much less traction, as evidence-based policies and cognitive arguments as well as the desire to stay apolitical carry stronger weight there. Facing both internal opposition in the ECB to the use of anti-cyclical measures due to fears of endangering the monetary transmission mechanisms by the financial markets division (such as was the case for anti-cyclical margins for Repos, see Thiemann et al. 2018b) and doubts of national central bankers in the EU skeptical regarding the scientific measurement of cyclical developments, his rhetorical interventions were unable to overcome the skepticism and achieved little in terms of actual interventions. While central banks are heavily engaged in measuring the cycle and determining means of intervention (see Aikman et al. 2018), there is yet little anti-cyclical central bank action.

Tarullo's Position

One reason for this timidity can be gauged from the speeches by the Fed representative, who after 2009 was responsible for designing macro-prudential policies for the banking sector. In contrast to Constâncio, Daniel Tarullo, FED governor responsible for banking regulation and financial stability, advocates a much more modest, structural approach to macro-prudential regulation that seeks to increase the resilience of the system rather than tempering the financial cycle. Tarullo distinguishes between measures that address pro-cyclicality and those seeking to increase resilience. He links the former to time-varying, discretionary measures, whereas resilience can be increased by non-discretionary, non-varying, that is structural measures (Tarullo 2013: 3). Based on practical problems as well as lacking certainty about the existence of the financial cycle and the appropriate metrics for mitigating it, he ascribes a limited role for discretionary measures that seek to lean against the wind and rather favors structural measures, which are non-varying and non-discretionary.

Appealing to the original intervention of Crockett in 2000 as path-breaking, Tarullo nevertheless pleads for a more limited agenda. In a first rhetorical step, he points to the uncertain epistemic status of the financial cycle, further cautioning that due to the concern of macro-prudential regulation with tail events, it is intrinsically difficult to generate sufficient data to test different theories regarding the propagation of systemic risk (Tarullo 2013). He admits that in theory time varying measures seeking to tame the cycle are "a conceptually appealing approach as the problem of the excessive upswing could be much better controlled by time-varying measures" (ibid.: 23). He further concedes that the structural through-the-cycle measures he advocates would be either largely ineffective dealing with increasing leverage or asset prices that raise macro-prudential concerns as would be monetary policy (ibid.: 16f).

However, he qualifies this approach that favors time varying, discretionary measures to temper the cycle as one that raises a fair number of significant issues regarding problems of the reliability of measures, calibration and speed of decision making coupled with the need to identify the competent authority (ibid.: 15). These are problematic from the point of view of the legitimacy of regulatory decision making, which in the case of the US demands an open due process and scientific backing for regulatory decisions to be legitimate (Jasanoff 2012: 12, 37). These facts lead him to favor structural measures, which have important advantages. While such measures still require judgment, they do not depend on timely measurement of the build-up of risks and can furthermore "proceed with the full opportunity for debate and public notice-and-comment that attends the rulemaking process" (Tarullo 2013: 23).

It is the capacity of structural measures to appear legitimate and not their adequacy to the task at hand which drives Tarullo's choice, avoiding the political dangers for central bankers inherent in the unrestrained application of their judgment. His intervention is hence characterized by an attempt to de-politicize regulatory intervention, bringing it into line with the norms of US policy making. This involves both the scientific underpinnings of action as well as the due process which allows for accountability (Jasanoff 2012). The speeches clarify the different characteristics of the policy tools connected to the two policy goals as well as their implications for the political exposure of central banks (see Table 39.1). Structural measures linked to the goal of resilience impose much more limited demands on metrics of systemic risk (see also Borio and Drehmann 2009: 9) and limit the vulnerabilities of regulators to political exposure. They can follow the method of due process and calibration rather than employing discretionary judgment that is prone to exhibit them to political attack.

These characteristics are important for the choice of central banks with respect to which policies they wish to pursue and are a further explanatory element in the partial implementation efforts of central bankers. For this community of technocrats (Riles 2018), the concepts and models and metrics are not sufficiently specified, nor is the competent authority which is supposed to enforce these claims. Caught within the iron cage of evidence-based policy, this community finds it difficult to enact counter-cyclical policies, instead choosing to merely raise the resilience of the financial system. Given these difficulties recent statements by policy makers declare the struggle over intermediate objectives to be over, with the goal of resilience having won the day. As the former Bank of England Deputy Governor Tucker put it in a recent working paper:

> Of the two types of social cost ... policy makers have prioritized the costs of financial system collapse over the costs of resource misallocation during financial booms. The assumption is that whatever the inefficiencies during the upswing, the destruction of wealth, jobs and productive capacity during busts matters more. ... the approach adopted by policy makers is not a regime for actively managing the credit cycle.
>
> *(Tucker 2016: 31)*

Hence, in the end, a policy program which initially sought to intervene in the financial cycle and constrain the expansion of finance was reduced to a set of policies seeking to reduce the impact of inevitable financial crises through measures that increase system resilience.

Conclusion

During the implementation phase of the macro-prudential paradigm, anti-cyclical measures that could limit asset price appreciation were largely not implemented. Instead, macro-prudential regulation has become a tool to stabilize, but not alter financialized capitalism (Casey 2015). Partial reasons for this omission are the frictions within the policy field linked to the lack of epistemic authority for the concept of the financial cycle and the lack of clear metrics (Thiemann et al. 2018). The reduction of macro-prudential goals to enhance the resilience of the system only can further be linked to the preferences of the US macro-prudential regulator for a continued depoliticized status, which made any international anti-cyclical measures difficult to envision. Its opposition in turn can be traced to the distinctive requirements of legitimate regulatory decision-making in the US (Jasanoff 2012), which puts value on scientifically backed decisions and due process. A Federal Reserve subject to oversight by Congress seems to be wary of taking decisions that might lead to political questioning. It is only fitting then that the ECB representative emerges as the most forceful voice for anti-cyclical intervention, given that democratic accountability is rather absent in this case (Jabko 2009).

The lack of measures further reflects the weakness of the anti-cyclical goal of macro-prudential regulation to operate as a unifying idea in the coordinative discourse among the group of technocrats asked to implement macro-prudential reforms. The lacking agreement among regulators to engage in anti-cyclical policies means that measures focus on increasing the resilience of the financial system, largely abandoning any attempt to tame the cycle. The domination of the goal of increasing resilience over the goal of being anti-cyclical means the rejection of a Keynesian/

Minskyan macro-management of the financial system in favor of an attempt to avoid a negative downturn in terms of GDP caused by financial markets in the downswing (see Dow in this volume).

The developments with respect to the macro-prudential policy program are particularly consequential for the fate of financialized capitalism, as the existing monetary policy framework seems particularly inept at constraining cyclical financial developments. Every time a bubble bursts, central banks intervene and flood the market with additional liquidity, feeding the next bubble which is even bigger than the previous one (Arestis and Karakitsos 2013). Central banks find themselves at this critical juncture partially due to their own prior decisions. While they engaged in anti-cyclical policies up until the 1980s, they withdrew from constraining credit, at least in the US, to avoid the political backlash it entailed (Krippner 2011; Elliott et al. 2013).

Re-imposing such controls now seems to be impeded by the same desire to avoid political confrontation. This means that meaningful anti-cyclical regulation, currently blocked within the technocratic expert community, can only come about if the discussion is shifted back into the public arena, where it needs to overcome the opacity of the topic and put the costs incurred due to both the booms and busts of financialized capitalism center stage. This political discourse can draw upon activist central bankers (such as Constâncio) to make its case, but it cannot rely on central bankers to take care of it.

In this respect, possibly the most detrimental effect of the containment of the debate over the purpose of macro-prudential regulation within circles of central bankers rather than a public concerned is that a public political debate over rising house prices and their potential implications for financial stability, the social purpose justifying anti-cyclical interventions is not occurring (Baker 2018) and that deepening financialization is not tackled. It is well possible that such a debate will only emerge after the next crisis, when we find that the tides of finance were higher than the dams built to protect us. A possibly more harrowing option is that the dams are indeed built high enough that financial crises can be contained, perpetuating the inequality aggravating effects of a financialized capitalism based on growing private indebtedness and house price appreciation.

Notes

1 A financial cycle as a macroeconomic phenomenon, based on credit expansion and asset price appreciation, followed by asset price declines and credit reduction lasts between 8–30 years, moving into bust when tail events, the unexpected realization of systemic risks occur (see Borio and Drehmann 2009).
2 This view, however, must contend with the much-reduced power of private actors in the immediate aftermath of the crisis (Young 2014).
3 See e.g. Tucker's contribution to a panel on macro-prudential policy, September 23, 2016, https://www.youtube.com/watch?v=R8XFULU5114 (accessed January 11, 2019).

Bibliography

Aikman, D., Bridges, J., Burgess, S., Galletly, R., Levina, I., O'Neill, C. and Varadi, A., 2018. Measuring risks to UK financial stability. *Bank of England Staff Working Paper* No. 738. London: Bank of England.
Arestis, P. and Karakitsos, E., 2013. *Financial Stability in the Aftermath of the "Great Recession"*. London: Palgrave Macmillan.
Baker, A., 2013a. The new political economy of the macro-prudential ideational shift. *New Political Economy*, 18(1), pp. 112–139.
Baker, A., 2013b. When new ideas meet existing institutions: Why macro-prudential regulatory change is a gradual process. In Moschella, M. and Tsingou, E. (eds.), *Great Expectations, Slow Transformations: Incremental Change in Post-crisis Regulation*. Colchester: ECPR Press, pp. 35–57.
Baker, A., 2014. Macro-prudential regulation. In Mügge, D. (eds.), *Europe and the Governance of Global Finance*. Oxford: Oxford University Press, pp. 172–187.

Baker, A., 2015. Varieties of economic crisis, varieties of ideational change: How and why financial regulation and macroeconomic policy differ. *New Political Economy*, 20(3), pp. 342–366.

Baker, A., 2018. Macro-prudential regimes and the politics of social purpose. *Review of International Political Economy*, 25(3), pp. 293–316.

Barwell, R., 2014. The macro-prudential voyage of discovery: No map, no specific destination in mind… no problem? In: Houben, A., Nijskens, R. and Teunissen, M. (eds.), *Putting Macro-prudential Policy to Work*. DNB Occasional Studies Vol. 12–7. Amsterdam: De Nederlandsche Bank, pp. 196–218.

Basel Committee on Banking Supervision (BCBS). 2015. Frequently asked questions on the Basel III Countercyclical Capital Buffer. Available at http://www.bis.org/bcbs/publ/d339.pdf

Belfrage, C. and Kalifatides, M., 2018. The politicisation of macro-prudential regulation: The critical Swedish case. *Environment and Planning A*, 50(3), pp. 709–729.

Birk, M. and Thiemann, M., 2019. Open for business: Entrepreneurial central banks and the cultivation of market liquidity. *New Political Economy*, pp. 1–17.

Bisias, D., Flood, M., Lo, A.W. and Valavanis, S., 2012. A survey of systemic risk analytics. *Office of Financial Research Working Paper* #0001. Washington, DC: United States Department of the Treasury.

Blyth, M., 2008. The politics of compounding bubbles: The global housing bubble in comparative perspective. *Comparative European Politics*, 6(3), pp. 387–406.

Borio, C., 2003. Towards a macro-prudential framework for financial supervision and regulation? *BIS Working Papers* No. 128.

Borio, C., 2012. The financial cycle and macroeconomics: What have we learnt? *BIS Working Papers* No. 395.

Borio, C. and Drehmann, M., 2009. Assessing the risk of banking crises – revisited. *BIS Quarterly Review*, March 2009. Borio, C. and Lowe, P., 2002. Assessing the risk of banking crises. *BIS Quarterly Review*, December 2002.

Casey, T., 2015. How macro-prudential financial regulation can save neoliberalism. *The British Journal of Politics and International Relations*, 17(2), pp. 351–370.

Carpenter, D., 2010. *Reputation and Power. Organizational Image and Pharmaceutical Regulation at the FDA*. Princeton, NJ: Princeton University Press.

Cecchetti, S. and Tucker, P., 2016. Is there macro-prudential policy without international cooperation? *CEPR Discussion Paper* 11042, January 2016.

Claessens, S. and Kodres, L., 2014. The regulatory responses to the global financial crisis: Some uncomfortable questions. *IMF Working Paper*, 14/46.

Constâncio, V., 2012. Shadow banking – The ECB perspective. Speech by Vítor Constâncio, Vice-President of the ECB, *Towards Better Regulation of the Shadow Banking System*, European Commission Conference, Brussels, April 27, 2012.

Constâncio, V., 2014. Where to from here? Remarks by Vítor Constâncio, Vice-President of the ECB, at the Federal Reserve Bank of Chicago 17th Annual International Banking Conference, November 7, 2014.

Constâncio, V., 2016a. Principles of Macroprudential Policy. Speech by Vítor Constâncio, Vice-President of the ECB, at the ECB-IMF Conference on Macroprudential Policy, Frankfurt am Main, April 26, 2016.

Constâncio, V., 2016b. Margins and haircuts as a macro-prudential tool. Remarks by Vítor Constâncio, Vice-President of the ECB, at the ESRB international conference on the macro-prudential use of margins and haircuts, Frankfurt am Main, June 6, 2016.

Crockett, A., 2000. Marrying the micro- and macro-prudential dimensions of financial stability. *BIS Review*, 76/2000.

Deutsche Bundesbank. 2018. Monthly Report: Housing in towns and cities still overvalued. Available at https://www.bundesbank.de/Redaktion/EN/Topics/2018/2018_02_21_monatsbericht_immobilien.html; last accessed January 11, 2019.

ECB 2009. *Financial Stability Review June 2009*.

Edge, R. and Liang, N., 2017. New financial stability governance structures and Central Banks. *Hutchins Center Working Paper* 32.

Ekholm, K., 2014. What should be the ambition level of macro-prudential policy? In Houben, A., Nijskens, R. and Teunissen, M. (eds.), 2014. *Putting Macro-prudential Policy to Work*. DNB Occasional Studies Vol. 12–7. Amsterdam: De Nederlandsche Bank, pp. 94–103.

Elliott, D., Feldberg, G. and Lehnert, A., 2013. The history of cyclical macro-prudential policy in the United States. *Office of Financial Research Working Paper* 008, Washington, DC: United States Department of the Treasury.

European Systemic Risk Board (ESRB). 2014. *Flagship Report on Macro-prudential Policy in the Banking Sector*.

G-20. 2009. Declaration on strengthening the financial system. London Summit, April 2, 2009. Available at https://www.fsb.org/wp-content/uploads/london_summit_declaration_on_str_financial_system.pdf, last accessed September 23, 2019.

Gabor, D., 2016. A step too far? The European financial transactions tax on shadow banking. *Journal of European Public Policy*, 23(6), pp. 925–945.

Hall, P., 1986. *Governing the Economy. The Politics of State Intervention in Britain and France*. New York: Oxford University Press.

Hall, P., 1993. Policy paradigms, social learning, and the state: The case of economic policymaking in Britain. *Comparative Politics*, 25(3), pp. 275–296.

Helleiner, E., 2014. *The Status Quo Crisis: Global Financial Governance after the 2008 Meltdown*. New York: Oxford University Press.

Hellwig, M., 2014. Systemic risk and macro-prudential policy. In Houben, A., Nijskens, R. and Teunissen, M. (eds.), 2014. *Putting Macro-prudential Policy to Work*. DNB Occasional Studies Vol. 12–7. Amsterdam: De Nederlandsche Bank, pp. 42–77.

Hood, C., 2011. *The Blame Game*. Princeton and Oxford: Princeton University Press

Jabko, N., 2009. Transparency and accountability. In Dyson, K. and Marcussen, M. (eds.). *Central Banks in the Age of the Euro-Europeanization, Convergence and Power*. Oxford: Oxford University Press, pp. 391–406.

Jasanoff, S., 2012. *Science and Public Reason*. London: Routledge.

Krippner, G., 2011. *Capitalizing on Crisis*. Princeton, NJ: Princeton University Press.

Langley, P., 2014. *Liquidity Lost: The Governance of the Global Financial Crisis*. Oxford: Oxford University Press.

Lombardi, D. and Moschella, M., 2017. The symbolic politics of delegation: macro-prudential policy and independent regulatory authorities. *New Political Economy*, 22(1), pp. 92–108.

McPhilemy, S., 2015. Financial stability and Central Bank power: A comparative perspective. PhD thesis, Warwick University.

Moschella, M. and Tsingou E. (eds.), 2013. *Great Expectations, Slow Transformations: Incremental Change in Post-crisis Regulation*. Colchester: ECPR Press.

Persaud, A., 2014. Central banks, monetary policy and the new macro-prudential tools. In Houben, A., Nijskens, R. and Teunissen, M. (eds.), 2014. *Putting Macro-prudential Policy to Work*. DNB Occasional Studies Vol. 12–7. Amsterdam: De Nederlandsche Bank, pp. 159–164.

Persaud, A., 2010. The locus of financial regulation: Home versus host. *International Affairs*, 86(3), pp. 637–646.

Riles, A., 2018. *Financial Citizenship-Experts, Publics, and the Politics of Central Banking*. Ithaca, NY: Cornell University Press

Schmidt, V., 2002. Does discourse matter in the politics of welfare state adjustment? *Comparative Political Studies*, 35(2), pp. 168–193.

Schmidt, V., 2008. Discursive institutionalism: The explanatory power of ideas and discourse. *Annual Review of Political Science*, 11, pp. 303–326.

Schmidt, V., 2011. Ideas and discourse in transformational political economic change in Europe. In Skogstad, G. (ed), *Policy Paradigms, Transnationalism, and Domestic Politics*. Toronto: University of Toronto Press, pp. 36–63.

Strassheim, H., 2015. Politics and policy expertise: Towards a political epistemology. In Fischer, F., Torgerson, D., Durnová, A. and Orsini, A. (eds.), *Handbook of Critical Policy Studies*. Cheltenham and Northampton, MA: Edward Elgar, pp. 319–340.

Tarullo, D.K., 2013. Macro-prudential regulation. Remarks by Member Board of Governors of the Federal Reserve, September 20, 2013. Available at http://www.federalreserve.gov/newsevents/speech/tarullo20130920a.pdf.

Thiemann, M., 2019. Is resilience enough? The macroprudential reform agenda and the lack of smoothing of the cycle. *Public Administration*, 97(3), pp. 561–575.

Thiemann, M., Aldegwy, M. and Ibrocevic, E., 2018a. Understanding the shift from micro- to macro-prudential thinking: A discursive network analysis. *Cambridge Journal of Economics*, 42(4), pp. 935–962.

Thiemann, M., Birk, M. and Friedrich, J., 2018b. Much ado about nothing? Macro-prudential ideas and the post-crisis regulation of shadow banking. *Kölner Zeitschrift für Soziologie und Sozialpsychologie*, 70(1), pp. 259–286.

Tsingou, E., 2015. Transnational veto players and the practice of financial reform. *The British Journal of Politics & International Relations*, 17(2), pp. 318–334.

Tucker, P., 2016. The design and governance of financial stability regimes: A common resource problem that challenges technical know-how, democratic accountability and international coordination. *CIGI Essays on International Finance*, 3.

Turner, A., 2015. *Between Debt and the Devil*. Princeton, NJ: Princeton University Press.

Underhill, G.R.D., 2015. The emerging post-crisis financial architecture: The path-dependency of ideational adverse selection. *The British Journal of Politics and International Relations*, 17, 461–493.

Wood, M., 2015. Puzzling and powering in policy paradigm shifts: Politicization, depoliticization and social learning. *Journal Critical Policy Studies*, 9(1), pp. 2–21.

Young, K., 2014. Financial Industry groups' adaptation to the post-crisis regulatory environment: Changing approaches to the policy cycle. *Regulation and Governance*, 7(4), pp. 460–480.

40

HISTORICAL PERSPECTIVES ON CURRENT STRUGGLES AGAINST ILLEGITIMATE DEBT

Christina Laskaridis, Nathan Legrand and Eric Toussaint

Introduction

When the failures of the financial system came to the fore, tides of discontent swept across Europe and North America. This chapter discusses the scope and strategies used by debt resistance movements to effectively challenge the power of creditors, which has grown with financialization. After the global financial crisis of 2007/8, private indebtedness became closely linked with public indebtedness as states intervened on a large scale to socialise the private losses of the financial sector of core economies (Toussaint 2015; see also Epstein in this volume). This led to problems for indebted states which Roos (2016), through the prism of the structural power of finance, shows how debt was used to constrain and maneuver specific policy choices by states. As suggested by Davis and Walsh, this had implications for households, which are "drawn into financialisation through a range of activities, from the securitisation and collateralisation of mortgage debts to the nationalisation of bankrupt banks" (2015: 667). The result of this was a higher concentration in public debt ownership and a reinforced unequal distribution of income overall (Hager 2015).

This chapter looks at some of the collective strategies of resistance against the excesses of financialization. We try to show that successful initiatives by debtors were those in which broad peoples' movements pushed directly or indirectly to question the legitimacy of the accumulation of debt. Viewed through the lens of the political economy of austerity we look at the "overlapping dependence" of the struggles in private and public debt (as in Montgomerie and Tepe-Belfrage 2018). We bring in the longstanding literature upholding debtors' rights, broadly drawing from the literature on odious and illegitimate debts (such as Mader and Rothenbühler 2009; Lamarque and Vivien 2011; Millet and Toussaint 2012) and illustrate the relevance for today of unilateral sovereign acts and debt repudiation throughout the history of the nineteenth and twentieth centuries.

The first section outlines extensions to the doctrine of odious debt to conceptualize the conditions in which repudiation and cancellation are legitimate. The second section provides an overview of historical examples where political support for repudiation bore fruit. The remainder of the chapter focuses on recent strategies used to challenge the power of creditors and asset holders. The scope of debt audits is elaborated and the official audits of Ecuador and

Greece are compared. Following from this, the chapter identifies key elements in other recent debt struggles that have proven to be successful: popular education, effective use of courts and direct action. The chapter draws out the broader conditions under which social mobilizations in the context of financialization may prove successful.

The Doctrine of Odious Debt

Successful repudiations by debtor states led a Russian conservative jurist, Alexander Nahum Sack, in 1927 to draft what would later be known as the "doctrine of odious debt." Although in favor of the continuity of state obligations after a change of regime, Sack acknowledged the fact that some states had successfully repudiated their debts. Interpreted as a way to warn creditors to avoid lending in ways that may legitimize the repudiation of loans after a change of regime within the debtor state, he defined the criteria which must be met in order for a debt to be considered odious:

> a) that the purpose which the former government wanted to cover by the debt in question was odious and clearly against the interests of the population of the whole or part of the territory, and
> b) that the creditors, at the moment of the issuance of the loan, were aware of its odious purpose.
>
> *(Sack 1927: 163)*

Sack does not consider the despotic nature of the debtor regime as a *sine qua non* condition for a debt to qualify as an odious one, widening the scope for the application of the doctrine to include debts contracted by democratic regimes. Despite important limitations of the doctrine, such as prioritizing creditors and the lack of consideration towards human rights, some debt resistance movements have adopted it and gone beyond it, using "that which is applicable and rejecting what is unacceptable and adding elements related to the social and democratic advances that have been made in international law since the Second World War" (Toussaint 2019: 129).

Indicatively, the definition adopted by the Committee for the Abolition of Illegitimate Debts (CADTM) (see Toussaint 2005 for an extended account), evolves the concept as follows:

> ...considering the development of international law since the first theorization of odious debt in 1927, odious debts can be defined as those incurred by governments which violate the major principles of international law such as those included in the Charter of the United Nations, the Universal Declaration of Human Rights, and the two complementing covenants on civil and political rights and economic, social and cultural rights of 1966, as well the peremptory norms of international law (jus cogens).
>
> *(Toussaint 2019: 131)*

Historical Precedents of Successful Repudiation

This section reviews some important examples of public debt repudiation to inform the subsequent discussion on recent debt struggles. Four vignettes from the USA, Mexico, Russia and Costa Rica indicate that historical precedents of successful repudiations hinged upon decisive political will and the vitality of social movements.

In the 1830s in the USA, four states – Mississippi, Arkansas, Florida, and Michigan – repudiated their public debts owed predominantly to British creditors. Alexander Sack wrote in this regard:

One of the main reasons justifying these repudiations was the squandering of the sums borrowed: They were usually borrowed to establish banks or build railways; but the banks failed and the railway lines were never built. These questionable operations were often the result of agreements between crooked members of the government and dishonest creditors.

(Sack 1927: 158)

The debt repudiations followed the 1837 banking crisis and occurred against a backdrop of strong people's movements in the 1830s. Creditors attempted to prosecute the states that had repudiated their debts in a US federal court, but had their lawsuits thrown out (Ludington et al. 2009).

In Mexico, Liberal forces came to power in 1855 but their reforms were met with hostility by the Conservative Party. In 1858, in the course of the War of the Reform, the Conservatives overthrew the newly elected Liberal president Benito Juárez, but enjoying widespread support, Juárez eventually came back to power in 1861. His government repudiated the internal public loans contracted by the usurpers between 1858 and 1860 and then suspended repayment of the public debt owed to London bankers as well as to Mexican creditors who had newly acquired French or Spanish citizenship in order to benefit from the protection of these European powers (Wynne 1951; Bazant 1995). In December 1861 and January 1862, Spanish, British and French troops invaded Mexico eventually leading to France seizing the capital and installing a Catholic monarchy with the support of the Mexican dominant classes whose interests as creditors were defended by France. In 1867, the French military expedition was defeated and Benito Juárez returned to the presidential palace. The debts contracted on behalf of the Mexican state by France's puppet, Maximilian of Austria, were repudiated and he reaffirmed the repudiation of the internal debt contracted between 1858 and late 1860 by the Conservatives (Wynne 1951).

In 1905, during the first Russian revolution, the Soviet of Saint Petersburg published the "Financial Manifesto" which exposed the illegitimacy of public debts contracted by the Tsar. These debts were contracted for the benefit of the Tsarist autocracy, foreign creditors and the few Russian capitalists that existed. The Manifesto proposed that these debts would not be acknowledged once the autocratic regime was deposed. The First World War accelerated the political unrest in Europe while also enriching banking and the military trade. Between 1913 and the October 1917 revolution, Russian public debt rose from £930 million to £3,385 million (Lienau 2014). In February 1918, all debts contracted by the Tsarist regime and by the provisional government which had continued the war were repudiated by decree by the legislative body of the newly formed Russian Soviet Federative Socialist Republic.

European powers, the USA, Canada and Japan's economic interests were jeopardized by this repudiation as well as by the revolution in Russia as a whole (Carr 1953). The international Genoa conference in the spring of 1922 hosted by five major powers attempted to force the Soviet government to acknowledge the debts it had repudiated and to cease calling for a global revolution if it wanted to revive its economy by taking out loans and attracting foreign investment. Russia refused and claimed that it was fully within its rights to repudiate Tsarist debt as the revolution had created a new legal order while the Russian diplomats at the conference mentioned the eighteenth-century revolutions in France and the USA as historical precedents (Mills 1922). No agreement was reached during the conference, but subsequently, the Soviet state was broadly recognized making the Russian debt repudiation broadly a success.

In January 1917, Federico Tinoco led a military coup that established a dictatorship in Costa Rica. Pressured by strong popular discontent, he left the country in August 1919 taking with him funds previously borrowed in his country's name from a British bank (see Ludington et al. 2009). The Constitution from the regime prior to Tinoco's coup was re-established, and in

August 1922, the Constitutional Congress declared null and void the contracts entered into between the executive power and private individuals, with or without the approval of the legislature, during Tinoco's rule. It annulled the law which had authorized the government to issue 16 million of local currency in paper money which had been taken by Tinoco when he left the country. While the new president, Julio Acosta, initially vetoed the debt repudiation law which was voted by the Congress in 1920 (Lienau 2014) arguing that tradition was to honor international obligations contracted toward creditors, the Constitutional Congress, under popular pressure, maintained its position and the President finally rescinded his veto.

These short vignettes exemplify that political pressure has a vital role in making debt repudiations successful. To further highlight a long historical lineage of successful debt cancellations or repudiations that invoked the argument of their illegitimate or odious character, we include a long but non-exhaustive list.[1]

Sovereign Debt Audits: Movements to Uncover Illegitimate Debts

The last ten years have created a wealth of experiences with popular mobilization challenging financialization. This section covers some of the tactics and strategies used and notes occasions on which opportunities to victoriously confront the creditors were missed. We first outline how debt audits can serve as a tool to challenge the power of creditors by raising into the public eye the illegitimate aspects surrounding debt accumulation, and then cover two examples of official audits, the case of Ecuador and Greece.

A new generation of debt resistance movements that placed auditing at the center of their activities have come into being, inspired by global debt justice movements over the past two decades, among others Jubilee 2000, CADTM, and Jubilee South.[2] Such organizations have long sustained public advocacy regarding the use and abuse of debt as an illegitimate transfer of resources, opening up *Who Owes Who* exercises to challenge and reverse the traditional notion that debtors owe creditors (Millet and Toussaint 2004). Over time, initiatives to cancel unjust public debts have accumulated a wealth of experience. Emblematic audit-based movements which inspired current debt struggles include official initiatives, such as Ecuador's Public Credit Audit Commission (Comisión Para la Auditoría Integral del Crédito Público, or CAIC 2008), or citizen-led initiatives such as those in Brazil or the Philippines (see Auditoria Cidadã Divida (n.d.) and Freedom from Debt Coalition (n.d.) respectively).

Debt audit movements emerged as a means to challenge the official narrative regarding the unyielding imperative that debts have to be paid. Although sounding technocratic, the objective of such an audit is not a routine accounting exercise but rather an attempt to initiate a broad movement of civic participation to empower democratic processes as means to confront entrenched power of finance. The "auditors" could include representatives of social and labour movements, employees, unemployed and so on. Looking into the public debt generating process has a broad educational objective facilitated by popular education about what are commonly seen as complicated, opaque terms and processes. Audits act as repositories of localized knowledge and means to exchange information about debt mechanisms operating in, for example, local councils, state owned enterprises, ministries and so build upon participants' different contributions. The educational process is a vital step to developing arguments and evidence to hold governments and authorities to account for their borrowing and lending, helping movements to articulate demands for cancelation or mobilize legal proceedings against unjust public debt, while assisting a spectrum of mobilizations in support of social justice (see Fattorelli 2014). The networking and dissemination aspects are key activities undertaken, as popularizing how the economy works enables articulation of more just alternatives that respond to real needs and interests of society, as opposed to needs of "markets," elites, and creditors (PACD 2013).

Table 40.1 Historical Examples of Public Debt Cancellations and Repudiations

Year	Sovereign debt cancellation	Circumstances
1837	Portugal	Queen Maria II repudiated a loan contracted by King Miguel in 1833 through an issue of sovereign bonds in Paris, arguing that Miguel was a usurper and therefore that the debt was illegitimate and illegal (Wynne 1951).
1865	The former Confederate States	After the American Civil War, the Federal government required the Confederate states to repudiate the debts they had contracted towards various international bondholders in order to carry on the war as they were illegitimate and illegal according to the 14th Amendment of the US Constitution (Ludington et al. 2009).
1898	Cuba	After the USA won its war against Spain, it argued that Cuba's debtor status was a fiction since the so-called "Cuban" debts were in reality Spain's (Ludington et al. 2009).
1919	Germany's former territories in Poland and Africa	The Versailles Treaty stated that the debt incurred for the German colonization of territories would not be transferred to these ceded territories. The European victors considered it would be illegitimate to request from the nations concerned to pay for debts which had been incurred in their oppressor's own interest (King 2016).
1920	Estonia, Latvia, Lithuania	Soviet Russia acknowledged the illegitimacy of the debt imposed by Tsarist Russia to the Baltic nations and recognized the right to self-determination (King 2016).
1921	Poland, Persia, Turkey	Soviet Russia acknowledged the illegitimacy of the debt imposed by Tsarist Russia to Poland, Persia, Turkey, and recognized the right to self-determination (Toussaint 2019).
1949–1952	China	Revolutionary China considered that it was not bound to the decisions of the regime it had overthrown (King 2016).
1956	Indonesia	After independence, Indonesia refused to acknowledge the debts contracted by the Netherlands to colonize the territory (King 2016).
1959–1961	Cuba	Revolutionary Cuba considered that it was not bound to the decisions of the regime it had overthrown (Lienau 2014).
1963–1966	Algeria	After independence, Algeria refused to acknowledge debts contracted by France to colonize the territory and wage war against the independence movement (King 2016).
1991	Estonia, Latvia, Lithuania	After the dissolution of the USSR, the Baltic republics considered that debts taken on their behalf by the USSR would not be paid because they had been illegally annexed (King 2016).
1994	Namibia	The post-Apartheid government in South Africa cancelled Namibia's debt as it considered it had been issued in the interest of the Apartheid regime for illegally occupying Namibia (King 2016).
1999–2000	Timor Leste	After independence, Timor Leste refused to acknowledge a debt towards Indonesia that had been contracted for its own subjugation under the Suharto regime (King 2016).

Year	Sovereign debt cancellation	Circumstances
2004	Iraq	After the US invasion of Iraq, the USA and other major creditors (including the UK, Germany, Russia, France, the World Bank, the IMF) cancelled 80% of Iraq's debts; the US government argued at the beginning of the negotiations among creditors that they were odious as they had been contracted by Saddam Hussein's regime (Toussaint 2017).
2006	Ecuador, Peru, Sierra Leone, Egypt, Jamaica	Debt cancellation by Norway, the creditor country, after a popular mobilization demonstrated debts were illegitimate (CADTM 2006).

A debt audit typically tries to analyse key characteristics and features of the public debt, and the borrowing policy followed by the authorities. Considering the pressures put on public budgets to prioritize the creditors, citizens are demanding the right to know how the debts were incurred and where the money was spent (see for example Laskaridis 2012 and 2014a). The kinds of questions asked may include: Were the debts used for their intended purpose? Who profited from the loans? Who are the creditors and what conditions do they impose? How were the decisions to take out loans made? What is the portion of the state's budget used to service the debt? How have private debts become public debts? How much did each bank bailout cost? Debt snowballing,[3] credit-pushers, loan sharks, bailiffs and the international multilateral lenders, can thus be exposed as working to maintain the sense of an unyielding imperative to pay, even though public debt accumulation may have not benefitted the collective objectives of a population. As the Spanish citizens debt audit initiative, PACD, put it:

> There are debts that imply violations of human rights or economic, social and cultural rights of the population; that threaten the development of a dignified life, that generate inequality, benefiting an elite and harming the majority of the population; that undermine sovereignty or that are the product of corruption or bad management of the government. These debts can be considered illegitimate, unfair or even contrary to international law principles.
>
> *(PACD 2013)*

It is precisely these aspects of debt accumulation that can galvanize political pressure to insist on debt cancellation.

Two recent official audits in Ecuador and Greece provide valuable lessons on the opportunities for success and challenges that audits face. The official Ecuadorian audit during 2007 and 2009 provides an example of an alternative means of dealing with sovereign debt problems. Ecuador implemented an audit with citizen participation while suspending debt repayment, which eventually led to a significant reduction of the country's external debt.

Rafael Correa took office in Ecuador in 2007 after being elected in the wake of strong social movements, including the campaign in favor of debt cancellation launched in 1997. Correa appointed as Finance Minister Ricardo Patiño, the leader of the anti-debt movement, who brought together Ecuadorian political officials, social activists and debt resistance activists from abroad in order to draw up the presidential decree, issued in July 2007, that instituted a debt audit commission (see UN 2010). On the basis of the results of the commission's work, Correa suspended payment of $3.2 billion of debts in commercial bonds, which had been sold on Wall Street and would mature between 2012 and 2030, arguing that these debts were illegitimate. The Commission found evidence, inter alia, of violations of the constitution, civil and commercial code, and documents in its pages all manner of abuses, including the abuse of legal rights, violation of public order, illicit enrichment, and disregard towards the administrative authorities (CAIC 2008). Correa suspended payment from November 2008 and was firm with the bond holders, withholding information on what Ecuador was planning to do next up until April 2009. In June 2009 the Ecuadorian government managed to arrange a buy-back of 91% of these bonds at a 70% discount. For a payment of $1 billion, Ecuador recovered bonds nominally worth $3.2 billion. Ecuador saved $2.2 billion, or with the interest that remained, a total of an estimated $7 billion (UN 2010). This was possible because Correa's government, with the support of social mobilizations, decided unilaterally to suspend the payment of the debt in November 2008 (CAIC 2008).

In 2011 the Greek Debt Audit Campaign was launched to demand a full examination of Greece's public debt with the aim of cancelling illegitimate, odious and unsustainable parts of the debt (ELE 2011 and ELE n.d.). The campaign worked to open-up the "black-box" of Greek debt, about which an extensive conditionality program led the country into a deep recession and a dramatic drop in the standard of living. History would have it that the opportunity for an official committee to be established was created several years later by the Hellenic Parliament during the first Syriza government in April 2015 (Hellenic Parliament 2015a). The undertaking of an audit in Greece had been recommended by the UN independent expert on the effects of foreign debt on human rights[4] following the 2013 mission to Greece and the creation of the parliamentary audit was subsequently welcomed by the independent expert in 2015 (UN 2015).

The Truth Committee on Public Debt (Debt Truth Committee) was established by the President of the Hellenic Parliament, Zoe Konstantopoulou.[5] The resultant Report outlined how the mechanisms devised by the official bailouts transferred their loans almost in their entirety to financial institutions, creating new debt whilst generating abusive costs, accelerating the privatization of public assets in Greece and deepening the crisis further (Hellenic Parliament 2015b). The report made novel discoveries regarding Greece's loan agreements and memoranda, describing human rights obligations breaches, and showing the way the reforms were coercively imposed, thus stripping the country of significant aspects of its sovereignty. "Conflicts with human rights and customary obligations, several indications of contracting parties acting in bad faith, which together with the unconscionable character of the agreements, render these agreements invalid" (Hellenic Parliament 2015b: 4). The Report exposed how the intrusive conditionality programs precipitated broad human rights violations, concluding that the impact of the measures "directly affected living conditions of the people and violated human rights, which Greece and its partners are obliged to respect, protect and promote under domestic, regional and international law" (Hellenic Parliament 2015b: 4). The Report documents how the imposed conditionalities affected the right to work, to education, to health etc., while generating high levels of social exclusion and poverty. This was a breach of Greece's human rights obligations but importantly, each of the Lenders as well. It documents the variety of violations in ratification procedures and the abusive clauses contained in the agreement and illuminates that the main beneficiaries of bailouts were not the general population but rather the foreign and domestic financial sector as well as creditor governments. The Committee's Report contained within it numerous possibilities for a case to be taken forward against the creditors. Options suggested included legal foundations for repudiation and suspension of the Greek sovereign debt, in particular the conditions under which a sovereign state can exercise the right to unilateral act of repudiation or suspension of the payment of debt under international law (see Bantekas and Vivien 2016; Bantekas and Lumina 2019).

In the end, the Greek government led by Alexis Tsipras did not use the results and the recommendations of the Debt Truth Committee's Report in 2015. Instead, it agreed on a program of macroeconomic adjustment designed by the creditors, the third one since 2010 (about which more information in Laskaridis 2014b, and 2015). Yet this outcome was not inevitable. With only a hollow approval of the Debt Truth Committee when it was launched, the government ignored the Committee's Preliminary report in June 2015 which put forward the case that Greece had the right to an alternative with examples of options. The final chapter of the Committee's Report is dedicated to the variety of legal mechanisms which states could rely on to unilaterally repudiate or suspend debts that are illegitimate, odious, illegal or unsustainable, thus providing legitimate means to reverse the balance of power and clear the decks of debt.

Elements of Success from Recent Debt Struggles

This section identifies techniques that were used to confront the power of creditors in the USA and in Europe since the global financial crisis. The elements that stand out are the effective use of courts and direct action, both accompanied by research and popular education tools. The first section covers effective use of courts in Iceland and Spain and the second section covers direct action for debt jubilees in the USA.

Use of the courts

In Iceland, the bank Landsbanki was nationalized in the wake of the 2008 economic crisis, but its foreign branch Icesave was precluded and was not bailed out by the Icelandic government. The Netherlands and Britain unilaterally compensated Dutch and British depositors of Icesave, and requested that Iceland cover the costs, which Iceland refused to do. After complaints were brought to the European Free Trade Association (EFTA) by the Netherlands and Britain, the EFTA arbitrated in favor of Iceland (see EFTA Court 2013). Iceland's refusal to pay and its decision to sue the people responsible for the risks taken by its banks were only possible because of the popular mobilization in the country, which included large petitions generating enough political pressure to bring about a referendum to reverse the government's initial agreement to the bailout (CADTM 2013).

Spain presents a second example of effective use of courts. As public rescues for corrupt and fraudulent banking practises sparked great discontent, several campaigns formed to expose banking scandals. One example of a campaign successfully ending bankers' impunity took place in Spain, surrounding the nefarious activities of Bankia. Accused of multiple offences such as mis-selling products to the public, false reporting when floating its stock and deep corruption in senior management, Bankia became Spain's primary symbol of financial scandal (Badcock 2016). Caja Madrid was one of six regional savings banks that formed Bankia in 2010, whose subsequent bankruptcy necessitated an EU bailout. Corruption and bribery in senior bank management tiers even after the obvious financial troubles facing the institution and its consequent merger into Bankia sparked wide-spread discontent.

On the anniversary of the 15M movement[6] in Spain, in 2012, citizens gathered in public squares and issued a plan to end the bankers' immunity (see Grueso 2012). Since no authority was willing to make an investigation or inquiry into the responsibilities for financial collapses, citizens began a process of self-mobilization to attempt by themselves, to hold bankers to account. Two activist networks, 15MpaRato and XNET, collaborated to create online platforms inspired by WikiLeaks, to facilitate people to pass on information and share citizens' complaints (15MpaRato 2014 and XNET n.d.). Bank employees, among others, deposited documents that would provide evidence of wrong-doing into an anonymous online dropbox, and activists launched a crowd funding campaign to raise the funds needed to pursue a legal case.

The citizen-led lawsuit aimed to uphold accountability for the crisis and was instrumental in collecting the necessary documentation to reveal fraudulent practices. After a dedicated pursuit,

Rodrigo Rato, a former Spanish Finance Minister (1996–2000), former deputy Prime Minister, and former Managing Director of the IMF (2004–2007), who was chairman of Bankia during this crucial period (2010 to 2012) was found guilty of embezzlement in 2017 and sentenced to over four years in prison (Reuters 2017), a sentence which was confirmed by the Supreme Court in October 2018 (Reuters 2018).[7]

Direct Action against Personal Debts

In the USA, a bold initiative has taken direct action for debt cancellation. A debt jubilee is cancellation that wipes the slate clean for those in debt bondage. The Rolling Jubilee project put such demands into practice by creating "a bailout for the people by the people," by forming a crowdfunding platform to raise money to buy the defaulted debts of individuals and cancel them (Rolling Jubilee n.d.). Up to 2018, over $700,000 had been raised and correspondingly over $31 million of debt had been cancelled by buying the defaulted loans in the secondary market and abolishing it. The campaign focused on medical debt; original lenders of medical loans at some point decide to stop pursuing repayment and sell defaulted loans on the secondary market at a high discount rate to debt collectors. Rolling Jubilee, contacting a debt buyer, navigated the secondary debt market to purchase and cancel a portfolio of anonymized defaulted medical debts. The immediate accomplishment is that debtors, at random, are freed from their debts and are no longer hounded by debt-collectors. The move highlights the predatory nature of the financial system, as although the banks may sell such non-performing loans and defaulted debts for pennies on the dollar, the buyers of these debts are trying to collect full amounts. The campaign exposes that debt cancellations are not only desirable but also feasible, boasting that "together we can liberate debtors at random through a campaign of mutual support, good will, and collective refusal" (Rolling Jubilee n.d.).

The Rolling Jubilee arose from the Strike Debt collective, created in the USA in the wake of the Occupy Wall Street movement (see Strike Debt n.d., and Ross and Taylor 2012). From the primary focus of fighting the distress that engrossed indebted individuals and households, it widened its scope. The Strike Debt collective is thus a debt resistance movement in a broad sense, fighting financialization as a whole, from private to public debts. In September 2012, it released the *Debt Resistors' Operations Manual*, which "aims to provide specific tactics for understanding and fighting against the debt system so that we can all reclaim our lives and our communities" (Strike Debt and Occupy Wall Street 2012: v).

Conclusion

The power of the creditors has grown with financialization, yet is far from stable or inevitable despite the fact that it is often presented by policymakers as something which is necessary and cannot be challenged. Historical examples of unilateral actions and popular mobilizations are relevant reminders to the discontents that financialization has bred. Numerous social movements emerged in the wake of the global financial crisis to effectively challenge the impacts of financialization. Citizens across Europe organized public debt audits to counter the broad austerity response that prioritized creditors over social need. In two case studies of official audits, in Ecuador and Greece, loans were found to have violated crucial obligations by states, including human right obligations. Where debts are illegitimate, odious, illegal or unsustainable, there is legal foundation to confront the creditors, as the Greek audit report showed, but pursuance of these rights rests on political support for them.

Nonetheless, to illustrate that with broad political support, successful confrontations with creditors against unjust public and private debts is possible we look at examples with an effective mixture of grass roots mobilization, use of courts and direct action. The example of Iceland serves to remind that bailing out the financial sector that many countries paid heavily for through austerity, was not inevitable. The immunity that those responsible for large scale financial collapse have often enjoyed was challenged in Spain with groups demanding accountability and justice. In the USA, the unequal treatment of debtors, where large corporations get bailout out whereas individuals get hounded by debt collectors, inspired a modern jubilee. These examples illuminate practices useful to the political challenges of financialization.

Notes

1 Ecuador (2007–2009) and Iceland (2008–2009) will be covered later in this chapter.
2 The International Citizen Audit Network was launched in 2012 and provided the space for sharing information on the types of audit or other types of debt struggles pursued (see ICAN 2012).
3 Debt snowballing describes the changes in debt to GDP ratios which arise, not from government expenditures being greater than revenues, but a positive interest rate-growth rate differential.
4 Full title is Independent Expert on the effects of foreign debt and other related international financial obligations of States on the full enjoyment of all human rights, particularly economic, social and cultural rights.
5 Scientific Coordination of its work was given to Eric Toussaint.
6 The 15M movement, also known as the Indignados movement, was named so because of its initial meeting day of 15th May 2011. It was a broad movement associated with calls for real democracy and anti-austerity.
7 The movement against illegitimate debts in Spain was furthered with the Oviedo Manifesto in October 2016 which called for debt audits of local administrations with citizen participation, leading to the municipal network against illegitimate debts and fiscal cuts (Red Municipalista contra la Deuda Ilegítima y los Recortes) (Duval and Martín 2017).

Bibliography

Auditoria Cidadã Divida, n.d. Website of the Brazilian Citizen Debt Audit. Retrieved from https://audi toriacidada.org.br/ [Accessed February 1, 2018].

Badcock, J., 2016. How Spanish activists landed ex-IMF head Rodrigo Rato in court. September 25, 2016, *BBC News*.

Balbuena, H., 2008. "La décision souveraine de déclarer la nullité de la dette ou la décision de non paiement de la dette: un droit de l'État" [The decision to declare a debt null and void or default on its payment is a State's sovereign right] (trans. CADTM) Retrieved from http://www.cadtm.org/La-decision-souveraine-de-decla rer [Accessed March 17, 2018].

Bantekas, I. and Luminas, C., 2019. *Sovereign Debt and Human Rights*. Oxford University Press: Oxford.

Bantekas, I. and Vivien, R., 2016. On the odiousness of Greek Debt. *European Law Journal*, 22(4), pp. 539–565.

Bazant, J., 1995. *Historia de la deuda exterior de México 1823–1946*. México D.F.: Colegio de México Centro de Estudios Históricos.

CADTM, 2006. CADTM applauds Norway's initiative concerning the cancellation of odious debt. *Press Release*. October 10, 2006, Belgium. Retrieved from http://www.cadtm.org/CADTM-applauds-Norway-s-initiative [Accessed March 17, 2018].

CADTM, 2013. EFTA court dismisses "Icesave" claims against Iceland and its people. *Press Release*. January 23, 2013. Retrieved from http://www.cadtm.org/EFTA-court-dismisses-Icesave [Accessed March 17, 2018].

CAIC, 2008. *Final Report of the Integral Auditing of the Ecuadorian Debt*. Ministry of Economy and Finance, Quito, Ecuador. Retrieved from http://www.cadtm.org/Final-Report-of-the-Integral [Accessed March 17, 2018].

Carr, E.H., 1953. *The Bolshevik Revolution (1917–1923)*, vol. 3. London: Macmillan & Co.

Davis, A. and Walsh, C., 2015. The role of the state in the financialisation of the UK economy. *Political Studies*, 64(3), pp. 666–682.

Duval, J. and Martín, F., 2017. Spain: The Municipal Network against Illegitimate Debt held a second successful meeting in Cadiz. CADTM. Belgium. Retrieved from http://www.cadtm.org/Spain-The-Municipal-Network [Accessed March 17, 2018].

EFTA Court, 2013. Judgement of the Court, 28th January 2013, Luxembourg. Retrieved from http://www.eftacourt.int/uploads/tx_nvcases/16_11_Judgment_EN.pdf [Accessed March 17, 2018].

ELE, 2011. Petition for a call for an audit commission on Greek Public Debt. February 19, 2011, Go Petition. Retrieved from https://bit.ly/2MXSwdk [Accessed September 1, 2018].

ELE, n.d. Archived website of ELE (the Greek Debt Audit Campaign), Athens, Greece. Retrieved from https://bit.ly/2zq5vkI [Accessed September 1, 2018].

Fattorelli, M., 2014. *Citizen Public Debt Audit*. Geneva. English Edition, Liège, Belgium: CETIM/CADTM.

Freedom from Debt Coalition, n.d. Website. Retrieved from https://fdc.ph/ [Accessed September 1, 2018].

Grueso, S., 2012. *15M: Excellent. A Wake-up call. Important.* Written and directed by: Grueso, S., produced by Madrid.15M.cc. Retrieved from https://vimeo.com/71961963 [Accessed September 1, 2018].

Hager, S.B., 2015. Corporate ownership of the public debt: Mapping the new aristocracy of finance. *Socio-Economic Review*, 13(3), pp. 505–523.

Hellenic Parliament. 2015a. *Press Release*. March 17, 2015, Athens, Greece. Retrieved from https://bit.ly/2xKTiF1 [Accessed September 1, 2018].

Hellenic Parliament. 2015b. *Preliminary Report of the Debt Truth Committee*, Athens Greece. Retrieved from https://bit.ly/2I92tnq [Accessed September 1, 2018].

Howse, R., 2007. The concept of odious debt in public international law. *UNCTAD Discussion Papers* No. 185. New York: United Nations.

ICAN, 2012. Coordinated efforts in Europe and North Africa to fight against debt and austerity, April 16, 2012. Retrieved from http://www.cadtm.org/Coordinated-efforts-in-Europe-and [Accessed March 17, 2018].

King, J., 2006. Odious debt: The terms of debate. *North Carolina Journal of International Law and Commercial Regulation*, 32(4), pp. 606–668.

King, J., 2016. *The Doctrine of Odious Debt in International Law. A Restatement*. Cambridge: Cambridge University Press.

Lamarque, C. and Vivien, R., 2011. Suspending public debt repayments by legal means. CADTM, Belgium. Retrieved from http://www.cadtm.org/Suspending-public-debt-repayments [Accessed March 17, 2018].

Laskaridis, C., 2012. Why audit the Greek debt. *Journal of Modern Education*, 168 (in Greek).

Laskaridis, C., 2014a. Debt mechanism. *Levga Periodical*, 14 (in Greek).

Laskaridis, C., 2014b. Greece: Europe's worst success story. In T. Philips (ed.), *Europe on the Brink*. London: Zed Books, pp. 150–189.

Laskaridis, C., 2015. *False Dilemmas: A Critical Guide to the Euro Crisis*. London: Corporate Watch.

Lienau, O., 2014. *Rethinking Sovereign Debt: Politics Reputation and Legitimacy in Modern Finance*. Cambridge, MA: Harvard University Press.

Ludington, S., Gulati, M. and Brophy, A., 2009. Applied legal history: Demystifying the doctrine of odious debt. *Theoretical Inquiries in Law*, 11(1), pp. 247–281.

Mader, M. and Rothenbühler, A. (eds.), *How to Challenge Illegitimate Debt Theory and Legal Case Studies*. Basel, Switzerland: Aktion Finanzplatz Schweiz.

Millet, D. and Toussaint, E., 2004. *Who Owes Who?*London: Zed Books.

Millet, D. and Toussaint, E., 2012. Citizen debt audits: How and why? Liège, Belgium: CADTM. Retrieved from http://www.cadtm.org/Citizen-debt-audits-how-and-why [Accessed March 17, 2018].

Mills, J.S., 1922. *The Genoa Conference*. London: Hutchinson & Co.

Montgomerie, J. and Tepe-Belfrage, D., 2018. Spaces of debt resistance and the contemporary politics of financialised capitalism. *Geoforum*, 98 (January 2019), pp. 309–317.

PACD – Plataforma Auditoria Ciudadana de la Deuda, 2013. What the PACD means by citizens debt audit and illegitimate debt. Retrieved from https://bit.ly/2QTCa8S [Accessed March 17, 2018].

Reuters, 2017. Ex-IMF boss Rato sentenced to jail in Spain over credit card scandal. February 23, 2017. Retrieved from https://reut.rs/2QU1coo [Accessed March 17, 2018].

Reuters, 2018. Spain court confirms jail sentence for former IMF chief Rato. October 3, 2018. Retrieved from https://www.reuters.com/article/us-spain-corruption/spain-court-confirms-jail-sentence-for-former-imf-chief-rato-idUSKCN1MD1FT [Accessed October 170, 2018].

Roos, J., 2016. *Why Not Default? The Structural Power of Finance in Sovereign Debt Crises*. Thesis Introduction, European University Institute, Florence.

Ross, A. and Taylor, A., 2012. Rolling Jubilee is a spark – not the solution. *The Nation*, November 27, 2012. Retrieved from https://www.thenation.com/article/rolling-jubilee-spark-not-solution/ [Accessed March 17, 2018].

Rolling Jubilee, n.d. Website. Retrieved from http://rollingjubilee.org/ [Accessed February 1, 2018].

Sack, A., 1927. *Les effets des transformations des États sur leurs dettes publiques et autres obligations financières* [The effects of the transformation of States on their public debt and other financial obligations]. Paris: Sirey.

Strike Debt, n.d. Website. Retrieved from www.strikedebt.org. [Accessed March 17, 2018].

Strike Debt and Occupy Wall Street, 2012. *Debt Resistors Operations Manual.* Retrieved from www.strike debt.org/The-Debt-Resistors-Operations-Manual.pdf [Accessed March 17, 2018].

Toussaint, E., 2005. *Your Money or Your Life. The Tyranny of Global Finance.* Chicago, IL: Haymarket/ Mumbai, India: VAK.

Toussaint, E., 2015. *Bankocracy.* London and Amsterdam: Resistance Books and IIRE.

Toussaint, E., 2017. *The Odious Iraqi Debt.* Retrieved from http://www.cadtm.org/The-Odious-Ira qi-Debt [Accessed March 17, 2018].

Toussaint, E., 2019. *The Debt System.* Chicago, IL: Haymarket.

Ueberschlag, L., 2016. The citizen guerilla that brings "banksters" to court in Spain. October 27, 2016, Retrieved from: http://networkcultures.org/moneylab/2016/10/27/the-citizen-guerilla-that-brings-ba nksters-to-court-in-spain/ [Accessed March 17, 2018].

UN, 2010. *Missions to Norway and Ecuador.* UN General Assembly, Human Rights Council, document A/ HRC/14/21/Add.1. Geneva, UN. Retrieved from https://www2.ohchr.org/english/bodies/hrcoun cil/docs/14session/A.HRC.14.21.Add.1_en.pdf [Accessed March 17, 2018].

UN, 2013. Mission to Greece. UN General Assembly, Human Rights Council, document A/HRC/25/ 50/Add.1. Retrieved from http://www.undocs.org/A/HRC/25/50/Add.1 [Accessed March 17, 2018].

UN, 2015. Press Release. June 2, 2015, UN Human Rights, Office of the High Commissioner, Geneva. Retrieved from https://www.ohchr.org/EN/NewsEvents/Pages/DisplayNews.aspx?NewsID=16032, [Accessed March 17, 2018].

Wynne, W., 1951. *State Insolvency and Foreign Bondholders: Selected Case Histories of Governmental Foreign Bond Defaults and Debt Readjustments,* vol. 2. New Haven, CT: Yale University Press.

15MpaRato, 2014. *Citizens against Corruption: The Story of a Citizen Lawsuit.* October 28, 2014, 15MpaRato. Retrieved from https://15mparato.wordpress.com/2014/10/28/story-citizen-lawsuit/ [Accessed March 17, 2018].

XNET, n.d. Website. Retrieved from https://xnet-x.net/ [Accessed March 17, 2018].

INDEX

accountability 5, 279, 283, 395, 469, 476–477, 489, 491

accounting 45, 47–49, 128, 225–228, 232, 327, 359, 382, 401–405, 407, 485; firms 33, 224, 232, 349; national 23, 25; social and environmental 215, 217, 219–220

accumulation: financial 150, 163–164, 166, 173, 303, 331, 353, 371, 469; regime/mode of 10; 21–24, 27, 39, 44, 126, 140–141, 180, 201–202, 209, 312, 381, 469

activist investors 270, 272–273

advanced capitalist economies (ACE) 10, 31–32, 35, 115, 121, 150–153, 155, 157–158, 177, 181, 193, 203, 206, 302–303, 330, 340, 448, 451–453, 455

aggregate demand 141, 149–150, 157–158, 178, 180–182, 384–385

Algeria 92, 99, 486

algorithm 217, 352, 375

alternative trading system (ATS) 256, 261

American see United States

Amsterdam see Netherlands

Anglo-America 2, 4, 8–9, 121, 277, 281–284, 304, 348, 350–351, 381, 383–386, 405

animism 219–220

anthropology 4, 9, 73, 92–100, 347–349

arbitrage 232, 360–361, 364, 429

Argentina 127, 165, 167, 170, 306, 313

Asian financial crisis 103, 164, 170, 470 see also financial crises

asset: -backed securities 35, 63, 116, 214, 242, 247, 363–364; -based welfare 335, 383; class 206, 215, 217, 253–254, 257–259, 290, 293, 337, 352; management 82, 88, 116, 189, 192, 194–195, 259, 263, 266–268, 271–273, 444; price inflation 33, 35–36, 149–152, 155–156,

162, 164, 171, 178, 180–181, 335–336, 384, 386, 465

auditors 88–89, 407, 485

austerity 33, 57, 88, 95, 97, 102–104, 108–109, 120, 154–155, 314, 336, 342, 382, 386–387, 396, 401–408, 482, 490

Australia 203, 302, 304, 337, 341, 392

Austria 34, 151, 153–154, 157, 203, 341, 403, 405, 484

bailout 103, 193, 384, 487–490

balance sheet: of financial institutions 202, 206, 242–243, 247, 359, 363–365, 459–461, 463–464; of households 127–128, 201, 380, 382–383, 386; of non-financial firms 117, 306; national 183–184, 193

Bangladesh 107, 261, 295, 305, 307

Bank of England 28, 50, 225, 243, 262, 437, 477

Bank of International Settlements (BIS) 166–167, 172–173, 202, 226–227, 302, 365, 470

banking 59–65, 142–144, 227–230, 358–365, 438–445; central see central banking; commercial 95, 137, 142–144, 193, 196, 243–244, 439, 445, 461–463; crisis 364, 439, 484; development see development banks; investment 35, 65, 439; private 242, 293, 445; regulation 244, 458, 472, 476; sector 34, 39, 115, 249, 358–360, 364–365, 406, 430, 462, 476; shadow see shadow banking; supervision 358–359, 361–362, 365; system 28, 63, 129, 180, 196, 242–244, 246, 302, 306, 441, 445, 461, 471

bankruptcy 206, 364, 374, 393, 397, 427, 489

Basel Accords 315, 358, 361–362, 365, 406, 470–471

behavioral economics 58, 106, 390–391, 396

Belgium 227, 230, 393, 404, 406

Index

women 95, 98, 102–109, 128, 296, 305, 326, 330, 332, 336, 338, 372, 382, 394, 440
work *see* employment
worker 11, 20, 37–38, 48, 85, 95, 119, 126, 129–131, 150, 155–157, 179, 182, 218, 265, 270, 292, 301, 306–307, 319, 324–342,

348–354, 373, 393, 413–419, 425, 443, 451; *see also* employment, labor
working class 37, 120, 203, 290, 302, 318, 341, 371–372, 375, 421
World Bank 92, 166, 215, 303, 313–315,
world system 138–140, 233